Also by Arlene Croce

Sight Lines
Going to the Dance
Afterimages
The Fred Astaire & Ginger Rogers Book

Writing in the Dark, Dancing in *The New Yorker*

Writing in the Dark, Dancing in *The New Yorker*

Arlene Croce

Farrar, Straus and Giroux

New York

Farrar, Straus and Giroux
19 Union Square West, New York 10003

Distributed in Canada by Douglas & McIntyre Ltd.
Printed in the United States of America
Designed by Jonathan D. Lippincott
First edition, 2000

Library of Congress Cataloging-in-Publication Data
Croce, Arlene.
   Writing in the dark, dancing in *The New Yorker* / Arlene Croce.— 1st ed.
      p.   cm.
   Includes index.
   ISBN 0-374-10455-7 (alk. paper)
   1. Dance—New York (State)—New York—Reviews.   2. Dance—
United States—Reviews. I. New Yorker (New York, N.Y.: 1925)
II. Title.

GV1624.5.N4 C79 2000
729.8′09747′1—dc21   00-035448

All the pieces in this book except one were originally published in *The New Yorker*. "On *Beauty* Bare" first appeared in *The New York Review of Books*.

Contents

Writing in the Dark, Dancing in *The New Yorker*

Writing in the Dark

Looking back over the events covered in these pieces, I can hardly believe they happened. That dance could ever have been as rich, as varied, and as plentiful as it was in the seventies and eighties now seems a miracle. When I was appointed *The New Yorker*'s dance critic, in 1973, I knew the hour was late: Balanchine was sixty-nine, Graham had left the stage, and any number of important careers were winding down. Still, there was enough activity to keep anybody interested, and what with Baryshnikov's defection in 1974 and Suzanne Farrell's return from exile that same year, there was more than I could keep up with. I was in the theatre nightly and sometimes, between Friday night and Sunday evening, I saw five performances. Companies often played side by side, and it was nothing to dart from one theatre to another and back in the course of a single performance.

The dance season had always been a congested affair. In my time, it reached such levels that I invented something called Ballet Alert, a fictitious telephone service for hyperactive balletomanes, and was taken seriously. This was probably because "Ballet Alert" was printed in "Dancing," my regular space in *The New Yorker*, and not in the front of the book where the "casuals" were. I should have warned my editors that I was perpetrating a hoax. William Shawn was not amused. I had broken an inflexible *New Yorker* rule: critics do not write humor.

But of course "Ballet Alert" was also a joke on *The New Yorker*—my parody of a Talk of the Town piece. To me it was so obviously parodic, and so patently silly (Cynthia Gregory's shredder?), I never thought it would be believed. But perhaps I underestimated the special idiocy which outsiders attached to the "ballet boom," a term invented by the media to cover their own delayed recognition of the ballet scene. In actuality, the boom had been going on since the thirties; by the late sixties, ballet was an accepted part of American culture—a covertly accepted part. You'd go to a party; if someone's eyes lit up at the mention of Balanchine's name, you'd made a friend. The excitement of ballet-going in New York was an undercover excitement. The outside world seemed to have no inkling of what was going on; it still thought that the balletgoing public consisted of little girls, mothers, homosexuals, foreigners, and outright nuts like my invention Carmel Capehart. A glance at the audience on an average night at the New York City, the Royal, or the Bolshoi Ballet would disprove the truth of this. Even Martha Graham drew a normal Broadway-theatre-going audience. Today, of course, as many kinds of people go to dance performances as play tennis, another "aristocratic" pastime of my youth. As for the ballet boom, the reader can judge the reality of it by the number of boomlets it inspired in the seventies alone—Bournonville, regional ballet, drag ballet, and that unique product of the times, the post-modern ballet.

The term "post-modernism" has an extra semantic layer

in dance: it means not only after modernism but after the modern dance. Post-modern ballet is a hybrid that came about when the ballet and the modern dance ceased to be hostile camps—ideology was dying out along with creativity—and began embracing each other. The ballet companies, with their rising popularity and longer seasons, needed choreographers, and because choreographers had yet to come forth from the academy in sufficient numbers, they came from the modern and post-modern dance. To Twyla Tharp, Laura Dean, Mark Morris, and a host of other young nonclassical choreographers, a ballet-company commission meant prestige, which meant bigger grants for their own companies from a new government agency, the National Endowment for the Arts. To ballet dancers like Nureyev and Baryshnikov who knew nothing of the ideological warfare in American dance, fraternizing with the moderns meant a chance to learn new techniques, which enabled them to extend their careers. A fair number of the premières I reviewed were of post-modern ballets, a development I took for granted at the time but now see as symptomatic of the forces that were struggling against depletion in the seventies and eighties. They are still struggling; the energy of the American dance renaissance that began in the thirties is not completely spent, but that post-modern ballet is a twilight (I almost wrote "Twylight") phenomenon I have no doubt.

Another thing that has changed, of course, is *The New Yorker*; its whole style was different in Shawn's day. The amount of freedom a writer enjoyed there may have been unique in American journalism. I never wrote on assignment, was never asked to cover this or that event—"coverage" as a conception did not exist. Once it was conceded that dance was a topic acceptable on a regular basis to *New*

Yorker readers, my choices of subject and deadline were
never even queried. When I thought I had to write, I would
reserve space, then file at the last minute. When, as frequently happened, I overran the space, more space was
found. And *The New Yorker*'s editing procedures were a
model of courtesy and scrupulosity.

But even though my options as a practicing critic were
practically limitless, my capacities still weren't enough for
my subject. It seemed that in those days I could never *write*
as much as I had *seen*—I mean in depth as well as diversity—and every deadline was an opportunity missed. I realized that what I wrote was always going to be at a certain
remove from the actual experience—I believe it was Merce
Cunningham who said that speaking about dance is like
nailing Jell-O to the wall—but getting comfortable with
that distance took some doing. It required accepting a possibility of success based on an inevitability of diminution. In
the course of writing about a dance, you invariably diminish
it; you change its nature. It becomes, or aspects of it become, utterable, therefore false. It is a real temptation to a
dance critic to prolong the illusion of utterability; art is, after all, a world of semblances—even dance tolerates falsity
to an extent. However, if you get to where the reader is saying to himself, "I guess you had to have been there," you
have gone past the point of toleration.

Did I take notes? Yes and no. Mostly I took them if I
felt my attention wandering, but I found it better, if I possibly could, to force my concentration in the hope of finding
an afterimage later. It is the afterimage of the dance rather
than the dance itself which is the true subject of the review.
To let an afterimage form, one has to give the stage one's
full attention, without the distraction of note-taking. This,
the greatest lesson I absorbed from the master, Edwin

Denby, was too strict to adhere to if it happened to be the weekend, I had to file on Tuesday, and I was not in my freshest mind. I evolved a method of minimal, disciplined, and, I hoped, risk-free note-taking, using a small memo pad on which I could get no more than two or three notes a page. It was okay when it worked. A white label pasted on the front cover was supposed to guard against getting the pad upside down in the dark, and by moving my thumb down the page, covering what I'd just written, I could at least hope not to scrawl one note on top of another. After the performance, I would jot the title and date of the event on the white label. I filled whole shelves with such pads in the course of a season, and I doubt that I consulted more than two or three of them when it came time to write the reviews. Some image would by then have formed, not necessarily an afterimage, but a cumulative impression more suggestive than "Jumps like a seal" or "Off the music?" In the end, all note-taking was good for was recording visual facts, like the color of costumes and the sequence of events, which I had trouble remembering. It made *New Yorker* fact checking easier.

Mistakes got in just the same, and I hereby absolve the checkers of all responsibility; the mistakes are mine, and most of them remain uncorrected; knowing something is wrong is not the same as knowing how to make it right. This may also be the time to make a full disclosure which will not come as a surprise to some people: I am a dance illiterate. I have never formally studied dance, never taken a music lesson, never performed on any stage except as a youngster, in school plays. My career as a critic is proof that one can come to dance knowing nothing of how it is done and still understand it, or understand it well enough to spread the news. This has to be because even the most highly cultivated form of dance, classical ballet, speaks directly to the prenatal instinct for movement and for rhythm, the thing that makes sense of movement. My own unsuppressible need to try to make sense of what I'd seen led to my becoming a writer of dance criticism; the folly, for me, of that undertaking was offset by my belief in the power of dance to communicate itself to others as it had to me.

This faith of mine was upheld during my reviewing years by all three of my editors at *The New Yorker*—Shawn, Robert Gottlieb, and Tina Brown. Without their support, I should not have known how to continue. Shawn loved the ballet. He never told me this for some reason; maybe he thought it would influence me. He never complimented me on anything I wrote except for the first couple of articles and one other, "The Dreamer of the Dream." Gottlieb, also a ballet lover, was volubly happy with my work even after he was fired by Peter Martins from the board of New York City Ballet because of a piece of mine, "Dimming the Lights."

It was under Tina Brown that I wrote my most notorious piece, "Discussing the Undiscussable." The idea was mine, and so was the rubric under which it ran, Critic at Bay. That and a few other traces of levity remain as vestiges of my first conception of the piece, which was as a Shouts & Murmurs, a one-pager complaining of trends in performance, some sinister, some absurd, which had the effect of limiting what a critic could decently say. (One of the things that bothered me was choreographers so loaded with antidepressants that you couldn't look at their work and distinguish their creative personalities from their medication.) It is amazing to me now to recall that my screed against victim art began in this semiserious way. I had been avoiding the subject, telling myself that victim art and its purveyors had been adequately covered by other writers, when suddenly I was faced with a direct challenge: the event called *Still/Here*. I have been asked whether, when I wrote the piece, I had any idea of the controversy it would arouse. I only knew it would make some people angry. Would I have written it differently? No, but I would have taken more time over it and weeded out the embryonic Shouts & Murmurs bits that embarrass me now. And I would have put in a sentence or two about the pornography of atrocity, which often goes hand in hand with victim art and by which we are insidiously seduced in such prestigious ventures as the movie *Schindler's List*.

As I said then, we live in hard times for critics. When I joined *The New Yorker*, the magazine was one of the loftiest critical platforms in the country, and I am enduringly grateful for the standards set by my colleagues in their writings about the arts—Pauline Kael mainly, and Andrew Porter and Harold Rosenberg and Whitney Balliett. There weren't as many cultural constraints on the critic as there are now, although I can recall even then having to defend in many a seminar or panel discussion the right of the critic to be "judgmental" in a democracy.

Although my reports tell a slightly different story, I think of 1989, the year Lincoln Kirstein, Robert Irving, and Suzanne Farrell retired and Mikhail Baryshnikov quit as director of American Ballet Theatre, as the last year of ballet, the end of the wondrously creative and progressive ballet I'd known all my life. What took its place was retrospective ballet: memorials, anniversary celebrations, tributes of one sort or another to the legacy of the past; as New York City Ballet once specialized in festivals of choreography, it now specializes in revival marathons. The retrospective spirit prevails even in Russia, our former adversary. Nineteen eighty-nine was also the last year of the Cold War and the beginning of the end of Communist Russia. One of the forgotten facts of recent history is the reality of the cultural Cold War and the way the United States and the Soviet Union were pitted against each other—seriously—as dance superpowers. But the dance capital of the world wasn't Moscow or Leningrad; it was New York—we addicts knew it then and the world knows it now. One cannot ask more of one's portion of history than to be there when it happens.

Most of the material in this book is from three previous collections of my work, now out of print—*Afterimages* (1977), *Going to the Dance* (1982), and *Sight Lines* (1987). All the pieces were selected by Robert Cornfield, who also chose the format. For his initiative and judgment, and for his generous devotion to every phase of this book, I extend loving thanks.

THE SEVENTIES

Joffrey Jazz

As its name indicates, *Deuce Coupe* is a vehicle for two companies, and as a joint presentation of Twyla Tharp's company and the City Center Joffrey Ballet it was the hit of the entire spring season. Now it's back in repertory with much the same cast as before and in even better performance condition. The audience loves it; I love it. But *Deuce Coupe* is more than a big hit, more than the best thing the Joffrey Ballet has ever done—it's the outstanding accomplishment to date of the ballet year.

For excitement and originality, none of the new works by major choreographers compares with it—not even Merce Cunningham's *Changing Steps*, which was given last March at the Brooklyn Academy. I say "not even Cunningham" because there may well be a genealogical link between him and Twyla Tharp. I won't attempt to trace Twyla Tharp's line of descent—she seems to have absorbed something from nearly everybody who moves well—but, like Cunningham, she is routinely classified as "avant-garde," and only a few years ago she was one of those choreographers who were working without music and in nontheatrical and open spaces—either out-of-doors or in museums and gyms. The only element that she did not eliminate was dancing itself, and in this she was unique—defying the exponents of nondance and antidance. The way she danced was unique, too. The open-space movement in choreography goes on, and Twyla Tharp now has her imitators, but at that time nothing like her had ever been seen before. The finest of the post-Cunningham generation of choreographers, up until *Deuce Coupe* she was thought to be also the most forbiddingly idiosyncratic. Even when, with her own small company, she started choreographing in more conventional surroundings to eighteenth-century music and to jazz, the burn of her intensely personal style didn't wear off, and her dancers seemed to be moved by a form of private communication which made them unlike any other dancers that one could see. I believe that the dances she has done for them—especially the great jazz ballets *Eight Jelly Rolls* and *The Bix Pieces* and *The Raggedy Dances*—are her best work. But *Deuce Coupe* is a good work, too. It isn't a great ballet, but it fills to abundance every need it was meant to fill, and, as far as ballet audiences are concerned, nothing like *it* has ever been seen before, either.

Deuce Coupe is a pop ballet and a great gift to the Joffrey company. Since 1968, when Robert Joffrey put his company on the cover of *Time* with a mixed-media/rock ballet called *Astarte*, it has been polishing its reputation as America's great swinging company. This is one half of the Joffrey company's Janus profile; the other is the image of custodian of modern-day classics from the international repertory. But the Joffrey's dual policy stretched the capacities of its dancers too far. Dancers live and progress on roles that are created for them. All those slick, empty, and violent ballets by Gerald Arpino that slammed the audience with the

Dionysian ecstasy of dance or appealed to the audience's political convictions and hunger for "relevance" certainly did contribute to the shaping of a style, but it was a style that rendered Joffrey dancers unfit for anything better. As classical dancers, the Joffreys have no touch; they look squat, badly placed, hectic, and unmusical. When Joffrey, who has excellent taste in non-Joffrey ballets, imports a classic Danish ballet like *Konservatoriet*, his dancers can hardly get through it. After seven years in residence at the City Center, the structure by which the company made its dancers grow was dead. Generally speaking, you can't feed dancers on imports and revivals. Imports and revivals please audiences; they seldom help the dancer, who can't be at his best in somebody else's repertory.

It would be too much to claim that *Deuce Coupe* has saved the Joffrey, but it does give the dancers something genuine to respond to—something that's exactly suited to their talents—and it tidies up the company's self-image. It's just as if Twyla Tharp had said, "So you want pop? I'll give you pop," but what she has given the Joffrey is so close to the real thing that part of the audience—the part that has decided what contemporary, orgiastic, youth-spirited, with-it ballet looks like—is taken by surprise. *Deuce Coupe* astounds by the utter unfamiliarity of familiar things. Its music is a tape collage of fourteen Beach Boys hits, starting with "Little Deuce Coupe" and ending with "Cuddle Up"—probably the last jukebox pop that *was* pop, and not Pop Art. Its décor is spray-can graffiti applied to a rolling backcloth while the ballet is in progress. And its dancing— that which gives it life and joy—is a peculiar Tharpian combination of classical ballet and the juvenile social dancing of the past decade. The ballet steps are like a primitive's-eye view of classical style, fascinating in their plainness and angularity, and the social dances are rich with crazy, campily corny suggestion. Neither type of dancing is what it would be in the hands of any other choreographer, and yet neither is what it ordinarily appears to be in its raw state—in the classroom, or in school gyms, ballrooms, and discothèques. Whatever the Tharp eye sees, it changes. (Even the graffiti, with their characteristic stilted lines, curly serifs, and locked edges, look as if they were intended for *Deuce Coupe*. And, oh, New York! Isn't it nice to see the stuff in a place where it belongs?) As a result, the whole ballet has this low-contrast choreographic weave that knits its separate scenes together, but there's so much action going on, and the action is so complicated and delicately timed, that the effect is never one of monotony. (There is one moment when the ballet seems to slump. At the end of "Don't Go Near the Water," we get one more roiling group instead of something we haven't seen before.) This complexity and delicacy can be undervalued. Most of the time in *Deuce Coupe*, the dancers appear to be behaving with such realism that we could believe they were making it up as they went along. People who don't often go to the ballet might recognize the validity of these dances at once and wonder why such a fuss was being made over them. People who go more regularly fall into the trap of their expectations, and *Deuce Coupe* looks formless to them—just taken off the street and thrown onto the stage. Actually, no one has put contemporary American popular dancing of quite this intensity and freedom on the stage before, and I am sure no one but Twyla Tharp would have known how to make these dances legible in the theatre. A hundred kids going berserk at a school prom is a powerful but not necessarily a theatrical spectacle. To be realized on the stage, such potency has to be objectified; the material has to be changed and heightened. In the process, it becomes beautiful, but "beauty" isn't the choreographer's object—clarity is. And Twyla Tharp does something that people dancing for recreation don't do: she makes a theatrical translation of the music. In "How She Boogalooed It," she doesn't give us the Boogaloo—she gives us something that looks more like snake dancing at top speed. "Alley Oop," "Take a Load Off Your Feet," "Long Tall Texan," and "Catch a Wave" are based as much on the lyrics as on the music, and include several obvious, Broadway-style jokes. In "Papa Ooh Mau Mau," the dancers mime smoking pot and freaking out. When the music isn't interesting enough, it's speeded up or two tracks are run side by side. We do get a long way from the school prom. The spontaneity and naturalness of the dances are a marvelous illusion, a secret of professional style. Everyone has had the experience in the theatre of the happy occurrence—some fantastically accurate inflection or bit of punctuation, so like a moment in life we think it couldn't happen again. Twyla Tharp's choreography is full of such moments that do happen again. In *Deuce Coupe*, I think of Nina Wiener's freak-out or Glenn White landing in fifth position right on the *pow!* of the downbeat in "Wouldn't It Be Nice." (The surprise is partly that you hadn't seen him jump.)

Deuce Coupe makes rather a special point of ballet versus pop dancing. In this, it's an extension of *The Bix Pieces*, which was composed two years ago for the Tharp company's formal Paris début. *The Bix Pieces*, named for Bix Beiderbecke, is based on jazz-band dance music of the 1920s. The dancing is a moody synthesis of the tap-toe-baton-acrobatic routines that millions of American children have been heirs to, and in the course of the work a narrator informs us, "The fundamental concepts of dance are few, but the stylistic appraisal of these concepts can produce infinite combinations and appearances. For example, 'slap, ball, change' is 'chassé' in ballet, or 'slap' ('tendu'), 'ball' ('piqué'), 'change' ('plié')." This is demonstrated, and the narrator goes on to say, "So, you see, all things can be profoundly and invisibly related, exactly and not at all the same." *Deuce Coupe* deals in a similar technical paradox—sometimes at too great a length. For example, it has a ballerina (Erika Goodman) performing a classical solo virtually all through the piece. Sometimes she's alone onstage and sometimes she's the eye of the hurricane, but she never stops dancing, and since there are other ballet dancers on the stage, I have sometimes wondered why she's there. She is eternal, the others are temporal? But I have never wished Miss Goodman off the stage while watching her on it. I like what she does, and she's doing it this season with unusual beauty. Erika Goodman is chubby and neckless, with big legs that wave in disproportionately high extensions. With her large-scale gesture and demonstrative warmth, she's becoming a baby Struchkova. But, like most of the Joffrey girls, she lacks something as a classical stylist, and her role—a taxing one, which consists of the ballet vocabulary performed alphabetically—is so Tharpian in conception that it really doesn't resemble classical ballet enchaînements at all. What we see in her random provocative movements is a parallel to the dislocated, familiar-unfamiliar movements that dominate the main action of the ballet. The two dance forms—ballet and popular—remain technically distinguishable but become stylistically fused. It's a Tharpian fusion, and the didactic point of *The Bix Pieces* disappears. All things are no longer so invisibly related.

There's a sense in which *Deuce Coupe* would be better if the Joffrey members of the cast were better classical dancers. Twyla Tharp has asked a lyricism of them, and a precision of épaulement, that they can't consistently supply. Yet in "Wouldn't It Be Nice," the most exhilarating of the Beach Boys songs, the steps are entirely classical, and this is the number I love best. From the opening port de bras to the quietly held preparations in fifth—held so long that when the jetés into attitude front start popping like molecules around the stage the pressure appears to blow them into the air—there is a tender mystery to the dancing which seems equal to the best of *The Bix Pieces* and to the best classical ballet I know. *Deuce Coupe* makes the Joffrey dancers look human (at the first performance I had trouble recognizing most of them); it rescues them from the curse of pseudo-ballet and gives them back their natural grace of movement. They look very much as they might have looked as children—which is right for the preteen, presexual world that the ballet invokes—and they are magically divested of their customary hard-sell performing style. Besides Goodman and White, the Joffrey dancers who shine most vividly in this new light are (in order of their appearance): Rebecca Wright, William Whitener, Beatriz Rodriguez, Larry Grenier, Gary Chryst, Donna Cowen, and Eileen Brady.

As for the Tharp dancers, their stage personalities are so alive that we can follow them like characters in the Sunday comics. Twyla Tharp herself, with her sorrowful-baleful semihallucinated stare, is the Krazy Kat of the bunch. Sara Rudner is the Mysterious Lady (her *Deuce Coupe* solo "Got to Know the Woman" is ironically seductive, like an adolescent's vision of sexuality), and Rose Marie Wright, the "Long Tall Texan," has an instantaneous impact on the audience—it applauds her on sight. Kenneth Rinker, the lone male, is a brotherly, somewhat taciturn corduroy-cap type, and the two other girls, Isabel Garcia-Lorca and Nina Wiener, have a fashion-model elegance. The group dancing of the Tharp company suggests a federation of individuals, and you can see the same kind of freedom in the group dancing of *Deuce Coupe*. But the restlessness and pain of American children are in it, too. The end of the ballet—the long, slow crescendo of tossing arms, lunges in plié, and backward bourrées on pointe, with here and there a fall to the floor—is half truth, half myth. It sums up a kind of schmaltzy romanticism that young people love to wrap themselves in, and it is absolutely true to our experience of their world. The crescendo is ingeniously stage-managed, gaining might not by mass but by intensity, like a hum that gets louder, and it ends in a masterstroke—a freeze-pose blackout into silhouette. The cliché is the only possible schmaltz-climax. Then, gradually, it loosens, Miss Goodman takes a few hops forward, and *Deuce Coupe* continues somewhere in space as the curtain falls.

Deuce Coupe is fresh and exciting because it is closer to its source in popular culture than most pop or "jazz" ballets ever care to be. The music is the kind of music for which a dance idiom already exists. The choreography is in part a parody of that idiom, but it is authentic. In two other ballets in the Joffrey repertory, Eliot Feld's *Jive* and Arpino's *Trinity*, the music is concert-hall jazz and evangelical rock, respectively: two forms for which the dancing has to be invented, and in both ballets the choreography is more synthetic than the music. *Jive* is set to Morton Gould's "Derivations for Clarinet and Jazz Band"—the same score that Balanchine used for a piece called *Clarinade*, which is remembered solely because it was the first ballet he created at Lincoln Center. The music doesn't work any better for Feld, who transforms it into a tight, cheerless, and ambivalent pastiche of the fifties, the period of Jerome Robbins wearing sneakers. It ends with the dancers lurching at the audience and crying "Jive!" *Jive* (a forties title) represents a good choreographer working below his form. *Trinity* represents a bad choreographer working at the very top of *his*. The work is all big jumps and running lifts, and it is consumed with the fake piety of the beads-and-amulets era. At the end, the dancers place peace candles all over the stage. In the context of these two ballets, and of the Joffrey repertory generally, *Deuce Coupe* is a masterpiece. Not only is it musically sound and poetically convincing—its emotions are the kind that make civilized contact in the theatre possible. It doesn't bludgeon us for a response; when it throws out a manipulative net, it does so with a grin. It doesn't pretend that we share the life it depicts, or make us feel that we should. It is completely objective, but, beyond that (*Jive* is objective, too, and dead), it respects its material. *Deuce Coupe* is an adult ballet about kids.

—*October 29, 1973*

Ailey and *Revelations*

When a choreographer can't follow up on a great success, it may be because he is not sure what success is made of. The Alvin Ailey City Center Dance Theatre has its one big hit in *Revelations*. It is always taking on new works and revivals, yet, year in and year out, nothing tops *Revelations*. Nothing that seems to have been intended to top it even gets halfway. And as *Revelations* looms in its increasingly solitary splendor, it becomes something that its admirers want to stay away from—a superhit that will win ovations and encores even when, as in this past season at the City Center, it isn't very well danced. At one time, *Revelations* was plausibly the signature work of the Ailey company, standing for what Ailey and his dancers could do best. Now it might almost be taken for a fluke. All the attempts to repeat its success have loaded the repertory with failures based on similar material. But the special power of *Revelations* doesn't come from its material, strong as that is; it comes from the structural tension and driving rhythm that Ailey built into the piece in the years when he was still working on the things that craftsmen care about. Ailey either doesn't realize or doesn't care anymore what makes *Revelations* so popular, and the work he now does is marked by an incredible inconsistency and slackness of design. However, Ailey is remarkably consistent in trying to capitalize on *Revelations* as if it were a *formula* success.

The bric-a-brac tavern set of *Masekela Langage* is unusually detailed even for Ailey, and the dancers lounging around in it, snapping at each other and playing South African jazz by Hugh Masekela on the jukebox, look as if they had specific characters to project. There is Sara Yarborough as a short-tempered teenager, Judith Jamison as a faraway Tennessee Williams–type lady, and Kelvin Rotardier as a debonair bum-about-town. *Masekela* might have ranked with *Blues Suite* (which it resembles) as Ailey's best work next to *Revelations*, but stylistic crudity and lack of coordination destroy it. Its big failure is that the dance monologues go on too long without developing characterizations. Rotardier is a mime of great elegance, in a class with Francisco Moncion and Derek Rencher. Ailey has given him lots of yardage here but no ball, and Rotardier can't keep *Masekela* from collapsing in the middle of his solo. Nor can Jamison pick up the pieces. Because of some extra poundage gained since last spring, Jamison did not dance effectively this season. There wasn't much for her to dance. Jamison has become a star because the audience thinks she should be one. None of the roles that have been fashioned for her really lets her deliver. In *Cry*, the nearest thing she has to a vehicle, Ailey doesn't use her rich humor or her exuberant shimmy style until the last moment, and until that moment she is forced to do an unconscionable amount of barge-toting and bale-lifting. (Some of the blackface stereotypes Ailey deals in would be jeered at if they came from a white choreographer.) The best dancing of the season was done by the talented Sara Yarborough, and *Rainbow 'Round My Shoulder* was worth seeing for her. This is another of the folk-song ballets and one of the better ones, although it can't be sat through very easily. The work songs of the chain gang were choreographed by Donald McKayle, and if you find the idea of chain-gang choreography repulsive you'd better not go. The prisoners come sidestepping on like a line of chorus boys. Within this gauzy frame there are a few sober vignettes about convicts and their dream woman, and one or two unforced moments of sweetness and pain, mostly contributed by Miss Yarborough.

The McKayle piece dates from 1959 and looks much older, as do portions of *Revelations*, which was first presented in 1960. The idea of combining folk songs or Negro spirituals with American concert-dance choreography wasn't new; the combination had been used by generations of dance recitalists. If you've ever seen one of those "Songs of My People" recitals, with dancers doubling themselves up to "Go Down, Moses" or earnestly miming their way through "He's Got the Whole World in His Hands," you know what the perils of the genre are. Black choreographers still embraced the expressionistic style at a time when white choreographers were abandoning it. Merce Cunningham and his descendants felt no need of that style, just as novelists of the fifties and sixties felt no need to write like Hemingway or Steinbeck. But the black choreographers did have a need for a "strong" statement of a "strong" theme, and they held on to the dance technique of the 1930s for the same reason many white choreographers were relinquishing it—because it was respectable. The dancing in the opening scenes of *Revelations* is neither fine art nor vernacular art, it's "cultured" folk art; and although I respond to the almost symbiotic attachment between this kind of movement and this kind of music, I can't escape feeling that the music is being subtly undermined, if not exactly cheapened. When I see that familiar pyramidal cluster, with the women planted straddle position and the many hands clasping and splaying to heaven while the choir sings "I Been 'Buked and I Been Scorned," I don't believe it. Images made of Dynel sackcloth don't fit the simple majesty of the song. The wide plié and the upward-straining gestures are, however, basic to a kind of tacky sincerity that is the only strength of cultured folk art. Genuine folk art shocks; cultured folk art appeals. There's a very appealing duet to "Fix Me, Jesus"—the best Ailey has ever made. The central image is of a woman braced and struggling to rise tall on a man's outspread thighs (plié stance plus yearning arabesque). In a good performance, it is clear that he is a preacher and she the soul he's trying to save, but *save* isn't the same as *fix*. Ailey has no imagery for such diction; his technique has to say "save." In the performance I saw this season, Dana Sapiro's high ballet extensions conveyed Ailey's point forcefully and she deserved every bit of her applause, but I feel it is worth pointing out that a great song like "Fix Me, Jesus" suffers a loss of power in proportion to its success as a dance number; it loses the humility of its sentiment as well as the precision of its utterance.

"I Want to Be Ready" is Dudley Williams in a series of perfectly pitched and controlled body lifts from the floor. He draws himself up and sinks back, never coming fully erect, never finding rest, and he finishes in a blazing star-pointed pose on one knee. This is dance metaphor on the level of "Fix Me, Jesus," but this time I find nothing wrong in it. It tells the story the song tells, and adds to it, because Williams's technique transfigures him and becomes, seemingly, the result of the religious idealism of the song—he *is*

ready. There is a patness in the number I don't care for, but
I can't pick it apart. The only trouble with "I Want to Be
Ready" is that by the time it comes on I have seen something better than what this studio-fashioned technique can
produce, even at its best, and that's the dancing in the bap-
tism sequence, "Wading in the Water." The staging is a little *faux-naïf*—blue and white veils stretched low across the
floor and shaken, white streamers, white netting, white
gowns, and one big umbrella draped in white—but it hardly
matters when Jamison is stepping through those waves and
undulating her torso, and Rotardier and Yarborough are
doing their forward-and-backward slow pelvic walk (and
their one lovely burst as the walk changes to a skip). There
aren't many times when one sits before the Ailey dancers
and wonders, How do they do it? This is one of those
times. The movement looks inimitable and untaught, like
the perky little strut downstage and up that is done in the
last two numbers—"You May Run Home" and "Rocka My
Soul in the Bosom of Abraham."

That casual, loose style hasn't been cultivated since the
decline of tap-dancing, and I know of no black choreographer who is cultivating it now. Ailey hasn't in years choreographed a gesture that looks colloquial or hip. His
pantomime, which once seemed a fascinating private language used by his dancers, has become decorative chatter,
done for us, not for them. Compare the stylized fight scene
in *Masekela Langage* with any of several rough incidents in
Blues Suite. In the former, the dancers appear to be always
looking over their shoulders, to see if we're watching them.
In the latter, they don't give a damn. There seem to be
fewer jokes, too, with less point to them. Nothing matches
the moment in *Revelations* when Ailey reverses the effects of
the polished, conscientiously strained, effortlessly effortful

style of movement by having the women turn their backs to us, go into their straddle stance, and slowly, slowly, fanning themselves the while, sit down on stools. That slow, heavy squat is good and rude, but Ailey seems to have lost interest in how people really move. There is no black colloquial dance in the theatre today. Most black choreographers are content to work in the received idioms of thirties-style expressionistic concert dance. Their forerunners aren't Bill Robinson or Buddy Bradley or Josephine Baker, or even Katherine Dunham, but Martha Graham and Doris Humphrey and Charles Weidman and, in Alvin Ailey's case, Lester Horton. One large reason for Ailey's success is that he has known how to profit from the gradual absorption of this generation's methods by Broadway. He is much more credible as the descendant of those choreographers who took over Broadway musicals in the forties than he is as a promulgator of the Horton technique. Expressionistic concert dance became respectable in Broadway musicals, as respectable as ballet. When choreographers began directing shows, the dance technique and the musical became more or less fused, and Ailey found that he was able to make his thirties-style religious dance suite as entertaining as a musical comedy. I never saw the original *Revelations* of 1960, but the printed program for its suggests that, in content, it did not greatly differ from the version we know today, except for the final section, which then included "Precious Lord," "Waters of Babylon," and "Elijah Rock." By 1962, these had been discarded in favor of the present selections—"The Day Is Past and Gone" and "Rocka My Soul." "You May Run Home" was inserted later, but "Sinner Man," originally a solo, had become a trio by 1962. It's in these numbers, plus "Wading in the Water," that Ailey's choreography breaks out of the church-basement dance-recital mold and attains the precision and showmanship that make *Revelations* a hit. When, to "The Day Is Past and Gone," the girls start coming on with their stools and floppy hats and palm-leaf fans, each girl wearing a long yellow gown that suggests the street dresses of the thirties, the heavy tent skirts and technique-laden dance movement of the opening numbers seem far away.

But all the scene-setting and music shuffling wouldn't have meant much without the tight organization. The original *Revelations* was forty-five minutes long. Now there isn't a wasted moment in the entire piece. The outline it has is that of a beautiful onrolling wave, rising to little crests of excitement and breaking just in time, or unfurling long climaxes that smash with an accumulated intensity. The "Rocka My Soul" finale used to leave audiences dizzy with happiness; now it—and sometimes the whole ballet—makes them dizzy with anticipation. Ailey keeps adding dancers to his finale, and the piece has become too much like a Broadway show, with too many dancers onstage punching their spirits too high. I think the audience lavishes its emotion on *Revelations* because it hasn't got anyplace else to put it. Ailey is a pop choreographer who no longer seems to train himself to the efficiency standards of popular art. He has made a few other pieces that look like Broadway shows, but they don't have the controlled energy of good entertainment, and his nonpop pieces are hopeless—all those overlong, attenuated lyrical ballets that seem to be taking place underwater. The boringly even rhythm and lack of tension are weakening the dancers, and Ailey doesn't have many good dancers to begin with. (He doesn't have one male dancer who can turn well in "Sinner Man.") The Ailey company is pressing its luck. It's loading up on religious and secular song suites, feeding its audience with a particular kind of material when all that matters is how that material—or *any* material—is assembled. With musicals slipping badly in recent years, the Ailey has been drawing a lot of people who think of it as a higher substitute for Broadway. They find what they are looking for in only one piece. It doesn't take them long to discover that *Revelations* is the higher substitute for the Ailey.

— *January 7, 1974*

Cunningham at Westbeth

It has been a fine if somewhat reclusive season for Merce Cunningham and his company, who are now in the midst of a series of performances at the Cunningham studio in Westbeth, which has a seating capacity of about seventy. Reservations are absolutely necessary and early arrival is recommended. The performance generally does not run more than seventy-five minutes, and there are no intermissions. Various sound accompaniments are provided, but, as is the custom with this company, they bear no relation to the dancing. On a Sunday evening recently, John Cage read a deranged version of portions of Thoreau's *Journals*, in a voice that sounded like Vincent Price performing in Kabuki. The only aural gaffe occurred during one of Cunningham's solos; as he strolled about shaking his wrists, a tape of a talk-show conversation about impeachment was played. It made Cunningham appear to be reacting to the remarks. The sound on other evenings has ranged from pleasant to tolerable, and its pitch seldom rises above a murmur.

Cunningham's hands are like chords of music; full articulation flows straight to the electric extremities. He really does seem to have more in his little finger than most dancers have in their whole bodies. And the diversity and specificity of nuance of which his body is capable, after more than thirty-five years of professional dancing, are amazing. His performing this season has been limited mostly to quiet solos of great tension and delicacy, though I recall vividly one burst of allegro when he danced against the group in a different rhythm. The solo I mentioned is called *Loops*; another is just called *Solo* but is commonly referred to as "the animal solo" because of a passage in which Cunningham seems to turn by degrees into a furry beast. No obviously representational gestures are made. Cunningham seems to get *inside* the animal and reproduce its senses in different states of consciousness. Nor does he lose his humanity; he could be an old man or a dreaming baby.

Because Cunningham choreography dissolves conventional stage space, it is best seen not in theatres but in big, open rooms. I also prefer it at close range. The Lepercq Space at the Brooklyn Academy is a fine location for a Cunningham dance, but there the audience, seated on opposite sides of the dance floor, was often forced to look through one dance to see another. At the Westbeth studio, the audience occupies a narrow margin along one wall, and it's easier to hold on to simultaneous dances when they're spread out in front of you. Like the Styrofoam molds that cushion appliances in custom-built packing cases, this grand, spacious room, its floor an expanse of inviolate maple (visitors must remove shoes before entering), its high ceiling hung with stage lights, its row of windows giving onto a skyline view, seems to contain the dances in their pristine beauty. *TV Rerun* and *Landrover*, two of Cunningham's recent works, had largely escaped me when I first saw them performed onstage at the Academy. In the studio they were both ravishing.

So far, no new works are being presented this season. Instead, Cunningham puts together sections of some of his recent pieces, changing the order from week to week. The performances are billed as "Events" and given numbers. That Sunday was Event No. 95 (Event No. 1 took place in Vienna in 1964), and it consisted of parts of *Canfield*, *Changing Steps*, *Signals*, and *Solo*. I regret the absence of Robert Morris's lighting design for *Canfield* and Richard Nelson's for *Signals*, which were among the most beautiful and ingenious of late years, but even out of the theatre *Canfield* generates its peculiar nervous force. The force hasn't a chance to collect, as it does in the theatre; already we are into the various duets and small groups of *Changing Steps*, performed two or three at a time. The dances are full of odd happenings (and odd steps, a couple of which seem based on *Giselle*). Two girls face-to-face do a solemn wigwag with squared elbows. A girl sits on a boy's back and remains seated as he rolls over. Later, the same girl (Valda Setterfield, who looks like a Van Dongen lady) is hilarious trying to interrupt or join a couple in a maniacal stomping dance. There is a pause as Cunningham completes *Solo*, which he had begun during *Canfield*. The dance is made almost wholly of tiny, slightly twitchy movements and stillnesses too active to be poses. Lying on his side, he makes one or two pawlike passes around his head, then another. Suddenly alert, he stares for a long, suspended moment into the forest. The room is in complete silence. Beyond the windows, which rattle in the wind, a helicopter passes.

The mysterious drama of this dance is unique in the Cunningham repertory at the moment. There are often implied situations and relationships in the dances the company does, but none that have a dramatic impact. Incidents aren't stressed; the dancers don't use that kind of timing. One is entertained solely by the formal values of dancing—by what Cunningham has described as "the passage of movement from moment to moment in a length of time." Those who aren't disposed toward this dry sort of interest probably shouldn't risk a night at Westbeth, but those who get pleasure from the sheer physical act of dancing and from its cultivation by experts will find their pleasure taking an endless variety of forms, and several times in the course of an evening, they may even be moved to ecstasy.

Cunningham's choreography has no external subject, and as an object it removes itself irrevocably and more swiftly than dancing that is set to music—music is a powerful fixative and memory aid. Although its basic vocabulary comes from classical ballet and its style is more precise than that of most ballet choreography, the dancing is by classical standards nonsequential. It faces in all directions. It does not draw toward and away from climaxes. At first, it seems to have no markers that pass the eye smoothly along. But soon the sense of it as a series of growing actions becomes deeply absorbing. Individual dancers begin to fascinate and can be studied like progress charts. The present company includes many new or newish dancers, among them two excellent boys, Chris Komar and Robert Kovich, who are sharply complementary. None of the girls have yet arrived in a class with Susanna Hayman-Chaffey, a magnificent dancer, whose look of luscious contentment in impossible positions never fails to astonish me. It is she who consoles me for the loss of Sandra Neels and the irreplaceable Carolyn Brown.

Performers like this, and choreography that attempts to rid dancing of familiarity, dullness, and inertia, antagonize some people. The company recently gave a lecture-demonstration at Town Hall. As we watched the dancers going through some new virtuosic combinations, an irritated voice called out, "We came here to see dancing. When are you gonna *dance*?" Cunningham has lost none of his power.

—*April 1, 1974*

The Blue Glass Goblet,
and After

Martha Graham has a gift for utterance, and now that she no longer dances, audiences are responding with renewed excitement to her eloquence as a public speaker. Her appearance onstage to introduce her company on its opening night at the Mark Hellinger Theatre was the high point of the evening and the season's most glamorous occasion. Her delivery is casual but precise; she seems to speak thoughts that have just come into her mind, but many of them obviously have been formed from a lifetime's meditation and are almost as well known as the passages she loves to quote from T. S. Eliot or St.-John Perse or the Church Fathers. "Theatre is a verb before it is a noun, an act before it is a place," she tells us, in her disconcertingly lazy, musical little voice, and although she also tells a lot of jokes (with enviable wit and timing), it is upon these philosophical heights that she places us for our view of her own work. Unfortunately, Graham's theatre these days is all too often a noun before it is a verb.

"Freedom to a dancer means only one thing—discipline," she also says, and one sometimes feels that she chose a dancer's life because of the severity of its discipline. It was the way of a puritan, and, at Graham's moment in history, it was also the way of an artist. Dancing, the domain of the frivolous, needed to be reshaped; the pull of gravity could not be denied; and discipline had to be revealed to the audience as a sign of the dancer's new vitality and her new seriousness. Under Graham's command, dancers now did onstage what they customarily did only in the studio—struggled, wasted themselves, fell, and rose again. Effort was not concealed, it was dramatized, and although the sense of toil in dancing was not Graham's invention, the sense of its drama was. Self-discipline in the dancer is spiritual as well as physical; Graham, most powerfully among her contemporaries, was able to relate that fact to the expressionist movement then taking hold of the American stage. In Graham Theatre, as purely and outstandingly American an artifact as Eugene O'Neill Theatre or Robert Edmond Jones Theatre, the drama within became a dance drama and the dancer became generically a tragic heroine.

But the tragic heroine is also a triumphant heroine. Implicit in the rigor of her self-discipline is the certainty of her reward—self-discovery. No Graham heroine dies unillumined. The difference between her and the fated heroines of nineteenth-century ballet—a Giselle or an Odette—is that the Graham heroine possesses, herself, the key to her mystery. She does not entrust it to the hero; she herself must unlock the inner door. In a Graham ballet, this is precisely what happens. The heroine, discovered at her life's supreme point of crisis, summons her forces, resolves her dilemma, and moves into the light. The arc of the narrative rises upward, sometimes looping backward to gather up evidence from the past before reaching its apex, which is the moment of illumination. On this moment the curtain falls. We always leave the heroine a step ahead of the point at which we found her. Clytemnestra, at the start of the action, has already died. In the Underworld, she meditates, relives her past, and pursues its meaning to an ultimate acceptance of her position among the dead. Like Jocasta (in *Night Journey*) and St. Joan (in *Seraphic Dialogue*), she must understand why she is where she is. The outcome of the tragedy is upbeat, and although the illumination, in the instance of Jocasta, is unbearable, it does constitute a victory. If one were to adopt a maxim for Graham Theatre, it would be the inscription on Apollo's shrine at Delphi: "Know Thyself." Even Medea, the blackest of Graham's heroines, by extinguishing her humanity discovers the essence of her being. In *Cave of the Heart*, she becomes the evil she feeds upon, and in the perfection of her translation (and its brilliant realization on the stage) hers may be the biggest victory of them all.

The tragic-triumphant heroine is a relatively late development in Graham's theatre, and I think it postdates the period of her greatest work. In the repertory the company is now showing at the Hellinger, that period is represented by *Letter to the World* (1940–41), *Deaths and Entrances* (1943), and *Appalachian Spring* (1944). In all three of these works, the dancing has that mysterious spiritual force that appears to arise from the discipline of Graham technique, but the heroine, who possesses more of it than anybody else, does not yet know the meaning of her inner treasure, and we in turn are not sure she will discover it before the curtain comes down. There is a looseness, an uncalculated tension, an openness to life in these works that is lacking in the so-called Greek period that began in the late forties and, for many people, epitomizes the theatre of Martha Graham. Perhaps the "Greek" works are esteemed because of the

grandeur of the Greek legends, but they're all a bit Hollywood, especially *Clytemnestra*, which is often spoken of as
Graham's masterpiece. (It's merely her longest work, with a
prologue and two acts—a Graham blockbuster.) Graham,
who made the dancer's self-discipline part of the poetic language of the theatre—who put effort on the stage as a posi-
tive theatrical idea—seems to have felt the need to establish
a dramatic corollary to her technique of movement, and
those moments of illumination and critical "instants" of
self-recognition began to proliferate until they became the
stock framing device of Graham drama.

The affirmative endings of *Letter to the World* and *Deaths
and Entrances* and *Appalachian Spring* are freely arrived at,
but already, in *Deaths and Entrances*, one sees the beginning
of the turn toward the symbolic and the second-rate that
was completed in the fifties. At the end of this long, marvelously charged, complex work, the heroine all at once decides to move a prop, a blue glass goblet, which she has
been toying with for the better part of an hour. The move is
entirely consistent with the woman's frenzied, impulsive
character as we have watched it develop through her dancing, but the telltale bit of symbolism gives the audience a
chance to perceive what it might not have noticed already—
"See! She has the courage to change!" And in her later
pieces Graham increasingly "explained" her movement to
the audience by further externalizing its implications, so
that we could turn to one another and say, "See, it means
this." In 1948, Stark Young could still write of Graham's
choreography, "We have the sense that, no matter what
has been left out, nothing has entered a composition that
has not grown into it organically." But by the fifties what
was growing organically into Graham's compositions was
Noguchi's props, and much as I admire Noguchi, particu-

larly the Noguchi of Graham's theatre, I find all the symbol-making a little deadening to sit through season after season. The ballets are tight and dry—exquisitely shaped and adamantly sealed. It is difficult for us to evaluate them, even with new casts, because so little of the drama can be affected by the different emphases of this or that dancer. Since the work "means" only one thing (what it says in the program), since it has been molded toward a predetermined end, the audience responds not to its moment-by-moment power but to the smoothness of its trajectory, which we observe from a distance. We aren't drawn mentally into the action, as we are in Graham's best pieces. We stand at the corner and wait for it to catch up.

Of course, even second-rate Graham may be immensely enjoyable, and I include in this category three other pieces in the Hellinger repertory that I usually enjoy—*Errand into the Maze* (based on the myth of the Minotaur); *Seraphic Dialogue*, which, though not one of the "Greek" numbers, can be classified among the more mechanically contrived Graham works; and *Diversion of Angels*, which has no plot but does have a gooey layer of desperately acted-out and dearly cherished emotion poured over the dances by the company. (It's good choreography; why can't it just be danced instead of hugged to death?) One clue to the inferiority of these first two pieces is that the heroine's big moment is not really there for an audience to see. Although I sometimes imagine I have seen it in *Errand into the Maze*, all that happens on-stage is that the heroine suddenly finds the strength to clobber her antagonist. Where this strength comes from is not explained. The transfiguration of Joan of Arc in *Seraphic Dialogue* is a plot event rather than a dance event, and so is the "rebirth" of Clytemnestra. The complicated dénouement of the *Oresteia* is too much to handle without words, and in

Graham's version Apollo and Athena preside at a tribunal that decides nothing. When Clytemnestra seizes the black scepters from Hades and dances out along the forecurtain, we're meant, I'm sure, to see that her spirit has attained peace at last, but Graham has no way of showing what she would like to show—that Clytemnestra's peace comes not from the vindication she sought but from a realization of her own guilt and complicity in the bloody system of retributive justice. In the latter-day Graham Theatre, it often seems that movement is trying, and failing, to take the place of words; in the epochal Graham Theatre of the forties, movement expressed what no words could.

The decline in the repertory is linked inescapably to Graham's own physical decline as a dancer. I don't think she began preferring props to dances, or grew rigid in her thinking, or became literary by choice; my point is that her physical technique, which once buoyed her through a series of theatrical adventures such as the world had never seen, was eroded with the years, and this erosion forced her to seek other means of expression and inevitably to invent on a lower level. This is not a tragedy; Graham's lower level would often be another choreographer's stratosphere, and one lesson the present repertory teaches us is that this most imitated of modern choreographers has seldom been imitated in the right things. Others have ripped off her style of gesture, her technical discoveries, her manner of presentation, her subjects, even her hairdos, but very few of her predators have learned to organize space and time as well as she has or trained themselves to build suspense abstractly, as she does in such a piece as *Deaths and Entrances*.

Possibly the most damaging aspect of the decline in her theatre has been the intrusion of all the clanging affirmations and moments of truth. Compare, for example, *El Pen-*

itente (1940), a gentle, sunny "minor" classic, with the Silver and Bronze Age "masterpieces," and you'll see the difference between a secure work of art, asking nothing, insisting on nothing, and a series of post-Victorian exhortations designed for the moral enrichment of mankind. Perhaps the temptation to exhort was always present in Graham, and I've suggested that a kind of doctrinal heroism is a special attribute of her technique. I'd also suggest that their invigorating moral atmosphere is what makes a lot of the second-rate Graham works so appealing; more than one observer has felt himself rising on the yeastiness of their good intentions. It's almost like being in church. But this "exalting" aspect of Graham is one, I think, that we should avoid enjoying too heartily. It builds up our worship of a gone world and keeps us from seeing the things in her art that are really liberating and contemporary. At times, Graham presents herself not as the first of the moderns but as the last of the Victorians. *Letter to the World* and *Deaths and Entrances* and *Appalachian Spring* are all views of the nineteenth century, but they're distanced views; the ballets themselves are of their own time, and some of the things in them may strike us, even today, as avant-garde. Of course, they've all been stolen blind, but this hasn't made them stale. The really amazing thing about them is that their freshness of feeling, which seems to come from behind the dances like a light, is still there after thirty years.

The only answer I can give to those who ask how much these pieces lose by not having Graham in them is that *Appalachian Spring* loses least. *Letter* and *Deaths* are portraits of woman as artist; *Appalachian Spring* is a portrait of woman as wife. Long ago, when Graham was still dancing the part of the bride, I thought she had miscast herself, and when Ethel Winter and then Phyllis Gutelius took the role over, I felt sure of it. Gutelius does it now with William Carter as the husband, David Hatch Walker as the preacher, and Janet Eilber in the mysteriously effective role of the pioneer woman. All of them are excellent; it's the cast to see. Gutelius fills out her role with suggestions of things that are not explicit in the choreography. She's refined and vulnerable—a city-bred girl, one feels, who has had servants, and the mother-to-be of children who will surely die. Nothing in her past has prepared her for the frontier except the necessity of making so hard a choice and the courage to see it through. Gutelius also does the principal sister in *Deaths and Entrances*, with more range than depth. In those powerful plunges into madness, she doesn't go down very far. But then this was unquestionably Graham's greatest role, and one can still contemplate the sheer size of it with awe, even though, in its present version, it seems to have been deliberately shrunken in scale. The roles of the two other sisters, taken by Eilber and Diane Gray, seem to have been scaled down proportionately. They're now conventional villainesses, like Cinderella's stepsisters.

There are works of Graham I no longer care to see, because of the flattening out of certain details. Medea does not feed the red ribbon into her mouth, as Graham used to do, but folds it into her bodice, and the famous solo looks altered in other respects. This was another role in which Graham tore up the stage, and the one Graham performance of which I have the most vivid recollection. The dancers who now do the role aren't able to extract the right dance values from it, and so miss its spirit. However much they squeeze and contort themselves, they never seem really pulled together inside and can't work up much more than a vague, catlike spitting and clawing, whereas Graham aimed and struck like a cobra, all in one piece. Graham as Medea didn't spill over into melodrama, yet the younger dancers always do. Because they don't have this gift for wholeness of emphasis in movement, they can't hold on to the seriousness of Medea. What would be called integrity in an actress is in a dancer a secondary virtue. Many of the Graham dancers have it, but not all of them have it as dancers.

Although Graham's program notes are almost as famous as her dances, sometimes it's advisable not to read them. The program suggests that *Deaths and Entrances* is about the Brontës, but "Emily Brontë" is really a Grahamesque metaphor for the anarchic female spirit struggling in a prison of cultural stereotypes. The four characters of *Embattled Garden*, a straight-faced suburban sex comedy, are identified as Adam and Eve and Lilith and the Stranger (i.e., the Devil); this throws off the dancers as well as the audience. But I'm afraid there's no getting away from the program in *Chronique*. With its St.-John Perse text read aloud from the orchestra pit, the piece is one long, bloviating program note. *Chronique*, a revision of last year's *Mendicants of Evening*, is one of two new works Graham is presenting this spring, and in it she seems to be giving us not so much a ballet as her ideas for one. It's like a living enactment of a page from *The Notebooks of Martha Graham*, the volume published last year to the sorrow and confusion of many of her admirers. Graham's mind is infinitely more fascinating than this anthology of scholarly jottings suggests, and the publication, together with *Chronique*, unhappily reinforces the present-day image of Graham as that of a bookish lady who puts on dances. Visually, *Chronique* is a swirl of draperies and fragmentary choreographic studies. It's not bad to look at, but it never comes off the page.

Graham's mind has been revealed to us first through her great dances, then through the ingenious but ever more restrictive means she found when her body could no longer speak for her mind. The Graham company does not contain Martha Graham, but, like a giant picture puzzle, it does contain images of her, and one must seek them out. Trying to authenticate those images amid all the distortions of the revived works and the compromises of the later ones is a hazardous job, and Graham, who will be eighty next week, is still choreographing. But for the final, authentic image of Martha Graham it is we and not Graham who bear the responsibility.

—April 22, 1974

Royal Jitters

With the Western world passing through a crisis of leadership, it hardly seems worthwhile to exaggerate the perils of the Royal Ballet under the direction of Kenneth MacMillan. Three times in the last three years, London has been agitated by a MacMillan production on which, we were told, the fate of the company depended. The first of these, *Anastasia*, was liberally mocked, but I didn't find it nearly as awful as the word from London had led me to expect. The MacMillan version of *The Sleeping Beauty* was so despised that the company hasn't taken it on its current American tour. And now we have the controversial *Manon*, opening the Royal's season at the Met. It is neither as good nor as bad as advance reports had suggested, and its smooth mediocrity is alarming only because it seems to derive from a fear of offending public opinion. Once the company recovers from its attack of the frights, it should survive *Manon* very well.

At its worst, as in Act III, *Manon* is like a bad opera. The chorus jumps into its dance, the stars jump into their climactic point-of-death duet. Irrelevant characters, inexplicably lingering on from previous drafts of the libretto, get their big chance minutes before the curtain falls. At its best—a pas de trois in Act I, in which Manon is sold by her brother to Monsieur G.M.; the brothel scene in Act II, with its rich collection of variations and group dances—the ballet really does seem to be giving us, in dance terms, some of the mood and tension of Abbé Prévost's story about the luxury prostitute who loved a poor man. Of that love itself, and of its consequences for Des Grieux, the ballet has virtually nothing to say. The several pas de deux for the lovers are the big washouts of the piece—nonsensically pure in form, unvarying in expression. We see a girl; we see her meeting a boy. He dances for her in adagio tempo, then they dance together in the same tempo. A moment later, they do it again. They are separated and come back together. Again they do their dance. The story content in all this is so badly focused that it might as well not be there at all. For some in the audience, and possibly for MacMillan, too, the content of these dances is filled by the performers. On opening night, when Des Grieux introduced himself to Manon, he seemed to be saying, "Madame, I am Anthony Dowell. Notice my turns, my perfect développé into attitude front." And her answer was "If you're Anthony Dowell, I must be Antoinette Sibley. Let's have a Sibley-Dowell pas de deux." And they did.

MacMillan's direction appears to suffer from two kinds of pressure—the need to support a star system with star vehicles and the need to maintain a progressive standard in choreography. Both kinds of pressure operate to destructive effect in *Manon*, because in his anxiety to satisfy public taste, MacMillan has brought them into conflict with his principal obligation, which was to tell a great dramatic story. International trends in story ballets decree that dancing shall replace mime. But in the best examples we have of mimeless drama the dances fill the dramatic purpose of mime; they don't wash the drama away. The audience that long ago stopped looking for literal meaning in dance movement has now stopped looking for *any* meaning. No matter how mechanical and inexpressive the dancing may be, as long as dancing is happening, it's a ballet. If dancing is not happening, it's dumb show, a silent movie, a museum piece. *Manon*, like so many other modern story ballets, panders to this prejudice. Its stars are so busy dancing they haven't time to fill out their characterizations or advance the plot. There's an absurd moment in the third act when Manon is being led by the jailer to his private lair and Des Grieux follows abstractedly along doing slow pirouettes. At least, audiences can't say they haven't seen Dowell (or Wayne Eagling or Rudolf Nureyev) *dance*. Or Sibley dance with him. (Or Jennifer Penney dance with Eagling, or Merle Park with Nureyev.) The big acrobatic pas de deux that brings the ballet to a close has so many running lifts and body flips and catches in the air that old-style, literal minded audiences might well have supposed that Manon dies of overexertion. And they might have wondered why the only bit of sex that occurs in any of the pas de deux is the hint of fellatio with the jailer.

It's the old story: Poverty of Means goes to the ball dressed up as Purity of Expression. We're supposed to be too sophisticated to notice the masquerade or to want anything better even if we do notice it. The cover for this is the theory that everybody knows the story anyway—from Massenet's and Puccini's operas if not from Prévost's novel—and people have paid to see dancing. But I don't know any people who would pay to see meaningless dancing, even if they don't recognize it when they do see it. And if it's true that we all know the story, isn't it likely that we know it because it's a great eternal story that people have never tired of hearing? Surely the pleasure the audience expects to get from a three-act ballet version lies in having *Manon Lescaut* told to it all over again in a new form. MacMillan leaves too much of the story out. He has discovered no means of conveying the sensuality and poverty that Prévost made seem mutually exclusive. Nicholas Georgiadis's basic setting for all three acts is a wall of rags, but this symbolic reminder of the poverty that terrifies Manon so is itself aesthetically appealing. The rags are beautiful, as stage rags always are. And MacMillan gives us nothing of the character of Des Grieux or of his corruption through his passion for Manon. He remains a sweet, innocent boy to the last. Without Des Grieux's fall, the story comes to little more than an account of foolish young people who wanted nice things.

The Royal fields its star teams with lavish ease. Of the two Manons I saw during the first week, Sibley was the more rapacious, Penney the more touchingly frail. Manon would have been a great role for Sibley if MacMillan hadn't been so timid about characterizing it in dance. Temperamentally, it suits her as well as anything she has done since Titania in *The Dream*, but MacMillan hasn't responded to her gifts as well as he responded to Lynn Seymour's in *Romeo and Juliet* and *Anastasia*. *The Dream* was the ballet in which Ashton launched Sibley's partnership with Dowell. MacMillan pays homage to that partnership in *Manon*; he hasn't analyzed or extended it, and Sibley seems a little imprisoned by her stardom. I can't help wondering what would have happened if the entire role had been choreographed on Penney. The most talented of the Royal's junior ballerinas, Penney is still in that overprolonged nascent stage of development peculiar to so many Royal Ballet dancers. It's time she had a big, custom-built role to make her a big star. Dowell, paraded about in his nothing of a part, looked handsome. Eagling, whose self-assertiveness shatters the Royal mold, did not look lost.

The ballet has been much abused for its music. My ear doesn't cringe unless it is attacked, and it approved the use of Massenet's "Elégie" as the lovers' theme song in three different orchestrations. The score, based on MacMillan's own scenario, is made up of miscellaneous Massenet pieces that include nothing from the opera *Manon*, and succeeds in sounding very much as if Massenet were working on commission for the choreographer—a feat for which MacMillan and his musical collaborators, Leighton Lucas and Hilda Gaunt, deserve congratulations. MacMillan's *Manon* is another in a series of attempts to extort from the nineteenth century the ballets it somehow failed to produce—a series that began with John Cranko's *Eugene Onegin*, set to music by Tchaikovsky which is not in the opera score—and each time I've seen one of these operatic ballets I've been impressed by their triviality in relation to the operas. Musically, the trick is turned, but dramatically there's no contest. Operas are able to encompass much more of the literary works on which they're based than ballets are, and usually, when a ballet succeeds in exploring literary material, rather than just defining it in dance form, it's because the choreographer has re-created the material. MacMillan's first-act trio is one example of this process, and the high point of the brothel scene, admirably set to the Nocturne from *La Navarraise*, is a dance for Manon and eight men—an emblem of her career as a courtesan which triumphantly compresses the repetitious incidents of the novel. MacMillan has also invented a mistress for Lescaut, Manon's brother, and given her two bitterly proud solos, in high contrast to Manon's fresh seductiveness. Many of MacMillan's surprises, though, are restatements of earlier works. *Romeo and Juliet* seems to have lent its marketplace to the opening scene of *Manon*, and Lescaut is very much a Mercutio figure. Act III, with its sad little deportees debarking at the Louisiana penal colony, and its "hallucinations" accompanying the final pas de deux, seems drawn from *Anastasia*.

Of the three full-evening ballets MacMillan has produced so far, *Anastasia* seems to me the best, not so much because of what it achieves as because of what it attempts. In *Romeo*, MacMillan had before him both Leonid Lavrovsky's version for the Bolshoi and Cranko's for the Stuttgart; in *Manon* he is again working à la Cranko. But in *Anastasia* he produced a personal fantasy about a global cataclysm entirely from nothing. I don't think he was being pretentious, and the insults that were showered upon him for missing the mark themselves missed the mark. MacMillan's taste, musical instinct, and technical skill place him first among those British and European choreographers whose careers began in the fifties. *Manon* shows a loss of confidence. The steely bravura of *Anastasia* is missing. But, at forty-four, MacMillan is just entering his maturity, and I think we have a right to expect him to fulfill it.

The Royal's first week also unveiled a friendly *Swan Lake*, shorn of most of the neologisms that disfigured it in the past. Yet again there was a puzzling reticence, a strange modesty, that marred the performance. Merle Park, the first of the Swan Queens, was letter-perfect, musically sound, and gratifyingly unaffected in style. But she wasn't very exciting, and the second act went as if she were determined not to scale heights but to remain humbly in the foothills of the role. As Odile, she brought out her Joan Greenwood personality, but it didn't project. Park has an "unclassical" physique, and in the British view of things she is a soubrette and nothing but a soubrette. I don't agree with this; typecasting may be as much a matter of psychological as of physical conditioning. Jennifer Penney, on the other hand, is one of those ballerinas who has the role of Odette by inheritance. No one can ever have looked more beautiful in the part, more marvelously right in every move—or more fearful of imposing herself on the audience. In the black act, she seemed unsure of herself. She doesn't lack bite, but she does lack something in tenacity. With her "Russian" back and higher-than-high arabesques, she represents a break in the line of ballerina-models that stems from Fonteyn, and the company would do well to encourage her.

The two Siegfrieds I saw, Nureyev with Park and David Wall with Penney, were both extremely pleasing, Nureyev steadily loosening and gearing up his style (and providing Park with deluxe support), and Wall acting and dancing with consistent, full-bodied spontaneity. Ashton's heavenly pas de quatre, which used to be given in Act I, has been moved to Act III, where it naturally becomes the highlight before the big star turn. Two objections: The sets and costumes, by Leslie Hurry, look as if they'd been taken out of cold storage, and the choreography for Act IV, restored to its old patterns, continues to disturb me with its naturalistic details—the kissing that goes on between the two principals, Odette being tugged back from the suicide brink by Siegfried, or being pulled between Siegfried and Von Rothbart. Just as the Count di Luna should never sit down (said G. B. Shaw), Odette should never be caught standing any way except pointe tendue back.

—May 27, 1974

Glimpses of Genius

Mikhail Baryshnikov, the legendary young star of Leningrad's Kirov Ballet, is making his first appearances on this continent this summer, touring in Canada with a contingent of Bolshoi dancers. Baryshnikov became a legend even before he was admitted to the Kirov, in 1967; he was the pupil—the best, many said, and one of the last, as it turned out—of Alexander Pushkin, the great Leningrad teacher who had trained Yuri Soloviev and Rudolf Nureyev. In 1970, the year Pushkin died, Baryshnikov appeared in London, and from the way the London critics threw around the word "genius" I began to get an uncomfortable feeling about him: either he wouldn't live up to his notices or he would so fully justify them that he'd be, as a phenomenon, unrecognizable. True genius doesn't fulfill expectations, it shatters them, and the initial experience of it can be disturbing. Now that I've seen Baryshnikov perform in Montreal, I can't remember what I expected him to be like. Something on the order of Soloviev, I suppose, only smaller, higher, and faster. (That would have been genius enough.) Well, Baryshnikov is all three, but he's unlike anyone else, and he

does things I've never seen any other dancer do. I was con-
founded, and the audiences at the Salle Wilfrid-Pelletier
were, too. Although they gave him ovations, I think they
really didn't get him. Probably they, like me, were bemused
by the purity of Baryshnikov's style. He carries the impeccable to the point where it vanishes into the ineffable. One
can't see where the dazzle comes from. When he walks out
onto the stage, he doesn't radiate—doesn't put the audience
on notice that he's a star. His body, with its short, rounded
muscles, isn't handsome; he's no Anthony Dowell. His head
and hands are large, and his face—pale, with peaked features
and distant eyes—is the face of Petrushka. He attends carefully to his ballerina and appears utterly unprepossessing.
When he dances, the illusion—its size and glow—comes so
suddenly that it takes you by surprise. You think from the
looks of him that he might be a maverick, which would
make him easy to accept, but he doesn't dance like one. Any
hope of idiosyncrasy or impertinence is dashed the instant
he leaves the floor. And yet there's no mistaking his phenomenal gifts. It's obvious that Pushkin has turned out not
the last of a line but a new and unique classical virtuoso.

Baryshnikov is able to perform unparalleled spectacular
feats as an extension of classical rather than character or acrobatic dancing. Lovers of flashy entertainment, of sport, of
raw prowess, may not take to him at once, but lovers of
classical style will go mad. He gets into a step sequence
more quickly, complicates it more variously, and prolongs it
more extravagantly than any dancer I've ever seen. And he
finishes when he wants to, not when he has to. Perhaps his
greatest gift is his sense of fantasy in classical gesture. He
pursues the extremes of its logic so that every step takes on
an unforeseen dimension. His grande pirouette is a rhapsody of swelling volume and displaced weight. He does not

turn; he is turned—spun around and around by the tip of his toe. Like the young prodigy Nadezhda Pavlova, whom the Bolshoi introduced to American audiences last year, Baryshnikov both summarizes and extends the resources of classical expression. The three performances I saw him give in Montreal were of standard pas de deux (two *Nutcrackers* and one *Don Quixote*), and while it would be absurd to judge his range on so short an acquaintance, one can certainly assume that he possesses many qualities he had no chance to display in Montreal. I can believe, for example, that he is the fine actor he's reputed to be, because of the way he altered his style to suit each of the pas de deux. In *The Nutcracker*, he was an image of elfin Mozartean grace; in the *Don Quixote*, he was diabolical, dancing with a livid force. And the dance pictures he produced in these different styles—particularly one of a high, slow jeté passé in which he arched his back at the peak of the jump—will linger long in memory.

His partner in the two *Nutcrackers* was none other than Irina Kolpakova, the Kirov's great prima ballerina, and she also appeared, unannounced and partnered by Nicolai Fadeyechev, in the Gluck *Melody*—one of those wafty adagios-with-a-veil that seem to mean so much (but what?) to the Russians. Kolpakova is the kind of star who does radiate, although when I last saw her, ten years ago, she had nothing like the rosy confidence and direct manner toward the audience that she has now. The lovely legs are as eloquent, the style as correct, the phrasing as musical as ever. Like Baryshnikov, and like her former colleague Natalia Makarova, she dances from a center of mysterious calm, and with an all but invisible attack. A knee injury prevented her from giving us her famous soaring jump in *The Nutcracker*, but she did breathtaking unsupported double pirouettes with arms en couronne.

A word about the company that Baryshnikov and Kolpakova are traveling with. Basically, it's a provincialized version of the one, led by Raissa Struchkova, that appeared in
American cities last summer, when it was augmented by an
array of new-generation talent. Except for Baryshnikov,
who comes late to these shores, Canadian audiences aren't
getting much in the way of new talent. Besides Struchkova,
Fadeyechev, Yaroslav Sekh, and two or three not very well-
prepared young soloists, the roster includes many of the
same aging second- and third-raters seen here last year, and
the company performs the same excerpts and divertissements from the Bolshoi repertory—but a less extensive and
demanding selection than it showed here. In its *Walpurgis
Night*, the four satyrs in fur breeches are oddly replaced by
four bacchantes (who then have to chase the nymphs); its
Spring Waters is far below standard; and it gives a duet
called *Dolls* that was actually performed in New York by the
children of the Bolshoi Dance Academy. (Another "highlight"—six girls linked together like the cygnets in *Swan
Lake* and bouncing to the "pizzicato" variation from *Sylvia*—is worse than childish.) Fadeyechev, now grown enormously fat in the hips, partners the younger women in the
second acts of *Swan Lake* (the hideous Gorsky version) and
Giselle (the great Lavrovsky version), and the backcloths for
the two ballets are flip versions of each other—dull-blue
swamps obviously rendered by the same incompetent hand.
Yet all the tackiness and substitutions don't kill the Bolshoi
spirit or its talent. Struchkova is in roaring form (especially
opposite Baryshnikov in *Don Quixote*), Fadeyechev still has
his spring (his big bottom seems filled with helium), and
the corps in *Giselle* shows its magnificent schooling in every
step. But it was Baryshnikov and Kolpakova I had come to
see. In their Bolshoi setting, the two Kirov stars cast a dis-
tinctively different, tantalizing spell. What artists they are,

and what a way to see them! If it weren't for the wretched Panov affair,* which wasn't resolved until the eve of the Bolshoi engagements in Canada and London (where the main company is appearing), they would be dancing with their own company in New York right now.

—July 8, 1974

---

*The case of Valery Panov, a Kirov dancer put under house arrest by the Brezhnev regime, had become an international *cause célèbre*.

Makarova's Miracle

A breathless week—in dance—for American-Soviet relations. Mikhail Baryshnikov, about whose appearances in
Montreal I wrote two weeks ago, defects in Toronto—the
greatest male dancer to have escaped Russia since Nijinsky
got himself fired by the Imperial Ballet in 1911. Three days
after Baryshnikov's break, Natalia Makarova's staging of *La
Bayadère* is presented by American Ballet Theatre. It is an as-
tounding success—more evidence that self-exiled Russian
stars have as much to give as to gain in the West. *La
Bayadère* (short for *La Bayadère*, Act IV: "The Kingdom of
the Shades") is an old Petipa classic of which most Western-
ers were unaware until the Kirov Ballet toured it in 1961.
When Rudolf Nureyev, who defected on the same tour,
produced it two years later for the Royal Ballet, it seemed
that a miracle of transposition had taken place. Makarova
has wrought an even greater miracle. She's not only reproduced a masterpiece of choreography, she's taken Ballet
Theatre's corps—hardly the most sensitive choreographic
instrument in the world—and recharged it from top to bottom. In place of the lifeless gray ensemble that has skated

through *Giselle* and *Swan Lake* all these many years, there is now in *La Bayadère* an alert, disciplined, and expressive corps de ballet, trembling with self-discovery.

The process of transformation is as yet incomplete, but never in my experience had the company danced a classical piece in so strict a style, on so broad a scale, and with such clarity of rhythm. Without these qualities, *La Bayadère* wouldn't be fun—it wouldn't even be *La Bayadère*—and what's *most* fun about this production is that every girl on the stage seems to be aware of the sensational progress she's making. When the famous single-file entrance down the ramp began, at the back of the State Theater stage, I looked at those unconditioned thighs and jelly waists and thought, They'll never manage it—their backs won't hold, their legs won't keep lifting free. But they did manage it, and not so much by force of will as by force of energy correctly sensed. If the bodies looked underbred, they didn't look strained, and the losses of control that appeared at one or two points were minor. It isn't easy for these girls to take a développé to the peak of a diagonal and hold it, unsupported, at full turnout. One day it will be easier and the backs will be stronger and more beautiful, too. What matters now is that the motor impulse is there, solidly pumping energy into the right channels.

Makarova's direction has been faithful and revealing. That motor impulse is basic to Petipa's exposition of movement flowing clean from its source. It flows from the simple to the complex, but we are always aware of its source, deep in the dancer's back, and of its vibration as it carries in widening arcs around the auditorium. This is dancing to be felt as well as seen, and Petipa gives it a long time to creep under our skins. Like a patient drillmaster, he opens the piece with a single, two-phrase theme in adagio tempo (arabesque, cambré port de bras), repeated over and over until all the dancers have filed onto the stage. Then, at the same tempo, with the dancers facing us in columns, he produces a set of mild variations, expanding the profile of the opening image from two dimensions to three. Positions are developed naturally through the body's leverage—weight, counterweight. Diagonals are firmly expressed. Returning to profile, the columns divide and flutter one by one to the rear. The final pose is of two long columns facing the wings with annunciatory arms. Now, to a collection of beer-garden tunes (the composer is Ludwig Minkus), Petipa sets dances for five soloists—a ballerina, a danseur, and three principal Shades—while behind them the vast, tireless corps responds in echoes, diverges, vanishes, regathers into garlands, into gateways, tosses, and freezes. The choreography is considered to be the first expression of grand-scale symphonism in dance, predating by seventeen years Ivanov's masterly designs for the definitive *Swan Lake*. But our first reaction is not to how old it looks but to how modern. Actually, the only word for this old-new choreography is "immemorial." *La Bayadère* (1877) looks like the first ballet ever made: like man's—or, rather, woman's—first imprint in space and time.

The subject of "The Kingdom of the Shades" is not really death, although everybody in it except the hero is dead. It's Elysian bliss, and its setting is eternity. The long, slow repeated-arabesque sequence creates the impression of a grand crescendo that seems to annihilate time. No reason it could not go on forever. And in the adagio drill that follows, the steps are so few and their content is so exposed that we think we'll remember them always—just like dancers, who *have* remembered them for a hundred years and for who knows how long before Petipa commemorated them in this ballet. Ballets, passed down the generations like legends, acquire a patina of ritualism, but *La Bayadère* is a true ritual, a poem about dancing and memory and time. Each dance seems to add something new to the previous one, like a language being learned. The ballet grows heavy with this knowledge, which at the beginning had been only a primordial utterance, and in the coda it fairly bursts with articulate splendor. My favorite moment comes in the final waltz, when the three principal Shades are doing relevé-passé, relevé-attitude cambré to a rocking rhythm, and the corps, seeing this, rush to join them in the repeat. They—the corps—remember those cambré positions from their big dance.

It's the corps' ballet—a fact the management should recognize by allowing a company call after as well as before the soloists have taken their bows. But the soloists in the performance I saw—Cynthia Gregory, Ivan Nagy, Karena Brock, Deborah Dobson, and Martine van Hamel—deserved their applause. Gregory was at her greatest. She took her grand port de bras the way it was meant to be taken—straight up out of the floor and through the body. Van Hamel, who may be the most talented of the company's younger ballerinas, did her variation the hard way by not coming off pointe until she was well up and into arabesque, and the excessively slow tempo made it even harder. Nagy has a way of filling a role superlatively without actually doing the steps. In his variation, he gathered himself powerfully and unfurled something that started like double assemblé and ended halfway to double saut de basque. In the pas de deux with the veil, he didn't parallel the ballerina's steps and poses—but this is one of the differences between Makarova's staging and Nureyev's. Another difference is that she doesn't stroke the upbeat, or break the path of a gesture in order to "point" it. The way these two have staged the piece corresponds to their styles as performers—hers, musically more fluid; his, more emphatic. The solos are arranged in a different order, and she ends the ballet with the corps stretched along the floor in a semicircle rather than back-bent in a sunburst. I prefer the Royal Ballet's orchestration, with its drumrolls and its protracted climax that accompanies the sunburst, and I think I prefer the sunburst, but apart from those things there's little to choose between these productions. They're both marvelous. Marcos Paredes's costumes for Ballet Theatre are in the Victorian style traditional to this ballet, and I liked his headdresses for the women—beaded circlets à la Anna Pavlova.

—August 19, 1974

The Two Trockaderos

The art of female impersonation, thousands of years old, enters a new dimension when the females impersonated are ballerinas. The basis of the parody is not gender alone but a stylization of gender, and the subject is—or properly should be—not Woman but Woman as Dancer. It was Mallarmé who said that a ballerina is not a woman dancing, because she isn't a woman and she doesn't dance. In this he was drawing a critical distinction between dancing and the ballet. The ballet, in Mallarmé's view, is dancing adapted to the theatre; it is "preeminently the theatrical form of poetry," and the ballerina is a metaphor, one who writes poems with her body, who appears before us as a vessel teeming with abstract preliterate suggestions—forever a symbol, never a person. For Mallarmé, whose ideal in dance was the purity of expression we have since come to recognize in great abstract choreography, the signature of the classical ballerina was her ability to summon up elemental visions—"a sword, cup, flower, etc." was the way he put it, and he didn't need to add that the ballet was not a mere business of noodling around on pointe. Drag ballet, or men on pointe and in tutus, has to be expressive in the same way as straight ballet is, or it loses the essence of its parody. There are two companies doing drag ballet in New York. I didn't go to either of them expecting to be reminded of Mallarméan first principles, but the difference between the companies is so basic that only Mallarmé's great paradox will do, like a gleaming cleaver, to separate them. In one company, the Trockadero Gloxinia Ballet, the subject is gender and nothing more; it's drag-queen display, dressing up, noodling around on pointe. In the other company, Les Ballets Trockadero de Monte Carlo, the subject is ballet. In the Gloxinia, the travesty is formless and unfunny. In the Monte Carlo, it is dead on target and hilarious.

New York, "the dance capital of the world," has long needed a company of madmen to break us all up, and until I actually saw it I half believed the Gloxinia was it. But it's really just one more bad ballet company, and its appeal as a drag act depends less, I think, on one's taste for such things than on one's willingness to put up with its pretensions as a ballet. And with all the murky lighting. The Gloxinia's is the art that conceals. In one of its rare lights-up numbers, four soloists take turns doing a little something to the "Four Seasons" music of Prokofiev's *Cinderella*. Each wears a Botticellian tunic, boxily cut and thickly layered to disguise the wearer's physique. You could almost swear you were watching girls, but you'd never think you were watching dancers. The Gloxinia is so good at being girls that, for me, it's boring theatre. There's not much difference between the show it puts on and a show by inept women dancers, but its ineptness isn't a comic ineptness; it's merely evasive and unaware.

The parody company we've been needing may have just arrived, with the Trockadero de Monte Carlo. Its début season last month, in a loft owned by the West Side Discussion Group, a homophile society on Fourteenth Street, could not have been more of a success, and it took everyone by surprise, not least the Gloxinia, of which it is a rebellious outgrowth. One evening with the Monte Carlo (the name, of course, is in memory of the Colonel de Basil–René Blum rivalry of the thirties) and you see the reason for the rebellion. The Monte Carlo is the creation of ballet fanatics. They've seen the performances, memorized the steps, read the books (this shows in the program notes), listened to the music (this shows in the editing of the taped scores), and turned the whole scorching experience inside out. If it weren't for the long white gloves, a Trockadero trademark, there'd be nothing the two companies have in common.

Unlike the Gloxinia, which aims for a chilly beauty, the Monte Carlo seems to have an affection for broken-down, touring-trunk, desperate-last-stand ballet (its *Swan Lake, Act II* owes something to the production of Denham's Ballet Russe de Monte Carlo, the survivor of both de Basil and Blum), and it believes in warhorses—not only *Swan Lake* but *Don Quixote*, whose third act is arranged to look like the entire ballet. The big surprise is how much of this standard choreography the company is actually able to present—more than you'd believe possible, considering its numbers (corps de ballet of five), its handkerchief-size stage, and the fact that only the two leading artists can dance on pointe and that in the classics one appears as the other's cavalier. A female performer appears in this company, too, but—wisely, I think—only in mime roles. The rest of the company totter, gallop, or bourrée in a flat-footed scuffle through the scene, or else lumpily decorate it in poses; although they do what they do brutally, they never do it sloppily. The Monte Carlo has a great ballerina in Tamara

Karpova (Antony Bassae), but by and large it isn't technically more proficient than the Gloxinia; it's only more—much more—observant of and faithful to its models. The Monte Carlo's sharp-eyed artistic direction constitutes its main technical resource. It's so damned all-seeing that I don't think anything in ballet can be safe from it for long. Take, for example, the miraculously compact *Don Quixote*—the way it casually opens, with its peppery, sullen señoritas doing their lounging walks around the marketplace, tossing away bits of over-the-shoulder mime, then suddenly grabbing brooms and sweeping the upbeat like maniacs for the first *danse générale*. No two mime scenes are alike, and no two dances; the whole gamut of classical-folk clichés is there, whirling on the head of a pin.

Though apparently she is not a born comedienne like Olga Tchikaboumskaya (Peter Anastos), La Karpova, "the black rhinestone of Russian Ballet," is a mistress of style and the finest of the travesty performers. She's built like a pug version of Lou Costello, and on pointe looks a little like a bulldog standing on its hind legs, but she's musical and soft and rounded in the *Swan Lake*, smoothly vivacious in the *Don Quixote*. And in the notorious *Don Quixote* pas de deux—notorious because it is always being performed and almost always *barbarously* performed—Karpova, I believe, gave a better performance than the Bolshoi's Nina Sorokina, who was at the time dancing it at the Met. Though the two performances are not to be compared technically, there was more wit, more plasticity, more elegance, and even more femininity in Karpova's balances and kneeling backbends than in all of Sorokina's tricks, and the way Karpova used her snap-open fan put Sorokina to shame. Antony Bassae's mimicry of a ballerina is not just a personal fantasy; it's an immaculately deadpan rendering of what a ballerina actually does, and at the same time a critical comment on what she should do. As a theatrical figure, Karpova has it all over the more fabled Ekathrina Sobechanskaya, prima of the Gloxinia (Larry Ree). Sobechanskaya styles herself after pictures of Anna Pavlova, but she does only the things she feels like doing, namely, walk a lot on pointe, take teetery little balances, and wave bye-bye to the audience. Ree's Sobechanskaya believes in herself; Bassae's Karpova believes in her role. The difference between them is the difference between the boudoir and the stage.

Watching ballet in drag can be instructive. If it really *is* ballet, it can have moments that are astonishingly close to the experience of straight ballet; the impersonality of it doesn't change, yet of course everything is wrong end to. Drag ballet provides one answer to the question of why men impersonating women are funny, while women impersonating men are not; it has to do with gravity. (A heavy thing trying to become light is automatically funnier than a light thing trying to become heavy.) And watching the two Trockaderos forced me to reponder certain aspects of sex in regard to ballet. It is partly because a ballerina isn't a woman but an abstraction of one that ballet attracts homosexuals in large numbers, but the Gloxinia may be partial evidence that at least some homosexuals think the ballerina *is* the woman and not an abstraction at all. Naturally, if you believe the powerful, supremely theatricalized being on the stage is Woman, you'll never understand much about real women. And like those feminists who feel that ballet traduces women, you'll never understand much about ballet, either. There are homosexual balletomanes who celebrate ballet for its distortions of women, while insulted feminists denounce it, but the two groups operate—from opposite ends—on the same scale of confusion. Both exaggerate the sexuality of ballet. Both are blind to ballet as a world of signs and designs. Because most of the great imagery in ballet has come to us through the courtesy of women's bodies, even people who aren't sexually prejudiced may grow confused and overconcerned with sex, but to impute sexist meanings to standard ballet usages (such as the supported adagio, which shows the woman as the man's puppet, Germaine Greer tells us, when, with equal prejudice and less paranoia, she might have seen the man as the woman's slave) is to indulge in fantasyland explorations at the Disneyland level. Ballet is fantasy, true, but even when it is erotic fantasy its transfigured realism reorders the sensations that flow from physical acts, and our perceptions change accordingly. The arabesque is real, the leg is not.

—October 14, 1974

Taylor and Nureyev
on Broadway

People in search of intelligent lyrical entertainment on Broadway could not have done better than to buy a ticket to the Paul Taylor company during its week at the Alvin. There were two programs—a mixed bill that included a new work called *Sports and Follies*, alternating with *American Genesis*, the evening-length ballet about our vicissitudes as a puritan nation. There wasn't a dull moment in either show. *American Genesis* has some structural flaws and it lacks the seriousness one might expect of its theme, but it is a fine example of Taylor's capacity to set a stage abundantly flowing with ideas by means of a few props and gestures he seems to have pulled out of a hat. The piece is good to see again when you've digested the ideas, which are not difficult. Then its rhythmic continuity becomes even more powerful and sensuously exciting.

Sports and Follies, a suite for uncertain athletes set to a Satie miscellany, is expertly made and silly, the kind of Paul Taylor silly I enjoy. Carolyn Adams has a jumping solo in which she never seems to touch down or take a breath. The high point of the week was a revival of *Churchyard*, a hypnotically morbid piece, as engulfing as a good horror movie. There were those long, rolling rhythms again, but here the ideas—if they are ideas—never come unstuck from the nightmare of what we're seeing: people piling onto and around each other in frenzies, their lower bodies covered with tumors. Taylor, who was abandoned years ago by the snobbishly avant-garde audience, has become the master of a kind of popular theatre without losing any of his integrity.

Yes, Rudolf Nureyev appeared with the Taylor company, and no, he is not a Paul Taylor dancer, but who ever said he was? Fifteen years ago, I would have given anything to see Taylor dance *Apollo*. He was not a classical dancer then, any more than he is now, and I don't think his presence in the ballet would have done it anything but good. Nureyev's presence in *Aureole* was a little like the Joffrey doing *Monotones*; he didn't get it all, but it was surprising how much of it he did get. And more impressive than his dancing was the way he put himself imaginatively at the service of the choreography and the company, even changing the way he takes his bows. Nureyev is the kind of dancer who causes categories to have a nervous breakdown. It's his personality rather than his technique that does it. He seems able to go anywhere and do anything, and even those who have never seen him on the stage have an impression of him as an extraordinary unconfined being. The impression stems, naturally, from his defection to the West, but he no longer seems especially Russian. He seems, instead, the man from nowhere, the man with an erased past and a completely restructured new life.

And when he arrived in the West, it was at a moment of upheaval in public morals and popular culture. Nureyev's behavior on- and offstage appeared related to a new trend, and he may even have instigated it, in part. It was amazing how many British rock stars suddenly turned up looking like him. He has never really belonged to the Royal Ballet; he has said that he is an interloper wherever he goes and that he will go anywhere if he is asked. I'm not even sure that he belongs to the dance profession, and it's always a bit of a surprise to see him turn up for his entrances on cue. A picture book devoted to his career would be dull if it were limited to pictures of Nureyev just dancing. When Nureyev comes out onto the stage, he brings this large, magical aura of freedom with him. It is greater than any gift he has as a dancer, and it is an aura very different from the one he projected when we first saw him, twelve years ago. Then it was his pride and idealism, which sometimes took the form of defensiveness, that were so moving. Nureyev has got the world to accept him exactly as he is, because that is how he accepts himself. There's plenty of showmanship in his makeup but not an ounce of self-deception. He has chosen to live as a gentleman of the West.

—*November 11, 1974*

Blind Fate

Balanchine's celebrated dictum "There are no mothers-in-law in ballet" may have stemmed from his experience producing Stravinsky's *Le Baiser de la Fée*. The hero of the ballet is a babe in arms in the Prologue. A fairy bewitches the baby with a kiss, and after he is grown to manhood she returns disguised as a Gypsy fortune-teller on the eve of his wedding. The young man awaits his bride; when she appears he lifts her veil and recognizes instead the fairy-Gypsy, who has come to carry him away with her forever. How to show that the bridegroom is the child of the Prologue and the Gypsy the fairy in disguise were problems that appeared to trouble Balanchine more than they did the audience. He has never believed in "mothers-in-law"—transformations and relationships that aren't clear in visual terms. In *Tyl Ulenspiegel* he showed Tyl and his enemy, Philip II of Spain, growing to manhood by having the two crouch behind a table as children and stand up as adults. In *Baiser* he had to appeal, impurely, to the audience's intellect. But audiences have always known that the baby of the Prologue to *The Sleeping Beauty* is the sixteen-year-old Aurora of Act I and that Odile is not Odette in *Swan Lake*. The libretto of *Le Baiser de la Fée*, drawn from Hans Christian Andersen, was intended by Stravinsky to be an allegory about Tchaikovsky ("the Muse having similarly branded Tchaikovsky with her fatal kiss, and the magic imprint [having] made itself felt in all the musical creations of this great artist"), and the ballet used elements from the Tchaikovsky ballet classics, including a snow scene that recalled *The Nutcracker*, to create a theatrical fantasy as Tchaikovsky himself might have imagined it.

In this sense, there *are* mothers-in-law in ballet—precedents so well established in the mind of the audience that they become part of a choreographer's inheritance. I can understand Balanchine's having reservations about the libretto of *Baiser* in 1937, when he first choreographed the ballet and when American audiences weren't as familiar with the full-length Tchaikovsky classics as they are now, but I can't understand his continuing to have reservations about it or about the staging of the ballet's final scene, which presented genuine technical problems both in 1937 and in subsequent revivals. For this scene, in which the fairy draws the boy farther and farther into her kingdom, Stravinsky composed an extended, slow-moving melody that flows on and on in the manner of one of Tchaikovsky's panoramas, and Balanchine has described the accompanying stage effect that he tried to produce: "The fairy should appear to be suspended and the bridegroom, just below her, must seem to be swimming through space, as it were, to reach her." Balanchine's various attempts to achieve this illusion, including the one that most people remember—the hero slowly climbing a cargo net spread across a giant glacier—met with no success, because the action was invisible to the part of the audience sitting in the upper house, and after 1951 he gave up on the ballet. It seems a pity not to have one more attempt at a time when Tristan and Isolde sail miles into the sky at the Met and John Neumeier (through American Ballet Theatre) gives us as the finale to his ridiculously encumbered and obtuse production of *Baiser* a tortuous zigzag around some traveling curtains strung on rods. Surely anything Balanchine might think up today would be better than that.

For his revival during the New York City Ballet's Stravinsky Festival in 1972, Balanchine used excerpts from the *Divertimento*—the concert suite Stravinsky made from his ballet score—and staged a suite of dances that had no reference to the libretto except for those who could find in the dances for Patricia McBride and a small female corps echoes of the ballet's bride and wedding attendants, and in Helgi Tomasson's moody solo an intimation of the hero's tragic destiny. The dances for the girls and the pas de deux are part of the wedding divertissement in the original ballet, and very likely they are what they would be in a full version of the ballet had Balanchine elected to stage it. But Tomasson's dance is something that probably couldn't occur in any other context—a statement that sums up, in nonnarrative, emblematic form, the eerie mystery of the ballet as a whole. And the staging of the finale, which Balanchine has added to the *Divertimento* this season, is also something that couldn't occur in the full ballet. For this music, which begins with Stravinsky's lovely setting of "None But the Lonely Heart" and continues into his extended slow "panorama," Balanchine uses only the material of his *Divertimento* ballet—the corps of girls, in their now incongruous peasant dresses, acting as impersonal agents of fate to separate the two lovers, the lovers weaving their way toward each other through the corps' diagonal, passing each other blindly and, still blinded, backing offstage in opposite directions as the curtain falls. Balanchine has managed this—the hundredth variation on his classic theme of blind fate—

more handsomely than I can make it sound. The new scene matches Tomasson's solo in mood; the question is whether it's just a bit of tacked-on drama or an extension into new territory that resets the proportions of the *Divertimento* as we've known it up to now.

After one performance, I couldn't see that anything had really changed, and I couldn't take the expanded mystique of a story, which Balanchine has provided instead of the story itself, any more seriously than the three haunted-ballroom scenes with which he regales us while we're waiting for *Theme and Variations* in the *Tchaikovsky Suite No. 3*. When *Suite No. 3* was first done, a few years ago, all the barefoot dancing and long hair, together with the schematic lighting the piece then had, seemed to mean something in relation to "Theme"; what that was I no longer remember. The sober truth seems to be that Balanchine these days often sets pieces of music he happens to like without making ballets out of them. The *Divertimento from "Le Baiser de la Fée"* has always been something more than a divertissement and something less than a drama, but within its hybrid structure it had, and continues to have, a formal distinction in the relation of its parts that *Suite No. 3* lacks. There's a great difference between the blind-fate episode in the *Divertimento* and the one in the first movement of *Suite No. 3* (which, perhaps not coincidentally, also contains a variant of "None But the Lonely Heart"). In *Suite No. 3* it's a stock situation, weak in dance impetus and dangerously close to kitsch. In the *Divertimento* it is developed directly out of Tomasson's earlier pas de deux with McBride. Balanchine has taken McBride's signature attitudes and distorted them slightly to reveal their dark implications. In the earlier duet, she dipped and turned in different directions, pirouetting with a powerful swing of her leg to lock her partner behind her. Now, in the new scene, she freezes in low-slung arabesque and, as he turns her, gradually knots herself about him until the two are fused. The bride of the original tale becomes the fairy, and this, too, recalls a traditional Balanchine theme—the heroine whose aspect flickers between vampire and goddess. The sinister-sweet elements in McBride's personality are perfect for the role. But if the new developments seem to grow naturally out of what has gone before, I can't see that their refocusing of the piece in the general direction of conventional Balanchine dramatics is any great gift, especially to those of us who would have loved a revival of *Baiser* complete. The *Divertimento* is one of the most superbly crafted pieces that have come from Balanchine in recent years, and McBride, Tomasson, and the girls always perform it with exceptional polish, but it's basically footnote material, a collection of thoughts about a lost work of art.

McBride continues to perform, in "Theme and Variations," a role that doesn't suit her. She's far happier meeting the terrors of *Tchaikovsky Concerto No. 2*—but what terrors they are! No sooner has the ballerina entered than a pit yawns at her feet—the piano cadenza to which she must perform pirouettes of utmost difficulty, including several ground-skimming double pirouettes on quarter-pointe which, in their problems of traction, momentum, and braking, are practically unique in the ballerina repertory. Merrill Ashley, making her début in the role, swept through the cadenza with startling ease and, gaining confidence, went on to have a great success. Ashley is a tall dancer whose main strength is in her legs and in their frank power in big jumps. Because of a long, narrow torso and an oblong, somewhat sharp face, she can sometimes look tight and clawlike. Although her movement is large, it isn't full. Lack of amplitude is at the moment her only deficiency.

—December 9, 1974

Over the Rainbow

Eliot Feld's new ballet, *The Real McCoy*, suggests a work in progress about show dancing of the thirties. For the most part, Feld chooses to evoke rather than imitate; there's no tap-dancing in the piece, and where the thirties spectacle was typically extravagant, Feld's is sparse—perhaps too sparse. The nature of *The Real McCoy* is fantasy—a finer thing than parody—but if the ballet lacks the smugness and the vulgar appeal that outright parody might have, it also lacks the sweep. It's weak the way so many of Feld's other ballets are weak—in the projection of a consistent poetic idea. Because the elements of Feld's thirties fantasy don't combine to form a clear statement and other elements seem to be missing, the foreshortened perspective of fantasy doesn't really appear, and the ballet just looks unfinished.

But even in this state it is worth seeing for the way it misses and then scores. Feld assembles the basic ingredients of a thirties-type show (the solo, the romantic duet, the production number), and he tries to re-create their essence by means of a few necessary figments (song-and-dance man, dream girl, male chorus). But Feld hasn't in every instance found the magic formula, which wasn't a formula so much as it was an imaginative process, that made these numbers vintage spellbinders. What's fascinating about *The Real McCoy* is that when Feld finally involves himself in that imaginative process he produces original, gleaming choreography—pure Feldian fantasy, or genuine parody so remote from piracy as to amount to the same thing.

The piece starts badly, like a tinny fake-thirties knick-knack. Feld, in contemporary sports shirt and slacks dons a topper, glances up at the rainbows on the backcloth, catches a cane thrown from the wings, and begins noodling ineffectually about the stage to a piano blues by Gershwin. The noodling continues, on wheels, when a rolling couch appears with a girl on it and Feld jumps onto it with her. The two glide and swivel around and across and all over the stage, with the piano playing the "Walking the Dog" number from *Shall We Dance*. The absurd, dreamy locomotion, smoothly timed to the music, is beguiling once it gets to you, but I think Feld intended it to be more. I think he intended a crystallization of the animate props and décor of thirties movie musicals, and I'm not sure he succeeds. For one thing, the couch remains a couch, whereas a thirties choreographer would have played "let's pretend" with it, turning it into a bandwagon, a sailboat, Washington crossing the Delaware. Feld can turn the couch into a canoe, but he certainly doesn't let his imagination run riot. Much of the strength in the thirties sense of design lay in the play of allusions and resonances; it was a marvelous bond between entertainers and their audiences, and we think of it as "thirties" only because it is dead. Doesn't a modern audience seek this kind of bond, too? Watching ballet especially, we cling to bits of references and build on them unconsciously. We look to the choreographer to control the way we're building his piece in our minds. When he doesn't give us enough to go on, we go on what we've got. For me, Feld's would-be Busby Berkeley couch became irretrievably cross-circuited with the driving rod of the engine that slowly bears Keaton and his girl away in *The General*. In the lulling, vacuous charm of what Feld put on the stage, I couldn't help what I was thinking, and when I knew I was thinking it I loved it. Feld has something Keatonian in his face and in his quick-wittedness as a dancer. I had never noticed the resemblance before, and I probably wouldn't have noticed it now if Feld hadn't cast himself as Fred Astaire. Aiming at Astaire in my mind, he hit Keaton. Although there *was* something of Keaton's character in the early Astaire—in his resourcefulness and total harmony with the universe—Eliot Feld is better at being tight and still and obsessive, like Keaton, than relaxed and mild and free, like Astaire. I don't know what he thought he was doing in that opening solo—it wasn't hoofing; it wasn't anything—but a moment after the couch disappeared he and the girl (Michaela Hughes) were presenting a very creditable Astaire-Rogers pastiche, and Feld seemed at last to have jumped over the rainbow into the thirties.

Whereupon the strangest thing happened: the thirties themselves disappeared and we were in Feld's own imaginary world of romance-as-illusion. There is a chorus of five men with walking sticks, turning, bending, pausing to tap the floor or probe the upper paths of air. They make a swing of their sticks, and Feld lightly seats the girl on it. Lightly he lifts her down, and the sticks continue to circle slowly, like a Ferris wheel. The gradual flowering of the image, set with great delicacy and precision to the Gershwin Prelude No. 2, is a great achievement for Feld, and the unforced sentiment is, coming from him, remarkable. Though he's been brilliant in the past and sometimes sweetly lyrical, too, he's never before given us a dance that spreads like slow honey, all in its own measure of attainment. The dance is evocative in a way that relates to the spirit of the thirties, but the meaning of it isn't confined to the thirties. Feld has titled his ballet after a Cole Porter song (although his music is drawn from the non–Tin Pan Alley Gershwin). The song, "At Long Last Love," runs, "Is it a cocktail, this feeling of joy, / Or is what I feel the real McCoy?" In other words, just how potent is cheap music? Do we fool ourselves by believing in the reality of its emotions and in the grace and beauty of the theatre they inspired? Is any of it good for more than nostalgia?

Feld hasn't given us his answers, because he hasn't handled the whole ballet with the degree of careful attention he's given to its parts. When the ballet is at its liveliest and most fertile, he actually seems to be drawing new substance from his subject. At other times, he's brash, familiar, and unconvincing. Maybe he started out to make nothing much and then ran into more; maybe he found his nuggets first and then couldn't find their setting. However it was composed, the piece has no internal consistency. After the Ferris wheel, the male corps do an obligatory chorus-boy routine. Feld doesn't define their relation to the girl or to himself, and he doesn't show us why Rouben Ter-Arutunian has dressed them like poolroom sharks. Nor does he account for the absence of other girls by making Michaela Hughes into the one girl who stands for them all. This final part of the ballet is set to the "Jazzbo Brown" music that was deleted from *Porgy and Bess*, and from the sound of it, it should have been the most exciting scene in the ballet. Feld gives us nothing to conjure with. The men vanish, somehow, along with the girl, and Feld time-travels back to the present, yearning before his rainbows as the curtain falls.

The Real McCoy is not all there, but it's an important ballet for Feld to have attempted. A lot of his recent work has been insular, dried-up stuff, and although he's built a repertory on the models of other choreographers, he hasn't often found the inner mechanism that made his model ballets work. In the atmosphere of the best American popular art he seems to have uncovered an instinct for formal allusion, and for the first time he makes a metaphor real on the stage. Many young choreographers haven't developed similar instincts, and I suspect it's because they're afraid of seeming decorative or dated. It may be that in its simplest forms of expression, allusion *is* a dead convention. But holding up a bunch of sticks and having an audience breathe back "Coney Island!" isn't such an easy thing to do, and Feld has done it, after years of waste motion. Encouragingly, he hasn't pushed it as a big moment; he's let it announce itself as the happy event it is. If he can do this, perhaps he can go on to richer and more complex forms of metaphorical expression. Perhaps he'll even make a coherent ballet out of *The Real McCoy*.

—December 30, 1974

New Boy in Town

Nothing galvanizes the general public like the advent of a new male star in ballet. Baryshnikov evenings at the American Ballet Theatre are sellouts and surpass in the feverish excitement they arouse even Nureyev's first American season with the Royal Ballet, in 1963. In those days, the hard ticket was Nureyev-Fonteyn. Nureyev by himself didn't sell out the Met until the Hurok office released its publicity barrage in 1965, and it must be remembered, too, that Nureyev's star had already ascended partly via network television. If Ed Sullivan and the *Bell Telephone Hour* were still in business, Mikhail Baryshnikov would be known to millions more Americans than know him today. As it is, he's on the verge of becoming a national household name, and only New York, Washington, Houston, Denver, and Atlanta have seen him. In the current City Center season, the clamor is as much for Baryshnikov solo in *Les Patineurs* as it is for Baryshnikov-Makarova or Baryshnikov-Kirkland in *Coppélia* and *La Fille Mal Gardée* and *La Sylphide* and *Giselle*.

So far, if I'd had to give my scalp for one ticket, I'd have given it for *Les Patineurs*. In this transcendent Baryshnikov performance (which, alas for the scalpers, he gave exactly twice), one didn't have to wait around for him to dance. Each appearance was an instantaneous string of firecrackers, a flaring up of incalculable human energy in its most elegant form. The Ashton ballet, thirty-eight years old, is still a model of construction. The central role is so well designed that a dancer can get by on neat execution alone. Baryshnikov embellished it like a bel-canto tenor, and as often happens, he made the choreography look as if he had invented or at the least inspired it. A now famous Baryshnikovism, the split tour-jeté, looked right for the first time in the context of this ballet about ice skaters, and Baryshnikov produced the step as none of his imitators so far have done—coming out of a double air turn. Curiously, in the performance I saw (the second of the two), the role had none of the brash extrovert character that is associated with it. It had instead a sense of spiritual dissociation, as if the Green Skater's isolation were to be attributed to his genius. He—the "character" as Baryshnikov assumed it—suggested a boy who builds dynamos in his attic; he had that kind of tragic happiness.

Up to now, *Patineurs* is the only role in which Baryshnikov's dazzling dance power and the diffidence of his personality seem to fit together, but it isn't the role Ashton created. (Not that it matters.) As it happens, Ballet Theatre already has a superlative show-off Green Skater in Fernando Bujones, and Bujones is dazzling in an altogether different way—sharp and arrowy, while Baryshnikov is soft and sinuous. With Bujones leading what is now the strongest male corps in American ballet, and with Natalia Makarova and Cynthia Gregory and Martine van Hamel leading a female corps that includes such exceptionally talented soloists as Kim Highton and Marianna Tcherkassky, the company didn't need Baryshnikov to put over its winter season. But it has got him, and it has Gelsey Kirkland, too, who left the dwindling Sugar Plums at the New York City Ballet to be the icing on Ballet Theatre's top-heavy cake. How Ballet Theatre was to handle its load of talent was a problem *before* Baryshnikov and Kirkland joined; the company's ability to attract stars isn't matched by an ability to attract choreographers, and the disproportionately small shareable repertory means that dancers are either waiting to get into a part or waiting to get out of one. A Makarova-Baryshnikov *Coppélia* this season wrung the material for all it could give, shook out a few extra gags (Makarova popping an elastic band under her chin), and wrung some more. Makarova's showmanship doesn't fail her even when her dancing does. Baryshnikov's dancing *is* his showmanship. His acting tends to be a cover for his personality, not a revelation of it. In comic roles, he's less guarded than he is in roles like James and Albrecht, in which he contorts his face and his playing is heavy and confused. He hasn't Ivan Nagy's gift, in *La Sylphide*, of putting the audience in his place. Nagy, the company's best actor in classical roles, is also Makarova's best partner. Makarova's solos were finer in the *Giselle* with Baryshnikov, but in the duets she didn't have the unearthly halation she had when Nagy lifted her.

And Baryshnikov is better with Kirkland. They did one *La Sylphide*, he in his kilt and Frankenstein makeup, she looking like a French chambermaid, yet it was wonderful—the evident climax of this first phase of their partnership. In the first act, Baryshnikov seemed to be trying out different interpretations of the role in a kind of Stanislavskian attempt to make sense of it. James is a character of stormy temperament, but his dances are light and airy. Ironies of that sort, which abound in Romantic ballet, make contemporary Russians impatient. They gave us a Stanislavsky *Giselle*, and they probably can't understand how we can live with that and the light insincerities of *La Sylphide* at the same time. In the second act, Baryshnikov actually forced a new element into James's solos. That element was passion. James's buoyancy and speed were overtaken by the fury of frustrated desire. This was dark "Russian" Bournonville, but it was very different from the undirected violence that marks Nureyev in the same part. No other dancer alive could have done it.

Kirkland's Sylph is the first great performance this production has seen since Toni Lander's. She has a lot of natural assets for the role—her size, her years, her baby face—and she has the boneless arms, the plastic waist, and the light, springy jump, which got lighter and higher as the ballet went on. But Kirkland wasn't only physically right, she was theatrically perfect. Unfortunately for the company's star-rotation system, not everybody was born for *La Sylphide*. Cynthia Gregory, for example, can outdance any other woman in the company, and her Bournonville style is admirably conscientious. In the second-act crescendo variation she was unbeatable. But the Sylph eluded her. The tilted head positions, the capricious transitions in mood, made her look dotty, and the character lost tension. Makarova gave us the lightest and most billowy jumps of all, and she's one of the finest actresses on the ballet stage. But although this season she was playing with a new simplicity and directness, she still looked like much too sophisticated a woman to be taking such a part. Kirkland has the total unity that one wants to see in a stage character. She's a true sprite—a particular kind of imaginary creature with an imaginary nervous system. No one else showed such musical mime, such distinct, untrivial pathos in the death scene, such an unclouded consistency of movement in every aspect of the role. A weakness at the moment is the vague port de bras in jumps, but this performance—as I had to remind myself forcibly throughout it—was, after all, a début.

The City Center is full of star-gazers, and this annoys some of the dance addicts. But the general public that buys into a dance event only when some new comet is passing across the heavens knows what it is doing. It is looking to have explained to it something about an art form which it has never understood. True, it can't be counted upon to "support ballet," but people to whom most dancing is meaningless can't be in on the struggle; they can only be in on the glory. The better dancing is, the more nearly universal is its appeal.

—January 20, 1975

Back to the Forties

~

If the number of fine ballets that American Ballet Theatre had to show for its thirty-five years of existence equaled the number of fine dancers it currently has under contract, its anniversary gala, on January 11, would have been a night to remember. But numerically and stylistically the equation is unbalanced. The handful of illustrious ballets that made the company's name can't support dancers like Baryshnikov and Kirkland and Makarova and Nagy and Gregory and Bujones, and even if it could, it's patently impossible to build a gala retrospective around *Fancy Free* and *Pillar of Fire* and *Romeo and Juliet* and *Three Virgins and a Devil*, all but the last created between 1941 and 1944. The creativity of that first decade had no sequel in the fifties, the sixties, the seventies. When you are seeing Ballet Theatre choreography at its best, you are almost always seeing a picture of the forties. The dancers of the seventies don't fit into that picture. The ballets are still interesting and they're a challenge to perform, but their aesthetic is dead. Often the sentiment is dead, too. Audiences can't get excited about them in the old way because the life of the period that produced them has receded and they're insulated from the way we think and move today. When they are presented as they were at the gala—deliberately disconnected fragments of the past—it's hard not to see their position in a contemporary repertory as an extended irrelevance. They're really "gala material" in a quite specific sense—not part of the ongoing gala that Ballet Theatre's apologists pretend its history has been, right up to the present.

The programmers for the gala didn't try to force a continuity between the company's bygone achievements and its current resources. Mostly, they exhibited Ballet Theatre as a performing collective that had once been a company. They gave us sections of Tudor's *Pillar of Fire* and *Romeo and Juliet* mimed by the original casts. They put on some of the earlier dancers, such as Igor Youskevitch and André Eglevsky and Agnes de Mille and Yurek Lazowski, alongside the present ones. They put on Miss de Mille in a speaking part as well. But apart from these indiscretions it was much like a usual night at Ballet Theatre. Bits from the current repertory (*Les Sylphides*, *Concerto*, *Etudes*, *The River*) were mixed with bits that might become current at any moment, such as Makarova and Nagy in *Spring Waters*. (The company's foreign stars customarily bring their old repertories with them; otherwise, they wouldn't have very much to dance.) Some of the programmers' intentions canceled each other out, among them the decision to impose four stellar but aging cavaliers on Cynthia Gregory in the Rose Adagio. She was understandably rattled, but in the excerpt from *Miss Julie* she danced with the relaxed intensity she always has in modern character parts. Erik Bruhn returned in this, flying downstage in one of his uniquely taut leaps, and won the great ovation of the evening. Baryshnikov in *Le Corsaire* was another miss; the choreography is simply too tame for him. But Kirkland's first shot at the ballerina role turned out to be a direct hit. So it went: a familiar Ballet Theatre progression of ups and downs. The look of Makarova standing and bending on her pointes in *Concerto*—the look of the leg, with its wonderful upward flow of weight, and the sense of a further weightlessness in the foot—was for me the dance highlight of the evening's first half; in the second it was Kirkland's undreamed-of pirouettes in *Le Corsaire*.

Between the halves, we got Agnes de Mille, pointing out that among performing companies in America only the Metropolitan Opera has lasted longer than Ballet Theatre but that, unlike Ballet Theatre, the Met had to go outside its walls to obtain its repertory. "This," she said, hurling an invisible torch to the ground, "is a *creative* institution." Agnes de Mille, arch-propagandist of the dance, regularly shills for Ballet Theatre, but even for her this is a new peak of chauvinistic bluster. Since 1950, Ballet Theatre has not commissioned one ballet of lasting merit. It has gone outside its walls for every useful ballet from Herbert Ross's *Caprichos* on (and for a lot of useless ballets, too). In 1965, Robbins did his version of *Les Noces* for the company, and Eliot Feld did *Harbinger*, his first ballet, two years later. Some would make exceptions of these pieces; I wouldn't. But the point is that neither Robbins nor Feld, both Ballet Theatre alumni, has found it possible to stay with the company long enough to give it his best. Since the beginning, Ballet Theatre has also made a point of producing the standard classics, but it really didn't get into the classics business until the midsixties. Its repertory is too small for the demands its huge roster of stars makes upon it, and the productions are insufficiently stylish. An original full-evening work has never been attempted. The company has relied more and more on big-name stars whom the public would see in anything, and

it hit bottom with this policy when it revived its dodo version of *La Fille Mal Gardée* for Makarova.

Fille is too big a price to pay to see stars, and the stars
have to pay as big a price to put it across—to make the characters real, the action coherent, the bumbling, tacky humor
seem like innocent zest. The piece has absolutely no dance
architecture. The stars slave to build a bit of momentum in
their variations only to have it leak away the next second
into the crevasses of the plot. If they did less, they'd look
like paper dolls. Even the *Coppélia* has to be treated by the
dancers like a theme for ever more expansive dancing and
acting improvisations. The more expansive Baryshnikov and
Kirkland become, the more recessive and moldy their surroundings seem. They dance at full height, so to speak; the
rest of the company at half height. But it's a pleasure to see
them trying to live up to the values this production merely
hints at. Ultimately, only Makarova, running wild this season, gets away with performing at the production's expense.
She has the wicked wit for it and the improvisatory flair, but
Kirkland, who has learned so much from Makarova, wisely
doesn't follow her lead in this. A pity that Kirkland's second
act, grown enormously more assured, had to be truncated at
her last performance because of an accident at the rear of the
stage. But we got to see Kirkland's instant cool reaction to
the accident (the collapse of a dancer who was one of the
puppets); she "played" it as part of her conversation with
Coppélius and swept on.

It may be because of the unreasonable load of responsibility he has to carry, as much as his unaccustomed intensive
performing schedule, that Baryshnikov is beginning to look
a little tired. The things he has to do in *Le Jeune Homme et la
Mort*, revived for him this season, are a pathetic waste of his
resources. The piece, one of those in which, at rise, a young

man lies smoking in a cheap room while electric signs blink, is B-movie aesthetics puffed to the pretentious limit of a Cocteau fable. Cocteau conceived it in 1946 for Jean Babilée, the angel-thug of Les Ballets des Champs-Elysées, and Babilée subsequently performed it for Ballet Theatre. The role is full of sustained acrobatic balances, some of them in slow motion, and baroque flights over the furniture. But the style of the piece is wearyingly brutal, and the choreography, by Roland Petit, is in raw, convulsed chunks that keep knotting at the same level of tension. Cocteau, in a famous radical departure, had Petit set the steps to jazz, switching to a Bach passacaglia at the dress rehearsal. The disparity isn't very poetic; because the choreography isn't really dancing, the music need be no more than background accompaniment, and the fact that it's Bach strikes me as one of the more mechanically fabulous gestures of the Cocteau of this period. Baryshnikov, more angel than thug, is physically so vital and radiant, so unstrainingly precise, that he unconsciously undermines the expressive intentions of the ballet. Bonnie Mathis, in Nathalie Philippart's role as Death, has to stand like a rock wall over this shining cataract of energy, and she hasn't the dominating presence for the job.

From *Le Jeune Homme*, as from so many other pieces in Ballet Theatre's repertory, I get the continuous impression of an incongruous enterprise. It's like listening to cracked 78-rpm records being played on the finest stereo equipment. But the forties are hot just now, and so is Ballet Theatre. How often we have had recalled to us the company's opening night, in 1940! (Who remembers New York City Ballet's opening, in 1948?) With so few other landmark evenings at their disposal, the company's publicists have had years to press this upon us. Miss de Mille went over it all again on gala night, trying hard to make the sequence of fortuities that constitute the company's history sound like a success story. For twenty-five years, Ballet Theatre's management has been inattentive to the growth of its dancers as artists so long as the public would buy them as stars. It has dedicated itself to devising ways for the company to survive, only survive. Survival is what Ballet Theatre is best at. It markets ballet but it specializes in the survival business, and this year business is very good indeed.

—January 27, 1975

Farrell and Farrellism

Suzanne Farrell, one of the great dancers of the age, has rejoined the New York City Ballet. She returned without publicity or ceremony of any sort, entering the stage on Peter Martins's arm in the adagio movement of the Balanchine-Bizet *Symphony in C*. As the long bourrée to the oboe solo began, the audience withheld its applause, as if wanting to be sure that this was indeed Suzanne Farrell. Then a thunderclap lasting perhaps fifteen seconds rolled around the theatre, ending as decisively as it had begun, and there fell the deeper and prolonged silence of total absorption. For the next eight minutes, nobody except the dancers moved a muscle. At the end of the adagio, Farrell took four calls, and at the end of the ballet an unprecedented solo bow to cheers and bravas. The Bizet was never one of Farrell's best roles, but it is probably the most privileged role in the Balanchine repertory. Returning in it, she returns to the heart of the company, and she could become great in it yet.

In that first moment of delighted recognition and then in the intense quiet that followed, the audience, I think, saw what I saw—that although this tall, incomparably regal creature could be nobody but Farrell, it was not the same Farrell. She has lost weight all over, and with it a certain plump quality in the texture of her movement. The plush is gone, and it was one of her glories. The impact of the long, full legs was different, too. If anything, they're more beautiful than ever, but no longer so impressively solid in extension, so exaggerated in their sweep, or so effortlessly controlled in their slow push outward from the lower back. The largesse of the thighs is still there, but in legato their pulse seemed to emerge and diminish sooner than it used to, and diminish still further below the knee in the newly slim, tapering calf. Yet the slenderness in the lower leg gives the ankle and the long arch of the foot a delicacy they didn't have before. And it shaves to a virtual pinpoint the already minute base from which the swelling grandeur of her form takes its impetus. Farrell is still broad across the hips (though not so broad as before); in pirouettes she is a spiraling cone. But it isn't that Farrell is so terribly big; it's that she *dances* big in relation to her base of support. The lightness of her instep, the speed of her dégagé are still thrilling. You'd think a dancer moving that fast couldn't possibly consume so much space—that she'd have to be more squarely planted. Farrell defies the logic of mechanics, and in that defiance is the essence of the new heroism she brought to Balanchine's stage a little over a decade ago.

Farrell's speed and amplitude were demonstrated more compellingly in *Concerto Barocco*, two nights after the Bizet. They are old virtues, and I am happy to see them back. Farrell doesn't look muscular or drained, as I feared she might, after five years in an alien and diseased repertory. In the upper body, she is almost totally different, and vastly improved. I miss the lift in the breastbone, and I think her sight line has dropped, but the shoulders, neck, and head have a wonderful new clarity and composure. The refinement of the arms and the simple dignity of the hands are miracles I didn't expect. And here is perhaps the best news of all: a Farrell who dances with a new grace of deportment and sensitivity of phrasing. Of all the changes that have come over her, this is the most significant, the most moving. Farrell sensitive? Back in the old days, in the seasons just before her departure from the New York City Ballet, she was the exact opposite—a superdiva who distorted every one of the roles she danced except those with distortions already written in. The absurd sky-high penchées, the flailing spine and thrust hips, the hiked elbows and flapping hands were as much a part of the Farrell of that period as the prodigies of speed and scale and balance that she accomplished. She wasn't joyously vulgar, like an old-style Bolshoi ballerina; she was carelessly vulgar, with no idea of the difference between one ballet and another. But the concept of differences in ballets was in general collapse, and one couldn't blame Farrell for what the company failed to teach her. Strangely, she returns at a time when those distinctions are beginning to be felt again—when the company can be seen at its best one night in *Tchaikovsky Concerto No. 2* and again another night in the utterly different *Stravinsky Violin Concerto*. But there's a collision in the making between Farrell's new, unaffected, clean style and the style of the dancers who've been replacing her all these years.

Farrell's great promise, in which Balanchine was immersed for so long in the sixties, marks the company to this day. It is saturated with her image. What Balanchine saw in her he has projected onto other dancers, but when she left, nearly six years ago, she was still evolving and obviously under fearful pressure. For many of the dancers who got chances after she left, the Farrell image in all its negative aspects has become rigidified as a norm—even intensified as a norm. Karin von Aroldingen and Sara Leland and Kay Mazzo are much worse than Farrell ever was; they're caricatures of the caricature she had become. Beside their wild, strained excesses, the Farrell of today looks almost conventional. Of course, compared to the ballets Balanchine made for her, *Symphony in C* and *Concerto Barocco* are conventional, and these are the only pieces we've seen her in so far. The rest of the Farrell story, which may well contain contradictions of what I've been saying about her, will unfold this season in *Jewels* and *Don Quixote*. But even without having the mature Farrell around to point up the difference, one can see that the Farrell image has been grievously misconceived. Swinging pelvises, baling-hook arms, and clawing hands have become the new, cruel orthodoxy, and there's a whole cluster of young girls in the corps—thin, long-limbed girls who look hysterically overbred: the ultimate degeneration of what might be called the Farrell strain. Heather Watts, whose hyperextended joints I rather enjoy, does Allegra Kent's old role in the Webern ballet *Episodes*, while Penelope Dudleston does Diana Adams's. The great breeding cycle of which Farrell's early NYCB phase was a part has long since run its course and is now exhausting itself in mutations. Bodies like Dudleston's and Watts's are redundant in ballets like *Episodes*; they're the bodies that mad, hyperbolic choreography is about, and they get no antipathetical play—no drama—out of the deliberate awkwardnesses and non sequiturs and extreme dislocations that Balanchine invented for the more resistant bodies of Adams and Kent.

Who Cares? is, like *Episodes*, a landmark ballet, and it, too, is showing signs of erosion. When it finally gets going (with the ten demi-soloists doing their relay of Gershwin hits), *Who Cares?* is a ballet I adore, but the moment it marks in the history of the company is a poignant one that I can't get out of my mind. It was Balanchine's first ballet after the break with Farrell, and in it you could feel the whole company breathing easier. Patricia McBride, who is still marvelous in it, was unexpectedly marvelous in it then; it was one of the ballets that consolidated her stardom. One of the reasons it's no longer fresh is that von Aroldingen has trashed the beautiful part Balanchine gave her—the part that for the first time made her look like an American ballerina and that might well have gone to Farrell if she'd stayed. It was as easy in 1970 to imagine Farrell in *Who Cares?* as it was in 1957 to imagine Tanaquil LeClercq in *Agon*, and that, perhaps, is part of von Aroldingen's problem. She's a hardworking, thoughtful, not overly endowed dancer who doesn't deserve the unseemly prominence into which Balanchine has forced her, and she hasn't borne up well as the prime custodian of Farrell's image. In her roles, one feels, Balanchine has been creating for Farrell by proxy and not really succeeding. Although on occasion (the *Violin Concerto*) he's used her and Mazzo very well, it's pretty obvious that what has been thrown up in Farrell's wake isn't a new wealth of opportunities for other dancers but a whole flock of surrogate ballerinas. Gelsey Kirkland was the one dancer to have arisen and progressed during this difficult period; when she resigned from the company last summer, only McBride was left to carry on as major star and full-time ballerina. As one of the witty dancers remarked, "Suzanne coming back is the best thing that's happened to us since she left." There are young dancers, as yet below ballerina level, who have escaped the influence of Farrell and Farrellism. Merrill Ashley and Colleen Neary (who is one of the thin, long-limbed girls, but with a soft, human core) are two of the most rewarding. It isn't amusing to speculate, even in private, on what may happen to these talented girls now that Farrell has returned, or to the less talented ones, or, indeed, to Farrell herself. The crisis is a serious one, and these are family matters. Farrell once precipitated a revolution in the company. She made audiences sweat, and indirectly, blamelessly, she's been making us sweat ever since. Remembering those revolutionary days, one can only look with helpless fascination to the days ahead. This is 1975, a new year in the life of the most adventurous, erratic, and valuable ballet company in the world.

—February 3, 1975

Free and More Than Equal

If George Balanchine were a novelist or a playwright or a movie director instead of a choreographer, his studies of women would be among the most discussed and most influential artistic achievements of our time. But because Balanchine works without words and customarily without a libretto, and because the position of women in ballet has long been a dominant one, we take his extraordinary creations for granted, much as if they were natural happenings. It is part of Balanchine's genius to make the extraordinary seem natural; how many contemporary male artists, in ballet or out of it, can compete with him in depicting contemporary women? Balanchine's world is pervaded by a modern consciousness; his women do not always live for love, and their destinies are seldom defined by the men they lean on. Sexual complicity in conflict with individual freedom is a central theme of the Balanchine pas de deux. The man's role is usually that of fascinated observer and would-be manipulator—the artist who seeks to possess his subject and finds that he may only explore it. For Balanchine it is the man who sees and follows and it is the woman who acts and guides. The roles may not be reversed. When the man sometimes does not "see" (one thinks of Orpheus, or the lone male figure in the Elegy of *Serenade*, or Don Quixote, who hallucinates), he continues blindly on his mission, passive in the grip of fate. But when the woman is passive and sightless it is because she is without a destiny of her own. She can belong to a man. This is what the Sleepwalker suggests to the Poet in *La Sonnambula*; it is what Kay Mazzo suggests to Peter Martins in *Duo Concertant* and *Stravinsky Violin Concerto*. In both these ballets, Mazzo is blinded by Martins in a gesture both benevolent and authoritarian. They are the only pas de deux of Balanchine's I know in which the man has a fully controlling role. Even the Sleepwalker does not surrender to the Poet she tantalizes. And even Allegra Kent, who in the roles Balanchine made for her was so supple she practically invited a man to turn her into a docile toy, was uncapturable. Think of *Episodes*, in which every trap her partner sets seems to contain a hidden spring by which she can release herself—or ensnare *him*; or her role in *Ivesiana* ("The Unanswered Question"), in which she is borne like an infanta on the shoulders of four men, lifted, turned in this direction and that, dropped headlong to within inches of the ground, delivered for one burning instant into the arms of a fifth man who is crawling wretchedly after her, and taken away into the dark whence she came. Like the Sleepwalker, she does not seem to belong to herself, yet she doesn't belong to her manipulators, either—they're a part of her mystery. (In the same ballet, another woman enters blind, groping her way forward; what seems to happen between her and the man she meets is rape.)

The image of the unattainable woman is one that comes from nineteenth-century Romantic ballet, but in Balanchine the ballerina is unattainable simply because she is a woman, not because she's a supernatural or enchanted being. He can make comedy or tragedy, and sometimes a blend of both, out of the conflict between a woman's free will and her need for a man; he can carry you step by step into dramas in which sexual relationships are not defined by sex or erotic tension alone, and in this he is unique among choreographers. He is unique, too, in going beyond the limits of what women have conventionally expressed on the stage. In *Diamonds*, the ballet that follows *Emeralds* and *Rubies* in the three-part program called *Jewels*, Suzanne Farrell dances a long, supported adagio the point of which is to let us see how little support she actually needs. There is no suggestion here of a partnership between equals, of matched wits in a power play such as there is in *Rubies*, with Patricia McBride and Edward Villella. In *Diamonds* there is no contest, and in a sense the conception is reactionary—the woman is back on her pedestal and the man is worshipful. But that is not the meaning of the dance as we see it today. There's much more substance to *Diamonds* than there was in the days when Farrell first danced it; then it seemed the iciest and emptiest of abstractions with, in the woman's part, an edge of brazen contempt. Farrell, a changed and immeasurably enriched dancer, in stepping back into the ballet has discovered it. She is every bit as powerful as she was before, but now she takes responsibility for the discharge of power; she doesn't just fire away. And whereas she used to look to me like an omnicompetent blank, she's now dynamic, colorful, tender. Her impetuosity and her serenity are forces in constant play, and one may see the action of the piece as a drama of temperament. It is a drama very different from the one I remember. Farrell's independent drive no longer seems unacceptably burdensome to her, and her mastery implies no rebuke.

And what mastery it is—of continual off-center balances maintained with light support or no support at all, of divergently shaped steps unthinkably combined in the same phrase, of invisible transitions between steps and delicate shifts of weight in poses that reveal new and sweeter harmonies of proportion no matter how wide or how subtle the contrast. Your eye gorges on her variety, your heart stops at the brink of every precipice. She, however, sails calmly out into space and returns as if the danger did not exist. Farrell's style in *Diamonds* (and the third act of *Don Quixote*) is based on risk; she is almost always off balance and always secure. Her confidence in moments of great risk gives her the leeway to suggest what no ballerina has suggested before her—that she can sustain herself, that she can go it alone. Unlike Cynthia Gregory, and many ballerinas less distinguished than Gregory, who perfect held balances, Farrell perfects the *act* of balance/imbalance as a constant feature of dancing. It is not equilibrium as stasis, it is equilibrium as continuity that she excels in. Although, as in her *Diamonds* performance, she can take a piqué arabesque and stand unaided, she's capable of much more; her conquests are really up there where the richer hazards are. In the Scherzo, going at high speed, she several times takes piqué arabesque, swings into second position and back into arabesque, uncoiling a half-turn that, because of the sudden force of the swing, seems like a complete one. In the finale, her partner (Jacques d'Amboise) is only there to stop her. She slips like a fish through his hands. She doesn't stop, doesn't wait, doesn't depend, and she can't fall. She's like someone who has learned to breathe thin air.

Of course, the autonomy of the ballerina is an illusion, but Farrell's is the extremest form of this illusion we have yet seen, and it makes *Diamonds* a riveting spectacle about the freest woman alive. The title is a misnomer. *Diamonds* finds its entire justification in a single dancer; apart from its presentation of the multifaceted Farrell, the ballet is paste. None of the ballets Balanchine created for Farrell were top-flight, and there is very little besides Farrell to justify the maintenance in repertory of his full-evening work *Don Quixote*. Farrell has little to do until the third act, where she fully recaptures her old brilliance and adds to it a new gift for dramatization. Up to that point she has outgrown the role, and the ballet is stale and boring. It was an interesting failure ten years ago, when it was new, but Balanchine's attempts to straighten out the strands that connect the Don's fantasies to the reality of persons and events around him have led to a succession of ever more futile revisions in the first act, and with the addition two years ago of a classical-Spanish divertissement he abandoned all efforts at mise-en-scène. The story of Don Quixote doesn't really get going until well into the second act, most of which is taken up with another divertissement. The ballet has always suffered from a lack of conviction; maybe it was on account of Nicolas Nabokov's music, maybe it was because giving overt dramatic expression to his theme of the elusive Ideal Woman betrayed Balanchine into unflattering revelations of self-pity. Although Jacques d'Amboise, taking over the role this season, gives the Don modesty and dignity, Balanchine seems to feel very sorry for him indeed.

Farrell's Dulcinea and her role in *Diamonds* suggest that, as a Balanchine conception, she's free and more than equal to any man. In *Bugaku*, she appeared in a contrasting role, one originally done by Kent. Here the woman is seen ribaldly as an object, and though there are moments of satire in the geisha-girl pantomime (as well as some nasty pseudo-Oriental mannerisms), *Bugaku* is the nearest thing in the New York City Ballet repertory to a Béjart ballet. Balanchine seems to have derived his inspiration for the pas de deux from Japanese pornographic prints. Farrell brought out some of the acid below the surface, but not enough. Kent can bring it all out—complicity carried to the point of mockery—so the piece becomes nearly a feminist statement; she can make the movements look insinuating and delicious at the same time. There is a close link between Kent and Farrell that Farrell's absence had obscured, but Farrell in Kent's roles rather emphasizes their dissimilarities.

—*February 24, 1975*

Going in Circles

To Steve Reich's very interesting musical composition called "Drumming" Laura Dean has now set choreography for eight dancers, with results that are often pleasant and sometimes powerful. The dance, accompanied by Reich's musicians, had its première in the Lepercq Space at the Brooklyn Academy; the sound was wonderful. The dancing is not as interesting as the music, but for the first twenty minutes or so (the piece lasts ninety minutes) it exerts a pressure of naïve excitement that would be ideal if it could be sustained. The flaw in the dancing is that it tries to be a mirror image of the sound, and though the music and the dance are alike in the simplicity of their processes, they are widely divergent in their resources. Reich's score consists of a single rhythmic pattern enunciated in turn by bongo drums, marimbas, and glockenspiels; to each of these bands are added male and female vocalises, whistling, a piccolo; in the fourth and final section all voices are heard together. Since the instruments frequently play out of phase with each other and introduce further variations in pitch and timbre, the effect is sumptuous—a multilayered sonic veil of which the dance is only able to pick up two or three threads. And Dean's choreography is hampered by the fact that her dancers are not, all of them, as keen as they might be; they're enthusiastic performers, well rehearsed but not well trained in any sense comparable to the musicians, and in a piece of this size they can't stay the course. The most they contribute to *Drumming* as a dance event is a lightweight, preppy charm.

Laura Dean, as she says in her program note, has been experimenting for years with "spinning, steady pulse, repetitive movement, and geometric patterning." To take spinning first: it's the most favored of her devices and the least effective. Dance sociologists may be able to make something of the present moment, which finds so many American concert dancers behaving like whirling dervishes; for me, the whole business is a bore. As soon as a dancer or a group of dancers starts to spin, my attention immediately drops by half, then slides to total indifference. It's like waiting for someone to get off the phone and back to conversation. The first Western dancer I ever saw do this kind of spin was Ann Halprin, in a solo called, I believe, *The Prophetess*. This was in 1955, and in those days even Halprin was conscious of borrowing from an exotic tradition. (Years before Halprin, Ted Shawn, in his *Mevlevi Dervish*, was said to be the greatest spinner of them all.) Nowadays, concert dancers spin for the sake of spinning, as ballet dancers turn pirouettes. But, unlike a classical pirouette, a dervish spin has no reality as bodily sculpture; its entire emphasis is on the dancer's interior state, and the pleasure of it belongs to the dancer alone. When, to the marimba section of *Drumming*, the Dean dancers go into their bobbin-like spins, their faraway trance corresponds to the remote whirr of the music, and their different bodily rhythms correspond to its multiplicity. But maintaining the spell becomes a problem for the spectator. There's no kinetic transference, and one has to struggle to keep the field of focus clear. Later on in the piece, there was more spinning—clockwise and counter-clockwise, or in crouches, or with changing arms. No matter how Dean varied the visual pattern, the *dance* effect was unintelligible.

What's surprising about these lapses into mystique is that they occur in the work of a choreographer whose other devices—"steady pulse, repetitive movement, and geometric patterning"—suggest a mathematically precise, even a severe turn of mind. But although she's one of the few really promising choreographers around, Laura Dean doesn't seem to have crystallized an attitude toward her work. She's rigid where she should be rigorous, slack where she should swing. From *Drumming* and from earlier works of hers that I've seen, I get the impression that she'd like to cut loose but can't—that she's trying for the kind of objectivity that will swallow her up. To lose oneself in one's work—is there a greater joy, especially for the performing artist? But Dean's choreographic range is so limited (by choice, it would seem) that as a performer she always looks as if she's holding something back. The few irreducibly basic steps to which she restricts herself—stamps, hops, shuffles, low kicks that barely part the legs—have the weight of intense scrutiny; only primary colors are used, and they're meant to burn us with their purity. In the early part of *Drumming*, the dancing also had a brightness of temper that kept it from looking like a ritual, but planned primitivism seems to be what Dean's work is all about. It's a paradox not easy to survive gracefully, and Dean's tension shows in her neck and mouth. She's not one of the best dancers in the company. At least two of the others throw themselves about with more quasi-mystical rapture. Dean dances like an agnostic in her own church.

Dean's ambivalence is just now the most interesting thing about her. I hope it means that she'll develop her material (along with her dancers). The dance to *Drumming* is far from intricate, but portions of it are already a big advance from *Jumping Dance*, *Stamping Dance*, and *Circle Dance*. The question of why a dancer of intelligence and skill would ever want to hold herself down to such an elementary level can be answered by a glance at the formless attitudinizing, the tackily derivative contrivances that constitute so much modern choreography. But it's not the whole answer. Choreographers of Dean's generation are heirs to the radical experimentation of the sixties, which took Merce Cunningham's rejection of literary and psychological content in dance and inflated it into a revolt against all established forms of dance. The alternative to dance was nondance—or, rather, ordinary movement construed as dance. The idea was so shocking that it captured—and paralyzed—a whole generation. As Steve Reich has described the situation (in his book *Writings About Music*), "For a long time during the 1960's one would go to the dance concert where no one danced followed by the party where everyone danced." Nondance concerts persist in the seventies, only now they are likely to consist of stylizations of ordinary movement rather than the real, raw thing, and to take place on a considerably reduced scale. Just as sixties nondance paralleled Pop Art, seventies nondance parallels Conceptual or Minimal Art. The ordered elements in it often have the look of baby's first steps, which are repeated over and over in wonderment, as if choreographers hoped to discover for themselves the secret of why on earth man dances. Certain dancers have elected not to dance at all.

Yvonne Rainer, the best-known of the sixties revolutionaries, has turned to filmmaking; the most recent concerts of Simone Forti and Kenneth King consisted of Forti and King reading. (Forti, widely acknowledged as a primary influence on the sixties radicals but seldom seen in performance, has amassed the biggest legend in absentia since Sybil Shearer.) The Grand Union, a group to which Rainer formerly belonged, counts among its current members Steve Paxton, David Gordon, Trisha Brown, Barbara Dilley, Nancy Lewis, and Douglas Dunn, all of them choreographers in semiretirement. An evening with Grand Union, like the one a few weeks ago at the La Mama Annex, is a free-for-all of improvised dialogue, shticks, and stunts, much of it funny on purpose, all of it inconsequential, none of it more than incidentally concerned with dancing. The format is so amorphous that no two performances are the same, and so discontinuous that no two descriptions of the same performance are, either. Grand Union is a slightly less conventional form of actors' improvisational theatre; its communal permissiveness makes it perfect campus-cabaret entertainment.

Implicit in all this seems to be the idea that unless dancing can be taken back to an embryonic state (before there ever was a Martha Graham, a José Limón, or a Merce Cunningham to impose environmental influences) it cannot be done. The only trouble with this is that the embryo never grows. Two years ago, Lucinda Childs gave a baby-step concert at the Whitney Museum; last month, she gave another, at a downtown loft, in which two of the Whitney pieces were repeated. As before, four girls marched forward and backward in circles to a basic count of six. As before, Childs appeared alone to measure the space, walking a slow back-and-forth path, row upon row, until the floor area was covered. The walk was embellished at regular intervals with a turn of the body, a turn of the head, an extended arm. In the circle dance, once you'd observed the tiny variations in recovery of impetus with which each of the four girls switched from forward to backward march, you'd observed all. What made Childs's walk dance interesting (minimally speaking) was nothing organic to the dance; it was, rather, that Childs is a striking-looking woman with a beautiful head. Even in minimal, equalizing, white-on-white dances, those dreaded élitist principles, that horrible star quality can't be ironed out. Like Dean, who in relaxed moments can look ravishing, Childs doesn't like to smile or look her audience in the eye. I was reminded of Rainer's mid-sixties manifesto of renunciation: "NO to spectacle no to virtuosity no to transformations and magic and make-believe no to the glamour and transcendency of the star image . . ." Childs and Rainer are exact contemporaries who helped make a revolution. Ten years later, it's no to dance.

The embryo never grows because the dancers do not build on one another's accomplishments—they work on as if nobody had ever done anything. And the audience has no memory. In the seventies, the "new" and "radical" choreographers who are repeating the experiments of the sixties play to a predominantly young audience—an audience that, having heard of the firebrands of the sixties, now sits cross-legged in lofts and discovers the scene unchanged. (Laura Dean's audience for *Drumming* contained many people who were evidently drawn by the music; it was a refreshingly adult crowd.) And the young audience gets no help from the dance critics, who are either unaware or forgetful of developments in other forms of theatre. Kei Takei, a young Japanese dancer, recently put on a five-hour disaster epic called *Light* at the Brooklyn Academy. It was full of nameless terrors and indefinable threats, and it was acclaimed as original and visionary. But it might have been produced, scream for scream and grovel for grovel, by the Living Theatre. Doesn't anyone remember the Living Theatre?

Modern dance, American dance, contemporary dance, new dance, free dance, or avant-garde—however you call it, it's currently a scene of chaos and devastation. Laura Dean's use of recognizable dance movement is the first breakthrough it has witnessed since the emergence of Twyla Tharp. Dean has her problems; she's overly possessed by the rudimentary, and when she describes her experiences with spinning she sounds like Isadora discovering her solar plexus. Nevertheless, she's dancing, and she's composing dances of rhythm and pattern. She leaves the others standing still.

—April 21, 1975

American Space

The New York City Ballet has brought its *Ivesiana* back to the stage of the State Theater, a year late for the Ives centennial but in plenty of time for the Bicentennial. The piece is one of those on an American subject in which Balanchine becomes completely an American choreographer—not the Stravinsky Balanchine, or the Balanchine of *Western Symphony* or *Stars and Stripes* who expresses America from a European point of view, but a Balanchine who sees us at the same distance from which we see ourselves. *Ivesiana* is about that American distance, that equalizing yet comfortless space which separates Americans from Americans under the neutral American sky. It is about the lack of perimeters, and journeys pressing onward despite that lack. It is about situations, not destinations, and in it the stage is a box with no sides. Dancers come and go and disappear and seem to fall off the edges into eternity. Each section of the dance gives us a concise picture of what might be happening in the real world, but the pictures, evocative as they are, are not fashioned after anthropological home truths. They are images of pure drama, disconcerting and melancholy, unlike any we have seen before, and *Ivesiana* is like no other ballet in the repertory.

Balanchine made it in 1954 as an homage to Charles Ives in the year of his death. The choreography reflects the music not in patterned dance sequences but in a kind of epic pantomime suspended in time. All but one of the ballet's four sections have this floating quality. The exception is "In the Inn," which comes the closest to an actual dance. "Central Park in the Dark" and "The Unanswered Question" move very slowly, at about the same speed. The finale, "In the Night," moves only a little faster. And all but "In the Inn" are placed far away in space, looming from odd corners or levels of the blackened stage, deep within their cave of orchestral sonorities. Yet dramatically the piece as a whole persistently throws you off course. When it's over, its shape is still unsettled; it goes on spreading its queer dissonances in your mind. This is wonderful, of course, but *Ivesiana*, which has never been a popular piece, ought to grip its audiences more than it does. In the form it has kept since its revival in the sixties (four sections out of an original six) it is too short—and too short on contrast—to do the damage it was meant to do. "In the Inn," a casual encounter between a boy and a girl who compete to the piled-up, off-center rhythms of many raggedy dances, is so different in mood from the other numbers that it practically throws you out of the ballet. Next comes the end, in which numbers of people walk in different directions all over the stage on their knees—nothing but that for a few minutes until the curtain falls. The particular insanity that the ballet mirrors is consistent. The crazy jazz couple who break off their involved game with a handshake and a farewell merge with the night stream of aimless yet obsessed wanderers who populate the ballet, but that point takes a while to sink in. At first sight, "In the Inn" seems to be a break in style.

The only other direct encounter in the ballet, a violently sexual one, occurs in "Central Park in the Dark." In a forest of bending and swaying forms, a girl cannot find her way. She touches a man's chest and crumples; he catches her up bodily in a lift and releases her in a groping descent; then they lose each other. There is a panic, a tumble, a suggestion of rape, and she is again lost and sightless as the forest shrinks back to the spongy cluster it was at the beginning. In another circle of Hell, another cluster emerges out of the dark—the totemic cortege of "The Unanswered Question." In this amazing, slow-motion adagio, a girl enters standing upright on the shoulders of four men, who then manipulate her body in a series of passes through space, high overhead or around their waists like a belt or low over the floor on which the questioner stretches himself, hoping for a moment's contact. It never comes—or, rather, she does come once into his arms, feet first, clenched up tight as a ball. With this, his erotic torment is complete. Soon, before the ritual can restate itself many more times, it is disappearing, moving off into the dark.

In Elise Flagg's performance I missed the security that would have enabled her to execute one of the more peacefully startling of the scene's incidents—the slow passé into attitude back, accompanied by formal port de bras, which is performed by the priestess atop her human pyramid. Deni Lamont as the questioner and Sara Leland and Francisco Moncion as the "Central Park" pair repeated the good performances they used to give years ago. Suzanne Farrell appeared in "In the Inn," her hair parted gothically and braided in pigtails, and gave a lighthearted, mischievous performance quite different from years ago. Victor Castelli paralleled her in stealth and wit as well as in some frisky high jumps. The costumes, which have never been credited and have always been effective, are practice clothes in a selection of pungent, subdued colors. Only Moncion's shirt, which looked like something a Technicolor pirate might wear, was wrong. The lighting has never recaptured the atmosphere that Jean Rosenthal once gave it, but it has been better than it is now—especially in "In the Inn," where a harsh, dirty-white light is used instead of the gold of New England on a summer afternoon.

—*May 19, 1975*

It's a Wise Child

By subtitling his version of *Ma Mère l'Oye* "Fairy Tales for Dancers," and by staging the ballet as a series of improvisations dressed in leftover décors and props from other ballets in the repertory, Jerome Robbins accomplishes several things at once: a joke about the New York City Ballet, a commentary on the concept of a ballet company in the act of paying "Hommage à Ravel," a peculiarly shrewd and touching rendition of the power of theatrical fantasy. Ravel framed his *Mother Goose* ballet with the story of the Sleeping Beauty, who dreams a suite of fairy-tale dances—Beauty and the Beast, Hop o' My Thumb, and the Empress of the Pagodas. In the end, the Prince appears walking down the avenue of brambles that part to let him pass, and the wedding celebration, attended by all the other fairy-tale characters, takes place to the tingling climaxes of the "Jardin Féerique." Ravel took his idea of the Sleeping Beauty's sleep from Perrault—who tells us that "(though history mentions nothing of it) the good fairy, during so long a sleep, had given her very agreeable dreams"—and the idea of her wedding (though history mentions nothing of it, either) probably came from the Tchaikovsky-Petipa ballet. Robbins follows Ravel's scenario closely, but by adding one element to it he colors the whole ballet to such an extent that it appears, from first to last, to be his own creation. He surrounds Ravel's frame with another frame, making the ballet a charade put on by dancers, whom he sees as the scamps of the theatre. This new frame by itself is nothing much; yet the ballet could not have been presented in just this form by any other company or by any other choreographer.

Because Robbins has so personalized the idea of dancers as precocious, amusing kids, in dozens of ballets and musicals starting as far back as *Interplay* and *Look, Ma, I'm Dancin'* and *Pied Piper*, he succeeds in turning *Ma Mère l'Oye* into a typical Robbins kid-style ballet. When the Sleeping Beauty enters skipping rope, or when the Good Fairy whistles on her fingers, these impudences specified by Ravel seem like Robbins's inventions. When he throws in chunks of classical mime out of *The Sleeping Beauty*, the satire fits right in. So does the general satire of the New York City Ballet and its uncommendable habit of mounting new ballets in the fittings of old ones. Here is that Horace Armistead garden drop yet again, here are pieces of *A Midsummer Night's Dream* (some of them hung backward), here is the *Nutcracker* bed, the French doors from *Liebeslieder Walzer*, the lanterns and grass stalks from *Watermill*. The whole company and its repertory are jumbled together in a salute to Ravel, but people who don't recognize the bric-a-brac won't miss out on the fun or the self-mockery. The elemental, poverty-pleading tackiness of the piece may be vintage New York City Ballet; it's also a more serious conception of Ravel's ballet, coming from Robbins, than a reverent incense-and-gossamer production would have been.

In the poetic style of *Ma Mère l'Oye*, Robbins returns to

those qualities which first defined him as a unique theatre artist. He's once again the New York play-school referee, the maestro of the slum kindergarten, the Peter Pan of arts and crafts. When Robbins speaks with a specifically local accent, when his boyhood origins and his eternal boy-genius sensibility are allowed to resonate with their natural color and size, his art seems universal. When he deliberately attempts big, grown-up, universal themes (as in *West Side Story* and *The Goldberg Variations* and *Watermill* and *Dybbuk Variations*), he becomes parochial, local in a reductive sense: Mr. New School Seminar or Mr. Broome Street Avant-Garde. *Ma Mère l'Oye* is bound to be underestimated because it looks so easy and hasn't a lot of dancing, but it's a New York artifact of wide significance. It catches up the beloved Robbins myth about dancers as children and relocates it in our current world of young dancers' workshops, professional children's schools, and incubators of the performing arts. The point of overlap is the ancillary myth, so real to the stagestruck kids of Robbins's generation, of puttin' on a show.

You can see this clearly in the datedness of the ballet's opening scene—its one bad moment. The corps kids are lying around the stage, propped up on trunks or bits of scenery, listening to Mother Goose reading from her book. Comden and Green are not far off. (At the première, Mother Goose was Mme Pourmel, the company's wardrobe mistress, in her blue smock; that shows how thorough Robbins's backstage-musical conception is.) Dancers and audiences everywhere, especially at the New York City Ballet, have outgrown this sentimental aspect of Robbins's juvenile fantasy. Besides, it violates practical reality. Why should a ballet company be sitting around? If they'd been warming up—doing their barres or stretching their muscles—instead of just listening raptly, the scene might not have looked so forced and coy. However, the fantasy rolls: theatre trunks are thrown open, hats with plumes come out, the scenery moves, the traffic rumbles; the tables, if there were any, would be turned. These dancers aren't wistful dreamers; they're sober technicians, as systematic as circus acrobats. They do not try to cajole you with an illusion of spontaneity; everything is mechanical, deadpan, precise, and twice as funny because of it. Twice as real, too, in the normal, everyday dimensions of a child's imaginings which Robbins intended the action to have. In the old movie musicals, child performers have no youth; the hysterical energy of vaudeville has ravaged them prematurely. The young dancers Robbins is using now are old and wise, too, but, unlike the monstrous theatrical children of the past, their youth hasn't been sacrificed to their learning. It's a conception that fits neatly into Ravel's world—the child as mandarin.

—*June 9, 1975*

Congregations, Criticism, and a Classic

The idea that ballet is a form of entertainment, and an extremely popular one, is making one of its periodic returns this season. As in former seasons, the television specials and magazine spreads coincide with a congestion of bookings in the big cities. The media scouts, naturally, make no distinctions in quality; to read them, one would think that an appetite for serious good dancing could be sated as well at the Bolshoi as at the New York City Ballet as at the Stuttgart. The dance audience, admittedly a growing one, is always being represented as wildly eclectic, when in fact it is divided into as many sects as nineteenth-century American Protestanism. Only the critics go to everything, and to sustain themselves in their exhaustion critics can get into a habit of condescending to audiences—of thinking, Well, this isn't for me, but it's all right for *them*, and then writing as if their personal reactions didn't matter. However, if you can't take dancing personally, chances are you can't take it at all. Most people take it very personally indeed, and when someone tells me how much he loves the ballet and then mentions something he's seen at the Stuttgart, I become very gloomy, because I imagine a pro-Stuttgart position to be at least as deeply held as my own anti-Stuttgart one.

To suggest further that some dancers aren't as good as others is an affront to personal taste. The sensations of the theatre are such that often one is in the grip of a helpless attraction, and it's painful to have the beloved ripped apart on technical points. But sometimes it seems that there's a conspiracy not to mention technical points. Everyone can see the superiority of a Baryshnikov; as for the others, they're all great fellows, great girls. Analyzing dancers is like cutting up their bodies. We tell ourselves that we're free to enjoy dancers now that we've suppressed puritanism. However, it's indecent to enjoy some dancers more than others, because this seems to imply that some bodies aren't as good as others. In our age of inverted prudery, when you attack the body you attack the self.

Then, since we also live in the age of the supereminent choreographer, it is presumed that bodies on the stage are largely the creations of the choreography; that dancers aren't really responsible for the way they look. This is a partial truth. No dancer can look consistently bad who is not a bad dancer. Recently, we have had two productions of *Daphnis and Chloë*, both awful. John Taras's for the New York City Ballet had Peter Martins and Nina Fedorova in the leads; Glen Tetley's for the Stuttgart Ballet had Richard Cragun and Marcia Haydée. Martins and Fedorova were used about as appreciatively as two mannequins; Fedorova really is a mannequin, but Martins really is a dancer—a fine one. Cragun and Haydée are performers with a big following in this country, but I'm unable to take them seriously as dancers. Cragun is an acrobat with a facility in turns, and all his dancing is light, facile, and dull. By "facile" I mean that he works off the top of his strength, not through the center

of it. His celebrated prowess in multiple turns has no fascination for me because it has none for him. It looks like rotework. Watching dancers like Cragun in the same season as
dancers like the New York City Ballet's Martins and Tomasson or the Bolshoi's Vasiliev and Gordeyev, I've begun to
think that a dancer's center of strength is seated in his imagination. Maybe it's the ability to imagine the full shape of
the dance their strength can produce which makes these
men dancers while Cragun remains a turner. (I once took a
friend, an athlete and a man who loved social dancing, to
see Villella. I thought he would enjoy the full-bodied force
that Villella had, and started to speak of it afterward, but my
friend, suddenly bright-eyed, said, "He has it *here!*" and
tapped his temple.)

I prefer Haydée funny on purpose, so I went this time
to see *The Taming of the Shrew*, hoping my bad memories of
it were an overreaction to the culture shock of the
Stuttgart's first New York visit, six years ago. But after the
second of the slapstick pas de deux I had to leave. Haydée
and the choreographer, John Cranko, had done it again.
Why do people sit in an opera house squeezing themselves
in delight over what they'd yawn through if they saw it on
television? Any Carol Burnett show is funnier, and in ballet
relentless emotionless farce just doesn't work. The farce formula for Haydée is that she walks a lot on her heels and
keeps her knees apart. Her timing is good, her chickeny run
is good (better here than in *Romeo and Juliet*!); but this Kate
has no wit, no womanhood, no pride for Petruchio to
wound. She's a little ogress and one hell of a spunky performer. Often at the Stuttgart I feel that what I'm seeing is
not a vision of ballet but an idea of what ballet could be as a
Broadway show. In a ballet of *Shrew*, the comedy to be really funny would have to be serious at its core, worked out

in terms of the characters and their emotions. Cranko
worked it out in terms of routines.

Daphnis and Chloë, by Tetley, with designs by Willa
Kim, was pretty as a picture. In fact, it *was* a picture, as flat
and expressionless as one of those Tonight the Ballet ads for
perfume in magazines of the forties. Tetley, who took over
the direction of the company after Cranko's death, two
years ago, makes dancing look linear in much the same way
Cranko did. It's the opposite of plasticity; the shape and
contour of a phrase don't count, the continuity does. The
dancers become animated line drawings who never stop
bending and twisting, and the perspective of the stage flat-
tens into a neutral backdrop. Without depth, the images
can't be felt, they can only be seen. Well-designed dancing—dancing that occupies and affects space—exerts a force
that passes through the spectator's muscle sense. The instinct for it in a choreographer corresponds to a dancer's
correct deployment of energy, and the loss of this mutual
instinct for form in big companies like the Stuttgart is a
tragedy of modern ballet. Neither Tetley nor his dancers can
make a ballet a more than visual event. Sometimes powerful
dancers can salvage weak choreography—as Martine van
Hamel very nearly does in Tetley's *Gemini* at American Ballet Theatre—but I watched *Daphnis* and Tetley's *Voluntaries*
and Cranko's *Initials R.B.M.E.* on the stage of the Met and
it might as well have been a movie screen. Looking for
drama (since there was no dance), I kept seeing lifts and
more lifts—solemnly portentous ones with the women
supine on a fortissimo climax, or real maulers, where their
bodies were twisted and wrung like hemp. No company
surpasses the Stuttgart in the strained ingenuity of their
lifts. They really ought to put out a catalogue. Leather-
bound.

Paul Taylor's new ballet *Esplanade*, set to the music of Bach, is twenty-eight minutes of dancing without a single dance step. The dancers walk or run, shifting direction with a light hop. There is one section composed of mimelike gesture, another in which the boys take the girls up in cradling lifts to dandle or swing them through the air. The choreography looks as though it could be danced by anybody with a little daring and bounce and with a knack for virtuoso timing; all other forms of virtuosity have been ruled out. Sometimes the dancers are on all fours, clustering like sheep; at other times they are flat on the floor, lying there or rolling convulsively. For this simplified vocabulary, the movement invents a silly-simple logic that keeps turning hidden corners. A boy lies on his side and a girl walks all over him, stepping from ankle to knee to hip to shoulder as from peak to peak of a mountain range. Then she steps off him, turns, and steps right back on. A little scherzo for Carolyn Adams is filled with pitterpat runs suddenly broken by a leap into Elie Chaib's arms. Or the logic accumulates a tidal force that pounds steadily at a single effect, as in the finale, which is a paroxysm of slides and rolls across the floor. When you think about it technically—about the materials it is made of—*Esplanade* involves the same negation of professional dance expertise that has preoccupied certain radical choreographers in the past decade. But *Esplanade* doesn't *force* you to think about it technically, whereas "minimalist dance"—or "people dance," to use a term in recent circulation—does, because it's often so cryptic. It's so grayly modest, so pure, that it leaves out the reason it was made. Taylor's piece engages the audience completely, so that we never have to think about what has been left out, and we know exactly why it was made. It has pristine beauty, elementary drive, democratic appeal—all of that. But when I

left the Lyceum Theatre, where it had its New York première, I wasn't thinking, How beautifully minimal! I was
thinking that I'd seen a classic of American dance.

The simple progression of the piece freshens the vision.
After the opening walks and runs, which clear a space in our
minds for the action that is to come (hence, I think, the title), we pass to another set of basics, in which we are shown
how, by lengthening or shortening the phrase line on which
an arm is extended or a head turned, gesture is made to assume the color of drama. There is no story here, just as the
differently accented walks and runs have no practical objective. Taylor is demonstrating the fundamentals of expression in choreography—a heavy thing to say, but he has
found the lightest way of doing it. At moments, he gets a
little light-*headed*—Taylor's blending of the blithe and the
serious is one of the most volatile compounds in theatre—
and yet it is just this giddiness, paradoxically, that steadies
him through the succession of tours de force that constitute
Esplanade. For the final two sections of the work he uses the
Largo and Allegro of the Double Violin Concerto in D Minor—the music of Balanchine's *Concerto Barocco*. Does he
crack that barrier? I think he does—primarily by producing
nothing remotely like *Concerto Barocco* or any other ballet.
His gift for sheer rhythmic propulsion has never been more
exciting.

The single program for the week's engagement, which
was a sellout, also included some of Taylor's best pieces:
Sports and Follies, *Three Epitaphs*, the duet from *Lento*, and
Private Domain. Taylor himself did not dance, but the rest
of the company performed with exceptional intensity. Playing to full houses every night seemed to have sharpened
them. They are very attractive in their new popularity, with
an unreal vitality, like cartoon animals. The new audience

for Taylor doesn't resemble the audience for any other company; yet another congregation has sprouted on the rim of Broadway. Its heartiest applause went to *Esplanade*, which may become the most popular work in the general repertory since Alvin Ailey's *Revelations*. The dancers, crashing wave upon wave into those slides, have a happy insane spirit that recalls a unique moment in American life—the time we did the school play or were ready to drown in the swimming meet. The last time most of us were happy in that way.

—June 30, 1975

Separate Worlds

American Ballet Theatre is launching its combinations of Russian and native stars in planned stages: Rudolf Nureyev and Cynthia Gregory in Nureyev's production of *Raymonda*, Natalia Makarova and Erik Bruhn (an ABT veteran star returned from retirement) in a new pas de deux, Makarova and Fernando Bujones in *La Bayadère*, and, in the last weeks of the season, Mikhail Baryshnikov and Gelsey Kirkland in the *Giselle* that New York has been waiting for, and in practically everything else except *Swan Lake*. The season is huge box-office with madness in the air—not only full houses but demonstrative ones that keep the madness going long after the curtain has dropped. Bunches of flowers are pelted across the footlights; shredded programs (a specialty of the Gregory fans) rain from the top balcony. Not every star-coupling has produced chemistry, and except in the case of Kirkland-Baryshnikov, who have already established themselves as a team, none could have been hoped for; it was simply the friction of star rubbing against star. Audiences may think they're getting more for their money when such mismatchings as Nureyev-Gregory or

Makarova-Bruhn occur and the size of the ovation is automatically doubled, but the excitement dies with the last bouquet, and sometimes it doesn't begin until the flowers start flying.

In *Epilogue*, the pas de deux created for Makarova and Bruhn by the American-born Hamburg choreographer John Neumeier, nothing happened until the curtain came down and the fans went into their act, but this wasn't the epilogue that Neumeier had in mind. Leaves falling one by one, rust-colored costumes, Makarova in a turban, Bruhn with his back to her—a neon sign spelling out "The Autumn of Their Relationship" couldn't have made the situation more obvious. We "read" the situation at a glance, feeling foolish because it's so easy but feeling apprehensive, too. Neumeier has set us up before with his literary concepts that go nowhere as dances, yet his choreography is so ingrown and painfully labored that it seems to spring from a revulsion against the very idea of literariness. It wants to get somewhere as dancing, but, for Neumeier, translating a dramatic situation into a dance seems to be chiefly a matter of avoiding paraphrasable content. He keeps emptying the dance of what the characters might be "saying" to each other and substituting the arduous anonymous relations of two dancers trying to work something out in a practice studio. The steps are meaningless; they look as if they could have been composed in any order, and to any music but the music we hear, which happens to be the Adagietto from Mahler's Fifth. At this level, Makarova and Bruhn are more interesting taking class. There's nothing wrong with a choreographer's being literary if he has guts, and although I prefer drama when it's revealed from inside the dancing, choreography that works with the drama outside (as in the best of Tudor) is just as difficult to bring off and just as rewarding when it succeeds. Neumeier starts by being Tudor, then crosses suddenly to would-be Balanchine. He plants a signpost, then rips up the path it points to. He's become a successful, in-demand choreographer because some of his concepts are almost magisterial: the use of Stravinsky's score combined with bits of Tchaikovsky to frame a story about ballet in *Le Baiser de la Fée*, the use of Nureyev in *Don Juan*, or Makarova and Bruhn dancing to the score of the movie *Death in Venice*. But Neumeier's concepts are always stuck on the page, like an undirected script. In his *Baiser* one could all but see the script indications for the blanks in the action which the dances were supposed to fill: "Groom dances with Bride"; "Bride dances alone." In *Epilogue*, it's "Middle-aged dancers dance."

Bruhn has always been an insular kind of star. Inwardly rigid, absorbed in his own perfection, he has never mated well with any ballerina, and his best roles were those that placed barriers between him and women—James in *La Sylphide*, Jean in *Miss Julie*, the Poet in *La Sonnambula*—or that accounted for the neurotic tension he projected, and still projects, onstage. Neither of his two new roles this season—in *Epilogue* or in *Raymonda*, as Abdul-Rakhman, the Saracen sheikh—accounts for Bruhn in this way. He remains Erik Bruhn, possibly the only major male star in ballet who can't walk toward a woman and appear to love her. In *Epilogue*, his role seems to be based on *Miss Julie*, which would be all right if Makarova's were, too, but she's all suppleness and entreaties, and when she stretches her lovely silken legs around him she seems to give him cramps. The two are temperamentally disparate dancers who have appeared together before mostly in ballets like *Giselle* and *Les Sylphides*. In a "strange," modern work built around their disparities they might have struck sparks at last, but there's no interest in seeing them unrelate to each other in a piece that doesn't have unrelatedness as its subject. It's the dancers, not the characters, who remain in their separate worlds.

Epilogue is the kind of piece that makes an unintentional joke of expressive form. It reveals by accident what the ballet should have been about. *Raymonda* betrays itself in much the same way, but on a far larger scale. Its accidental subject is the destruction of the ballerina; it should have been titled "Putting Raymonda in Her Place." Nureyev, who appeared as guest artist during ABT's first week, is wrong for Cynthia Gregory not only because he isn't tall enough but because he hasn't any use for her as the heroine of his ballet. This is the version of *Raymonda* he originally produced three years ago for the Zurich Ballet, with Marcia Haydée as Raymonda and with scenery and costumes by Nicholas Georgiadis. Nureyev in recent years has avoided putting himself up against dancers of Gregory's strength and stature; it's been Haydée or Karen Kain or Merle Park or the aging Fonteyn, and he has adopted an unseemly high-handed approach to his classical revivals. *Raymonda* is the most egotistical show he has ever put on and as a work of custodianship the most licentious.

Even without Nureyev's participation, *Raymonda* would have been a dubious addition to the Ballet Theatre repertory. It is a long and prolix work, with a foolish story and a score lacking in theatrical momentum. Petipa conceived it, in 1898, as a series of dance suites bridged by a thin scaffolding of pantomime. The suites—classical in the first act, character in the second, a combination of both in the third—are best seen in excerpt form: a fact acknowledged by every major ballet company in the Western world, including ABT, which until a few years ago gave the old

Balanchine version of Act III under the title *Grand Pas Glazunov*. About the only case that one can make for a full-length *Raymonda* (did ABT try making it to Nureyev?) is that it has a great ballerina role. Arranged for Pierina Legnani, the Odette-Odile of the St. Petersburg *Swan Lake*, the role is large and glorious, with a superb entrance that recalls Aurora's in *The Sleeping Beauty*. After running down a flight of stairs, the dancer bends to the floor and rises into high attitude, scooping up six roses in turn. Petipa's detailed notes to the composer warned, "You must pay special attention to this entrance. It is for the first dancer." Poor Cynthia Gregory! In her *Raymonda*, the first dancer is Nureyev, and he enters to her music, leaving her to scoop up her roses almost as an afterthought. Raymonda has no entrance—she's onstage when the curtain rises, fooling around the back of the set in the warm-up-the-house scene. Nureyev leaves her her five variations (he himself has four—three more than Petipa and Glazunov planned for), but he never surrounds her with light and space. The role is that worst combination in theatre: it is difficult and it is drab. The production doesn't build up a special picture of a romantic heroine, or even a star ballerina. Petipa's heroine was passive and dreamy, but Nureyev makes her a masochistic nitwit. He has reworked the plot elements so that an uncomfortable amount of the action takes place in her mind, and the triangle of Raymonda, the heroic knight, and the Saracen sheikh becomes tense with ambiguous confrontations in the manner of modern-dance drama. Neither man is characterized so as to make a choice possible, and the girl is badly pulled about between the two to no expressive purpose. I mean literally pulled about: Nureyev never leaves her alone except in her solos. In their big first-act pas de deux, he partners so incessantly that she hasn't room to expand, and he keeps her bouncing like a marionette. Where is the adagio in this adagio? Bruhn partners in the same callous manner—"Oh, here's an ankle," and he grabs it and cranks her into a turn. None of this is meant to be dramatically expressive, but it says a great deal. As in *Epilogue*, the dancing takes on implications that lie outside the ballet; it tells us more about Nureyev's unconscious than about Raymonda's.

Boxed in by Nureyev and slowed by the conducting of Akira Endo on the first night, Gregory gave an exhibition of virtuosity drained of vivacity. At the next performance, David Gilbert's tempi were more reasonable and the steps were brightly produced, but with a sense of personal dissociation, and with no surge through the body. Nureyev's dancing was like his production—eccentric, excessive, overworked. At this point in his career, Nureyev probably feels he must show as much of himself as he can to his audiences, and his audiences obviously feel the same way. But Nureyev's interests, which mesh with the interests of companies in difficulty at the box office, clash with Ballet Theatre's. It doesn't need Nureyev vehicles; it needs vehicles for its own stars, and it badly needs authoritative coaching in the styles proper to classical revivals. What remains of the Petipa tradition in the first two acts of this *Raymonda*—a string of variations, the choreography for the female corps in the Valse Fantastique, one or two of the character numbers—isn't enough to offset the chaos and gloom of Nureyev's staging. The famous Hungarian divertissement in Act III is by far the best part of the show, but like the show as a whole it's inferior to other versions Nureyev has produced. (It includes a particularly incoherent solo that Nureyev has fashioned for himself to the processional music, and the Apotheosis begins with a slow-motion wrestling match between him and the ballerina which, in a sense, apotheosizes their odd relationship.) Ballet Theatre keeps on buying pigs in transparent pokes. Did no one fly to Zurich to see what this production was all about? Since the company was not to get out of it what it most coveted—a long, rich role for Gregory—one wonders why it didn't save its money and revive *Grand Pas Glazunov* instead.

Ballet Theatre is weak in middle-rank female soloists— another reason it should have thought twice before putting on *Raymonda*. Only Martine van Hamel, a principal dancer cast in a supporting role, floated above the storm; her several classical variations were fully pronounced and glowing in tone, and her intrepid Spanish number was the salvation of the exotic "character" suite. In *La Bayadère*, the three women's solos were disastrously handled; we did not get van Hamel (nor are we to get this season her magnificent performance in the leading role). But there was continued improvement in the work of the corps, and Bujones danced with javelinlike precision, though with perhaps a little too much deliberation in the heroic Russian style. Makarova's Nikiya, the best I have seen from her, was troubling in its remoteness and lack of bite until I remembered that Nikiya is a ghost in a world of ghosts and Makarova the kind of dancer who would insist on that. Her way of taking charge of the meaning of an entire ballet and not just her own role in it is one of the traits that make her an artist as well as a star. I happen to disagree with her Nikiya, but not with her Chekhovian Caroline in *Jardin aux Lilas*, where her sorrow encompasses all trapped creatures. And she continually renews herself. This year's *Swan Lake* did more than last year's by doing less. The dual portrait was ravishing in its subtlety and mystery—with an Odile neither wittily wicked nor corrupt but guileless in the purity of her evil—and an audience that had come to stamp and yell was cooled to stillness and attention. Makarova did the impossible at Ballet Theatre: she calmed the beast.

—July 28, 1975

An American Giselle

Last summer, Mikhail Baryshnikov made his American début partnering Natalia Makarova in *Giselle* with the American Ballet Theatre. Makarova "sponsored" Baryshnikov in that performance, and a year later almost to the day Baryshnikov did the same for Gelsey Kirkland in her New York début as Giselle. In different ways, both débutants enjoyed a triumph that seemed guaranteed in advance. There was nothing to do but wait for the performance to bring it about. Baryshnikov would have had his triumph in any role that let him soar, but in Kirkland's case it was the perfect apposition of star and role that was a fait accompli. In the nearly forty years that we have had *Giselle* in the American repertory, we haven't lacked great interpreters, but we have lacked a great American-born Giselle. Kirkland may be the first totally credible American Giselle since the ballet was first danced here, in the nineteenth century. The role has been taken by brilliant American ballerinas, but none seems to have fit inside its Russo-European tradition as Kirkland does. And this isn't just because, partnered by Baryshnikov and modeling her conception on Makarova's, Kirkland has made herself look almost as if she, too, came from the Kirov; it's because she's a natural Giselle, whose chrysalis is the immediate influence upon her of these two great Russian stars. I wouldn't be surprised if, as she grows accustomed to the part, she were to shake off some of the more pious Kirovisms, such as the very slow tempo of the second-act adagio. A deliberate act of emulation, the performance is already impressive for its lack of excrescence. Kirkland has borrowed only as much as conforms with her instinct, and that instinct is profound. I predict that when she reaches her full wingspread in the part, she will have made the connection between the Russo-European Romanticism of the ballet and the romantic mythology of American melodrama even clearer than it is now.

Kirkland is a natural Giselle the way other Americans are natural Myrthas—by reason of Freudian biological destiny. But it's not only that the role underscores her airiness and fragility; it also enhances the archetypal echoes in her personality. As Giselle, Kirkland is more Lillian Gish–like than ever; she even seems to be playing a Gish role. She also has, again by nature, a plainness and stringency of manner in the way she presents a role, a fastidious taste that withdraws before "romantic" excess. All this has, I think, a peculiar appeal to Americans, especially to young Americans new to ballet. For old-timers, Kirkland just now brings no burst of originality to the part, but that is as it should be. She doesn't jar the marvelous singular clarity of the picture she presents; she awakens an extinct cameo image and lets us play with its reverberations. There is no suspense over "interpretation." She forgives her Albrecht as she dies, and that's that. Though it by no means sets the capstone on what she has achieved as an artist, Kirkland's appearance in *Giselle* is a promise fulfilled.

In the first performance, there were a few technical uncertainties, most of them having to do with the spacing of entrances and exits within the set. Erratic conducting marred the first-act solo. There was a moment at the start of the solo when eye contact between Kirkland and Baryshnikov lapsed, but it's an indication of how well they were performing together that the lapse should have been felt. I expect that by the second performance these errors had been corrected. So, too, the descent from the two overhead lifts, which on the first night was chancy both times. Baryshnikov is a much more relaxed Albrecht than he was a year ago or even last winter. His acting is free and unguarded, yet rhythmically taut, and there's a new and keener flow of volubility between him and Kirkland, which also showed in their *La Sylphide* this season. The dancing pours out of the mime as if in a fever of pent-up eloquence. The diagonal of brisés toward Myrtha with open, pleading hands has never been stronger in its emotional impact, and the lily-strewn ending, with its symbolic transference of Giselle's spirit into the bouquet that scatters, never more lucid.

The third member of this superb cast was Martine van Hamel. Tall and luscious, van Hamel dances Myrtha as the great ballerina role it is. The grandeur of her carriage makes even a simple rhythmic port de bras, such as the one she does standing in a cluster of Wilis, an exciting dance experience, and when she advances on a majestic tide of sautés en arabesque those treetop arms of hers both clear her path and cross it in momentary blockages. She gives Myrtha a divided nature—she's no one-dimensional dry-ice villainess.

Van Hamel is the company's most dramatic classical dancer. She shows us the drama of classicism as a drama of poetic suggestion, not a drama of peril. At Ballet Theatre, you frequently see dancers, gifted and ungifted, trying to reduce classical phraseology to one bright element—the piqué balance or the extra twirl—that the audience can read as a blanket meaning. They have acrobatic daring, but they don't have the large understanding that van Hamel has of the compound imagery of a classical phrase—its ability to express several meanings at once. At times, at ecstatic peak moments, van Hamel gets swept away on the crosscurrent of her text; she goes emotionally high on the movement and, apparently, regrets it later. Recently, she told a *Soho Weekly News* interviewer that she felt her Black Swan was "too young and too happy." But the multidimensional logic of classicism allows for van Hamel's happiness, and we're as happy as she is that she can express that logic so well. Van Hamel uses her weight and size fearlessly to magnify the fluid changes of balance and proportion of which she is such a mistress. She is the perfect Petipa dancer—squarely based, obliquely reinforced, yet temperate, rounded, and soft. In the title nonrole of *Raymonda*, she made sense of every moment that fell to her; and every moment that didn't—and there were quite a few—found her cheerfully content. Van Hamel's movement is big and honest. Very beautifully, she showed you the exact point of all the *Raymonda* variations and also the exactness of the monotony with which they are arranged. She couldn't save the ballet, but it was one of her largest and sunniest performances, and at the end there was an ovation. As the season closed, the audience seemed at last to be catching on to van Hamel's magic. Several fans even threw flowers—a sure sign.

—*August 18, 1975*

The End of the Line

The Broadway shows *A Chorus Line* and *Chicago* are dance musicals in the sense that both were devised and directed by choreographers—*A Chorus Line* by Michael Bennett and *Chicago* by Bob Fosse. I don't think anyone is going to the shows just for the dances, because these aren't distinguished and, curiously enough, they don't aim to be. Choreographer-directed shows, in which the choreography works as an element in the staging, have been with us for a long time, and so has the choreographer as a triple threat—not only arranging the dances and directing the show but also in whole or in part "conceiving" it (as the credit line usually says). But not until now has the viewpoint of the choreographer-director-conceiver taken over the function ordinarily assumed by the writer of a show's book. *Chicago*, which is based, not very soundly, on Maurine Watkins's 1926 play of that title, has a book by Fosse and the lyricist Fred Ebb, but anyone who has seen such former Fosse productions as the film *Cabaret* and the show and film *Sweet Charity* will immediately recognize in *Chicago* the imprint of Fosse the *auteur*. And the circumstances that led to the creation of *A Chorus Line* are already famous. In a *Times* interview shortly after the show opened, downtown at the Public, Mel Gussow printed the following:

> Mr. Bennett, who began his career dancing in the chorus (at seventeen in *Subways Are for Sleeping*), met with twenty-four dancers. "We danced for hours," he recalled, ". . . and then we went into a room and talked about it. I wanted to know why they had started dancing. In a sense, I wanted to know why I had started—and hadn't I lost something along the way?"
>
> From this original, long rap session gradually grew *A Chorus Line*. Before a word of the show was written, he chose his cast . . . "It is their lives," Mr. Bennett said, referring to the performers, "although they are not necessarily telling their own stories. A couple of stories about my youth are there." From this material and their own imaginations, James Kirkwood and Nicholas Dante began fashioning a book.

The book that Kirkwood and Dante fashioned may be said to have the banality of truth, but it also has the banality of show business. The show takes the form of an audition: seventeen dancers line up, give their resumés, and answer questions put to them from the dark by the choreographer-director (Robert LuPone) about why they started dancing. This inquisition is never rebelled against; one might almost think it part of any Broadway open call. And in fact it has been a part of Bennett's continuing auditions for replacements in the show and for second casts. A *Times* follow-up story reports, " 'How did your family feel about your being in theatre?' Michael Bennett, who conceived the show and was running the audition, asked." In the real as well as the staged audition, the dancers respond to Why did you start? and How did they feel? with the stock answers: I used to dance in front of the mirror. I put shows on in the garage. I got interested in my sister's dancing classes. My mother pushed me into it. My parents were unhappy. I had to get out of Buffalo. I saw *The Red Shoes*. But this small change of dancers' biographies grows into the common currency of commercial theatre when the contestants start hitting the "truth" part of the game. In quite a few Broadway and Off Broadway shows of recent years, the action consists of people coming together in tight situations and confessing. In Harold Prince's *Follies*, a musical that was choreographed and co-directed by Michael Bennett, the characters spent a great deal of time raking up the past and accusing themselves and each other of misspent lives. *A Chorus Line* is nothing like this orgy of disembowelment, but it takes its cue from it, both in the setting (a dark, empty theatre) and in the assumption that recitals of past humiliations are synonymous with character revelation. The dancer-characters of *A Chorus Line* are in their twenties or just past thirty, and what they reveal of their lives are their childhood encounters with sex or the pain they felt at being "different" or their resentment of parents and teachers who did them dirt—all fairly innocuous stuff by Broadway standards but mediocre stuff by any sterner standard. When the show is over, we have our choice of two conclusions—either that we haven't discovered who these people are or that they're actually as shallow as the show makes them out to be. Those who go to *A Chorus Line* hoping to learn something about chorus dancers, their life and work, will gain approximately as clear an insight as could be had from the *All About Eve* musical adaptation *Applause*, in which the same sort of energetic, desperate, hard-bitten youngsters were on view playing supposedly fresh and charming chorus boys and girls. *A Chorus Line* is a little like *Applause* crossed with *The Boys in the Band*; as in the latter show, there's an array of representative types—the cast is a statistical sampling of ethnic and geographical origins, class divisions, and levels of professional experience—but all this variety has no expression in the performances. Nearly everybody is overearnest and strained or cute-tough; the only character who doesn't fit the Broadway-juvenile mold is the cool, wisecracking Miss Been Around, and she's a fixture of long standing in the backstage musicals we used to know.

The powerful illusion of this show and the source of its appeal are that dancers are onstage playing out their own lives. Bennett keeps the pressure-cooker intensity of the audition building even unto the final judgment, when the dancers who are asked to step forward turn out to be the ones who have been rejected. (Good old false suspense; it worked in *The Red Shoes*, too.) One illusion the show can't sustain is the worthiness of a dancing career on Broadway; especially at the chorus level, conditions haven't been so bad since the days when show dancing consisted of hack routines that the able-bodied could pick up overnight. Vocational miseries creep into the show in the plight of Cassie (Donna McKechnie), a failed star trying to come back by starting again in the chorus, and in the plight of Paul, who loses his place in the lineup when he injures his knee, and in the plight of all of them when they hold a solemn symposium on the subject "What do we do when we can't dance anymore?" (with lines like "Dreams don't pay the rent"). There's a polemical tinge to the aggrieved feelings that pile up, and Edward Kleban's lyrics—which, together with Bennett's staging, are the best element in the show—make sardonic use of these feelings in several comedy numbers. One girl sings about a Method-acting course that nearly destroyed her, but nobody sings about the aesthetic content of the dancing that they are asked to do. It doesn't take more than a few visits to musical shows to see what the real tragedy of the dancer is. He's inherited a vacuum. His training, compared to what it was even ten years ago, is weak, his tunes are uninspired, his choreography is stale, and his performing style is corrupt. *A Chorus Line* is one of the shows that reveal this sad state of affairs, and one of the saddest things in it is the dancers' vision of Broadway as a refuge for talent, a haven where you can still shine even though you won't become a ballerina or a star. The emotional tone of the show isn't rousing—it's sweaty and sad—and when the cast recovers its spirits with a hymn to the theatre which is meant to wipe away all anxieties and regrets ("What I Did for Love"), and when those spirits are pumped still higher in the grand finale ("One"), I don't believe in it.

This finale and a solo for Cassie are the only two real efforts at choreographing dances which Bennett makes, and his craft is nothing a dancer can live on. "One" is a conflation of Rockettes-style line dancing and the kind of super-cool mannerisms that are primarily associated with Fosse (in fact, it looks very much like a Ben Vereen number from *Pippin*). The solo, in which Cassie tries to prove what she's got if only she can have a chance to use it, is one of the sorest letdowns of the show. The choreography is frantic and unfocused, and McKechnie, who has the most evenly developed technique in the company, *can't* show what she's got. The firm, lifted upper torso, clear waist, and columnar neck that look so lovely when she's standing still are never brought into play by the dance, and she stiffens her back against the jagged phrasing. The other dancers are technically weak in every kind of movement that they can't use peak force to control, such as a high kick or a turn; they have neither an easy rhythm nor a convincingly nervous one. The Fosseisms, which glue the feet to the floor and keep the center of the body pinched against the pelvis, conceal their awkwardness, but they're also seen competing in the various combinations that form the obstacle course of the audition (ballet, Latin jazz, tap). These combinations are given just the way they would be in a real audition. In the ballet combination, which is taken across the floor four dancers at a time, each lurching quartet performs a gag extraneous to the dancing, though it would be more honest to let the dancing be the gag. For a show built around dancers, *A Chorus Line* is loath to release any of its meanings through dance. Perhaps Bennett doesn't feel much of a commitment to dance as a source of expression. There's a terrible dialogue scene, painful in its factitiousness, in which Cassie and the choreographer-director, who are former lovers, have one of those career-versus-romance quarrels, and he tells her she never understood what his career meant to him how if he succeeded he wouldn't be "stuck just making up dances." The dances in *A Chorus Line* show us exactly how dreary a fate that would be.

Bennett's talent is evident in the tight pace of the show and the smooth integration of the various confessional arias. Some of these are spoken or sung without interruption; in others the staging splinters and intercuts the material in such a way as to transcend its bathos. And Bennett's staging of "One" transcends his own trite choreography. His device is repetition. So many repeats take place before Robin Wagner's mirrored backdrop (which reverses to disclose a gold-and-silver sunrise) that the formula steps are dramatized into an eternal ritual, an apotheosis of routine. The chorus line seems to stretch into infinity doing its same dumb dance—the only dance that Broadway knows.

Although the limitations of Bob Fosse's dance style became obvious long ago, it is still the pervasive style of Broadway. Its method of closing down and hugging the figure so that the only way it can move is by isolating and preciously featuring anatomical parts makes it a good vehicle for narcissistic display and slithering innuendo. *Chicago* cheapens the style even further, but the style is only part of the décor in a generally cheap and vicious show. The tale of a dizzy chorus girl who shoots her lover and then showboats to fame on the publicity surrounding the trial might have made an excellent musical; the song-and-dance styles of the era come practically ready-made. In the 1942 film *Roxie Hart*, Ginger Rogers danced the Black Bottom. But Chicago in the twenties was probably too easy a subject for Fosse to get wound up in. He has expanded the yellow press and the shyster lawyers of Cook County's worst decade into malign forces with perennial roots in American life. You won't catch anyone doing the Black Bottom in Fosse's *Chicago*; this is a universal allegory, and Roxie Hart is Arturo Ui.

Even with this preposterous overload to carry, the story might still have worked if there had been some wit and tension in the writing, but there isn't one line that scalds, one clever characterization or turn of plot. Instead, there are wormwood jokes in the staging, like the one about the innocent imprisoned girl who goes up a circus ladder while the band plays merrily and then swings from the gallows in silhouette. *Chicago* goes beyond *Cabaret* in the putrescent horrors of the life it puts before us; I think it goes beyond any other show I have ever seen. Fosse tells us that we not only permit evil to flourish in our midst but actively enjoy it and love making stars out of scheming whores like Roxie Hart. In both its shock imagery and its scabrous text, the show is a frontal assault on the audience. The lawyer (well played by Jerry Orbach) sings a song called "Razzle Dazzle," the burden of which is that with a little glitter before its eyes the public can always be fooled and any no-talent can get by if he knows the tricks. When Roxie and her girl friend from murderesses' row reach the big time in their vaudeville act at the end of the show, they toss roses to the audience because "you made us what we are." The cynicism is appalling, but the audience takes the bait and applauds as if it were really being complimented. Fosse knows all the tricks; does he want us to think he's a no-talent whose success has been too easy?

With Fosse, as with many choreographer-directors, the image seems to come first, then the meaning that will support it. Many of his images in *Chicago* are unsteadily supported because he is trying to force a correspondence between Chicago and pre-Nazi Berlin which has no basis in reality. Roxie's husband, a sad fat man, is given a solo in a clown rig that makes him resemble Emil Jannings in *The Blue Angel*. *Chicago* is full of odd, elusive conceits like this, which keep it from being boring and may cause people to think of it as a well-staged show, but it's really an over-staged show—the height of theatrical decadence; everything that we're meant to react to is in the staging. It's strange to think of Fosse as the last German Expressionist—strange that his own decadence as an artist should take such a visually alien form. With Liza Minnelli in the role of Roxie for the next few weeks, the link to *Cabaret* is strengthened, but Liza Minnelli is so easy to take that Fosse's conception of the role is vitiated by her presence. Minnelli is a warm, happy performer whose eagerness to please the audience contradicts Fosse's intention of affronting it. She just can't offend. When she throws the roses, at least part of the applause is a response to her personally. I haven't seen Gwen Verdon in the part, but she doesn't seem to have had much dancing to do; all the strenuous stuff is handled by the hard-working, cheerless Chita Rivera.

Dancers and choreographers were once credited with raising the standards of the musical, but that was in an era when those standards were already high. Music on Broadway has declined along with dance; the two are interdependent. When an art form is in trouble, its practitioners may grow self-serious in an effort to assert the stature of their work. Many show people are looking deep into themselves for something to say and finding that the only subject they know is show business. *A Chorus Line* and *Chicago* are about show business, and each reflects an attempt to make the subject rise to some level of significance above mere entertainment. Musicals are proclaiming their stature; now they're being taken with solemnity by people who never could take them at all.

—August 25, 1975

Momentous

A masterpiece by definition transcends its time, but even masterpieces are created in response to some need of the moment. Perhaps it would be more true to say that a masterpiece doesn't so much transcend its time as perpetuate it; it keeps its moment alive. In *The Four Temperaments*, revived at the New York City Ballet after some years out of repertory, the moment is luminously there. This was 1946, and Balanchine was in the midst of one of his most fertile periods. What a monumental decade the forties was! Balanchine by then was established in America, but not solidly established; from *Concerto Barocco* and *Ballet Imperial* on through *The Four Temperaments* to *Theme and Variations* and *Symphony in C* he is on the attack. His objective: to make plain to American audiences the dynamics of classical style. In each of these ballets, the dancing grows from simple to complex structures, and every stage of growth is consequentially related to every other. It is partly because of their structural logic that his ballets make such great sense—or such vivid nonsense—to us years after they were completed, but it's also because such logic isn't the featured attraction; it's only the means by which a particular kind of entertainment is elucidated. What *is* featured is human variety.

This is true even of *The Four Temperaments*, one of the earliest works in which the elements of logic are arrayed in a form so brilliantly consequential that they nearly become the whole show. The relation between the continuity of the piece and its subject, which is the four varieties of human temperament (melancholic, sanguine, phlegmatic, choleric), is truly a magical one, consisting of a dance logic Balanchine has made look uniquely ritualistic. It isn't ritualistic in an exotic sense, it is ritual achieved by the most radical exposure of classical style Balanchine had provided to date. *The Four Temperaments*, created in 1946, marks one of Balanchine's several "beginnings," and, like *Apollo*, his first collaboration with Stravinsky, and *Serenade*, his first ballet for American dancers, it is a messianic work, which conveys to this day the sense of a brilliant and bold new understanding. Hindemith's score, subtitled "Theme with Four Variations (According to the Four Temperaments) for String Orchestra and Piano," was written to Balanchine's commission in 1940, but it was not until the formation of Ballet Society, following the Second World War, that Balanchine composed his choreography. After years of working on Broadway, in Hollywood, and for ballet organizations not his own, he was again in charge of a company, and in his first ballet for Ballet Society (the direct predecessor of the New York City Ballet) he made a fresh start, re-establishing the bases and the direction of American dance. Nowadays, *The Four Temperaments* (carelessly billed without the *The*, as if there could be more than four) doesn't appear novel in the way it did to observers of that time; its "distortions" and "angularities" have been absorbed into one important stream of Balanchine ballet and have been imitated the world over. But its style, in both root and blossom, is so consistent and so consistently keen to the eye, and the scale on which it flowers is so active in its leaps from tiny to enormous and back again, that one follows the progress of the ballet in wonder; it never fails to surprise and to refresh. And so it is new every time.

Going back to basics in 1946, Balanchine concentrated his attention equally on the smallest details and the largest resources of classical dance and on clarifying transitions from one to the other. When, in the opening statement of the ballet—the first part of the Theme—we see a girl, supported on her pointes, turning from side to side and transferring her weight from one foot to the other as she turns, we see her do it with a finicky grace: she lifts and lowers the free foot, curls it around the standing leg, and carefully flexes it before arching to full pointe. We see, in short, a foot becoming a pointe—nature being touched to artificial life. The detail looms for an instant, then quickly takes its place in the grand scheme of the ballet. The Theme is full of elementary particles, jostling, caroming, crisscrossing space in strokes that define the boundaries of the territory Balanchine will invade. In the Theme's second statement (there are three such statements, each a pas de deux), the side-to-side turns have become full revolutions, rapid finger-turns marked off by the girl's pointe as it taps the floor. In the third statement, the finger-turns are taken in deep plié with one foot held off the ground in passé position. The weight on that one supporting pointe looks crushing, but as we have seen, there is something about a woman's pointe that makes it not a foot—that makes it a sign. The image created by the third girl as she is spun is blithe, even comical; could Balanchine have been thinking of the bass fiddle the forties jazz player spins after a chorus of hot licks?

The developing sense of the passages I've cited is analogous to the process that takes place in the molding of a classical dancer's body. The "story" of *The Four Temperaments* is precisely that story—the subjection of persons to a process and their re-emergence as human archetypes—but these citations may make it seem as if that process happened all in close-up, and if that were true we would be in a crazy man's world. The world of *The Four Temperaments* is wide and swarming with possibilities, yet if we could pass the choreography through a computer to see how many core gestures there actually are, there would probably not be more than six—maybe eight. Balanchine has built a large and dense composition on a handful of cellular motifs, and it's this economy that allows us to perceive the ballet and survive it, too. There are gestures that seem to cluster in family relationships and that recur subtly transformed. How many elaborations are there on grand battement en balançoire? How many derivations from, adaptations of, combinations with? Some of these we see clearly, others hang just at the edge of vision. There are gestures that do not change at all—they're like stabilizing props that keep back the tide. One of these is the "Egyptian profile" with squared elbows; another is the women's splits across the men's thighs (but this, too, is an evolution—from the first pas de deux: the girl dropped in a split to the floor and slid into the wings). Balanchine's control of the action's subliminal force allows us the most marvelous play in our minds; we're torn in an agony of delight between what we see and what we think we see. Metaphoric implications flash by, achieve their bright dazzle of suggestion, and subside into simple bodily acts. The way the women stab the floor with their pointes or hook their legs around men's waists or grip their partners' wrists in lifts—images of insatiable hunger, or functional necessities? Balanchine gives us a sharp pair of spectacles to see with, but he occasionally fogs one of the lenses. If he didn't, we'd perish from the glare.

And that lens we see with—isn't it a moving lens, a camera eye? Darting in for details, withdrawing to lofty heights, it views the dance from as many perspectives as the body can indicate in its manifold placements within space. Space itself is liquefied, and planes on which we observe the dance rise, tilt, descend. Sometimes we are launched and roving in this liquid space; sometimes we are pressed, riveted, to the floor. Out of these volatile perspectives drama is made. In the first variation (Melancholic), we have an expansive field of vision, but the solo dancer does not seem to know how much room he has. His space is penetrated by menacing diagonals for the entries of the corps. The corps is a few small girls, a small menace. But they are enough to block and frustrate his every attempt to leap free. He leaps and crumples to earth. We recognize this man: his personal weather is always ceiling zero. (It's a nineteenth- rather than a seventeenth-century conception of melancholy—Young Werther rather than Robert Burton.) In the Sanguinic variation, for a virtuoso ballerina and her partner, the vista is wide, the ozone pure and stinging. The ballerina is an allegro technician; she is also a character. She enters and pauses. Her partner is expectant. But she pauses and turns her gaze back toward the wings. For a moment she seems to wear a demure black velvet neck ribbon, and then she is bounding like a hare in the chase, an extrovert after all. The Sanguinic variation takes us to the top of the world, and twice we ride around its crest, its polar summit (a circuit of lifts at half-height). In these two thrilling flights, the camera eye pivots on the pinpoint of a spiral, once to end the trajectory, once to start it. We see, as in some optical effect of old cinema, a scene spread from the center of its compass, then respread in reverse.

The topography of the ballet shrinks in the Phlegmatic variation to the smallest it has been since the Theme. Phlegmatic is indolent, tropical, given to detached contemplation, to pretentious vices. The male soloist languishes, and loves it. Slowly he picks up invisible burdens, lifts them, and clothes himself in their splendor. Slowly, self-crowned, he picks up his right foot and studies it. His little dance with the corps includes cabbalistic gestures toward "his" floor, and he hovers close to the ground, repeating his mumbo-jumbo (a syncopated time step) as if he expected the ground to answer him. The confined, floor-conscious world of Phlegmatic and Melancholic returns redeemed in the next section, when Choleric, that angry goddess, executes her climactic ronds de jambe par terre. Here we have the traditional dénouement of an eighteenth-century ballet (or such a nineteenth-century one as *Sylvia*), in which Mount Olympus hands down a judgment on the mess mortals have made. Choleric enters in a burst of fanfares and flourishes, kicking the air. Her fury must be appeased, assimilated by the ballet's bloodstream. The entire cast collaborates in the process. Key motifs are recapitulated in tempi that charge them with new vitality. We are racing toward the finality of a decision, and then it comes. Those ronds de jambe are a space- and air-clearing gesture. Three circles traced on the ground: it is the most wonderful of the ballet's magic signs; the vastness of it incorporates all bodies into one body, all worlds into one planet. After a silence in which nobody moves, the great fugue of the finale begins its inexorable massed attack. All the parts the ballet is made of are now seen at once in a spectacle of grand-scale assimilation. Apotheosis. We see a succession of sky-sweeping lifts; we see a runway lined by a chorus of grands battements turned to the four points of the compass. The lifts travel down the runway and out as the curtain falls.

As a conception for a ballet, the four temperaments, or humors of the blood, have been realized with a profundity that doesn't depend on the intellectual powers of either the audience or the dancers. Balanchine has interpreted the subject in the form of a dance fantasy, but never so literally or so schematically that we need fear, if we miss one element, having missed all. We can trust the ballet in performance because it is built of the things that dancers as a race know about. No small part of its moral beauty comes directly from the dancers, from their fastidious concentration, their ghetto pride. Yet in *The Four Temperaments*, as in every ballet, casting does make a difference. This season, the perfect cast was Bart Cook in Melancholic, Merrill Ashley in Sanguinic, Jean-Pierre Bonnefoux in Phlegmatic, and Colleen Neary in Choleric—all of them new to their roles, and all hitting new highs in their careers. For dancers and audience alike, the ballet represents the cleansing and healing that Robert Frost speaks of in "Directive" when he says, "Here are your waters and your watering place. / Drink and be whole again beyond confusion."

—December 8, 1975

More or Less Terrific

⚋⚋

The big question about Twyla Tharp's *Push Comes to Shove*, for the American Ballet Theatre, is whether it is a very complex, very radically evolved piece of choreography enjoying itself as a send-up of conventional ballet or whether all its ingenuities of construction only go to service a few jokes about the style of *Giselle*, *Swan Lake*, and the institution of ballet in general. After two performances, I believe it is a real work of art and an entrancing good time in the theatre. But the play between the primary and secondary interests of the piece—the real invention versus the spoof material—is maintained in so careful a balance that, as in one of those optical illusions that can be looked at with equal conviction from two perspectives, I have difficulty deciding which end is up. *Push Comes to Shove* (the title is no help) is to Ballet Theatre as *Deuce Coupe* is to the Joffrey Ballet—it's a comment on the company as well as a gift to its dancers. But in *Deuce Coupe*, in both the première version and the one that Tharp prepared for the Joffrey repertory, there is a subject that carries the piece home to audiences who know nothing of what it comments on. That subject is popular songs and

dances, and what audiences are not expected to know or
care about is how it pertains to the Joffrey's self-styled pop
image. In the Ballet Theatre piece, the subject is more elusive. The ballet satire is double-edged. It works for a general
audience but not, I daresay, in its freshest form. And in its
freshest form—the embedded jokes of construction—it
ceases to be satire and becomes pure wit.

Tharp's wit is literally devastating. She finds so many
ways for the dancers to keep moving it's as if she had no
time to keep order. This illusion—and it is a brilliant illusion—widens into the spectacle of a ballet company in the
process of a breakdown, and Tharp several times reinforces
the point with moments swiped from the classics: the Wilis'
arabesques voyagées, Giselle leading Albrecht into the villagers' dance, the dance des coupes from *Swan Lake*. The an-
thologizing of such moments is good fun; we know why
they're there, and we know why in the middle of the last
section of the piece we suddenly get the ritualistic curtain
calls that are part of any evening at the ballet. But I don't
think we experience the comedy of these things as a product
of the highly original eruptive force that produced the ballet; they're really no different from the standard gags about
ballet that people of far less talent than Twyla Tharp have
been pulling for ages. When Martine van Hamel goes into
her hard-to-partner act with Clark Tippet, it's funny all
right, but the funniness is too far up front—too far from the
nervous center of the piece. Tharp at her best—and she is
here at her best about eighty-five percent of the time—produces an audacious logic out of dancing which is its own
form of comedy. In *Push Comes to Shove*, some of the gag
material goes beyond the discipline and self-sufficiency of
her style, and despite the abundant flow of creative juice
throughout the piece, the final impression it makes is a bit

slender. When Twyla Tharp gives us more than she has to, she actually gives us less than we want.

Still, she gives us a lot, and she spreads it around. Tharp has a logician's mind and a vaudevillian's heart. The tension between the two is her hallmark, and if it occasionally leaves traces of ambiguity in her work (as I think it does here), it gives her a tremendous advantage over every other young choreographer working today: she can be as abstruse as she wants and yet reach the big audience. *Push Comes to Shove* takes a very odd form, but it would be odder coming from anyone but Twyla Tharp. She has composed as if the form had been suggested to her by the title of the company that hired her. What's American about American Ballet Theatre? What's ballet to it, or it to ballet? What's left over that has to be theatrical? Isn't American Ballet enough? So the piece starts with an American rag—Joseph Lamb's "Bohemia," of 1919—and a shuffling turn in front of a forecurtain by three entertainers whom we recognize as the ballet dancers Mikhail Baryshnikov, Martine van Hamel, and Marianna Tcherkassky. There are Tharpian shrugs, slouches, and pelvis bumps for Baryshnikov ("Tharpian" because no one else uses this defunct style of black American dancers in blues performance), and there's also a derby hat that the girls keep stealing from him. When you've seen van Hamel deliver a high développé kick from under the hat, you've seen the beginning of the synthesis that is Tharp's answer to the proposition "American Ballet Theatre." The synthesis involves an amalgamation of high and popular art which no other choreographer except Balanchine has achieved in this country. Tharp's creative bent in recent years has been toward rephrasing the whole process of amalgamation in her own terms. That may be why she follows the rag with Haydn's 82nd Symphony. They have nothing in common except formal lucidity and refinement. But Tharp likes rags and she likes Haydn; she has used both before. And in the 82nd, subtitled "The Bear," Haydn was becoming the master, as Charles Rosen notes, of a "deliberately popular style," incorporating the folk songs and dance rhythms which up until then had been marginal to his inspiration. What Haydn achieved, Rosen says (in his book *The Classical Style*), was "true civilized wit, the sudden fusion of heterogeneous ideas with an air paradoxically both ingenuous and amiably shrewd," and it's what Tharp achieves in passages of this new piece, with her omnivorous dance wit. Some of the heterogeneous ideas come right off the wall. In Baryshnikov's solo to the opening movement of the symphony, in between all the sensational power-packed spins and jumps and off-center balances, he stands with folded arms and contracts his middle, or else walks around in circles running his fingers through his hair. The dancing gives us more of Baryshnikov, the twentieth-century "American" Baryshnikov, than anything else he has done so far, and the "rests" give us more of him, too—more than we normally see in the walking and posing that come between the step sequences in a classical ballet. His personality does not go behind a cloud, as it often does when he isn't dancing; it continues to radiate.

Tharp takes offstage behavior and rehearsal behavior and choreographs them into the dance. She does it again in the Allegretto, when the corps of girls change place in mid-dance merely by walking across the stage (having previously proved how nicely they can *dance* into place). The contrast may be delicate, as it is here, or violent, as in Baryshnikov's stop-and-go solo; it is funny both times. And it makes the sane point that ballet can be as much as a personal style or as little as a habit of performance cultivated by real people.

The lifelike, humane manners of the piece are one way Tharp shows her class as an artist. And she shows sound audience sense by providing something besides dancing for people to look at. We can follow that derby hat (which shortly becomes two hats) all around the stage. We can enjoy the farcical speed of the jokes, the unpredictable timing of entrances and exits, the differentiated roles of the stars, the happy zest with which the entire company performs. Although no one else could dance Baryshnikov's part, the piece is not a personal vehicle. His is the igniting spark that starts the ballet on its steep ascent, but then the others—van Hamel particularly—carry it up and away.

Once aloft, it never looks back—or, rather, it never stops to look back. What I have called the subject—the comedy of big-time ballet conventions—keeps advancing while the structural motifs organize themselves more and more tightly around the music's core. It feels like being caught in a whirlwind. Those of us who care about dance values have to look sharp. The big symphonic ballet in the Allegretto is a space-filling geometrical composition in the style of a drunken Petipa. Yet it's also a triumph of the daintiest musical craftsmanship. Like all of Tharp's group choreography, it is best seen from upstairs (where, at the Uris, the orchestral sound is stronger, too). In the finale, the stage is an arena of profuse activity—a ballet circus. There is a great deal to see as the piece rushes by—too much to take in at once. In between movements there are choreographed episodes danced in silence or to a nattering metronome which stretch the time the ballet happens in (not just its running time but also its temporal landscape); even so, it seems to be all gone in five minutes. Fortunately for us all, it is a great big hit, and it will be around for a while. On the first night, there were ovations for everyone—for the dancers, for Santo Loquasto, who designed a charming and curious array of costumes, and for Jennifer Tipton, whose lighting ranged from pastel brights to her warmest darks. The corps de ballet, which has its most exacting task since *La Bayadère*, was cheered. But the loudest roars were for Twyla Tharp. She has given Ballet Theatre a flash act and left us yelling for more.

—January 26, 1976

Two by Balanchine

Balanchine's two premières of the season, *The Steadfast Tin Soldier* and *Chaconne*, came in that order and without an intermission on the same program. They are two well-contrasted pieces, even contradictory. If you like me, says one, you can't possibly like the other. But the New York City Ballet audience, which seems to have grown more acutely responsive in the past year, wasn't drawn into that game. Despite some blurriness of intention toward the end of the first ballet and a prevailing blurriness in the second, it welcomed both warmly. *The Steadfast Tin Soldier* comes from the same confectionery as *The Nutcracker* and *Harlequinade* and *Coppélia*. Based on an Andersen tale, it tells of a dancing doll and a toy soldier who carry on a hearthside flirtation. The flames of passion leap higher, a gust of air blows the doll into the fire, and there is nothing left of her but her red enamel heart. Bravely, the soldier mans his post. Although it's only an excuse for a pas de deux, the story might be stronger than it is. I think Balanchine means to tell it earnestly but blithely, without sentiment. However, it isn't clear that the doll runs into the fireplace because she's blown there; nor is it clear that she's incinerated. The music (the galop from Bizet's *Jeux d'Enfants*) contains no motive for the doll's death, but properly staged, it could sound the exact note of heartless whimsy the piece is aiming at.

Doll dances have a perennial fascination. The overt simulation is a release from the conventions of theatre; it plays upon our need to judge empirically, rather than through a tolerance of fiction, what is "real." And every doll-dancer invents her own pseudo-personhood. Patricia McBride has invented one pseudo-person called Coppélia. She now invents another, without a name, warmer and sillier than Coppélia. The mechanics of the part are not undertaken as a great feat (unlike those mannequins in store windows which really set out to fool you), and they soon vanish into conventional fiction: we must take flesh and bone for wood and sawdust, when a moment ago we were mesmerized by the proposition that wood and sawdust were plausibly there. *The Steadfast Tin Soldier* is a dance and not a puppet show. The dance is continuously absorbing, stringent even in its moments of coyness, and McBride brings an ageless vitality to the doll's character. She has the sparkle of an experienced soubrette. Playing opposite the relatively inexperienced and still tentative Robert Weiss, she resists the temptation she often yields to when her partner is not a match for her—the temptation to compensate for him by exaggerating her own authority. It is a beautifully tempered performance.

The Steadfast Tin Soldier had its world première last summer in Saratoga. It is not a new ballet but a revival of part of *Jeux d'Enfants*, set by Balanchine and other choreographers to Bizet's complete score in 1955. David Mitchell has designed flattering new costumes and a new set, showing a sketchy Victorian parlor with toys piled on the hearth and a row of life-size cardboard sentinels in forced perspective.

The choreography for the ballerina looks as witty to me now as it did in the fifties except for one small detail: then she applauded herself *after* the audience applause had begun. The Soldier has entirely new choreography, and it is this role, made for Peter Schaufuss, that should really justify the revival. I regret not having seen the Saratoga performance; Schaufuss has been out with an injury since the start of the season.

Chaconne is not a new piece, either. It is a suite set to the ballet music from Gluck's *Orfeo ed Euridice*, and it derives from a production of the full opera mounted by Balanchine at the Hamburg State Opera in 1963. Gluck customarily ended his operas with dance finales in the form of a chaconne; they are seldom staged today. Balanchine's score was the Paris version of 1774, which Gluck had expanded by adding dance numbers from his other works. In 1973, Balanchine restaged the production, with cuts in the chaconne, at the Paris Opéra. Rouben Ter-Arutunian's Louis XIV–inspired costumes for Hamburg were replaced by Bernard Daydé's in the style of Gustave Moreau. Costumes—especially eighteenth-century dance costumes—are strongly implied in the line and sense of the choreography, but the New York City Ballet *Chaconne* uses plain white tunics for the women, white tights and shirts for the men. (This is the company's impartial "Greek" look.) Suzanne Farrell, in an overpowering role, wears an off-white chiffon shift.*

We begin with Farrell, her hair unbound, and Peter Martins alone on a dark-blue stage. Their dance—a romantic "swimming" duet to the flute solo from the Dance of the

---

*Karinska later designed an effective set of white-and-blue costumes, and Balanchine added a prelude with nine girls pacing the stage in toast chiffon.

Blessed Spirits in Gluck's second act—is less a prologue to
the ballet than a puzzling preliminary. What follows is completely different in style—a rococo divertissement with entries for the corps de ballet and demi-soloists. (The scene in
the opera is a court ballet in the Temple of Love.) There is a
gracious and supple, long-limbed pas de trois in which the
boy holds an invisible lute or mandolin. (In Hamburg, the
instrument was actually carried.) Two more courtiers have a
vivacious and somewhat taxing pas de deux. A pas de cinq
to music that sounds like the chirping of birds would be
more interesting metaphorically if we could tell that the five
short girls are cupids—cupids with wings. But then Farrell
and Martins return, and the court ballet fades away, to be
continued by other means. Farrell (now with hair classically
knotted) is high-rococo expression in every limb and joint.
Architecturally and ornamentally, her dancing is the music's
mirror, an immaculate reflection of its sweep and buoyancy,
with no loss of detail. Farrell's response to music is not to
its moment-by-moment impulse but to its broad beat, its
overarching rhythm and completeness of scale. When people speak of her as the perfect Balanchine dancer, this is
what they mean. The blurriness I complained of is not in
what she does. The trouble is simply that such poise, such
angelic transparency, is a law unto itself. What happens in
the middle of *Chaconne* is that a whole new ballet crystallizes, a new style in rococo dancing appears which in 1963
was unknown. Balanchine turns the clock ahead so suddenly
that if it weren't for Farrell's and Martins's steadiness we'd
lose our bearings. Their first pas de deux gave no hint of
what was to come. Now, in a minuet, they present a solemn
façade or gateway to the variations for them both that follow in a gavotte. These are like sinuous corridors leading
one on and on. It is excess, but it is controlled excess—

never more than one's senses can encompass, yet never less. Farrell's steps are full of surprising new twists; her aplomb is sublime. And Martins achieves a rhythmic plangency that is independently thrilling. (When people speak of him as the perfect partner for Farrell, this is not all they mean, but it's part of it.) Together, from the gavotte onward into the concluding chaconne, these two dancers are a force that all but obliterates what remains of the divertissement. Balanchine's ensemble choreography here is musically focused, but visually it is unrhymed. His yokes and garlands and summary groupings don't quite manage to gather and contain the new material for Farrell and Martins within the shell that remains from Hamburg-Paris. Evidently, Balanchine has restored the musical repeats he cut in Paris, but instead of giving them back to the corps (or, as seems more likely, to the demi-soloists), he assigned them, with new choreography, to Farrell and Martins. The two-sidedness of the ballet is a problem.

On première nights, the audience always applauds persistently, waiting for Balanchine to take his bow. After the double première, on January 22, he came before the curtain wearing one of his sprucest blazer-and-silk-scarf combinations, and it was hard to believe that it was also his seventy-second birthday. Not merely because he didn't look his age but because, measured against his accomplishments, his age seemed not nearly great enough. How many in the audience could remember what ballet was like without him? Generations of dancers, of audiences have received his imprint. The epochs unreel in their diversity, showing where he's been and with whom: Diaghilev and Cochran's Revue; Sam Goldwyn and Tchelitchev; Stravinsky and *Cabin in the Sky*; *Where's Charley?* and *The Nutcracker* and again Stravinsky. *Chaconne* reminds us of his many encounters with Orpheus: not only the two European productions of Gluck's opera but Offenbach's operetta and Stravinsky's ballet. Last December, he staged the dances—minus the chaconne—for yet another *Orfeo*, at the Chicago Lyric Opera. And there was his production in 1936 at the Metropolitan, from which only George Platt Lynes's photographs remain: a ballet-pantomime with offstage voices, hell pictured as a concentration camp, allusions to judo and nudity, and an attendant scandal in the press.

In those days, Balanchine had just started to build an American ballet company. He must have been as unpredictable then as he is now. Where he stands today, what aspect of his art he will emphasize next are questions to which the two "new" pieces he has just given us don't supply answers. Probably they weren't meant to. But the split in *Chaconne* reflects a vast impatience to be moving ahead. There's a motor racing inside this vehicle which is determined to shake it to pieces, and as a goad to performers what could be more exciting? A week after the première, I saw another performance. There was such euphoria onstage and in the pit that the final chaconne, loose ends and all, came together and held as if by miracle, and stars, demis, corps, orchestra, and audience were wafted together into Tiepolo skies.

—February 9, 1976

Home to Bournonville

The Guards of Amager is one of the dozen or so works by the nineteenth-century master August Bournonville which survive in the repertory of the Royal Danish Ballet. Until the company presented it here at the tail end of its Met season, the ballet had never been seen in New York. Visits by the Royal Danes are rare (the last was in 1965), and although one can see more or less authoritative performances of Bournonville ballets danced by other companies or by student groups, there's nothing like seeing a "new" Bournonville danced by Bournonville's own company—danced and mimed. The Danes bring a quality to miming that endows that sick art with new life. This isn't simple declarative mime in *The Guards of Amager*. This is visual conversation, paragraphs of it, running in counterpoint, overlapped and interrupted to complicated beats. It is done in ensembles all over the stage at once, or in intimate duologues or triologues, and so fast that if you drop your eyes you miss a vital narrative link. Yet it isn't what the characters are "saying" that tells the story—it's the characters themselves. The story that is being told is an operetta-ish af-

fair about the skirt-chasing commander of the guards and
his wife, who by way of reprimand seduces him at a masked
ball. There are two lovely moments in this story. When the
wife finds the sheet of music her husband has been playing,
she touches her temple and nods, as if saying to herself,
"He's been thinking of me." When she discovers that he's in
fact faithless, and later when he faces her, unmasked, at the
ball, neither of them takes it big. Louise and Edouard are
grown-up gentlefolk, a species we seldom see on the ballet
stage.

The Guards is late Bournonville; he made it in 1871, six
years before he retired, and eight years before he died. It has
the wisdom and buoyancy of old age, a fragrance of nostalgia that still penetrates. The frontcloth bears the subtitle
"An Episode of 1808." The prologue consists of five spotlit
scenes, each shorter than the one before. First, the guards
stationed on Amager are seen in unguardly attitudes surrounding their commander, who plays a spinet. To their
left, we see a sewing circle; to their right, townsmen dip-
ping snuff. Next, a huddle of gossips. A line of villagers
skips through the darkness, and then a doorway in Copen-
hagen lights up: two ladies in Empire gowns receive a letter
from a postman. Louise will visit the garrison. Almost before we have taken it in, the scene blacks out, the scrim rises,
and the ballet proper begins at a daunting pace. It never
slackens. The whole first scene is played in what looks like
the vestibule of an inn. Though poorly executed in places,
this set and the following one, of a provincial ballroom, are
good contemporary pastiche of nineteenth-century semi-
realistic design. Scene I combines an effect of mullioned
windows and painted woodwork with overhead borders
and side pieces covered in a floral pattern. A large hole in
the back wall reveals a winter landscape; it is not a doorway.

Through the actual door troop more characters than most companies have in their entire repertories. They're quirkily individualized characters, but they aren't farcical; they have interior as well as exterior life. And the ballet doesn't tell us all there is to know about them. It leaves some of its life behind the scenes.

In the ballroom scene, Bournonville gives us a set of social, folk, and demi-caractère dances, ending in a classical ballet number for two girls and a jester. Louise (Vivi Flindt) appears in disguise: first as one of a quartet of vivandières, then in a coquettish solo with a veil. Henning Kronstam, who plays Edouard, changes his costume to dance a hornpipe with two other sailors, but the lack of a plot motive for the change suggests that this may be a performance tradition. Possibly, too, Louise's masquerade was originally limited to the veil solo. It's unlikely that the ballet we see today is the same in every respect as the one Bournonville composed. Unfortunately, there was no opportunity to sort it out. *The Guards of Amager* was a novelty of genuine interest—the only novelty, in fact, of the Danes' entire season. New York got two performances. Washington had four. That speaks ill but, I fear, all too truly of New York. It is in New York that the Danes encounter steep prejudices about what does or does not constitute ballet. In the coarsest New York terms, *The Guards* doesn't qualify as ballet; it has too much mime. The more elegant and responsible New York attitude holds that *The Guards* is simply old-fashioned— very dear and charming in its way and, because it once *was* a ballet, worth preserving. You could probably raise more support for a Bournonville Landmark Preservation Society in New York than you could in Washington, but you still couldn't get four performances. Worth preserving, yes, but not worth inhabiting as a theatrical experience.

On the question of mime: Mime is a legitimate resource of the dance theatre (and not only of the dance theatre). The impatience of audiences when faced with extended mime sequences reflects a suspicion that the meanings being expressed so directly in such easy-to-read sign language are superficial, and that if the characters had something important to say to each other they'd be dancing. The idea that dancing makes a profound statement and mime doesn't may arise in somber ballets with a tragic expression, like *Swan Lake*, but even there, where the fantastic plot is only a pretext for a dance entertainment, it does no harm to refer to the plot now and then in mime. I find that it refreshes concentration. However, in most modern story ballets if the plot is to be taken seriously the choreographer avoids mime. Often these ballets are weak because he does no more than that. He doesn't invest the dances with dramatic content; he relies on the dancers or the audience to translate dance figures into stylized description. Modern audiences are as pleased to puzzle out these bottomless riddles as audiences of former days were to guess the meanings in a well-wrought mime passage. Formally coded mime of the "unless I marry I die" variety is not the only kind of mime there is. There's the Bournonville kind, which the choreographer himself defined as "a harmonious and rhythmic sequence of picturesque attitudes taken from nature and classic models, suitable to character, costume, nation, and epoch. The sequence of postures and movement composes a type of dance, but without the turnout (en dehors) of ballet. Its attitudes are aimed at effects of plasticity and characterization entirely apart from virtuoso academic technique." One might add that *The Guards of Amager* is a comedy deeply rooted in the life and lore of its time, and the lively and differentiated pantomime that fills out the whole of its first scene is as much an expression of the Bournonville ballet d'action as the lively and differentiated dances of the second scene. There is no question of frivolous mime versus earnest dancing. The whole ballet is consistently light and consistently vivid in terms of its characters and setting.

On being old-fashioned: Bournonville is well aware of the degrees of theatrical intensity on the scale between pure mime and pure dance. The ballet exploits the whole diapason, from the opening vignettes to the climactic classical pas de trois. The delay in the outbreak of dancing is a calculated effect. When the hero takes a girl on each arm and flirts with her, it's almost but not quite a waltz. The second scene is almost but not quite a straight divertissement, for it is danced by the characters of the ballet, and the plot reaches its dénouement in the dances. This is really a very modern approach. Perhaps what people mean when they say the ballet is old-fashioned is that, for what it is—the prototype of ballet bouffe—it isn't very exciting. It doesn't swirl with uniforms and petticoats. It doesn't make temperatures soar. Apart from the classical pas de trois, the only dance image that stays with you is the amusing side-to-side chassés in the hornpipe. It's also true that the Met is much too big a place for it. But that many of the cultural references in the mimed action are obscure is not a reasonable objection. There is one very broadly played character, a large nursemaid or granny who trundles mechanically like a mama doll. A Danish audience undoubtedly recognizes her; I took her for some ancient folk figure (though her fame may have originated in the ballet). The action occurs during a Shrovetide festival, as in *Petrushka*, and the significance of the few customs that aren't familiar is easily guessed. (One, the blindfolded swatting of a container to release a shower of goodies, is related to the Mexican piñata game.) But the larger point to be made about all this is that the Danish cast, which includes dancers, ballet children, and character mimes, plays with such precision that a time and place of which one knows nothing are brought spiritually to life. Because the ballet has meaning for the Danes, it has meaning for us. (It is this kind of life, incidentally, that is missing from all performances of *Petrushka* I have ever seen. Until it is done by a Russian company—if it is not too late for a Russian company to do it—I may never know why the ballet, not just the music, is a classic.) Ballet bouffe is a dead genre, buried by the Ballet Russe in gobs of Viennese schmaltz. *The Guards of Amager* is indigenous art. Perhaps that's why, after a hundred years, it remains a theatrical image one can believe in.

The rest of the Bournonville repertory consisted of *La Sylphide* in a new production, with a very beautiful forest set, and the dance portion of the third act of *Napoli*, in its same old glorious set. Filled with Danes young and old, it still creates one of the happiest stage pictures in all theatre. And there was Niels Kehlet, still dancing the central role and still producing his sensational jump at the indecent age of thirty-seven. Peter Martins returned to his home company in *La Sylphide* and showed how, with his ample, easy rhythm, clear beats, and command of natural gesture, he could have become the dominant James of our day. The production differs in several respects from the American Ballet Theatre version—musically and rhythmically it is superior—but the other differences weren't as interesting as I'd hoped they'd be. Sorella Englund was a waiflike Sylph, with the beginnings of impressive style. There were no other ballerina prospects, and despite two very good young men, Arne Villumsen and Ib Andersen (and Johnny Eliasen in mime), the company seemed to be losing ground in

Bournonville. The young women have all learned to jump like Russians; none could produce the grand jeté in attitude that is one of the glories of the Danish school. Technique aside, the appeal of Danish dancing has always been partly philosophical. It's the appeal of a kind of ballet that is not a branch of show business. In the overheated climate of professional ballet in New York, the Danes can't really compete. They tried to, but the season was not hot box-office, and since that might have been predicted it is a pity the company did not go down fighting, with a complete *Napoli*, with *Konservatoriet* instead of *Etudes*, and with perhaps one or two more of the Bournonvilles that have never left home. Danish dancers have been struggling to get into the twentieth century almost as long as there has been one, and they've tried every kind of wrenching alternative to their own classical style and repertory. Yet of all the dancers who have visited New York in the last decade the Danes have changed least. Doing what they do best, they are still the gentlest and most tasteful dance company in the world.

—June 21, 1976

Isadora Alive

In *Homage to Isadora*, a solo made a year ago for Lynn Seymour, Frederick Ashton staged from memory a dance image he had often cited in speaking about Isadora Duncan—the image of the dancer releasing a stream of rose petals from either hand as she ran forward. Ashton set this to No. 15 of Brahms's Waltzes, Opus 39. It was the briefest of homages. Now the dance is the last of five numbers, all drawn from Opus 39; under the title *Five Brahms Waltzes in the Manner of Isadora Duncan*, the extended solo was the highlight last week of American Ballet Theatre's gala at the State Theater. Ashton's dances are not reconstructions but evocations of a personality and a style. Unlike the actual Duncan studies that Annabelle Gamson performs so vividly to the same music, they do not reveal a technique. Neither do they conceal it. But without being any less simple than Gamson's performance Ashton's choreography places far less emphasis on the symmetrical oppositions, the big, plain contrasts by which Duncan dance demonstrated its constancy of motivation from the body's center. Those things, stated in the most instructive way by Annabelle Gamson, tell us how Duncan saw dance. Ashton tells us how she saw herself. For him, "the manner of Isadora Duncan" is inseparable from the person of Duncan, and it may be that at the time he first saw her—1921, when she was past forty—she was giving a less active and clear-edged account of what was purely prescriptive in her work. The Isadora of *Five Brahms Waltzes* asks to be taken on her own terms as a magnetic performing artist, and because she is danced by Lynn Seymour that is how we do take her.

Seymour's rightness for the part isn't measured only by her magnetism. If there had been a poll in the dance world on the question of whom to cast in the movie of Duncan's life that was made a few years ago, the choice would have been Lynn Seymour—Seymour the actress, the performer of epic daring, but most of all Seymour the dancer. She has always possessed the roundness and fullness of contour, the plastic vigor, and the coherent rhythm to express the sculptural depth that Isadora's dancing must have had. Beautiful in classical effacé positions, Seymour is heroic in Duncan plastique. The back yields, the chest lifts, the arms expand and float, and then from this open aspect the figure suddenly withdraws in a crouch or a stance braced and turned in on itself. The reversal seems miraculous each time because Seymour is so securely centered. She doesn't have to stop and relocate, and she doesn't tighten up or rigidify or signal ahead; she simply arrives in one piece, loosely disposed, the arms coiled about the head, the hips angled, the turned-in knee relaxed. The whole scroll-like motion is carelessly light and free, yet it's indelible. Ashton's and Seymour's Isadora is a virtuoso.

Duncan at her recitals often had pianists of renown; Seymour's accompanist at the gala was Malcolm Frager. After a short prelude, the curtain rises. A scarf of pink silk hangs from the piano, and in a pink puff-peplum tunic, Seymour lies on the floor, one knee cocked, one hand toying with invisible pebbles. Like the costume and the tousled red hair, the monumental thigh is Isadora's. The pebbles are on Nausicaa's beach. The image recalls the photographs of Isadora ensconced in her Grecian mood, but then, as Seymour rises and advances in slow balancés with outspreading arms, the photograph suddenly liquefies and becomes three-dimensional. And, from there on, stage space becomes the landscape of the performer's imagination. At first, it's that Homeric beach where nymphs play; then it's the abstract architectural void redeemed and dramatized by its lone tenant. Seymour "acts" the drama of space as if such a drama had never occurred before, as indeed it hadn't. Isadora's recitals marked the advent of the dancer as a personage encompassing all scenery, all events in a series of autonomous gestures. The vault of space expands or contracts and the dancing figure itself becomes voluminous or tiny, sheltered or exposed, as if by impulse. One variation on the theme: the silk scarf held aloft in a headlong run becomes "this canopy the sky"; in the next moment, it sheathes the body, a second skin. Then, when it is cast decisively aside, it is as if intimacy with nature had been checked, and the august impersonal world returns. That the dancer can alter the proportions and the investiture of space without the aid of a corps de ballet, without scenic decoration, is a presumption with metaphysical implications that would repay serious study. There are historical implications, too, in the fact that this idea dawned in a period when, despite Darwin, people still believed in man's hegemony over nature. But what an enthralling theatrical idea it still is. Ashton and Seymour have brought it back alive.

—July 26, 1976

Baryshnikov's *Nutcracker*

One of the drawbacks to staging *The Nutcracker* without children is that the dancers who take the children's parts look too old to be playing with toys. One of the advantages is that the "children" can then take over the adult roles — growing up into the Sugar Plum Fairy and her Cavalier. Although this gives the ballet a unity it doesn't have when it is cast with children, there is a danger that the dancers, by extending their roles, will stretch the ballet's story beyond its limits. Growing up in *The Nutcracker* means changing a fantasy of childhood into an adolescent romance. And while that change can perhaps be justified in terms of the story's source, it can't be justified in terms of the score. Tchaikovsky's *Nutcracker* is his vision of childhood — of small, orderly, and unstained lives that can be touched by magic. He commonly announced the principal emotions and concerns of his ballets in the overtures: *Swan Lake* begins with a plaintive utterance rising to anguish; *The Sleeping Beauty* brings Carabosse into immediate conflict with the Lilac Fairy; the *ouverture miniature* to *The Nutcracker* is a hovering bubble filled with small scurrying creatures and tingling ice. The lone outburst of passion in *The Nutcracker* occurs in the Sugar Plum adagio. Petipa had asked for "colossal effects," and Tchaikovsky leaves us in no doubt that here, for once, are big people, grand emotions. The young hero and heroine of the ballet may step into these climactic roles, but they have to do so without preparation. Tchaikovsky provides no accompaniment to their growing up.

Tchaikovsky wrote his score to fit a scenario fashioned by Petipa, who ended the narrative portion of the plot with the end of Act I. In Act II, the children enter the Kingdom of Sweets and become spectators at a divertissement. American Ballet Theatre's new *Nutcracker*, which had its première at the Kennedy Center, in Washington, is like most productions that dispense with children—which is to say most productions. The choreography, by Mikhail Baryshnikov, tries to keep the story going in the second act. The sections of the Sugar Plum pas de deux—which is, of course, danced by the two young lovers—are rearranged so that the adagio comes last and is converted into a pas d'action: Drosselmeyer, the impresario of Clara's dream and the architect of all the transformations in Act I, returns to claim her; a struggle of wills ensues, with Clara and her Nutcracker Prince winning out over Drosselmeyer. The victory is celebrated in another transposed dance (Buffoons), and the happy couple lead the company in the final waltz. But at Tchaikovsky's transition to the Apotheosis the scene becomes phantasmagoric, with background figures from both acts appearing and scattering in the dark. The Prince vanishes behind Drosselmeyer's cloak, and Clara is left alone facing the streaming sunlight of dawn.

Since neither the manufactured crises nor the rational "mature" ending is supported by the music, the production leaves an impression of musical insensitivity. But when

Baryshnikov isn't forcing his story effects, his choreography is musically sound—simple in construction, sometimes to the point of humility, yet not unconfident. He has less success with ensembles than with solos and duets, but in a first attempt at choreography that is nothing to be ashamed of, and his directing and coaching of the dancers are on the highest level. Several of the duets in the suite section (the Spanish and Shepherds' Dances, and the Russian Dance, which is really a double solo) are good to look at and good for the dancers who perform them, and there are one or two effective solo passages for Clara. Choreographing for himself as the Prince, Baryshnikov shows us nothing about his gifts that he hasn't already revealed (in, say, *La Bayadère*); though his own performance galvanizes the entire production, the choreography is well within the limits of the Soviet "hero" style, and his duets with Marianna Tcherkassky as Clara are models of Stakhanovite vigor in the lift-leap-and-lift-again tradition. (Says the horse Boxer in *Animal Farm*, "I will work harder.") This is the tradition that Baryshnikov has grown up in, and it is the classic Soviet *Nutcracker* that he gives us, with all its sentimental vitality, its tribute to noble youth, and its insistent drawing out and rationalizing of psychological meanings in the libretto—meanings that are better left latent. Baryshnikov occasionally tries to draw out metaphoric meanings. His duet with Tcherkassky in the Fir Forest, to the "journey" music that precedes the snow scene, includes a progression of lifts in which she does fishtail beats and dives—a reminder that in the original story Clara and the Prince traveled to the Kingdom of Sweets in a seashell drawn by dolphins. The only trouble with the image is that Tchaikovsky disagrees with its placing. His "water" music opens the second act.

Like Nureyev's production, which has been performed

here by the Royal Ballet, Baryshnikov's appears to have based its story elements on the standard Kirov version produced by Vassily Vainonen in 1934. Nureyev retained one Vainonen number by way of homage, and Baryshnikov does the same in a Snowflakes Waltz whose chief charm is the mechanical efficiency with which it uses thirty-two girls to cover the stage and beat time like so many chorines. They do a zoom-on entrance like airplanes, a shuffle-off exit up a ramp, and very little in between. (If this is Baryshnikov's model for ensemble choreography, he's lost.) The original 1892 choreography, by Ivanov, had been abandoned, and it was apparently Vainonen who shoved the most influential wedge between the seams that bonded Petipa's scenario to Tchaikovsky's score. Petipa had drawn upon portions of "Histoire d'un Casse-Noisette," the version of E.T.A. Hoffmann's "Nussnacker und Mausekönig" which the elder Dumas had written for French schoolchildren. As W. H. Auden noted in his essay on *The Nutcracker*, Hoffmann was "haunted by nostalgic visions of a childhood Eden" and also by "terrors and visions of evil." "Nutcracker and Mouse King" may be understood on one level as a study of sexual hysteria in puberty, and though Hoffmann's principals do grow up, after a fashion, and get married, choreographers looking for material to flesh out a story of tender adolescent love had best look elsewhere.

There is no question that Petipa softens and dilutes Hoffmann's story almost past recognition. Nureyev's has been the most clinical *Nutcracker* to date, and the most horrifying. His mice were rats who tore off the heroine's skirt. Baryshnikov's mice are somewhere between Balanchine's skittering zanies and Nureyev's monsters—they're mice studying to be rats. The Nutcracker doll is broken not by the heroine's naughty brother Fritz but by a tipsy adult guest at the party. Later, this guest returns as the Mouse King, and the other male guests return as the mouse army to be defeated in battle by the Nutcracker, grown to life size and capering about on a wooden horse much as Fritz had capered about at the party. And the Nutcracker's army is composed of soldiers who recall the little-boy guests who had played soldier at the party. During that party, Drosselmeyer had staged in a puppet show a kind of preview of the duel between the Prince and the Mouse King, and Fritz had reacted by leaping up with a toy saber and looking for someone to fight. But in the transformation scene after the battle the Nutcracker doesn't turn out to be Fritz (Warren Conover); he's a completely new boy, who leads the heroine to the Kingdom of Sweets.

In its doubling of real and dream images, Baryshnikov's staging is very much like Nureyev's, and a puppet show occurs in both productions (as it does also in *Don Quixote*, with the Don reacting much like Baryshnikov's Fritz). Although the standard view of the Nutcracker Prince is that he's a projection of Drosselmeyer, Nureyev may have effected one transformation too many when he had Drosselmeyer actually turn into the Prince, taking both parts himself. Baryshnikov's suggestion that the Prince is a sublimation of Fritz is not quite as queasy. However, it does leave him with the problem of solving just who Drosselmeyer is and what he wants. In the climactic pas d'action, does Drosselmeyer (Alexander Minz) want to return Clara to reality or keep her for himself? Since this production is one that explains the inexplicable, we look up and are not fed.

But then the confusing Drosselmeyer doesn't really fit into the picture that Baryshnikov is trying to produce. The keynote to the Vainonen production was struck by one of its mentors, the composer and musicologist Boris Asafiev, when he wrote that the music depicted "the ripening soul of a little girl, at first playing with dolls, and then arriving at the dawn of love through dreams of a brave and manly hero—in other words, the process of the '*éducation sentimentale.*' " Baryshnikov's ballet comes out looking just the way those words sound—sweet, dull, and forced. Vainonen's idea was that Clara should change into a ballerina and dance the Sugar Plum adagio, and Asafiev seems to be looking for a reason to have that happen. Baryshnikov doesn't follow Vainonen's plan (he does refer, elsewhere in his choreography, to Vainonen's adagio, when Tcherkassky is thrown upward by a line of men), but he accepts Asafiev's thesis, possibly because it's the only one that would have allowed him to fit himself into the ballet. And he had to fit himself into it. *The Nutcracker* plus Baryshnikov is the ABT formula for a superhit. Playing superman in a superhit is probably not the best way to start out as a choreographer, but Baryshnikov has managed everything honorably and with a generosity of spirit that carries one along. Of the several Soviet or Soviet-style *Nutcracker*s that we have seen, this one is the best.

The mechanical side of the production is undistinguished. Boris Aronson's Christmas tree is an affair of interlocking parts, and it grows without astonishing us. His second-act set is in sour colors laid on as if by smudged block prints or bubble-gum transfers. Frank Thompson's operetta-ish costumes are relatively sweet, and some of them are as cloying as the Kirov's for its Tchaikovsky ballets.

—January 17, 1977

Notes on a Natural Man

As revolutionaries grow older, they are supposed to turn into conservatives. Merce Cunningham, who radicalized an entire generation of American choreographers, is fifty-seven; his company has just given its first solo season in a Broadway theatre (the Minskoff); and he has not begun to change. He is still a radical, still a classicist, and still a great actor. He has been widely understood as a radical, grotesquely underestimated as a classicist, and barely considered an actor at all. Yet each of these three claims—I base them not only on the Broadway season's repertory but on all I know of Cunningham's work—deserves and supports the others. Cunningham's radicalism at first consisted in divesting dance of all content that did not irreducibly belong to it. As time went on, he manipulated formal propositions, breaking open kernels of academic wisdom and here, too, discarding all but essence. In a way, he saved classical dancing by showing what it could be reduced to and still work. He innovated but he also renovated. *Summerspace*, the oldest work in the Minskoff repertory, was made in 1958 and is a highly conscious reconstitution of several very old ideas about classicism. Its subject moves as far back in time as a Poussin landscape peopled by nymphs and fauns (and even farther, for that was itself a reconstitution) and as far forward as the thousand dells and glades of Denishawn. Cunningham's dancers not only appear and vanish at irregular intervals and move at different speeds but are also seen from multiple viewpoints—not boxed, as in the nineteenth-century theatre. We are comfortable with the continuity of *Summerspace*, with its random pattern and "flow-through" action; we sense its closeness to us and feel its rehabilitating effect. Of course, the lucidity of *Summerspace* is more real to us than the antique subject it contemplates, and so we think of that lucidity as its "real" subject. Cunningham probably does, too. Dances that are their own subject have been his specialty for thirty years.

That a dance be, as he once wrote, "unprompted by references other than to its own life" is a prime requirement of classicism. Cunningham has eminently satisfied it. Two other requirements—academic legibility and virtuosity—are also part of his canon. Most of the works in the Minskoff repertory—*Summerspace*, *Rebus*, *Signals*, *Torse*, *Sounddance* —make nonsense of the statement in a recently published dance reference book that Cunningham "works with isolated movements, far from the academic dance." But, at the same time, he has recognized that dancing is not a pure and finite activity enclosed in its own system of perfection—that it includes drama simply because it reminds us of life. And there is a drama unique to Cunningham, which consists in the play between essential and existential insights—between the sparkling polished gems and the gritty, more or less accidental processes that surround and sometimes disclose them. It is not this drama that I am thinking of when I call Cunningham a great actor, although his extensive development of it throughout his repertory suggests that he is, at the very least, a great actor-manager. During the years when Cunningham was creating and performing the vigorous roles he now allocates to younger dancers in his company, his gifts as an actor were not widely spoken of. He was an actor the way Chaplin was a dancer—no less vivid when asserting this secondary talent, but still asserting it as secondary to his main performance. At this moment, though, Cunningham's acting abilities seem to encompass him. In *Solo*, which he made for himself only four years ago, he comes as close to Stanislavskian realism as the structure of his work can ever have allowed him to come. This is the quiet, hypnotic dance in which he shows us the life of one forest creature after another. Cunningham devotees are not surprised that he has taken his dance from nature or that he isolates, tenses, and relaxes his muscles with animal-like control, but we are startled to find the animals really there. The kind of empirical description that is more characteristic of Cunningham's performance stops on the brink of specificity, summarizing several events in one charged instant or allowing one event to obscure another before we've had a chance to name it—like a cloud cover or a setting sun.

The impression of fleeting phenomena, of mutability, that we get from so much of Cunningham's work is the controlling metaphor of his theatre. It's so easy to understand—there's no way *not* to understand it—that one is baffled by people who find the Cunningham spectacle baffling. His idea of nature-in-the-theatre rests on the flux that is common to both nature and the theatrical performance; as he says of one of his ballets, "the continuity is change." And in his various impersonations Cunningham has rung changes on the archetypes that in his own person he irresistibly suggests: the faun, the clown, the athlete, and—for those special man-made environments which his theatre sometimes incorporates—the mechanic (in mechanic's overalls). However, Cunningham sometimes *is* baffling. Nothing else in his repertory is as obscure as his own role in *Rebus*. If *Solo* spells out the powers that lie behind the faun archetype, *Rebus* gives us a glimpse of what may lie ahead of the athlete. But that glimpse—who can say what we see there? The man-made environment of *Rebus* reminds one of a studio where the dancers assemble for company class. And, as far as one can see, what takes place *is* a company class or a rehearsal. Only Cunningham seems out of step. *Rebus* is everyday life broken by dream incidents that verge at times on nightmare. And Cunningham, who is isolated from the group but at the center of this dream, acts one of his strangest roles. It may be a direct transcription of life in his Westbeth studio (where it was shown while it was being made), with Cunningham playing the choreographer-teacher marking steps, instructing, guiding, but never really participating. At the end, where his own great solo should be, there are just blurs of activity, as if Cunningham were articulating through a fog. *Rebus* contains the handsomely developed ensemble choreography that Cunningham has been producing lately; there's more of it in *Torse*, a lighter-weight companion piece, in which he does not appear at all. In *Rebus* he manages very nearly to disappear while remaining onstage. I take the title to be a reference to his role and to be literally descriptive. In *Rebus* he is the key to a puzzle we and perhaps he himself cannot solve.

It may be that the time has come to concentrate less on Cunningham and more on the Cunningham company. At the Minskoff, this was hard to do. The company is no longer a group of soloists but a collective, as the Russians say, and in recent years there has been a high rate of turnover. The stage is a magnifier; on the Minskoff stage there were too many inexperienced dancers. Of the pieces that featured steady, intricate dancing in large groups, *Rebus* and *Torse* suffered from this weakness. *Sounddance*, though, emerged as a triumph, and the season's biggest hit. Why this happened brings up another way in which the company has changed: the matter of Cunningham's collaborators and his modus operandi with or without collaborators. The Minskoff season marked the first time in five years that New York had seen Cunningham works in repertory. Instead of repertory, we have been seeing his Events, which often present new choreography as part of a continuous performance of repertory excerpts. In Events, new and old dances alike are performed to music different from the scores that were commissioned for them, and often without their rightful costumes and without décor. To see *Rebus* or *Torse* as part of an Event is to see substantially all there is to see (although *Torse*, a fifty-two-minute work, has never been given in its entirety). At the Minskoff, the entrances and exits were upstage left, just as they were (and had to be) at the Westbeth studio, and the only décor was a clothes rack for *Rebus*. Events sound, too, is likely to be better than the dreary scores that were provided for both these works. *Sounddance* has lavishly exciting choreography; and with its décor and lighting by Mark Lancaster and sound by David Tudor, it forms a complete entity. The entrances and exits are made through a center slot in a draped curtain that extends the width of the stage. Each dancer appears, is immediately caught up in the vortex of the dance, and at the end is hurled by centrifugal force back through the slot. The effect cannot be captured in an Event, nor does it seem likely that any other score could do for *Sounddance* what Tudor's *Toneburst* does—raise its energy level to volcanic fury. It is largely because of its sound that *Sounddance* emerged as one of Cunningham's more fearsome works, like *Crises*, *Winterbranch*, and *Place*, though probably what accounts for its popularity is that *Toneburst* has a beat that now and then coincides with the rhythm of the dancing and seems to drive it on. If Cunningham's idea is that any sound can accompany any dance anyplace, I think that events as well as Events prove him wrong.

Squaregame and *Travelogue*, the newest Cunningham productions, are "game" pieces rather than dance pieces. *Squaregame* has the most beautiful of theatrical-natural sets—the stage bared to the brick wall, with wings exposed and the whole area flooded with white light. A white floor cloth flanked by moss-green borders and stacks of white duffel bags are Mark Lancaster's décor. Buffalo leaps, contractions, backward scuttling runs are the choreography's motifs. There are two outstanding moments in *Squaregame*—one a Cunningham solo with extremely precise movements of the arms and torso (very unlike what goes on in *Rebus*), and the other a duet in which he supports the most talented of his new dancers, Karole Armitage, in some buttery slow falls and then shadows her in an undulant walk on half-toe. In *Travelogue* Robert Rauschenberg returns to Cunningham's stage after a thirteen-year absence and rather overwhelms it: the colors are like candy, but all those chairs, bicycle wheels, color wheels, silk flags, and paint cans are sweets of sin. John Cage's score is in the same overwhimsical vein—a collage of telephone-service tapes, like Weather, Time, Rare Bird Alert, and Dial-A-Joke. *Travelogue* is an escapade in the style of *Antic Meet*, with nothing on its mind. *Antic Meet* (1958) has a little something. Although Cunningham's humor tends to be arch, like Martha Graham's, the best bit in the new piece is his. He enters, furtively snatching up a girl's dropped veil, and in a twinkling becomes both Nijinsky and the kid with the blanket in *Peanuts*.

—*February 7, 1977*

A Hundred Ways
to Make a Dance

Twyla Tharp, in her season at the Brooklyn Academy, included parts of old and new dances in an anthology piece called *The Hodge Podge*. The new dances are a solo by Tharp to Paul Simon's singing of "Fifty Ways to Leave Your Lover" and a quartet to a Simon medley, and they represent the current Tharp style at its most casually seductive. It would have been interesting to see, along with these dances, something more representative of the early Tharp than eggs plopping to the floor, a chair being smashed, a hoop turning as someone walks inside it. There were those nondance incidents in Tharp's work of the sixties, and there were antidance incidents—like the relevé in second held during the playing of Petula Clark's "Downtown"—but reviving those antics today in the form of a montage tells us more about the taste of an era than it does about the emergence of Twyla Tharp.

It was in her *dances*—particularly her austere, intricate group dances—that Tharp distinguished herself during the sixties. *The Home Phrase*, from a 1969 piece that was made to be presented in museums, is intricate, all right (the dancers exchange clothing and take turns reading aloud while executing the phrase), but it isn't the kind of thing that made Tharp a supremely different choreographer even then. I can't help feeling that the showy performance of it in *The Hodge Podge*, which would never have been given in 1969, was an attempt, like the selected bits of Dada, to eliminate any suggestion of severity in the works of Tharp's past. But, of course, they were severe. The best of them (*Generation*, *Group Activities*) were inwardly directed, too—entertaining us only as a consequence of entertaining their dancers. In the present repertory, *The Fugue* has that kind of inwardness, and *Cacklin' Hen*, a piece new last year, has it. Such pieces strike a necessary balance with the more extroverted ones, like *Country Dances* and *Sue's Leg*. I don't mean that the dancers enjoy doing the latter works less than the others or that the others are less enjoyable to us; it's a question of aesthetic emphasis. And a work composed with one emphasis doesn't shift easily to the other.

In *The One Hundreds*, a dance of 1970, Tharp began to deal in compressed exposition of movement and in space-time ratios. The work is composed of a hundred phrases performed in silence, one after another. The phrases vary widely. Some involve the whole body in far-flung bursts of activity, others are sparsely constructed—a shoulder, a hip, a turn of the head—and cover only a few feet of ground. All the phrases, no matter what they consist of, take exactly eleven seconds each, with four seconds for recoveries in between. Since there are no transitions from phrase to phrase and no music or aural cues of any sort, the dancers have to keep the whole catalogue in their heads. Performance is a feat of mental memory as much as of muscle memory. *The One Hundreds* was originally performed in three sections designed to expose all the material in decreasing lengths of

time. Two dancers did fifty different phrases simultaneously. Then five dancers did twenty. Then all the phrases
were represented in one grand eleven-second finale as a
hundred persons (who didn't have to be dancers) appeared
and did one phrase apiece. Practically speaking, the finale
was often impossible to achieve (though it could be faked:
thirty people appearing for eleven seconds can look like a
hundred). The more manageable cut-down version called
Half the One Hundreds that was performed in Brooklyn is in
two parts: a solo consisting of fifty phrases followed by fifty
persons doing one apiece—or at least appearing to be doing
one apiece.

Whichever version you see—and there have been other
variations in format—*The One Hundreds* is a fascinating exercise in perception. Tharp once described it as "a study in
deterioration." In the way that it sums up many of the leading themes of avant-garde dance in the sixties, it is very
much a key work. The importance then of eliminating all
gaps between how a work is made and how it is to be performed is a theme we can still respond to today. In works
like *The One Hundreds* (and like the "task"-oriented movement games devised in that period by Yvonne Rainer and
Deborah Hay), performance as a concept apart from execution is ruled out. The works were so constructed that just to
perform them correctly was to explain how and why they
were made; the choreographers were, in Susan Sontag's
phrase, "against interpretation." Tharp's break with that tradition was also a confirmation of it. In 1971, she began
working with music, and to *The Bix Pieces*, composed that
year, she added a lecture-demonstration explaining "Why
They Were Made." But the explanation turned out to be extraneous to the performance. We learned that in order to go
against interpretation (of the Bix Beiderbecke–Paul White-

man music) Tharp had first composed a seventeen-count phrase and elaborated it into movements, which she then set to Haydn quartets. The actual *Bix* dances were Haydn dances transposed and rephrased, and thus (in Tharp's view) safeguarded from the tame interpretative responses that (again in Tharp's view) would have resulted if she'd choreographed directly to the jazz music.

Tharp's *Bix* lecture made public a formal problem that the public had never heard of before, and it proposed a solution that nobody in the profession (except perhaps Merce Cunningham) had ever heard of before. It was a way of explaining to people why Tharp dancing is as good for Haydn as it is for jazz. *Push Comes to Shove*, created five years later for American Ballet Theatre, explained that correspondence one more time. The explanations in the *Bix* lecture may seem mildly defensive today, but we must remember the fears that avant-gardists of the sixties harbored of repeating anyone else's method of making a dance, and we must remember, too, their explicit fear and defiance of the audience. Tharp sometimes goes overboard in accommodating the audience: she lets her theories be known; she fudges her past; she takes on a few too many "celebrity" collaborators; she ingratiatingly performs the *Half the One Hundreds* solo as if the phrases were dramatizable material. But Tharp has in fact achieved the dream of all the sixties purists by making dances that speak, in new accents, entirely for themselves. Her dances have reconditioned our values and swept away the ideological dividing lines between "classical" and "modern" and "pop." We don't need to be told why they were made—much less how. We can see it happening.

The Bix Pieces, a central work in the Tharp canon, has an introvert-extrovert dual identity that will always be slightly confusing. (Its mixture of subtlety and earnestness confuses the audience these days into laughter at the wrong moments.) But it may be for just that reason that it is especially dear to those who have followed Tharp's career. It was at its best this season when Tharp took over the narrator's role after performing the opening baton solo (and relinquishing the rest of her role to Shelley Washington). The script is in her speech rhythms, terse and flat, and much as she may try to give it a "platform" quality, it doesn't elevate to false heights as it can so easily when spoken by others. Other things also helped make this the definitive staging of *Bix*: the dark-gold lighting; the onstage musicians partly concealed by a scrim; their rendition, led by Dick Hyman, of the Whiteman arrangements. Among the dancers, it was good to see Sara Rudner and Kenneth Rinker in their old roles. Rinker returned also to *Sue's Leg*, and Christine Uchida made a fine impression—fluffy, rascally—in Tharp's role.

—May 30, 1977

White Turning Gray

When a classic is lost—not forgotten but lost, right there on the stage in front of our eyes—we think one of two things must be true: either the performance is totally destructive or the work was not a classic to begin with. I watched Martha Graham's *Primitive Mysteries* (1931) die this season in what seemed, for the most part, to be scrupulous performances. The twelve girls looked carefully rehearsed. Sophie Maslow, who had supervised the previous revival, in the season of 1964–65, was again in charge. Everybody danced with devotion. Yet a piece that I would have ranked as a landmark in American dance was reduced to a tendentious outline; the power I remembered was no longer there. And some new and disturbing element had taken the place of the original content of the piece—a content I have largely to take on faith because the performances I knew were only partial indications of it. Still, those performances had conviction, and what we see now is affectation—a portrait of a rather claustrophobic girls' troupe and its self-martyred leader. Undoubtedly, the piece always had undertones of preciousness. The undertones have become overtones.

We know that Graham's own performances are past recapturing, and we know, too, that the earlier Graham works, which were made on bodies that hadn't been pre-stretched and refined by ballet technique, are impossible to reconstruct without compromise. When *Primitive Mysteries* was last revived, with Yuriko leading the cast, the same things were said about it that had been said about the revival of 1947—that its performance was weak and inauthentic. But the Yuriko revival was one of the big events of the sixties for the younger members of the audience, whose only contact with the Graham of the thirties was the white-hot intensity of Barbara Morgan's photographs. *Primitive Mysteries* was Graham's first masterpiece of group composition, and it *is* very "white"—a few incisive strokes on a shadowless plain, organized to music by Louis Horst that sounds like a singing bone. It came about after a stay in the Southwest had exposed Graham and Horst to Mexican-Indian Catholic culture and the vestigial paganism of some of its ceremonies. The work, dealing with rites surrounding the Virgin, is divided into three parts—Hymn to the Virgin, Crucifixus, and Hosanna—which correspond to the Joyful, Sorrowful, and Glorious Mysteries of the Rosary. In 1964, as the dance unfolded on the stage, one could settle into it and begin to understand the "pioneer" vision that the Graham of those days shared with Willa Cather and Georgia O'Keeffe. The formal rigor of the groupings in the Morgan photographs came to life with the force of revelation—no matter that the bodies weren't right. In the sixties, we could be impressed by the power of structure alone; perhaps that isn't enough now. Perhaps there's a statute of limitations on how long a work can be depended upon to force itself through the bodies of those who dance it.

One can pick at flaws in the present revival. The tempo,

particularly of the crescendo in the Crucifixus, when the bison leaps turn into runs, seems too fast. The new ending, with the light fading on the final group pose instead of on the group's exit, is too romantic. And Janet Eilber as the Virgin floats about in her white capelet like a prom queen. Phyllis Gutelius does it better; with her dour white face tightly concentrating and her stick arms held out in archaic attitudes, she suggests one of those Mexican candy skeletons. But trying to say exactly why *Primitive Mysteries* doesn't work this time is like trying to say why Natalia Makarova isn't right in *Firebird*. She should be precisely that "filmiest and most fairy-like actress-dancer" whom Carl Van Vechten in 1917 demanded in Fokine's ballet, but in spite of a new commitment to the role she just looks dutiful. And that's how the Graham dancers look in *Primitive Mysteries*—dutiful and a little hysterical. Luckily, a film of the Yuriko version was made, which shows something of the vitality the piece had.

—*June 13, 1977*

The Godmother

Many dancers, when they retire, could take up acting, yet few of them do. Dancers do their "acting" in the classes they teach; their powerful temperaments and techniques of coercion are used on their students. But put them before an audience and they'll blaze again. Alicia Markova and Anton Dolin, presented by Walter Terry at Town Hall last month, reminisced about Diaghilev and their past triumphs, then got up and did mime scenes from *Swan Lake* and *Giselle*. Sitting down and talking, or moving through the patterns they'd traced long ago, Markova and Dolin were casually spellbinding: Markova with that porcelain calm, that concern with "arrangements" which marked her last (late-Victorian) phase as a performer, and Dolin looking as he had never looked—wild of hair and eye, shrewdly dyspeptic of manner, a character out of Beckett.

Like Dolin, Alexandra Danilova seems suited by type to certain acting roles, and like Dolin she has had some acting experience. (Dolin, a predecessor of Rudolf Nureyev, made movies in the thirties.) In 1948, she had a speaking part in one of her ballets, *Billy Sunday*, and toward the end of her career she appeared in a Broadway show, *Oh Captain!*, with Tony Randall. But in the nearly twenty years since then she has busied herself teaching and staging ballets, leaving us to imagine the Mme Ranevskayas and Arkadinas she might have given us. In the new movie *The Turning Point*, she has a small part, representing the eldest of four generations of dancers. As the coach Dahkarova, she's elegant and charming still, and she suggests the class that the next generation (as played by Anne Bancroft and Shirley MacLaine) doesn't have. Class, apparently, is something you can't hand down the years. But you can't do without it, either. It's the big missing ingredient in this well-stocked but half-baked movie about ballet.

The main issue in *The Turning Point* is age. Looking ahead to a life of coaching like Dahkarova's, the aging Emma (Bancroft) sees herself becoming extinct. Looking back, her friend and former rival Deedee (MacLaine), who has chosen marriage and children, regrets the career she never had. This middle-age crisis stifles the interest we might have taken in the movie's one serious theme—the necessity for continuity in the ballet tradition—and in order to precipitate the crisis the movie concocts an outlandish story. It shows a young dancer, sixteen or seventeen years old, leaving Oklahoma City, coming to New York to join a company described as "the best in the world—well, in this country anyway," getting the lead in an important new ballet, and dancing the *Don Quixote* pas de deux opposite Baryshnikov, all in one summer. Children's books about ballet often indulge in such fantasies, although the most popular of these books, Noel Streatfeild's *Ballet Shoes*, takes a fairly sober approach to its subject. But whereas juvenile fantasies in books don't seem to have caused much mischief, *The Turning Point* may raise temperatures around the country, with countless young aspirants seeing themselves as the Emilia of the film. The goddaughter of the prima ballerina Emma, Emilia doesn't depend on the link to get ahead, and though she sleeps with Yuri, the Baryshnikov character, that doesn't help her career, either. She succeeds on merit. But was merit ever—in real life—so swiftly rewarded? *The Turning Point* doesn't come out and say that in ballet you can sleep your way to the top. Nor does it come out and say that prima status can be won by operators like Emma, who bulldozed her best friend out of a key role. But the movie doesn't gainsay those things, either. And because it seems knowledgeable and hard-nosed, an insider's report on backstage realities, it leaves the impression that the Eve Harringtons and Sammy Glicks can have ballet anytime they want it.

The Turning Point is a Beverly Hills view of professional ballet. Trying to use backstage life as material for a realistic, "mature" drama, the script doesn't even develop the aura of truth that clung to melodramas like *The Red Shoes*. In *The Red Shoes*, which starred Moira Shearer, the real-life story that was the basis of the script (that of Diaghilev and Nijinsky) was already so bizarre that we didn't question the absurdities piled on top of it. The movie was made from the viewpoint of infatuated outsiders; it had an appetite for magic. In *The Turning Point*, we can't help wondering why the life decisions of the two self-involved heroines are irrevocable. Dancers have married, borne children, and gone on with their careers. Emma's case is so exaggerated that it appears to have been taken from *Camille*. Looking for a way out of her misfortune, she humiliates herself before her "protector," a dreary businessman played by Marshall Thompson (a former juvenile actor cast so that we can see how he has aged). The movie puts its characters in a mun-

dane setting where we can evaluate cause and effect. When
to the question of what she wants out of life Moira Shearer
answers "To dahnce!" she has already entered another
world, and it isn't Emma's. Hardened pros in the ballet
business can't be magnified into legends. Their real-life stories may be touching, but as the stuff of drama they acquire
the coarse unedifying texture of gossip. The real-life story
used in *The Turning Point* is partly that of Leslie Browne,
who plays Emilia. Leslie Browne, a soloist with American
Ballet Theatre, is the daughter of two former ABT dancers,
Isabel Mirrow and Kelly Brown, and she's the goddaughter
of Nora Kaye, the executive producer of *The Turning
Point*—the same Nora Kaye who had her first big success in
the Tudor ballet *Pillar of Fire* in 1942 and who became
ABT's great dramatic ballerina. In the movie we are told
how Deedee's pregnancy (with Emilia) imperiled her
chance at the leading role in an epochal Tudorish ballet, and
how by encouraging Deedee to have the baby Emma
snagged the role and began her career as a great dramatic
ballerina. In actual fact, Isabel Mirrow joined Ballet Theatre
some years after Nora Kaye had become a star. But it
doesn't matter whether the gossip is true or not—what matters is that it's *only* gossip.

Emilia's breathless ascent to stardom, during which
Deedee and Emma renew their rivalry by fighting over her,
is based on the career of Gelsey Kirkland, who was to have
played the part. Even Kirkland had to put in her years of apprentice work, but with her in the role of Emilia the movie
might have seemed less preposterous. Leslie Browne is still
an unknown, who has done only one big role so far—*The
Nutcracker*, with Baryshnikov. Her perfect School of American Ballet body photographs beautifully, and camera illusion helps her dancing withstand Baryshnikov's onslaught.

(Classical dancing on film may be unintelligible but it is also sensational. The camera increases a dancer's speed and heightens the physical glamour of stretched limbs. You can imagine what it does for the spectacle of Baryshnikov.) Her best moment as an actress is a little drunk scene in a bar, but then the movie has her come to the theatre drunk and be nursed through her paces as a Wili by Emma, standing in the wings. Typically, the movie invents this highly implausible situation to launch another Deedee-Emma skirmish. It's also typical that, in one of the few scenes that come close to being fun, the fun is secondhand. The drunken-Wili number looks like a resetting (uncredited) of the Mistake Waltz in Jerome Robbins's ballet *The Concert*; no balletgoer can miss it. Herbert Ross, the director of *The Turning Point* and Nora Kaye's husband, is a former choreographer. He staged the *Swan Lake* parody in *Funny Girl*, but he hasn't used his own ideas in any of the dances in this movie, and he hasn't extended ballet metaphorically to support the story. The little *Romeo and Juliet* passage, cutting from Emilia and Yuri in the MacMillan pas de deux to Emilia and Yuri in bed, is as far as Ross goes. An Ashton solo devised specially for this film is danced by Leslie Browne under the end titles, when the film is all over, and Emilia's first starring role turns out to be the Vortex solo from *The River*, by Alvin Ailey. This number represents the progressive abstract ballet that an Eliot Feldish choreographer (played by Daniel Levans) has created, much to the annoyance of dancers who would rather feel music than count it. Feldish is not conceivably Aileyish, and neither one is the avant-gardish genius the script wants here. (Isn't it a bit late for the abstract revolution in ballet to be taking place?) There's no equivalent in the film to the *Red Shoes* ballet, and maybe there couldn't be. The story emphasis isn't on how ballerinas are made, it's on how they die. Even though the art of older ballerinas can be expressed more effectively in the movies than the art of young ones, we don't have any active older ballerinas in the movie. (Bancroft, a nondancer, demonstrates Emma's greatest role by collapsing under a cloak.) And even though the movie is full of quotes from well-known ballets, it doesn't view them selectively, with an eye to their dramatic relevance. The most beautiful shot occurs under the opening credits, as dancer after dancer steps into frame in close-up. It's *La Bayadère*—could there be a better symbol in dance of the continuity of the classical tradition? All the fuss about aging dancers could have had at least this much dignity. The film might have said that all dancers are godmothers. But once we've made the transition from the credits to Oklahoma City, where the story begins, we never return to *La Bayadère*. Eve Harrington had her progeny foreshadowed in mirrors at the fadeout of *All About Eve*. *The Turning Point*, a film made by and about dancers—those people who spend their lives before mirrors—cannot reflect its own world.

—November 21, 1977

Prose into Poetry

In choreography, if you can't be a genius, then you must be ingenious. Pilobolus Dance Theatre, I would have said a year ago, is simply ingenious. Now I'm not so sure that the gift of ingenuity isn't capable of once in a while surpassing itself, so that we are shaken out of admiration into awe.

Pilobolus is already in several respects a phenomenon. The performers create their own material. What they create is good, it is unique, and it is a big box-office hit. The world of Pilobolus is, in fact, a magical world where fairy-tale success actually can occur. Usually, the price of fame is a movement from the complex to the simple. The larger the audience, the greater the need to be understood. But the size of the following that Pilobolus has acquired in recent years seems only to have emboldened it. The company has just finished playing its first Broadway season. Business was excellent. In the repertory at the St. James Theatre were old pieces that have been shaped up and newer ones that have struck out exploratively. Two programs were presented; in both one could trace an impressive growth chart. *Ocellus*, the oldest piece in the repertory, looks back to the early seventies, when the company consisted of four men. Hypnotic but limited, it repeats motifs without expanding its vision. *Ciona*, revised to include two women, has more variety, but like *Ocellus*, it shows us athletic exuberance undistilled. The great step in the group pieces was taken in 1974 in *Monkshood's Farewell*. Is the title a reference to the addition of the two female members? Alison Chase and Martha Clarke have distinct, and distinctly different, styles both as artists and as performers. I think it was their individual qualities of style, and not just their sex, that changed the troupe and made it complete. *Untitled* (1975) belongs to them; they are gargantuan virgins sailing around a pastoral landscape on men's legs, giving birth, swallowing men whole, even swallowing each other, yet abiding serenely to the end of days.

Pilobolus is, of course, a company of acrobatic mimes rather than dancers. They do not step to a beat but move to a system of cues arranged like a musical sound track. Often they move in silence. However, it isn't the lack of an audible measure that makes their "dance" strangely unpredictable. The secret lies in the way the pieces are constructed out of mime continuity rather than dance continuity, and it lies, too, in an increasing urge toward the nonliteral image. *Monkshood's Farewell* is crammed with specific pictorial events that pyramid from the simplest of physical premises—the one that we're familiar with from the kindergarten game of "I'm a little teapot." The company starts with a medieval tournament in which linked limbs and torsos conjure up horses, riders, lances. Gargoyles abruptly appear to herald a sequence of random virtuoso pictures: shoes, bicycles, frogs, monkeys. Then the men all become hunchbacks, lascivious and gentle at the same time. As they look on happily, Martha Clarke is carried away by St. Vitus's dance. This is the funniest headless-chicken act since

Imogene Coca's sewing-machine girl went berserk back in the fifties; Clarke, with her large dark eyes and rubber mouth, resembles Coca, too. The fadeout comes on an unexpected note of pathos as three figures are seen bearing on their bent backs three others, who lie upside down and stiff as boards. It's the only nonrepresentational image in *Monkshood's Farewell*, yet—perhaps because it seems related to those dear hunchbacks—it's oddly moving. A lot of the imagery in this brilliant episodic piece suggests Bruegel; in *Untitled* and other dances, it's Edward Lear who comes to mind. *Untitled* has a nonsensical scenario that seems to have been hatched not from literary ideas but from props and acrobatic maneuvers. Making "sense" is a secondary object of the performers; their primary object is to keep going. By the time the piece is over, the women's long skirts, the men's bare or clothed bodies have been used like interlocking parts of a puzzle to build a complete design. *Untitled* never gets explicit in its reference to life, and it doesn't tell us what it means, yet we know wordlessly what it means. The design is there not to dictate our reactions but to set us free.

The St. James repertory included a number of solos and duets. In his solo from *Eve of Samhain*, Robby Barnett, wearing satyr-like shaggy leggings, stalks a steel snake lying on the ground. It whips itself around him; he frees himself, retreats offstage, and reappears in a pouncing leap from a height. The struggle grows intense. The snake dies as it is swung in ever more graceful, ever narrowing arcs. Finally, draped across the hunter's shoulders, it is caressed. In *Alraune*, the illusions are fostered entirely through anatomical manipulation. Moses Pendleton punches his head down into his torso, and later he holds Alison Chase's head so that it appears to float in midair. The Chase-Pendleton duet in which their bodies merge has become a staple of the repertory. It reaches a new peak of refinement in *Shizen*. Here, before the merger takes place, the two remain for a long time apart, holding positions of extreme difficulty. There are bits of mime that suggest (but never specify) a landscape of waving grass, a waterhole, the passage of tall birds. As soon as Chase locks herself around Pendleton's body, the two are one being, and they seem to keep evolving as one being. There is a sequence in which slight separations occur—enough to show the twinship of sexual intimacy. And at the end they are alone again, bent like peasants to the earth. *Shizen* passes as slowly as an Ozu film, to the sound of a bamboo flute. A pure object of contemplation, it marks a decisive advance in Pilobolus style; it's the movement from prose to poetry.

A dance troupe seldom achieves wide success until it is well into its second or third generation and its original brilliance is gone. The Pilobolus company we see today is still in its first generation. As first generations tend to be, it is a mixed band of individuals whose separate talents enrich the common enterprise and add to it the spice of potential dissent. Some of the solo turns look like decompression chambers. Jonathan Wolken's *Pseudopodia* is a wonderful tumbling solo in which his own foot is the hub of the wheel that turns him. It would look right at home in *Monkshood's Farewell*. But his *Renelaugh*, performed in fencing mask with foil, is entirely a private vision. Martha Clarke's solos undersell Martha Clarke. A rigorous form-follows-function comedian, she's constantly trying to build fires from a few carefully selected twigs—a veil and a baggy black dress in *Vagabond*, tin buckets and a floppy Pierrot suit in *Pagliaccio*. Though *Vagabond* isn't as precious as *Pagliaccio*, it's still a bit too choosy in what it reveals of Clarke's range. Yet in her selectivity she can be emotionally precise. The sadness of the moment when she "captures" Chase in *Untitled* could only belong to a very abstemious clown.

All the Piloboli are clowns—even Alison Chase, a statuesque, clear-browed beauty who functions most often as the troupe's indispensable straight woman. The glinting satyr Pendleton and the wolfishly jovial Wolken are just enough alike to set each other off; they could be brothers brought up by different tribes. The remote, poetic Barnett and the handsome Michael Tracy round off a perfectly balanced set. When a Pilobolus evening is over, one leaves the theatre with a complete experience, refreshed by the company of six of the most extraordinary people now performing.

—December 19, 1977

Adagio and Allegro

In *Ballo della Regina*, the new ballet that Balanchine has made for Merrill Ashley, she carries bravura allegro dancing to a peak it may never have reached before. The adagio, partnered by Robert Weiss, requires the singing line that Ashley doesn't have and is dispatched with typical efficiency, but her polka variation, whirling to a close with hops in fifth on pointe, cuts like flying glass. Balanchine seems to have taken Ashley's role in last year's *Bournonville Divertissements* as a sketch for the brilliant new material he has given her, and he has orchestrated the Ashley "theme"— her strangely characteristic ability to move her tall, straight body through rapid and complete changes of shape. Ashley doesn't combine different shapes in the same movement, but she can achieve counterpoint through juxtaposition, and she's so fast she can even appear to be in two places at once. The dances for an all-girl corps (four demi-soloists and an ensemble of twelve) are as spontaneous and fresh as the dances for Ashley. Balanchine has designed them for contrast—her fleet footwork against their wide striding and turning, their plasticity against her square-cut, erect style.

All this is allegro in range, although as Balanchine allegro it is unfamiliar. Those high, sailing jumps, for example— where did they come from? The ballet makes the audience very happy, especially at the end, when, to slamming final chords, Ashley takes three or four flash poses on the way down from a supported position in second to a kneel: it sums up her phenomenal high-speed accuracy.

In spite of the show put on by Ashley, Bonita Borne, Sheryl Ware, Debra Austin, Stephanie Saland, and the ensemble, *Ballo della Regina* doesn't add up to much. It lacks conviction as a ballet. Weiss's role is trumped up; musically there doesn't seem to be a real place for him, and he gets wedged into corners. (Flat and stiff as he looks, it's still unfair treatment.) The music is the seldom-performed ballet from Verdi's *Don Carlos*, written to a libretto that Balanchine has disregarded. Musical echoes of that libretto remain, nevertheless, in passages (*azione mimica*) that don't easily support the straight dancing that Balanchine has choreographed to them. In another ballet to music by an opera composer, *Donizetti Variations*, Balanchine has drawn a sharp, and sharply satirical, picture of Donizetti. But he doesn't appear to have had Verdi's qualities much in mind, perhaps because the music has no particular Verdian savor. (It was one of the composer's attempts to satisfy Parisian taste.) Balanchine's *Ballo della Regina* is a quarter-hour discourse about the qualities of Merrill Ashley.

When Suzanne Farrell dances an allegro role and brings to it an adagio color, as she did this season in *Allegro Brillante*, she creates a complex and interesting event. Farrell wouldn't be interesting in *Ballo della Regina*, since for the most part the role completely blocks out any adagio quality. The prima role in *Divertimento No. 15* doesn't need her, either, as one none too successful fling with it last year showed. For Farrell to captivate in allegro, the role has to be porous. For Ashley, it has to be airtight. *Allegro Brillante* isn't, and she probably wouldn't be terribly exciting in it. It took the enormous range of Farrell to show me that *Allegro Brillante* could be danced, with no loss of allegro values, as an adagio part. (I mean all the way through, not just in sections.) But the big Farrell occasion of the season so far has been her dancing in *Chaconne* the night of the *Ballo* première. To watch Farrell stretching a Farrell part is a frontline experience; dancing just does not go further. On this night, there were quantitative embellishments of all sorts: quadruple pirouettes, sixes instead of quatres in the entrechats, even triple soutenu turns. But quantity is not the end of virtuosity. What Farrell achieved was a heightening of all those fluid transactions between extreme ends of her range—between allegro and adagio—which Balanchine wrote into her role. And though she advanced to the very limit of the ballet's style, she never toppled into distortion.

—January 30, 1978

Broadway Downbeat

Book musicals are dying, revues are dead. One-man shows and chorus lines survive, with nothing in between. No-star ensembles are in, along with "theme" collages instead of plots, and the choreographer is still king of Broadway. Bob Fosse's *Dancin'* actually congratulates itself, in a spoken prologue, for dispensing with plot and characters, just as if every other musical in town were stuffed with boys meeting girls. The trend toward the reductive, the skeletal, the downright monomaniacal has been in motion a long time. It's a natural consequence of expecting one omnipotent soul—generally a choreographer—to be responsible for not only how a show looks but what it is about. Fosse himself provided the content—such as it was—of *Chicago*, a few seasons ago. For a book show, *Chicago* was as near to decadent abstraction as it could possibly get, and by eliminating the book altogether *Dancin'* takes the logical next step. Supposedly, in showcasing Fosse's talent as a choreographer rather than as a choreographer-*auteur*, *Dancin'* frees him from the taint of decadence, because if decadence is style trying to do the work of substance, surely whatever substance there can be in an all-dance show is more than accounted for in the style. The position of most reviewers of *Dancin'* has been that it's perfectly fine as a dance show if dance is what you want, but not if you want a real musical. I agree that it's no substitute for a musical, but I don't agree that Fosse's kind of dance show is the best you can get. Is it because Fosse's style has dominated show dancing for so long that we've come to accept them as synonyms? Fosse *always* puts style in place of substance, even when the substance is dance. In *Dancin'*, as in *Chicago* and other shows, he doesn't work in dance terms—he works in images. Fosse's images don't arise spontaneously out of links and contrasts between dance shapes, they're locked into those convulsive, writhing movement-chunks he habitually makes his dances out of. His choreography is without wings—literally and imaginatively grounded. But it always makes instantaneous contact with an audience.

Few choreographers have succeeded without a sense of the kinetic. Massine, the most successful choreographer of his day, was one. Fosse, with Broadway and Hollywood at his feet, has been successful beyond anything Massine could have approached, and now, as if demonstrating his freedom from the compromises and restrictions that go to make a commercial success, he stages on Broadway the kind of event that belongs more properly to the world that was once Massine's. But even in that world the choreographers who can sustain a whole evening by themselves are few.

Fosse knows his limitations, and he knows how to make them look like powerful artistic choices. He even throws us off the scent by claiming to have chosen the only course open to him. More breathtaking than his claim to have got rid of plot lines is his inclusion of a "tour de force" in which the dancers nail their clogs to the floor and perform a whole number without moving their feet. Footwork has about as much to do with Fosse style as lariat-twirling: gyrating body shapes are the essence of that style. Shoulders roll, pelvises grind, and knees boggle; the feet aren't in it. "A Manic Depressive's Lament" is about someone who's glad to be unhappy. The song ("I've Got Them Feelin' Too Good Today Blues," by Jerry Leiber and Mike Stoller) and the dance that goes with it *seem* to go against tradition, but Fosse's movement, which is nothing if not a tradition, is naturally manic-depressive. It suits the ambivalent mood of show business today, and it turns perennial "up" numbers like the strutting top-hat-and-tails routine into downers. (The latest example of the up-downer occurs in *The Act*, a show starring Liza Minnelli, with dances by Ron Lewis.) Buoyancy, gaiety, optimism are beyond the limits of this strenuous low-down technique. When Fosse wants to get happy, he's still strenuous. Squeezing out happy juice, he gets syrupy. The most wistful number in the show is "Dancin' Man," a tribute to Fred Astaire. The dancers, instead of tapping, slap their thighs numb. We know it's the best they can do.

Fosse's dancers often seem to be winding themselves around a core of wistfulness. Inside his dance is a better one trying to get out. Some of his coolest images are impressions of the effect that truly elegant show dancing has upon us: they're externalizations of a feeling about dance. The feeling is openly presented. The dancers look out at us; they trust us to know what they mean. A number such as "Recollections of an Old Dancer" is disarming and boring at the same time. Boring because it doesn't move like a dance, disarming because it speaks right up and says it never meant to. "Recollections," a quasi soft-shoe, is relatively gentle. Fosse's dancers strike attitudes as representative as public statues, and in the hard-punching numbers they can seem to grow to frighteningly huge, pythonesque proportions. They're like big photo-realist paintings come to life. At their cheapest, they're editorial cartoons. The would-be satirical closer, "America," is wearily efficient rather than scathing. Although it's one of the show's two big mistakes, a moment in it has conviction—American women pictured as infantile sluts. It's as appalling as anything in *Chicago*. "The Dream Barre," in which Charles Ward as a timid ballet student fantasizes his seduction of the girl next to him in class, is the other big mistake—it's off base as satire. Nobody except Ward looks like a ballet dancer.

Jerking from one stance to the next like flip pictures, Fosse's dancers are best when they are backed up by a pounding beat. "Percussion," a fast, slick suite of dances to drums, cymbals, and other noisemakers, is a demonstration of your classic Fosse twitch-and-slink. The big killer in the show is "Benny's Number," staged to an arrangement of "Sing, Sing, Sing" as recorded at Benny Goodman's 1938 Carnegie Hall concert. The music is a powerhouse that shakes Fosse loose from some of his mannerisms, but he really responds only to Krupa's beat. In the musical passages, he is dismayingly literal. When Goodman slides to his famous high C above A, what do we see but the boys sliding their hands up the girls' thighs, and for Jess Stacy's (equally famous) odd and delicate interlude he uses a curious sidling tap duet that mimics the music. "Benny's Number" looks like something Fosse has meant to do for a long time, and you can't watch it without wanting with your whole soul to see it work. Fosse succeeds in putting it over—but as a conventional show-stopper, with ladders and trapezes in the finale. Fosse's experience is with show music. He hasn't developed the range for the jazz epic that "Sing, Sing, Sing" is. With the relatively modest big-band forces of "Big Noise from Winnetka" he's on safer ground, and he turns out another Fosse classic—one that resembles his memorable trio "Steam Heat." The "Winnetka" number doesn't sink in—it's little more than a crossover during a stage wait. But the throwaway may be a deliberate reminder of the stage wait in *The Pajama Game* that made "Steam Heat" possible.

Fosse's involvement in the material he uses for *Dancin'* is inescapable. The show discloses and focuses his personality and his abilities as no other show yet has; it's practically confessional theatre. It confirms and defines his talent, while aiding our suspicion that he is a driven and cynical man, but it also reveals a degree of self-knowledge that isn't given to many in the entertainment field, and here I include Fosse's peers in the "artistic" branch of the profession. Only two doors down the street from *Dancin'*, Rudolf Nureyev is appearing, for the first part of his stand at the Minskoff, in dances by Murray Louis. Of course, there's no one in the cast of *Dancin'* like Nureyev or with any real star wattage to speak of, and Murray Louis has credentials as an artist which Fosse doesn't have. Yet when a Broadway engagement in the glare of Nureyev's publicity holds those credentials up to the light, Louis comes off as knowing a lot less about his craft and his capabilities than Fosse does about his. Louis is a twitcher, too, and the quality of the movement he gives his dancers—rigid above the hips, spongy below, as if they were so many beanbag ashtrays—may be no worse in its way than Fosse's patented slither. But the follow-the-bouncing-ball choreography is, I think, a good deal worse, because it's habitually set to Ravel or Bach or Schubert. When it's set to Cole Porter songs (arranged by William Bolcom), it tells obvious jokes; we can laugh, because we know it isn't art anymore.

The name of Louis's Cole Porter ballet is *The Canarsie Venus*, and the action is reminiscent of the 1943 musical *One Touch of Venus*. It has a Walter Mitty type (Nureyev, if you please) being seduced by the goddess (Anne McLeod), who has been washed up on a beach crowded with litterbugs. Fosse, in *Dancin'*, may be aspiring to the crown of choreography, but he hasn't given up being a showman. Showmanship in Louis's case means that his usual crudity turns into fatuous sleaze. The simple little story of Nureyev changing from mouse into lion under the goddess's touch isn't made clear. As a comedian under Louis's direction, Nureyev is vacant and heavy. It doesn't hurt his popularity with the audience. Like Liza Minnelli, he's impervious to flops. Nevertheless, it's sad to see him, too, hitting Broadway in a down show.

—April 24, 1978

Arts and Sciences
and David Gordon

One of the most controlled and sophisticated performance artists is David Gordon. His current work is characterized by brilliantly elliptical dialogue or parodies of real conversations. Whether it's delivered by the performers or by taped voices, this verbal material is balanced and coordinated with choreographed movements that reveal the same flair for selection and for lifelike imitation. Gordon's type of dance movement is the simple, technically ungroomed movement that was promoted in the post-Cunningham rebellion of the sixties by Yvonne Rainer and others. Gordon, who worked with Rainer, is the first to use this movement nonideologically. He seems to see it paradoxically—as being interesting in itself but also somewhat absurd in its presumptive amateurism. Valda Setterfield, his wife and partner, is a former member of the Cunningham company. A trained dancer, she's particularly good at projecting the double edges in the material. Because he is by nature a satirist and a critic, Gordon has instinctively developed into an avant-garde comedian. The subject of his new evening-length piece, *Not Necessarily Recognizable Objectives*, is performance. By the end of the evening, the inference that he is criticizing his own performance—as dancer, choreographer, scriptwriter, and host (the event was held in his loft on lower Broadway)—as well as the conventions of performance has grown into a certainty.

The piece begins as Gordon and Setterfield circle the space slowly in a jog-walk. They wear satin gym pants, white shirts, jogging shoes. An atmosphere of trial, of self-tempering, begins to gather. Meanwhile, a voice catalogues, casebook-style, the perils of performance. Another voice (Agnes Moorehead's in *Sorry, Wrong Number*) pleads with an operator to dial a wrong number on purpose. Soon we find ourselves unable to distinguish the planned accidents from the real ones. The action pauses momentarily and an ingenious floundering conversation takes place—ingenious because we can plainly see that it's being read from posters on the wall. But, in spite of the cue cards, there's a place where the talk takes off on its own. We grasp this when the entire conversation, which deals with the course the performance is to take, is repeated with the roles reversed and we come back to the improvised section. Whether we recognize it or not, Gordon has made a point about perception and about conventional ways of listening and reacting in the theatre. He can be quite ruthless in pressing this point. Later in the action, a similar incident occurs after three other members of the troupe have joined the principals and become confused about the next step to take in a walking pattern. Somebody says, "Oh, now I know what to do," and instantly the line and the gesture (hand clapped to head) are incorporated by all five dancers into the pattern. Was the confusion real? Of course not. Gordon now springs his trap. On the next repeat, "Oh, now I know what to do" is said not with dancers smiting their brows but with them holding their noses, and even as we begin to laugh Gordon takes the laugh out of our mouths and puts it in the mouths of his dancers. The line becomes " 'Oh, now I know what to do' [laugh]." And to this demonstration of indifference to our reaction we *really* don't know how to react.

Gordon creates a triple-distilled mixture of dance, drama, and words. The text develops an almost insidious relevance to the movement, and the movement keeps commenting on itself. Specific sequences take on new aspects when they're done faster or more slowly, by different people, in different directions, or with as little as one element in the sequence varied. A bewitching women's trio, which follows a simple loop pattern of slowly descending to the floor, rolling over, and getting back up, is complicated by the tightest unison possible: the women are pressed one inside another the whole time. Gordon adds a final variation to the roll on the floor and accompanies it with the sunrise music from *La Fille Mal Gardée*—a touch that mingles humor and erotic mystery. Another movement sequence is a series of dashes broken by abrupt directional shifts and off-balance skedaddling whirls. It runs like a spine through the piece, alternating with its companion motif, the slow jog in a circle. Gordon keeps this material so clearly focused that we easily see it turning over on itself, its effects as differentiated as the words in the dialogues. Gradually, within its limits, the piece develops a disarming openness. We know that if anything can happen, it surely will.

David Gordon does not look like a dancer. He has an actor's weight and presence, fierce black hair and whiskers that set off a sleepy expression, and a resonant voice. He is soft and shaggy in texture and sensuous in movement, with an overall look of ovals slipping within larger ovals. Sometimes in motion he looks as if he had popped out of Max

Fleischer's inkwell. His personal peak in *Not Necessarily Recognizable Objectives* is reached when he does a solo, first having told us on a tape how aware he is of the egocentric temptations of soloing, how he has arranged to undercut these by having his group comment as he performs, and how we mustn't be fooled into thinking *he* thinks this will do anything but force us to pay all the more attention to "his person" (Gordon talks of himself Mailerishly). He does the solo, which appears to be made up of all the movement material in the piece so far, to the accompaniment of remarks that send up crowd psychology, cultural fetishes, dance criticism—everything that performers have nightmares about. And dreams of revenge, too. How to end? The four remaining dancers are given the same solo to do in the form of a round, ending as Gordon ended, by slipping behind a sliding door. Thus we conclude with another recapitulation in a different form, which makes it a fresh statement.

—May 15, 1978

On Video, On Tap

As the curtain rises on *Fractions*, the dancers are posed facing in different directions, and their stillness is charged with the kind of tension peculiar to Merce Cunningham. It is a memorable, emblematic opening, and *Fractions*, as it unfolds, has the concentrated energy of a great signature work. When it is over, it seems to have summed up everything important in the Cunningham canon and yet to have weighed not an ounce. *Fractions* was conceived as choreography for television. As seen on tape, the dance is divided by four cameras; in the image that we see, quotient and remainder appear side by side and change constantly. In the past, Cunningham has experimented with split screens and chromakey arrangements. Here he simply sets up TV monitors in the studio to catch the overflow from the main image. Along with solid-color panels, by Mark Lancaster, which are positioned around the space in a different relation to the dancing from what we see in the stage production, the monitors are part of the set. They may show close-ups of the dancers being photographed or they may register background action or action not within the range of the main camera. The multiple viewpoints may suddenly contract to a partial viewpoint and the entire frame may be filled with, say, Karole Armitage seen only from the hips up as she goes through the maze of an elaborate pas de deux. Her partner, Robert Kovich, becomes a mysterious erotic presence. Cunningham, alone of the choreographers who have worked with video, has assumed that defining TV space is necessary to the projection of a dance in TV terms. (Twyla Tharp's brilliant *Making Television Dance*, for PBS, was about television more than it was about dance; it was electronics commenting on itself.) And Cunningham's acute sense of how to use video is related to his theatre choreography. The diffused focus, the interchangeable perspectives, the simultaneous play of discrete elements are readily translated to fill the TV void. The same factors that make Cunningham choreography as interesting to watch close up as from a distance make it televisable; as in figure skating, which is also a good show on television, space is fluid. To watch the videodance *Fractions* is to watch the medium find its dancing master. Is it just a coincidence that Lancaster's scenery for Cunningham's latest solo, *Tango*, is a tuned-in (but silent—John Cage provides the sound) television set?

The stage version of *Fractions*, which was first given last winter in Boston, is so reorganized and replotted that only in the content of the choreography can we recognize it as the same dance; even the dancers seem transformed. No monitors are to be seen. (Occasionally, someone will appear over to one side, taking up a position on invisible chalk marks and then walking off. It is typical of Cunningham to take away the cameras and leave their subjects.) *Fractions* may be the most successful of Cunningham's videodances because it's really about dancing, and "television" is metaphorically present in its conception—a part of the real world of change which Cunningham believes in and makes dances about. Unlike *Westbeth*, a former video experiment, *Fractions* isn't fancy and self-conscious, with one eye on the lens; it's a natural happening, whether you see it on the tube or on the stage, and it may be the closest any choreographer has yet come to working with absolute integrity in two media at once. If I prefer the theatrical version, that's because I prefer the theatre. Even Cunningham hasn't shown me where the poetry is in television, although he has shown me its wit. The closing minutes of *Fractions* build to an ensemble section in which the dispersals and regroupings are punctuated by the repetition of a single phrase: three pliés in rhythm followed by plié-hold. On television, credits were flashed over the holds as if they were frozen frames. But there can be no TV equivalent of the moment when, onstage, a group freezes to isolate a solitary leap. There doesn't seem to be any such thing as "solitary" on television—not even when Karole Armitage is alone in her pas de deux. People are either on camera or off. In the theatre, Kovich's supporting role in the pas de deux is, of course, fully seen, and it is still almost entirely "below frame," but the beautiful poses he takes as he leans away from Armitage's hovering body or embraces it from underneath place the action clearly on two planes. Armitage, with her amazing high extension, is as secure in her upper realm as she would be on pointe; no ballerina was ever more gracefully or daringly cantilevered. And the drama of it is Kovich's also.

It is impossible to discuss Cunningham's choreography these days without discussing his dancers, many of them newcomers. There was another influx this year, and some former members—Louise Burns, Catherine Kerr—have returned. But for the first time since the turning-over process began, about two years ago, the company has lost its raw-recruit look, and among the girls especially there is a new, sharp sense of style. Armitage exemplifies it; Lisa Fox, Kerr, and the others reveal it, too. It's based on the high, free-swinging leg extensions they all seem to have under admirable control from the inner thigh. What thunderous grands battements these women produce, and what floating footwork! Cunningham loves to skew classical standards, to be oblique where ballet is direct and direct where it's oblique. Seeing legs whip straight back from a zigzag fouetté into penchée arabesque is like crossing a divide when the bridge is gone; you feel the full impact of what hasn't happened in between. There are many such moments in Armitage's solo in *Fractions*. (Fox does a slightly different version.) As she kicks, turns, and strides in huge seconds and fourths, she seems in a very real sense to be breaking ground. Old structures crumble; air rushes up. A lot of the material in *Fractions* is not really new; it's canonical. Perhaps working with television and with so many new dancers made Cunningham want to recover and restate his foundations. In any event, *Fractions* enters the repertory at precisely the right moment. It's a stabilizer. Wonderful as Cunningham's recent work has been, a concise, limpid experience like *Fractions* hasn't happened in some time. The piece doesn't fall into sections; neither does it become monomaniacally urgent, like *Torse*. In its organic development, its suspenseful configurations, *Fractions* reminds me of the older works, which are represented in the current repertory by *Summerspace* and *Rune*—works in which the dancers are as sensuously alert and free as forest creatures in a clearing.

Inlets also has some of this characteristic nature poetry, with unusually small, elegant transitions. Beautiful Giacometti distances, too (there are only six dancers), and a few curiosities: a recurrent "Greek" pose, a broken-footed walk in relevé, a group tableau that looks like a climax. But I'm not sure it's the dark, enigmatic piece that the décor, by Morris Graves, makes it out to be. The big shiny "sun" that travels slowly across the backcloth, the scrim that makes everything misty, even the very handsome sulphur-by-day, cobalt-by-night lighting, by Charles Atlas, press far too hard. The choreography is Cunningham at his most gently uninsistent. Another curiosity is the Graves poster that was offered for sale during the season. It links a big solar semicircle to two coiled serpents. The colors are the same as those we see on the stage, but the pronged, writhing shapes are far from the earnest romanticism of the set. Animal imagery appears in the costumes—unitards dyed in patches of dark gray and worn with rhinestone dog collars. Cunningham, in addition, has one white and one black foot, which throws his famous parallel position into high relief.

Jasper Johns has also made a striking set of costumes for *Exchange*. Together with his lighting, the gray-over-pastel coloring suggests a theme of shadows and smoke. The choreography, though, comes in a thick flow of exuberant invention. *Exchange* is a cornucopia: some of the dances look like points of origin for things in *Fractions* or *Inlets*, and the piece as a whole looks as if it could furnish an entire repertory. I wish I had been able to watch it more closely, but my concentration broke about halfway through under the battering of David Tudor's score. Cage's water and fire music for *Inlets* didn't get in the way of my enjoyment, and Jon Gibson's flute solo for *Fractions* enhanced it. If the tenebrous décors for *Inlets* and *Exchange* were discordant, they were not destructive. But how can you watch a dance with V-2 rockets whistling overhead? Of all the aspects of the Cunningham revolution, music remains the most problematical. Some of the dissociated-sound scores that Cunningham uses are more interfering and dictatorial than planned settings would be.

Quite a few young women are clacketing around in tap shoes these days, showing off techniques learned from the jazz dancers of a former generation—men like Stanley Brown and Charles Cook and Honi Coles. The new tappers are all white, and almost all are displaced modern dancers; a disconcerting number of them have performed with Meredith Monk or had their interest whetted by Twyla Tharp's use of tap. They want not so much to revive a bygone era as to develop tap into a contemporary art form. But at their concerts one tends to hear pre-rock jazz and see the dancing that went with it. Jazz dance was largely the province of black male hoofers, and it was primarily acoustic; it seldom got off the ground and into the air. There were also spectacular "flash" acts, like the Nicholas Brothers, but women did not often venture into virtuoso hoofer territory, because, whether in the air or on the ground, the technique was physically unflattering. It still is; in tap-dancing, a woman has to work hard to avoid looking like she's working hard, and those who study with aging hoofers have to beware of absorbing their heaviness. A young woman doesn't need a low plié; she needs height in the upper back, loose hips, more flexibility in the ankle than in the knee. And she needs to develop something in the way of a body line for her audience to look at. I'm aware that these sexual distinctions probably don't interest the new breed of female tap-dancers, but who could be interested in the low-primate stuff they're turning out now? Some of these women are very articulate students of jazz-tap history; they're trying to rescue a dying art. But almost none of them have seen how to re-create the art in respect to their own needs and gifts.

Gail Conrad is an exception to all this; she may be the

only woman choreographer in the currently expanding tap field whose objective isn't laying down irons like a man. It was through watching Conrad perform with her group last month at the Theatre for the New City that I began to see what the others were missing. Conrad's carriage is consistently buoyant, her line is attractive, her sound is delicate and full. A small, active redhead, she casts herself slightly tomboy, but this is plainly her adaptation of a musical-comedy convention—she has none of that neutered look the other tappers seem to think is appropriate. Conrad's personality is clear, sweet, and strong, and the four members of her company are just as vivid as she is. In this single fact may lie her greatest accomplishment as a choreographer, for as the evening passes it becomes evident that only Seth Tomasini, the gangling leading man, and Conrad herself have a high-grade technique. Bob Duncan, though a practiced performer, is not yet in their league as a tap-dancer. Anny DeGange and Muriel Favaro can best be described as enlightened amateurs. Conrad's choreography presents her performers at their various levels of strength without revealing inequalities that might hamper the show. With all of them dancing up to capacity in their tailor-made roles, the show becomes transparently and engagingly a set of full-length "character" portraits.

One way to vary a tap step is to travel it. Conrad calls her hour-long show *Travelers: A Tap Dance/Epic*, and the dances are strung on a thread of a story about a mixed bunch of travelers in South America. So fine is this thread that the show was half over before I saw where it was going. No other tap choreographer I know has attempted a whole show on a single theme. Conrad has done it, but how much scope dancing of this sort can impart to a theme is a question. At times, Conrad seemed to evoke the curious unmoored sensation of foreign travel, and the evening took on an avant-gardish hallucinatory tinge; at other times the atmospheric bits about tourists reading maps and going to the beach and taking pictures seemed intended as nothing more than rests between dances. I wouldn't be surprised to learn that *Travelers* took the form of a Latin American travelogue because of the music. Not only are the sambas and rumbas and cha-chas good for tap-dancing, they also avoid the dilemma of having to choose between a jazz stereotype and a rock experiment. A swinging five-man ensemble played the music (when it was not on tape) and entered good-naturedly into the show. *Travelers* was that rare success—an intelligently staged homemade fantasy. It kept you off balance—no tricks, no hit material—yet happily absorbed.

—*October 23, 1978*

The Spoken Word

Robert Joffrey keeps adding laurels to the crown he wears as uncontested master of revivals. *A Wedding Bouquet* is the prettiest thing he has done since *Les Patineurs*. Both of these ballets, by Frederick Ashton, revived from the original Vic-Wells productions of 1937, are decorated in a freshwater palette that seems to have slipped away with the war. William Chappell's lantern-lit forest in *Les Patineurs* has a honey-toned glow; its intricately laced branches have been marvelously reproduced in cutouts, which give a burrowing depth to the forest. Some of Lord Berners's pastels in *A Wedding Bouquet*—a "spring" counterpart of Chappell's "winter"—appear to have gone slightly acid, but his mild, floral-scented country air is still delicious to breathe. Although *A Wedding Bouquet* is not as well performed as it is well produced (like most Joffrey revivals), something of the past is alive in it; in its way, the ballet is as evocative of its time and place as *The Green Table*, *Parade*, *Rodeo*, and *New York Export: Opus Jazz* are of theirs. All these pieces are in repertory this fall, being as faithfully kept up as if each and every one were a classic. The Joffrey restorations are uncomfortably jostled by the Now ballets of Gerald Arpino, which have a way of becoming Then almost before their first season is out. Last season's *Suite Saint-Saëns* is unconscious self-parody; I don't want to dwell on it except to suggest that the time may have come to divide the dancers into two wings—one to do Joffrey's revivals and the other to do Arpino's ballets. No company can serve two ballet masters. Dancers whose style has been coarsened by Arpino cannot be expected to perform Joffrey's Ashton. *Monotones II* (to Satie's *Gymnopédies*), which used to be given a respectable performance, has now faded; *The Dream* has yet to be mastered. Even *Les Patineurs,* which doesn't present nearly as many difficulties, is roughly handled by nearly everyone in it. The dancers are most at ease with the calculated vulgarity of *Jazz Calendar*—their high is Ashton's low.

In *A Wedding Bouquet*, the problem is more elusive. Its dance style is not as critical to its expression as are the manners and customs that the style elaborates. One might describe the ballet, which concerns the cast of characters at a large, frilly provincial wedding at the turn of the century, as a set of Anglo-Saxon attitudes, even though its locale is a French village and one of its authors is Gertrude Stein. *A Wedding Bouquet* is as preciously English as the English ever get. Whatever it was understood to be in 1937—some saw it as a satire of *Les Noces* or *Jardin aux Lilas*; others called it the ripest comedy of manners that English ballet had produced—it is no more than a brittle period toy today. What we get from this revival is a picture of the fashionable and precocious minds that created it—Berners's and Ashton's and Constant Lambert's, mostly. Gertrude Stein's seems to have been conscripted. Berners, who wrote the music and designed the scenery and costumes, was the senior member of the trio. Ashton and Lambert, who both helped with the scenario, were the bright young things. Since the ballet has no reality now apart from the particular atmosphere of creativity which it evokes (in which even the dancers shared: the young Margot Fonteyn as Julia comes back to us; Julia the character does not), it was a happy stroke on Joffrey's part to arrange Anthony Dowell's guest appearance as the Narrator. The Narrator is outside and inside the ballet at once, and he seems to be imagining it as it goes along. Besides standing for its creators, Dowell stands for the whole Royal Ballet. As he talked, my mind went back—not to that wedding but through the years from the Royal to the Sadler's Wells to the Vic-Wells Ballet and its talented young men, down for a weekend at Berners's country house, throwing themselves about in transports of inspiration while their sly host sat at the piano, swooping now into a tango, now into a waltz. Dowell, taking the part that Lambert created, contrives the faint suggestion that he's playing Lambert's puppet, sitting on a gargantuan institutional knee, with his voice piped in from afar. Normally radiantly handsome, he slicks back his hair for this role and makes up his face like a wooden doll's whose eyes and teeth flash as if hinged together at the back. Dowell makes no attempt to force connections between the words and the action; the voice, as warm and flat as (one suspects) the champagne he sips, is engaged but noncommittal. Getting delicately plotzed as the ballet rolls on and letting his head loll slightly like a dummy's is a good idea, too.

The Joffrey is the only company other than the Royal and its affiliates to revive this ballet in recent years, and I don't think that even the Royal would try it today without Ashton there to coach the dancers. The characters are all his inventions; though the cues come from Gertrude Stein's text, they are Stein cues. (What must a dancer make of

"Thérèse. I am older. Than a boat"?) The Royal choreolo-
gist Christopher Newton does a good job, but he misses
important details, like the joke about Julia's dog coming
and hogging the foreground in the group portrait. The
dancer should strike the kneeling arabesque pose from the
opening tableau of *Les Sylphides*—not just fling her leg in
the air. Besides Dowell's, there are two outstanding performances—by the endlessly resourceful Gary Chryst as the
Groom, and by Lynn Glauber, a new member of the company, as the Bride. The others are not bad; they're just not
there. And neither is the ballet.

When the Narrator says, "Webster was a name that was
spoken," we understand him to mean Webster the officious
maid—the role that was modeled on Ninette de Valois and
danced by her in the first production. In the Stein play from
which the line was taken, "Webster" refers to Daniel Webster. How Daniel Webster came to be a name that was spoken at a French country wedding is a mystery that must lie
coiled within the greater mystery that was the art of
Gertrude Stein. She had her house in the French country-
side, and when Ashton came to visit her after the ballet was
produced she took him on a tour of the village, pointing
out the originals of the characters she had in mind when she
wrote the play. (I have this information and most of the
foregoing facts from David Vaughan's admirable study
Frederick Ashton and His Ballets.) To these characters she
gave equivocal or non-French names, like Josephine, Julia,
Ernest, and Guy. Was Stein really writing about her French
neighbors "in English" or was she writing, as so often seems
the case in her other work, in English for English's sake,
taking in this instance her neighbors as a pretext? Stein
claimed that her native language had become more precious
and meaningful to her in France. It had become in fact a

dream language—a secret garden that she cultivated by digging up roots. In "They Must. Be Wedded. To Their Wife"—the main source for *A Wedding Bouquet*—the language is all porous description and cryptic epigrammatic observation that could be applied to any fluster-prone social occasion anywhere; even the fact that it is a wedding must be largely inferred.

Language so majestically impartial has power in the theatre—maybe only in the theatre. Especially when allied with music, it can produce an effect of queerly formal continuity, of harmony on top of chaos. This chemical reaction of words and notes was Virgil Thomson's discovery. Not until her collaboration with Thomson, in the opera *Four Saints in Three Acts* ("Pigeons on the grass, alas"), was it Gertrude Stein's intention to compose another kind of music, much as Edith Sitwell had done in *Façade* ("Daisy and Lily, lazy and silly"). According to David Vaughan, Berners originally composed *A Wedding Bouquet* for a singing chorus, and that was the way it was performed at first. I've never heard the sung version, but the change to a spoken narration must have altered the relation of words and music from something like Thomson's setting of *Four Saints* to something more like William Walton's setting of *Façade*. (Ashton, of course, had made the choreography for both those works.) The speech that rattles along in rhythm to the music in *A Wedding Bouquet* has an inescapably English, Sitwellian ring. The frivolity is all wrong for Gertrude Stein. In spite of Anthony Dowell's untheatrical voice and deadpan delivery, the effect is incongruous, like tying ribbons on an elephant.

—*November 6, 1978*

Balanchine's Petipa

Harlequinade is a two-act Petipa ballet of 1900, remade as inconspicuously as possible by Balanchine. To illustrate what I mean by "inconspicuously," take the last of the episodes that make up the action. Harlequin sets a trap for Columbine in the Enchanted Park, where, having just signed a marriage contract, they will spend the rest of their lives. The trap is a portable birdbath; it spins like a top—three little harlequins keep it turning. Birds flutter around the small silver cascade, and Harlequin shoos them away. Then Columbine comes to take a long drink, bending low in flat-footed arabesque penchée. He captures her, and their pas de deux explores that deep penchée as, reperched at his arm's length, she dips and swoops close to the ground. A moment later, Harlequin is himself spinning like a top, one leg extended like the point of a compass, the spangles on his diamond-patterned costume throwing off light. For an instant, this whirl of light and the other whirl it reminds us of—the fountain—plus the corps of birds and the long-throated birdlike image of the girl are made to contain each other loosely in a structure of mutual celebration. It's Balanchine springing *his* trap, creating one of those crystal moments of pure captivation out of the oddly assorted events he has set before us. Harlequin's spin isn't just one more event, it's a catalytic explosion, and Mikhail Baryshnikov's cyclonic grande pirouette has never had a more appropriate setting.

Yet the structure of correspondences, all but subliminal, does nothing more than captivate. Like Harlequin's capturing Columbine only to set her free, it dissolves as soon as we see it, without celebrating itself. The nascent imagery of the scene, which another choreographer—Ashton, for one—would have developed, is left undisturbed. Balanchine, like Petipa, is content with its suggestive drift—more than a tender conceit yet less than a metaphor. He gives us a kind of parable of forms—naïve, with rough edges. He doesn't coach us for a response. As the sequence builds up, it accumulates elements of harmony and elements of contrast and relief (those birds have one of the dizziest entrées right in the middle of it), and all we're conscious of as we watch it is the pressure of concentration. Nothing so official as a "meaning" is ever delivered—here or anywhere else in the ballet. *Harlequinade* is one of Balanchine's most innocent and vulnerably affectionate works, and one of his least popular.

The Harlequin of the ballet is the eternal Harlequin of mischief and protean tricks. Contemporary audiences may see him as unsympathetic, and the harlequinade as coy fantasy or rootless frivolity—which it very often is. In any case, there are people who have never seen the ballet and don't want to go, because they're pretty sure they won't be amused. Balanchine's way of seducing these people over the years (the piece was first done in 1965 and was revised in 1973) has been to give them more of what they don't want:

more children, more merrymaking (which really *is* rootless), gaudier costumes. But even the hard-core ballet public resists *Harlequinade*—I suspect because it isn't "Balanchine." That is, the traditional material isn't sufficiently filtered and doesn't express a "contemporary point of view." What's deceptive about *Harlequinade* is that Balanchine's re-evaluations occur within the material, not outside it in the form of a commentary. The steps may not be Petipa's but their quality of expression is. And is Balanchine's at the same time. For a comparison, see his *Swan Lake*, in which both the surface and the depths of an old ballet have been organically reconceived. The expressive mode of *Harlequinade* would be recognizable to Petipa; a modern-day "reinterpretation" probably would not; one that searched out pithier characterizations and metaphors certainly would not. Perhaps it's a question less of craftsmanly connection than of spiritual identification. When Balanchine is dealing directly in the Petipa tradition, as in *Harlequinade* and *The Nutcracker* and *Raymonda Variations* (and in his other variations on *Raymonda*), he works in a nonaggrandizing way. He converts the material to a new purpose, makes it serve new dancers, without stamping it with a new personality. This leads to accusations that he doesn't revise as well as he copies. There's nothing in *Harlequinade* like the Waltz of the Flowers, but then we love the Waltz for the way it appears to spring directly from its music and its period. Although it originates in the same period, nothing in *Harlequinade* was destined to be as wonderful as that. Petipa, too, knew the difference between Tchaikovsky and Riccardo Drigo, and valued them both. As far as metaphors go, it is enough for Columbine to be a bird—when she isn't being a doll—as it is for Harlequin to be a cat.

The ballet's stylistic precedents are somewhat hazy. Russians saw harlequinades at the *balagani*—the covered stages at the Russian fairs. Alexandre Benois, who commemorated the *balagani* in his décors for *Petrushka*, writes, in *Reminiscences of the Russian Ballet*, about the harlequinades he saw there as a boy, and he describes the same Harlequin figure who, in some of the same episodes, found his way into Petipa's ballet. If, as Benois writes, "Harlequin was given exactly the part that he played in our old *balagani*," either the ballet must have reflected the people's theatre to a degree unsuspected by historians of the Petipa years, who always picture the Imperial Ballet enclosed in a bubble of sanctity, or the people's Harlequin represented the francophiliac culture of St. Petersburg, which also seems unlikely. The Imperial Theatres were under the direction of I. A. Vzevolozhsky, a typical product of that culture, and it was Vzevolozhsky, as Benois also informs us, who conceived the Harlequin ballet, drawing on his memories of the féeries he had seen in Paris. Petipa, a Frenchman, would have known all about that; both men had, in fact, turned to the féeries a decade before, for *The Sleeping Beauty*. The style of the ballet *Arlekinada*, or *Les Millions d'Arlequin*, as it was also known, conformed to the sophisticated taste of the capital. It was romantic, pretty, "French." The Pierrot was (and is) the lazy, woebegone mooncalf popularized by French mimes. But as the servant of Cassandre, Columbine's father, he's a fink, ratting on the lovers and creeping into the audience's affections only by bungling most of his servile assignment. He doesn't have a great deal in common with that other hero of the *balagani*, Petrushka, who was a Russian Pierrot so well assimilated that he is still universally accepted as a symbol of the Russian soul. Drigo was, of course, Italian. His music for the ballet is contemporary with *Cavalleria Rusticana* and *Pagliacci*, and sounds that way. For an Arlecchino who is youthful and elegant, both poet and lover, he composes a lace-doily Serenade, the hit of the score. Balanchine stages it with a minimum of dancing as if to draw our attention to the mandolins in the pit. But when a nuptial anthem is wanted at the end of the ballet, the orchestra bursts into the French drinking song "Malbrouck s'en va t'en guerre," which is known in this country as "For He's a Jolly Good Fellow."

With all this for a background, it's not surprising that the style of Balanchine's production is polyglot, a merry jumble of Russian, French, and Italian influences. Rouben Ter-Arutunian's scenery, modeled on the Pollock's toy theatres of Victorian England, adds a fourth influence and reminds us of the long and rich tradition of the English harlequinade. Ter-Arutunian's lighting has always seemed unatmospherically dim in Act I, and in Act II the stage is blatantly sidelit, so that leaping shadows are thrown on the wings by the dancers' entrances and exits. The shadows can be excused as magic-lantern effects suitable to a toy theatre, but although there must be moonlight in Act I if there is to be a Serenade, the moon ought not to be clouded over. Ter-Arutunian does not provide a Pierrot moon, perhaps because the bulk of his scenery was designed not for this production but for a New York City Opera *Cenerentola* in 1953. The part of it that belongs to *Harlequinade* is the house of Cassandre, with its twin turntables, which allow the statue of La Bonne Fée, Harlequin's protectress, to come to life and Harlequin himself to be miraculously restored after he's been dismembered in a rout. There's also a balcony that lowers itself to the ground. (I thought I'd seen all the scenery's magic tricks when suddenly, this season, Baryshnikov made an exit through the wall of the toy theatre.) The choreography in Act I is concerned mostly with getting the cast into and out of the house and Harlequin together with Columbine, who has been pledged by her father to a wealthy fop. It's all business, a farcical ballet d'action, but it isn't busy, and the perfection of its shape cracks only once, when Balanchine abruptly introduces a stageful of revelers from a nearby carnival, which is never alluded to again. The variations for the principals—Columbine, Harlequin, Pierrette, and La Bonne Fée—and the smoochy Columbine-Harlequin pas de deux are seamlessly joined to the action. The only "divertissement" number (apart from the tarantella-fugue of the revelers) is the pas de quatre done by the four ladies of Harlequin's entourage in espresso-black seventeenth-century outfits. This pas de quatre, currently undersold in performance, is one of the gems of the repertory. Stylistically, it embraces both the art and the life of Petipa's period, it comes from deep inside the ballet, and it smiles. If there is a Waltz of the Flowers in *Harlequinade*, this is it. But the pas de quatre is unique in Balanchine in being designed for larger, seemingly older, and slightly fatuous women, who do needlepoint steps that insist on propriety. Balancing it is the march of the drunken foot patrol, which used to arouse a steady ripple of laughter and applause. Now the *carabinieri* are too obviously drunk, and they don't seem to know of any propriety to insist on.

The plot of the ballet is a series of happenings stitched together by Petipa, probably from evenings at the *balagani*. Harlequin Serenades Columbine; Harlequin Meets les Sbires (minions of Cassandre, visually recalling the devils of the *balagani*); Harlequin Wins His Baton (precursor of the slapstick?), His Money, His Columbine. The story ends early in Act II and is followed by one more set piece: Harlequin and the Birds. After that, it's all dancing. According to Russian historians, Petipa's Act II went on too long and dragged. The same could be said of Balanchine's, which has two extensive divertissements—one performed by squads of children, the other by principals. Children, revelers, Scaramouches, and a flock of birds make four separate corps de ballets; the little stage becomes overstuffed. And Drigo's charming, voluble score grows garrulous. (He could write bird music by the yard.) The events in Act I and the start of Act II are continuous in time, but Patricia McBride is no longer deterred by that fact from changing her costume. (To clinch the joke, the wrap that Pierrette follows her with should also change. And what prevents the trickle of gold coins from the Fairy's cornucopia from becoming a real flow? The ushers might take up a collection.) One of McBride's finest moments is in this ballet—the second-act solo, with its long, long, and slow déboulés on pointe ending in a curtsy and three blown kisses. Her partnership with Baryshnikov has yet to rival the vitality of her partnership with Edward Villella, who created this Harlequin, but her Columbine, made of ovenproof porcelain, endures. Deni Lamont as Pierrot and Shaun O'Brien as Léandre, the foppish suitor, after all these years give undiminished performances. This season, there were two new Cassandres. Frank Ohman's was only moderately effective; he betrayed the primary failing of the amateur mime—going dead when he didn't have a "line." But Andrei Kramarevsky's—bluff, violent, yet humane—was the best Cassandre we have had. Elyse Borne was the perkier of two new Pierrettes; Stephanie Saland acted extremely well, but her dancing lacked flair and her dusky glamour looked wrong in the role. The glamour role in the ballet is La Bonne Fée, though occasionally it is good to see it well danced, as by Colleen Neary. (This role is full of flat-footed penchées, but unlike Columbine's they don't speak bird language. Balanchine's steps take their color from situations and contexts; that's why he can change historic choreography—which he says was always changing anyway—and stay within a historic style.) Sheryl Ware currently leads, or misleads, the Alouettes—a vibrant, springy dancer in a part that calls for a brittle, flighty, almost edgy quality. At a matinee, Daniel Duell made a début substituting for Baryshnikov. Duell as Harlequin was a bit like Saland as Pierrette, only he was plainly much happier dancing than acting. Harlequin, who doesn't really dance much, needs mercury in his blood. Baryshnikov and Villella have it. When Duell turned away from the audience, launching his Serenade toward Columbine's balcony, his back didn't sing. Jean-Pierre Bonnefoux, a great character dancer, made Harlequin live almost entirely through plastique—he was as stealthy as a cat burglar.

—*January 22, 1979*

Repertory Dead and Alive

The final weeks of a long, exhausting, and exciting season such as the one the New York City Ballet is now having take their toll in injuries and illness. Scheduled dancers drop out, replacements must be prepared, sometimes at short notice, and pretty soon there aren't enough rehearsal hours left for next week's programs. The ballets that do not appear on the bills until late in the season—particularly if they're unusually complex or delicate ballets—may have to be sacrificed as the emergencies pile up: either canceled or put on in an under-rehearsed state. So far this winter, only two ballets and several pas de deux have had to be pulled—a not bad record for a company that maintains a year-round active repertory of more than fifty ballets. Not bad, that is, until we consider that the canceled ballets were *Tchaikovsky Piano Concerto No. 2* and *Divertimento No. 15*—two of Balanchine's greatest. The loss then is far greater than the numerical facts can express.

When you talk about the ways ballet companies are run, you're talking about ways to rationalize the irrational, and a great deal of superstition enters the talk. At NYCB, one good argument for maintaining an enormous repertory is that disrepair tends to strike hardest at ballets that are not performed every season. Yet staples like *Symphony in C* and *Serenade* can be performed year in and year out and still go through drastic fluctuations in quality of performance. Ballet is intrinsically inefficient. Just when you've got optimal accuracy costed out in man-hours, something magics it away.

Another problem is that until the sixties the company's repertory was formed for smaller stages than the one at the State Theater. Some of the Balanchine classics have been expanded since the move to Lincoln Center; others look troublingly small in their current productions. Perhaps the time has come to set up a second company, to perform the older, smaller works that have resisted the transition to the larger stage. What would we not give to see *Liebeslieder Walzer* again, danced in its full original décor on the stage of the Juilliard Theater? There, too, ballets like *Divertimento No. 15*, *Agon*, and *Donizetti Variations* could regain their proper dimensions. And new ballets might be born that could never be conceived at the State Theater.

Orpheus came back into the repertory this season—its first revival since the Stravinsky Festival in 1972. For the occasion, which marks the thirtieth anniversary of the founding of New York City Ballet, Mikhail Baryshnikov made his début as Orpheus, and Francisco Moncion appeared in his original role of the Dark Angel. Kay Mazzo was Eurydice, and there were two other débuts: Heather Watts as the leader of the Bacchantes and Adam Lüders as Apollo. Baryshnikov gave a strong, thoughtful, deeply committed performance, wrong in every move. It wasn't his fault; he had canceled two performances in order to rehearse a role to which he is ill suited. Orpheus is passive, turned-in—a

mime rather than a dancer. The role, like the ballet as a
whole, is cast in the hieratic mime of the forties. Baryshnikov's mime was in the modern Russian tradition of dance-
acting; he sniffed out the dance implication in every gesture
and gave that full play. For the first time since he joined the
company, he looked a stranger. His Orpheus is a romantic
hero, a protagonist. Balanchine's is a disinterested artist,
submissive in the grip of fate. The role was drawn on the
loose line and introverted stance of Nicholas Magallanes—
hardly a prototype for Baryshnikov. The production itself
came on looking like a scrappy dress rehearsal. The second
performance was smoother, but again there were accidents
and mistakes. The projections that mirror the rocky landscape in the first scene rose on the horizon as we began the
descent to Hades; they reappeared, as they should have, on
the return trip; but as Orpheus regained Earth they rose
again, instead of sinking. The great white silk curtain that
drops like a veil of mist to envelop the principals on their
journeys is a notorious hazard. In the first performance, the
dancers had to fight clear of it; in the second, Moncion was
cut off from his downstage exit. But these things have gone
wrong before without affecting the tragic mystery of the
ballet. This time, there was no mystery and no intimation of
one—just a sketchy recital of events that were once part of a
treasured ballet. *Orpheus* in its present form is a token reminder of the past, not a serious revival. Composed in an
unemphatic narrative style, the ballet is an ashen meditation
permeated by the sweetish odor of death. The veil dropping
between Earth and the Underworld is the shroud of the
dead. The effect is derived from Tchelitchev's décor for an
earlier ballet, *Errante*; it is related to the veil in *La Bayadère*.
Orpheus at Eurydice's grave begins the ballet; Apollo ends
it by conjuring from blood-soaked ground a flowering

branch that bears the immortal lyre heavenward. But this production seems to have been pervaded by a death wish. Perhaps we should read as its reigning symbol the fact that the twist of ivy that should hang from the branch is missing.

There are many people who hold *Orpheus* in beloved memory, not least because its première, in 1948, was a turning point in the fortunes of American ballet. After the première, which Stravinsky conducted, Balanchine and Lincoln Kirstein were invited by the City Center to form New York City Ballet. Kirstein includes the sequence *Apollo*, *Orpheus*, and *Agon* among the fifty historic masterpieces in his book *Movement and Metaphor*. And there are countless personal testimonials to the ballet's impact. I never shared in the apocalypse that was *Orpheus*. By the end of the fifties, when I saw it for the first time, it was embedded in a triumphant New York City Ballet repertory. It looked unique (and still does)—a distant relative of a Martha Graham piece—and the pas de deux was impressive then and for many years to come. But one could be critical. What about the Furies scene, where some people moved rocks while others did vehement high kicks and wagged their elbows? Later, I found my objection, and much more, in a laudatory review by Edwin Denby ("A pity the Furies' dance in Hell is of no value"), and Denby was at the theatre on the first night of the current revival. He remembered vividly being overcome by his first impression of the ballet; during intermission he'd sat slumped in his seat, attracting the concern of ushers. He described Maria Tallchief as Eurydice—her large, handsome head and her shoulders, her dramatic weight and torsion in the pas de deux in which, climbing Orpheus' back, winding her legs about him, she seemed to drag him heavily downward. The erotic urgency of this passage I had witnessed myself. ("Eurydice writhes at her husband's feet

like a mountain lioness in heat," Denby had written.) By
contrast, Kay Mazzo was as light as a stick of balsa. Dramatically and sculpturally, Baryshnikov's chunky contours were
unrelated to her skeletal ones. Denby also spoke nostalgi-
cally of the Epilogue. Apollo appears bearing the severed
head of Orpheus and drawing from it eternal song—a rite I
have never seen performed with anything like the evocative
power that seems to have been intended for it. But in a
more intimate house you could begin to guess what it
meant. The idea of performing the small works of the repertory on a small stage like the Juilliard's is Denby's; I pass it
on eagerly. It might be the way to a restoration of *Orpheus*.
In 1972, the company went to some trouble to present
Noguchi's famous décor in a revised and rescaled version,
and the look of the whole production dropped a notch in
meaning—from barren to desolate, from provocative to eccentric. Now the scuba-diving helmets and hoses, the bodies decorated with ropes and pancakes just seem a curious
anticipation of High Tech. The Bacchantes still have their
1972 wigs, which look like Orlon sea grass, and unfortunately they dance not wildly but flamboyantly, like the
corps in *The Cage*. But the moment when Orpheus and Eurydice join hands for the journey home and a pale ribbon
slashes the wall with a glimpse of sky is still magical.

Sometimes, as with *Orpheus*, we see performances that
are really dress rehearsals. Other times, we see a very different thing: a performance in which experimentation and
danger are present to a degree that no rehearsal could have
anticipated, and the ballet is, in effect, created before our
eyes. In a penetrating interview in the current *Ballet Review*,
Suzanne Farrell says that performances can't really be rehearsed—that "a performance is a process, an enactment
that must be done in accordance with the speed and dynam-

ics of the music on a given night." Three performances in one week of *Vienna Waltzes* were stations on the road to that kind of spontaneous perfection. Because of the "process" that its performances have been revealing, this ballet seems to me the current pinnacle experience to be had at New York City Ballet. It's the great ballet of the repertory right now, and I say that with full appreciation for the resurgence of established classics like *Symphony in C* and *Serenade* and *The Four Temperaments* and for the canny estimate of current company strength that Robbins offers in *The Four Seasons.*

Vienna Waltzes is what it is partly because it is a still new portrait of the company. The novelty may be wearing off, but not the validity of the characterization. And it is designed as a full-company vehicle. It's a big statement, munificently set on the big stage, using all the company's resources: its wonderful orchestra, its roster of principals (pre-Baryshnikov). But it has stature as well as scope and panoply. *Vienna Waltzes* was, from the first, taken much too lightly as box-office bait, a kind of Viennese counterpart to *Union Jack*, which had been a great hit the year before. The suspicion that a multitudinous nonballetgoing public was waiting outside the gates of Lincoln Center for Balanchine to make an hour of Strauss waltzes was enough for people who should have known better to dismiss the ballet in advance as unserious. But then the dancing itself was condemned: not complex enough, not inviting choreographically, not *dancing*. It is always strange to see the example of one kind of Balanchine ballet set against another, as if there were a "good" (progressive) Balanchine who needed to be separated from a "bad" (commercial) Balanchine. There are bad commercial ballets by Balanchine; it is more challenging to try to distinguish them from the good ones, like *Vienna Waltzes.*

However, *Vienna Waltzes* is only in part a good commercial ballet. The opening, "Tales from the Vienna Woods," may properly be described as a commercial masterpiece, and when the dancers learn how to perform it better it could become something more than that. The men in this section wear their mustaches and uniforms a little bit as if they were embarrassed by them. Their courtship of the women is lacking in ceremony, spirit, dash. Hussars used to be fixtures on the ballet stage; our boys have never seen Hussars. (Couldn't the Film Society of Lincoln Center arrange to screen Max Ophuls's *Liebelei* for them?) "Voices of Spring" had to be done this season without Patricia McBride, who has in it her ripest role. Merrill Ashley is too tall for Helgi Tomasson to partner comfortably; by the end of the week the disparity was barely noticeable. Ashley had caught on to the carefree, heady Romantic style, and Tomasson, whose grasp of style has about it an almost moral tenacity, seemed to tower. The role is Oberon as King of the May. Despite an inappropriate costume (it's that same Fauntleroy suit he wears in other ballets), Tomasson understands the artificiality of the conception. He sweeps sedately through his glen, and we know that he rules a gaslit-and-muslin forest. "Voices of Spring," more delightful and enriching each time I see it, is not the great composition that the last section, "Der Rosenkavalier," is, but it can lay claim to a status just below the first rank. It's *Valse Fantaisie* lifted to the level of, say, *Allegro Brillante*. The exuberantly coarse little polka and the "Merry Widow" scene may be chocolate-boxy, but I find no fault in this. Mazzo's entrance as the Widow seems to have finally settled on a definitive staging, and as the central couple waltzes (to Lehár's "Gold and Silver") the small corps spreads and retracts itself like a fan. Peter Martins has the gift of magnifying his partner. His complete absorption as he turns her

across the floor, his way of leaning back slightly, as if daz-
zled, are indispensable to the illusion that Balanchine wants
to create. Sean Lavery in the "Vienna Woods" section has
adopted Martins's manner toward his partner; it's less
striking in Lavery only because his torso is shorter. Lavery's
gallantry is in his long greyhound legs and precise foot
positions.

The period style of *Vienna Waltzes* is deliberately fantastic. Lavery and the rest of the Hussars waltz to music written in 1868, but their costumes suggest a much earlier
period. The "Merry Widow" women's dresses are turn-of-
the-century, while their escorts wear the frock coats of fifty
years before. But if the men, too, were matched with the
date of the music, they'd look like bankers. Karinska has
produced visionary costumes that enhance the spirit of the
time and not the letter. Balanchine's survey of various waltz
eras extends from the Congress of Vienna, in 1814—the congress that waltzed—to an elegant ballroom in the heart of
Europe a hundred years later. This is the night the waltz
breaks down; tomorrow the guns of August will open fire.
The history of three-quarter time up to that point is sum-
marized by what Lehár and the younger Strauss could invent at their most inspired. (Would we really have preferred
Balanchine to make a documentary survey to possibly less
sumptuous sound?) It is music written for dancers. The disintegration of waltz time, as imagined by Richard Strauss,
has never before been danced, as far as I know. To get
through the piece, with its steep rubatos, its dizzying fad-
ings and revivals of impetus, the entire company must be
alert to "the speed and dynamics of the music on a given
night." And so, this season, they have been. Much depends
on the conductor. My performances were led first by
Robert Irving and then by Hugo Fiorato. The flickering

changes of step and momentum in Farrell's own great performance were different every night. So was the moment of "immolation," when her exit becomes the signal for the flooding of the stage with light and with waltzers.

In this finale, the music was so transparently alive, the dancers so restively responsive, that a mood of anxiety arose in the audience which did not entirely evaporate when the curtain went down. Balanchine does not soothe us—he shakes us and threatens us with catastrophe. The atmosphere of the "Rosenkavalier" waltz goes way beyond *La Valse*; in fact, there's a breathtaking moment when the men whirl and rush forward in a diagonal line that reminds us of *La Valse* and its boundary of virtuosity. The men cross that boundary. From then on, as the ballet repeatedly slides and skitters over thinnest ice, the tension starts to mount, and there's no relief from it. The big swirling stage is a spectacle of controlled hysteria. *Vienna Waltzes* is no longer getting the ovations of its first months. Whether that's because the audience has changed or because the ballet's intentions are more exposed, I cannot say. But those who see in it nothing but a big simple hit are as estranged from it as those who want nothing but a big simple hit.

—*February 19, 1979*

Nureyev as Nijinsky, Babilée as Babilée

In the Ken Russell film *Valentino*, Nijinsky kept popping up, almost as if the casting of Rudolf Nureyev as Valentino had thrown Russell into a dreamy quandary over which legendary male star he really wanted to make a film about. In the first reel, Valentino taught Nijinsky to tango, and in another scene Valentino posed as the Faun for what it was hinted were lascivious photographs taken with his wife, Natacha Rambova, at the instigation of her friend Alla Nazimova. With a few changes in character and circumstance, Russell's fantasy could have centered on Nijinsky; poor Nazimova appeared to be playing Russell's conception of Diaghilev. On the face of it, Nureyev as Nijinsky would seem to be good casting (Anthony Dowell played Nijinsky in *Valentino*); in his Faun costume, he looked more at ease than he did in Valentino's sheikh or gaucho gear, and the glimpses we got of him in Faun plastique were tantalizing. Surprisingly, when Nureyev made the film he still hadn't danced the role; he is dancing it for the first time in his current season at the Mark Hellinger, where, with the Joffrey Ballet, he is performing a program of Diaghilev revivals.

His Faun is as pictorially attractive as it was in the movie. With his wide shoulders, tapering waist, and low-slung hips, he is able to make the planar oppositions in the role clear without strain. But the performance is too heavily anchored in static oppositions, and their delicate, fluid force is retracted as soon as the Faun changes his pose. Nureyev moves from pose to pose as if from one living picture to another; the sense of the choreography as one long unbroken gesture is imperfectly sustained. And the sense, too, of the Faun as the depiction of adolescent sexuality. Nureyev doesn't luxuriate in the movement; when he lies on the rock or tenses his prone body in the air, he doesn't give us a feeling of blood-heat steeping his vitals. To judge from the photographs, Nijinsky had a thickness and grossness in this role which the elegant Nureyev doesn't have. But critics have often compared the two dancers, and there is a creaturely warmth that exists like a bond between them. Nureyev's power in slow motion, which he displayed so lavishly in his younger days, was his strongest link to the Faun. It was this extraordinary power—Nureyev could even jump slowly—that made people use Nijinskyesque language about him ("animal magnetism," "elemental force," "pantherine"). The Faun is cast in slow motion but not broadly cast in space. Nureyev's dancing years ago lost its broad arc and separated into dozens of small peaks. But that doesn't explain why it still cannot recover its span when circumference is not a problem. What does explain that, I think, is Nureyev's deficiencies as an actor.

A generation ago, the Faun was danced perhaps too much as a mime role, but when a dancer as gifted as Nureyev fails to make obvious connections between continuity of phrase and dramatic motive we can see how large a part pantomimic skill played in Nijinsky's conception. Because Nureyev doesn't grasp the "why" of the Faun's movements, he turns the plastique into something arbitrary, to be dropped or caught up as a token reference to another age. Nureyev's dance instinct tells him that Nijinsky didn't hold himself perpetually twisted between profile and en face—he's free enough with that overprized aspect of the role. But the Faun's responses (to the Nymphs, to the veil) and the graphic sense they gradually make within the total ritual of self-absorption which those famous flat poses enclose—these aspects slip through the cracks that are literally breaks in a regimen of poses.

Nureyev stays on the surface in his two other Nijinsky roles, too. He is a truly terrible Petrushka—waggling, flapping, hunching like a small boy in need of a bathroom, and turning up a piteous little face. It takes something for Rudolf Nureyev to become as a little child, and his effortful bad acting is inflamed by pathos—he's a sob-sister Petrushka. It happens that the finest Petrushkas I've seen—Gary Chryst, Michael Smuin, George de la Pena—were not only Americans but good actors. They also *danced* the part of a spineless rag doll with bobbling head and sightless eyes; acting and dancing were not for them separable phases of the role. Although American ballet hardly bothers with such distinctions, these dancers are character dancers. Nureyev appears to have been typed early in his career as a danseur noble, and the Russians, with their insistence on types, would never have expected him to act any role but that of the prince. Nijinsky did do prince roles but, as his biographer Richard Buckle tells us, they were not in his line.

Born into an age of resurgent male dancing, Nureyev the cavalier demands Nijinsky roles as his rightful legacy, but Nureyev is as out of place in Nijinsky's repertory as Nijinsky would have been in his. Nureyev's career may be understood in part as an attempt to gain and hold center stage without a repertory that places him there. So he has become the usurper, encroaching on the ballerina's territory with extensions of the prince's role. In *Le Spectre de la Rose*, he dances a part that Nijinsky himself came to loathe as "too pretty." Apart from its exotic aspect, *Spectre* is a danseur-noble role carried to an extreme of virtuosity and endurance—virtually a nonstop allegro solo offset but hardly interrupted by passages of doublework. The Specter guides and shadows the ballerina; it's too much to say that he partners her. Yet from the moment he enters through the window until he jumps out again, it is implicitly a partnering role. The evening I saw him, Nureyev did his most vigorous and sustained dancing in this. His energy was higher than it had been for some time; he connected his phrases; he didn't sag in a landing or reprop himself after a finish. In an effective costume by Toer van Schayk—a modified petaled cap à la Nijinsky and a unitard of dark rose red tapering to flame points of greens and grays—he looked slim and handsome. Yet his port de bras was sketchy, and he danced almost totally without reference to the girl. The lack of arms—those enveloping Art Nouveau arms which it is hardly possible to exaggerate—is less crippling to the role than the notion that the Specter, supplicant, imploring, seductive in every move, could be dancing by and for himself. Nureyev's insularity reached its peak when, while Denise Jackson waltzed around the stage, he held a high relevé in fifth with his gaze fixed on her empty chair. But that was no worse than the moments in the other ballets which showed a Nureyev fundamentally out of sympathy with the artist and the era he celebrates.

In dance encyclopedias, the "B"s begin with Babilée, Jean, b. Paris, 1923. Never having seen Babilée dance and never expecting to know firsthand how he looked at the height of his fame, which was in the late forties and early fifties, I went to see what, on the opening night of the Maurice Béjart company's run at the Minskoff, had been billed as *"une surprise"*—a new ballet starring Babilée. A personal appearance made by an aging dancer was all I hoped for; with any luck, it would be no more damaging to the dancer's reputation than the silly Isadora vehicle fashioned by Béjart for Maya Plisetskaya a few years ago. Well, the curtain went up on a semidarkened stage, and there, behind a box-shaped jungle gym, stood Babilée, a shortish, compactly muscled man in a sweatshirt and baggy jeans. Stepping inside the box and grasping its supports, he began a few elementary exercises in which one saw the speed and economy of motion of a perfectly conditioned athlete. Then, quite suddenly, with no handhold to speak of and no sign of exertion, he rose up the side of the box and hung in space, and one saw Babilée. And went on seeing him—not only the Babilée of the complex acrobatic feats in *Le Jeune Homme et la Mort* (one of which simulated death by hanging) but also the galvanic Babilée who could flash from stillness to violence in *Till Eulenspiegel* and even the classical Babilée who danced a fabled Bluebird. And (the lights having brightened) one saw the commanding head, with its noble aquiline face so like that of an American Indian, and the silky shock of hair—a slightly creased Cocteau drawing come to life. It was, of course, a Babilée whose spectacular powers are operating now on a diminished scale. Yet they are no less vivid for that. Babilée makes not one false move, nor one that is hasty or incomplete. His aura is tragic but equanimous—not intense, like a young man's. Most miraculously, among all his qualities the one he was loved for, his reposeful violence, is still there. In the midst of a spasm his center is always calm. And in the midst of calm he appears ready to explode.

Béjart calls the ballet *Life*. It seems to be about an isolated man of middle years who may not want to end his isolation. Babilée is partnered by a young beauty, Catherine
Dethy. Her comings and goings are keyed to his moods,
and with her last entrance, far upstage and behind him,
comes the moment of decision. Babilée makes their sudden
exit together inevitable yet impulsive. I saw two performances: he took her hand two different ways; both ways
were enigmatic. But Babilée is an enigmatic artist, and he
performs as if the heart of his mystery were at stake. Because
of him, one could watch the whole ballet attentively and
have something to ponder when the curtain went down.
What is a star for, if not to shed light? I imagine that many
in Béjart's audience had never heard of Babilée. But whether
you watched the ballet to see Babilée or Babilée to see the
ballet, you had a real experience.

The rest of the Béjart programs were polyester. People
speak of Béjart as if he were a choreographer. He is, rather,
a purveyor of sensation, like the movie directors Russell and
Fellini, and ballet is just one of the glutting effects he uses.
And yes, he *uses* dancers—hollows them out and consumes
them. Every time I see the Béjart dancers, they've lost more
muscle tone and added more makeup. The company these
days is more openly a drag show than it used to be. As
W. C. Fields says of the city (in *The Fatal Glass of Beer*), "It
ain't no place for women, but pretty boys go there." Béjart's
other guest artist this season is Judith Jamison. Béjart has
put her to work in his version of *Le Spectre de la Rose*, one of
a number of pieces (others are *Gaîté Parisienne* and
Petrushka) that take famous ballet scores and substitute
phantasmagorical effusions for the original choreography.
Another formula has the phantasmagoria set to "shocking"
collage scores—Schumann lieder, say, alternating with bits
of Nino Rota, or Bach alternating with tangos. Those who

can't defend Béjart's choreography will still praise his the-atricality. But what Béjart's sense of theatre comes down to is an addiction to greasepaint, flashy costumes, masks, boys cast as girls, dual and triple identities, and silences broken by hideous bursts of laughter. The same chunks of leaden diablerie churn senselessly through one ballet after another, usually with some young man at the center pressing his fists to his temples. True, the continuity is always jarring, but it's so deliberately, preeningly inconsequential that after five minutes it has no punch. Béjart shapes his ballets with a channel selector, and he's learned to be derisive toward seri-ousness. The solemnity of the hippie-ritual ballets of the six-ties has been displaced by the cynicism of the seventies. When a genuine event happens on his stage, it's almost as if he weren't responsible. *Life* has the silences, the jagged dis-continuities (Bach and bongos), and Babilée gets a migraine at one point. But it also has a performer in whom grandeur of style is so much a personal attribute that it shows itself helplessly. In such surroundings, after so many years, *c'est vraiment une surprise*.

—*March 26, 1979*

Ballet Alert

I talked last week to Carmel Capehart, the founder and chief
operator of Ballet Alert, a new telephone service (dial
BALLERT) that supplies up-to-the-minute information on
the local performance schedules of all the major companies.
"It's a real godsend during the peak of the dance season,
when it's hard to keep up with who's doing what," said
Miss Capehart, a vigorous-looking gray-haired woman in a
dirndl and a National Dance Week T-shirt. "Before Ballet
Alert got going, last winter, those of us who attend lots of
performances would have to depend on the grapevine for
last-minute cancellations and cast changes. We'd spread the
word like a chain letter—only, of course, by phone. Once, I
remember, three ballet companies were playing side by side
and a festival of major moderns had just opened in Brooklyn when an epidemic of Asian flu hit. Trying to monitor
that situation took seventeen of us, between Staten Island
and New Rochelle, and we'd be on the horn all day long.
Add that to the cost of tickets, taxis, and drinks après-ski
and you're getting into some heavy expenses." Miss Capehart and some of her friends found themselves cutting back

on their floral tributes to ballerinas. They even sold the program-shredder they'd used to make confetti for Cynthia Gregory ovations. But it was not economy that drove them to start Ballet Alert so much as sheer frustration. "There was the time Kyra Nichols was out of *The Four Seasons*, then in, then out again, all in one day," said Miss Capehart, with a sigh. "Sometimes who'll dance isn't decided until the performance is about to begin. Of course, we can't even now keep up with things like that, so we're always careful to give the time along with our information, just like the weather report."

Miss Capehart, who received this year's Adidas Award in public relations for her down-to-the-wire bulletins, maintains her contacts with balletomane inner circles. "Without their input," she told me, "I couldn't keep up. There are people who knew when Mikhail Baryshnikov was going to do *Tarantella* even before he knew himself. On the other hand, everybody thought Stephanie Saland would do *Swan Lake* this season, and that didn't pan out. Of course, I release nothing without the confirmation of company managements, even though it's sometimes hard to get it in time. When there are cast substitutions, the management people are often the last to know. The waiters in O'Neals' and Dazzels have known for hours. I try not to make a habit of calling up the dancers themselves—especially the ones who've been taken sick or who've been injured. I did call Patricia McBride to see if she was dancing *La Source* with Helgi Tomasson and was told that she'd gone to the theatre to rehearse. Well, in the meantime Merrill Ashley and Peter Martins were announced, and we put that on our tape. In the event, Ashley did it, but with Adam Lüders, not Peter Martins, so we were half right. We did catch Kevin McKenzie, though, going in for Patrick Bissell in the third act of

The Sleeping Beauty. Bissell had pulled a leg muscle the night before and suspected he might not get through the whole performance—which was a pity, because it was his New York début in the role. But we didn't call him, he called *us*. And when Gelsey canceled the rest of her season at American Ballet Theatre recently, she put a message for us on her answering machine before she left town."

I asked Miss Capehart what her biggest scoop had been.

"No doubt about that," she said. "Baryshnikov's début in the Costermonger pas de deux in *Union Jack*. He did it twice in one day without telling anybody. If we hadn't caught wind of it, nobody would have been there but the audience."

We settled down over steaming glasses of Russian tea, and Miss Capehart talked a bit about Ballet Alert's early days. "We had to overcome a credibility gap," she said. "Ballet Alert retains, I think, the pizzazz of good old word-of-mouth, but in the beginning that was a liability. Some people weren't sure our information could be trusted. The breakthrough came this spring when we found out Jolinda Menendez was going to do the lead in *La Bayadère* instead of Martine van Hamel. Nobody believed us. They went anyway. Menendez did do it, and they believe us now, all right. Most of our reports have to do with cast changes. So far, we haven't had too many changes of program this season. New York City Ballet actually got *Tchaikovsky Piano Concerto No. 2* and *Divertimento No. 15* on, I'm glad to say, though not always with the scheduled casts. And there were only two major program disruptions at Ballet Theatre, both because of an injury to the same dancer. God knows, a ballet dancer's life is fraught with hazard. But few people realize the hazards that ballet-*goers* have to face. For example, there're those one-shot performances that sometimes crop up out of emergencies; balletomanes learn to look for them. One man, a fan of Yoko Morishita, dialed us from his office in Boston, learned that Morishita was substituting for Kirkland in *La Bayadère* that night, and flew in on the shuttle. Just as his cab reached Columbus Circle, there was one of those cloudbursts we've been having a lot of recently, and the motor stalled. When he got to the Met, it was one minute past eight, the performance had started, and the ushers wouldn't let him take his seat. He had to watch *La Bayadère* on television in the viewing room, and the reception was so poor he couldn't tell Yoko Morishita from Janet Shibata. That's not as bad, though, as the story I heard about the lady who came to the New York première of *Désir*, John Neumeier's pas de deux for Natalia Makarova and Anthony Dowell, and got Peter Gennaro's soft-shoe duet for Dowell and John Curry instead. Of course, the change was announced, but it somehow failed to register. She thought she was seeing Makarova in a top hat. Well, we exist to forestall that sort of confusion. And I may say that, with the current season as chaotic as it is, we're rapidly becoming indispensable to the city's ballet life."

—*June 25, 1979*

Blue and White

In a poem he once wrote about New York City Ballet, Kenneth Koch referred to ballets like "the blue-white sea / Outside the port-hole: Agon, or Symphony in C." The image came back to me in the closing weeks of the spring-summer season as, one by one, *Chaconne* and *Square Dance* and *Tchaikovsky Piano Concerto No. 2* appeared, all part of that same blue-white vista, all island realms, cloud-capped Illyrias. The nacreous grotto of *Ballo della Regina* is part of it, too. With its sparkling aquatic imagery, this ballet is an abstraction of the underwater ballet in *Don Carlos*. This past season, it emerged as one of Balanchine's freshest visions—transparently a mid-nineteenth-century neoclassical seascape, with bravura waves and naiads surging through the foam or glowing like pearls in the deep. A streaking cataract named Merrill Ashley holds the whole thing together. It isn't unusual for Balanchine ballets to hit their peak a year or more after the première; the miracle is that they don't take longer. *Vienna Waltzes* has a huge ensemble and a long, rhythmically complicated finale. Yet the ballet arrived last winter, having taken no longer to find its form than the compact little *Ballo*. An exceptionally talented group of girls a year ago graduated into the company from the School of American Ballet. This influx has given the company not only the youngest but perhaps also the strongest corps in its history, and very likely it's what has made possible within the same six-month period the fully developed *Ballo* and *Vienna Waltzes*—ballets that fill very different expressive purposes. For these revelations and for restoring *Agon* and the *Tchaikovsky Concerto* to form after several disquieting performances last year, one must also thank the assistant ballet mistress, Rosemary Dunleavy. The contributions of a fine corps and régisseur wouldn't mean much, though, if it weren't for the italicized achievements of individual dancers—those who lead all the rest. The ones I'm about to name aren't part of any breed or class; they're just the dancers whose progress or prominence has impressed me most in the past two months.

The characteristic look of Merrill Ashley in the midst of one of her exciting and highly specialized dances is a look of angular intensity. She dances with even force yet with a naturally oblique expression; even en face she seems half turned away from you. Or, about to turn away, she'll square off with a suddenness as disconcerting as a full-in-the-face glance from a passerby. Her allegro is filled with rapid-fire monosyllabic interjections; through the brilliance of it audiences sense an understated, all-business style that is specifically and flatly American. This year, Ashley began to open out and show us a more than cordial warmth; she has freed her head so that it floats graciously; she's beginning to get a real ballerina glow. Her phrasing is just as clipped, her angles just as severe, but something about the way she presents herself makes us happy to see her. We can tell she's aware of her sharp edge and ready to use it provocatively.

The technician who demanded the audience's respect has become a performer who commands it. In *Ballo della Regina*, *Square Dance*, and the last movement of the *Tchaikovsky Concerto*, there's even a whiff of comic self-enjoyment.

But though Ashley has developed her performing style, her dance style hasn't changed. Last winter, there were moments when she'd suddenly expand in a slow movement—prolong the start of a phrase or the length of its connection with the next phrase—and she'd look unguardedly beautiful. I haven't seen any of those moments recently. In adagio passages she still shows a too-crisp attack, a tendency toward overswift completion of a phrase, and an unwillingness to depend on her partner for support. It's a little as if Ashley thought that her punctuality and surgically clean execution were all that keep her from being a dull dancer—as if speed and more speed could make of her angularity an object of wit. There's more, technically speaking, to *Emeralds* and the *Symphony in C* adagio than she's interested in exploring right now. There's more to Merrill Ashley, too.

Apollo, *Tarantella*, the revival of *Orpheus*, and the Costermonger pas de deux in *Union Jack* called forth from Mikhail Baryshnikov what certainly must be the widest range ever demonstrated by a male dancer in a single season. Baryshnikov's feat was all the more impressive in that it included the mastery of a role in which he'd been miscast last season, Orpheus. I still don't think Baryshnikov is the right choice for the part; it's against-the-grain casting of the kind that isn't productive, even for the audience. Nevertheless, after his overemphatic performances of last winter Baryshnikov returned to the ballet with a style so changed and subdued that it looked like a conversion. But then his assimilation of new and radically different styles has been amazing from the start of his career in America. As the Costermonger, he instinctively improvised his way through a role that, again, did not need him and that already has two very able interpreters. Baryshnikov wasn't like Jean-Pierre Bonnefoux, who is handsome and fatuous, or like Bart Cook, who plays a wizened Cockney. Baryshnikov's personal style is really more Cagney than Cockney. But not even *Push Comes to Shove* prepared me for how funny he was. I expected diabolical glee; I didn't expect such a showering of gags or such a spirit behind it—the wriggling, ecstatic, outrageous, pandering spirit of vaudeville itself. He not only got the gags going, he got Patricia McBride to respond delightfully, and the two worked together better than they have in anything else. In *La Sonnambula*, McBride was the Sleepwalker and Baryshnikov was the Poet—another mime role, but one that I believe he is mistaken to perform as passively as Orpheus. Perhaps he appeared passive only because the role, with its links to the tragic heroes of *La Sylphide* and *Swan Lake*, doesn't cut across our expectations of what he's like onstage, the way Orpheus does. In any case, as nondancing roles go, the Poet seemed to me the lesser achievement.

Suzanne Farrell went back to the principal allegro role in *Divertimento No. 15* and, for the first time, captured it. She did it by scaling down her attack on the variation and rephrasing it musically. The adagio portion of the role, which is all short lines, small jumps, and supported figures, she lengthened by dancing it as connected events in a single phrase. In the Sanguinic variation of *The Four Temperaments*, another unaccustomed role, there was smooth performing and a fertile array of ideas, which will undoubtedly be developed in further performances. Farrell also returned to the *Tchaikovsky Concerto*, a ballet she used to dance in the sixties, and by the end of her first solo had repossessed it.

After her solo, the ballerina goes off, and she keeps coming and going all through the ballet. Perhaps because we're used to seeing her hold the stage for long periods and build extended structures, the *Concerto* doesn't seem to give us enough Farrell. But it could become another of her azure kingdoms, somewhere near the polar regions of *Diamonds* and *Vienna Waltzes*. If it doesn't—if there were no other ballets for her but those two and *Chaconne*—Farrell would still have a repertory. Her performances are occasions for unique and unrepeatable happenings and have to be spoken of as one-time events: "The *Diamonds* of Saturday Night Closing Weekend," "The Great Saratoga *Chaconne*." Recently, I watched her give the minuet in *Chaconne* with an attack I'd never seen before, brightening each step like sunlight behind a cloud. And the delicacy of this effect of illumination came from a dancer who can, when she wants to, lift a leg and hurl it like a bolt of lightning.

One of the most commented-upon aspects of Farrell's technique is her aplomb—for example, in the big battements that send her off balance while she hurls those bolts, or in the supported adagios where she doesn't seem to need the man's support. What one notices upon further study is that Farrell doesn't place herself or her partner or her audience at the mercy of her facility in these matters. The battements are an element of syntax, not a separate event thrown in for its own sake, and Farrell often does rely on her partner. Even when she doesn't—when she's thrilling us by not needing his assistance—she never suggests that she doesn't need *him*. The illusion of the ballerina's independence—or of any feat in dancing—will always count for more than the mechanical proof of it.

Sean Lavery. Tall, strong, angelically correct, he is perhaps the finest example of the pure danseur-noble type to have been produced by American schooling in a generation. (Not the School of American Ballet this time but the independently run New York School of Ballet.) It's true that at times he dances as if he had all that and more to uphold. Lavery is still very young—only twenty-two—but his propriety makes him look younger and greener than twenty-one-year-old Patrick Bissell, at American Ballet Theatre. This season, in the Stravinsky double bill *Monumentum/Movements*, a light seemed to go on inside Lavery. Partnering Farrell, he began to use his upper-body weight like a man's instead of a boy's. He continued to do it as the cavalier in *Ballo della Regina*, and it only increased the fantasy of the role: he seemed to belong to the same order of mythical creatures as the women—he was a Triton, not a mortal interloper. My other picture of the new Lavery comes from *Dances at a Gathering*—the role that is usually done these days by Peter Martins—and there was a premonitory flash earlier in the season in the *Tchaikovsky Concerto*, his most becoming role to date. Maybe this is the role he will grow up in.

A blond daddy longlegs of a dancer with Danish classical technique, Adam Lüders seemed an eccentric blend of Bournonville and Hans Christian Andersen when he joined New York City Ballet a few years ago. He was tall and a good partner—assets never to be discounted in Balanchine's company—but it seemed that he would never work out as a dancer in Balanchine's repertory. In addition to his recalcitrant physical proportions, there were serious infirmities of placement and coordination. His looks and a noticeable flair for acting seemed to stamp him a character dancer, of limited usefulness to Balanchine. If Lüders ever does play Coppélius or Drosselmeyer, it won't be because he has to. He's unquestionably a dancer and this has been his year. Oddly enough for a dancer with character sense, his two biggest achievements have been in classical roles. Who ever thought four years ago that one day he'd take Martins's place in *Divertimento*? Or in *Chaconne*? That it would be he and Farrell meeting in that silence and dancing like two snow leopards?

Stephanie Saland is physically a larger Gelsey Kirkland, and though she's not as gifted a dancer she is sometimes presented as if she were. She did *Square Dance* with Helgi Tomasson, a charming performance overcast by the lengthening shadow of G. (for gargouillade) Kirkland. (Although Kirkland never actually performed *Square Dance*, it would obviously have been her part if she'd stayed with NYCB.) Saland, though, had by the time of *Square Dance* established her individuality in a dozen varied repertory roles, and except for Lüders she's the most improved dancer in the company this year. Long before this phase of progress began, Saland was compulsively watchable because of the elegant carriage of her head and arms and her warm, glamorous presence. She's still very much an upper-body dancer. The port de bras in the Violette Verdy solo in *Emeralds* looks second nature to her. Maybe a few more *Square Dances* are needed to sharpen her footwork. Saland is an instinctive actress, and her sense of theatre makes me think of Jillana, a dancer of the fifties and sixties whom she also physically resembles. As the Coquette in *La Sonnambula* (a Jillana role), Saland was all soft malice, and she was also astonishingly precise last winter as a last-minute substitute for McBride in Costermongers.

Judith Fugate, who did the other ballerina role in *Emeralds* (you couldn't miss her pear-shaped pointes), is always pleasant to see: accurate, musically sensitive, daring. In *Dances at a Gathering*, she took the most acrobatic of the women's roles. She was one of a host of débutantes in the ballerina roles of *Divertimento*, and she may have been the best. Fugate doesn't project the way she dances; if she did, we might appreciate her even more. Heather Watts, who certainly does project, has been getting a number of ballerina roles lately. She looked happiest, to me, in the McBride part in *Dances at a Gathering*—really relaxed and happy, as if it were dancing she loved and not competing with other dancers. But the competition is part of the fun of watching New York City Ballet—fun for the audience, at least. I like to see dancers like Lourdes Lopez, Sandra Jennings, Carole Divet, and Nichol Hlinka get parts. I'm dashed when a potential soloist like Peter Schetter leaves the company and quits dancing, buoyed when he suddenly returns. He's had no brilliant opportunities yet, but wait until next season. Repertory is destiny.

—July 23, 1979

Kylián and His Antecedents

It's not often that a choreographer can make audiences sit up and forward in their seats and watch the stage with shining eyes. I didn't find as much to watch in the ballets of Jiří Kylián as I did in his demonstrative audiences. It was a spectacle of enjoyment that had something self-conscious about it, as if people were watching themselves watch Kylián and being doubly tickled: not only was Kylián wonderful but they were, too, for responding to him. Kylián, the thirty-two-year-old artistic director of the Netherlands Dance Theatre, was making his New York début with eight ballets. A ninth, *Return to the Strange Land*, as slickly confident but not as ambitious as some of those in the Netherlands repertory, had been given a few weeks before by the Stuttgart Ballet at the Met, and its reception had been ecstatic. The press had already turned Kylián into a conqueror, but the audiences who attended his company's two-week season at the City Center weren't just bowing down on cue. I think they were genuinely stimulated by what they saw and relieved not to be reacting to a critical hype. One might interpret the reception of the company as the return of feeling, yet the feeling was not without a disturbing element. The people who adored Kylián didn't seem to want just to applaud good work; they wanted to celebrate their sense of personal gratification. The applause was peppered with those falsetto woofs that seem to be taking the place of bravos. Why should the sound of people going into a tizzy be changing in this way? Is it another mark of the Me generation? Bravos, olés—all the traditional audience vocables—say, "*You* were wonderful"; they're directed to the performer. These wordless woofs say, "*I'm* wiped out."

Kylián, born in Czechoslovakia, studied Graham-style modern dance in Prague and ballet in London. He joined the Stuttgart Ballet and worked under John Cranko. Four years ago, he became resident choreographer of the Netherlands company, which had an eclectic modern repertory of European and American choreography. As I recall that company from its previous American tours, it moved on an identifiable classical-ballet base and had ranking soloists. Kylián has transformed it into a welded ensemble, an instrument as responsive to his idiomatic personal style as Eliot Feld's and Paul Taylor's companies are to the personal styles of Feld and Taylor. There are no soloists—indeed, there are no solos. Kylián's smallest unit of expression is the duet, and he prefers his duets doubled. A duet that is not doubled is as likely to be a double solo as a standard pas de deux. These devices widen the magnetic field of the action at the same time that they ensure anonymity. You watch nothing for its singularity, everything for its duplicable speed, shape, and finish. Though the company is not large, it seems to be a marvel of universal conditioning, every dancer formed inside the same bubble and impelled by the same breath. And the other things one notices are in line with this impression—the tiny vocabulary of steps, the repetitious patterning, the men's and women's roles evened by unisex choreography. The Netherlands makes a fetish of impersonality, but so do many American modern-dance companies. What interested me was the extent to which the company's blank, impersonal, controlled look became expressive in Kylián's hands and affecting to his audiences. I'm speaking now of his all-dance ballets, the most potent of which—*Sinfonietta*, *Symphony of Psalms*, and *Glagolitic Mass*—accounted for the success of the whole season. The nondance ballets were parables of modern life in which impersonality is simply a reflection of moral and social chaos. Everyone must have seen at least one of these bric-a-brackish happening-ballets by now, done by other choreographers. *Children's Games*, a Kylián version of that white asylum where people move slowly and portentously, crawl around in cages, try to build something, fight, make love, and are all the while pursued by death figures, seemed to take in every influence, from Anna Sokolow and Alwin Nikolais to Robert Wilson and Kei Takei. It even threw a few of Mahler's *Kindertotenlieder* into the noise-band sound track. Against this vision of clutter and noise and rebuke, the clean, smooth dance shapes of *Glagolitic Mass* were like a balm, wiping away the sins of the world with a few incantatory passes through space. The faceless crowd reappeared in redeemed form. I don't think I'm making too much of the juxtaposition.

Kylián's art, modeled on the trim, organic shapes of so much American dance, is very differently motivated. Where most American dance is nontendentious in its aesthetic choices, American-derived European dance is not only tendentious but specific. The few steps he uses are chosen for their impulsive, urgent look. A Grahamish rond de jambe cross step that keeps pulling the body off its center is invariably the takeoff for the careering flight of the Kylián dancer.

A typical sequence will go cross step, jump, cross step, jump-jump. And there are signature dances as well. A favorite form of pas de trois is the woman pulled and dragged on a steeplechase course between two men. It stands for rape, for exaltation, for fun; presumably, it's the music that determines the mood. Kylián likes liturgical music; it's easy to see why the most common adjective his admirers use is "exultant." The word attaches itself to all the runs and rushes and bucking leaps and up-and-away lifts.

But not all of Kylián's movement is captioned. Like that other choreographer-prophet Maurice Béjart, Kylián likes occasionally to preach sermons of ambivalence. Although he reintroduces the easy emotional correlatives that most advanced American choreographers have sought to avoid for the last thirty years, he doesn't make quite the suggestive references one might expect to the texts of Stravinsky's psalms or Janáček's vernacular folk Mass. I don't mean that there aren't penitential postures in the Stravinsky and pietàs in the Janáček and cruciform lifts in both; Kylián deals freely in the nondenominational religiosity of expressionistic modern dance. But one sees these gestures primarily as token allusions to the nature of the experience that is taking place in the music, not as part of any parallel to that experience which is taking place in the dance. Forget that we really don't need to see a dance parallel; would it be worse than the cheerful tastelessness that uses psalms—*these* psalms, especially—or Masses as neutral sound tracks for dance fantasies? Which is worse—clunky José Limón–style piety (see his setting of Kodály's Missa Brevis) or Kylián's ambivalent theatrics? One of Kylián's most forceful passages of choreography comes at the end of his staging of *Symphony of Psalms* where Stravinsky has set words of praise and jubilation glowing to contemplative, slow-moving harmonies. Kylián's response is a protracted view of his dancers inching their way upstage into a gulf of blackness, with their backs to the audience. Is it distractingly effective or effectively distracting? If any words fill our minds, they're more likely to be Eliot's despairing parody of Milton—"O dark dark dark. They all go into the dark"—than the words we are actually hearing: "*Omnis spiritus laudat Dominum*" ("Every spirit praises the Lord"). Is it that Kylián doesn't understand any kind of exultation but the leaping-up kind? More likely, it's that he understands how to flavor the juicy feeling we long for with a little of the modern skepticism we can respect.

The décor of the Stravinsky ballet is a wall of Oriental carpets hanging in layers, as in a showroom. The wall dissolves into darkness at the end. We understand that the carpets are "unrelated," as in a Merce Cunningham décor, yet when they dissolve at the same moment the choreography is giving us its "wrong" response to the music, we may feel that we're getting a statement about Kylián's uncertainty as an artist. Ambivalence, skepticism, uncertainty: they're practically a summation of the situational aesthetics that have guided the Netherlands Dance Theatre. Although the carpet décor is by an American, William Katz, it has the same enigmatic menace as all those coolly disengaged backdrops by the Dutch master of the form, Jean-Paul Vroom, and by other Dutch artists. The sensibility of the Dutch loads Cunningham's simple idea of disassociation with intimations of anxiety and estrangement. Vroom's art is familiar to us from the ballets of Hans van Manen, one of the original members of the Netherlands company. Kylián's choreography echoes or extends many of van Manen's devices, and he also shares with van Manen an attachment to heavy concert-hall scores—music of profundity and of questionable suitability for dance. In the thirties and forties, Massine made vaguely programmatic ballets about Man and Fate to music by Brahms, Shostakovich, and Beethoven. The dominant school of contemporary European choreography, which was fomented by the Dutch and by the German-based Cranko and maintained by such practitioners as Kylián and John Neumeier, has tried for twenty years to match big-scale, Massine-style significance to choreography that is as musically responsible and coherent as Balanchine's—a case of wanting to eat your cake and cut your calories, too, and a task made insuperably difficult if, like Cranko and Neumeier, you were unmusical to begin with.

Stravinsky's rhythm seems to have dictated a subtlety one doesn't find elsewhere in Kylián's work. For the most part, Kylián's rhythm is cadential, and that may be why I can't feel it as dance rhythm. Dance rhythm implies momentum, an elastic continuity. Kylián uses a sharp cadence that keeps falling back on itself and repeating. The sensation of force is additive rather than cumulative. *Glagolitic Mass* is a series of dances; one or two of them start out on irregular counts, but before long they've become caught in strings of reflexive ongoing cadences. And it makes no difference whether two or twelve dancers are onstage; there is no change in pressure or scale. Each dance starts at zero and gallops right up to the level of the previous one. Kylián, like so many choreographers, thinks to hold our interest by keeping the shapes as large and open as possible. But he doesn't set "large" and "open" against anything that might make us appreciate those choices as dance values. If one were to arrange dynamic options in terms of contrasting pairs—say, big/small, heavy/light, hard/soft—Kylián would most of the time choose Column A, seldom Column B, never a little of both. Big/light and heavy/soft are beyond him. But then they're beyond most choreographers, American or European.

Kylián reminds me of many people. He uses a tiny assortment of steps, like Paul Taylor, though without Taylor's variety of effect. (His idea of dynamic contrast is to use women as lighteners, doing the same steps as men.) He is as much a cultist of music visualization as van Manen, though not as depressingly bent on step-for-note literalism. He turns music into emotion, sort of like Jerome Robbins, by means of punchy rhythmic devices. And one would have to go all the way back to Kurt Jooss to find another Central European choreographer who has attained the same level of success. The choreographer whom Kylián most resembles, though, is Doris Humphrey. Humphrey was a structuralist who could reduce a Bach concerto to a nest of mixing bowls. Kylián, also by simplification and reduction, pretends to lay bare the intent of music; he doesn't care about structure, he cares about sensation. Just as Humphrey could always squeeze out one more mixing bowl, Kylián can keep his motorized ballets charging ahead as long as the music holds out, on and on into the dark.

—August 6, 1979

Theory and Practice
in the Russian Ballet

The first season of the Bolshoi Ballet in America, twenty
years ago at the Metropolitan Opera House, consisted of
Giselle, *Swan Lake*, *Romeo and Juliet*, *The Stone Flower*, and a
batch of excerpts and short ballets which made up two
"Highlights" programs. *The Stone Flower* was the sole modern work; at least, that is the way it was presented and, in
large part, received. It was also the sole work with choreography by Yuri Grigorovich, who is now the company's artistic director, and that must have been the reason it was
chosen to open the current Bolshoi engagement at the State
Theater, which is not only an anniversary season but also a
Grigorovich retrospective. The choice is otherwise inexplicable. If *The Stone Flower* is remembered here at all, it is for
the performances of Vladimir Vasiliev and Ekaterina Maximova in the two leading roles. Maya Plisetskaya, a heroine
of that first season, was from all reports (I saw Nina Timo-
feyeva) an engaging Mistress of the Copper Mountain.
None of these dancers from the original Bolshoi cast are
with the company in New York; in fact, they're part of an
anti-Grigorovich faction that has been touring indepen-

dently. Reviving *The Stone Flower* under these conditions draws attention to the existence of controversy and the hollowness of the ballet's importance.

One of the subjects of the controversy is the new Grigorovich production of *Romeo and Juliet*, which starts its run here this week. The separatists are saying that Grigorovich intends to replace the standard version, by Leonid Lavrovsky; Grigorovich says that both versions will be retained. It's unlikely, though, that the Lavrovsky *Romeo* will ever again be toured. Turn back to 1959, which was the last time it was seen here, and New York opinion is overwhelmingly negative. Ulanova's performance was praised, but the production was judged to be old-fashioned because it contained long stretches of the kind of melodramatic pantomime that hadn't been seen on a New York stage since the days of David Belasco. This is not a point on which local opinion is likely to have changed. *The Stone Flower*, coming at the end of that riotously successful début season, was given what might be called an indulgent reception. It, too, had a Prokofiev score, but a much inferior one. And it had a thin and unreal story about a stonecutter who has to choose between making art for the people and pursuing ivory- (or, in his case, malachite-) tower perfectionism. The story is unreal not just because you know how it will come out but because it is, in dance terms, incomprehensible. Grigorovich used three kinds of dance: lyrical-adagio, character-folk, and, for the scenes in the glowing green underground kingdom of precious stones, a spiky type of *ballet moderne* the like of which hadn't been seen here since Adolph Bolm was staging his city-symphony/iron-foundry ballets in the early thirties. In none of his chosen modes could Grigorovich express the dramatic point of the libretto that was outlined in the printed program or work up the least bit of suggestive atmosphere. Yet because he *didn't* use pantomime the Russians claimed the ballet was an artistic advance, and some American critics fell in with the claim. After all, what did we know in 1959?

When Grigorovich succeeded Lavrovsky as artistic director, he continued to make no-pantomime the signpost of progress. But in the whole course of Russian dance history, as recorded by Russian dance historians, it is hard to find a native choreographer who is *not* progressive in this way—even Lavrovsky is extolled for his promotion of all-dance expression. Only, of course, what looks all dance in one era looks a lot less pure later on, and in the pages of history the same choreographer turns into a reactionary the minute the next promoter gets ready to "reform the ballet." In a country where the story ballet is the only type of ballet tolerated, the use or non-use of mime is kept dangerously alive as an issue. Grigorovich really does choreograph everything as dance action. His trouble is that he must go on doing it for three hours, and after about twenty minutes the glad-sad-mad-bad slots tend to get all stuffed up. Twenty years later, *The Stone Flower* is still rigidly inarticulate, although, compared to the samples of Grigorovich's work we have seen since, it comes off as inoffensively naïve. The second-act suite of folk dances includes some entertaining Gypsy nightclub antics, and the act ends with the scene that in 1959 had audiences at the old Met yelling: the evil bailiff, lured by the Mistress of the Copper Mountain, is swallowed by the earth. The yells were for Vladimir Levashev, the great character dancer of that period, whose thrashings as the trap took him down and down ran up and up an emotional scale from bewilderment to panic to insane terror—an effect that the perfunctory heaves of Yuri Vetrov on opening night this season didn't begin to suggest. Anatoli Simachev was a more imaginative villain on the next night, but emotionally he embraced about half an octave. Along with Simachev, Andrei Kondratov as the stonecutter and Svetlana Adirkhayova as the Mistress of the Copper Mountain performed with more authority than the first-night cast, Leonid Kozlov and Valentina Kozlova, though they were no better as dancers. Kozlova, stylistically gauche, has solidity and power; Adirkhayova has layers of polish over technical weaknesses. Neither has the acrobatic precision or the spirited charm the part needs if it is to be rescued from the comic strips. The Mistress of the Copper Mountain is a slit-eyed slitherer. (In the original tale that the libretto comes from, she's a metamorphosed lizard.) She docs all her chaînés with angled elbows, and at the end of the ballet she tries several times to persuade the hero to stay by leaping on him from a crouch. This young man is also a stereotype—the bluff, honest folk hero in a tunic—and his chaste girlfriend, who wears an ankle-length nightie through the whole ballet, is an active bore. Dramatically and symbolically, the role of Katerina is absurd—at one point she defends her virtue against the villain with an upraised sickle—and choreographically it is feeble. Grigorovich relies on his favorite step, renversé in attitude, and a few other things that can be done in a nightgown: low arabesques, hobbling on pointe, or, in a lighter vein, hobbling on pointe backward.

The sacred/profane polarity in feminine type-casting seems to be standard Russian practice. Grigorovich used it again in *The Legend of Love* (Shirin/Queen Mekhmene-Banu) and *Spartacus* (Phrygia/Aegina), Lavrovsky used it, and both men could probably claim antecedents in *Giselle* (Giselle/Myrtha) and *Swan Lake* (Odette/Odile). In his production of *Swan Lake*, though, it isn't the ballerina roles that interest Grigorovich; he turns his good/evil polarization formula onto Siegfried and the sorcerer, von Rothbart, and tries to suggest, through many a renversé in attitude performed *à deux*, that the two are alter egos living inside the same character. The suggestion has no expressive purpose; it's just there to be fooled with, like a new tassel or drape. This *Swan Lake*, I understand, is a modified, censored version of the radical production Grigorovich wished to put on. Nevertheless, it contains its share of experimental follies; it's about the most senseless of the novelty *Swan Lake*s that are still around and, with its bleary unit set and swamp-gas lighting, the ugliest. However, the Bolshoi is the Bolshoi, and a maladroit *Swan Lake* is preferable to a *Stone Flower* for showing off the company, its style and its school. About two minutes into Act I, the impression of dull and absent performing left by *The Stone Flower* was dispelled by the big ensemble waltz. Here were young men and women visibly connected to a tradition. I have faint but stirring memories of Act I as it was in the former Bolshoi version— of an elegantly framed vision of haughty young aristocrats disporting themselves in a Botticelli autumn garden. And that vision comes back to me in the present production even though the garden is gone along with its frame of animated onlookers. The dancing shows such sensibility, so many details of step and accent which the eye picks out like metallic threads through a great tapestry, that one begins to grow a little afraid, as if in the presence of numbers of strangers all with finer instincts than one's own. What one is seeing is style—style as a system of preferences that has to be bred into a company. That's why the sight of it is scary. But isn't part of the reason we go to the ballet the tragic thrill of seeing so many accomplish what for one would be remarkable? Particularity of behavior elevated to group expression is what draws us to the great companies with the great corps, like the Bolshoi, especially when they do *Swan Lake*. It's the expectation of seeing in the tragic action of the ballet a logical parallel to what has already been fulfilled in the creation of a corps de ballet and the creation of a ballerina. The ballerina is the principle of the particular within the general, and the corps is the principle of the general within the particular, and each is achieved tragically, out of the depths of human pride.

One can't have cheap artistic direction and still have tragedy on the grand scale appropriate to ballet. From the way the Bolshoi dances *Swan Lake*, I'd say that its artistic direction is mainly benevolent—negligent or partial at worst. The great waltz in Act I is an adaptation of what I can recall seeing in the sixties; Grigorovich's fussing has mostly to do with pointework. I think the women used to wear heeled shoes in this number—the men, too—and the effect of that is still there, and so is the delicate balance of the whole figure as it waltzes. The women show becoming oppositions in neck, waist, thigh, and ankle; they're moderately vivacious while the men are moderately aggressive.

But the medium temperature is calculated against the extreme rigor of the lakeside acts. When the transition to the lakeside begins (the two acts are played consecutively), Grigorovich destroys the mood right away with his "conception," and he undermines the entrance of the swans by rushing them out of nowhere into a formation at the start of the act. But when they make their traditional entrance, in flying sautées arabesques, the show resumes its proper perspective. The Bolshoi is still the greatest turned-in ballet company in the world, and its swans, as usual, draw their bigness of scale from the instep and lower leg rather than, as Western swans do, from an open hip and mobile thigh. But then there is the wonderfully alive Russian back. Those backs and those strong and pliant feet somehow collaborate in a look of strain and confinement which has nothing to do with technical inadequacy. This is swan deportment in Bolshoi terms. And the suspense of Bolshoi phrasing—behind the beat, with linking steps inordinately inflated, climaxes unpredictably tossed away—adds its baffling fanciness to the total worked-over, slightly sweated weight of Bolshoi style. When these swans are in their human form, they're sitting in clammy castles making lace.

Natalia Bessmertnova is the Swan Queen who bears out the corps in its most ponderous aspects, but she's really not released in the role. With her beautiful turned-in plastique, Bessmertnova makes rapturous broken-winged pictures in this ballet; when she flies, though, she flies right out of it into another world. Her second-act adagio is so evenly accented and molded, and every bit of it is so heavy, that it seems twice as long as it is. In Odile's variation, which appears to have been made on her, she has a bright moment, and in the last act she has another, riding around the stage in huge jetés. Bessmertnova danced two performances with two different Siegfrieds, both of them talented and accomplished young dancers. Alexander Godunov, whom we last saw here in 1974, may be the more accomplished. From a rawly energetic performer he has developed into a classical dancer of distinction, and his personality has sweetened. Although Alexander Bogatyrev has, as they say, filled out, his listless attack and casual demeanor make him a pipe-and-slippers Prince. In the finale to Act I, he violated Grigorovich's idea of a Siegfried who does nothing but dance by actually appearing to sight swans overhead. Both of these performances of *Swan Lake* were graced by Irina Kholina's light and speedy solo in the first-act pas de trois—except for this plum an unexcitingly arranged piece of choreography.

From its low point on opening night, the company has slowly, very slowly, begun to come alive. We are still waiting for Nadezhda Pavlova and Vyacheslav Gordeyev in something other than *Spartacus*. For many of us, these two dancers have been among the world's legendary performers ever since we saw them and Semenyaka and Godunov make their startling New York débuts six years ago. *Spartacus*, in which Gordeyev must be tigerishly heroic and Pavlova kittenishly consoling, doesn't allow much more than a glimpse of what artists like this can do. But that glimpse was enough to touch off pandemonium in the audience.

—August 20, 1979

Trooping the Colors
at Covent Garden

From my hotel in London, which was on the Strand, I could walk two ways to the ballet at Covent Garden. One was straight up Bow Street to the front of the Royal Opera House; the other was around the back, across the large square next to the site of the famous evicted market, now under restoration. Both routes had their rewards. The marketplace, temporarily void and silent, flanked by Inigo Jones's church and what remains of his colonnade, presented a classical perspective that cleared the mind for the performance to come. As one neared the stage door, the narrow streets filled with people and small cars inching their way, providing a delightful agitato overture. The great thrill of approaching the theatre from the front was the sudden sight of its pediment and white columns jutting from the ramble of streets and shops—as surprising as finding a four-poster in an upper berth. The Covent Garden district is still a dream landscape, though no longer so inhospitable after dark. New galleries, boutiques, and late-hours restaurants add their sparkle to the jumble of vistas. The Opera House, placed on a height, faces nowhere in particular and is im-

possible to approach head-on. Unlike the Paris Opéra it is
not a magnet; one comes upon it and its counterpart the
Theatre Royal, Drury Lane, amid the swarm. These great
structures reassert the idea of a theatre embedded in life, not
artificially remote from it. The Opera House, especially, appears extended and involved in the affairs of the city yet
with just enough of a break in logic to command authority.
Our old Met was a bit like this; the new one could have
been more so if it had been built on the same spot.

On a violet evening in September, Covent Garden was a
pleasant place to be, with the façade rising above the
tootling traffic and letting in quietly chattering crowds.
Close to curtain time on opening night of New York City
Ballet's season, Balanchine was seen sauntering alone and
serene among the crowds. I imagine the pleasures of the
place have spoken to him many times; contrasts in scale,
leaps in logic are to be found in his ballets, and the style of
New York City Ballet—serious, self-challenging—implies a
seamless connection between the practice of classical dancing and our common human fate. Locally, the company
brings out aesthetic connections as well; we know it speaks
of and for New York—the best of New York—and we are
eager for that to be understood abroad. But the sense in
which ballet is important to us in New York is not understood abroad. Old World opera houses are built to human
scale; they're designed for the kind of experience our own
expensive, overscaled, ice-cold theatres can only contradict.
The New World cannot afford these theatres intended for
an élite; we have to build for the acquisitive audience. Yet in
cities like New York the dream of middle-class affluence has
clouded over. New York City gives me sustenance in the
form of New York City Ballet, but I can't afford to live
there—live, that is, in one of the enclaves that keep the

frightening realities of city life at bay. Lincoln Center is an enclave within an enclave. When it was built, it seemed to reflect the philistine notion that art is outside life, an excrescence. Now it reflects the sense that art is outside life, a refuge. It has never stopped being a monument to middle-class values, but only if you're a beleaguered middle-class New Yorker can you know what it truly stands for.

It may be because we were driven to create these monster theatres out of economic need and greed that we prize what goes on inside them so highly—it's all we've got. Art in America comes very dear; art anywhere does these days. The new theatres are almost always as ugly as they are unserviceable. One has only to cross the Thames to see what a horror of a modern cultural complex can be constructed in London, a city of theatres. Covent Garden may be old-fashioned, but few other theatres are as perfectly focused. The audience, upstairs and down, sits collected, stretching its two arms toward a brimming stage. There are slightly over two thousand seats. At the New York State Theater, there are slightly under three thousand. One might suppose that in that difference lies the sacrifice of intimacy to grandeur, but the Opera House at Kennedy Center in Washington, where New York City Ballet is playing now, is closer in size to Covent Garden and somehow it misses both intimacy and grandeur.

The State Theater, which was supposed to have been a gift to Balanchine, has instead been a problem—one that he has worked tirelessly to surmount—and the staging of his repertory at Covent Garden revealed further aspects of his resourcefulness in dealing with the State Theater's recalcitrant proportions. There were, of course, ballets that simply looked better on a smaller stage because they were made for one—ballets like *The Four Temperaments* and *Square Dance*, which were created before the move to Lincoln Center. *Stravinsky Violin Concerto*, a State Theater ballet (but a re-make of a 1941 work), assumed a more concise power in its new setting. To my surprise, such recent "small" works as *Ballo della Regina* and *Kammermusik No. 2* came over much as they do at home, and *Chaconne*, which I had expected to change quite a lot, looked absolutely itself. The biggest difference came in *Jewels*, of all pieces, which suggests that when he made it, early in his State Theater career, Balanchine hadn't quite attained mastery of the new space. A smaller stage enhances it. At Covent Garden, *Diamonds* was majestically ample, less effusive; *Emeralds* took on a hothouse glow; and *Rubies* was positively scandalous. *Vienna Waltzes* and *Union Jack*, the two blockbusters, appeared cramped. The blah reaction to them of the British public was less predictable. At Covent Garden, the audience sits close enough to see its own face in the mirror in *Vienna Waltzes*. But the intensity of that experience had to be exchanged for a more confined surge of massed waltzers in the finale. The quintessential State Theater ballet, *Vienna Waltzes* had other problems, too—the same ones it has in New York. An hour of waltzes was thought frivolous and boring, and the spectacular scale of the work was scarcely more appreciated than the reduced one of *Liebeslieder Walzer*, also an hour long but with a cast of only eight dancers. The ballet, long out of repertory in New York, had failed when the Royal Ballet produced it earlier this year. *Liebeslieder* in New York was never a hit; it is not, as *Vienna Waltzes* is, made of hit material. But in London it wasn't a critical success, either. The British critics, who differ in their views of Balanchine, are virtually united in the opinion that he and his dancers are not "romantic," not "lyrical." For some of the older and more insensitive reviewers, when a

Balanchine dancer is really "in," he or she is said to be fit for the Royal Ballet—it's the ultimate accolade. Fortunately, there are now critics who avoid evaluating one company stylistically to the detriment of the other. The American accent of the Jerome Robbins ballets was readily appreciated. Spotting the American Balanchine behind some of his disguises proved more difficult.

Although *Union Jack* was also made for the big stage of the State Theater, it seemed destined for Covent Garden from the start. Opening with a sustained flourish of Scottish pageantry, it next brings on the Pearly King and Queen in a highly idiosyncratic music-hall turn, and concludes with an extended hornpipe festival danced by the entire company. The use of British popular and folk material involves no pretense on Balanchine's part; he sees it all from the outside, and the humor of impertinence is as much a part of *Union Jack* as the tribute of parody. The Colonel Blimps of the London press who chose to get huffy over such solecisms as "The British Grenadiers" and "Colonel Bogey" serving as hornpipe tunes ("We must bear firmly in mind," wrote one of these wattles-shakers, "that they *mean* well") were in the minority. Most of the negative reaction had to do with Balanchine's apparent willingness to waste a company of splendid dancers on trivialities. In New York, the curiosity of seeing seemingly authentic folk dances performed by *those* dancers makes *Union Jack* a double-barreled exotic attraction. To Britons, the Scottish suite may be long-drawn-out and lacking in consequence. To Americans, it has a ritualistic simplicity not unlike some of our more austere avant-garde dance. And what could be simpler than the chorus of signal flags wigwagging "God Save the Queen" while the band thunders out "Rule Britannia"? This must surely be the greatest nondance finale that Balanchine has ever arranged, to the greatest of Britain's ceremonial hymns. (Only "Pomp and Circumstance" seems to me as nearly great.)

There are two points I should like to make about the supposed shallowness or inferiority or irrelevance of *Union Jack*. One is that emotional experience in the theatre is indivisible and is not necessarily finer for having come about through pure dance than through pure mime. The ending of *Union Jack* is palpably an expression of the same mind that conceived the endings of *Symphony in C* and *The Four Temperaments*; if Balanchine does not discriminate among his poetic resources, why should we? The other point is that here, at last, we have a keenly characterized folk-style ballet that asks of its dancers something besides dancing. Could not critics who for years have categorized, and castigated, the New York City dancers as anonymous instruments of choreography sense the moment that signifies a change? (The Blimp I quoted a moment ago realized that there was something different going on but concluded that Balanchine failed whenever he stepped outside his pigeonhole.)

In *Union Jack* the dancers are asked to be Scottish or English, with an American accent, of course. It is assumed that the imposture will be funny. I suppose it's possible to miss the point if you yourself are Scottish or English; and humor is less often a bond than a wedge between nations. Another divider is classical style in dancing. Although *Union Jack* doesn't contain any classical dances, it is danced by classicists, and it gathers its impact almost entirely from that fact. There's a whole series of Balanchine ballets that might be labeled "A Classical Choreographer Looks at——." The series includes not only *Union Jack* but such ballets as *Stars and Stripes*, *Who Cares?*, *Square Dance*, *Tzigane*, *Western Symphony*, and *Scotch Symphony*. Sometimes the titles

reveal the material that Balanchine is looking at, or "classi-
cizing," sometimes not, but the ballets are all part of a
process of analysis that ends in the annexation of new territory for classical dancers. *Union Jack*, the most radical of the
series, goes another route. It anatomizes classical values in
its subject without making a classical ballet out of it. It
seems to stand alone, yet if it were to be presented at
Covent Garden all by itself or by another company, it
would not make nearly as much sense as it does in repertory. It is as vivid a portrait of New York City Ballet as any
of the other pieces I have named. It is not, and was not
meant to be, a portrait of Britain.

Very wisely, Balanchine did not present *Union Jack* until
the third and closing week of the Covent Garden season,
when it was part of a gala attended by Princess Margaret.
Patricia McBride and Bart Cook danced the Pearlies; in the
hornpipe section, Suzanne Farrell and Peter Martins were
sharper and funnier than they had ever been before; all the
dancers were warmly applauded. But the piece was accepted
at face value as a deliberate counterfeit or an engaging trifle,
or else not accepted at all. I was reminded of New York's
initial reaction, in 1958, to *Stars and Stripes*. Once again, Balanchine's innocence was being equated with the naïveté of
his material. That innocence of his does not hesitate to
probe the mundane. In routine it finds variety, in well-worn
clichés it finds a seductive secret. The material is transformed. British parade-ground performance is in actuality
more exhilarating to me than Balanchine's use of it in *Union
Jack*. It's the principle of it that he has caught—the mesmer-
izing power of mass locomotion. *Union Jack* was at Covent
Garden the week of the funeral of Mountbatten. The drag
step of the brigadiers in the funeral procession, merely by
slowing down and stressing the toe with a delicate batte-

ment tendu, indicated the gravity and sensitivity of the occasion. Balanchine's regiments do not imitate this or the regular British-soldier march step—hard on the heel with the feet apart and the belly out. That just seems to go with the boots of soldiers, not the slippers of dancers. Strict protocol for slow tempos calls for marchers to hold their arms stiffly at their sides. Again, Balanchine has chosen a style more appropriate to dancers. And we should look at his regiments against the background of dance style in the repertory at large. When we do, *Union Jack* gets sweeter and funnier (and shorter), and Balanchine's face comes out from behind his ostensible subject, be it Highland flings, reels, or military marches. What the British call his "personal classicism" is the quality of emphasis he gives to enduring elements of dance that are, like configurations in a picture puzzle, hidden in the real world of movement. He has taught us to see these elements—us, the American people. And I would have hoped that by this time the term "personal classicism" could have given way to "American classicism" or even "classicism." It happens that at the moment no one else is practicing in that shop on such a scale of consequence or such a level of responsibility.

Union Jack, made in the year of the American bicentenary, salutes Great Britain. It also commemorates and capitalizes on *The Triumph of Neptune*, a ballet about Great Britain that Balanchine had arranged for Diaghilev fifty years before. Then twenty-two years old, he had also danced a featured role. His collaborators were two Englishmen, the composer Lord Berners and the writer Sacheverell Sitwell, but we assume that what the ballet mainly expressed was Diaghilev's idea of a Victorian pantomime. *The Triumph of Neptune* opened at the Lyceum Theatre (where last month the American Friends of Covent Garden gave an opening-night party for New York City Ballet) and was a success. The scenery was based on the traditional toy theatres of Pollock and Webb, and the costumes adapted national dress with what one recent writer has called "Diaghilevian whimsey." *Union Jack*, presented in London in the fiftieth-anniversary year of Diaghilev's death, uses as part of its décor a drop curtain modeled on the red swags of the British toy theatres. When it was lowered at Covent Garden, it touched a chord of association that it could never sound in New York. Balanchine, the last of Diaghilev's choreographers and the only one who is alive today, is seldom sentimental, but I believe he has always had a soft spot for England. Repeatedly, during his visit, he praised English manners and customs to interviewers. If he hoped to be praised in return, he didn't let on. To the veteran dance critic Alexander Bland he admitted that his not settling in London many years ago was probably a good thing because he isn't dignified enough for England, where "if you are awake it is already vulgar." A small enough joke, to which Alexander Bland returned the comment: "Though technically fastidious, he certainly lacks the regulator of good taste, which is one of Britain's hallmarks." And he didn't smile when he said it.

Sniffy good taste—chauvinism, in other words—has certainly regulated relations between Balanchine and British ballet in the past. On this visit, New York City Ballet's first in fourteen years, most commentators held their tongues on the subject of costume and décor. New York City Ballet is badly underdressed and the Royal Ballet is badly overdressed; but the subject of discussion this time was dancing. Every country recognizes two classical traditions—its own and Russia's. Where British observers warmed to New York City Ballet, they tended to see resemblances to the Kirov, if not to the Royal. Mikhail Baryshnikov's presence helped strengthen that connection. But to an American the existence of a Russo-American New York City Ballet is as incredible as that of an Italo-English Royal Ballet. Roots and blossoms should not be confused.

It takes time to be able to make those distinctions in a foreign company. For reasons that are not entirely clear to me but have mostly to do with money, it has not been possible for New York City Ballet to have regular London seasons. As a result, Americans know far more about British ballet than the British know about ours. There used to be a feeling around the country that, owing to its many U.S. tours, the Royal belonged partly to us. If the Royal's influence here is on the wane, it may be because American companies are at last making their way in cities outside New York and establishing a tradition of their own. In return for elevating our standard of judgment, the American audience gave the Royal Ballet dimension; it's what the company lacks now. The Royal is sinking into a cozy provincialism. I hate to see it happen—it offends my proprietary instincts. Yet those instincts tell me that there may be some clue to salvation for the Royal in the example of New York City Ballet. Not, certainly, a stylistic example, but a functional one. There is, for example, no tradition at the Royal Ballet of choreographers who also teach. That sets it apart not only from NYCB but from nearly every other dance institution in its period of greatest growth. There is also—and here more sensitive areas must be approached—no record anywhere in the history of ballet of ballerinas being formed by a matriarchy. The English ballet world is rife with its Mims and Madams—blessed, brilliant ladies of iron convictions and awesome accomplishments. But perhaps not the right kind of vision just now. Sir Frederick Ashton, who like Balanchine is seventy-five this year, takes curtain calls with regularity and always with emotion. The British are lavish with their celebrations. Of Sir Frederick they ask nothing but that he bask in their applause. Yet too much of the Ashton repertory has been lost owing to the public's indifference through the years. At Sadler's Wells Royal Ballet, I saw revivals of *Les Rendezvous* and *The Two Pigeons*—ballets that in successive eras have defined British classical style. It's another world; just compare Ashton's Gypsies in *The Two Pigeons* with *Tzigane*. But it is still the world that used to be American by adoption. Watching these ballets, I was impressed all over again with Ashton's long and patient effort to get dancers and audiences used to metaphoric rather than literal associations in dance gesture. He goes at times against the grain, for British dancers are almost all by nature good mimes and British dance critics are by custom devotees of acting and susceptible to coquetry—what one of Balanchine's ballerinas calls "eyebrow dancing." I also saw two new ballets made for the hardworking Sadler's Wells company. Kenneth MacMillan used the native gift for histrionics in a consciously overwrought and not very fresh mime drama called *Playground*. David Bintley, a talented young choreographer, made an old-fashioned pantomime-style piece called *Punch and the Street Party*. His music was the Berners score for *The Triumph of Neptune*; his story was new. I liked the piece a lot, but it did appeal to the tourist in me. A company must guard against doing too often what it does best. For American dancers whose capacities as actors are small, *Union Jack* is a character ballet. It shows that going against the natural tendency of an expressive gift can sometimes bring out an intimate truth. The colors it flies are our own.

—October 15, 1979

THE EIGHTIES

Swing Street Revisited

Fancy Free, the Jerome Robbins–Leonard Bernstein ballet about three sailors on shore leave, takes place on a hot summer night in 1944, the year of the ballet's première. The side street in Manhattan and the bar where the sailors drink were designed in Sunday-comics colors by Oliver Smith; their real-life counterparts were probably somewhere along the Hudson River piers, but the setting of the ballet has always seemed to be Fifty-second Street, or "Swing Street," as the block between Fifth and Sixth is now designated—the street of the jazz clubs that, like roistering sailors on shore leave, are with us no more. The ballet begins with a blues record playing in the dark; the song is "Big Stuff," by Leonard Bernstein, and in the American Ballet Theatre production the voice on the record has been Billie Holiday's for thirty-five years. I had never been able to tell what the song was—it was just a snatch of sound that preceded the overture. In the new production that Robbins has just supervised for New York City Ballet, Dee Dee Bridgewater sings in a specially made studio recording, and the record plays on long enough for us to identify the melody as the same one Bernstein uses in the pas de deux. When the curtain rose on the New York City Ballet production, I expected more revelations, and in fact the performance did resemble a newly scrubbed painting. Hard lines and colors appeared in place of soft edges and allusive pastels; vague contours and pliant, careless brushstrokes were erased. But the high definition wasn't a return to the original style; it was totally new, and it did strange things to *Fancy Free*. The central situation—of sailors picking up girls—seemed tense, the humor fell flat, with larky bits of business clinging to the stage like the edges of a damp soufflé. The dancers tried hard—maybe too hard. The breeziness and the innocence of the piece eluded every attempt to nail them to the ground.

A character ballet with musical-comedy overtones, *Fancy Free* is not at all typical of New York City Ballet, but at last year's School of American Ballet benefit performance the three solos were successfully performed by Jean-Pierre Frohlich, Mikhail Baryshnikov, and Peter Martins. At this year's benefit, the whole ballet was given, fully dressed in Smith's décor and Kermit Love's original costumes, and with Bart Cook in Baryshnikov's place and Stephanie Saland and Lourdes Lopez as the pickups. Last week, it went on the NYCB bills, where it joins the largest selection of Robbins ballets in active repertory, including the two that stand beside it as his masterpieces—*Afternoon of a Faun* and *Dances at a Gathering*. I would add *Interplay* to that list but for the fact that after all these years the eight dancers—who must be eight *young* dancers to be believable in the juvenile roles Robbins created—are seldom able to rise evenly and with full force to the technical demands of the choreography, which is classical and acrobatic with jazz accents. The current NYCB casts are probably the best classical dancers that *Interplay* has ever had, and their classical correctness has

the effect of enclosing their 1945 hepcat roles in amused
quotation marks. The dancers, though young, seem discriminating where earlier generations of NYCB dancers just
seemed square. But *Interplay* celebrates its antique groovi-
ness a little too thinly for comfort. I believe in the dancers'
emphasis on correctness; I think it gives the ballet a clearer
and truer sentiment than some of the show-bizzy interpretations we have seen. But that choice is helpless. Unlike the
dancers of the forties and fifties, current casts aren't prey to
the jive; they aren't familiar with any developed dance vocabulary outside the ballet. They're classical because they
know no other technique.

Interplay and now *Fancy Free* point up the coincidences
in the dance styles of an era—instances of momentary correspondence that flow across the board from the most academic to the most colloquial dance forms and that may be
extended into parallels capable of nourishing the most academic, if not the most colloquial. Classical academic ballet
goes on when the Lindy, the shag, the twist, and the boogaloo are gone. But classical style is also mutable from generation to generation. The steps in the syllabus may be the
same, but even the mechanics of execution bear the imprint
of an era. In old ballet films, that imprint leaps out at you.
The ballet dancers of the forties appear to have had more in
common with the samba line at the Copacabana than they
have with ballet dancers of today. Whatever that common
impulse was, it is unrecapturable. The great overlapping
wave of popular expression in dance and song came in the
first fifty years of our century; we are still drifting in the hollow of that wave. And, in the absence of any comparably
strong popular dance tradition, classicism today is impover-
ished. Our era dotes on the beauty of classical style at its
purest and most austere. But it can also be an anemic purity,

bled dry of support material, cut off from any enlivening influence of the vernacular. In the NYCB *Fancy Free*, the dancers' idea of a pop style is heavy and swaggering—the opposite of their own classical style and the opposite of the pop style of the forties, which was also lightly objective. They make the same kind of mistake singers make when they try to do the old popular songs; the words are doled out as if they belonged to the singer and not the song.

Different dance forms in the same era are more closely related than the same dance forms in different eras. We can imagine Balanchine's counting on the appeal of his *Serenade* to an audience that had seen Astaire-Rogers and Jessie Matthews movies. But photographs of *Serenade* taken in the thirties are disconcerting. Had the ballet not been kept in repertory, it might have had to be wholly re-created. Changing its shape now subtly, now radically, *Serenade* has over the years maintained its place and its essence: it has always been recognizably *Serenade*. The hope of perpetuation and continuity lies in repertory; so does the expectancy of permissible change. Without a continuous record of performances, even Ballet Theatre might find it difficult to stage an authentic *Fancy Free*.

NYCB dancers have no skill in throwaway gesture. When the sailors tease the girl with the red shoulder bag, the action that at Ballet Theatre can look ad lib is so precisely set and executed that it becomes harsh: these boys might be muggers. And Martins and Saland massage the tender little pas de deux into an explosive sexual encounter. Saland in any case is too knowing, too seductive, and Lopez is too patrician for the streetwise but "nice" girls that the ballet is supposed to be about. The casting of the men is off, too. As characters, Martins and Baryshnikov might have been plausible buddies, with Frohlich as a kind of mascot.

Now Martins, especially since he's been given the pas de deux, looks like the star of the show, with Cook and Frohlich in support. Cook dances the second, lyrical variation with a great deal of charm and care, but he has the same misfortune that he has in *Stravinsky Violin Concerto*, of being unequally cast against Martins. The second cast was better balanced. Judith Fugate and Delia Peters are both believable white-collar working girls. Fugate is as knowing as Saland but more vulnerable, and Peters sets the comic tone the instant we see her long, droll face appearing around a corner of the set. Douglas Hay, Christopher Fleming, and Joseph Duell, performing the variations in that order, weren't—except for Duell—as brilliant as the first cast, but their spirits were higher, their control of the ballet's moods was much more secure, and they looked like high school–age sailors. If virtuoso dancing is what *Fancy Free* is really about, Robbins has been lying to us all these years.

—February 11, 1980

Doin' the Old Low Down

No Maps on My Taps is a sweet, reflective, back-alley movie about three aging hoofers in Harlem—how they live and, when they can manage to get a gig, how they work. Chuck Green, Bunny Briggs, and Howard (Sandman) Sims are all former headliners. Chuck Green was the dancing half of Chuck and Chuckles, the appointed heirs to Buck and Bubbles. Bunny Briggs became famous in the twenties as a child star. Sandman Sims began as a boxer, cutting steps in the resin box; he did his sand dance at the Apollo for seventeen years. All three men are fine dancers still. The film shows that, and it depicts them as the last of a great line—artists who would like to pass their tradition along but know there are no takers. Although the tap-dance revival that began in the sixties has lately risen to a peak, its dominant mood is elegiac; it fits in with the recycled old musicals, the fads for forties clothes and hairstyles and furnishings, and the Preservation Society reverence in which we now hold the popular art of the past. Chuck Green and Bunny Briggs and Sandman Sims, along with a dozen other veterans of the swing-bebop era, are being seen and celebrated these days by new audiences. Tap-dance studios are full. But as an art of the people tap barely survives; it is a subcultural expression, like jazz. In *No Maps on My Taps*, Sandman Sims blames rock for the ruin of tap, and he tells the manager of the Apollo, "Rock closed this theatre." The manager quietly replies that rock is what people get on their radios. Times change. "For the three of us, it's probably the last hooray," Sims says. One wishes it weren't true.

One wishes, too, that the last hooray weren't also, for so many in the audience, the first one. Many of the black dancers of Sims's generation have had to wait until now to become known to white audiences. And it is, by and large, the white audience that has rediscovered tap. The performance scenes in the film, at Small's Paradise, were staged by the filmmaker, George T. Nierenberg; it had been years since Small's had booked tap-dancers. On Harlem streets, we are introduced to dancers who have never been seen downtown and probably never will be. But when Sims speaks of the talent walking down the street going to waste, he doesn't mean these obscure older men, some of whom have never had professional careers; he means the young people who aren't plugged in to the tradition. Sims thinks that all you have to do is show them what they've been missing—not an Astaire or Kelly movie but an old-time Apollo show, with a band, a singer, a dancer, and a novelty act. Well, the show might be a hit, but how many new tap-dancers would it produce? White boys didn't need to see and hear white musicians to know they wanted to play jazz; they wanted jazz—it was the air they breathed. A young black today would have to adopt tap as a conscious artistic vocation and practice it in isolation. Some young blacks have done so, but too few to count.

In another new film, *Tapdancin'*, the current tap scene is

so exhaustively presented and analyzed that one wonders about the dancers who are left out and the questions that aren't answered. It's sad to hear a great performer like Honi Coles say that he believes he could have done better but for racism; it sounds logical, as when Sandman Sims says of the young, "They never see a black dancer dance where it relates to them." But what are we to think when the camera turns from Coles to pick up some passing teenagers? There go the disinherited? Hollywood couldn't make a star of Paul Draper, and it was probably because Draper (who is one of the dancers *Tapdancin'* omits) had a style that in its own terms was as pure as the style of the blacks. There were other white dancers who came closer to what the blacks actually did. These white men had no impact comparable to Astaire's and Kelly's, because they weren't musical-comedy dancers, and musical comedy was what Broadway and Hollywood produced. A large grudge can be held against commercial theatre and film on racial grounds; the record is bad enough without incriminating the future, too. If kids don't want to tap-dance anymore, there are plenty of reasons, and they're probably the same for whites as for blacks.

The decline of tap is linked to the decline of big-band jazz and jazz-affiliated pop. If music for dancing is being mass-produced today, it isn't the listenable, rhythmically intricate music that tap masters understand. *Tapdancin'* (a Christian Blackwood film) seeks out some of the new tappers, but only one, Camden Richman, has something to show and something to say. Camden Richman, like nearly all this younger generation, is female and white, and she may be the best technician of the lot. In her film interview, she makes the point that tap technique, following bebop, developed such complexity that by the late forties it wasn't mass-marketable. Richman may be correct on the historical evolution, but I think that the reason for the decline in mass appeal wasn't what came into the music but what went out. Richman's model is Honi Coles (you can hear the resemblance), and it seems that she has also based her performance on her idea of historical jazz dance. She dances with the Jazz Tap Percussion Ensemble, consisting of two other white dancers and an instrumental group, also white. It's a cool, laid-back bunch; at its best, the dancing provides a discreetly absorbing panorama of sound. The nuances are a little overstarched, just as the sensibility is a little modern-dance frugal. The musical-comedy approach, which includes sex, glamour, high spirits, is ruled out. Comedy is not done, though one may be witty. Richman, in addition to her technical ease and personal elegance, has a sense of play. But JTPE tends to embody an attitude or a theory rather than a style. It brings to mind all those theses on the pressure of the big cities and its influence on jazz. Maybe the postwar decline of the cities had something to do with making tap dance obsolete (or driving it underground); we're growing conscious of it again now that we're restoring our cities. Blacks, of course, could never afford to give up the city. For them, tap is an urban art and an art of urbanity. It started on the levee; today, we think of pavement under tapping feet.

The Brooklyn Academy of Music this month repeated its program called *Steps in Time*, bringing out not only Sims and Green and Briggs and Coles and Gregory Hines and the tap fraternity known as the Copasetics but also the Nicholas Brothers, who are in a class by themselves. Except for Hines it was a grandfatherly assortment. But the Nicholas Brothers couldn't be anybody's grandfathers; they still look like uncorked genies. They came on late, introduced by film clips of some of their greatest numbers. In

Stormy Weather they were seen descending a giant staircase in air splits, brother flying over brother and landing on every other stair—no, not landing: *crashing* fully split to the floor and then twist-squeezing himself upright. When they got to the bottom, they squeezed up one last time, did a couple of pirouettes, raced back up the stairs, and slid down two ramps toward the camera, and at that point the live Nicholas Brothers stepped through the screen. (One of the delights of the two new tap movies is their inclusion of old Hollywood footage—Buck and Bubbles in *No Maps on My Taps*, the Four Step Brothers in *Tapdancin'*, Bill Robinson in both.) I had seen the Nicholas Brothers a few years ago, looking like the fatigued and distracted old-timers they had every right to be. In Brooklyn, though, they were really on: whizzing through their pirouettes, flashing the flashiest hands ever. One can't say they actually, miraculously, *danced* those old tap routines, but how they performed! Maybe the electricity of the other dancers got to them: the dry-bone delicacy (never arid) of Honi Coles clicking out light, dense confettilike taps while standing virtually motionless; Coles and Henry (Phace) Roberts donning Bojangles derbies and levitating through "Doin' the New Low Down"; Buster Brown bouncing, careering, mincing, skating, and losing a tap (Coles yelling, "You always wanted to be Peg Leg Bates"); Bubba Gaines tap-jumping rope to "Perdido," then double-timing to "Who?" A tap fest can easily grow tiring, but not when sparks are flying and each performer dances in rapport with all the others. Not when what they do transcends its technical mystery and becomes an evocation of life. *Steps in Time* is biographies, inescapably, of black men. The lives are so intensely lived onstage that after the show we don't speculate about them—whether the dancers drink beer like us and shop at the Safeway. Although we may well wonder how some of them pay the rent.

Steps in Time is not, as some tap evenings have been, an informal, improvised affair; it's a finely tooled, professionally mounted vaudeville-style show. In the finale, Harold Nicholas performs two of his signature stunts—sliding across the stage through a tunnel of legs (which he originally did at the suggestion of George Balanchine) and back-flipping into a split. Earlier, Sandman Sims, another dazzler, had shown his enormous range (of which the chugging, scuffing dance in the sand is only a portion), his exhilarating grand-scale dynamics, and his flair for comedy. In *No Maps on My Taps*, Sims is the sparkplug, inciting and sustaining much of the continuity, actively enjoying his newfound celebrity. Briggs is sociable on camera, but he's basically indifferent to its presence, a sealed-off, haunted man. When his mother, who died several years ago, is mentioned, he neither hides nor demonstrates his grief. His dancing in the film is winning, totally committed; on the stage it also has an edge of melancholy. In Green's eyes, there is fire and despair. He looks more frail in the film than he does on the stage, and though we linger on him at the fadeout, he's the least communicative of the three. How does he like being put in a Hall of Fame perspective after years of neglect? We never find out.

It was Green and the late Baby Laurence, they say, who fomented the tap revival in Harlem, drawing dancers together who hadn't seen each other in years. Green is now the esteemed elder of the tribe, the one all the others refer to as "a giant" or "a genius," but when he talks long-distance to his mentor, the seventy-eight-year-old John Bubbles, he's the dutiful protégé. "How you doin'?" demands Bubbles. "You creatin' any?" Green's solution to any problem is what one imagines it must have been for fifty years: "More jobs in better places." The title of the movie comes from a song he sings to himself with that half-hallucinated glint in his eye. Like Briggs, he seems unmindful of the camera, but once, when Sims deliberately provokes him and he cries out dramatically, "Don't tetch me!," one isn't sure. Green, as he grows older, grows stronger and purer, breezier and more precise. Age completes him; he's the King Lear of tap. *No Maps on My Taps* captures the quintessential Green, dancing one of his favorite routines to "Caravan." In Brooklyn a couple of weeks ago, he surpassed this exhibition. In his boxy tuxedo with the vented coattails and the ankle-length pants, in long bump-toed shoes, Green looks twice the eccentric he really is, but his style is sui generis, no doubt about it. The gunboat shoes stay flat-footed through a maze of stiletto taps, and we don't see the heel drops that sound like washtub thumps. When Green wants to get visual, he gives us air turns with heel clicks, ungainly hops with cartwheeling arms, ungainlier swooping pivots in a crouch, coattails awhirl. Or he skids back and forth, one foot flat and the other swinging. What Green does can be imitated but it can't be learned. It's soul food for the senses.

—April 28, 1980

Le Sacre without Ceremony

‚‗‗

When Paul Taylor was working on *Scudorama* in 1963, he used a record of *Le Sacre du Printemps* as a rehearsal score; new music was composed in time for the première. A few weeks ago, at the City Center, he presented his production of *Le Sacre* and had the hit of the season. Although Taylor is the logical choreographer for this mighty music, he has staged a completely unpredictable dance work to the two-piano reduction that Stravinsky made for Nijinsky's use in rehearsing the original ballet. If Taylor's *Sacre*, which he calls *Le Sacre du Printemps (The Rehearsal)*, has any resemblance to *Scudorama*, I missed it. And I wouldn't have looked for derivations from Nijinsky's ballet, but those flattened, two-dimensional body positions, angled limbs, and parallel feet are immediately apparent in Taylor's choreography. Taylor may be commemorating a rehearsal period in the life of two companies—his own and the Ballets Russes. When the curtain rises, to an unfamiliar tinkle of familiar notes, a dance company is onstage warming up. This turns into a formal rehearsal, and then into a frame for the action, which has nothing to do either with Stravinsky's scenario or with any *Sacre* scenario ever devised. Instead of tribal rituals and human sacrifices (which Taylor had given us in *Runes*), we see a farce composed of scenes from crime melodramas of the silent-movie era. The characters include a private dick in Harold Lloyd spectacles, a mother, a kidnapped baby, and a slew of Oriental villains. The melodrama may be the ballet the company is rehearsing or it may represent something going on backstage or it may be simple parallel action; the way the scenes are intercut with the rehearsal makes any interpretation possible. Taylor's associative links seem random—*are* random—but he never loses control. All the pieces are designed to fit together in a jigsawlike pattern, and the pattern, no matter how tenuously matched, is unbreakable. The jigsaw shapes seem hewn out of the dancers' bodies. There are opaque moments here and there, but even as we flounder we feel the tug of stylistic consistency.

The integrity of this *Sacre* is a Taylor miracle. A past master at building multilevel allusive structures, Taylor knows that you can swing from branch to branch as long as it is the same tree. In his *Sacre*, the Nijinsky references are reinforced by their implicit Taylorishness; they look so ingrown that we can choose to see them as products of Taylor's long association with the painter Alex Katz. Katz's forays into two-dimensional "depth" have been represented on Taylor's stage in such pieces as *Private Domain* and *Diggity*. Taylor as a dance-maker shares some of Katz's major concerns; he's very nearly Katz's dance double. But when he's expressing those concerns, as in *Le Sacre* or in another new piece closely related to it, called *Profiles*, Katz is not the designer; there's no need for him. John Rawlings's designs for *Le Sacre* are in a starkly cinematic palette of black, white, and gray with one or two splashes of red. Linear motifs—Art Deco circles and grilles—indicate a bedroom or a bar or a jail. The pulp Expressionism of the costumes and décor, the "screenplay" plot, and the dance style seem to blend in one great crashing image. The blunt, thick bodies cringe and lurch, hurtle and bound, dense with impacted energy. These loaded silhouettes with their pump-handle arms and swiveling heads are, perhaps, Taylor's comment on the "perverse" inventions of Nijinsky; he shows us how vivid a dance shape can be by reducing the body's options for extension and directing its energy toward rather than away from the core. As with all theories of polar opposition, this anticlassicism makes a classical statement—it gives us the irreducible essence of expression. And to a master of the irreducible like Taylor, the simplifications and limitations are so many opportunities for virtuosity.

But Taylor's *Sacre* is also a comedy, and Taylor's comic sense is not really located in his cartoon-classical body shapes. *Profiles* uses the same shapes and many of the same movements that make up *Le Sacre*, but it is a grave, lyrical essay with no plot. What makes *Le Sacre* a comedy is the music. By stripping the score of its orchestration, Stravinsky exposed its pistons and gears, and it's this mechanistic aspect of the music that Taylor responds to. He hears the tick-tock ostinato that winds up those massive charging rhythms—hears it as the music of automatons chugging to their doom in a deterministic universe. He can even risk a certain amount of overdeterminism: the kidnapped baby, who is thrown around like the baby in a Punch-and-Judy show, expires along with the rest of the cast, stabbed reflexively by the last man to die in a climactic piling up of corpses. Taylor isn't funny at the music's expense; he works *with* the music and is twice as funny in his straight-faced way as a consciously irreverent parodist would have been. Maybe Taylor himself got wound up in the coils of the music; there's an inevitability, a rightness, about this *Sacre* that seems to issue from a musical mind of the purest sort. By the time we come to the Dance of the Chosen Maiden—the peak moment in the original 1913 production—we have so completely forgotten the 1913 libretto that we're jolted when Taylor reminds us of it. He has Ruth Andrien launch herself into the dance the minute her baby dies, and it's a real twister, filled with irregular phrases none of which accord with the music's irregularity and all of which must be attacked at the highest energy level. Andrien dances in a delirium of precision—between the bar lines, so to speak—and maintains unwavering rhythmic accuracy: a marvelous performance.

Along with the pleasure of musical transparency that this *Sacre* gives us, there is the pleasure of diagrammatic visualization, which leads the eye through the thickets of the scenario. Some of these visual clues are identifiable Taylor fantasies and some are imponderable in origin. Wherefore these "Chinese" configurations and how could Taylor have known they'd make perfect sense to us? Taylor takes us back beyond the silent films to the primitive superstitious imagery that those films tapped. Along with Warner Oland and Anna May Wong and the tong wars in the streets, he gives us a kind of fiercely grinning terroristic "Orientalism" in the very physique of his dances. Those are jigsaw ideograms that pass before us. The omnipresent impassive rehearsal mistress played by Bettie de Jong in Cossack dress is quite obviously a fate figure who fits into the Ballets Russes picture. But she also reminds us of Big Bertha, the malevolent life-size music-box doll Taylor created for de Jong in 1970.

Big Bertha was revived this season with de Jong as pitilessly terrifying as ever, and with Thomas Evert giving a powerful, harrowing performance in Taylor's old role as her chief victim. One might compile a sizable list of Taylor works under the heading "Motiveless Malignity"; it is one of his favorite themes. *Le Sacre* would be on the list, and not merely on the strength of the de Jong character. (Curiously, de Jong is the only mechanical figure in *Big Bertha* and the only nonmechanical one in *Le Sacre*.) Unlike *Big Bertha* or *Nightshade* or *Dust*, *Le Sacre* is too cheerful, too impersonally efficient to be disturbing. It is a work that sweeps us deep into Taylor's world and honors its preceptors at the same time: Nijinsky, Martha Graham (who once danced the Chosen Maiden in choreography by Massine), and, not least of all, Stravinsky. It is very likely the best *Sacre* we shall ever see, and we can only regret that the composer is not here to see it, too.

—May 19, 1980

Slowly Then the History
of Them Comes Out

First it was Louis Horst and Martha Graham. Then it was John Cage and Merce Cunningham. Now, it seems, Philip Glass and Robert Wilson, between them, are filling the role of mentor to the choreographers who are shaping the most pervasive new dance aesthetic. Glass, like Horst and Cage, has composed for dancers—notably for Lucinda Childs and Andrew deGroat, with whom he began to work after collaborating with them and Wilson in 1976, in *Einstein on the Beach*. Wilson, except in the most informal sense, does not choreograph, but as a writer and director of esoteric visionary plays and as a teacher of movement he has been the biggest influence, after Cunningham, on choreographers working today. These young (or young*er*) choreographers—among them Childs and deGroat and Meredith Monk and Kenneth King—are reflecting different aspects of Wilson's work, just as Trisha Brown and Steve Paxton and Douglas Dunn are reflecting different aspects of Cunningham's work. They all belong to the generation commonly referred to as "post-modern," although "post-Cunningham" would be a better term. The various streams of activity which they represent, Wilson's included, are all ultimately traceable to the climate of inspiration which was established by Cage and Cunningham thirty years ago. Even the big idea that seems to divide the mysterians from the mercists—the idea of a return to music—isn't really as sharp a break with the older tradition as it seems. (That secession was actually launched some time ago by Paul Taylor and continued in due course by Twyla Tharp.) Cage and Cunningham taught that a musical accompaniment and a dance have nothing in common but the length of time each takes to happen. Of course, they have much more in common— the theory of aleatoric structure was never denied, either in the dancing or in the music. A dance to a Glass score is also likely to be constructed according to the same laws as the music—laws of "repetitive structure and modular form," to quote a recent program note—but whether it then goes its own way or not is open to question. Besides principles of construction, there is a very heavy beat tying dance and music together and usually, although not always, there is a cryptic, spectral, incantatory atmosphere. These two elements—the beat and the misterioso atmosphere—aren't much, but they're enough to create a new sensation in dance. And they're beginning to crop up all over the place.

In recent weeks, I have seen a deGroat work choreographed to Glass music; a new ballet presented by the Alvin Ailey company to a portion of the score of *Einstein on the Beach*; a film about choreographers which incorporated part of Lucinda Childs's *Dance*, with its score by Glass; a Dance in America TV show in which this trend was represented by Laura Dean dancing to her own music; and a live concert by Dean, again dancing to her own music. Before she took to composing her own scores, Dean collaborated with Steve Reich, the country's other best-known composer of loop music, or music of incessant repetition. Terry Riley and Sergio Cervetti have also worked with dancers in this form. But it is Glass who has come to dominate the dance field. When Laura Dean composes, she sounds not like Reich but like Glass; and Meredith Monk, who has been producing her own sound for a long time, has done several remarkably Glass-like scores. School of Glass tends to feature electronic keyboards, eerie harmonies, pulsing rhythms, and vocalise; it is very loud. Like rock, School of Glass is meant to engulf you. As Andrew Porter wrote in his review of *Einstein on the Beach*, once the listener realizes that the endless repetitions are actually going somewhere, Glass's music is easy to take for quite long spells. Glass habitually works in long forms: a piece called *Music in Twelve Parts* lasts four hours. "The mind may wander now and again," Porter adds, "but it wanders within a new sound world that the composer has created." To be within that world is to experience music as a succession of instants. Glass has asked that his listeners surrender their usual equipment of memory and anticipation. Perhaps the reason he is attracted to dance is that dance is a present-tense art form with no precise way of recalling or predicting itself. Glass's hammering beat seems to drive dancers ever onward into the outer space of unanticipated movement.

This doesn't mean that the movement will be new; it means that the sensation of the movement will be new. In the work of Childs and deGroat and Dean, the steps are elementary, with no embellishments of technique. The repetition aims at creating a cumulative effect of movement beyond the movements that you see, and the total experience of action and sound can be all-involving. To those who are susceptible to this intangible process, there are degrees of abstraction and purity even within the ultimate high that it provides. Lucinda Childs's choreography is a maze of footpaths laid out with Euclidean austerity. To her followers, she was the first—some say the only—choreographer to elevate the sensations of the form to the level of an aesthetic. They may be right, although in actual fact the aesthetic came first. Childs worked for years cutting her school figures in silence. When she added music, the figures took on a brightly sensuous elegance, a change she acknowledged with a switch in costume: corduroys were discarded for flowing silk and lamé. But basically Childs does what she has always done. The atmosphere of chic that envelops her performances these days can be as irritating to those who know why she does it as to those who, like me, don't. Childs has evolved something that looks like prehistoric ballet. The erect, springy carriage, the walking and skipping and hopping patterns seem to want to accumulate technique. I see nothing in their logic to prevent their turning into actual dance steps. Maybe they will, and we'll see the first SoHo Civic Ballet.

At the moment, Childs's work is closer to that of her fellow minimalist Trisha Brown than it is to her fellow cultist Laura Dean. Dean, like deGroat, like William Dunas, like the intramedia specialists Monk and King, and like numerous other choreographers from unallied schools (Kei Takei, Phoebe Neville, Anthony LaGiglia), is a mysterian. The shadows and strategies of Robert Wilson hang heavy over them all. Brown isn't like that. Her work is sunny and open, with a practical base easy—fatally easy—to penetrate. If she uses music at all, it's usually an afterthought: a bit of country-and-western sing-along or early rock. Like Steve Paxton's, Brown's concerts resemble workshops in which the audience is taught movement logic. The leap in logic which takes us from the studio into the theatre is never made. (When Brown gets a theatrical idea, it usually pertains to production, not movement. At her most recent concert, her company danced through clouds of steam.) For a while, Brown and Childs and Dean were alike in having intensively systematic methods of producing choreography as an end in itself. Childs and Dean have customarily presented surface as substance. But in Dean's latest work, *Music* (at the Brooklyn Academy), the naïve, plainspoken little phrases seemed to dissolve back into a motive for doing them, which was apparently to put the dancers into a trance. I found myself looking not at a dance but at a rite. Perhaps the resemblance to the Gurdjieff dances in the movie *Meetings with Remarkable Men* was intentional; perhaps not. Dean's dances have always had their trancelike sections, their protracted sequences of dervishlike spinning which put me off; *Music* is the first dance to start building up a trance with the first step. Instead of developing her formal choreographic devices, Dean seems bent on evolving ever more extended exercises in concentration for her dancers. The first forty or so minutes of *Music* (the whole piece lasts seventy-five minutes) were devoted to a slow-motion legato exercise performed by the group of six in unison while an orchestra consisting of piano, violin, and synthesizer sustained an unbroken wave of chords. It looked like t'ai chi stuck in a groove, and the audience expressed its disgruntlement by walking out in numbers. The choreography turned to individual variations in canon, then to an allegro section, where it settled into the familiar spinning patterns. One couldn't just close one's eyes and spin in a "new sound world"; Dean's music for *Music* is as compulsive and lethargic as her dances. Fellow worshippers in the audience gave the company an ovation while those of us who'd stuck it out tiptoed up the aisle.

DeGroat began his performance series at the Midtown Y with a film of himself spinning with a rope; the film was projected as deGroat in person performed the same rope dance in the dark. Then several dancers did some low-grade ballet steps to a tape of Chopin. By the time the ensemble threw itself into a scrimmage of runs and lifts while a voice intoned and spelled out "Brick Brintzonhofe" over and over, we were well versed in deGroat-style mysterianism. It seems to take something from everybody; the aspect I am most uneasy about is its celebration of the work of Christopher Knowles, but I may be guilty of humanistic overreaction. Knowles is afflicted with brain damage; the things he does with typewriters and tape recorders (for example, the "Brick Brintzonhofe" spiel) also inspire Wilson, who considers him a poet. The way deGroat dances suggests that he may have adopted Knowles as an alter ego. DeGroat often looks uncoordinated and inarticulate, yet he also has assurance and control. The mixture of rough and smooth in his choreography seems to have been planned by a master. It's apathetic yet alert—heads-up ritualism. *Red Notes*, the work to the Glass score, is an anthology of influences. DeGroat in one way or another sums up the whole of the post-modern scene for which Glass and Wilson have acted as co-mentors, and throws in a few clues to *their* influences. Not that there are any surprises; instead of a Knowles text, *Red Notes* ("Read Notes") has one by Gertrude Stein, the patron saint of the avant-garde, and it includes the lines from *The Making of Americans* which could be the epigraph of post-modernism: "Slowly everything comes out from each one in the kind of repeating each one does . . . Slowly then the history of them comes out from them."

If Stein were talking about dancers and repertory, her meaning could not be clearer. My quarrel with post-modernism is not with repetition—it's with ritualistic repetition. Ritualistic repetition—ritualized ritual, in other words—makes repeating more important than "the history of them." It sentimentalizes the process of repetition by attributing to it more power than it possesses. "Natural movement" is enshrined, yet movements that are paltry and meager cannot make history no matter how many times they are done. When virtuosity is absent, personality counts for more than it perhaps should. The whole post-modern movement, from Yvonne Rainer onward, has been anti-personality, yet at this moment it is teetering on the brink of star worship. Childs and Glass are stars of increasing magnitude; Dean is amassing a cult. DeGroat's work, on the whole, has a force and variety that Dean's doesn't have, but it's also more ambivalent, heading toward then steering away from a broad-scale popular approach. The grossest appeal that the Glass kind of music can make is to the audience for head music. At its most coyly surrealistic, deGroat's choreography is head dance. In *Red Notes* there's the dissociative structure, the bits of sacerdotal imagery, and such light-show whammies as a giant shadow of a hand drawing arrows on a movie screen as the dancers beneath troop back and forth in lines. Above all, there's the pounding beat that binds one thing to another—that makes a monotonous, few-toned, desultory set of dances into a unified work of orgiastic vivacity.

Kathryn Posin's *Later That Day,* done for the Ailey company, is set to Glass music, but because it isn't inside the world of the music it manages to do more with it than the house choreographers so far have dreamed of doing. Where Childs and deGroat have used Glass as if his were the only kind of music there is, Posin catches up his peculiarities and accounts for them in her choreography. *Later That Day* doesn't resemble *Einstein on the Beach*; if it resembles anything, it's *Les Noces*. Dancers enter in a long line while a chorus repeatedly intones a five-note phrase. A couple (bride and groom?) crouches to one side on a platform. On the other side, Dudley Williams, in a three-piece suit, sits reading at a lectern or stands and waves his arms like a signalman. Preacher, guests, and bridal couple compose a triad; all are dressed by Christina Giannini in sleek playclothes of the 1920s. The guests pose and move in antiphonal harmony with the couple, like a Greek chorus. The action is entirely static, but at the end some new element has recharged the proportions of the triad. The element is time; Williams stands looking at his watch, amazed. As the response of a more conventional choreographer to the incitements of "new" music, *Later That Day* is highly suggestive. Without condescension or undue simplification, Posin manages to relate Glass to the world outside electronic circuitry and afflatus. She has found ritualistic images that match the sound, but she hasn't followed the sound to a land's-end depletion. And, by the looks of things, she has had an easier time of it than the post-moderns have had with their windy ongoing mystique.

Repetition is the sacred right of performing artists—actors, dancers, musicians. Performance art is a category in which nonperforming arts may be endowed with the repetitive, mutable aspects of music or dance. You have to see a successful performance artist like David Gordon to believe that it can work. Gordon's areas are dance, words, and sometimes photographs; that everything comes together on a high level of interest has to do not with the power of one or another medium, or even with their power in combination, but with the personalities of Gordon and his partner, Valda Setterfield. Their most recent concert, held in their loft, was a "performance collage," made up of previous works assembled in a new format and framing sections of new work. With Gordon the creative process is always retrospective. The evening was a pleasure both in its novelties and in its recapitulations, but I want to bring up instead two recent movie productions in which Gordon appears among his colleagues as post-modernism's most articulate spokesman. In both *Beyond the Mainstream* (in the PBS Dance in America series) and *Making Dances*, a documentary on seven post-modern choreographers by Michael Blackwood, the importance of personality in work of this kind is accidentally stressed. Although plain, small-scale post-modern movement is easier to convey on film than other kinds of dance, the experience of a performance is, if anything, harder; it may take a whole evening to build up. The camera can show neither transitions nor highlights comfortably, but it feeds on interviews. Here, and in the cinéma-vérité-style studio rehearsals, is where we form our impressions of the choreographers. Gordon rises to the top not only because the film medium magnifies his personality but because he is used to having his personality considered a major element in his work. The David Gordon who talks to the camera is the same David Gordon who appears as a character in David Gordon/Pick-Up Company presentations. To be sure, he usually appears at some point in the evening as a talking character, but curiously neither *Beyond the Mainstream* nor *Making Dances* captures that aspect of his performance. The chief interest, for me, of both these films was the bafflement they reflected. A lot of post-modernism is baffling to me, and I was looking to them for enlightenment. Instead, the burden of explanation was for the most part on the choreographers and what they could think of to *say*.

One of Gordon's provocative comments (in *Making Dances*) is an analogy with the movies. While moviegoers of the Joan Crawford generation now enjoy *Coming Home* and *Saturday Night Fever* even though the new movies are written, photographed, and cut in an entirely different fashion, "the way people approach dance is peculiarly conservative," he says. "I love *Sleeping Beauty*, too, but I don't have to see only it for the rest of my life." I see the point, but to me the style of dance that Gordon represents is more like television than like new feature films. Audiences have no trouble accepting new ballets, but not many people are willing to take the prosaic, uncultivated look of post-modern dance seriously. Fewer still are willing to relate the materials of this kind of dance to their sources in classic art. In his piece called *The Matter*, Gordon stages a parody of the Entrance of the Shades in *La Bayadère*. "I like it because it repeats itself many times," he says (in *Beyond the Mainstream*). "One ballerina enters, and then the next one enters, and then the next one enters, and it goes on forever. I mean, that ballet was made a very long time ago. And that audience is willing to sit in an opera house and watch forty-some-odd ballerinas come in one at a time, forever."

One reason may be that at the end of forever audiences know they're going to get a ballet. It's not just the glamour or the rhetorical style of ballet that accounts for the difference in acceptance. The diminished scale of modern and post-modern choreography—the fact that it can't project over opera-house distances—will always limit its appeal. This is why what Gordon calls "art disco"—amplified, big-beat walking music—is getting popular with dancers. It's fantasy-scale stuff, bigger in terms of time than any music, to compensate for dance that is smaller in terms of space than any dance. It goes on forever, and why not? Monotonous repetition, a feature of the folk art of all nations, has also been a factor in the popularity of art of all kinds, high and low. It's the "infinity factor" that keeps Ravel's *Bolero* on the Hit Parade, along with the Triumphal March from *Aida*, the first movement of the "Moonlight" Sonata (a particular favorite of Robert Wilson's), "Mack the Knife," and the Entrance of the Shades in *La Bayadère*. Mysterianism could produce the next masterpiece in kind.

—June 30, 1980

Heart of Darkness

Chivalrous, embattled, euphoric, distraught: the figure of Robert Schumann comes before us where we might least expect to encounter it—in a Balanchine ballet. Seen for the first time during the closing weeks of the season, the ballet is set to *Davidsbündlertänze* ("Dances of David's Band"), eighteen piano pieces in which Schumann's compound personality is characterized in musical dialogues of such quicksilver fascination that it or, rather, they call out to be presented in dance form. That no ballet has been successfully achieved before is probably owing to the problem of constructing a stage world for David's Band. This anti-Philistine league was composed of Schumann's multiple selves, to whom he gave fanciful names; it first appeared in his critical writings and it turned up as part of the supporting cast in *Carnaval*. But how much easier it must have been for Fokine to imagine dance roles for Florestan, Eusebius, and the other Davidites in his ballet *Carnaval* than for Balanchine to transcribe *Davidsbündlertänze*. In *Carnaval*, Schumann had established a theatrical setting of masks and guises. *Davidsbündlertänze* (a sequel, despite its earlier opus number) is introspective, its drama latent, its personae restricted to the dynamic Florestan and the contemplative Eusebius, who, as always, represent the two sides of the composer's nature. There is a clear musical kinship between *Carnaval* and *Davidsbündlertänze*, but it is not one that a choreographer may easily exploit. To put the difference in Schumannesque terms, *Carnaval* was written by Florestan and *Davidsbündlertänze* by Eusebius.

Of course, in the original manuscript the Davidite dances were ascribed to one or the other and sometimes to both. In the second edition of the score Schumann expunged all the bylines, together with most of the stage directions—such as "Here Florestan stopped and his lips trembled sorrowfully," before No. 9—and he even dropped the word "Dances" from the title. Between the first (1838) and the second (1850) edition, the major event that occurred in Schumann's life was his marriage to Clara Wieck. *Davidsbündlertänze* was written to her. Schumann noted in a letter, "My Clara will find out for me what is in the dances; they are more her own than anything else of mine." Clara could and did read Schumann's secret language; once they were married, he seemed content to let the music stand on its own.

Balanchine has obviously followed the second, "pure" edition. But he has also treated it as program music of the most personal kind. The ballet has four couples, all of whom portray aspects of Robert and Clara. At the same time, the dances can be seen simply as dances. There is no more mystery for the viewer to solve than there is in the music—music that, as Schumann hinted, even he found enigmatic. To Balanchine, the characters of Florestan and Eusebius are less important than the idea of duality which they represent. The ruling emotions of the ballet are neither-nor: happy-sad, light-dark, hot-cold. This is not un-usual for a Balanchine ballet. However, in its quality of expression the ballet *is* unusual. Continually and confound-ingly, it is forthright and evasive at the same time. The double or duplicit meanings in the dances aren't in any troublesome recondite allusions—they spring from the ma-nia of Romanticism to encompass all the feelings of life in one music. Schumann relished his mania. "If ever I was happy at the piano," he said of *Davidsbündlertänze*, "it was when I was composing these." But at the head of the origi-nal edition he placed a German proverb on the eternal link between *Lust* and *Leid*—pleasure and sorrow.

What strikes most people about the new ballet (to which no name has been given—it is listed in the program as *Robert Schumann's "Davidsbündlertänze"*) is Balanchine's use of a demonstratively dramatic style of choreography. Ru-mor had predicted another *Liebeslieder Walzer*, the beloved Brahms ballet that is no longer done in New York, but in-stead the dances are in a style similar to that of *Meditation* and parts of *Don Quixote*. While the format of the piece fol-lows *Liebeslieder* to a certain extent—the four couples danc-ing a succession of duets to an onstage piano, the women changing from pumps to toe shoes in the course of the dances—the choreography seems to take Schumann's dele-tion of the word "Dances" as its cue. There are scarcely any dance steps in the *Liebeslieder* mold, and the choreography makes no distinction, as *Liebeslieder* did, between social dancing and ballet. Compared to almost any other piece of Balanchine choreography, even compared to *Meditation*, the ballet has almost no intricacy or sweep of phrase. Instead, we see dancing used as an extension of a dramatic situation: steps are repeated over and over or protracted into poses or connected not by other steps but by walks, runs, hesitant

gestures, glances. The lack of density and the free look of
the timing make us feel we're witnessing a series of short,
probing conversations. And along about the fifth or sixth
dance (when pointe shoes are adopted), the dancers begin
to develop the psychological dimensions of real characters.
The four couples are divided into two pairs of "twins." The
more prominent pair—Suzanne Farrell and Jacques d'Amboise, Karin von Aroldingen and Adam Lüders—perhaps
represents Clara and Robert as they were in art and as they
were in life. Farrell is Clara the artist and also Robert's
(d'Amboise's) muse; von Aroldingen is Clara the bride and
wife, while Lüders, who has the most colorful male role, is
Robert the victim of hallucination and derangement—the
mad poet who died before his time. Heather Watts and
Peter Martins are paired with Kay Mazzo and Ib Andersen
as identical twins who may possibly be Clara and Robert as
lovers; twice all four appear in mirror-image dances. If
d'Amboise and Lüders are Florestan and Eusebius as posi-
tive and negative forces in Schumann's nature, Martins and
Andersen are those forces in balance, symmetrically justified
by Schumann's union with the perfect woman.

There are three solos. The first and most eccentric is Farrell's, to No. 12. Schumann marked it "mit Humor"—but
there are other humorous or good-humored dances in the
suite. What distinguish Farrell's are, first, its direct, unclouded emotion—it's the only "warm" dance that doesn't
contain some icy portent, some hint of its own undoing, either choreographically or musically—and, second, its connection to *Apollo*: the dancer ends poised in attitude with
one finger pointing ahead—the gesture of the Muses and of
Dulcinea and of the Fairy in *Le Baiser de la Fée*. The solos for
von Aroldingen and Lüders both belong to the "biography"
of the historical Schumann. Clara searches and weeps,

Robert struggles with his devils and throws himself into the
Rhine. In Lüders's solo, No. 15, we are again reminded
of *Carnaval*—the "Chopin" episode. Schumann had been
ridiculed for his impetuous review introducing Chopin to
German music-lovers: "Hats off, gentlemen, a genius!"
Against the forces of smug reaction David's Band took up
arms. In Balanchine's staging, the Philistines make a brief
appearance as static figures in black carrying their giant poi-
son pens. Perhaps this is one Schumannesque figment that
we don't need to be shown, but visually the inky silhouettes
do suggest something of the fantasy of Schumann's polemical style and the influence upon it and upon his music of
such writers as Jean Paul (Richter), E.T.A. Hoffmann, and
Heinrich Heine.

Lüders's off-balance wheeling pivots, runs to and fro,
and tight turns on a diagonal are the bombastic high point
of the ballet, and the emotional climax has yet to arrive. But
first there is a sudden switch in tone and all four couples are
dancing a quadrille. As in an earlier "party" scene (No. 13),
only more formally pressed, the suggestion is of a moment
of grace outside the tensions of private life. When all partners have been exchanged and returned to their places, a recapitulation begins, and as the music gets slower and grows
more hushed, the stage is gradually cleared. During this recapitulation, which signals the start of the ballet's long descent to its pianissimo close, the audience gets restless; there
have been too many radical transitions and we still haven't
reached the ballet's heart. It is at this moment that Balanchine steers straight for troubled waters—those indecisive
harmonies and lingering suspensions in the music. Into the
vacancy drops the wandering melody of No. 2—the most
haunting melody in the score. Farrell and d'Amboise
are alone; her off-center half-turns en promenade recall

Lüders's anguished pivots, and as they continue we know we're wandering far off course. Is nothing going to happen? Well, there is an acceleration, a rush, a sudden pause capped by a lovely slow-motion exit, but even as you watch, it seems inconclusive. The last dance is Lüders's farewell to von Aroldingen on a darkened stage; it's like the end of *Duo Concertant*—as inscrutable as that. The piece is not a hit; it doesn't want to be. It mirrors the passion of Robert Schumann, his intransigent daemon, his lust for the unknown. Like his music, it wears its heart on its sleeve even when there's no arm inside.

—July 14, 1980

Sub-Balanchine

Although it wasn't until 1940 that Balanchine started making his all-dance ballets in pure classical style, he is generally credited with fathering the dominant modern movement in choreography. The so-called abstract ballet had in fact been established by Massine and Nijinska, but *Les Présages*, *Choreartium*, *Rouge et Noir*, and *Chopin Concerto* haven't survived, and for all practical purposes it is to Balanchine that we look to make and break the rules of the genre. Most choreographers under Balanchine's influence, which is now global, don't respond to music sensitively enough to make absolute lyrical expression a real possibility for twenty or thirty minutes at a stretch. And this is only the first requirement.

Choo San Goh is the prolific young maestro of a sub-Balanchine type of plotless ballet; he's *so* prolific that his influence is rapidly getting to be global, too. But if Choo San Goh's product resembles Balanchine's it is only in negative particulars: no story, no props, no scenery, neutral costumes. Goh's titles usually refer to the music or to some aspect of Goh's methodology or technique: *Casella 1, 3, 4*, *Double Contrast*, *Fives*, *Momentum*. As it happens, his latest piece is called *Helena*; of course, there is no Helena in the ballet. I took this to be a comment on ballets named *Paquita* or *Sylvia* in which no Paquita or Sylvia appears, modern audiences having long since lost the taste for the narratives that held up those nineteenth-century shows of dancing. But stripping away excess does not guarantee purity. After seeing six or eight of Goh's works in various repertories, I'm persuaded that Goh hears music not as an aural landscape but as a permissive sound track with cues for changes in the action. He responds not to shape, structure, or sound but to volume, texture, and mood, and he doesn't make dynamic qualitative changes in the action, he simply switches gears. Goh appears to have thought out his ballets beforehand and to be using the music only to tell him when to go with this or that effect and when to stop. If a score's divisions don't accommodate his plan, he overrides them. In *Double Contrasts*, which has Poulenc's Double Piano Concerto playing in the background, the choreography several times ignored the play between the orchestra and the solo instruments. And Goh's choreography frequently ignores things like climaxes and diminuendos; it has its own highs and lows. Yet it's so exactly fitted to the bar lengths that it *seems* musical. And because it's independently driven it seems to be making a poetic statement—to be fulfilling the second of the requirements for absolute lyrical expression, Balanchine style.

Goh was born in Singapore and had his dance training in Europe. As assistant artistic director of the Washington Ballet, in Washington, D.C., he has since 1978 become the hottest young choreographer on the American scene. The Washington Ballet played Brooklyn College recently, bringing three of his works. The dancers were not very strong technically, but Goh's choreography made them look strong, sleek, capable. With dancers happy, audiences thrilled, and managers satisfied, why should anyone care that none of it has a thing to do with dancing? We've reached a new point in the history of modern abstract ballet—a point of near-computerization where coded options make choreography. Next to Goh's smooth calibrations, ordinary bad choreography looks paleolithic. Bad choreography usually has some personality. Goh's has none. What it does have is cachet—the equivalent of a designer label.

—*December 1, 1980*

Mythology

The revised, enlarged edition of *Orpheus* at the New York City Ballet works surprisingly well. There have been no extensive changes in choreography—only the Furies scene is new—but the piece looks different from the revival that was mounted two years ago for Baryshnikov. It looks different from the way *Orpheus* has ever looked. Peter Martins is Orpheus, and with a commensurately tall and blond Karin von Aroldingen and Adam Lüders as Eurydice and the Angel, the ballet is persuasive in a whole new set of terms. The enlarging process began with Isamu Noguchi's scenery in 1972, when the ballet was restaged for the Stravinsky Festival. The new dimensions and the use of coarser materials thickened the atmosphere. The current Viking cast breathes this air comfortably. Even the Bacchantes seem to be Valkyries who have stormed down the Thracian peninsula from the Rhine. Balanchine has prolonged the life of a ballet once presumed lost by giving a new life to its characters. In the old, small-scale *Orpheus*, first produced in 1948 at the City Center, Nicholas Magallanes was the poet, frail and limp, with a muscular, barrel-chested Angel (Francisco

Moncion) to support and guide him on his way to the Underworld. Martins is a physically powerful Orpheus whose passive grieving is all the more moving because it seems unnatural to him. And his Angel, Lüders, is a spidery androgynous intellectual.

Lüders's vigilance and delicacy are different from Moncion's massive calm; the quality of tenderness in the Angel's support of Orpheus is different, too. Moncion's quality was animal warmth; Lüders's is pure intelligence—it doesn't get mixed up with sympathy. Lüders is extraterrestrial austere. The "Greek" austerity, the Mediterranean tinge of religious ritual, is missing from this revival, and it's largely because of the way he looks and moves. In addition to the thick ropes wound around his limbs and torso (which Orpheus now also wears—formerly, he wore a few flat strips), the Angel has on a black skintight helmet with an elephant trunk hanging down the middle of his face. The design is an extension of the black rope that bisects him from cranium to crotch when he first appears. Orpheus' mask reminded Stravinsky of a baseball catcher's. Lüders's headgear makes us think of a spaceman, a scuba diver, or an anesthetist, and it keeps his bisected or dual nature constantly before us. When he lunges close to the ground or braces the body of Orpheus, his long legs are like grappling hooks; the men are two mountain climbers yoked together, first with that black rope or air hose, then with Orpheus' lyre, slung between them.

Martins has never been as quiet and slack and listless as he is in the first half of *Orpheus*, yet he's rhythmically charged. The nondance character of the role is not a negation of his dance energy; neither was the nondance role of Junker Ove in *A Folk Tale*, which Martins performed recently with the Royal Danish Ballet. His Orpheus, like

Baryshnikov's (once he got the hang of the part), comes out of the operatic-mime tradition. The role as originally conceived seems to have come more from the modern dance. Balanchine and Lincoln Kirstein had the year before sponsored the première of Merce Cunningham's *The Seasons*, which had décor by Noguchi. Not that there's necessarily a connection; however, the larval passivity of Orpheus is unlike anything a ballet dancer is trained to express. The reconstituted "classical" Orpheus has been achieved without changing a step.

The Furies, though, have always had weak choreography. Noguchi designed them with quills sprouting all over, like porcupines. Stravinsky set them quivering in perpetual agitato. Balanchine arranged a rhythm chorus of high kicks in relevé and pumping elbows. If Noguchi had not done the décor, the only conceivable visual style would have been seventeenth-century Renaissance, in keeping with the Monteverdian roots of Stravinsky's score. Shallow grotesquerie would have been appropriate if Hades had been a Renaissance court; demons in doublets and allegorical masks were a constant feature of the seventeenth-century *ballet à grand spectacle*. Balanchine's Hades is Halloween. The new staging, by Peter Martins, eliminates a lot of the jollity, expands the corps of Furies, and puts it more aggressively to work on the Lost Souls, who cower beneath their rocks or out in the open, making little mounds to be jumped over. The head Fury, with his egregious split jumps, has been deleted. Now it is Pluto who joins the hands of Orpheus and Eurydice. But the Pas des Furies is still a lightweight affair, irretrievably athletic. It's a relief when the scampering feet are stilled and Pluto, affected by Orpheus' song, wheels slowly to reveal the captive Eurydice pinned to his back.

Eurydice's solo, with its leggy contrapposto, its hesitations, its anguish, its fleeting Arcadian moods, is one of the sweetest Balanchine has made; it ranks with—and gesturally resembles—Calliope's solo in *Apollo*. Karin von Aroldingen dances it about as well as she dances Calliope badly. Eurydice's earthiness and womanliness bring out her best qualities. Von Aroldingen is wrong for the sprite Calliope; her forte is gravity, and in recent seasons she has come to symbolize a kind of humanity I don't recall seeing in any other Balanchine ballerina. Von Aroldingen's triumph as Eurydice came just before her Clara Schumann in *Davids-bündlertänze*. She is Clara the faithful, Clara the wife. Like Eurydice, she is at the center of her husband's affections, but is she at the center of his art—his obsessed mind? That is the question. It is the answer to this question which, in Balanchine's interpretation of the Orpheus myth, brings on the poet's tragedy. In von Aroldingen's interpretation, it's the mere wifeliness of her presence. She isn't imperious or devouring, as other Eurydices have been; she's so modest that her demands on Orpheus as they journey home come to seem something he can easily satisfy without tempting fate. After all, she only wants him to recognize her, his wife—how can he deny her this? Her sensuality has about it a submissiveness so trusting that we feel Orpheus is driven to rip off his mask as much by pity as by physical craving. She doesn't ask much, yet the little she does ask kills her. The death shroud swallows her up.

The Orpheus-Eurydice pas de deux before the shimmering silk curtain is justly celebrated. She follows in his footsteps (his arabesque, then hers, a beat behind), coils herself about him, whispers seductively in his ear, recalling their past life. With his eyes averted, they dance one of their little dances—a 1948-style Lindy. (In *L'Après-midi d'un Faune*, the Faun and the Nymph do a 1912-style tango.) She dies as in the myth, before the upper world is reached. Orpheus wanders in Limbo. He's lost his lyre—lost all his secrets. The sky turns red, foretelling his own bloody death. The Bacchantes appear: one, then several; then he's surrounded. Hanging on to his mask for protection, he tries to evade the swarm. The scene must be carefully done to avoid seeming like touch football. This season, it looked reblocked. The Bacchantes, led by Florence Fitzgerald, killed with stiletto precision. The blondly radiant Sean Lavery or the darkly soulful Victor Castelli made a good Apollo, though the Apotheosis has lost a lot of its mystery.

—December 15, 1980

Harlem's Fokine

Fokine's *Schéhérazade* is not about the Sultan's faithless wife who told stories for a thousand and one nights to stave off a death sentence. It isn't about one of her stories. Nor has it anything to do with the titles for the parts of Rimsky-Korsakov's tone poem—"Sinbad's Ship," "Festival in Baghdad," etc.—that provide the score. The faithless wife in the ballet, Zobeide, wriggles impatiently while her husband prepares to go hunting. The minute he's out of sight, Zobeide and the rest of the harem ladies bribe the Chief Eunuch to release the slaves. A door opens and out slithers a flock of glistening young men in harem pants and jeweled shackles. Another door opens: more slitherers. A third door opens and out pops Nijinsky. What happens next brought on fevers in Parisian audiences seventy years ago—so all the books say. In no time the Shah returns, scimitars flash, and the orgy becomes a massacre out of Delacroix. Zobeide's favorite slave, cut down in midair, falls headlong and thrashes the floor, Cocteau wrote, "like a fish on the bottom of a boat." (His leap, equally spectacular and very dangerous, from a platform ten feet high, is something of which history has not told.) This convulsive molto agitato death is followed by a droopy legato one: Zobeide, resisting the Shah's henchmen, plunges a dagger between her breasts as the curtain falls.

The books don't say when the thrill of *Schéhérazade* stopped rolling through audiences. By the middle of the thirties, the ballet had become an object of parody (by Balanchine, in the musical *On Your Toes*). But the Ballet Russe de Monte Carlo touring production of the forties was popular with American audiences. Frederic Franklin, who was the Golden Slave to Danilova's Zobeide in those days, has now revived the ballet for Dance Theatre of Harlem on the very stage, at the City Center, where the Monte Carlo used to dance it. A theory worth testing holds that no ballet revival goes back more than forty years in authenticity. Visually, this seems to be true of the new production. The Bakst scenery that stunned Paris looks all too Maria Montez. The colors seem to have burned out—the fabled greens and blues have an ashy tone. The dancers have been fitted with a new set of sherbet-colored costumes designed by Carl Michell. Their freshness is preferable to 1981 Bakst knockdowns, but a still better option would have been the commissioning of an original production retaining only the Fokine choreography, which turns out to be much stronger than its reputation would allow.

A program note by Karel Shook, co-director of DTH, rejects the idea of new choreography that "might possibly appeal more to the tastes and sensibilities of the current public than the original"—rejects it on the ground that "only a master of master choreographers could accomplish anything which would come close to Fokine." He's right. The movement is part of the music and part of the style of its era, which Shook identifies as Art Nouveau. And it is deliberately designed movement, not the programmed spontaneity that one reads of. The annals of *Schéhérazade* ripple with wavelets of the ballet's own abandon and give the impression that much of it was formless pantomime, and much of *that* improvised. But the way the orgy scene breaks out, drowses, revives, relapses, breaks out once again, and stops dead on the peak of a crescendo when the Shah's men return is dance construction in the grand manner. The dead stop freezes the stage picture as Rimsky's sea music goes on heaving. Then the picture cracks, and the climax passes over into the slaughter. The ensembles could be diagrammed with absolute mathematical precision. The Golden Slave leaps over and over on one spot in one wide rhythm while the company whirls around him in another. The orgy duets wend their way on a downstage diagonal; when the slaughter commences, everyone rushes in waves on an upstage one—rushes out, then back in, falling down and getting up, flooding the stage and damming it. The stylized sexiness of the dancing is of course ludicrous—the skipping in crouches, the continuously weaving backbends. And there are sets of people, as in *Firebird*, who do one little step—like prancing with stiff vertical arms and horizontal palms. One hardly knows which is more amusing, the decorousness or the commotion. But though the style of the choreography tends more toward perfected show dancing than toward classicism, one knows its maker for the polyrhythmic, architectonic Fokine of *Les Sylphides*.

The most one asks of a revival, especially one coming seventy years after a sensational premiére, is that it not embarrass history too much and that it furnish a few particulars of the sort that eyewitnesses always seem to leave out. Even Fokine, in *Memoirs of a Ballet Master*, when he describes Ida Rubinstein's Zobeide as she stood waiting for her lover's entrance, says only that "she waits for him with her entire body." Virginia Johnson, the DTH Zobeide, gives us the exact stance: legs braced in deep fondu, body arched backward in a swoon of anticipation. The moment doesn't slip by. We see what Fokine meant, even though the psychology of 1910 doesn't permit us to feel it. Although he's more Douglas Fairbanks than Nijinsky, Eddie Shellman's Golden Slave also satisfies our expectations. But any revival, no matter how bad, would give us enough information to color the blanks in our mental picture of the ballet. The value of the DTH *Schéhérazade* to me is that it colors blanks I didn't know were there. I don't see a company straining to interpret ancient psychology and dead aesthetics; I do see dancers performing with unaffected good sense and making the most of Fokine's gift whenever it accords with their own. The dance core of *Schéhérazade* is a discovery few companies could make.

—January 26, 1981

Think Punk

It is seldom that a young choreographer makes a début doing a new thing that is exactly the right thing. Karole Armitage's début, two years ago, was so startlingly new and so right—for her, for her dancers, for dance—that one drew back cautiously, wondering whether one had seen a real début or a fluke. Armitage has gone on working, giving concerts in the usual downtown places (the City Art Gallery, The Kitchen, the Dance Theater Workshop) as well as in the less usual ones, and though some of her experiments have been inscrutable, all of them have been marked by an underlying consistency, a clear sense of pattern and direction, and a flair for discovery. These are qualities that were embryonically present in her first piece. What that event is remembered for, though, is its audacity in bringing concert dance together with punk-rock music. It took place in a high-school gym on West Sixteenth Street—an enormous, brightly lit space with a platform at one end, where the band (called the The) was stationed. The gym stayed brightly lit from start to finish of the performance; apart from some neon tubes strewn around the place, no attempt was made at stage lighting or décor. The dancers came through a door at the far end of the gym and gradually made their way toward the audience, which was seated at the other end. Their movements were almost all violent, flung-out, harsh, and all on the largest possible scale—that is, on the borderline of distortion. The figures didn't appear swollen with excess and the movement wasn't hysterically jammed; it was limpid even at flailing speeds and with magnum-force attack. With minor diversions, the choreography kept to its main path across the floor, and the steady oncoming diagonal course toward the audience was like a slow crescendo. As they came toward you, the dancers—there were only three of them, including Armitage—seemed to accumulate the power of a mass image, almost a monstrous one. The band, firing intermittent blasts without warning, acted as an additional magnifier. Some punk rock, I take it, does cross the border into distortion; at the volume the The played, sounds appeared within sound, echoing the light-on-light of the neon tubes. And, to round out the reverberant picture, the dancers were dressed in some sort of punk-chic scroungewear made of pilled-out synthetic fur in Day-Glo colors. How it ended I don't recall; I think the dancers just found another door close by the audience. I do remember that at the end of the concert the band played encores for anyone who cared to get up and dance. Most of the audience had just enough inner-ear coordination left to get home.

Karole Armitage is one of Merce Cunningham's dancers, and one of the best he has ever had. Before joining the Cunningham company, she danced in Europe with the Grand Théâtre de Genève, which has a Balanchine repertory. She seems to me just now the only dancer besides Balanchine's own Suzanne Farrell who is capable of prodigious bodily feats of scale and balance, although even in these admirable extremes she doesn't resemble Farrell so much as she resembles a former Cunningham dancer, Viola Farber. As choreographers, Armitage and Farber are alike in their fascination with violence, but Armitage isn't uncontrollably fascinated, as Farber sometimes has been. Armitage's control of her theme, like her personal control of her technique, has the power of drawing audiences in. I care for nothing I know about punk rock and its world, yet I'm absorbed and persuaded by an Armitage concert; I find reality in the ugliness and the terrorism, and beauty in their conversion to raw expression. The need of dancers of Armitage's generation to be raw in just this way is a subject that can be debated. Armitage has never struck me as a dilettante. To me, she's applying Cunningham's aesthetic to conditions as she finds them, making a connection to the outside world, making order out of chaos.

Armitage may also be the only one of the latest post-Cunningham generation of choreographers who's as self-aware as Cunningham is. Not only self-aware as a soloist, with certain specialties, but also self-aware as a classicist with a commitment to classicism's physical integrity of expression. Armitage keeps testing that integrity by mocking it—reducing its means, abrading its textures, pitting it against grinding distractions, placing it in faddish, conceivably unwholesome contexts. Her most recent evening, held at the Dance Theater Workshop, was called *Drastic Classicism*. It was every bit of that: classicism in hellish straits, handed over to the dark powers. Yet it transcended its own wildness to become a vindication of formal values in dancing. And it did so not eventually, as the evening ripened, but immediately, the minute Armitage and Chris Komar along with four other Cunningham-descended dancers swung into action in a room pulsing with the roar of four guitars and a set of drums. The key to Armitage's success is surely her understanding of her own power as a dancer and her ability to use other dancers with the same understanding. Komar, a brilliant dancer who normally looks pent up even in Cunningham pieces, was released here. Michael Bloom, who has performed here and there but is scarcely a professional dancer (in Armitage pieces he always keeps his glasses on), also gave a perfect performance in his own range. The two parts of the evening, divided by an intermission, were basically the same set of intensive inventions for dancers, with a volatile scenario allowing for costume and makeup changes, exits and entrances. At one point in the second part, children entered and took flash pictures of the dancing. Armitage began the evening in white tights with a sawed-off black tank top and ended it in a blue tulle tutu over baggy pants, looking like two Toulouse-Lautrec clowns put together. The dancewear of the studio and the punk-style street costumes were jaggedly intercut, as if both styles were masquerades and one could plausibly begin where the other left off. Dancing and punk behavior collaborated; dancers and musicians intermingled, sharing the stage, everybody dressing up funny, with painted faces. Dancers braced themselves against guitarists for their high battements or picked up guitars themselves. Where there was proper choreography, it looked like stringent classwork, taking up one obsession after another: staccato phrases, legato phrases, staccato/legato attacks on no phrase whatsoever. All this to a perfectly vicious din. (NO PHRASE, I wrote in my notebook as the walls shook.)

In its overall effect, *Drastic Classicism* was an extension and a refinement of the gym event of 1979, a retrieval of classical dance values from their irrelevant mold of decorum. Decorous music, decorous costumes, decorous body positions and steps were thrown out, together with the notion that all these should be decorously related. Relations were expressed (as in the best of Cunningham) but not decorously. Each separate element—the visual design (by Charles Atlas), the music (lead guitar: Rhys Chatham), and the choreography—advanced similar notions at different times or different notions at the same time of what the other elements were up to; one felt the force of a controlling idea without being able to say precisely what it was. And beyond this Cunningham-style presentation lay something that we could identify as Armitage's own discovery— the annihilative fury of rock music as a scourge analogous to the flaying of the systematic and the habitual in the dance. The horrific sound of the electric band was void of musical content; no melody, no apparent harmony (though the guitars were carefully tuned), not even, at times, a beat—just amplified chordal strumming. Just as sound opened within sound and tones braided with overtones, the dancing risked organic destruction to promote organic regrowth; it had its own qualities of fission and density.

And play. I don't for a minute believe in the punk image of Karole Armitage; I do believe in her appropriation of it as a guise and an occasion of fun, much as I believe in Balanchine's appropriation of "Gypsy" character work for Farrell. Armitage's punk dandyism is her means of expression.

—*March 9, 1981*

A New Old *Giselle*

Somebody else's version of an old folktale is never as magical as the one we grew up with. Though the meaning is the same, the details are different, and it's the details that capture the imagination and bring the meaning alive. One of Mikhail Baryshnikov's first acts on taking over the direction of American Ballet Theatre was to throw out the company's production of *Giselle* and substitute a close approximation of the version he used to perform in Russia with the Kirov Ballet. This wasn't *Giselle* restudied—it was a simple exchange of one set of details for another. The Kirov's *Giselle* traces itself back to Petipa, and Baryshnikov believes devoutly in its authenticity, but it turns out to have less edge to it than ABT's late-1960s model; it looks scrappy, capricious, reduced. Because no great amount of thought lies behind it—nothing much lies behind it but taste—there's not a great deal one can argue with. It's a case of My *Giselle* against Yours.

ABT's production, by David Blair, introduced a sympathetic Hilarion, brought on the Peasant Pas de Deux (then a novelty for ABT) at an opportune moment, and in other ways extended and sharpened the dramatic logic of the first act. All this took time, and much of it was waste motion. The whole purpose of Act I, as its authors realized, is to set up Act II. Baryshnikov's speed, though, is the speed of impatience, not of economy. To say that Act I sets up Act II is not to say that the plot doesn't bear telling. In Baryshnikov's treatment, the ballet opens in the manner of the Kirov and the Bolshoi productions: Albrecht and Wilfrid run on and hide, followed by Hilarion, who runs on and hides. In the first minute, three men have entered who look alike and act alike. In a play, this would be excusable; in a ballet, it's a minute wasted. There are more absurdities in the staging. Hilarion should not have to enter Albrecht's cottage by the window when the door is unlocked. Immediately after Bathilde and Courland go into Giselle's cottage to get some rest, the villagers, with their wine festival, set up a racket right outside the door. This is probably unavoidable; it happens in every *Giselle* I have ever seen. We accept it, just as we accept the improbability of a royal hunting party putting up in a hut.

The Mad Scene is an extended absurdity that an incurable cultish sentimentality has elevated to the status of a touchstone. Unlike the operatic Mad Scenes on which it is modeled, it is a descent into naturalistic bathos. (No one would think of performing it out of context.) Yet it has no psychological depth. The ballerina is confronted with a stark contrivance, and we watch to see how she will bring it off. Théophile Gautier conceived the ballet *Giselle* after reading about the Wilis in Heine's *De l'Allemagne*, but he left the writing of Act I to a skilled librettist, Vernoy de Saint-Georges, whom he afterward commended for bringing about "the pretty death we needed." Dying prettily yet persuasively exercises a ballerina's tact rather than her art.

Baryshnikov prefers the Russian staging of the scene where Albrecht first sees the specter of Giselle, then kneels and prays for it to return. I like it, too—much better than the flitty comings and goings of the previous version (and Albrecht's "tawt I taw a putty tat" reactions). The atmospherics, though, are really shabby: for *feux follets* two stage-hands shake clusters of lights from the wings. Although there weren't enough Wilis on the stage (there never have been, at ABT), they danced better than I had ever seen them dance. This is a Baryshnikov triumph not to be underestimated. But he has chosen to incorporate it in this home-style production which does little to advance our understanding of the ballet and in some respects even retards it. Is Baryshnikov getting ready for a new look at *Giselle*—a possible break with tradition? He gives no hint of an original perspective here. And when we look up his thoughts in his book *Baryshnikov at Work*, we find such discouraging assertions as "The dramatic material of *Giselle*, Act II, is not rich in substance, but with careful preparation and thought it can be meaningful." This is certainly in line with Baryshnikov's own performance in this act, which is unsurpassed but is overwhelmingly a dance performance; one would call it rich in passion but not in drama. He sees the second-act drama in simplistic terms: "Albrecht fights to hold on to Giselle and fights to live." It is the Russian view, the view that has prevailed in the West ever since the initial tours of the Kirov and the Bolshoi showed us their monumentally pure second acts, heavily contrasted with the verismo of Act I. With Rudolf Nureyev's performances and then with Natalia Makarova's, the dramatic web of the second act was reduced to a single thread—the bond of love between Giselle and Albrecht—and the only suspense lay in whether the Wilis would get Albrecht before dawn. That's the way it is in Baryshnikov's current production; the bond between the lovers is even stronger, because there's less of Myrtha to make demands upon it.

The deterioration of *Giselle* as a dance drama is reflected in the demotion of Myrtha from a ballerina's role to a soloist's. It has been a gradual process, down and down over the years. Now Baryshnikov excludes her from the Wilis' adagio. Her entrance is limited to a single diagonal of bourrées to a downstage exit, after which she reappears almost immediately from the same downstage wing and begins the solo with the myrtle scepters. Myrtha's stage-skimming crosses, her re-entries at unexpected points, the weighty incantation of her dance along the ground were all intended to describe her authority in that space, on that spot of earth, and under it. These are graves on which she dances, and they are, as we see in a moment, the graves of dancers. Myrtha prepares the drama. Anyone who has not experienced the thoroughness of her preparation has not felt the icy breath of *Giselle*. None of the three Myrthas I saw this season did more than warm up the house for the stars. None gave clear directions to the lovers beyond a peremptory "Dance!" or "Continue!" Without Myrtha's influence on the course of action, the action doesn't make sense. Who would know from watching the ballet that Giselle's dances as Albrecht stands by the cross are dances of seduction—that as an instrument of the Queen's will she's trying to lure him out of his sanctuary? Who would even guess there could be a motive behind the solo adagio with which she opens her dance? Much less the duplicitous motive we find in Gautier's description of how Giselle "sought to disguise her powers of attraction, and merely made a faint and languid pretense of dancing, fearful of beguiling her lover from his post." But dancing was ever Giselle's temptation, and so she passed from adagio to allegro:

> The inexorable Myrtha compelled the shrinking Giselle to
> dance with greater energy and animation; and, obeying
> the mandate, she gave herself up to the full delight of the
> moment,—flying, bounding, floating, as it were, upon
> mid air; while her lover, forgetting the certain destruction
> that awaited him, flew to her side, took part in her dances,
> her attitudes, deeming himself but too happy to die for
> one so dear.

Gautier's account, one of the essays in *Les Beautés de l'Opéra*,
was written after the ballet had become a hit. If it sounds
like the fond author supplying ingenious motives after the
fact, how much closer we come, through Gautier's words,
to the intention of the ballet d'action than we ever do in a
performance. Surely, if the role of Giselle is what its devotees claim—the supreme test of the actress-dancer—that test
comes in the second act, when the ballerina must act
through her dancing. And which would we rather see her
aim for—the outer limits of virtuosity, as defined by Gautier, or the undemanding generalizations of Ballet Theatre's
synopsis: "Giselle resolves to protect him. She dances with
him until the clock strikes four, at which hour the Wilis lose
their power"? We don't see much more than this in what
happens on the stage. We even see contradictions. When he
walks her lightly over the ground in a series of supported
temps levés en arabesque, it isn't clear that she's covering for
his exhaustion; it looks more the other way around. The
conception of *Giselle* as a dance drama is badly served
by presenting the eventful second act as a ballet blanc
surrounded by a plot. The Wilis, deprived of their bridal
wreaths and veils, wearing their new long bell-shaped
gowns, could be the corps de ballet of *Serenade*. Isn't it a bit
late in the day to be streamlining the classics? The old Kirov
prejudices that this production reflects are as insupportable

as the underlying assumption of the Blair version that Act I is fascinating.

Inspired Giselles are possible even within the vaporish terms of the role. I saw none this time. Cynthia Gregory contributed an effectively wrought Mad Scene, and she has at last stopped trying to look petite and fey. But though she danced up to scale, she still kept the dynamic range short; an impression of bubble-lightness set in and never varied. Magali Messac has inherited Gregory's tall-girl jitters. She shrank her dancing, erased the bracing line of her shoulders, and out of numerous droopy arabesques extended doggy paws of devotion. I left thinking Giselle just wasn't her role (whereas, with decent choreography, she'd be a marvelous Myrtha). But Messac is an uncommonly fine dancer and an intelligent actress, and I've loved her in all her roles this season, even *Theme and Variations*, to which she really is unsuited. She ought to be encouraged to try Giselle again without corrupting her style. Dancers often confuse correct style with conformity to a physical type. A film of Spessivtseva (whose type is closer to Messac's than, say, Makarova's is) shows her to have been a forthright Giselle, with big legs and a fat braid hanging down her back. Gelsey Kirkland, though heavy and off form, is still the perfect waiflike Giselle, and she is still capable of giving a transporting performance. On this occasion, she performed better than she danced, and she trouped better than she performed, and at every stage Baryshnikov was there to match her. When, toward the end of the second act, her strength began to give out, he doubled his; he flew, he bounded, he soared through Gautier's catalogue, and the roles of the two principals were for once consciously reversed.

—May 18, 1981

Son of Pilobolus

I get lost in the imagery of Crowsnest, sometimes pleasurably, sometimes blankly. Crowsnest, which consists of Martha Clarke, Felix Blaska, and Robby Barnett, has been in existence for two years, but it just made its début in New York. I got seated late at the Public Theater, and the show began before I'd had a chance to look at the program. It didn't matter; in a few seconds I recognized the place, and I was held by it for some time before the drifting and dreaming set in and the spell broke. The three were onstage when the curtain went up. Some jazz started playing, and they began walking fast in circles, first alone, then together, then alone again. Clarke wore a short black velvet dress with her hair frizzed, Barnett was in tails, and Blaska, with a goatee, had on a black raincoat. They wore blue shoes and walked against a painted backcloth by Robert Andrew Parker—a composition in misty blue and gray blocks that suggested a city. It was a rich, full illusion: New York or Paris on a sodden spring night, back streets filling with the smoky sound of the old Duke Ellington band and with the scent of danger. (The piece is called *Don't Mean a Thing*, after the

Ellington tune.) There's a certain inevitability in what happens: Clarke seems to be a prostitute, and she has some rough encounters with the two men; Blaska is a flasher. But one is absorbed by the larger spectacle of people living intensely in their own worlds. Barnett, who is elegantly drunk, contrives to suggest that he has slept in his suit of tails but not rented it. Crowsnest is the offspring of Pilobolus Dance Theatre; although there's less emphasis on acrobatics, the mime is still dazzlingly, physically brazen and almost completely abstract. The sense of persons and places comes about through vibration, through resonant gesture. When a concrete idea arises—from, say, Clarke's getting too roughly handled and landing on the floor like a rag doll with her legs spread—I could wish it were less banal. Then, too, the physicality limits expression. It can be a happy limitation, as when Barnett and Blaska go careering around the stage side by side as if Blaska were riding in Barnett's sidecar. But there is also a tendency to trust blindly in the truth of appearances, to go on joining bodies, to mistake friction for vibration.

Crowsnest is not your average mime troupe. Clarke and Barnett, along with the rest of Pilobolus, practically invented free-association abstract mime, and they're aware of the dangers of going too far or of just going on, which is the greatest temptation of all. After about ten minutes, *Don't Mean a Thing* dissolved into scattershot effects (though Barnett on his motorcycle brought it briefly back). *Haiku*, composed of many short movement sketches separated by blackouts, was formally far more of a success. It was neat and clean; it avoided diddling in the materiality of the form. But for Crowsnest it felt like a concession. The great Japanese mimes Eiko and Koma achieve their supreme epiphanies through the intensification of a single effect.

Crowsnest aims for constancy rather than unity, and its habit is to proceed from one effect to another in a more or less continuous line. The line cut short is not a real method; it's a dead end.

The first group piece that Crowsnest made, *The Garden of Villandry*, was presented last, as if in the hope that we might see it as an extended haiku. The cast is in turn-of-the-century summer whites. The men walk very slowly on a tilt with their hands in their pockets; they hold the woman's body canted into space; they turn and glance; they hold modest arabesques. In the film *Martha Clarke Light & Dark*, also shown at the Public, we see this piece in preparation, and it works better in close-up than it does on the stage. Like the other Crowsnest scores, the slow movement of Schubert's Piano Trio in B Flat is used for pace and atmosphere but not for structure; lack of structural definition makes the piece seem vagrant from the start. By this time, too, the triangularity of Crowsnest's group compositions has become oppressive. Why always one woman and two men? That casting is practically a haiku in itself. There's not much leeway dramatically. No matter how neutral the terms are in partnering, there's always an odd man out, and the sexual dynamics within the group cannot go far beyond the variations presented in this program. Another problem is that Clarke and Barnett are much stronger performers than Blaska and are constantly trying to dispel that inequality by subordinating themselves to the group. Barnett does it naturally and gracefully. With one of the most riveting presences in all theatre, he rivets when he wants to. He seems to love fading out of himself, escaping in full view, and he's as content on the sidelines as he is in the spotlight.

When Clarke fades into the group, she looks happier there, and is it a coincidence that in both of her solos her face is masked? Clarke shares Barnett's virtuosity. She contains the same range of contradictions: heavy-light, monstrous-fey, ugly-glamorous. She has the same kind of sensitive, slightly battered clown face. The two of them (in Pilobolus they were often teamed) appear to have been born for theatre in the same minute. But Clarke seems uneasy about being the apex of the triangle. Maybe she rejects the easy domination her position gives her; maybe there's a group ethos lingering from Pilobolus days. But Crowsnest isn't really a group; it has no identity as such, and that's largely because Clarke is unwilling to state her presence unequivocally. In *Nocturne*, she performs barebreasted, wearing a bulky tulle skirt and toe shoes, and with her head wrapped in gauze. The costume is adapted from Adolphe de Meyer's enigmatic photograph *Woman with a Mask*, and Clarke seems to want to tell the story behind the photograph. I'm not sure I understand her story. Once her terms are grasped—and they're fairly obvious (she has made the woman a decrepit ballerina)—one is left to ponder their meaning; no further light is shed on the subject.

Nocturne is one of a series of melancholy "women in theatre" studies, and as a ready-made pictorial image it's also a companion piece to *Fallen Angel*, in which Clarke is a bird-woman out of Max Ernst's book of collages *Une Semaine de Bonté*. Clarke, completely hidden in a blue silk gown and a beaked head, gives us another baffler. The costume tells all. The costume tells nothing. The movement inside the dress serves only to restate the dress. Who are these headless women? Is there a thing going on about heads? Recently, Clarke directed the actress Linda Hunt as Elizabeth I in *Elizabeth Dead*, by George Trow. A lot of Elizabeth's monologue was quite graphically concerned with the beheading of Mary, Queen of Scots, and Clarke's staging was in the clinical-grotesque style that she is increasingly favoring for her own solos. One wouldn't know from an evening with Crowsnest how glowingly expressive her face is.

Martha Clarke is as complete a theatrical artist as any woman performing today, but in Crowsnest, which was her idea, she leaves a meager impression. (You'd never guess, either, that she's one of the funniest women alive.) For one who can suggest so much to cut herself so far back is a waste, painful to witness. The final image is one of self-mutilation.

—June 15, 1981

Tchaikovsky

The New York City Ballet's Tchaikovsky Festival began with Suzanne Farrell, in a formal tutu of solemn black, floating downstage on her long, sensitive pointes, her hands joined in prayer. And it ended pianissimo, with an image of a giant's heart beating its last under a black shroud, followed by the blowing out of a single candle on a darkened stage. It was as if Balanchine, in bracketing the whole festival with *memento mori*, were deliberately overturning the moral of the Stravinsky Festival, held a year after the composer's death, at the end of which Balanchine came onstage and drank a jaunty vodka toast in the Russian fashion "to the health of the guy that died." Farrell's prayer, set to the Preghiera from the fourth orchestral suite (*Mozartiana*), was preceded by a short concert, conducted by Robert Irving, of dramatic compositions on themes of love and death: the *Romeo and Juliet* Overture-Fantasy, with its closing cantilena that slowly withdraws in lingering contemplation of Juliet's bier; Lisa's aria from *The Queen of Spades*, sung as she waits by the canal in which she will drown herself; Lensky's aria before the duel in *Eugene Onegin*; the love duet for tenor and soprano from the abandoned opera *Undine*, which lent its music to the second act of *Swan Lake* and its dramatic situation to the fourth act. On the final program of the festival, the Elégie from *Suite No. 3* and the Andante Elegiaco (pas de deux) from *Diamonds* paved the way for a presentation of three movements from the "Pathétique" Symphony, in which Tchaikovsky is thought to have meditated on his own death. The Allegro con Grazia, with its mysterious five-beat waltz, was set by Jerome Robbins as a pas de deux for Patricia McBride and Helgi Tomasson with an ensemble of ten girls. Irving then led the orchestra in a brisk, unpompous rendition of the March. The Adagio Lamentoso, which ends the symphony, was done by Balanchine in the gothic-horror style in which he treated Schumann's misery and attempted suicide in his version, last year, of *Davidsbündlertänze*. The hooded processions in *Adagio Lamentoso* also recall the death of Don Quixote, until now Balanchine's most opulent staging of the artist's martyrdom.

All this didn't make the Tchaikovsky Festival itself a lugubrious affair. *Mozartiana* was Balanchine's fourth production of Tchaikovsky's homage to Mozart. After the ceremonial moment of the Preghiera had passed, the ballet evolved into the spiciest that Balanchine has done in some time. His other festival pieces were the "Garland Dance" from *The Sleeping Beauty* and *Hungarian Gypsy Airs*, a setting of the folk ballads that Tchaikovsky orchestrated in the last year of his life. Robbins, also in sprightly form, produced a pas de deux for Darci Kistler and Ib Andersen to the middle movement of the First Piano Concerto. His major work for the festival and its biggest hit was *Piano Pieces*, for which he returned to the most appealing vein of *Dances at a Gathering*. John Taras, Peter Martins, Joseph Duell, and Jacques d'Amboise fulfilled their festival assignments, for the most part, by celebrating the music and exercising institutional aesthetics. In all, fourteen ballets were introduced in ten days and shown alongside the company's regular Tchaikovsky repertory, which is the world's strongest. If most of the premières were not even potential contributions to this repertory, it was still a Tchaikovsky Festival—business as usual, in other words, at New York City Ballet. The only difference was that Day One and Day Ten were hung with crêpe.

In the marvelous ballets of the Balanchine-Tchaikovsky repertory—*Diamonds* and *Piano Concerto No. 2* and *Serenade* and *Allegro Brillante* and *Suite No. 3* (including *Theme and Variations*) and the single-act version of *Swan Lake*, and even "Waltz of the Flowers," which was the festival's sole excerpt from *The Nutcracker*—Tchaikovsky's melancholy is always accounted for, not only as the pervasive mood of his Andantes and Elegies but as a persistent aura edging even his brightest moments. In "Waltz of the Flowers," the appearance of the third melody, in B minor, has an effect of sudden estrangement—an effect that is answered in the choreography by the soloist's isolated entrance against the corps. It's such a wonderful, surging moment that it doesn't feel strange—it feels like a pang of elation. This complex, elating melancholy in Tchaikovsky is something no other choreographer has captured, just as no other choreographer has demonstrated more clearly the difference between exalted emotion and obsessive brooding in the adagio sequences. By custom, Balanchine has stayed away from the heavier symphonies, the more overwrought symphonic poems and overtures. For the purposes of choreography, Tchaikovsky is best without the introspective thickening to which he was sometimes prone.

When Balanchine has yielded to Tchaikovskian introspection, it has usually been to stage vision scenes of a more
problematic nature than the one in *The Sleeping Beauty*. Yet
compare the Andante of *Piano Concerto No. 2* with *Meditation*. In the former ballet (christened *Ballet Imperial*), he
took an unwieldy nondance composition—the first movement is inordinately long, broad, and melodramatic—and
made a great ballet out of it. The key to his success may
possibly be the fact that nowhere in the concerto does
Tchaikovsky look inward and shed tears. There is a certain sweetness-of-pain in the Andante, but the overriding
emotion is one of dignified resignation. Sweetness-of-pain
comes back in *Meditation*, together with nostalgia, regret,
and some central enigma one would have thought impossible to depict in dance. With Farrell's help, though, Balanchine did it. *Meditation*, a pas de deux with d'Amboise
created in 1963, is about lovers who are completely involved
with one another yet never meet—never become one. The
music is dedicated to Nadezhda von Meck, the great bene-
factor of Tchaikovsky whom he never met; possibly Farrell
in the ballet is an echo of von Meck, and her relation with
d'Amboise may be, in part, an evocation of the patron's
relation with the composer—benevolent, loving, all-
comprehending, dependent, yet distant. In *Meditation*, Farrell wears a draped costume and loose hair. In Balanchine
iconography, flowing hair and dress have come to signify
the muse of the Romantic poet: see *La Sonnambula*, the Elegy of *Serenade*, the first part of *Chaconne*, and the finale of
Walpurgisnacht Ballet.

In *Suite No. 3*, the stage teems with girls in long hair
and streaming chiffon. Under the influence of festival
Tchaikovskiana, it was impossible not to see them as a parade of the women in Tchaikovsky's life. In the Elégie, the

glamorous, inscrutable creature who steps out of the crowd and then back into it, leaving the hero in despair, could be the ideal woman whom Tchaikovsky worshipped but never found. She could be Désirée Artôt, the soprano with whom he was briefly in love; she could also be his mother, who died when he was a boy. In the Valse Mélancolique, the ballerina is like a siren or a witch holding the man under a spell. Antonina Milyukova, the woman who pursued Tchaikovsky until, disastrously, he married her, was probably mentally unbalanced, but in Tchaikovsky's all too suggestible mind she seemed to have been identified with Tatiana in *Eugene Onegin*, and that may be why her reflection in the ballet is not an altogether sinister one. In the Scherzo, the two principals dance freely, side by side. Is the girl Tchaikovsky's sister, whom he adored, and for whose children he wrote some of his most famous compositions? The weakness of *Suite No. 3*, apart from its involvement of Balanchine with the more subjective Tchaikovsky, is that there's no connection between the scheme of the first three movements and the classical ballet (choreographed twenty-three years earlier) that follows, to the Tema con Variazioni. The classical ballerina is, like all such Balanchine creations, a character in her own right. Since she is based on Aurora in *The Sleeping Beauty*, it is tempting to interpret the progress of *Suite No. 3* as a mirror of the process of sublimation by which life is transformed into art. In this interpretation, Tchaikovsky lived a life of Romantic chaos, which he distilled into Classical art.

In two ballets made for the festival by Joseph Duell and Peter Martins, this view of Tchaikovsky is upheld. Duell's *Introduction and Fugue* (the opening movement of the Suite No. 1) is a condensation of the action of *Suite No. 3*. The composer (Adam Lüders) is visited by amorphous forms that coalesce in the shape of a cathedral arch. The divine calling of the artist then gives way to his creation, which is a large and formal classical ballet, much like *Theme and Variations*. It hardly matters whether Lüders's artist-alchemist-priest is Tchaikovsky or Balanchine (Lüders was also Schumann in *Davidsbündlertänze*), or that the idea behind the ballet is imitative and naïve. Duell has worked it out gracefully without imposing on the music more pressure, second by second, than it can accept. I don't believe his Romantic-Classical, Life-Art antinomies (I don't believe them in *Suite No. 3*, either, if indeed they are there), but I think he was right to try for some kind of extramusical dramatic continuity. His mistake was in trying to make this extramusical continuity the story of the music. The ballet doubles back on itself in an extremely dubious way. In Martins's ballet, arranged to the First Symphony (minus the first movement), the notional content is secreted in continuity that is stiffly formal and, when we get to the "ballet" part of the ballet (Martins, like Duell, has had to set a fugue), is even more so. The choreography, beguilingly well knit, is modestly presented; it calls our attention to the music, to the ballerina (Kistler), to the costumes ("Romantic" tutus, switching to "Classical" ones for the fugue), even to the set—never to itself. In its reticence, its calm good nature and workmanship, *Symphony No. 1* is Martins's most "Danish" ballet. (Even the waltz in the third movement recalls a waltz in the Danish ballet classic *A Folk Tale*.) In the finale, the stage empties while blue and white lights play for a full minute on the extraordinary transparent-plastic set designed for the festival by Philip Johnson and John Burgee. The effect doesn't quite come off; there aren't enough lights to make this aurora borealis the climax that the "Winter Dreams" Symphony demands.

But a fancier light show would have needed a more aggressive ballet.

Johnson and Burgee's Crystal Cathedral, in Garden Grove, California, was the inspiration for their "ice palace" Tchaikovsky set, designed at Balanchine's request. The architects have done what no modern stage designer I know of has yet accomplished—enclosed and defined stage space with a neutral décor capable of assuming as much or as little presence as may be demanded by individual ballets. Its ice-white color and striated forms were put through nearly two dozen variations in the course of the festival and can be put through many more—indeed, must be, since festival programs are to alternate with repertory for the rest of the season and the set cannot be flown in and out. Like any theme-and-variations scheme, the set is a systemic thing, and one would not like to see it overused. It places everything in a fantastic and geometric universe, where not every ballet—not even every Tchaikovsky ballet—belongs. *Serenade*, to me, needs the pristine, unbounded territory of a bare stage, and festival performances of *Divertimento from "Le Baiser de la Fée"* only served to italicize its mixed nature—part divertissement, part drama—and its need of a fluid background in which an unreal "ice" décor could be contrasted with a snug domestic one. (Alexandre Benois, who originally proposed and designed Stravinsky's Tchaikovsky ballet, surely derived his Alpine setting from *Manfred*.)

The company also made a special effort in the matter of costumes. Every ballet was dressed, and only the "Garland Dance" was noticeably in hand-me-downs. Leotards and T-shirts never made an appearance. What the festival seemed to be saying visually bore out one of the problems of festival choreography: that Tchaikovsky cannot be expressed in absolutist abstract terms. Balanchine has known this all along, but the House of Balanchine, which is run on doctrinaire formalist principles, was thrown into insoluble dilemmas by the moods and dramas in Tchaikovsky's music. John Taras, a house choreographer of long standing, elected the either/or treatment: stretches of pure dancing interrupted by mime scenes. The treatment worked, or might be made to work, in the waltz from *Eugene Onegin*, which concluded the program called *Tempo di Valse*. The company's apprentices, for whom Taras staged the number, had no idea how to move when they weren't dancing full tilt, but that didn't impede the waltz, which went with a fine sweep. Taras has a touch with ensemble set pieces; last year he staged some sparkling dances from Glinka's *A Life for the Tsar* for the School of American Ballet. His big festival ballet, *Souvenir de Florence*, was placid as dance and inscrutable as drama. The large cast, in all-white Russian native dress by Ter-Arutunian, seemed to be acting out a story by Erich Maria Remarque about a field hospital in the Crimea. Jacques d'Amboise's *Concert Fantasy* involved some cadets at a prom where the Three Fates were keeping a vigil. By the second performance, this jumble had been cut in half. D'Amboise did two other numbers. In *Scherzo Opus 42*, a heavily impudent vaudeville skit for McBride and a group of men, one barely recognized New York City Ballet, but *Valse-Scherzo* touched on a continuing NYCB puzzle: Who are Kyra Nichols and Daniel Duell, and why are they so often paired? The two are husband and wife, but neither temperamentally nor physically are they a stage couple. And despite Duell's slight stature and his skill in low leaps with quicksilver retiré changes, he's not really a jester type. Robbins choreographs for him as if he were; d'Amboise does, too. Nichols, of course, is one of the strongest bravura ballerinas in the company, but the feats she performed in *Valse-Scherzo* barely registered, and in Robbins's *Piano Pieces* I didn't think she functioned as well as the two other principal women, Heather Watts and Maria Calegari. Give Nichols a Balanchine role, though, and the uncompromising terms in which she dances are lucid and complete. In a Balanchine-Tchaikovsky ballet like *Piano Concerto No. 2* or *Theme and Variations*, she springs to life. The festival was lucky to have her.

It didn't have Farrell, and but for a few token appearances it didn't have Merrill Ashley, whose recovery from a hip injury last year is still incomplete. In the première performance of *Mozartiana*, Farrell hurt her foot, and though she finished the evening neither she nor the ballet has been seen since. *Meditation* also had to be withdrawn. (The *Diamonds* pas de deux as done by Ashley was a curiosity—as remote from Ashley's style as *Ballo della Regina* would have been from Farrell's.) Another ballet that came and went was *Hungarian Gypsy Airs*, for Karin von Aroldingen with Lüders and a mixed ensemble. This, until *Adagio Lamentoso*, was the strangest event of the festival. Patterned after the *Tzigane* done for Farrell and Martins in the Ravel Festival (1975), it could hardly fail to arouse invidious comparisons. That it did not also defeat them seems untypical of Balanchine; one left thinking that he *must* have some tricks up his sleeve which a single performance failed to reveal. Since von Aroldingen was also dancing her première with an injury, it was hard to tell what he intended.

Balanchine's "Garland Dance," clearly a pièce d'occasion, may also disappear—unless, of course, he decides to surround it with *The Sleeping Beauty*. Its borrowed finery notwithstanding, the dance is a living rebuke to the Royal Ballet version and to the Petipa exhibits at American Ballet

Theatre—especially *Jardin Animé*, with its stolid rhythm and its miles of nonfunctioning garlands. Balanchine weaves the floral arches into the dance, and he uses them as colonnades for the entrance of the children's corps, just as Petipa must have done. (The Bolshoi's "Petipa" production of *The Sleeping Beauty* has this same entrance.) When the children have been put through their paces with the adult corps, and when it seems that every permutation of garland and dancer, grown-up and child has been run through once, Balanchine brings on nine more girls with nine rope garlands, and you know what a full stage really is, and what world enough and time are in choreography. The "Garland Dance" is essentially a background, scene-setting configuration, not a showpiece. It's a ponderous carousel that might have been designed by Watteau. The formations are all circles and grids—no dramatic diagonals or wedges, as in "Waltz of the Flowers"—and there are only about three steps, all obligatory. My favorite waltz step is the Duncanish scuff-kick into attitude front; the children do it deliciously, and toward the end they break formation and rush dizzyingly to place from opposite sides of the stage. The stage picture freezes, a human pyramid yoked with flowers. Balanchine is not in the picture—Petipa is.

Or so we think. Yet, just as *Mozartiana* is Mozart for ears that have heard Tchaikovsky, so this "Garland Dance" is Petipa for eyes that have seen Balanchine. It was so, too, with Stravinsky on Tchaikovsky in *Le Baiser de la Fée*. Following the *Divertimento*, we were given Tchaikovsky songs by the festival soprano, Karen Hunt, among them "None but the Lonely Heart," from which Stravinsky fashioned the climax of his ballet. This was a festival in which precedents were exposed and honored. The last and grandest of the selections in *Mozartiana* is the ten variations on a theme that

Mozart took from Gluck. Balanchine follows suit, setting a string of alternating solos for the ballerina and the danseur, as he did in the gavotte of *Chaconne*. Ib Andersen danced opposite Farrell. The variations are about male and female strengths polarized in allegro rhythms, and they devastate certain hallmarks of Balanchine style, especially Balanchine style for Farrell. Her step sequences and timings are irregular and unforeseen, yet not uncharacteristic; she looks like a tape of herself run backward. Andersen beats and flies in the bonny manner that Robbins exploits so well in *Piano Pieces*, but with an effect of greater science and power.

—*June 29, 1981*

The Royal at Fifty

Ars longa, vita brevis. In ballet, that dictum could be reversed—dancers outlive their creations. At the Paris Opéra, a special box is reserved for *anciennes étoiles,* from which, presumably, they gaze in wonder and dismay at the transfigured glories of their youth. The perpetuation of a dance tradition is no simple task of preservation but, rather, a constant effort of modification and renewal guided by the estimation and re-estimation of constituent strengths in the flux of time. The passion for the exotic was a constituent of the classical tradition into the twentieth century, but once the New World had contributed its cowboy and jazz ballets, it was discarded. Guardians of tradition are vigilant lest some strength be surrendered before its time. After a central feature has been eliminated, it is very hard to get it back. It is especially damaging to eliminate features of style, since the way a company dances is the result of conditioning both conscious and unconscious. At peak expression, the conscious elements of style are absorbed by the unconscious; this has an almost moral force of persuasion in performance. It is, in fact, the only kind of style to have, because the collective force of it is always greater than the cumulative details of a regimen or the sum of individual talents or the scope of choreography. Looking at the Bolshoi, one sees certain traits of style that we in the West reject; one sees, in fact, a whole different gamut of stylistic permissiveness. Yet these traits aren't lazily selected, and the Bolshoi's style exists above and beyond the terrible ballets it dances; it's a unanimous expressive urge that is there for us to respond to, whether we like the ballets or not, or even whether we like the technique or not.

If a company has the grand style, has this collective moral elegance, chances are you don't think about the technique, so unconscious and unwilled is it. Watching the Royal Ballet do the great classical ballets it brought to New York this season, my eye was repeatedly drawn to the dancers' technique, because the technique simply wasn't doing what the dancers needed it for. Like dancers everywhere, they tried to make up for it with extroverted performing; the result was that they were both vivacious and dim.

In a fiftieth-anniversary year—the company was founded in 1931—one doesn't want to have to talk technique about the Royal Ballet. Technique is the quantitative, style the qualitative source of the impression a company makes. Each company sets its own standards of technique and style, though for companies that play in opera houses the technique as a general rule conforms to opera-house scale. I don't think—near-capacity audiences obviously disagreed with me—that the Netherlands Dance Theatre has enough technique to play the Metropolitan Opera House; its means are insignificant on the great stage. And though there were full houses for the Royal Ballet, which preceded the Netherlands company at the Met, I didn't think the

Royal made the total impression it should have. It was sad to see how far the company had wandered from its sense of the grand style in the classical tradition. In that style, formed by Frederick Ashton out of Petipa and brought to a pitch of perfection in the sixties, the company used to dance *The Sleeping Beauty* and *Swan Lake*. In these same pieces this season, the corps was still a model of uniformity but no longer a model of strict discipline. It wasn't the corps that had danced *La Bayadère*. And how many of the soloists struggling to come to terms with Aurora or Odette or Florestan or the Bluebird could have been mustered for a performance of *Monotones* as crystalline as the ones we used to see? Even without the two great signature pieces of the sixties, the repertory chosen for New York was a constant reminder of the grandeur that was. Former dancers were missed, but the collective impression they made was missed even more. Memories of Margot Fonteyn were inescapable in *Daphnis and Chloë*; otherwise, the ghost has been laid. But the loss to a great company of its stylistic sense is a loss of—not identity, precisely, but something critical to it. The Royal, in the last ten years, has lost its superego.

Ashton and Ninette de Valois were present for the season. The third of the trio of founders, Constant Lambert, died in 1951, leaving a vacancy as musical director that has never been adequately filled. (His protégé, Robert Irving, went to New York City Ballet.) But now, with both Ashton and de Valois in retirement for more than a decade, the artistic policy of the Royal Ballet shows signs of revolution. The directors of the seventies—first Kenneth MacMillan and now Norman Morrice, with MacMillan as principal choreographer—have turned English ballet away from its native classicism and toward the turgid expressionism in force on the European continent from Stuttgart to Amsterdam, from Paris to Hamburg. In her foreword to *The Royal Ballet: The First Fifty Years*, by Alexander Bland, de Valois writes of the need for periodic change and recommends that change be carried out "with a detachment producing a calm contemplation of any temporary moments of stagnation." Is this her attitude as she sits nightly in her box watching the institution she created drift into the Stuttgart whirlpool? Is detachment what Ashton feels as he contemplates the stagnation—temporary?—of the style he forged? It may be that expressionistic tendencies were always implicit in English ballet. They were there in some of MacMillan's early work with Lynn Seymour. John Cranko, who mobilized the Stuttgart Ballet, was a Royal alumnus. Morrice is a product of Ballet Rambert. Marie Rambert, who in the sixties turned her company into a workshop for the Continentals and their followers, had sponsored the first efforts of Frederick Ashton and Antony Tudor. It was Ashton who proved to be the more fertile of the two, and it was his pearly classicism, in *Symphonic Variations*, that got English ballet back to classical principles after the war. One of the wartime hits, Robert Helpmann's *Hamlet*, was revived this season. Perhaps it stands as an example of the kind of thing Ashton was getting away from, but its compressed pantomime is so futile and at the same time so juicy that it appears quite harmless. At any rate, English ballet is not now being threatened, as it may have been then, by actors rampant in tights. The danger is from this new religiose preoccupation with the human body and its contortions which is now so pronounced in MacMillan's ballets. Although MacMillan has shown his winged abilities as a classicist in traditional academic terms, he seems to have abandoned that whole side of his talent. As the leading artistic influence on the Royal Ballet, he could not have made a more drastic decision. It wasn't supposed to, but the Royal season showed the effects of that decision.

What might be called the Tudor strain—thick, dark, Teutonic, quasi-dramatic—is now in the ascendant in MacMillan's work, and it has claimed the Royal dancers and their technique. Ashton was represented by five ballets, ranging from *Symphonic Variations* to his newest piece, *Rhapsody*. His fourth act of *Swan Lake* was also shown, along with his interpolations in that ballet and some of his choreography for *The Sleeping Beauty*. The company danced it all with a shaky gentility, whereas the performances of MacMillan's three ballets seemed to come from a core of strength. Ashton's sole triumph was the fourth act of *Swan Lake*; the choral spread of it looked beautiful on the Met stage. Earlier, though, we'd seen his Pas de Quatre, and even his Tarantella, vanquished by inadequate performance. The Pas de Quatre comes from the high sixties, but the decay of the Tarantella—one of those perennial Royal highlights—was quite unexpected. A comparable shock in *The Sleeping Beauty* was the Puss in Boots episode: the sweetness is gone. The divertissement is now a series of painful descents—Florestan pas de trois, Bluebirds, cats.

Why should the Royal be failing in the standard items of its classical repertory? To an American observer with three weeks of ill-served Petipa and ill-chosen Ashton to guess from, the answer must be that it is no longer a classical company. Royal technique used to be faulted for its rule-book moderation and lack of scale. Although it hasn't changed a lot, it's not so much small as it is incomplete. One sees partial turnout, lazy thighs, unstretched knees, sketchy footwork. The lower body is underworked while the upper body is exaggeratedly braced in épaulé. The old ideal of épaulement was to oppose head to shoulder and shoulder to spine with the continuous tension of a garland wound around a turning column. The Royal now produces a wide chandelierlike yoke hung with bunchy ornamentation, all twisting fervently around a vertical axis of tallow. The eel plastique of the MacMillan ballets influences "classical" épaulement in alarming ways. One Florestan trio yanked itself about so wildly that it swam out of focus.

There have always been certain features of Royal ballerina style that I've found unappealing, like the excitability in allegro. It's fine for fairies and coquettes but not for serious women, unless, as in *A Month in the Country*, it has a dramatic motive. And with the loss of firmness and fullness in the technique a kind of blowsiness has crept in. Genesia Rosato and Rosalyn Whitten managed to make this quality attractive in the small parts that they were given, but, again, it isn't serious. The beauties of the English style are almost all in adagio. The lift up and out of développé in Odette's variation, especially when it unfolds into arabesque, always made a heroic image when the English did it. But the marvelous poetic understanding that Fonteyn brought to the Rose adagio hasn't been passed on to the current generation. And the current production of *The Sleeping Beauty* is a heart-twisting disappointment. It has been revised a couple of times since the première in 1977. Act II is now decently concluded to the music that Tchaikovsky wrote, the egregious "Awakening" pas de deux has been dropped, and there is only a brief pause before the house curtain reopens on Catalabutte in the throne room. Is it madness to go on insisting on an *onstage* transition when the sequence following the Panorama, which involves several onstage transitions, is still a dismal failure? In the old days, it was seen as if from the Prince's point of view. Now it's from the point of view of a stage manager with a stopwatch in his hand.

Considering how little importance is attached to the Prince, the Sarabande he does in the second act seems a conspicuous waste of time. The intrada to the bridal pas de deux, which involved a unison mime speech by the courtiers, ought not to have been omitted. The lesser of Ashton's two Garland Dances is still the one being used.

Shall I go on with this? It's like straightening the pictures in a room that has been bombed. When you've seen all the Auroras and they're either sturdily dull or helplessly weak, when the best performance in the Prologue is given not by the dancing fairies but by Monica Mason's Carabosse (her stentorian presence was fine, too, as Gertrude in *Hamlet*), when the first thing you see in Act III—Leslie Edwards's Catalabutte—is also the last thing that will remind you of third acts gone by, why suppose that *The Sleeping Beauty* is anymore the symbol of Royal Ballet excellence? Staged by de Valois and revised by her in what seem to have been ever more wishful attempts to recapture a lost vitality, this *Beauty* starts gloriously, but the evening goes on and the vision keeps receding. It's a mirage. We never do reach the castle.

—July 27, 1981

Connections: Taylor and Tharp

In Paul Taylor's *House of Cards*, Bettie de Jong has another of those Bettie de Jong mime parts that place her firmly at the center of events yet mysteriously outside them. The title role in *Big Bertha* may have been the prototype of these disquieting impersonal instruments of fate, which de Jong has played ever since. Although de Jong's presence in *Esplanade* magnetizes the action without exactly controlling it, we still are unsettled by her, and "the shepherdess" or "the sheltering mother"—however we may privately characterize her role—is the most benign variation on the de Jong character up to now. As Big Bertha, the clockwork doll that drove the other characters to their doom, de Jong was malevolent; in *Le Sacre du Printemps (The Rehearsal)*, she was inscrutable. In *House of Cards* she's inscrutable in a different way; we just don't know who she's supposed to be or why she has to be there. The rehearsal mistress in *Le Sacre* is so neatly jigsawed into the pattern of the choreography that we may not notice how marginal the role really is—it's the most tenuous of Taylor's jokes in this piece. But the fact that de Jong is also the rehearsal mistress of the Paul Taylor Dance Company seems to be all there is behind her role in *House of Cards*; she seems to be making a guest appearance as a performer.

The piece, a highly tentative affair, deals in a Taylorishly oblique way with culture and the arts in Paris at the time of the music, which is Darius Milhaud's *La Création du Monde* (1923). De Jong's role is as static as one might imagine an Ida Rubinstein role of the same period to be, and her costume, by Cynthia O'Neal, seems designed to inhibit her even further: a stiff flaring jacket over a long skirt that maintains its bulky silhouette no matter how de Jong moves—or, rather, is moved. For although she makes the commanding Big Bertha gestures that dictate what the rest of the cast does, she is most often a passive figure, constantly being lifted and carried idol-like, or en cortège, or with straddling legs as the others pass beneath her. In her gown and her turban sprouting egret feathers, she's a period reference, while the others are neutrally clad in formal renditions of everyday dancewear. Her link to the period is clear when she's being obeyed or "celebrated"; then we see her as an all-powerful society hostess or patroness. But when she's a fallen statue we don't know what toppled her. Perhaps Taylor intended a lament for lost times and for lost ladies like Misia Sert. He doesn't follow the scenario of Milhaud's ballet, although he casts a sidelong glance at it now and then, and de Jong could be a parallel to the totems worshipped in the "tribal" dances of the old ballet. As iconography, the role is clear enough. Psychologically and structurally, it's opaque.

That de Jong's presence isn't as well integrated with the surrounding action as other de Jong roles have been is a real flaw. Yet it's also characteristic of the way the piece has been made. *House of Cards* (the title may be telling us something) is exceedingly fragile in construction, full of loose hinges and unmoored conceits. Nothing really holds together. The dancers are introduced to the mournful and sluggish "up from the slime" music at the beginning. As they roll one by one out of a revolving huddle in the dark, they groggily sketch out "period" identities that range from the broadly familiar (Linda Kent as a Charleston dancer) to the obscure (Karla Wolfangle as a marionette). These bits are like an orchestra tuning up, but the piece goes on being bits; it's always building up to a breakdown. Maybe that's why de Jong is there—as a focal point around which to assemble the sparse motifs and the discontinuities of the score. As Misia Sert or Lady Ripon or whoever, she's at her most obviously focal in the frantic group dances of the party scenes, but the focus she provides keeps dissipating, just as the groups do. At the end, everyone goes off single file, as if to affirm the linear, noncollective nature of the action we have just witnessed.

The fragmentation in *House of Cards* might be unbearably baffling if there weren't a strong foundation to support it. As often happens with Taylor, the foundation is the music. There isn't a moment of choreography that isn't musically justified; there isn't an image that doesn't have *some* light shining behind it. When we connect the dots of light, we begin to see *House of Cards* as one of a series of recent pieces in which Taylor seems to be meditating on historic eras of dance. From *Images* to *Profiles* to *Le Sacre*, similarities can be traced which incorporate two lines of descent— from historic American modern dance and from the era of the Ballets Russes. *House of Cards*, set to a renowned jazz ballet by a European composer (which was originally produced in Paris by Ballets Suédois), concentrates on the taste of the twenties for particular kinds of colloquial art. Not only the Afro-Americanisms of Milhaud's score are here, along with fragments of his scenario (the Adam and Eve figures are retained by Taylor and danced by Christopher Gillis and Ruth Andrien); we also find *Petrushka* and *Parade* and *Les Biches*—all ballets to which street songs, café Dixieland, tea dances, and bal musette in one form or another made decisive contributions. Here is the Hostess from *Les Biches*; here, in Karla Wolfangle's puppet, is Petrushka; Gillis and Andrien are also the acrobats in *Parade*—a ballet that for Taylor seems to be a key source of ideas. With its looseleaf impressions of a chaotic scene, *House of Cards* may be distantly modeled on the "vaudeville" structure of *Parade*. (And did not the Chinese Conjuror in that ballet find his way into Taylor's *Sacre*?) It follows from these precedents that Taylor's choreography for Milhaud's music is inspired mainly by the parody Charlestons and tangos in the score. Where most settings of this music ignore the colloquialisms or render them as straight demonstrations, Taylor gives us the chivied Charlestons, the tormented tangos of his own invention. When he comes to the miasmic interlude following the party, he stages a dazed morning-after scene as a slow-motion tumbling act for two men (Gillis and Daniel Ezralow). If the method invokes the music hall by way of Pilobolus, yet there's madness in it. Scott Fitzgerald's ghost is not far off.

House of Cards isn't major Taylor—it's an omelette by a master chef with a piece of eggshell stuck in it. The de Jong role is pardonable, but like the pineapple in Twyla Tharp's *The Catherine Wheel*, it causes more confusion than it is really worth. Alternating Taylor evenings at the Brooklyn Academy of Music with Tharp evenings at the Winter Garden, I came this season to have a new respect for the links between these two marvelous artists—links that Tharp's dramatic emergence a decade ago had obscured. At that time, one saw only the novelty in Tharp; dances like *The Fugue* and *Eight Jelly Rolls* made Taylor look mustily old-fashioned. Today, in such a piece as *The Catherine Wheel*, with its analogous systems of meaning and effect, Tharp seems very close to Taylor. The concept of *The Catherine Wheel* owes much to his *Orbs* and *American Genesis*. How strange that in the same season Taylor should have commissioned Mimi Gross's scenery for *House of Cards*—a strip of painted canvas which unrolls during the dance in the manner of the graffiti strips in *Deuce Coupe*. And that his dancers should be costumed by Mrs. O'Neal in the variations on practice dress that Santo Loquasto introduced in *Sue's Leg*. Tharp doesn't compose like Taylor; although she once danced in Taylor's company, there is no way one could mistake one of her dances for one of his. But her choreography is like his in its seamless continuity and elasticity of phrase. I heard Tharp compared this season with Jiří Kylián—the comparison was meant as the highest kind of praise—for her nonstop rhythm and use of a dramatic subject, not only in *The Catherine Wheel* but in *Short Stories*. But I find that Kylián's rhythm isn't really nonstop and that he doesn't use it in support of drama, as Tharp does. His line is full of breaks, which the dancers push themselves through, and his drama is pictogrammatic statements that spell out emotions. Kylián's roots lie in Central European modern dance; Taylor and Tharp inherited the miscellaneous legacy of American dance at a time—the fifties and sixties—when it was flowing with riches. Martha Graham, Cunningham and Cage, and the School of American Ballet were all at separate peaks of power and influence. A lively student could leap from peak to peak. Taylor eventually positioned himself at the end of the line that stretches through Graham back to Denishawn and Denishawn's contemporaries. He is the sentinel of modernity and, as his recent recherché work shows, its keenest and most circumspect analyst. There is in *House of Cards* an avidity for the past but also an unwillingness to probe beyond the barrier of retrospection. Taylor isolates a few motifs and monuments and hangs them up for scrutiny. The only conclusion he draws is a sighing "They don't look like much now, do they?" He's resigned to the vulnerability of history—history as a house of cards.

Tharp has always been an eclectic choreographer. Her omnivorous sweep tosses aside self-contradictions and mows down categorical shalt-nots. I don't see how anyone can resist the electric crackle of *Short Stories*—especially the first part in which degrees of relaxation and tension are so finely calibrated that drama becomes a creation of pure rhythm. Is Tharp returning the dance theatre to psychologically paraphrasable movement? In *Short Stories*, some teenagers at a dance quarrel almost for the sake of quarreling. The jealousies and rivalries the quarreling engenders aren't a byproduct of a social evening, they're the whole point of it. I see this and say this easily enough, yet the ritual as Tharp stages it is inexplicable; one really doesn't know why these things happen. We see the inarticulate rage and, at the same time, the strategies that keep it going. Then we see one girl who seems to take it all seriously—who becomes the victim from whose viewpoint the story is told. The switch from the general to the particular, from omniscient to subjective narration, is only one of Tharp's achievements. Another is her control of our comprehension of the words of the rock song she uses as accompaniment. Supertramp's "Lover Boy" is played twice; the first time it's just background, but the second time it applies cuttingly in every note and syllable to a single person. Whether the girl (Mary Ann Kellogg) is raped or murdered, whether she dies an actual or a spiritual death are questions that are transcended by the reality of an individual drama. Compared with this piercing vignette, the second part of *Short Stories*, set to a Bruce Springsteen song, is only an effective treatment of the same theme—quarreling—among grown-ups.

In *The Catherine Wheel*, the family scenes are all done allegro-staccato and reprised legato by the chorus. The antiphonal effect is gradually narrowed until, just before they disappear, family and chorus are down to echoes being batted back and forth in two spotlights. The staccato attack is a metaphor for irritation; it's used in gobs of literal Me Tarzan–You Jane pantomime, in on-the-beat dancing of all kinds, in sexual brawls timed like the wrestling on TV. The only explanation I can think of for that strange moment when Jennifer Way as the Mother tap-dances across the stage and exits is that it's the most staccato—the most irritating—thing she can do at that point. When the Mother and the Father (Tom Rawe) are momentarily reconciled, they do a ballroom duet that is all adagio swoops. And in one of the most extraordinary scenes in the whole show the frightened little Maid, played by Shelley Washington, docs a Kathakali-like mime solo in which she proceeds with slow and deliberate care through an extensive catalogue of ferocious grimaces; the timing makes our hair stand on end. The grimacing solo that Sara Rudner executes at top speed is completely different in effect. Rudner is the evil genius of the show, a kind of kinetic Bettie de Jong who directs its grand design without regard for moral consequences; all that matters is the flow of energy. The interesting thing is that the moral consequences are shown: bad and good are depicted as coexisting forces arbitrated by chance. The equanimity that Tharp shows is quite different from Taylor's American-puritan view of good and evil, but what other two choreographers could be discussed in these terms? Some observers of *The Catherine Wheel* were upset by the fact that there's no way out of the impasse of existence; they missed the catharsis that could have elevated the lyrical coda called "The Golden Section" to a point beyond wish fulfillment. It seems to me that the catharsis is there in the rhythm. The transition from the fallen world to the celestial regions occurs first of all in the music, with its lengthening and steadily broadening crescendo. Meanwhile, the pulse of the stage action has diminished to a terse rondo pattern—two patterns, in fact, which pit the family and the chorus against each other as twin points of jabbing intensity. When the stage picture finally changes from black to gold, there's a wonderful catch-up effect as the dancers enter on the new momentum the music has created.

Tharp also showed an earlier piece, *Assorted Quartets*. It contains the kind of roughhouse material that she was to use so explosively in *Short Stories* and the family scenes of *The Catherine Wheel*, but its tone is genial. Since there have been complaints about Tharp's violence this season, it seems fair to cite this work in rebuttal, along with Susanne K. Langer's observation that "the feeling in a work of art is something the artist *conceived* as he created the symbolic form to present it, rather than something he was undergoing and involuntarily venting in an artistic process." *Assorted Quartets* is much more than a footnote to the towering works it was seen with, and I trust it isn't its comparatively sanguine temper that makes me want to overlook it critically this time. This is the season, after all, that has shown Tharp entering a new phase. Next to what she's doing now, *Assorted Quartets* looks all too Bennington.

—*October 26, 1981*

The Return of the Shades

The Palais des Congrès, at the wrong end of the Bois de Boulogne, is where the airport buses drop their passengers. Above the garages are dozens of shiny boutiques where no one shops; outside are high-rise hotels and office blocks, glass and concrete, dust and desolation. Neither urbia nor suburbia, it's the worst possible introduction to Paris. The Palais also houses the largest theatre—around four thousand seats—in the city. Here, since April 17, the Kirov Ballet, from Leningrad, has been performing *Swan Lake* and *Giselle* and *Chopiniana* and *La Sylphide*, among other works, on a stage too wide and shallow and to the accompaniment of its own excellent orchestra, which has to be miked. The palatial bleakness, to New Yorkers, recalls the Uris or the Felt Forum. It was strange to be in Paris seeing the ballet at such a place, but the Kirov, with its reputation for bureaucratic intrigue surpassing even that of the Opéra, and with its recent history of scandals and defections, is hardly a distraction from negative modern realities. Things have been pretty quiet since the Panov affair; nevertheless, the company has not ventured in force to any Western capital but

Paris since 1970, when it last appeared in London. The Mitterrand government is hospitable, and the company enjoys a lively trade with French ballet—Béjart and Petit for productions of Petipa. Even so, a two-month engagement in Paris is being sustained at half strength; not all the dancers who were announced for the season have appeared, and some who have been left at home are said to be among the most interesting the company has recently developed. Pro-Solidarity demonstrations disrupted the opening-night performance of *Swan Lake*; leafleteers from Amnesty International have kept up a nightly vigil. But there is no feeling of unrest around the company. Outsiders are welcome to observe classes in the large rehearsal rooms below the theatre; interviews are freely granted. Perhaps the remoteness of the neighborhood—remote from the heart of Paris as well as from points East—makes this possible.

How long it has been since the Kirov was seen in New York was borne in on me by a single event: the discovery of a new and gifted young ballerina who was only three years old when the last New York season took place, in 1964. But this discovery did not dominate my impressions of the company for the simple reason that the newcomer was not starred in Paris. Altinay Asylmuratova was a name that was spoken—or, more often, misspoken. Other ballerinas were having their day. Barring this one revelation, and the disappointment of seeing two monuments crumble—the Shades scene and the *Paquita* divertissement—I found the Kirov much as I had remembered it. It is a great company afflicted by isolation. Even in the sixties, it had a tendency to be narrowly ingrown. That tendency has not been remedied by the relatively enlightened policies of the current artistic director, Oleg Vinogradov. Russia is a closed society. Vinogradov may take Western ballets in; he may not let dancers

out. Although it is difficult to judge the company's condition on nine performances in a foreign city, the lack of a
true contemporary direction was painfully evident. There
was no good modern choreography. The swans swam in
stagnant waters. The genius of the company lay in its Romantic revivals. But all this was true two decades ago. I
make my report, the rest of which will appear next week,
hoping that the Kirov's dancers will one day soon see New
York again. They need us as much as we need them.

May 26 and 27. The great revelation of the Kirov's first
Western tours, in the early sixties, was the Shades scene
from *La Bayadère*. It changed our notion of the Petipa corps
de ballet from that of a decorative frame for the principals to
that of a participant in the action. In the single-file entrance
of the corps and in its ensuing communal rites, Petipa is
closer to the true eschatological spectacle of the Romantic
ballet than he is thirteen years later in the Vision scene
of *The Sleeping Beauty*. Compared with the former ballet,
the Vision scene is inspired pastiche—a vision of a vision,
like Fokine's *Chopiniana*. Rudolf Nureyev's staging of *La
Bayadère* for the Royal Ballet introduced an exaggerated
slow tempo, which raised the hypnotic ritual to a stupor of
excitement; Natalia Makarova's staging for American Ballet
Theatre is also exaggeratedly slow. The ideal opening tempo
is probably somewhere between this and the unwontedly
brisk pace at which the Kirov dancers descended the ramp
in Paris. To be sure, there were thirty-two of them to be got
on, but there was not safety in numbers. Despite the faster
clip, quite a few of the protracted balances were seen to
wobble. In the subsequent dances, brisk became brusque.
The three soloists barreled through their variations. Olga
Chenchikova and, on the following night, Elena Evteyeva
picked distractedly at the ballerina role, as if they could af-

ford not to maximize its opportunities; they chewed gristle and threw away meat. The role of Nikiya is not glorious: the two adagios run together make up a blurry image, and the variations contain no felicities of invention comparable to the soloist variations. Nikiya is a hollow assignment that needs to be filled by an adagio technician with some—not too much—allegro twinkle. The Kirov ballerinas are legato technicians, and very monotonous about it, too. Evteyeva, less powerful than Chenchikova, is technically more finely bred. Chenchikova has been spoken of as the company's great new classicist. In the linked adagios, I see a monolithic grandeur but no discernment. In the slow variation that ends in an allegro flourish, instead of lightening or soften- ing her tone she just switches gears. Both women are part- nered by Eldar Aliev, who does not dance a solo. It strikes me that the Russians have seen the slightness of the balle- rina role and sought to disguise it by suppressing the male variation (which was Chabukiani's interpolation anyway— not *echt* Petipa). The stratagem doesn't work. The remedy for a weak Nikiya is a strong dancer.

A set of modern works comes next. The Kirov is not the first classical company to mistake its direction in contempo- rary choreography, but it may be the first to base its mistake on the assumption that "classical" and "contemporary" are contradictions. There is not the slightest sense of form in two pieces by Boris Eifmann, a young house chore- ographer—not even the elementary form that orders our sensations so that we may perceive shape, continuity, consequence. About all that's distinguishable is genre. *A Deux Voix* is a porno pas de deux; *Adagio* is one of those nameless-terror pieces in which a sinister group disgorges a soloist, lets him emote nakedly for an hour or two, and re- turns to pick him up. It is conceivable that a Russian audience sees meaning in these works—sees, for example, a victory over officialdom in the blatant sexuality of the pas de deux and its use of the music of Pink Floyd. I prefer to think that such gratifications exist despite the work and not because of it. Was any good cause ever served by bad art? Eifmann seems to have taken Béjart as his model. In the pas de deux, Galina Mezentseva reproduces to uncomfortable perfection the look of a libidinous hornet which is a specialty of Béjart's danseuses, and in *Adagio* Evgeny Neff dances his Jorge Donn–like role with more conviction than absolutely necessary. Two of Béjart's own works, *Webern Opus 5* and *Bhakti*, are also danced, and are actually made to look good—better, that is, than Béjart's own dancers can make them. In *Webern Opus 5*, Chenchikova wears a white unitard, revealing her retracted pelvis, which diminishes the power of her thighs and makes her upper and lower body look tenuously connected. Chenchikova is scrupulously careful about her footwork, and once you get used to the odd line of her neck and shoulders and her jutting head, which is a Kirov trait, she is also very striking in épaulement. But I find her plastically inexpressive, with no flow-through to relate and enliven the various poses and steps she executes perfectly; she's like a singer with perfect pitch who hasn't learned to sing a song. Instead of fluency, Chenchikova uses the cascading legato she used in the Shades scene; it is attack doing the work of rhythm. But *is* it attack? Is it legato or lethargy?

The most puzzling item on this mixed bill is *Variations on a Theme of the Thirties*, a miniature by another Kirov choreographer, Dmitri Briantsev. The music is by Shostakovich—the light Shostakovich of the ballet scores, which were indeed written in the thirties and denounced for their decadence. Fyodor Lopukhov, one of Shostakovich's choreographers, became an unperson. Later, Lopukhov reflected bitterly, "The thirties were a turning point not only for my personal fate but in the life of Soviet ballet." He meant by that the sanctions imposed on all forms of artistic expression not in line with socialist realism. Briantsev's little ballet is untranslatable; the two characters, who appear to be a peasant and his girl, may recall a period when light-hearted folkloric comedies were popular and the collective farms could be satirized, as in the Shostakovich-Lopukhov *Bright Stream*. But Briantsev's comic style is in the leaden tradition of Soviet kitsch; the boy is lunkish, the girl a doll-faced twit, and what we are to make of their dancing—their lunging tangos, the grands jetés that he performs while gripping the forward ankle, her incessant pas courus—is never clear.

The portion of the program called "Chorégraphies Anciennes" introduces another puzzle—the everlastingly inscrutable Petipa legacy. There are three Petipa fragments that I have never before seen the Kirov perform: "Grand Pas Classique" from *Carnival in Venice*; "Pas de Six" from *Esmeralda*; and "Divertissement" from *Paquita*, which is almost as renowned a Kirov specialty as "The Shades." The program states whose version of Petipa we are seeing in each case. Agrippina Vaganova, though, is given sole credit for the *Esmeralda* excerpt; Petipa's name doesn't appear at all. This may be true to the facts of authorship; nevertheless, Vaganova's *Esmeralda* turns out to be the most persuasively *ancienne* of all the relics and the most like Petipa in both shape and substance. But before buckling down to these matters we are given the pleasure of seeing Irina Kolpakova perform with Sergei Berezhnoy a little pas de deux from Offenbach's *Le Papillon* arranged by Pierre Lacotte. Kolpakova's only appearances this season have been in the

Romantic revivals and pastiches of the repertory. In her late age—she is now fifty—she has become the queen of sylphs; her grand impalpable style has never seemed more secure. Kolpakova does not offer us illusion in place of a technique that she no longer possesses; she offers us the mysterious extension of that illusion which her technique has always sought to fulfill, even at its height. When Kolpakova lands from a grand jeté and throws up her back leg to make us think she has jumped higher, we are instantly pleased by the illusion, and we don't think of the jumping she used to do twenty years ago. Now, as then, the separate facets of her technique are precisely in scale one to another. Like Ulanova at the same age, Kolpakova makes you concentrate on what she does, not on what she doesn't do. She judges every effect, and yet she appears to dance with the freedom of the day she was born. Kolpakova refreshes my faith in Kirov ballerina style and its possibilities of expression. The generation just below her—the one that startled New York—is dispersed (Natalia Makarova) or unrepresented in Paris (Alla Sizova, Gabriela Komleva). Evteyeva and Natalia Bolshakova (whom we saw in *Bhakti*) are younger still, and retain some of the qualities of training and expression of their predecessors. But between this level and the next there seems to be a wide gap. The airy flickering variety of Kolpakova and the workmanlike precision of Chenchikova have nothing detectable in common. In an adagio, Kolpakova seems to float; Chenchikova works with mass, volume, cantilevered weight. I suppose there is room for both. But not in my heart.

"Grand Pas Classique" gives us still another of the current ballerinas—Svetlana Efremova, who is all candy floss. I find that by the end of the excerpt she has given me a toothache. Or maybe it's the choreography—the ugly anachronistic lifts, the coy and unseemly recapitulations of Aurora's dances in *The Sleeping Beauty*. It is not unlikely that Petipa repeated steps from role to role—all ballet masters do that. But to repeat himself unthinkingly—and to caricature himself—is the way not of a ballet master but of a confused regisseur hoping to recapture some lost essence and settling for literal repetition. When Efremova does her variation, four men with lutes appear behind her, recalling not only the four suitors who partner Aurora in the Rose adagio but also the four friends with lutes who in some productions become involved with the suitors. In "Grand Pas Classique," nobody becomes involved with anybody; the men do some double air turns and that's that. The giveaway is that the music is in fours: would Petipa have passed up such an opportunity?

A corrective comes in the very next number—*Esmeralda*. Vaganova may have designed it, but she built upon Petipa just as surely as Petipa built upon Perrot (and Saint-Léon and Mazilier and Taglioni). The pas de six is, like the Rose adagio, a pas d'action. The heroine, partnered by a man she does not love, must dance for the man she loves and has lost. Petipa, having made his dance for Virginia Zucchi, demanded of Kchessinskaya, who coveted the role, "You love? You suffer?" The story is drawn from Hugo's *Notre-Dame de Paris*. Esmeralda, the street dancer, is partnered by Gringoire. Not Hugo but Drigo is responsible for the chorus of Gypsy girls who dance a perkily irrelevant pas de quatre. (These semidetached female foursomes—Drigoettes?—turn up also in *Harlequinade* as staged by Balanchine and *The Magic Flute* as staged by Peter Martins.) The high point is the pas de deux, in which Esmeralda's heartbreak, her faltering courage, and finally her unquenchable high spirits and love of dancing are depicted. Tambourines, which are played by all hands, are woven into the emotional fabric of the dance. In the adagio, a tambourine held over the heroine's head becomes a token of the enforced levity that draws her onward. She grasps the tambourine (arms en haut), bends low in arabesque, and, in a gesture of pride and submission, completes a long slow penchée promenade. In the variation, she reaches a peak of euphoria only to end slumped in dejection. Yes, what a role. And what a dancer. This is Asylmuratova (Ah-sill-moor-*ah*-to-va), and until this moment I had never heard of her, nor had I ever seen what she showed me: emotional highs and lows depicted with the unbroken tension of idyllic lyrical dancing. One doesn't know whether her impulse is musical or dramatic; the sense of consummation, of wholeness and richness, is there before you in everything she does. The other Kirov ballerinas dance on as large a scale, but they don't have her burning vitality or her musical momentum or her range. Asylmuratova can be huge, as in the yawning stretched-through arabesque allongée that she takes on entrance in *Esmeralda*. Or, slipping into épaulée attitude, she can show a delicious Kolpakova-like subtlety. (She slips the forward shoulder farther forward without strain or distortion.)

She was born in Kazakhstan. Both her parents and both her mother's parents were dancers, and she was brought up in theatres, which may account for her near-atavistic sense of drama. She began her training at the Kirov school at the age of ten and joined the company at seventeen. Vinogradov predicted jokingly that she would dance *Swan Lake* her first year in the company; her début came this year. In Paris the week before I arrived she danced *Swan Lake* unscheduled; it was her second performance of Odette-Odile. Olivier Merlin filed a dithyramb in *Le Monde*, comparing

her to Makarova and going on about her Greek nose, cherry
mouth, and Circassian sloe eyes. She also had the most gently curved bosom, voluptuous arms, long legs, and the
loveliest feet in the world. To people who had not seen her,
it sounded like a grab for attention on behalf of a company
whose ballerinas up to now had not thrilled Paris. But Asylmuratova is the real thing. And she is a great beauty. I saw
her give her Esmeralda performance again; the second time
she was slightly broader and twice as wonderful. She was
also one of the fiancées in the ballroom act of *Swan Lake*,
and she appeared in the corps of *Chopiniana* and *La Sylphide*. That was all I saw of her. In his review, Merlin said
that rapid promotion of young dancers is unusual at the
Kirov. It isn't in the case of unusual talent. Makarova
danced Giselle and Sizova Aurora at twenty-one. But I
agree that Asylmuratova is the most prodigiously endowed
ballerina the Kirov has shown us in twenty years.

Vinogradov restaged the *Paquita* excerpt, which was
danced before a drop portraying the audience at the Maryinsky in the 1880s. The variations (except the ballerina's)
were deleted, the man's role was reduced to partnering, and
the "choral" pas de deux, in which the ballerina's supported
poses are echoed and complemented by the unsupported
poses of the corps, was as evasively presented as it was in the
Makarova version given in New York two years ago. I suspect the great aesthetic divide between Kirov and Western
style is over the question of adagio. What the Kirov dances
in this *Paquita* pas de deux is not what we would call an
adagio—that is, a connected succession of slow movements;
it is a succession of fast movements performed in a slow
tempo. The time between movements is either filled in with
poses until the music catches up or bridged by legato leak-
ages that do not sustain connections so much as they avoid

posing. It may be that Petipa's point was to show precisely the difference between dancing and changing poses when he set supported and unsupported versions of the same steps. Whatever he intended, there is little substance here. The Makarova version, which was said to derive from the Kirov, tended to diminish the stature of the ballerina. Here she dominates. But, as in "The Shades," she does so at the expense of the other roles. Chenchikova danced with overwhelming strength and authority—especially in her solo, when she knocked off high-attitude en-dedans spins that ended in perfectly controlled hopping arabesques. In the coda, she started turning her fouettés with a triple. I think I see what others mean by calling her a classicist—it's her impeccability in the execution of steps. Tatiana Terekhova, who also danced *Paquita*, is even cleaner than Chenchikova and to my eye more comfortably centered. Unfortunately, she has a hard stage face. One can see the importance of these dancers in the development of Kirov ballerina technique. The great promise of Asylmuratova rests in the fact that she's not a throwback; she incorporates the Chenchikova strain and loops it back to Kolpakova, if not all the way back to Zucchi.

—June 21, 1982

The Kirov Abroad,
Stravinsky at Home

Palais des Congrès, Paris; May 28, 29, and 30: To anyone who has seen American Ballet Theatre's *Swan Lake* recently, the Kirov production is not eccentric. Except in the overture, which begins in a long-drawn-out moan of anguish, the tempos are not slower; they're only *as* slow, and often they're faster. The action is tautly paced; the peak is reached in the last act. Oleg Vinogradov has supervised a freshened version of the Konstantin Sergeyev production that has served the company since the fifties. Igor Ivanov has dressed it well: the swans as they cross the lake are reflected in deep-blue water; the throne room has stone Gothic arches and tapestries; everywhere, there is light and space. I would like to see the *Sleeping Beauty* that this designer could do. The costumes, by G. Solovieva, are unaffectedly beautiful, with faint references to early German Renaissance painting. (ABT's late-German Holbein-and-Bruegel look is too plummy.) The show opens badly, with a dozen courtiers doing sautés to the pantomime march, but this is not to be a series of scènes dansantes, like the Bolshoi production. Indeed, one of the most attractive aspects of this *Swan Lake* is its traditionalism; it even eliminates the Prince's variation with the crossbow, which years ago the Kirov introduced. The intrusive jester is still there, performing his misshapen grande pirouette after the hazing of the tutor. Of course, there is no Benno, no speech by the Princess Mother about choosing a wife, and no organized hunt. The two ensembles in the first act are both performed by nobles (no peasants) in a sprightly, small-stepping style that suggests sixteenth-century court dance. In the pas de trois, the man's solo opens with three sissonnes battues facing the downstage corner; Evgeny Neff, who danced in all three performances, had to adjust his tombé landing each time. The steps done at ABT, no less awkward, are in fact the opening steps of the Third Shade's variation at the Kirov. Wires are constantly crossing in Petipa revivals. The attitude balance that the Kirov's Odette takes standing on the Prince's thigh at the end of the coda is a vestige of the Benno version of the pas de deux; the customary high lift has been transferred by the Kirov to the end of the Black Swan pas de deux.

Swan Lake has come down to us a patchwork, and a patchwork it will probably always be. The Kirov version is the smoothest that one can see; the power of it keeps rising all evening long. The national dances are not a boring interlude before the pas de deux; taken at a tearing pace, they are performed with devotion and even pleasure. These dances have long been a point of pride with the Kirov, as has the work of the corps in the swan scenes. Kirov swans are more elegant than Bolshoi swans; no other swan corps I know is comparable. The Russian companies possess a collective style for *Swan Lake* which has existed as long as the ballet has. While I admire the Kirov's style as sheer accomplishment, I don't find it very appealing. The whole company, from ballerinas down to littlest cygnets, dances a beat behind the orchestra. But this first point of connection to a phrase of music may also be the last. It's as if correct execution of a step mattered more than musical transparency. The efforts of dancers and orchestra to get together take certain ritualistic forms. The orchestra often slows down the end of a number. Odette's variation is played as well as danced legato. The fidgeting of the corps as it forms up in this act is inexcusable—who cares whether they stand left or right pointe tendue back. None of the three ballerinas I saw—Olga Chenchikova, Tatiana Terekhova, Galina Mezentseva—was able to make the stylistic prerogatives lovely. (Right behind them were eight young demi-soloists any one of whom might have done the job.) The corps was best in the last act, performing its grand-scale orchestrations of Lev Ivanov's themes. At the end of the Valse Bluette, the dancers walk toward the audience in ranks, their arms around each other's waists, and there is a slowing down that, for once, has a real effect. As the Russian dance historian Yuri Slonimsky described it, "Their walk becomes slower and slower until, in accordance with the last measures of the dying-down music, the group of black swans stops on its last drawn-out step, as if throwing to the auditorium a whispered 'All has ended.' " Unfortunately, all hasn't; Soviet custom still requires the tearing off of the sorcerer's wing and the lovers united in life.

If I haven't mentioned the men of the company, it's because up to now they haven't done much. In truth, they're not asked to do more than partner, perform their solos in an appropriate style, and in general present a good appearance. Sergei Berezhnoy in *Le Papillon*, *Swan Lake*, and *La Sylphide*, Vladimir Petronin in *Paquita* and *Swan Lake*, Vladimir Bondarenko in *Chopiniana*, Eldar Aliev in "The Shades" and *Esmeralda* (also a good Rothbart), and one or two others whose names in last-minute loudspeaker announcements were unclear did all they were asked. Kirov men are not as rigorously trained as the women. The technical precision of a Nureyev, a Baryshnikov, a Yuri Soloviev is not emulated, though the Baryshnikov "look"—boyish, tousled, angelic— is still popular. Konstantin Zaklinsky took many of the leading roles, and it is easy to see why: he is tall, with exceptionally long and handsome legs, and with some of the Rudi-Misha magnetism. In modern roles, he has a feral power, but in the classics his dancing and deportment are unpolished. Valery Emets is an evidently important dancer whom I didn't get to see enough of. Neff, on the other hand, was all over the place. A rising young man, he looks as if he hadn't the energy to rise much farther. Limpness, translated into Romantic lassitude, was his main quality as Albrecht in *Giselle*.

June 1: The company has an excellent character dancer in Vadim Gulyayev, whose serenity at the center of Vinogradov's ballet on Gogol's *The Inspector General* was very nearly heroic. The piece is a whirlwind of unrealized conceptions or else of realizations—such as the use of dancers in paper costumes to represent currency or letters—that should never have been conceived. Ninel Kurgapkina, who will be remembered from the American tours, and Natalia Bolshakova appeared as comic ladies, and there was an enormous cast of stomping, storming, reeling, prancing, and mincing actor-dancers in grotesque makeup. I admire Vinogradov's effort to reintroduce narrative into Russian ballet without resorting either to standard mime or to currently popular all-dance formulas. But he chose an impossible vehicle. Words or some form of linguistic expression is essential to *The Inspector General*. Vinogradov may have suspected as much when he constructed the "conversation" in which Gulyayev and another dancer hurl syllables like "ah-*hah*, ah-*hee*" at each other.

June 2: *Chopiniana*, *La Sylphide*. Less than a week *chez* Kirov, and I have fallen into the company's thought patterns. Romantic ballet is one style, classical is another. *Chopiniana*, *La Sylphide*, and *Giselle* are Romantic; *La Bayadère* is Petipa, hence classical. Whatever they mean by these categories, there is no question that Romantic ballet is home to Kirov dancers. *Chopiniana*, the Fokine ballet that we know as *Les Sylphides*, is every bit as wonderful as I had remembered. The tempos do not drag; the performance— *spirituel*, not soulful—is vibrant with belief, fantasy, fun. Elena Evteyeva gives her liveliest performance of the week in the mazurka and the waltz pas de deux. A kind of pantomimic suggestiveness lies beneath the skin of these dances. Would that I could have photographed it and taken it home to Ballet Theatre. Bondarenko's performance as the Poet had some of the insularity that has long disturbed me in Nureyev's (why do they stand there gazing into their armpit while bien-aimée is dancing?), but I liked his vigor.

Vinogradov was right to acquire the Bournonville *La Sylphide* instead of Pierre Lacotte's mishmash of Taglioni. Apart from a tendency to mime too forcefully, the company's behavior is charmingly correct, and it dances as well as it does in anything else. The production, staged after a version by Elsa-Marianne von Rosen, has been tailored here and there to local taste; if it is un-Danish, it is never dull. Irina Kolpakova's dancing ripples with wit, and the sylphs, more impish than their Danish sisters, are adorable. There are four demis, led by one who in her solo takes some inappropriate développé-balances à la seconde. The program identifies her as Olga Likhovskaya, tomorrow night's Giselle.

June 3: Olga Likhovskaya turns out to be somebody else. The question is: Just who is she? This is the most boring Giselle I have ever seen, and it's opposite the most anemic Albrecht—Neff. Likhovskaya is young and pretty, but she has no conception of Giselle beyond the one that seems to have been handed to her, like a text, to study and master. The Kirov ballerinas are apparently expected to play their roles according to a set interpretation; even where you think the flash and fire of individuality could hardly be avoided, they are all alike. I saw three different Odiles stamped from the same mold. And you think of Makarova confined in this prison and then escaping to cut and polish numberless facets of the one or two gems in her native repertory. Likhovskaya is a good girl who has been to Giselle school. In the second act, she takes the damnable legato phrasing so seriously she seems to be moving underwater. Well, no matter: the production is marvelous—not in Act I, which plods and temporizes, but in Act II.

Let me add one more qualification: what's marvelous is the corps. *Giselle* originally had two choreographers: Perrot is thought to have done Giselle's dances and her pas de deux with Albrecht; Coralli is generally credited with the Wilis and all that end of things. In Russia, Petipa overhauled the whole ballet, and through the ages it went on being subtly redesigned until it became what it usually is today—a star vehicle, with the roles of Myrtha and the Wilis scaled down to a supporting chorus. The Kirov production, which might be called "Coralli's Revenge," restores Myrtha and, even more impressively, the Wilis to full dimension. When the Giselle and Albrecht are as uninteresting as they are tonight, the performance can still offer excitement in the staging of the Wilis' dances: in the ghostly materialization out of the night mist of Myrtha, in the equally ghostly materialization of the corps, which appears halfway out of the wings wearing bridal veils and pauses there as the veils are whisked away—an effect accomplished without raising the laugh that has caused it to be deleted from Western productions. (It's a matter of timing; the Kirov also manages a dignified introduction for its dummy Swan Queen at the start of the lakeside scene.) Then there is the excitement of the big waltz over consecrated ground which prepares Giselle's entrance, followed by the concerted sweep of the dances that ensnare first Hilarion and then Albrecht in their fatal web. The diabolical choral symmetry of the choreography is thrilling to behold on the wide stage of the Palais des Congrès. Thirty Wilis, each with an obdurate shoulder, compose a diagonal line as solid as an executioner's wall. And the dramatic sense of the choreography is carried out in the "dialogue" between the principals and the corps. Albrecht is directed to his doom not just by Myrtha but by all the Wilis; the slow half turn that waves him up the line is a turn through the shoulder. Then, as Giselle appears, running down the line, it re-forms itself in reverse, as if it had changed its mind. In the Hilarion episode, the corps masses behind him doing fouettés sautés in arabesque, which he clumsily tries to approximate; as in no other production, we actually *see* the Wilis compelling his moves, and when he collapses and they add the upflung arm that completes the step (we have already seen it in the waltz) it's like a cry of victory.

Some flying effects at the start of the act don't quite work. After her materialization out of the dark, Myrtha vanishes, to be flown by wire across the back of the stage; later, when she appears to Albrecht, Giselle is flown in the opposite direction. Likhovskaya and Neff, for all their dullness, manage a persuasive set of apparitions, most effectively climaxed by her launching herself into the slow lift that coin-

cides with the repeat in the melody. There are some parts of
the *Giselle* canon to which the Kirov gives peculiar emphasis. The Wilis, stationed on the sidelines, constantly change
their stance, like sentinels, but in one such change they repeat the pas de bourrée from their big dance, unsettling,
then resettling, then re-unsettling themselves in a way that
looks crazed with exhaustion. Why this restless flexing and
shifting of the feet should have expressive effect in *Giselle*
when a similar fidgeting in *Swan Lake* has none is something to puzzle over. But then a far greater puzzle is the disparity between the two ballets as the Kirov performs them.
Swan Lake, for all its handsomeness as a production, is
dead—dead in its dance core—and *Giselle* is alive.

June 4: Galina Mezentseva's head juts out farther, her
tempos are slower, her legato is gummier than anybody
else's. In her *Giselle*, as in her *Swan Lake*, she turns adagio
into adagissimo; even her mad scene is slow. In Act II, her
pointes, which seem arched only from the metatarsus down,
dig into the stage like claws. But Mezentseva puts on a big
face, *souffrant* and semiblind, and wins big applause. Those
feet of hers are an extreme version of the inflexible pointework one sees in the corps—consistently bumpy relevés,
nothing like the smooth rolling up to or down from pointe
which American dancers cultivate. The "sick" feet may be
part of what I love in the *Giselle* corpswork and reject in
Swan Lake. On second thought—tonight brings me a second thought—the big difference may be in the music. The
orchestra produces more emotion in the mad scene than the
dancers do. In the second act, it works hand in glove with
the corps. The emotion is enormous—Tchaikovskyan. But
the corps and the orchestra that carry *Giselle* lag and drag
and natter when it comes to the tempos and rhythms of
Swan Lake. In the second act, they give you the feeling that
they want it as much like *Giselle* as possible. The way every-

body hits the waltz phrase—with a retard, with a lurch, with a swoon—looks quaint, and quaintness is not the most desirable characteristic in *Swan Lake*. *La Sylphide*, with its charming, tractable score by Løvenskjold, can aspire to the condition of *Giselle*, but *Swan Lake* is musically light-years beyond them both. Slonimsky, who, along with Vinogradov, was responsible for the present production of *Giselle*, has written books on all three of these ballets which undoubtedly provide clues to their treatment by the Kirov, but the books have yet to be translated.

Performance tradition is so strong in the indisputable masterpiece of the repertory that tonight the ballet again succeeds despite its cast. Zaklinsky plays Albrecht as a heedless, ardent boy; the caddish Albrecht of former days seems to have been banished. But although he performs earnestly, Zaklinsky really doesn't know how to give the role shape and stature. The peasant pas de deux is attractively performed on both nights by Irina Chistyakova, who was thanklessly cast in the Briantsev piece I mentioned last week. The better of her two partners, and one of the most elegant male soloists I have seen all week, is Andrei Garbuz. Why don't the Kirov dancers spot their turns? Tonight's Myrtha, Olga Iskanderova, spins herself dizzy for lack of a spot. Jerome Robbins includes a joke about this habit of the Kirov in his *Other Dances*, made for Makarova and Baryshnikov. But without its crotchets the Kirov wouldn't be the Kirov. When a company has as much to show us as this one still has, crotchets can become as significant as any other element of style.

New York State Theater, June 10: New York City Ballet's main crotchets of style are in that big Stravinsky beehive it keeps returning to, sometimes making honey, sometimes just buzzing around. This evening, the Stravinsky Centennial Celebration is inaugurated with two trumpeters playing the "Fanfare for a New Theatre," which was composed for the opening of the house, in 1964. Then Jerome Robbins leads on forty-eight little girls in his clever *Circus Polka*, and the orchestra plays *Fireworks*. Finally, the first new work—*Tango*, conceived by Balanchine with a laconic wit that the dancers, Karin von Aroldingen and Christopher d'Amboise, seem unable to get hold of. *Tango*, like *Circus Polka*, reflects Stravinsky the vaudevillian, and *Piano-Rag Music* (the ballets, as is the custom of this company, are named after their music) continues the theme. Peter Martins's choreography is a set of trim acrobatic configurations for Darci Kistler and four men. Kistler, in black satin and rhinestones and with her hank of blond hair swinging, reminds you of the intrepid heroines of the musclemen acts. She doesn't in the least mind being pulled and hauled about—she thrives on it (Kistler grew up with four brothers who were wrestlers) and gives it style. And, as always, Kistler's sense of style is not derivative; it's her own invention. An amazing performer. Soon afterward—I keep to the premières on the program—Jacques d'Amboise's *Pastorale* presents Kistler effectively in quite different terms. But this brief lyrical pas de deux with Christopher d'Amboise might have more impact some other time; the Martins is a tough act to follow. John Taras's *Concerto for Piano and Wind Instruments* is his third and most successful treatment of this score. Its imagery recalls the first version, *Arcade* (1963), in its dual suggestion of the circus and the cloister. Kyra Nichols and Adam Lüders are a chaste couple in white, flanked by the profane forms of Wilhelmina Frankfurt, Peter Frame, and Mel Tomlinson. These three are actually among the lankiest and most llama-like dancers in the company; watching them career through

Taras's stride-stretch-strut ensemble sections is a pleasure, like watching an unusually well-matched precision drill team.

June 11: *Noah and the Flood*. In 1962, much publicity surrounded the collaboration of Stravinsky and Balanchine on a work commissioned by CBS Television. *The Flood*, as it was then called, was billed as a "dance-drama." Staged tonight, in scenery and costumes by the original designer, Rouben Ter-Arutunian, it is much more a drama-oratorio with incidental action and one dance. This dance, a convoluted corps-de-ballet number, is recognizably Balanchinean, but it is unrecognizable as the descriptive action that the scenario identifies as "The Building of the Ark." (Stravinsky wrote that he had visualized the builders as dancers—"the men pulling over their shoulders on imaginary ropes, the women bending, tugging, dragging." Balanchine seems to have cocked an ear and visualized pure-dance scintillation.) The Flood itself, in which some dancers roll invisibly under a black sheet while others are carried along on top of it, is the only passage with the kind of *faux-naïf* fantasy that Stravinsky appears to have had in mind. The other bits of action, which involve Adam and Eve, Lucifer as a scorpion and then as a thirty-foot serpent, and Noah and his family, who wear dummy heads and mime dialogue spoken by the narrator (John Houseman), do not require the services of a choreographer. Nor does the parade of the animals to the Ark, which is rendered here not by dancers but by dancers carrying cutouts of animals. Robert Craft conducts the performance, which includes members of the New York City Opera Chorus. The fragment called "The Building of the Ark" was reconstructed from CBS tapes and is typical of Balanchine's serial-music period, which ran intermittently between 1957 and 1966.

June 12: *Norwegian Moods*. New York City Ballet does not need to import Stravinsky ballets. This production of a Lew Christensen piece that was originally done for San Francisco Ballet salutes an old colleague who, forty-five years ago, was Balanchine's first American Apollo. *Norwegian Moods*, a pas de deux, also happens to be a good piece of choreography, structurally unorthodox, rhetorically inventive. Christensen hits off a skittish resemblance in the music to the bridal dances in *Le Baiser de la Fée*. The dancers, who perform glowingly, are Nichol Hlinka and NYCB's *Baiser* hero, Helgi Tomasson.

June 13: *Elégie*, a viola solo, is danced by Suzanne Farrell alone, in a filmy white dress. Kneeling, she begins what appears to be a conventional dance of mourning but then turns into something unconventional, unforeseen, and perhaps, when it is given again, unrecapturable. Emotionally, the dance is not extreme; it is, for Farrell, rather quiet. And, because it describes a singular more than a general condition, it is also noncathartic; it leaves you hanging. *Elégie* could become a solo version of *Meditation*, which in the great performances Farrell used to give with Jacques d'Amboise was always a singular experience, different each time it was seen.

In *Concerto for Two Solo Pianos*, Peter Martins casts two male soloists—Ib Andersen and Jock Soto—against a female ensemble. He also casts Heather Watts between Andersen and Soto, and his use of her determines the shape of the whole ballet. This is the first time I can recall Martins making a ballet that was not exclusively, or even primarily, about its music. The twenty-minute *Concerto* has a conscious dramatic subject, which it projects through the music—a very different thing from letting the music dictate what the drama will be. Watching the *Concerto*, you don't hear the music so much as absorb it. It makes exactly the right sound for every second of what you see, but you aren't directed to listen. Sight and sound come naturally and plausibly together.

This is an impressive advance for a New York City Ballet choreographer to have made, and from the evidence of his choreography I would guess that Martins knows he has made it. He pushes the drama all the way; he makes it uncomfortable for us. Not that it is comfortable to begin with. Here are the men in Stravinskyan split focus, there the tidily metrical, apian corps. Then Heather Watts walks on (shuffles on, really—has any classical ballerina ever made an entrance like it?), and the drama immediately begins. The choreography for Watts takes into account the thorniness that has made some people dislike her as well as the qualities of quick intelligence and serious dedication that have won her respect. Watts has worked very hard these past few years and progressed remarkably as a dancer, and it has changed her temper; she seems more open and genuine, happier to be right where she is, more obliging toward her audience. Yet she hasn't lost the almost bitter honesty that made her original indifference noticeable. Martins's ballet is in part about a destructive kind of honesty in the heroine. In a pas de deux with Andersen, Watts dances in a continual whorl of indecision; no move she makes looks wrong or bad, but she keeps on moving, keeps testing alternatives. You sense her outstripping the man—or his patience—and finally alienating him. A second pas de deux, with Soto, was less intricately fascinating in this première performance, and I am uncertain of the weight of the various solos in the piece as a whole. The female corps is both unnecessary and indispensable. Like the female corps in *Movements for Piano and Orchestra*, its function is to reflect and summarize aspects of the ballerina's role, and the ballerina's role, as Martins has understood it through Watts, is to illuminate a general condition through a process of self-exposure. Watts projects the kind of tension that is felt today by many women. She becomes part of the spectacle of our world and time. The role makes her a star. This uneasy, brilliant ballet is the first substantial work of the Stravinsky Celebration.

—June 28, 1982

Anna Pavlova

The Imperial Ballet of St. Petersburg in its last flowering produced a pride of ballerinas who, when their days of glory were done, lived on into illustrious old age. Lopokova died only a year ago; Spessivtseva, the last of the great pre-Revolutionary ballerinas, is still alive. The exception is Pavlova, who amassed the greatest legend of all. She died at fifty, on tour, a blazing comet that had burned itself out. Her death, from pleurisy, was headline news the world over, and she was mourned by a vaster public than any dance star had known before—or has known since. Her millions did not come to her; she came to them, traveling some four hundred thousand miles over six continents. Pavlova was a titan in an age of titans; even so, the facts of her career continue to amaze and appall. She endured the most arduous life a dancer can lead—a life on the road—and the bulk of her touring was composed of one-night stands. A new and valuable book, *Anna Pavlova: Her Life and Art* (Knopf), reprints the itinerary of her North American tour of 1914–15. Keith Money, the author, writes, "Just to look at it was to recoil with fatigue." *Was?* Here she goes, across the map of America, night after night stopping in a different city. Shrewd and ruthless bookers put her into the biggest halls they could find—three- and four-thousand-seaters— packed them solid, and then shot her on to the next Masonic hall or Shriners' auditorium. But Pavlova was indefatigable. When after nine months the tour ends in Chicago, her company rests. She herself films *The Dumb Girl of Portici*, goes to the West Coast for more filming, returns to Chicago, and begins a new tour, with the Boston Grand Opera, during which she performs, among other items, the opera on which the film is based. As Money remarks of a later and similar tour, "For the most part it was arrive, unpack, show, pack, travel—all in a twenty-four-hour span."

She did it, he thinks, because her restlessness and avidity gave her no choice. The Russian Empire was crumbling when, in 1909, Pavlova launched her Western career. Had she remained in Russia, she would have faced compulsory retirement at thirty-five, but even if, as in Preobrajenska's case, this rule had been relaxed and she had been allowed to continue, she would have had to deal with the stultifying regime at the Maryinsky. Not only Petipa, the ballet's principal architect and Pavlova's sponsor, but also her teacher Cecchetti had been dismissed, and the creative resources of the rising generation had already been corraled by Diaghilev for an assault on the West. There was a moment when Pavlova might have become the permanent prima ballerina of the Diaghilev company and Nijinsky's partner; Diaghilev let that moment pass. Butterfingers, Money suggests. He also suggests that Pavlova perceived an essential truth about the Diaghilev enterprise—that it was not primarily dedicated to dancing. This attitude betrayed her into some lapses of judgment (she rejected the title role in *Firebird* because she could not hear the dance pulse in the music), but it also fortified her on the missionary course her career took. She became in the world's eyes the absolute classical dancer, the singular representative of the Russian dance academies, the true successor to Taglioni and Elssler, the one and only great ballerina, the Swan.

Pavlova's art was so new in most of the places she went that reviewers and promoters had to search out a vocabulary to describe it. In the more sophisticated capitals, she was known as a "Russian" dancer; Isadora Duncan and Maud Allan were "classical"—i.e., "Greek." The word "ballet" meant nothing. When Pavlova arrived in America, her performance was billed as "ocular opera," and Carl Van Vechten wrote his famous laborious description of a traveling arabesque: "With her left toe pointed out behind her, maintaining her body poised to make a straight line with it, she leapt backward step by step on her right foot." Her physical appearance was new, too. For a dancer, she was thought to be unusually tall and thin, and she was not considered beautiful—not "exquisite" or "bewitching," like Adeline Genée. On behalf of her beloved *Giselle*, she fought the accumulated prejudices of her era. A New York reviewer found that "the ballet is just about as interesting to ordinary play goers now as looking over the files of *Godey's Lady's Book* for 1858 might prove." She danced it in London with Nijinsky. "The little jerky 'tunes' are unendurable. No! *Giselle* will not do!" It was the age of modernism, of expressionism, much too wise for the Wilis. "Who could really be alarmed by these nice young ladies in their white ballet-skirts?"

It may have been in response to criticisms like this that Pavlova began presenting her Wilis in Duncan-like draperies. Ultimately Pavlova triumphed. Her votaries

stamped *Giselle* with her image, and it dominates the ballet
to this day. Money's book, with its wealth of documenta-
tion, makes Pavlova credible as a forerunner of the classical
revivalism of our time. He dwells on such episodes as the
Hippodrome production, in one act, of *The Sleeping Beauty*.
This was in 1916, five years before Diaghilev attempted his
own full-length revival in London. Both Pavlova and Diaghilev were forced to dismantle their productions before
the runs were up. Pavlova's, a jewel-box fairyland concocted
by Bakst, is far less known than the Diaghilev version, also
by Bakst. But then less is known about Pavlova than about
Diaghilev and everything connected with him.

Anna Pavlova: Her Life and Art is an attempt to correct
the record. It is an elaborate testimonial to tireless research,
to single-mindedness, to connoisseurship of the most involving kind. Money, who has also done a book about Margot Fonteyn, obviously adores Pavlova, and sometimes his
scholarly discipline has to strain against an instinct to protect her, to make her be all things good. He cites her spon-
sorship of two Fokine ballets to prove that her taste in art
was not unsophisticated. (Perhaps only her taste in music?
The ballets were to Liszt and the nonentity Spendiarov. She
turned down Fokine's *Le Coq d'Or*, and it was produced by
Diaghilev.) He uses her activism in the reform movement at
the Maryinsky to suggest that she was politically avant-
garde. (But later, when Isadora became a Red sympathizer,
Pavlova was enraged.) If she slapped her partners, there
must have been a reason. She was not jealous of Nijinsky or
any other dancer. She paid her dancers well and gave expensive gifts. She loved children, small animals, and birds, especially swans. Although Money gives the impression of being
able to place her accurately on almost every day of her life,
he does not pretend to be omniscient. He speculates on her

character without subjecting it to analysis. That she was a lonely woman with an enigmatic sex life is something Money accepts. It was her lot. (Victor Dandré, who attached himself to her in Russia and remained until the end, was possibly her husband; if so, Money believes, there was no sexual union to speak of.) The Pavlova legend has always had about it the odor of martyrdom. Her genius, her toil, her power over the multitudes, and her early death seem to spell sacrifice and tragedy. There was sacrifice, perhaps, in dying at fifty. Implored to stop touring, Pavlova would say, "But my company! What will become of them?" Yet most dancers are dead as dancers by that age. What else but dancing could Pavlova have lived for? There was certain tragedy in the thinning repertory that was also her lot. Pavlova's wanderings began when she was twenty-eight; she had already conquered the standard ballerina repertory, had already claimed her signature roles (Giselle, Nikiya in *La Bayadère*, *Chopiniana*) and her personal vehicles (*The Swan*, *Autumn Bacchanale*). For the rest of her life, she was not to create another artistic success. Instead, she circled the earth repeating ancient triumphs, adding more dragonflies, more autumn leaves, more bacchantic veils to the diaphanous train of vanity ballets that sustained her. In India, she refreshed herself with Hindu dancing, and she performed awhile with Uday Shankar. But even this was a return of sorts—to *La Bayadère*.

She pushed on: Egypt, Japan, Australia. Money says of her obsession with touring, "Her body and mind were so programmed to this routine that the thought of abandoning it opened up black chasms of the unknown that terrified her more than the remorselessness of further touring." Perhaps it was to distract herself from such thoughts that she waged one of the most intensive personal publicity campaigns of the period. She endorsed face cream, silk stockings, pianos; she gave interviews by the score; she posed for endless photographs, many of which are reproduced in this book. There is not a bad one in the lot. Like Abraham Lincoln's, Pavlova's face is archetypal; it is changing and changeless at the same time. It responds to the lens as inventively as any movie star's, and it burns with inner life right from the start of the book—from the moment, to be exact, that she becomes a dance student. Its expression is irremediably tragic, but not bleakly so. There is pride in the way the head lifts itself above the tapering pedestal of the neck. And what vitality in that neck! How she flaunts it in her "grand" roles and guards it in her coquettish ones! Even in close-up, Pavlova's discipline proclaims her a dancer. She becomes pathetic only in the photographs that were taken in her forties—when she knows the search has ended. In one photograph, she appears to be offering her hands to the camera and not her face, but her face is caught anyway, wearing a look of grief. In a portrait on the same page, the chronic depression she suffered from is evidently upon her. Money's caption is "By now Pavlova was less inclined to force cheerfulness for the camera's benefit."

What makes the book valuable is that it isn't keyed to Pavlova's gloom. It projects a multifaceted picture: Pavlova as celebrity, sacred monster, symbol of the dance, artist, and star. The woman was fun, and Money has realized it. It takes some slogging to get through his text, but then Pavlova was a slogger. As the details pile up (enormous pains are taken to sort out her for the most part piddling repertory), we begin to sense something of the pain and joy of hard work, the bliss of sheer continuity, that Pavlova must have felt. Wholeness of mind and body must surely have been her salvation. In the fashion photographs, there is no affectation. There is artificiality, to be sure, along with elegance, wit, and style. In the dozens of dance photographs (some, with unretouched pointes, escaped Pavlova's vigilance), she shows the protean sensibility of performers of her era; she is always creating roles. But, unlike Karsavina or Nijinsky, she does not disappear into them. No matter the role or the circumstance, onstage or off, the eyes look out with an expression that says "I have found my life."

—December 20, 1982

Ordinary People

In the time-honored genealogical tradition of modern dance, choreographers are bred from other choreographers. A dancer in one company gets interested in making dances and starts another company, which produces dancers in a different style, some of whom will get interested in making dances. And so it goes: different and yet again different. But not always new and exciting. The tables over the years show a proliferation of companies; they don't show a proliferation of great choreographers. Choreography takes talent of a kind that not even the most accomplished dancers may possess. However, the tables also show that the best choreographers we've had, from Martha Graham to Twyla Tharp, have been electrifying performers; one could bank on that, just as one could bank on the expectation that sooner or later a good portion of our finest dancers would lose their potential simply because they didn't know how to choreograph, even for themselves. The one thing they'd have left was authority. Even though they weren't turning out remarkable dances, they'd still be the best dancers in their own companies—the system of succession compelled them to be, and the system was inviolable. So one would have thought until about a decade ago.

Sometime in the early seventies, the principle of the choreographer-leader fell into disrepute. Performing collectives sprang up which attributed choreography to the group. Ad-hoc performances were arranged by one person who would convene a group, which would then have the option of sticking together or disbanding. There were groups that did stick together and didn't renounce the idea of the choreographer-leader, but the choreographer-leader was no longer invariably the outstanding dancer in the group. He or she was a conceptualist. The time had come when one could no longer identify the key person in an unfamiliar company merely by picking out the best dancer on the floor. (The first time I saw Andy deGroat's company, I thought Garry Reigenborn was deGroat.) The antistar system of the seventies hasn't entirely succeeded in erasing stars, but it has succeeded in erasing dancing as the basis of stardom. By choreography alone—in their capacity or noncapacity as choreographers—we are asked to recognize the stars of today. If the old system was élitist, the new one is emphatically democratist. Under the old system, star performers would produce self-designed choreography, and if it worked for them, frequently it wouldn't work for anybody else. The problem with the new choreography, which looks as though it were designed at computer terminals, is that just about anybody can do it. Untrained dancers and rudimentary modes of expression are concomitants of computer choreography. Where trained dancers are used, as in Jim Self's company, they're kept busy trying to articulate the demands of an inarticulate printout. (The printout may be read in Self's own blurry performing.) It was different when a choreographer had to rationalize his theories of movement on his own body. At least there'd be *one* good performance to watch. Now that the choreographer-dancer-leader has been conceptualized out of existence, one can only watch good dancers struggle or weak dancers triumph.

The anybody-can-do-it school arose in the sixties as a reaction to exclusive personal virtuosity and self-display. This reaction was only partly dance-related. Deeper impulses lay in the countercultural politique, which was formed largely by progressive-school whiz kids trying to get in step with the underprivileged. Paradoxically, the idea of a programmed minimal vocabulary executed by trained or untrained dancers came about just as the shift occurred in social dancing from learned dances to improvisation. In discothèques around the country, "ordinary" people were making art for recreation; in modern-dance studios, professional dancers were doing Arthur Murray–like box steps. This may explain why the minimalist revolution never attracted much of an audience. Rooted in populist assumptions, it was out of phase with popular feeling. Besides, when ordinary people went to see dance performances they overwhelmingly chose the ballet, where spectacular lyrical dancing flourished. (To understand the dimensions of this rejection, try to imagine opera enjoying a wave of popularity while Barry Manilow and Elton John compete for government grants.)

The new choreography of today broadens and to some extent coarsens the egalitarian sentiments held by the minimalist vanguard of the sixties. Steve Paxton's "people dances" were like the life-size plaster casts of human bodies one began seeing at that time in art galleries. The dances and the sculpture were statements about how people actually move and look as opposed to how they were made to move and look in the theatre and the museum. It must be remembered that a big factor in Pop Art philosophy was the notion of things in unaccustomed places. Putting ordinary people making ordinary movements on a stage was like hanging a picture of a Campbell's Soup can in an art show. The idea was that the location would do the work of transfiguration which persons and objects normally underwent to become artworthy. As the sixties turned into the seventies and Pop Art polemics eased up, it was possible to see fruitful work—choreography that reaffirmed dancing as a natural human act. This accomplishment, though, was independent of prevailing stylistic trends, and it wasn't until later that these trends put their stamp on the era and decided the human temper of the dances that were being done. People dances had given way to structured choreography of a minimal nature. The beat returned to dominate what had seemed to be random movement in unfigured time. And then music came back—music marked not only by a heavy beat but by incessant rhythmic and melodic repetitions. The beat and the repetitions became characteristic of the new post-modern choreography. By the end of the seventies, it seemed that every new choreographer was presiding over some form of mechanized motion. Choo San Goh was doing it in ballet, and Molissa Fenley, following Lucinda Childs and Laura Dean, was doing it in postmodern dance. However one chooses to interpret the original impulse of the sixties—a symptom, a shock of the moment, or something finer and more lastingly significant—it is hardly possible to deny its conversion into a cult in the seventies. The regulating effect that cults have on creativity is well known. What we're seeing now is regulated *material*—literally, sports and games.

In post-modern dance, as the metrics got tighter and the repetitions more insistent, a new kind of content evolved—

one that superficially resembled the pedestrian tasks that were assigned to dancers by the older choreographers (like Yvonne Rainer's lugging of mattresses and Trisha Brown's manipulation of sticks). Charles Moulton's dancers stood or knelt in static groups and passed balls back and forth in complicated patterns. Or they flipped color squares in the manner of a cheering section in a stadium. These precision games of Moulton's were not, like the "tasks," designed to reveal something about movement; they were substitutes for movement. As a cheerful naïve form of entertainment, they were very winning, and audiences took to them. But they were only a new version of artists following box-step diagrams. Moulton is not as limited as I have made him sound, and he keeps on experimenting with popular dances and investigating specific dance forms. He's tried tap; he's even tried old-style expressionistic dance. But the results so far have been a little clinical. Moulton's use of old forms highlights the enormous change that has come over the pop sensibility in recent times. The cornerstone of popular American music and dance has been rhythm, and the rhythmic expression of American masters is an idea of freedom. But Moulton, like every other member of his generation, doesn't think of rhythm as something that gets larger and lighter; he thinks of it as getting tighter and heavier. In the dances of Johanna Boyce, which seem to have taken a lot from Moulton, minimal style is a kind of childishly gleeful overdeterminism. It's tiddly-pom with a vengeance.

Boyce's work doesn't just reduce the idea of minimalism—it makes reductionism a whole new principle. It completes the reduction of rhythm to metrics, and of plastic relationships to functional ones, and it goes further: it cuts away the supports of basic bodily gesture—it cuts into the *bone* of dance. The point of minimalism was to clarify and if possible to revitalize basic bodily gesture, but Boyce doesn't bother with basics; she hurls people around and lets the gesture take care of itself. She gets hold of one step combination (say, a hop-skip-jump) and repeats it, varying only number and direction, in a rhythm that gradually becomes deadening. In *Kinscope*, she has her company skip from one end of the piece to the other, throwing and catching and bouncing balls as they go. It sounds like fun, but it's so pressured and rhythmically so unrelenting that it becomes an endurance test—a black-humored marathon. The audience gets into the spirit and, at the end, cheers like the audience at *Rocky* or *Chariots of Fire*; the dancers have come through their ordeal. Team sports have fed choreographers ideas for a long time, but until now no one had thought to convert a sporting event into a dance. As choreographer (or games mistress), Boyce doesn't make the conversion complete. Things get wobbly the minute the dancers have to do two things at once or in two rhythms or speeds. In *Kinscope*, they each have to do an arm-whirling windup before throwing the ball, and very few of them can do it without looking frantic and smearing the movement. The idea of basic gesture, firmly supported from the base of the spine and cleanly delivered, is tossed away as casually as the ball.

It's rare to see so little discrimination brought to bear upon fundamentals. The last time I saw anything as heedless as this was in Molissa Fenley's solo concert last fall, in which she performed almost continuously at a brisk pace for over an hour. It was almost as naked a sports event as some of Boyce's work. Fenley tossed off a small repertory of dance steps, bringing to them about as much plastic energy, refinement, and variety of expression as she would have needed to cross a finish line. (Fenley is a runner who works out in gyms instead of taking dance classes.) Like Boyce's, her dynamics are confined to a single choice between fast and slow. But whereas Fenley tries to create a lyrical effect, waving her arms and flinging back her head (she reminds me of gymnasts who add ballet "finish" to their performance), Boyce seems to value gracelessness and cloddishness. The heavy inflexible rhythms are as deliberate as the tackiness of the costumes she designs, which are mostly shapeless T-shirts and shorts, rendered in a nightmarish assortment of floral prints. She also uses a number of people who aren't dancers, so that the bodies lumber where they might float, and look awkward and vulnerably sexual when stripped (for a nude sequence), unlike dancers' bodies. I have never understood the appeal of unskilled labor in the performing arts; still less do I understand why the unskilled should wish to appear unattractive. There's a vein of truculence through all of Boyce's work that I've seen. I wish I felt that she took more pleasure in her work and wasn't so determined to prove something. I wish, too, that she'd give up her evening-length autobiographical pieces, which come too close to being a form of personal mortification. It's interesting, though, that when Boyce did her solo in the latest of these epics, *With Longings to Realize*, she left the balls and batons and hockey sticks out of it and did a slow, brooding dance with flailings of the arms and little twitches, rather like—wistfully like—one of Merce Cunningham's solos. Was this the real Boyce, and how did it fit in with the clunkiness of all the rest? Boyce may need more time to emerge fully. Just now she's like a physical-education instructor trying to borrow a little status from the dance department.

—February 21, 1983

Theatre as Truth

Why is the new Paul Taylor–Alex Katz ballet called *Sunset*? A sunset is not part of Katz's décor; Jennifer Tipton's lighting does not imitate one. It is the time of day in which the events of the ballet take place, not so much in real time as in remembered time—time in the abstract. But the ballet doesn't have the sunset glow of memory; it has the chill of an actual experience on which the light has died, leaving the meaning of the experience suspended. And the feeling of suspension in the observer is perfectly pleasurable; we don't want to disturb it with explanations. Yet we can't deny that some part of the pleasure we feel comes from having, already, enough complexity of emotion to deal with. It's not just a feeling of being sated; it's a feeling of being sated and off balance. So the experience haunts us. There is some kind of trouble going on here—something unique, which the events of the ballet sharply qualify without naming. It calls out to be named, and there is no name. Under the circumstances, *Sunset* is as good a title as any.

Most of the pleasure we take in dance is purely private and has for sanity's sake to be defended from scrutiny—

our own as well as others'. But usually this pleasure doesn't ask to be defended. With *Sunset*, it does. Taylor and Katz have done more than make a piece filled with inscrutable sensuous-kinetic allure. They've taken our awareness of this allure and made it a condition of comprehension. What goes on inside us as we watch *Sunset* is normally the commotion that attends our responses in retrospect, and that's why, in retrospect, the ballet makes trouble for us. Thinking back on it is like probing a sore tooth. The sensation of the performance can dimly be re-created in memory because it sinks in deep from the start—it's like memory to begin with. We start with some soldiers in a park, whiling away the last hours of what probably was a weekend pass, and then the girls come in. The fact that the piece has a dramatic situation—that it isn't *pure* dance and therefore a comparatively pure memory—seems to me a masterstroke. Just the banality of it is a joy. But right away we are thrown off balance by the soldiers' unrecognizable uniforms with shoulder patches that we can't read, and red berets. Then there's the park itself. We see what must be a lookout promontory, but only a corner of it. The scenic view is cut off by a screen of Katz foliage—dabs of aqua and green—bordered by a metal guardrail. The screen meets another, taller one to form a sharp upstage angle; on this are painted more dabs, with the pattern ending where the treeline meets a patch of blank sky. Katz has thus walled off the back and one whole side of the stage, leaving the dancers no way in or out but stage left. Such a drastic modification of stage space might be expected to create a drastic effect. In fact, it looks modest and comfortable; the adventure of it dawns gradually as Taylor lays out his own modest bombshells.

When the curtain goes up on the men lounging by the guardrail, the whole stage picture has the disarming angular intensity of an Alex Katz painting; it is a natural scene from his special point of view. (It has the same selectivity that makes him paint only the upper story of a house, for instance, or a lakeside vista from behind a tree trunk.) And Taylor accomplishes the kind of miracle we hardly ever see in the theatre. He brings the naturalness and strangeness of this vision to life, and he even moves it through several levels of meaning and changes of tone without sacrificing its intensity as an image. The piece continues to look like an Alex Katz painting all the way through. The final pose—the frieze of women in their white summer dresses standing by the rail while another girl holds a beret that one of the soldiers has left behind—is another beautiful picture, and a complement to the first one. The movement of the ballet between these two images is motionless motion; nothing really seems to be happening but the rippling of a surface. Taylor achieved something of the same magical stasis a few years ago in *Nightshade*, his piece based on Max Ernst's collages in *Une Semaine de Bonté*. The violent stresses of Ernst's surrealism immobilized Taylor in a churning whirlpool of discontinuities. The new Katz ballet has a contemplative rather than an obsessive stasis. And things connect. Beneath the sweet, dreamlike surface, there's the conclusiveness of a social commentary. The agreeable dance manners of the piece are drawn from the social manners of the men in uniform. The elaborate listlessness and nonchalance they assume as a mask for loneliness are casebook attitudes. So is their behavior when the girls enter: without shifting their chewing gum, they become tense as young bulls. The moment has almost a generic fatalism, and the women are just women of the genre—nice city girls, as in *Fancy Free*. But in another minute the action diverges from genre ballets about servicemen, and diverges so significantly that it almost seems to be commenting on theatrical as well as social stereotypes. The women catalyze the change in the men; they themselves don't change (although they may be beginning to when the curtain falls). Taylor is very clear: this is a piece about men and men's responses to women.

Taylor has often shown us the power of his men dancers. It's unlikely that Christopher Gillis, Thomas Evert, Kenneth Tosti, David Parsons, Elie Chaib, and Daniel Ezralow have ever before set off the vibrations that they do here, in their awkward military uniforms. The boxy shirts and the belted pants with pockets that stick out give the wearers a kind of lumpish virility that prepares us for the situations they get into. Becoming involved with the women (Kate Johnson, Lila York, Cathy McCann, and Karla Wolfangle) releases a flow of reactions that the men don't seem to have under full control. Now and then, they lurch into dream situations, and we bob along on a tide of male subjectivity. At other times, the action is as prosaic as a street conversation. The littlest woman (York) is lifted and swooped through the air, more to the men's delight than to hers. Gillis makes a special moment of gallantry out of carrying her on his shoulder, and the others love bouncing her around. When she climbs over a mountain formed by their obliging backs, Gillis assists her, holding her by the hand, and at one point his hand clasping hers is between her legs. The climb, besides, is precarious; York doesn't attempt to disguise it. She doesn't make an issue of it, either, or of that indecorous handclasp. If we get the feeling that she's not too happy playing the part of an adorable little thing, it's no more than a shadow brushing the sun. Feelings like this come seldom. The women are happy with the men, and happiest of all with Chaib, who lets them pamper him and carry him about. (Unlike York, Chaib revels in being manipulated.) The others pair off to mutual good effect. One soldier (Tosti) is left out of the mating ritual, and his predicament pulls the ballet farthest from its pleasant prosaic center. Taylor has Tosti lie flat downstage during Chaib's idyll and appear to spy on it. This bitter moment is enlarged subsequently by Tosti's wrenching body lifts and slides on the floor. He's so much the odd man out that he almost falls out of the style of the piece. But the moment of near-expressionistic bravura passes, and, in one of Taylor's most tactful transitions, Tosti is restored to the amicable world we now know he doesn't belong to.

The finest of all Taylor's transitions occurs late in the action, during a dance for Kate Johnson and the six men. The absence of heat from this dance puzzled me at first. Johnson is the most elegant and the most demurely provocative of the women, and I was expecting some climactic development in the drama. But Taylor is already beginning to draw the men and the women apart—the day is ending. Johnson is there among the men, but she's not on their minds. They begin to form soldierly rows around her, and the neutrality of the arrangement persists when she is joined by the other women. At the end of this passage, the men take off their hats impassively in a farewell gesture. Then they march off in formation (dropping one hat), wanting clearly as much to be where they are going as where they have been.

Taylor's choice of music is oddly inspired: Elgar's Elegy and Serenade for strings. The dying embers have never seemed so nobly plaintive. In the Tosti episode, the music is interrupted by a tape of the cries of loons. This may seem unbearably sensitive to someone who wasn't there.

The things we take away from *Sunset* for the sake of conversation and criticism are the least interesting things about it. Whatever the piece "says"—about women as a part-time

need of men, or about the fatuity of male assumptions in regard to women, or about love versus duty, honor, and
country—is inconsequential beside the shimmering ambiguity of the vision it holds before us. Emotionally, no moment is unmixed, and the continuing delicacy and subtlety
of the piece trains us as we watch it. A simple response is
impossible. The short way of saying this is that *Sunset* invents a new realism in the theatre. Taylor and Katz have
taken the measure of the emotion we invest in the transitory
phenomena of dance and extended it to transitory phenomena in the real world. Edwin Denby, reviewing the première
of *Fancy Free*, recognized the ballet as "a superb vaudeville
turn," but he also could write, "Its sentiment of how people
live in this country is completely intelligent and completely
realistic." *Sunset* derives from painting rather than from
vaudeville; it, too, is a serious document of the way people
live. You can study it for the changes that have occurred
in human nature in the last forty years—or, rather, in our
stageable perception of human nature. Still, the fact of
change isn't as important as the motion of it. *Sunset* changes
before your eyes.

—April 25, 1983

The Legacy

In the first week of life without Balanchine, it was good to have New York City Ballet to go to, and especially good to have so many performances of great works like *Divertimento No. 15* and *Concerto Barocco* and *Symphony in C*. All honor to the dancers who performed so gallantly in such trying circumstances. Because of them, the darkest week in the history of the company—in the history of ballet in America—was not also a desolate one. Ballets don't exist unless they are danced; to see Balanchine's danced at such a time by his own company was to have the best possible assurance that they can endure as his monument. Which of them are masterpieces is a question that we do not have the luxury of deciding. Let posterity make the choices. For the moment, it is more important to know which are most perishable and therefore in need of closest attention from those now in charge of preserving Balanchine's repertory. Of the three I have named, *Divertimento No. 15* strikes me as the most fine-spun, the one most likely to snap under the strain of insufficient rehearsal or inadequate casting. Even when the dancers are good and are well prepared, things can be set wrong with a flick of an indifferent conductor's baton. In contrast to the *Divertimento*, *Concerto Barocco* is hewn from rock, yet it, too, has its vulnerable points. Overscrupulous and unmusical execution such as one sometimes gets from other companies that perform this work makes its marble surface gritty; in the long cantabile phrases of the pas de deux, lapses in stamina open fissures that Balanchine did not intend.

Concerto Barocco was made, along with *Ballet Imperial* (now called *Tchaikovsky Piano Concerto No. 2*), for a tour of Latin America in 1941. As companion pieces, they present balanced views of Balanchine's roots in imperial Russian ballet and of the flowering of the new ballet in America. *Concerto Barocco* could also have been called *Ballet Imperial*; New York is the Empire State. This small ballet (ten women, one man) to the Bach Double Violin Concerto has the epic power of some such new colossus as the Manhattan of the thirties. Power, cruelty, exhilaration (the colossus rising) are offset by baroque scrollwork and unexpected bursts of jive (the colossus as habitat). As in those black-and-white photographs taken by Lewis Hine or Berenice Abbott from the tops of skyscrapers, one sees detail and depth with contrapuntal clarity. "It amazes me," Balanchine said, "that some people never notice the tops of buildings."

It is difficult, seeing these ballets just now, to avoid thinking of them as landmarks in time—as milestones if not masterpieces. The conjunction of *Concerto Barocco* and *Symphony in C* on many of the past fortnight's programs repeated the historic first-night bill of New York City Ballet in 1948, at the City Center. (The middle ballet was *Orpheus*.) *Symphony in C*, another architectural marvel, had been unveiled the year before in Paris, under the title *Le Palais de Cristal*. Balanchine, reviving an early composition of Bizet's, staged it on commission from the Paris Opéra. So successful were the Balanchine evenings in Paris that he was urged to stay and assume control of the Opéra ballet. He might well have been tempted—it was the prize post in Western ballet. Balanchine returned to America. The following spring, instead of new triumphs at the Opéra there was *Orpheus* at the shabby City Center. As for the Bizet ballet, it has come to symbolize not the Paris Opéra but New York City Ballet.

Balanchine is widely and justly ranked with Stravinsky and Picasso. Unlike them, he lived and worked in New York and chose to consider himself a New Yorker. The city furnished him with inspiration right through to *Who Cares?* and *Stravinsky Violin Concerto*. Belatedly—not until the sixties—it provided a showcase theatre and a home for the School of American Ballet, which was Balanchine's first enterprise in partnership with Lincoln Kirstein and the foundation for all the others. To function properly, New York City Ballet and the School of American Ballet must be mutually dependent: the school feeding the company new dancers; the company, through its choreographers, feeding the school new ideas of dance style. (Balanchine also liked to say that style comes from the stage to the classroom, not the other way around.) This ideal exchange has not been consistently maintained. For one thing, Balanchine's new ideas were not always readily assimilated, even by his company. But in the school's annual workshop performances the soundness of the system proclaims itself. The reciprocal process works on a day-to-day, nonapocalyptic basis.

The school performances this year, as always, offered a range of work. Besides the Balanchine *Valse Fantaisie* and *Western Symphony* revived by Suki Schorer, and the Bournonville pas de deux from *Kermesse in Bruges* revived by

Stanley Williams, there was a selection of Morris folk dances from England, staged by Ronald Smedley and Robert Parker, of the Royal Ballet School. Even in a country-dance minuet or a four-hand reel, there is such a thing as correct style; indeed, the more elementary the form the more exposed are the basic principles of expressive dancing. In this respect, the SAB students were better exponents of minimalism than some of our professional postmodernists. The new ballet on the program was a setting, by Helgi Tomasson, of dance music by Messager, mostly from the opera *Isoline*. Tomasson has done one other work for the school; his *Ballet d'Isoline* is by far the more successful. The more ambitious, too. Tomasson hasn't yet found a personal style; his choreography keeps saying "Not by Balanchine" much the way the Messager music keeps saying "Not by Delibes." But the ballet is a skillful, confident, even venturesome piece of work. The House of Balanchine is turning out to have more rooms than one may have supposed. *Ballet d'Isoline* will be produced by the company, and there'll be more to say about it then, especially if it is revised. At the moment, it is strongest in the ensembles and male variations, weakest in the pas de deux. Here the choreography loses its grip on the music and meanders. A male quintet is the high point; Tomasson seems to have exercised recondite aspects of his own formidable technique as a soloist. The pride of the workshop series was the group of young male dancers who were featured in Tomasson's ballet and in the Balanchine pieces. It is unusual to see so many good boys in one year. But the level of achievement was a high one overall.

The fresh young performing in *Valse Fantaisie* and *Western Symphony* made me want to see both ballets in repertory—*Western* with its long-missing third movement restored. The version of *Valse Fantaisie* was the later one, choreographed in 1967. It shares a few steps with the 1953 version, but it is a different ballet. In expanding the male soloist's role Balanchine seems to have drained off much of its poignance. Once a ballet about a man and three women, *Valse Fantaisie* became an extended pas de deux—actually, two pas seuls—with a backup group. The first program announcements by the school erroneously gave the ballet's date as 1953. Maybe next year. There are not many other ballets retired by Balanchine which would be worth restoring to active repertory. *Gounod Symphony* would be, but not *Clarinade* or *Variations pour une Porte et un Soupir*.

Symphonie Concertante was unaccountably dropped in 1952 and forgotten for thirty years. When American Ballet Theatre revived it from dance notation last winter, one could only be grateful for the recovery of a lost treasure. But the performance seemed wrong then, and it still seems wrong. The principal roles, arranged to the violin and the viola of Mozart's concerto symphony, are still being danced by Cynthia Gregory and Martine van Hamel with the concern for trivial technical perfection and the unconcern for dynamic shading and musical transparency which marred the première performances. They were followed by Susan Jaffe and Magali Messac: same irrelevant display of technique, same unmusicality. If Gregory and van Hamel, senior ballerinas with ironclad performing styles, were miscast, their juniors were miscast and misguided. Jaffe was plainly taking Gregory for her model, while Messac's virtues were never meant for Balanchine. Stiff where they should be crisp, weak where they should be soft, persistently on the beat and off the music, all these ladies danced as if they thought Balanchine and Mozart were a more concentrated version of Petipa and Minkus. Patrick Bissell, the cavalier in the first cast, seemed to know better but not to have passed his knowledge on to his successor, Ross Stretton. After four months of breaking in, ABT's noble experiment in resuscitation looks very much like a failure.

Does the failure reflect incapacity on ABT's part or is there something the matter with trying to revive a ballet as complex as *Symphonie Concertante* from notation with no other memory aid? ABT has long possessed a Balanchine jewel in *Theme and Variations* and would on occasion perform it to the hilt. I saw some wonderful *Theme*s as recently as a year ago. This ballet stems from the same creative period in Balanchine's career as *Symphonie Concertante* and *Symphony in C*, and although it is set to Tchaikovsky and not Mozart, it supplies clues to Balanchine's musical thinking which could have been pertinent to the reconstruction of the unknown Mozart work. But the two ballets as staged come from two different worlds. And, as if to create the widest possible contrast between them, ABT has revised its production of *Theme and Variations*, substantially reconceiving the ballet in the process. The stage is dark; the pas de deux is now a nocturne. The slow tempo doesn't make it more romantic; the legato attack only blurs and sentimentalizes the beautiful dance poem that Balanchine was able to create while contriving an ingenious simulation of adagio effects for the allegro technician who danced the première, Alicia Alonso.

Baryshnikov is presiding over a new Ballet Theatre—one in which every corps member performs impeccably. A clean style is always pleasant to see. But scrubbing away impurities isn't enough to make dancing interesting. I am sure Baryshnikov knows it. He is assembling a dream repertory of works by Balanchine and Merce Cunningham and Paul Taylor and Twyla Tharp that do make dancing interesting, but in completely different ways. A mixed repertory has ever been Ballet Theatre's policy and ever an impractical one. No company in the world could master all these styles at once. Ballet Theatre excels in *Push Comes to Shove*, which Tharp created on commission (and keeps restudying). It is credible in *Airs*, a piece that was begun by Taylor on ABT dancers. But its version of Cunningham's *Duets* suffers because ballet dancers aren't trained in Cunningham methods of torsion and attack. Drawing ballets from here and there is chancy even when choreographers are commissioned.

No known system records the synchronization of steps to music with anything like the precision it takes to dance Balanchine. Ballet Theatre enlisted several Balanchine associates in its preparation of *Symphonie Concertante*, and at one time or another Tanaquil LeClercq, Maria Tallchief, and Diana Adams were invited to have a look. Even for the remarkably retentive memories of dancers, thirty years is a long time. What wouldn't we give now for a notated score of *Caracole* (or *The Figure in the Carpet* or *Transcendence* or *Cotillon*, and so on back through time)? Isn't it reasonable to suppose that style can be reconstituted once a text exists? Or, inasmuch as Balanchine style *is* the text, wouldn't a reconstitution by the School of American Ballet or New York City Ballet have a better chance of success than one by American Ballet Theatre? Probably. But Balanchine thought his ballets were for the world, not just for his own dancers—he gave them away free. (In a moving opening-night tribute to Balanchine, Baryshnikov said, "Mr. B. doesn't just look out for the company across the plaza. He looks out for us and for all companies.")

The ultimate issue then becomes what Balanchine is in the world's eyes—the dance world's, I mean. Has he taught it to dance Mozart? And what of the audience? The eye-

and ear-filling experience that is a Balanchine ballet—that is any Balanchine ballet—simply isn't being delivered in the monochromatic rotework of *Symphonie Concertante*. Yet the audience applauds; the company has a hit. I think the applause would be much greater if the ballet were done right, but I've seen too many imitation-Balanchine pieces go over with audiences to believe that style genuinely matters. The agreeable sight of dancers in tutus demonstrating classical decorum seems to be enough. *Symphonie Concertante* began life as a student piece, and it does reflect the regimentation of the classroom. Performing the ballet, Tallchief has said, "was like taking your medicine every day." The hygienic spectacle that is ABT's version may reflect *some* classrooms. Not Balanchine's.

New York City Ballet maintains the world's largest active repertory, but it has never hesitated to retire pieces for long periods because Balanchine would be there to remind the dancers how to do them. If the pieces no longer served, he would replace them. His whole operation as a ballet master looked so simple that up until the last decade of his life Balanchine was taken pretty much for granted. The absence of ego in his work and the protean forms it took tended to make people think they were responding not to one man's genius but to the genius of his medium. The artist disappeared into his art. When I came to New York as a college student in the fifties, the first theatre I happened to see was a performance of New York City Ballet—a company I knew about only because it had been featured in *Life*. I saw *Symphony in C* and thought it one of the natural wonders of New York, something in no way extraordinary except as ballet itself was extraordinary—and New York, too. On the way out, I heard a man greet someone he obviously hadn't seen for a while. "Oh, I couldn't miss *Symphony in C*," said he. "It's my bread and water." That made sense to me, and since I was eager for caviar and champagne, I didn't go to the ballet as often in those years as I might have. I missed *Metamorphoses* and *Opus 34* and *Roma*, and they have not been done since. I certainly didn't miss *Concerto Barocco*. With the arrival of *Agon* I became an addict.

In recent seasons, NYCB programming has been going slightly overboard in the minor Balanchine; there are too many pas de deux and tin soldiers and Russian scherzos. A program in which Balanchine is represented only by *Swan Lake* and *Kammermusik No. 2* is one I won't attend. But what about five years from now? A few nights ago, when *Concerto Barocco* was put on in place of *Ballo della Regina*, I felt a qualm. What if we should never see dear little *Ballo* again? Who cares if it isn't great? The greatest Balanchine ballet is the one you happen to be watching.

—*May 23, 1983*

Reflections on Glass

One of the commandments of choreography is that there shall be dances to music by Philip Glass. The primordial simplicity of Glass's music makes choreographers want to construct clean statements in space and time. Yet there's also a neutrality: the music has the capacity to reflect whatever the choreographer wants to do. The possibilities—narrow but densely woven—are extended by the combinations and permutations that Glass keeps introducing as organic developments of his style. In his latest work for New York City Ballet, Jerome Robbins uses a Glass score; he even uses a modicum of the minimalism associated with Glass choreographers such as Lucinda Childs and Andrew deGroat. The stage is hung with a plain beige sheet, lined like graph paper; most of the dancers wear practice dress and jazz shoes. It all has the look of some new, pristine adventure, yet what Jerome Robbins comes up with is a Jerome Robbins ballet. Exactly what the music ordered.

Glass Pieces is in three parts. The first two are built on selections from the CBS record *Glassworks*; the third uses the opening instrumental section of the opera *Akhnaten*, as yet unrecorded. As a Glass sampler, the pieces are well chosen. They give us hard- and soft-core Glass. But they also give us his strengths and weaknesses. "Rubric," laying down deep chords of steam-whistle-like sound over a burbling, pulsating accompaniment, is followed both on the record and in the ballet by "Façades," a smooth and serene intertwining of two melodies, one wavering, one steady. "Rubric" and "Façades" are the most seductive tracks on *Glassworks*, and for Robbins they work together as classic audience psychology—stir 'em up, quiet 'em down. "Rubric" has radical heat and energy, while "Façades" lingers on the borderline of convention. The pounding drums of the *Akhnaten* excerpt, to my ear, cross that borderline and end deep in jungle-movie-sound-track territory. And the extended finale that Robbins has devised to that music is the weak part of the ballet. He doesn't give in to the convention—he can't, because of the peculiarly restraining rhythm—yet he's uncomfortable with the alternative, which is to pretend that Glass is being as pure as he is in "Rubric."

Like the rhythm of rock, Glassian rhythm is static; as movement, it takes you everywhere and nowhere. Its sensibility is Eastern; its mode is ritualistic. To a Western romantic like Robbins, rhythm is abstract or anecdotal. He succeeds in making anecdotes of "Rubric" and "Façades": he tells us the story of the music. "Rubric" opens pell-mell with a nondescript horde of dancers walking—barreling—around the stage in various directions. Into this rush-hour mêlée drop two ballet dancers (assemblé descent), to be lost in the swarm, then recovered in time for a brief pas de deux in conventional ballet syntax. The horde returns, and two more aliens arrive, clad like the other two in Milliskin tights and toe shoes. The four of them are together in a double duet, then the horde fills the stage again. The filling and emptying of the stage, the arrival of the aliens (three pairs in all), their disappearances and reappearances—all this fits perfectly with the alternating strands in the music. The traffic pattern occurs four times, with slight variations each time; by the last repeat we see quite clearly that the process could go on forever, at which point everything stops and the scene blacks out.

Choreographers of Glass's generation (he was born in 1937) don't try to explain the peculiarities of his music— they just accept them. Older choreographers may see the music's strangeness as a subject in itself. For Robbins, the fact that the music is sunk in a ritualistic mode means that a story can be constructed about it—a story that seems to tell us something of the impervious, aimless rushing about we do in our lives, never stopping to notice the wonders in our midst. In "Façades," the ritual is again double-stranded. One melody oscillates like the path of a moonbeam on the surface of a lake, and the other melody spans it in slowly shifting single-note progressions carried by the high winds. Robbins translates the slow melody into a floating, rather mindlessly beautiful pas de deux for Maria Calegari and Bart Cook, while the all but motionless oscillation becomes a line of shadowy figures inching along in profile at the back of the stage: the piddling continuity, as it were, of daily life. Robbins doesn't ever mix the two motivic strands (though Glass does); his pas de deux could have been done for any other ballet. But then his point is that the wonderful events in life are different in kind from the ordinary events. They may interpenetrate, as in "Rubric," but custom prevents us from seeing this. In "Façades," beauty is enclosed in an entirely secret realm. Calegari and Cook at one point run to the line of figures and break through it; it goes on as if they'd never touched it. Yet it's the humdrum background, not the ravishing foreground, that one wants to watch. Robbins's minimalistic choreography includes about a dozen steps, all as tiny as the inchworm shuffle that gradually carries the line off, and the way the minutiae accumulate, with a sidestep or a kneel or a pause added for every repetition of the sequence, makes a hypnotic spectacle.

As dance music, Glass's compositions call up ancient associations not only with Oriental (specifically, Indian) ritual dance but with old ballets like *La Bayadère*. It is also head music and, as such, conspicuously a product of the sixties, that era of drug-incited revelations and rock ecstasy. None of this matters or has to matter to Robbins and his Glass ballet. The fact that a choreographer of his stature chose to involve himself just now with Glass's music set me pondering the whole Glass phenomenon. And *La Bayadère*, revived once more this season by American Ballet Theatre, seemed a more than ever relevant link to that phenomenon and to the consciousness of that generation.

Philip Glass and *La Bayadère* have both transcended the sixties. With his own ensemble, Glass performs in high-decibel rock clubs and is a major figure on the art-rock scene as well as on the concert and opera scene. It seems to me that as a composer for dancers he has done something very like what Delibes (in *La Source*) and Minkus (in *La Bayadère*) did—namely, filter the ethos of the East through popular Western idioms. For Delibes and Minkus, the idiom was the waltz, as intoxicating in its day as rock was in the sixties. *La Bayadère*, set in India, describes the travails of a Hindu temple dancer. She dies, and her Nirvana is (as Ted Shawn would have noted) in three-quarter time. It is also a paradise of grand-scale minimalism. This vision of infinity, the "Kingdom of the Shades," is beheld by the hero in an opium trance. A key element in the choreography is ritual repetition, which also marks the work of Glass and his colleagues in music, theatre, and dance. It only remains for *La Bayadère*, a work of major significance in ballet, to take its place on the fever chart of the American sixties. That was the decade and the climate of its American début, and the repercussions are still being felt.

—June 6, 1983

In Your Face:

Home Thoughts from Abroad

Love Songs, presented by the Joffrey Ballet, works very hard at affronting the audience, and in fact part of the audience at the Joffrey's opening in Los Angeles last spring *was* affronted; the other part applauded demonstratively. In New York, the piece plays to a different public—one whose sensibilities have been conditioned by the Joffrey's trendiness. *Love Songs* has to do with women's anger. It's a suite of dances, mostly solos and duets, that focus on women, and because it uses a lot of flailing paroxysmic movement that doesn't make the women look attractive, some observers concluded that its intentions were antifeminist. The choreographer, William Forsythe, may well lack sympathy for the women he depicts, but his manner of depicting them is so inflexibly violent that it couldn't express a viewpoint if it wanted to. The ballet has nothing to say about women except that they are angry; it takes a theme that has persistently resounded in the media and exploits it on the most reckless media-inflamed level. *Love Songs* (the ballet uses a score consisting of songs recorded by Aretha Franklin and Dionne Warwick) is as shallow and self-celebrating as

Astarte and *Trinity* and all the other Joffrey ballets that have plugged into the audience's awareness of and identification with media issues and pop fashions. These productions don't deepen our understanding of the issues and the fashions; all they do is inform people that the attitudes circulating throughout our culture can also be found at the ballet.

The Joffrey attracted a new audience with this kind of product, and it has held on to the more serious-minded by offering revivals of famous old ballets and premières of works by new—radically new—choreographers. A Joffrey choreographer can appeal to more than one public. It happens that only one, Twyla Tharp, has ever done so successfully. *Deuce Coupe*, her Beach Boys ballet, fed the company's early-seventies preoccupation with the youth cult and was at the same time a wild and witty, genuinely novel piece of work. Ten years later, we have Forsythe regaling us with the sex war and doing it in an idiom that is transparently Tharp's own—one that embraces her Joffrey period (not *Deuce Coupe* so much as *As Time Goes By*) along with her current essays in movement terrorism. Forsythe's version of Tharp is highly simplified, to be sure, and is colored throughout by his ballet background. He likes the cliché of long runs ending in a split jeté quite as much as he fancies the Tharpian off-balance twist-pirouette in low arabesque, and he doesn't pass up the opportunity to make the women's pointework look as painful as Cossack toe-dancing. Still, a Joffrey audience can justifiably murmur, "It all comes from Twyla."

It's interesting—a sign of the times—to see idiomatic Tharpisms turning up as normative expression in a Joffrey protest ballet. It would have been more interesting to see these usages absorbed by a choreographer of means (as Paul Taylor absorbed certain usages of Martha Graham's).

Forsythe is all short, sharp thrusts, blatant jumps, loops within loops within whorls that maunder unstoppably. A short plumpish girl does the first flailing solo and is followed by a long lanky girl doing much the same thing, with no modification in shape or attack. Later a young hopeful girl dances against the grain emotionally but the movement keeps to the same repetitious pattern. In the two pas de deux, the men are brutal, and the single male solo is just the tables being turned: observed by a woman (as the women were observed by men), this man grinds his pelvis, lashes into his turns with the same pent-up fury as the women, and ends with a by now predictable gesture of contempt toward the watching lover. The Joffrey dancers work as conscientiously as they did for Twyla Tharp, even though the movement makes them all alike. Tharp investigated movement; Forsythe incorporates results of those investigations. I'm not suggesting there's anything illegitimate in that—the growth of the art, after all, depends on a steady process of incorporation. And Tharp isn't the main influence on *Love Songs*. I only wish that she were—that Forsythe, an American-born choreographer, could show himself closer to the roots of the idiom he has tapped here.

Forsythe's "school" isn't really American dance. Though he's a former Joffrey dancer he established himself as a choreographer in Europe, working for companies like the Stuttgart and the Netherlands Dance Theatre, and his sense of characterization and continuity has Jiří Kylián stamped all over it. *Love Songs*, his first production for an American company, is an adaptation of a ballet originally done in Munich. The New York première was followed by a Joffrey commission, *Square Deal*, in which Forsythe continued his confrontational tactics. *Square Deal* uses dancers as facets of a cubistic configuration involving lights, voices, sound, words, and nonwords. There's a set composed of portable screens on which headlines are fleetingly projected, and the action jerks along in discontinuous fragments punctuated by blackouts. It all seems to be a parody of the cuteness and smartness of the avant-garde, or rather the avant-garde audience. The scenario appears to revolve around the creation of the piece we're seeing, and Forsythe has his mouthpieces onstage deliver running critiques, such as "It's a blend of the new realism and the old artifice," as if this were what the audience is thinking and aren't we fools. *Square Deal*, this season's daring new work, was probably meant to antagonize New York the way *Love Songs* antagonized Los Angeles, but all it garnered was a few boos and a weary round of applause. The fastidious technological effects with which the piece was equipped deserved a great deal more.

Carolyn Carlson is another American choreographer who has made a name working in Europe—mainly at the Paris Opéra, and now at La Fenice, in Venice. With her company from the Fenice she made her local début, at the Brooklyn Academy of Music, dancing an evening-long piece called *Underwood*. The set suggested an American pastoral scene; the Italian voices that called out from time to time suggested it was not to be taken literally. Perhaps Miss Carlson was going back in her mind to Oakland, her birthplace; perhaps there is a place in Oakland like the one portrayed on the stage, where women run about in their slips and try to dump each other out of rocking chairs. Or perhaps Miss Carlson is interested in the Theatre of Exorcism, in which a great many American women choreographers have run about in their slips casting off emotional burdens. One spends the evening at *Underwood* slipping from one vagary to another: Where are we now? What doing? What's in those boxes? Who's that in the rocking chair? One seeks clues to a puzzle, and one is wrong to—these are only formalist conceits. At any moment, the simple mad folk on the stage may erupt into squads of robots doing one step over and over hard on the beat, for all the world like the step done just last week at this very theatre. Nobody here but us post-modernists catching the Next Wave.

Underwood is constructed out of two—at least—incompatible systems of movement. The implication that there is a repetitious ritualistic content in expressionistic dance and an emotive force in the plain ritualistic walking, stepping, and running of radical antiexpressionistic dance is not unfascinating, but Carlson's amalgamation of the two systems is highly indecisive. Sometimes she just appears to have settled arbitrarily on one system for instituting dramatic meanings and another for taking them away. Which does which is a toss-up; this choreographer puts *all* terminology in doubt. In Act II, she comes out in a floppy straw song and sings a hat.

A former Nikolais dancer, Carlson still performs for the most part in a style that keeps the extremities in play with no noticeable motivation from the center of the body, and her long thin limbs and long thin torso make a further spectacle of the style. As *Underwood* goes on, she becomes more and more isolated (the other dancers are far from capturing her movement) and more and more fraught with possibilities, but she stays fraught. She has made what in old-fashioned modern-dance terms would be an Ophelia piece. The bouts of minimalism, the ritualistic pieties, the chopsticks music—all that is Ophelia's new clothes.

—December 5, 1983

A Balanchine Triptych

Balanchine used to deny that he wasn't interested in male dancers; when he said "They are very important as princes and attendants to the queen, but woman is the queen," it was, he insisted, because of the woman's greater technical capacity. A woman can do more; consequently she makes more demands on a choreographer. Balanchine reiterated the point three years ago in an interview in Paris. "It is easier to make dances for men—they jump, they turn. A woman is more complicated, that is the only reason they are a priority." Maybe so for other choreographers, but for Balanchine? One gathers from his ballets that women would have been a priority in his universe whether he had been able to design a step or not. Pressed to explain what special pains he took with his ballerinas, he resorted, typically, to metaphor: "They are fragile like orchids. You have to know exactly how much sun, how much water, how much air and then take them inside before they wilt."

A full-evening Balanchine ballet called *Flowers* is not unimaginable, nor is one called *Horses* or *Birds*—images more or less conspicuously floral or equine or avian are

strewn throughout his repertory. In 1967, the three-part ballet called *Jewels* was made, and it is still unsurpassed as a Balanchine primer, incorporating in a single evening every
important article of faith to which this choreographer sub-
scribed and a burst of heresy, too, to remind us that he will-
ingly reversed himself on occasion. Edward Villella was
then as much a priority as the ballerinas who composed the
original cast—Violette Verdy, Mimi Paul, Patricia McBride,
and Suzanne Farrell—and so, in between *Emeralds* and *Diamonds*, we have *Rubies*, with a smashing male role, more
than prince or attendant, at its center. The exception proves
the rule about technical capacity; only a man who could do
the things that Villella could do would have deflected Balanchine from his preoccupation with female dancers. Still,
there the role stands, in lonely eminence, flanked by male
roles that are virtual definitions of the consort and the cavalier. These men are not just links in the chain of jewels.
They are active presences, courtiers of rank and sensibility,
and they are the means by which Balanchine focuses our
thoughts on the women and creates a setting for them. The
men embody the choreographer's point of view; those who
partner the ballerinas in *Emeralds* and *Diamonds* are what
Balanchine's male dancers often are—stand-ins for Balanchine himself. But the roles are so beautifully differentiated—lover and poet in *Emeralds*, knight in *Diamonds*—that
they can be interpreted as fully as the more richly developed
jesterlike Villella role in *Rubies*. And *Jewels* includes a fifth
principal male role—that of a youth in *Emeralds* who dances
between two young princesses in a pas de trois and whose
choreography gives opportunity to any soloist of mettle.
(The original soloist was John Prinz, then the company's
most promising male dancer.)

Designed as a company showcase and as an introduction

to Balanchine, dressed in glittering costumes and scenery, christened with a real title hinting at a pretext if not a plot, *Jewels* remains New York City Ballet's most powerful box-office attraction after *The Nutcracker*. The audience is told in three ballets a great deal about Balanchine and what he stands for; it is *not* told that he disdains male dancing — on the contrary.

As a popular hit, *Jewels* has had to withstand charges of expediency. Balanchine, newly settled at Lincoln Center and needing to lure an unaccustomed public, had contrived the theme of jewels to link three unrelated nonstory ballets. Actually, couldn't you call any three Balanchine ballets *Jewels* (or *Flowers* or *Horses*)? It's true that *Jewels* isn't about jewels. Although Claude Arpels is said to have originally suggested the mining and cutting of gems as a scenario to Balanchine, the geometric dazzle connecting classical ballet and precious stones could have occurred to anybody. (A less facile connection to Oriental carpets was made several years earlier in *The Figure in the Carpet*.) Even as a metaphor, *Jewels* doesn't quite work. By 1967, Balanchine's style had evolved beyond the kaleidoscopic manipulation of strict classical forms for which he was chiefly known. He was less interested in the chiseled severity of footwork than in the weight and shape of the body as it posed or plunged in cubic space. *Rubies* and *Diamonds* both take their stylistic cues from the bravura of their stars, which was as much curvilinear as rectilinear, while *Emeralds* is a floating island, its softness of contour an anomaly in Balanchine's repertory then and now. Yet "jewel" imagery is not neglected; it depends on where you sit. From high in the house, the loops, strands, and pendants that emerge in the changing patterns of the corps may be distinctly seen in all three ballets. The weakest choreography of the evening is the section that comes the closest to foursquare geometrical precision—the opening of *Diamonds*, set to the second movement of Tchaikovsky's Third Symphony. From orchestra or first-ring level, it is boring to look at—a plodding ensemble waltz that lasts forever. Seen from above, it shows you diamonds, diamonds, diamonds. This is Balanchine as Busby Berkeley, thinking up ways to eat up space on the large new State Theater stage. The sparkling footwork throughout *Tchaikovsky Piano Concerto No. 2* is more properly diamantine.

Balanchine took his titular metaphor seriously enough, but he took even more seriously another kind of imagery—one that seems to have come to him from the imaginary world of ballet. For Balanchine, who inherited it from Petipa, it is not only a feminine microcosm but an actual stage world. *Emeralds* and *Diamonds* are each a conflation of *Swan Lake* and *Raymonda*; they bring back the medieval pageantry and chivalry of those ballets, complete with their glow of post-Wagnerian mythomania. *Rubies* is a sharp (not to say malicious) commentary on the anachronistic survival of the myth into the twentieth century; it's the New World—Stravinsky, jazz, America, sexual equality—pitted against nostalgia for the Old. Both *Emeralds* and *Diamonds* are about queens and the courts they rule; in *Rubies* the royalty is like that in a deck of cards; and it is all part and parcel of the toy kingdom of ballet. The leading male roles in all three ballets are Maryinsky stereotypes, but what Balanchine does with them is something else again. Amid these reverberant depictions, the female roles assume the substantiality of a continuing lineage stemming from the Maryinsky and beyond the Maryinsky, for what was the late-Petipa era of Russian ballet in Petersburg but a revival of the era of Romantic ballet in Paris, with its Gothic inspirations? The roles in *Jewels* are made of memories of memories. They are also, of course, living portraits of their originators as they were in 1967, and though this makes them difficult to keep in repertory, their archetypal connections ensure that something is left over when the originators are gone. There is probably no ballet more closely identified with Suzanne Farrell than *Diamonds*, and Farrell's performances of it this season seemed to set on it the ultimate seal of ownership. Yet when Merrill Ashley took it over, it became intelligibly another construct. The pas de deux without Farrell can still be performed as an Odette fantasy (with hand-behind-head poses reminiscent of Raymonda); Ashley handled this aspect extremely well. And without Farrell's all-absorbing presence it was easier to concentrate on the structural ties that make *Jewels* a true triptych.

The choreography's binding theme is walking. The walking on pointe that is done in the most memorable pas de deux in *Emeralds* reappears with a different emphasis in the *Diamonds* pas de deux, but it is recognizably a theme that bridges the evening's three sections. In *Emeralds*, the walk is paced to the pulse of the music; it follows the turns and twists of a melody that gives no hint of how it is to end. It is as a dance virtually patternless; nothing occurs in it that might call forth a consummation, and so it is as an image virtually motionless, too. It wanders on, beat by beat, until, to a sudden sighing cadence in the music, it passes away into the night. Balanchine is not often given to such stylization, and for him to keep the dance so still is also unusual. He even has the dancers underline the regular beat of the walk with stop-motion poses of their limbs while they're standing still. The consequence is that we pay closer attention to the music, but the music, which is indeed beautiful, does not entirely explain a choreographic treatment that for Balanchine verges on pedantry. Fauré's score was written to accompany a French adaptation of *The Merchant of Venice*, and this Nocturne was heard under Lorenzo's speech to Jessica about "the sweet power of music." "Mark the music," says Lorenzo, and Balanchine does—literally! (I believe the stylization of the dance also derives from the somewhat stilted conceits in the Lorenzo-Jessica love scene a page or two earlier—the lines beginning with six repetitions of the phrase "In such a night.")

Some years after the première, Balanchine added to his choreography for *Emeralds* another pas de deux and an epilogue the effect of which introduced a fatal symmetry but also enlarged and integrated the ballet's images. The braced and straining arabesques in the new pas de deux become in the epilogue a linked series of such arabesques spread like an ornamental chain across the back of the stage. We see the necklace one last time before it dissolves into fragments to be folded and put away for good. The music for the dispersal is the funeral march from Fauré's *Pelléas*; it ends as the choreography has reverted to walking steps for the three cavaliers, now bereft. On a final note, they kneel in tribute to a vision lost in time.

Balanchine followed Fauré's musical pattern in the portions added to *Emeralds*, just as he had throughout the ballet, but he ascribed his own meaning to the pattern, and that is the procedure he seems to have followed all through *Jewels*. The heraldic horns in the Fauré link up with the mournful French horns in Tchaikovsky's symphony, and we hear the horns the way we see the walking—as a motivic element in the structure of the work as a whole. (In *Rubies*, the horns are heard in the brassy whoops of a neoclassical score, and the walking becomes running and prancing.) In *Diamonds*, when Farrell walks on pointe she stretches her feet in a slight pawing motion and we hear a horn call. The

echo seems to come from way back in the forest of *Emeralds*—from that wonderfully youthful pas de trois and its air
of freedom, of an outing in the woods, perhaps a hunt.
(The young man several times extends one arm to lift the
two women in light sautés—like a trainer testing two mares
in dressage.) Hunt scenes from old ballets rise up invisibly
to reinforce that sound and that image, now transferred to
Diamonds, but Farrell's "Odette" wears no plumage. Rather,
she flexes her long feet, places her delicate pointes on the
earth, and arches her neck like a white steed—like the one,
in fact, she gives us in a pawing, head-tossing passage in
Monumentum pro Gesualdo, the ballet to Stravinsky's setting
of sixteenth-century madrigals (in which, as it happens, Balanchine also uses a necklace construction). And when she
bends her head low and stretches both arms out above a forward extension of her leg, "horse" passes into "unicorn,"
and the "hunt scene" becomes an allusion to the unicorn tapestries. Farrell is both the lady and the unicorn, and in a
sense she's the hunter, too, on the scent of her own mystery.
The long *Diamonds* pas de deux is really a monologue; the
man is privy to secrets the woman reveals to herself. That, at
any rate, is how I read it when it is danced by Farrell and
Peter Martins. Its relation to the walking pas de deux and
the two intensely private women's variations in *Emeralds*
seems to me unmistakable.

One could parse Balanchine's language for further correspondences; I have named only the most obvious. But even
a casual glance at *Jewels* shows it to be composed not of
three unrelated ballets but of two matching panels and a fla-
grantly dissonant middle panel, which, however, keeps a
connection with the two others by extending and upending
their formal logic. Without *Rubies*, Balanchine must have
reasoned, *Jewels* would be a bland evening. By way of de-

scribing the ambiguous but compelling logic of abstract ballet, our greatest dance critic, the late Edwin Denby, used to like to cite a line of Mallarmé's about poetry that is made up "of reciprocal reflections like a virtual trail of light across jewels." *Rubies* refracts instead of reflecting; it does its job in the total scheme of things, and it may be the evening's masterwork.

Balanchine carried out his tripartite scheme to the music of three different composers. It is the music that determines the instant-by-instant progression of his choreography, its accent and impetus; and the music is what gives the evening its pleasing symphonic shape—a broadly flowing andante prelude, a red-hot scherzo, a maestoso finish. If I had to guess how the piece was made, I'd say that Balanchine worked backward from the pas de deux of *Diamonds* and from the scherzo that follows it, in which Tchaikovsky burrows into the magic forest of Mendelssohn's *A Midsummer Night's Dream*. As we saw in the pas de deux, Balanchine makes it a tapestry forest, but basically it's the same forest that he planted with Fauré's help in *Emeralds*. Music is widely supposed to be the beginning and end of Balanchine's concern with expression. *Jewels* shows how effectively he could use music to pursue concerns of his own.

—*December 19, 1983*

Mark Morris Comes to Town

Curly-haired, androgynously handsome young dancer-choreographers who look like Michelangelo's David have been a feature of the dance scene for some time. Unlike the shaggy hippies whom they replaced, they can be found in ballet as well as in modern dance, in Europe as well as in New York and other American cities. They seem to have come in on the wave of seventies glamour—unisex, it was called then—that is now at flood tide among the young. It's a look I can do without, and I wouldn't be bringing it up except for the fact that Mark Morris, who closed the fall season at Dance Theater Workshop, has that look without the aureole that puts me off. Morris is a serious choreographer. He has talent and, along with his self-awareness, the self-possession that makes the androgynous-youth look stand for something besides dime-store narcissism. Actually, he does sometimes make it stand for that, but it's a precisely identified attitude—one can smell the popcorn in the air.

Morris, whose ringlets are brown—not blond, like the other michelangelini—has some of Sylvester Stallone's droopy-lidded sultriness, but he's saved from absurdity by

toughness of mind. He doesn't use his soft, pretty-boy
looks on the audience. He doesn't flash camp messages with
his eyes, or messages of any kind—not even when he does a
turn in drag. The meanings are all in the movement. From
up close, which is how you see him in DTW's loft theatre,
his eyes while he dances are blind with fatigue; they have
the permanently bruised look of insomnia. And he dances
with insomniacal energy. His large, wide-hipped body, his
big legs and feet are all over the place, lunging, clomping,
skittering. Every movement is clear and precise, yet bluntly
delivered; strong, yet with a feminine softness. Even the big
Li'l Abner feet are never rough. Prepared to laugh at the
drag act, the audience is silenced by the lack of imposture in
it. It isn't an act; it's Morris declaring an aspect of his nature
as matter-of-factly as the Japanese *onnagata*—female imper-
sonator. It's impersonal impersonation. He defuses dangerously gaudy material by shaping it into a dance that presents
itself—presents *dance*—as the true subject. In the second of
two concerts, he performed a companion piece in a business
suit, discarding jacket and vest as he entered. The differences in the quality of the movement were in structural,
technical, and musical details, not in sexual ones. Morris
turns the transsexual chic and the frivolous passions of his
generation into pretexts for dances. He's committed to his
time and place, he seizes on the theatricality of it, but he
doesn't try to be anything more than a good choreographer
and a completely sincere theatre artist.

Morris works in the time-honored tradition of the modern-dance choreographer who breeds a company and a
repertory entirely out of his own dance style. His performing background includes ballet and modern, post-modern
and folk dance. His dances, among which solos number far
less than pieces for large and small ensembles, blend all

these influences into an indefinable Mark Morrisian brew. His own physical versatility is the model for the group (seven women, six men), but he doesn't set up unfair terms of competition. Much of his choreography is plainly set out, and all of it is musical. The sharp musical timing gives the dancers another standard to aim at; they aren't lost if they can't move just like their leader. But they have to be able to handle radical dynamic changes (Morris shows more variety here than any five other choreographers his age) rung on a restricted range of steps. Not easy to make so little count for so much. Morris's inflections of a single step or his combination of many steps in a single phrase are a real test of virtuosity. He sometimes loads a phrase beyond his dancers' capacities—requiring them, for example, to fall splat and spring erect on one count. But Morris is a witty taskmaster who can make a virtue of sloppy recoveries. His invention is at its richest in the exigencies that come about through having to create choreography for other people. *Bijoux*, his solo for the small, light, and agile Teri Weksler, filters her style sympathetically through his own. I was able to see only a first-night performance of this piece, when Weksler was slightly less in command than she usually is. The music, a suite of nine brief songs by Satie, was on tape. Live, it might have exerted less harrowing pressure. So musical a performance—such musical choreography—needs accompaniment that breathes.

The occasional impression of steppiness I get from this and other Morris pieces is an effect of density created from limited means. He really doesn't have a lot of steps, and though he may not think so, he doesn't need them—neither does Paul Taylor. (Morris's combination of musicality, sprawling energy, and sparse vocabulary may remind you of Taylor; to sharpen the resemblance, Morris also has a flair for comedy. But his originality defeats comparisons.) In another Satie piece, he reversed the proportions of *Bijoux*: instead of many brief packed solos for one dancer, a woman, he created, to the music of *Socrate*, an extended slow-moving frieze of discontinuities for six soloists, all men. Draining his line of the high-contrast dynamics that gave it shape, color, and texture, Morris offered us the nothingness of steps. *The Death of Socrates* was a parched and static vista peopled by boys in Greek tunics. As a picture, it had life and thought; its intentions were clearly stated. But as a dance it was inert.

What does Morris do that's funny? Well, he always includes one or two mime pieces to pop music on his programs. I like them less than his dances, particularly when the music is country songs with long spoken inspirational texts. Audiences find these semicaptioned displays of Morris's hilarious. I prefer the Thai or Indian numbers, where the expostulatory gestures chatter alongside incomprehensible ditties and aren't upstaged by a corniness already familiar and complete in itself. Best of all are the pieces that blend mime and dance, and the best of these—Morris's "masculine" solo and *Dogtown*—are both funny and unfunny. In *Dogtown*, done to the quizzical songs of Yoko Ono, Morris actually makes dogs. He contracts his palette to a few crouching, crawling, prostrate forms interspersed with frisky leaps, usually by one dancer upon the unsuspecting rump of another. But the amazing thing about *Dogtown* is that it doesn't operate literally. The dogginess of it all is a continual shadowy implication in movement as finely drawn and cunningly interlocked as the pattern on an ancient Greek jar. In the title number, the rhythm of forms is so beautifully controlled that it wins laughs from the sheer electricity of its timing. It's the *design*, not the subject, that becomes funny.

This mastery of mimetic implication in the logic of forms is a mark of wisdom as rare in choreography as musical mastery. No other choreographer under thirty has it; the few of those over thirty who have it have been great. Like musicality, it is a gift, and it appears right away. (No use waiting for other bright young choreographers to get the idea through observation or experience. If the things that root their art in life are not instinctively understood, they are not understood at all.) Morris comes from Seattle, where he will return later this year to teach at the University of Washington. His first New York concert was held in 1980. I encountered his work two years later, and the wonderful effrontery of it still hasn't left me. Nothing in his biography, training, or performing history explained how he could have come by such technical sophistication. This year's concerts show him using and flexing his technique with even greater assurance. *Canonic 3/4 Studies*, a parody of human beings in ballet class, is one evolutionary step beyond *Dogtown*. In its investigation of three-quarter time and in nearly every other way, it is an improvement on 1982's *New Love Song Waltzes*, the piece that most of Morris's admirers love best and the one that stunned me with its precocity. Seen again this year, much of it seemed too big and splashy for the Brahms liebesliederwalzer it was set to. It remains Morris's purple moment, his burst of excess before the reining in that signifies the start of true growth. Next to *New Love Song Waltzes*, *Canonic 3/4 Studies*, to an arrangement of ballet-class tunes, appears cautious, but it is the more secure piece by far—less in need of contrapuntal commotion and shock effects to keep the audience in a state of excitement.

There is a tendency in Morris's current work to make each piece a batch of exercises or lampoons that don't quite add up to a complete entity with a point of view (though the suite *Dogtown* comes close). Instead of a conclusion, he reaches an arbitrary cutoff point. It is obvious that he is still learning, but it is also obvious that no one is teaching him. His technique is something he was born with. The raw gift of choreography may be the most individualizing of all gifts to experience. Those who possess it are enclosed in a kind of sanctuary. No word or sound contaminates the freshness of their language, and dance language as we have known it— old academic or antiacademic usage—falls from their bodies like rags. In its place are new sights, which we perceive with a thrill of recognition. The Mark Morris experience is like nothing else in dance but quite like a lot of things outside it—especially in the streets and shops of lower Manhattan. I imagine that the younger you are, the more of these things you recognize. For me, Mark Morris is a dance-maker and a spellbinder. That is enough to make him transparently a symbol of his times.

—January 2, 1984

Tharp's Sinatra

Frank Sinatra records may not seem much of a basis for serious choreography, but in *Nine Sinatra Songs* Twyla Tharp has made them work excitingly for her and her superb company. The dance style is ballroom-acrobatic, and it's very different from her original, rather arty approach to this music back in 1976, when she and Mikhail Baryshnikov worked together in a duet called *Once More, Frank*. The three songs she used then—"Somethin' Stupid," "That's Life," and "One for My Baby"—are represented in the new ballet, along with "Softly As I Leave You," "Strangers in the Night," "All the Way," "Forget Domani," and "My Way." ("My Way" is used twice, in two different versions.) It's certainly a mixed bag. Tharp hasn't tried to separate the connoisseur's Sinatra from the Vegas brawler, and in that I think she's been true to the nature of her material. In pop music, one can flash from the shallows to the heights without warning. Tharp confronts what Sinatra stands for in all its aspects (though when we get to the "dooby dooby doo" section of "Strangers in the Night," she lifts the needle; there does seem to be a limit to her tolerance). She emerges with something like a panorama of Middle America in middle age. The generation that came of age in the fifties probably knows Sinatra best. It spans his bobby-sox era and his ring-a-ding-ding and Paul Anka and Stephen Sondheim eras, and it was one of Tharp's most perceptive decisions to set "My Way" both times as an ensemble dance instead of as a duet. The graying masses have throbbed to this valediction ever since Sinatra first recorded it. As staged by Tharp, with first three, then seven couples wheeling and sweeping across a stage lit by a turning silver ball, it has an anthemic power.

Oscar de la Renta's ball gowns are fifties-ish without being archaic, and with the exception of the one for Sara Rudner, which looks like two bibs hanging back to back, they aren't examples of egregious chic; they're what wives and girlfriends might reasonably dream of wearing on New Year's Eve. The great Rudner is also given the most labyrinthine acrobatic choreography—a tortuous series of slithers, blind leaps, upsy-daisy lifts, and ass-over-heels floorwork, to "One for My Baby." With excellent support from John Carrafa, Rudner makes it all lyrical. The sexual frankness of Tharp's choreography may surprise people who haven't seen exhibition disco recently. But the discos know nothing like Tharp's wit. Her roughhousing is as tautly controlled, as systematically applied as her boffo effects. The two tactics come together in Song No. 8, "That's Life," when Sinatra sings "Pick myself / Up and get / Back in the race!" and a supine Shelley Freydont is yanked to her feet by degrees. The audience starts to yell because nothing as brutally obvious and as funny has happened up to that moment. Then Tharp tops it by having Freydont hurl herself through the air at Tom Rawe before he has quite finished putting on his dinner jacket. He makes the catch. Uproar.

Nine Sinatra Songs hits the audience very hard—it can barely keep still. Nearly every number is met with groans and giggles at having these old family albums brought out and plunked down right in front of everybody. Even if you haven't grown up with the songs, the mixed emotions they induce are apt to make you slightly queasy. Tharp toys with the audience's susceptibilities, but she doesn't take undue advantage. The straight numbers are perfectly straight. "Strangers in the Night" is a militant tango done by a serious, straight-backed team, Mary Ann Kellogg and John Malashock. In the up-tempo division, we get two surprises. The newest and youngest-looking woman in the company, Barbara Hoon, dances "Somethin' Stupid" in puffed sleeves with Richard Colton and captures the essence of dopey Junior Prom ecstasy. "Forget Domani" is Jennifer Way and William Whitener wagging their heads roguishly and practicing their flamenco—the essence of dopey middle-aged escapism. I wouldn't care to choose among such riches, but when I think back on *Nine Sinatra Songs*, "Forget Domani" is the one that makes me smile.

Technically speaking, the main interest of the piece is its adaptation of professional ballroom dances. Tharp has dissected the style with her usual care. Her tango parody is a knowledgeable one. Her aerial work in "Softly As I Leave You" is a beautiful development of exhibition-dance heroics. There's a whole stack of dance manuals as well as a few cruise brochures behind "Forget Domani." She knows how to feature the women without shading the men. Even the roughhouse has its model in the knockabout ballroom acts; it's crème de l'apache. In another area of technique, her work here can be admired for its resourcefulness in setting steps to long vocal lines and chunky ones, to rigidly regular rhythms and overplangent orchestrations. Although the spectacle of *Nine Sinatra Songs* seems utterly familiar, people never actually danced to Sinatra records. Tharp's choreographic line is like a wide silk ribbon winding through the plush of the ballads. When I first heard of her Sinatra project, I wondered why she wasn't using a virtuoso jazz singer like Mel Tormé, whose way with a pop song strikes me as more nearly equal to her own methods than Sinatra's. Possibly there would have been too even a match—silk on silk. As it is, *Nine Sinatra Songs* joins *Sue's Leg* and *Baker's Dozen* and *Eight Jelly Rolls* as a masterpiece of Americana.

—*February 13, 1984*

Visualizations

Alwin Nikolais's theatre has lately become less illusionis-
tic—concerned less with costumes and props than with the
exposed bodies of dancers dancing. When he makes a nifty
piece of choreography these days (like the opening of *Litur-
gies*, which churns out a great froth of insect visualizations,
from beetles to centipedes), his conceits are likely to be
purely anatomical. The company is trained to this kind of
expression, and it's no longer as good at disappearing into
the décor as it used to be. Looking at the older pieces in the
current repertory—three out of four were revivals from the
fifties—I was struck by how often they seemed to require
(as much of their audience as of their maker) a hermetic
concentration on form and no interest in the real world. In
Nikolais's work then and for a long time to come, a decorative object that looked like an onion or a trumpet was never
used to remind us of onions or trumpets because, I suspect,
references of that sort were thought to be at best utilitarian
and at worst anti-art and just too Disney. Though Nikolais's
abstractions may have corresponded to the mood of the
fifties, particularly to the ethos of some Abstract Expres-

sionists, their lack of resonance makes them look pointless
and trivial today. Whereas Disney (to invoke the archfiend
of those years) has started looking really bright and consequential. Right after a Nikolais matinee, I saw *Fantasia*,
which was playing just across the street, and I kept thinking
of Nikolais—of his affinities with Disney and his lack of interest in them. In the Chinese dance in Disney's *Nutcracker*
episode, the dancers are mushrooms with coolie hats.
Everything you see and think about because of what you see
is intended to be there, and the impudent associations
(China, dope, mushrooms, trance) are sweetly sent up by
the innocence of the music. The same thing happens on a
slightly lower level in the Arabian dance, only here it's the
visual image that sends up the music. The parody of the
classic belly dancer (she appears in both the Ivanov and
the Balanchine productions of the ballet) in the form of a
guppy wearing lipstick and mascara is not apparent unless
you know *The Nutcracker*, but you don't have to know it to
enjoy the ineffable rightness and silliness of the image and
of the choreography, which in a series of fishtail twists and
turns captures amazingly the slumberous and sinuous
movements of belly dancing. It even adds an exit no dancer
on any stage could duplicate—a zigzag flick too fast to be
seen as more than a blur that leaves a dazzle of bubbles behind.

The worst part of *Fantasia* is the dull opening—a display of fireworks and some wisps in the sky which look
like UFOs, set to the Bach-Stokowski Toccata and Fugue
in D Minor. This is a watered-down version of designs
submitted to Disney by Oskar Fischinger, the German
avant-garde filmmaker. The compromise seems to have
dishonored everyone concerned. As music visualization,
this overture to *Fantasia* is surpassed by the Waltz of the

Flowers, with its whirling leaves, its glistening, pollen-skirted Toumanovas, its snowflakes, and its ice-skating Tinkerbell. The sections of the movie that work best are, as one might expect, those that are set either to ballet music or to music that has a visual conception built into it, like *The Sorcerer's Apprentice* or *Night on Bald Mountain*. The Arcadian clatter that goes on to Beethoven's *Pastoral* was originally meant to be accompanied by Gabriel Pierné's *Cydalise et le Chèvre-Pied*, a two-act nymphs-and-satyrs ballet first presented by the Paris Opéra in 1923. Extracts from *Cydalise* became a staple of the light-concert-music repertory. Had Disney gone through with his plan to use this score, he might have made a more seemly spectacle, but then generations of schoolchildren might not have been introduced to the Beethoven who is reflected in the lordlier aspects of Disney's creation. That business of Zeus rolling over in his cloud blanket after his thunderstorm of a tantrum has died down is wonderful, and the further business of his fishing out from underneath him a stray lightning bolt and tossing it casually to earth (where it detonates, an echo of the dying storm) is *really* wonderful. I venture to say Beethoven would have loved it.

I first saw the film, which was originally released in 1940, about twenty years ago. It seemed to me not nearly as bad as people said, and I thought the Stravinsky episode was actually exciting; but on the whole *Fantasia* impressed me as a film made for children by children. It used to be fashionable to praise the comedy portions—especially the still hilarious ostrich-hippo-alligator-elephant ballet to Ponchielli's *Dance of the Hours*—and deplore everything else. Stravinsky's animadversions on the use of his *Rite of Spring* seem to have been more anti-Stokowski than anti-Disney. Leopold Stokowski, who not only conducted the sound track of the film but collaborated with Disney on the production, made some cuts in the *Rite* and changed the order of some of the sections. The scenario, of course, was completely different, but since the original scenario is regularly abandoned in productions of the ballet nowadays, that seems no great violation. Between them, Disney and Stokowski almost manage to persuade us that Stravinsky's music is about the creation of the planet Earth, the emergence of sea and animal life, the appearance and disappearance of the great reptiles (the tyrannosaurus seems to have been inspired by King Kong), and the formation of the continents and the topography of the earth as we know it. The real problem is that this story has no place for the final cataclysm that in the ballet accompanies the dance of the Chosen Victim, so Stokowski cuts this music and substitutes an ending of his own, for which Disney's artists provide some rather inconclusive dun-colored views of the planet from outer space. (Too bad they didn't know about the blue-and-white marble.)

The strength of the *Rite of Spring* sequence—the strength of the film as a whole—is the appositeness of the music and the movement. The visualization of the *Rite* is apposite in *scale* to the music; the visualization of the *Pastoral* is not. What appears appallingly out of scale is the treatment of the conductor. Stokowski is most often seen silhouetted against the blaze of a thousand suns. Conducting, as always, without a baton, he subdues his legions of musicians and molds music out of thin air. It's the Führer conception of the conductor, but in the end *Fantasia* transcends this unwelcome reminder of thirties cultural propaganda. It gives us Mickey Mouse conducting the elements in *The Sorcerer's Apprentice*—a deliberate satire of Stokowski. Then it gives us a less ingratiating and possibly less conscious parody in the towering bat-winged devil who dominates the revels in *Night on Bald Mountain*. *Fantasia* is a big enough movie not to be dragged down by its inequalities and its gaffes in taste. It is big enough to parody itself—to suggest that the play of forms within forms is, after all, finite. Thus an omnipotent conductor is both Mickey Mouse and Satan, and the lascivious alligators who swoop down on the hippos in the *Dance of the Hours* are the pterodactyls of the *Rite* in disguise.

Fantasia is now being shown with a completely re-recorded sound track, synchronized to Stokowski's and conducted by Irwin Kostal, and with the addition of a foreword dedicating the reissue to Stokowski's memory. It is not at all the naïve movie I remembered.

—*March 12, 1984*

Three Elders

Radical ideas, if repeated long enough, become traditional ideas. They don't even have to be widely imitated to lose their original eccentric force. This season at the City Center, the Merce Cunningham company marked its thirty-first year. Cunningham's philosophy of movement has been more extensively adopted than his actual language of movement, yet that language—one might call it a protestant classicism, with its grammar of dissent—no longer seems strange. It has become traditional to Cunningham, and we accept it along with other formerly disconcerting features of his canon, like the relevant-irrelevant sound. Everything looks so sanely irrational on Cunningham's stage that we can fail to notice new peculiarities when they creep in. Some of the recent pieces seem organically connected, as if they were segments of a larger, ongoing work or variations on a theme. It's easy to see these connections when they're imagistic, as in *Quartet* and *Gallopade*, and when they fall into discrete patterns, as they do in those two works. But then there are the nonimagistic works—*Trails* and *Coast Zone* and *Pictures*—which haven't a clearly defined "closed" structure and simply progress from one thing to another until the curtain falls. I don't suppose that Cunningham has never used linear progression before, but I doubt if he has ever used so much of it at one time. Because nothing appears to repeat or return in these dances, they are all but impossible to grasp as entities.

In *Pictures*, the newest piece, some of the dancers fall into poses and hold them while the others keep moving, but these poses are all different and completely contradictory in their makeup—sometimes strikingly arranged, sometimes beautiful, but more often unresolved or off balance. Whether the stopped action has any intelligibility as a pose seems a matter of luck, like a snapshot taken at the right time. And the meaning, if any, is purely formal; these aren't images in the poetic sense, and they have no cumulative power. But they do give us handholds—literally points of rest—that keep the flow of movement from dissolving into chaos before our eyes. I can imagine a younger Cunningham who would have relished such a dissolution. But *Pictures* is a gently inquisitive work; at first glance, it doesn't seem to be up to very much at all.

Pictures may have evolved from *Coast Zone* (1983), which may in turn have come from *Trails* (1982). *Trails* is a succession of entrées in which no fewer than two and no more than five dancers are on the stage at one time. (There are ten dancers in all.) The entrées are fairly long, fairly virtuosic, and they build. But they do not build one upon another, there is no climax, and once the piece is over you realize that it is centerless. *Coast Zone*, similarly constructed for twelve dancers, seems not only centerless but spineless. Each event lasts less than a minute and is wiped away by the succeeding event. The structure is so restlessly episodic that it seems to be all transitions. Cunningham even breaks up the one constant factor: the dancers who keep running in and out suddenly about halfway through the piece change into other dancers; one cast is wiped away by another. I believe this happens in *Pictures*, too; it contains all the dancers in the company, and a most effective entrance late in the action is made by Cunningham himself. Once the dancers come on, they tend to stay on for long periods; my memory is of a stage almost constantly full of various kinds of slow-winding activity. Cunningham comes close to Chinese landscape painting.

The other of the season's new works, *Inlets 2*, is a new version of an older piece. Cunningham has created new choreography from the same material, deleting his own role in the process. He has also deleted the Morris Graves décor, but not the John Cage score, which sounds like a faucet dripping in a bucket, then like a campfire. These noises and some vivid animal imagery are all I recognized of the *Inlets* of 1978. The soft-edged sectional design and the quietly unfolding moods were closer to *Pictures*. Both in *Inlets 2* and in *Pictures*, the choreography employs doubling devices—people sharing a phrase by performing it in unison or in canon or splitting it between them—in a marked way I don't recall seeing before in Cunningham's work. But the more I see of his work the more unfamiliar it looks. The chain-smoking phase he seems to be in now, igniting one dance with the tip of another, emphasizes similarities in his work that were probably there all along. It also reproduces the essential Cunningham experience on a new plane. Out of what first seems to be undifferentiated spectacle themes appear, objectives appear, and continuity assumes familiarly strange proportions.

There is a characteristic moment in all Jerome Robbins's best ballets which I can't help looking for in each new ballet he does. It's the moment that crystallizes the secret of the ballet's excitement and reveals the innermost workings of Robbins's gift. Invariably, it's a tiny thing, like the moment when the cast of *Moves* appears, sinks into fifth-position plié, and extends a line of tendues forward along the floor. In *Dances at a Gathering*, the moment comes when the partners in the Opus 42 waltz stand hand in hand with their backs to the audience and do a string of relevés passés and sautés passés. At this moment, they are good little ballet students striving their hardest to please some stern invisible teacher, and Robbins seems to open his heart to them and to us. In its simplicity, this passage is diametrically opposed to the clever lift that comes a moment later and is applauded by the audience. *Dances at a Gathering* is filled with clever lifts, clever exits, clever choreographic schemes that never fail to impress us. The plain old relevés passés, coming at such a crazy moment in the music (Chopin seems to be rushing his coda, like a child saying his prayers in a hurry to get out of church), have a disproportionate grandeur, a beauty of aspiration by which in a single flash of recognition we come to know, judge, and accept the ambition that lies at the heart of the whole ballet.

Robbins's greatest ideas are nearly always revelations of the commonplace. He gives us something we've seen a million times in the one form in which we think we've never seen it before. He's able to do this, I think, because he's an outsider who came to ballet relatively late and for whom tensions and barriers as well as the most magical correspondences exist between ballet's fantasy world and real life. When Robbins is expressing familiar things in ballet terms, as in *Fancy Free* and *Interplay* and *Faun* and *The Cage* and *Moves* and *Dances at a Gathering* and *Mother Goose*, he has a quality of insight like no other choreographer's. No one else gives us these flashing nuggets that light up in memory and reactivate whole ballets. Take the moment when at the start of the lift in *Faun* the girl drops her head. She turns away from the direction of the lift and also, we feel, from her usual self. For once she doesn't look into the mirror (which is to say out at the audience) to see the effect of a movement, she feels it inside. She yields as a woman, not just as a dancer, to the boy's hands on her body. And yet the turning of the head in one direction while the body sails in another is only classical logic; the movement that looks so intimately revealing could have been taught. The gesture calls up the whole disturbing mood of Robbins's ballet because it crystallizes the ballet's discovery of a correspondence between realism and artifice—a correspondence that it was Robbins's genius to arrive at as if it were a natural coincidence and not something derived from a study of the Nijinsky original. In Nijinsky's *L'Après-midi d'un Faune*, the dancers move in profile, with the feet going straight ahead and the torso twisting to the front. Why they do that is still a question, but in Robbins's *Afternoon of a Faun* if we think about Nijinsky we find that Robbins answers the question in his own terms. It's because dancers are self-absorbed beings who are always looking in a mirror. Nijinsky's profile stance is modified by Robbins to fit the preoccupied behavior of dancers who, even as they hold and caress each other, constantly look away into a mirror. It's faces front all the time—no getting away from it. If Robbins is proclaiming that Nijinsky's Faun was a direct descendant of his Narcissus, he is persuasive. His ballet is the best critical essay that has ever been composed about *Faune*; it shows conclusively how, by invoking a commonplace of *his* time (what Lincoln Kirstein calls "the Maryinsky's 'Egyptian' style"), and investing it with a novel tension, Nijinsky could have brought off his 1912 explosion. And, of course, the Robbins *Faun* is in its own right a masterpiece which we have admired for more than thirty years.

Last season, Robbins returned to Debussy and the Greek nymphs of Debussy's (and Nijinsky's) period. In its dances for eight women, *Antique Epigraphs* even revived Maryinsky profiling. But this time Robbins had no comment to make. It was merely a pretty world that he showed us—one uncertainly situated in time. Was this the Greece of the Belle Epoque, was it the Greece of early American modern dance, or was it the historical, unimaginable *Greece?* The ballet suggested a little of all three. Florence Klotz's gauzy long shifts, cinched under the breasts, made the dancers look heavy—an effect Robbins may have intended (to judge from the weightedness of his choreography) or, then again, may not have (to judge from the toe shoes he had the dancers wear). Sadly, this indecisiveness is typical of Robbins's work these days. If he had come right out and said that these women were imagining themselves Greek, as the dancers of *Faun* imagine themselves in love, the ballet might have worked.

Robbins and Merce Cunningham are in their middle sixties. Martha Graham will be ninety in May, and she, too, is still producing—at least, her company is still producing, with her advice and consent. As part of the birthday-year celebration, it announced a production of *The Rite of Spring*, to be presented at the State Theater, in costumes by Halston. I went expecting nothing more than a glimpse of the thinking that had allowed Graham to say in press conferences that she was returning "to hallowed and terrifying ground." I assumed she meant the terrain of *Primitive Mysteries* and *El Penitente* and *Dark Meadow*, although some press releases had her saying what could not easily be believed: "Dancing

the role of the Chosen One in the 1930 revival of the Nijinsky ballet was a turning point in my life." (It was Massine's,
not Nijinsky's, choreography that was being revived, and
Graham's clashes with the choreographer on that occasion
are still legend.) No, by "hallowed and terrifying ground" I
hoped that Graham was speaking of her own turf, on which
she would now erect not—preposterous expectation—another
work of art but perhaps a sign or two of her understanding
of the primitive rituals of the Southwest. I imagined her
dusting off old notebooks and reading aloud to her dancers.
These notes would, of course, be similar to the anthropological jottings in *The Notebooks of Martha Graham*.

And she may well have given readings, and she may have
dictated every gesture in the rehearsals and supervised every
stitch of Halston's costumes. The results are still as trifling
as we had every reason to fear they would be, and they are
inauthentic besides. The outlines of Stravinsky's libretto are
vaguely impressed upon a locale that could be Santa Fe,
Samoa, or Haiti. The Chosen One, topless in a black
sarong, is trussed up in thick white cable, then immediately
untrussed. She thrashes and dies under the Shaman's gor-
geous cape. More cloth is flung down, and that's the rite.
Even if the rhythms of the music were deployed in the
choreography, even if the dancers were stronger than they
are, the ritual drama of catharsis could not occur, because
the Graham technique—that supreme instrument of theatrical catharsis—has now faded to the point of ineffectuality.
The only note of authenticity is an occasional reminder of
old Graham dances: in the relationship of the Shaman and
the Chosen One there are echoes of St. Michael and Joan of
Arc, and some of the choral episodes recall *Dark Meadow*.

I suppose it is something that a production as large,
long, and expensive as this can actually be put on by a

woman in her ninetieth year. That it is devoid of content will not disturb people whose knowledge of Graham's work begins with her Halston period. Older pieces on the program do not show it up, since there's scarcely anything left of them. It used to be that only those in which Graham herself formerly danced were being misrepresented. Now, because of lobotomized performing, we're losing works like *Seraphic Dialogue* and *Embattled Garden*—works that Graham never appeared in. The stage of the State Theater, twice too large for such pieces, does its own job of burying them. In *Primitive Mysteries*, the dancers had to take about fifteen steps to get from the wings to the center of the stage. Because they exit and re-enter so many times, *Primitive Mysteries* became a piece about walking. (It was, however, the most scrupulously rehearsed of the old works.) The audience was justifiably puzzled by these curiosities. As soon as the curtain rose on an *Andromache's Lament* or an *Acts of Light*—pieces made on a big scale in the eighties and furnished in posh fabrics and gilt—you felt the atmosphere change. These new synthetic products have nothing to say, but they project. People relax and start to applaud. The worst is *Phaedra's Dream*, in which Phaedra and a male rival (designated The Stranger) compete for her stepson Hippolytus. It carries the anonymity and the bombast of the eighties to a new level of violation. The action, which takes place in Noguchi's old set for *Alcestis*, is filled with a kind of coarse realism—lurchings and couplings and evil stares —that I have never seen before on Graham's stage. I'd thought nothing could be worse than the caricature of Graham exercises which appears in *Acts of Light*—all preening postures and flaccid dynamics. *Phaedra's Dream* is worse than a distortion—it's a sham.

—*March 26, 1984*

The Search for *Cinderella*

Mikhail Baryshnikov has brought his *Cinderella* to the Metropolitan after a four-month break-in tour. Box-office has been pretty much what it was on the road: big. The most expensive production in the history of American Ballet Theatre, *Cinderella* has already recouped its costs four times over. Baryshnikov achieved this success without dancing in the ballet himself. Apparently, the public has trusted him to put on a show it wants to see—a show called *Cinderella*. But is *Cinderella* a hit? Hits in ballet are not made of money. From the moment that *Cinderella* was announced, Baryshnikov's artistic prestige was on the line, and now that the financial returns are in, it still is. The out-of-town critics wrote reviews balancing the show's flaws and merits. In New York, the press was mostly negative, and also captious, inattentive, unjust. Baryshnikov doesn't consider himself much of a choreographer and has said so. The New York critics seemed determined to take him at his word and go him one better: he's not only not a choreographer, he's a vandal. His victim is the beautiful, beloved fairy tale of *Cinderella*. He and his accomplices, Peter Anastos and Santo

Loquasto, have drained the innocence and the magic out of it and turned it into a heartless burlesque.

In mounting such a line of attack, the critics have made two mistaken assumptions. One is that the ballet they want is the ballet Sergei Prokofiev wrote. (Does the public share that assumption? We shall see.) The other is that Baryshnikov and company have deliberately set out to undermine the romantic and sentimental values of the fairy tale. Prokofiev's ballet, written in Stalin's Russia during the forties, is not a conventional, sweet storybook romance; it is a brooding, disjointed affair. The domestic scenes are broad farce; the court scenes are farce and satire; and the love scenes are emotionally overscaled, as if by exaggerating their passion Prokofiev could make Cinderella and the Prince transcend a world they obviously don't belong to. The out-of-this-world aspect of the love duets has its negative reflection in the ballroom music. Cinderella's home life isn't bad enough; her social life is characterized by sour tunes and clashing tonal colors. The sinister "fate" music builds out of the ballroom waltzes in such a way as to suggest that the heroine is imperiled by the society she finds at court, not by her own forgetfulness.

Prokofiev's musical imagination in *Cinderella* is to my mind livelier and less neurotic than in *Romeo and Juliet*, but at times he seems to be casting Cinderella and the Prince as star-crossed lovers. The crescendos in the love duets are so huge they run the risk of alienating Cinderella from her own aspirations. Love on these terms isn't something she has dreamed about—it's a whole new reality, troubling in its size and importance. But then going to the ball isn't wish fulfillment. What girl could hope for happiness as the princess of this crass, petit-bourgeois kingdom, with its dinky little court? And doesn't Prokofiev's sarcasm infect the love duets? Listening to the score several times over at the Met, I found that what used to seem full-throttle emotion sounded more like bombast: a dream of pure love is inflated with hot air. The producer of *Cinderella* has no choice but to go along with it, hoping by some ingenuity of staging and choreography to convey a sense of grandeur and poetic isolation. The Baryshnikov production doesn't do this; its effects are too modest. But it isn't trying to drain the ballet of romance—only of pomposity. If Baryshnikov does in fact undermine the spirit of a fairy tale, his chief accomplice is Sergei Prokofiev.

Prokofiev affronts the child in us who wants to see Cinderella enter the same beautiful world of privilege her sisters are part of. The sisters are ugly, and so is their world. As an alternative to materialistic greed, the scenario proposes the wealth of nature. Birds, flowers, the changing seasons are represented in a divertissement presided over by the Fairy Godmother, and Cinderella goes to the ball not as a social-climbing impostor but as Rousseau's naturally good human being in search of a nonbrutalizing environment. She doesn't find it. (The Fairy Godmother should have known that, but she's naïve.) Instead, Cinderella finds another child of nature, the Prince, who, even as she, has miraculously escaped environmental conditioning, and the two of them are united in the starry idealism of a world to come.

This fatuous moralism is what passes for a fairy tale in Prokofiev's version. Half the time, he doesn't seem to believe it himself. The Western version of *Cinderella*, with its practicality, its fantasy of social conquest and revenge, and its vindication of the individual, can't be imposed on the Soviet fable without considerable sleight of hand. If Cinderella is made to dream of love and beauty and good times and to find them all at the ball, then Prokofiev's satire of a corrupt society is out of place. If she doesn't find these things at the ball, there's no point in her going there in the first place, especially when she's given no moment in which to awaken from her delusion. We're supposed to believe in a differently motivated Cinderella, purer than the one we know. Baryshnikov and Anastos, who together choreographed the ballet, have been criticized for making Cinderella the scullery maid too cheerful. She dances contentedly with her cat instead of moping by the hearth. Taxed beyond endurance by her stepsisters, she stuffs their dirty laundry in the oven. I find this conception of the heroine the one instance of compatibility between the traditional and the Soviet versions. A Cinderella who doesn't accept her lot meekly yet doesn't waste time repining is sturdy enough to resist worldly temptations. She'll marry the Prince not because he's the Prince but because she loves him. She'll deserve the title of Princess because she really is one and knows it. (Actually, she's Mary Pickford, whom Russians of Prokofiev's generation adored.)

The Baryshnikov-Anastos-Loquasto production doesn't want to change the Soviet *Cinderella* so much as it wants to make it more agreeable. Loquasto's aluminum-foil backdrop stays in place for all three acts; in the second act it has a coppery glow and in the third act it is punctured by stars. Of course, Loquasto's designs are the first thing you see, and they are anything but sweetly pretty; they're in fact the key to the ideological style of the whole production. How to satirize luxury without violating standards of good design or insulting the taste of the audience: that was the problem, and Loquasto has handled it gracefully for the most part. He has received little credit. Nearly every review has either commended the production's Trump Tower opulence or bridled at its "glitz." The problem faced by the choreographers was no less difficult. Inexperience, impatience, unruliness show in their work. But not bad taste, cynicism, profligacy, lack of intelligence. If anything, Baryshnikov and Anastos have been too intelligent, too tasteful. In the Ugly Sisters' scenes in Act I, their touch is light, but the pacing is slam-bang, as if buffoonery were something that needed to be got through as quickly as possible. In this respect, the production is light-years away from the Frederick Ashton–Robert Helpmann scenes in the Royal Ballet's *Cinderella*. These were deliberate, unhurried clowns, and funnier for it. They were also two distinctly different people. ABT's Sisters are different, but not different enough. At this speed, they can't get much character distinction out of the dressing up and primping scenes. Instead of being fussy and fastidious as only female impersonators can be, they're nervous, squalling prima donnas too much of the time. Yet they dance well; the pas de trois with the Dancing Master is a real business of getting up on pointe and into arabesque. We'd like to see more of the Sisters at the ball—there's a place for them to pop up in the mazurka—but Baryshnikov and Anastos rein them in. They don't even let us see what the Sisters might make of Cinderella's appearance as the belle of the ball. (If they don't recognize her, we ought to see that they don't.)

In a story ballet, story points have to be brought out at every opportunity. Not enough happens at this ball, and what does happen tends to be underplayed. When, for example, the Sisters enter, one of them falls down the stairs. Huffily, she refuses assistance. Then she notices that someone else is wearing the same gown she has on. Two blows before she even gets in the door! The trouble is, the audience sees only the first blow. It's a performance slip of a kind that occurs often. We don't really register Cinderella's dreaming in the first act—she takes so little time over it. The moment is there in the choreography; it's up to the dancer to frame it—a close-up, as it were. Earlier, Cinderella's scene with her father is just roughed in. There are no mime details to convey that the picture he shows her is of her mother, that it *is* a picture and not a mirror, and so forth.

The production gives us a conception of Cinderella but not a living character. This may be one reason we forget about her so quickly when the Prince comes on in the second act. Suddenly he takes over, and it becomes his ballet. As in *The Sleeping Beauty* and *Giselle* (as Baryshnikov plays those classics), love transforms a playboy. There are few things in the ballet more genuinely romantic than the Prince's single-minded search through the kingdom for the owner of the slipper. I suspect that if this production is gratefully remembered it will be for its handling, witty as well as romantic, of a sequence that is usually cut. The Prince visits the home of the Bourgeois Gentilhomme, where he is besieged by three rapacious daughters, in waltz time. He goes to the garden of *Le Nozze di Figaro*, Act IV, where he has an assignation with a Masked Lady who he hopes is Cinderella. (The ploy is no more cynical than Siegfried's mistaking Odile for Odette.) These conceits that, perhaps undeservedly, relate Prokofiev's ballet to other works of art are effective in more than one way. They give Loquasto relief from the cottage and the castle. They suggest that there's some further dimension to the world of folly and wickedness evoked by the ballet. The idea is not that Prokofiev's satire is on a level with Molière and Beaumarchais but that it's in the same tradition. Has any other production of the ballet been as generous to the composer and his librettist? Ironically, Baryshnikov has had to be generous at Prokofiev's expense. The music that was composed for the travel episode, a trashy montage of exotic scenes, has been replaced by waltzes from *War and Peace* and the film *Lermontov*, which were written at about the same time as *Cinderella*. The fact that this outstanding sequence is an interpolation tells much about the production and its struggle to come to life. The fact, too, that it is an episode in which Cinderella does not figure.

Cinderella and her purity place a great strain on the narrative of the ballet, particularly in the overblown love duets. How shall they be danced? The solution has usually been to import the content of a climactic pas de deux in some other ballet. Ashton's choreography is based, none too persuasively, on *The Sleeping Beauty*. The Konstantin Sergeyev production for the Kirov went right along with the music's suggestion that the lovers were really Romeo and Juliet. In a recent version for the Chicago City Ballet, planned around Suzanne Farrell, Paul Mejia spirited in touchstones from several Farrell roles choreographed by Balanchine. Baryshnikov and Anastos go so far as to switch the order of the duets in Acts II and III, putting the more pompous one last (it sounds as if Cinderella were marrying Alexander Nevsky), but the choreography is vacuous. The woman's role has no repose but also none of the drive that Farrell's Cinderella had or Irina Kolpakova's in the Sergeyev production. We are told no story in these dances, nor can we make one up while we watch. A chance to set up a story is missed in Act II by having Cinderella and the Prince declare their love as soon as they meet. They waltz in and out among the guests, and the dance subsides in a pretty tableau with the ensemble framing the principals, already deeply in love. They ought really to be only on the threshold; the big pas de deux that comes up a few minutes later brings them over. Prokofiev's pattern here is very much on the lines of Romeo

meeting Juliet at the masked ball, contriving to find her in
the crowd and dance with her, and only gradually disclosing
his fascination with her (not his love—*that* comes in the balcony pas de deux). By the time the lovers in *Cinderella* get
to their all-alone-in-the-night pas de deux, they've already
said it. This isn't why the pas de deux is empty; this is why
it would take much better choreography not to *seem* empty.

The third-act pas de deux is now preceded by a scene in
which the Prince unveils Cinderella before her tormentors
and they react with appropriate amazement and mortification. The story is thus rounded off and the lovers can be
alone to display their technique at no cost to verisimilitude.
There are other such improvements and at least a half hour's
worth of deletions. Cinderella's solos are less tepidly
Fonteynish. (I accused the choreographers of attempting a
link to Margot Fonteyn's Aurora. Ashton attempted it
first.) I question the wisdom of retaining an unidentifiable
entourage for Cinderella in the ballroom scene. Who *are*
these daughters of Denishawn wafting about the premises?
What were they to Cinderella in Act I? Why don't they attend her in Act III? An apotheosis has also been left intact in
which, to the sweetest music in the score (which the composer marked "Amoroso"), all the characters of the ballet assemble and parade about an empty stage till we get the
point that they're no longer characters—the story is over.
Like all such built-in company calls, this scene makes the actual curtain calls anticlimactic and puts a damper on applause. But Baryshnikov and Anastos also seem to be
offering an image of collective redemption. Are they saying
that (1) a hypocritical, ostentatious society doesn't anathe-
matize the individual after all or (2) we can only wish that it
didn't? However you take it, it's daring, but then much
about this production is daring. They really should be call-

ing it *Zolushka*—Russian for *Cinderella*. After all, *our* Cinderella isn't in the ballet, and Ballet Theatre happens to have nobody who can make us think so. Maybe the right ballerina could sweep up all the contradictions and soar to glory. There are things that could be done to make the production more worthy of her, should she ever be found. It could be made more dramatic, but it could never become a sweet, simple fantasy. That is not its style.

—*May 21, 1984*

Life Studies

David Gordon's pieces, dancier and less verbal than they used to be, are fascinating in their devious logic. The new, expanded dance portions are not interludes intended to relieve the spoken portions; they're parallel constructions that soak up the content of the speeches and redistribute it in abstract form. Not that the abstraction is immediately recognizable; at first, you just look and listen delightedly.

Parallel composing in words and movement has been Gordon's method for some time. As a general rule, the intelligibility of movement takes a lot longer to grasp than the intelligibility of words, and one way he has dealt with the disparity is by playing with common everyday speech patterns, using puns and non sequiturs and stringing them out casually in rhythmic sentences that slow down thought, bend it, or trip it up. "I hate the word 'out,' " a Gordon character will remark. "It's everything 'in' isn't." A long monologue plays on the colloquial use of "go" for "say." "He goes 'Move over.' I go 'Hold it.' He goes 'Hold what?' I go 'Very funny.' I go 'Ha ha.' He goes 'I'm going.' I go 'Go.' " Lately—in *TV Reel*, in last year's *Trying Times*, and now in *Framework*—Gordon has been experimenting with different qualities of impetus in dance movement. He now has three or four speeds, from the near-stasis of contact improvisation (or its simulation) right through to straight lyrical dancing. He has also developed with the designer Power Boothe a kind of portable décor that is flexible; a Masonite panel or a picture frame made of wooden strips can be different things at different times. It is this highly operative, integral décor that gives *Framework* a controlling metaphor as well as a title.

Framework is an evening's discourse on the way we compartmentalize ourselves as social beings. The panels and picture frames are objectifications of the alienation, confinement, or conventionalized rapport that we feel in our daily relations with fellow workers, lovers, and friends. They objectify good feelings, too, such as closeness in marriage, but the prevailing tone of *Framework* is wry, and its theme of manipulation, at first amusingly plaintive, darkens gradually to end the evening on a note of desperation. Manipulation isn't only a function of the décor. It's a requisite in dancing, where it functions as the inverse of dependency. The choreographer manipulates and depends on his subjects; partners manipulate and depend on each other. Added to the social picture that Gordon gives us—the absurd behavioral patterns, the pressures, the distractions—these purely formal biomechanical situations, played out to the pounding of rock records, take on a certain psychological realism. Gordon is careful not to press meanings on us, but he does keep attacking. It's as if his manipulation theme acquired its malign shadings as a corollary of his versatility.

Gordon has expanded his technique and his subject matter at the same time. He's no longer content to expose the surface ambiguities of limited movement. Moving more, he sees more. In the manifold machinations of *Framework* he sees tokens of the subtle monstrosity of human relations. And since he seems to be adducing evidence from his own life—the life of a harried, hardworking artist—we're invited to see him as part of the monstrous scheme and ultimately, when he trudges slowly, slowly across a stage filled with indecipherable hubbub, a victim of it. There may be something too notional in all this. When an artist's theme is what it is simply because of the number of ways it finds to express itself, the artist may feel that he hasn't chosen it—it has chosen him. He feels trapped, while we in the audience want to rejoice in what looks to us like a virtuoso performance. The last word in *Framework*, an unspoken pun, is Gordon saying "I was framed." We're showered with droplets of self-commiseration. There was always a moralizing taint to the earnestness with which post-modern dancers went about their anti-technique revolution. I don't think David Gordon believes that technical sophistication is corrupting. But the self-deflating ending of *Framework* may be the last vestige of post-modernist morality in his work.

The emotional ending is surprising, because nothing about *Framework* is facile. The boards and frames (which first appeared in *Trying Times*) sound like clichés until you see how Gordon has used them. In the first of several long pas de deux, Gordon and Margaret Hoeffel put a frame against a board and keep the two moving between them like a sliding door. They slip the frame ahead and step into the opening, close it up, and step in on the other side. This develops into variations, no two alike, in which they take turns setting and eluding traps, supporting each other's weight on the board, or disappearing behind it. The "board" pas de deux is offset, in the second act, by a "frame" pas de deux, in which Gordon holds a frame for Valda Setterfield to step through as she executes a fluid adagio in classical style. In neither case do the man and the woman touch. The nature of the relationship in the first duet is defined by the way each perceives the other's "space." In the Setterfield duet, the frame is her barre, her home, her Platonic halo. Possibilities multiply and crisscross. It is the hoop that her husband the choreographer puts her through even as it is the image of his adoration.

Like every other David Gordon piece, *Framework* is a total system discharging interior meanings. But it is also a view of real life. We recognize the times and the customs, the clothes, the postures, the lingo. The music sounds as if someone backstage had turned on the local rock station and let the dial drift, so that wisps of Chopin now and then float above the beat. Gordon keeps the dualities so delicately balanced that we can be lulled by the formal beauty of the piece into ignoring signs of its double life. When, at some point in the action, the dancers pause and sum up "the story so far," we're startled, because so much of the action has been abstract. Are these dances staged to look like social rituals or are they social rituals staged to look like dances? The content seems at all times reversible, and though the suggestion of a "story" is partly ironic, it is serious in its urging of a noninsular, nonrelativistic point of view. In fact, the spoken synopsis turns out to be a completely acceptable literalistic interpretation of the borderline drama of the piece. ("Margaret and David had a falling out," etc.) For a moment, we get to see things in the "framework" of a story, then back to the mirror world. The wonderful "I go 'Go'" monologue, vivaciously delivered by Susan Eschelbach to five other dancers as they group themselves around, behind, and beneath a panel (a table, a door, a bed), seems to open up another story. Whether or not it is one depends on how you read the pas de deux of Eschelbach and Paul Evans which immediately follows. Gordon is a collagist. Many of his dances and set pieces (like Eschelbach's monologue) can be lifted out of context and combined with new material to make a new impression. The pleasure we get from Gordon's work is the pleasure of synthesis. The integrity each new piece has is always a surprise. We go to see how the collagist's beads and shells and feathers and pinwheels will work this time and what new things have been added to the collection.

For me, the outstanding novelty item in *Framework* is a group dance that goes to the song "Fresh." A sextet that frequently divides into three couples, "Fresh" has a momentum unlike any other ensemble that Gordon has done; it keeps on unrolling itself like surf as the dancers spin, dive, re-dive, tumble, shove, and toss each other into the air. Then, with a shift into slow motion, it seems to plunge underwater and go on traveling. This five-minute dance, which ends the first half of the show, sums up many of Gordon's movement motifs; it's awash with seashells and pinwheels. It's exciting—new and old at the same time—and somehow I think I'll be seeing it again.

If Gordon is a collagist, Douglas Dunn is a draftsman who keeps sketchbooks. His sketches are admirable; each has a life, a secret of its own, a brilliantly opportune idea that seems to lead the eye. The trouble is, Dunn's ideas don't extend themselves for more than a few seconds; they keep erupting, ever new. While we long to scan a landscape, to see large configurations develop and details recede, Dunn keeps showing us page after page of motifs. There used to be a fidgety, short-winded quality in his movement. The newer numbers in his recent concerts at the Joyce showed very little of this. In *Elbow Room*, Dunn's phrases have lengthened, and they've never been more beautifully formed, more inventive than they are in *Pulcinella*. But they are still fragments. Dunn originally staged the Stravinsky score on commission from the Paris Opéra Ballet. The New York production has a drop cloth by Mimi Gross showing a sunbaked Bay of Naples, and an array of crumpled white silk costumes, also by Mimi Gross, that suggest a down-at-heels *commedia dell'arte* troupe. There is no plot. The dances ramble along in the disorderly fashion and with the diffuse impact of a street festival. Stronger continuity could have made the image a valid one, but though Dunn's phrases are set on the music, they have no adhesive power, and forty minutes is too long a time to deal with fugitive impressions.

Dunn himself is a gifted dancer and a highly civilized artist. His too-assiduous imitations of Merce Cunningham's performing style are an obstacle. A former Cunningham dancer, he was also a member, with David Gordon, of the choreographers' collective known as the Grand Union. His style is nervous, sensitive, refined, but inconsistent. Some steps in a sequence are perfectly pronounced, but others are tentative. Gordon, who lacks Dunn's phrasemaking talent, is technically cleaner and more precise. As a choreographer, Dunn remains a soloist, and he heads a company of soloists, augmented for the Stravinsky ballet. He danced a frazzled, hallucinated Pulcinella. Karole Armitage made a guest appearance doing odd, violent, high-tension solos that seemed to relate more to her own work than to Dunn's.

I also saw at the Joyce two programs by San Francisco choreographers. Brenda Way's choreography struck me as energetic but crude, and I found nothing to admire in her costumes or lighting. Margaret Jenkins's pieces aren't much on the production side, either, but I was held by a succession of ideas mounted in long, full, rhythmically taut phrases. *Max's Dream*, suggested by images from Max

Ernst, was something in the surrealistic line; the choreographer wandered among her dancers wearing a tuxedo, her upper body encased in a huge cabbage rose. What the dancers did was more penetratingly eccentric, more Ernstian: a woman was inserted head downward through the arms of an embracing couple; a woman dove down a man's back into the wings. Partners holding each other by the hand swung apart and together in wide, whipping loops. Jenkins likes to counter flowing big-scale body movement with small staccato gestures of the head and arms; here these looked like the manic chattering of puppets.

—June 18, 1984

Bad Smells

At the Brooklyn Academy of Music, the Pina Bausch company was the height of chic. The visual effects echoed fashion-magazine layouts; the politics did, too. Pina Bausch plays right into feminist paranoia; it's her most consistent theme.

The rhythm of a Pina Bausch piece is obsessively regular. Bursts of violence are followed by long stillnesses. Bits of business are systematically repeated, sometimes with increasing urgency but more often with no variation at all. At every repetition, less is revealed, and action that looked gratuitous to begin with dissolves into meaningless frenzy. *Café Müller*, which opened the Bausch season and set the tone for it, is thirty-five minutes long and feels ninety; its subject is duration, and repetition is its only device. The café—apparently it is meant to resemble a real place—seems to be the canteen of a mental hospital. A small cast of inmates gives us intermittent doses of violent/apathetic behavior while a woman who may be a visitor scurries noisily about in high-heeled shoes. Music from Purcell's operas drifts over the loudspeakers, doing its best to solemnize the goings on. *Café Müller*, with its thin but flashy shtick, is a how-to-make-theatre handbook. It enshrines the amateur's faith in psychopathy as drama. Bausch herself is in it, entering the set at curtain rise and remaining onstage throughout, a thin, spectral figure in a nightgown. Sightlessly she creeps along a wall and huddles in the dark until the end, when she staggers downstage and starts bumping into the furniture. It takes a considerable ego to cast yourself as a pathetic, sightless, wandering creature. When I saw Bausch playing the blind princess with the sad smiles in the movie *And the Ship Sails On*, I thought she was a typical Fellini invention. But Bausch evidently sees herself as this wan, wasted Duse; the blind-seeress act is perfectly in keeping with the inverted Romanticism of her theatre.

There have been numerous clinical analyses of Bausch's Theatre of Dejection; they're beside the point. Bausch may have her hangups, but basically she's an entrepreneuse who fills theatres with projections of herself and her self-pity. Since there's nothing between us and her—no mediating dramatic rationale, no technique to transfigure and validate raw emotion—we think that she's somehow authentic, that her suffering, at least, must be real. She *can't* be just acting po' faced. Bausch's power lies in having calculated audience voyeurism to a nicety, and those sad smiles have a way of curling up contemptuously when it comes to her favorite theme of men and women. In Bausch theatre, men brutalize women and women humiliate men; the savage round goes on endlessly. The content of these bruising encounters is always minimal. Bausch doesn't build psychodramas in which people come to understand something about themselves and their pain. She keeps referring us to the *act* of brutalization or humiliation—to the pornography of pain. Presumably, the superficiality of it all is what allows the

Wuppertaler Tanztheater to call itself that; *dance* is something it hardly ever shows us. (One of the great jokes of the season was the choice of this supremely unathletic company to open the Olympic Arts Festival.)

When the Wuppertalers do dance, they're strangely inhibited. They usually begin by standing in place and stretching and swerving the upper body this way and that, their hands locked over or behind their heads. They don't move their feet much except when they run, and then it's usually pell-mell. But it seems they only run in order to halt. Either they halt stymied (by banging into something or somebody) or they halt dead, feet planted apart, eyes cast down, as if they'd suddenly realized they were violating the ground by running over it. The run motifs and the halt motifs are used in Bausch's version of *Le Sacre du Printemps*. Running in herds (the Tribe) is opposed to running alone (the Sacrifice). The catalogue expands to include sweating, heavy breathing, clammy bodies slapping against each other, and peeling wet clothes from clammy bodies. We'd already seen these motifs in *Café Müller*, but there the stage was completely filled with little black tables and chairs, and in the *Sacre* it's covered with packed-down dirt, like a camping ground or like a Peter Brook set. Bausch's covered floors have become famous, and I imagine the clinicians really do have something to say about this need to fill the floor end to end and wing to wing with objects or foreign substances: dead leaves are used in *Bluebeard*, live grass in *1980*. By getting sweaty dancers dirty, the earth floor adds an element of yuck to *Le Sacre* which the other pieces don't have, but the dead leaves and the grass are bad enough: they made the Brooklyn Academy, which isn't air-conditioned, smell like a stable. Naturally, you don't *dance* on such stages.

In spite of its yuckiness, the *Sacre* remains in memory as the only tolerable Bausch piece. But if the Stravinsky score sets limits on her tendency to maunder and repeat, it also amplifies and energizes her theme of female persecution. This must be the tenth or twelfth *Sacre* I've seen in the past five years. Every one but Paul Taylor's has used the score to whip up an excitement the choreography could not have sustained on its own. Bausch's version, which is about ritual murder with no reference to fertility, has no feel for the rhythms of the score. In the Sacrificial Victim's dance, it reaches its wit's end before the music runs out. If Bausch has a choreographic technique that she disdains to use in her "theatre" pieces, here was the place for it. But she produced a run-of-the-mill *Sacre*. The only moment of tension—I found it agonizing—came when the choice of the Victim seemed about to settle on one of the little fat girls in the company. The Bausch troupe contains quite a few members who don't look like dancers and are none too prepossessing physically. They look their best in *1980*; the women dress up and comb their hair and put on makeup, and even the men seem civilized. When the whole cast of eighteen comes on like a chorus line, snaking through the audience and grinning in all directions, we can see that they mean to be likably batty, but then they go on to do vaudeville turns and little skits reminiscing about or reverting to their childhoods, and they're corny and tiresome. The casting is so determinedly egalitarian (everyone gets a chance to bore you) and the material is so clownish or so literally childish (actual children's games and songs, actually played and sung) that the fact that some, if not all, of these reminiscences are biographical has no weight. And why is it that everyone seems to have had a sad childhood? Because everyone belongs to the Theatre of Dejection, that's why. *1980*, named for the year it was first put on, suggests what life in the Bausch company must be like: *Animal House* with Weltschmerz.

The Theatre of Dejection builds down from the Theatre

of Absurdity and the Theatre of Cruelty and other manifes-
tations of the sixties; the cycle has come back to the raw
pulp of abuse it started with. It is hard to believe in mental-
asylum metaphors twenty years after *Marat/Sade*; in audi-
ence-involvement techniques fifteen years after the Living
Theatre; in bleak despair, in the prankishly surrealistic, in
monomaniacal simplicity, and in all the affectless contrivances of avant-garde fashion which Bausch puts on the
stage after two full generations of American modern
dancers have done them to death. She is a force in European
theatre, and perhaps that explains everything. (It explains
quite a bit of Carolyn Carlson, an American choreographer
now working in Europe, in the European mode.) To judge
from the Eurotrash that has poured in on us in recent seasons—a partial list would include Peter Brook's *Carmen*,
Maurice Béjart, Jiří Kylián, and Patrice Chéreau's *Ring*—
there is not much resistance to such a force.

I can't say I was surprised by anything I saw done by the
Wuppertaler Tanztheater, but there was one element I was
surprised not to see. Bausch's publicity has exaggerated the
amount of sex in her work. Some mild ribaldry, some rather
unappetizing nudity are all she has. As a theatre terrorist,
she gets her main effect by repetition. People throw each
other against the wall not once but many times. Women are
caught in a sling and swung round and round and round
not once but many times. Men are undressed, paraded
naked, and smeared with lipstick not once but so frequently
and maliciously that the point reverses itself, and Bausch's
vengeance becomes seemingly that of a woman who not
only has hated to expose herself for male delectation but has
feared to. Body shame is a subtheme of the female-
exploitation theme. In *Café Müller*, *Le Sacre du Printemps*,
and *Bluebeard*, the women wear filmy slips without bras,

which makes them look like a bunch of sad sacks, and they use a characteristic Bauschian gesture: they hang their heads and let their hands creep up the front of their bodies, lifting the garment exhibitionistically as they go. Skirts are sometimes lifted without implications of shame but never with implications of pleasure, and it's typical of Bausch's males that they show no interest whatever. It's typical, too, that when they strip they have nothing to show *us*. I was unable to hold myself in the theatre for more than an hour of *Bluebeard*, the most concentrated of Bausch's feminist tirades, and an hour and a half of *1980* (which was four hours long), but I should be surprised to learn that Bausch was able to turn out one credible, attractive image of masculinity. Having made women look worse on the stage than any misogynist ever has, she is under no obligation to men.

—July 16, 1984

"Giselle, ou La Fille des Bayous"

Dance Theatre of Harlem has presented its first full-length classic: *Giselle*. The first act is set on a Louisiana plantation, with a white porch and white barns overhung with Spanish moss, and with a black farm girl betrayed by a rich landowner's son, also black. The second act takes place in the bayous. Like some other DTH transpositions, the production is pictorially and emotionally so satisfying that we gladly excuse a few implausibilities. And, anyway, what are a few more implausibilities in *Giselle*? The music isn't what you'd have heard in the American South of a hundred and fifty years ago, but we listen to the score of *Giselle* less for its local color than for its melodrama and sentiment. The only passage of music and dance that seems wrong in the Harlem version is the peasant pas de deux, a traditional interpolation that takes its flavor from folk-based steps. In the context of this "Creole" production, the effect is the reverse of what it usually is: instead of two field hands showing off to the local gentry, the dance seems to be displaying imported Paris finery—the steps themselves look gentrified. (Maybe a few tambourines banged on the sidelines à la Bournonville

would reinforce the intention.) There are some implausibilities the production would be better off without. The fine
folk for whose benefit the pas de deux is danced: shouldn't
they all be invited by Mme Berthe to sample the scupper-
nong? Instead, as in the traditional production, a meager
glassful is doled out to the two kingpins while their "court"
stands about stiffly. On this point and on several others
concerning the manners of Act I, I agree with Deborah
Jowitt's review in *The Village Voice*. Albert's sword is
sheathed in a gold-headed cane, but it's hardly the mark of
caste that Albrecht's sword is. And why, confronting Hilarion, should this same Albert grope for a missing sword at
his hip when he doesn't carry it that way? The staging, by
Frederic Franklin, makes almost no concessions to the new
setting, and thus passes up several good opportunities to
reinvigorate a stereotype.

According to copious historical notes provided by the
company, caste among the free blacks in the Louisiana of
the 1840s was determined chiefly by the number of generations a person could count up from slavery. Though Giselle,
whose mother was born a slave, is three rungs lower than
Albert, the difference between them is not so great as the
difference between a peasant girl and a duke, and a Giselle
who goes mad and kills herself when it turns out her fiancé
is engaged to the belle of Plaquemines Parish is insecurely
motivated unless it can be shown that she's unbalanced to
begin with. Or pregnant. The pregnancy-of-Giselle theory
has long been entertained by some students of the ballet.
It's the real reason, they think, that Berthe keeps cautioning
her daughter against dancing. I doubt if anyone has actually
played out this interpretation on the stage.

Carl Michel, who compiled the historical background of
this version and designed the sets and costumes, and evi-

dently was very much a moving force, achieves his greatest coup in the second act, with Albert being poled through the swamp in a flat-bottomed boat toward the tomb of Giselle looming through the wisteria. (It is set above the ground, Michel tells us, like most Louisiana graves, because of the high water table.) The scene recalls the river Styx with Charon the ferryman—an image appropriate to a ballet whose libretto parallels the descent of Orpheus and his encounter with the bacchantes. The whole second act moves in the heavy dead air of "Thanatopsis." There would appear to be a tomb for Myrtha, too, with her statue mounted over it like a civic virtue, grim in crown and scepter. Instead of ballet skirts, gray tattered shifts are worn (Giselle, the novice, is in white), with an effect of shrouds. Michel has omitted nothing.

But his colleagues have. The lighting (by Shirley Prendergast) is weak in those atmospherics which should startle the villagers at the beginning of the act, and totally negligent when dawn arrives to save Albert from the Wilis. Act II should be a ballet d'action from start to finish, not the abstract ballet with a few set pieces of narration which we are used to seeing. Franklin's staging of the choreography is routine. Beyond those set pieces, it rationalizes none of the action from a dramatic point of view; it omits the traveling in Myrtha's traveling arabesques, has her declaim the same mime speech over and over, has Giselle enter before Albert is finished praying for her to do so and then fudges the steps she performs on entering, has Hilarion enter, chased by Wilis, before the stage is clear, and has the women push him so sedately up the line and off you'd never guess he was being thrown to the crocs. Franklin also poses his Wilis with their hands fanned out behind their backs, as if indicating the waist wings their costumes don't have. The

gesture is a throwback to ancient productions in which the
Wilis were flown on wires. (They're called Wilis in the program, by the way; the term derives from a Slavic word for
"vampire" and is probably too indelibly associated with the
ballet to change. Myrtha's two lieutenants are called Miseries.)

The two casts of principals are thoughtfully balanced.
Virginia Johnson, delicate and dutiful, is paired with the
forceful Eddie J. Shellman; Stephanie Dabney's fervor is
modulated by Donald Williams's reserve. All of them dance
better than they mime, perhaps because the direction makes
so little of its chances dramatically. But Cassandra Phifer is
one of the best Berthes I've ever seen; she mimes colloqui-
ally. Lowell Smith and Keith Saunders both do a dignified,
manly Hilarion. Theara Ward is Bathilde, in a top hat
wound with a veil, a wing collar, and a riding habit with a
full white skirt; she looks ravishing but acts unassertively.
(Michel, who also composed biographical sketches of the
ballet's characters, may have put her off with his suggestion,
unnecessary to the action, that Bathilde is capricious and
hard to figure.) Ward is one of the company's big, handsome women. Her counterpart in Act II is Lorraine Graves,
who plunges bare-legged through the role of Myrtha and
fills the stage with untrammeled power. Graves is so beautiful in arabesque it's a shame to deprive her of those voyagées. She heads a corps whose collective performance is the
triumph of the production—huge in scale, avid in attack yet
plangent in rhythm. Dabney's Giselle reflects the corps' vo-
racity, and she has some marvelous impulsive moments.
Bolting from the wings into the supported temps levés en
arabesque, she actually brings off the illusion of displacing
her partner's faltering strength.

Agon, the Balanchine ballet, was danced as a curtain-raiser, and I'm sorry to say that it's no longer the shining, taut *Agon* we used to see this company do. Taut has become stiff; formerly elastic phrases have hardened, fractured, and been rejoined in odd places. The mock-ceremonious manners of the piece are exaggerated. Ward and Shellman are physically magnificent and technically able in the pas de deux, but their timing is gauche and the moves are all out of shape. Ward has a quality of excess that's exciting. It's not the dry stylistic exaggeration we see in other dancers—it's sheer anatomical abundance flowing in all directions, not all of which are appropriate to Balanchine's choreography. A good coach could edit the flow, but for the moment I'm almost glad to see it bursting out; it distorts Balanchine, but not as much as it defeats the rigid controls on expression now being imposed on the dancers in this and other classical ballets. The imposition is carried out, I am sure, in the name of discipline, and I don't know what to make of it. It's both benevolent and hurtful. It energizes a wonderful Wili corps in *Giselle* but tightens the life out of *Agon*. Dancers seem caught in a vise—encouraged to dance on a generous scale but also with a prissy correctness. Attending DTH these days can be a bewildering experience. It's exuberant—flamboyant, even—one night, dauntingly respectable the next. Respectability is no substitute for elegance. This talented company is being made to mind its manners too much of the time.

—October 22, 1984

Strangers in the Night

Persons to whom "Dancing in the Dark" is a ballad by Arthur Schwartz and Howard Dietz and not Bruce Springsteen will be pleased to hear of a new dance company called American Ballroom Theater, which just made its theatrical début at Dance Theater Workshop. The four couples who make up the company are all of Springsteen's generation, and they perform the old dances with an ease and a zest and an accuracy that bring them alive again. The sensibility of American Ballroom Theater is what might be called neoclassical eclectic. The traditional step patterns of the fox-trot, the lindy, the rumba, and so on are revived and invested with a new vitality based squarely on the energy and the imagination of the dancers who perform them. We see *real* dancing—not dancing that's been depersonalized and embalmed by overconscientious reconstruction. I hate to watch young people reverently revisiting the past or trying so hard to score points in dance competitions that they overscale the steps and flatten the dynamics. American Ballroom Theater gives the dancers room to entertain themselves. And it entrusts them with the key to the life of these dances: differentiation. The dancers as they move keep differentiating particles of rhythm, of pace; they keep the shape of a step moving and changing and catching new lights; they make you see that the fun of discriminating among fine details is the whole fun of dancing.

In American Ballroom Theater many historic strains are joined and evoked by implication: the Savoy, Roseland, the Harvest Moon Ball, the Latin hot spot, the dinner club with the specialty act whirling in a spotlight, the intimate revue with the wisecracks, and the big jazzy stage show with squads of exhibition dancers trucking in front of the band. For such a panoramic sweep to succeed, there has to be a measure of specialization among the dancers, and there is. Pierre Dulaine and Yvonne Marceau, who are the company's artistic directors, are an exceptionally elegant acrobatic-adagio team, whose lifts (and descents) are prodigious without being arduous. Gary and Lori Pierce are the more lyrical, John and Cathi Nyemchek the more bravura of two exhibition-dance pairs. (The Nyemcheks, shorter and more chunkily built than their colleagues, are glittering stylists; they brought down the house with their quickstep to "Anything Goes," and they reprised the head-to-head circuit of turns in "The Carioca" with a manège of barrel turns wrapped in each other's arms.) Then, there are Wilson Barrera and Margaret Burns—handsome, unstereotyped Latin dancers. But all the dancers are handsome; and all of them do the complete repertory—that's what makes them a company. That, and the choreography of John Roudis.

Ballroom dancing is a salon art, hard to expand in theatrical space. These days, we see it mostly in movies or on ice; the medium does the job of expansion without destroying the intimacy of the style. Roudis began his dancing career in vaudeville in the twenties, and his staging has the nimbleness and musical fluency of a golden era. In the American Ballroom Theater performance I was interested to see how the elasticity of the dancing kept adjusting space-time ratios, and how the staging followed through on that, shifting the focus from one couple or one dance to another, separating and reuniting couples, splintering numbers into segments, and in general applying whatever theatrical tactics seemed natural and useful to the form. The result was a show that opened up on its own terms. The stage at Dance Theater Workshop was actually too small for it.

A more serious impediment was the musical sound track, which consisted mostly of pop records. The records were fine, but they kept forcing the transitions between numbers into awkward holding patterns. This is a problem for the new company to iron out. I can't see that it has much else to worry about. It is personable and talented. It has a unique identity and (if the reception at DTW was any indication) a waiting audience. It encourages individuality in the dancers, yet is firmly centered in exhibition ballroom dancing. The few times it ventured into additional material I thought it was wrong to. The swirling bullfighter capes in the "flamenco" section were especially distracting. And in what classy boîte of yesteryear would a male dancer have been permitted to play his partner's bottom like a bongo drum? Sometimes the dances were encased in the kind of fervent sentiment one doesn't see anymore outside of Dracula movies. There's no need of it. American Ballroom Theater is saying that classical social dancing is still good to see and do; one doesn't have to strike poses.

—November 19, 1984

Championship Form

Mark Morris didn't call his latest concert "The Modern Dance Till Now," though he well might have; the three numbers on the program took us from Bennington through Judson to Morris's own era in ninety minutes (with intermission). When it was over, it seemed as if Morris, in summing up his tradition, had placed himself in charge of it and could now take it wherever he liked. He's the clearest illustration we have, at the moment, of the principle of succession and how it works in dance: each new master assimilates the past in all its variety and becomes our guide to the future. The present is the only known tense in dance, so the spell cast by a Mark Morris is the illusion of a perspective—seeing the past and the future simultaneously contained within the present, seeing Then as Now, Now as Forever. And within this perspective there is the no less fascinating spectacle of Morris's own evolution. I felt that *Gloria*, the earliest work on the program, was not quite the whole Morris, yet it has things—a musical score, for one, most sensitively treated—that the latest piece doesn't have. And it is a kind of modern-dance compendium in itself.

The rhetorical style of *Gloria* is in the main a recapitulation of an early pietistic phase in modern dance which has actually persisted in the work of Alvin Ailey and some others. Set to Vivaldi's Gloria in D, the choreography is full of the sky-sweeping arms, canting torsos, and ecstatic, relevé-triggered spiraling "falls and recoveries" that were dear to the heart of old Bennington. But the piece is also a postmodern testament: there is the odd gesture, the convulsive accent, the mild strain of dissonance; one person shoves another, hands grip crotches, a whole bunch of people fall to the floor and crawl forward on their bellies.

If the "uplift" movement recalls at times the puritanical fervor of Doris Humphrey (at other times the unction of Ailey), it also hints at the radical simplicity and frankness of Paul Taylor. But the breezy impenitence of it all summons up the robotic era, just past, of motiveless motion and dissociative gesture typified by such choreographers as Laura Dean and Andy deGroat. These echoes appear not as a nice neat set of discrete evocations but as a scrambled-together cacophonous mass of material. Maybe to Morris the past is all one piece of goods, and it could be that what I see as a historic survey (the religiosity of the thirties generation superimposed on the ritualism of the seventies, or the other way around) is only his response as a choreographer to a certain kind of music. He danced for several seasons in the company of Hannah Kahn, who sets pleasantly anachronistic joy-of-dance movement to classical music. Like Morris's, Kahn's technique is highly kinetic, and she uses the same kind of wide stance, broad upper body, and round, full phrasing. Morris also danced with Dean, who was possibly a more potent influence. At all events, he hasn't turned out a pastiche. The fact that he has made a very successful new version of a modern-dance staple shows that an instinct for the new can coexist with a taste for the perennial. (This may seem a cliché, but count up the "new" choreographers and see how many there are to whom it actually applies.) Even if Morris was as conscious of his past in making *Gloria* as I was in watching it, I think his impulse must have been to make it as if no one had been there before him. I also suspect that, seen at an earlier stage of his development, *Gloria* (which is in fact a reworking of a 1981 piece) would have been the evening's high point—the event that revealed *the* Mark Morris. It wasn't this time, and not because the two newer pieces were without doubt the weirdest to be seen on any stage this season.

The second work on the program was a twenty-minute solo that he performed himself. Twenty minutes is a long time for a solo, but not for this tour de force. Morris has adapted to his own purposes classical Indian dance forms, which with their typically protracted time sense and repetitive structures have inspired a whole body of avant-garde music and dance in America; even as he danced, *Einstein on the Beach* was being rehearsed in another part of the building. Yet *seeing* Morris in the guise of an Indian classical dancer was something of a shock. He appeared in a loincloth, with his shoulder-length curls unbound and with his palms and the soles of his feet anointed with red paint. These trappings were assumed quite unaffectedly, and in twenty minutes Morris established two points of connection with the past. First, he is the link, missing until now, to the mid-seventies and the cult of Eastern music and dance which began flourishing then. Second, he transcends cultism and becomes, indeed, a kind of corrective to the cult. Instead of a score by Glass or Reich, Morris uses a tape of "O Rangasayee," a raga by Sri Tyagaraja sung by M. S. Subbulakshmi. She has a soft, supple, velvety voice, and Morris produced movements that were a mirror of her inflections, even of the texture of her sound. Some of his movements—the warrior stances, the one-legged Shiva-like poses en face with cocked knees and angled arms—were traditional; others appeared to be freely invented, though close enough to the tradition to seem part of it. (If there were an indigenous modern dance in Southern India today, it might look like this.)

In what he attempts here, Morris evokes another tradition—that of Ted Shawn and his dances of the Orient. Shawn, however, Westernized his models; one can't imagine him performing a twenty-minute raga or, if he ever did, observing its structural pattern. In one section of *O Rangasayee*, Morris does about fifteen repeats of a passage on the diagonal, which he varies occasionally with lateral sorties at the rear of the stage. Every time Morris repeated the diagonal sequence it was different. He followed a basic pattern: holding himself in profile, he would back upstage in small, delicate emboîtés, then abruptly about-face and walk the rest of the way squarely erect, waggling his head. Whirling and continuing to whirl, he would come back downstage in a wide-striding crouch. The sequence was a loop, and as one watched it one saw shortened and lengthened phrases, phrases thickened and attenuated, accents shifted, attack altered. But one saw these things with one's second sight; primarily, the experience of the passage was a purely rhythmic pleasure with incidental pleasures along the way. The head-waggling became ever more mysterious, the emboîtés ever more delicious (Morris would vary the depth of his plié and the drumming of his feet as they traveled upstage). The catch step that resumed the emboîtés became, like the metal clasp on a necklace, a small event in itself, unwearyingly familiar, to offset new sparkles in a constantly changing configuration.

In his bearing, Morris has a relaxed and powerful physicality. He's voluptuous but not narcissistic. He gives the impression of dancing for his own pleasure, but without vanity. Not a small man, he's not all soft edges, either. Previous solos of his that I've seen have played on his androgynous quality, but *O Rangasayee* went beyond them all in its reconciliation of masculine and feminine aspects in his dancing. It excelled, too, in its labyrinthine rhythm and its dynamic use of antithetical energies (stasis-kinesis, abandon-control). Reconciliation of opposites was, in fact, the solo's poetic theme. East and West, tradition and the avant-garde as well as sexual ambiguities were brought to new harmonious resolutions, and it was done through the manipulation of abstract dance forces. In the solos in last year's New York concerts, Morris had shown himself to be a remarkable personality, with a sense of form and a flair for self-presentation. Afterward you wondered, Who is this guy? After *O Rangasayee*, I still wonder at Mark Morris's mystery. But that he is one of the world's marvelous dancers I have no doubt.

Somewhere in his being, Morris is a philosophy major. Last year, he gave us a piece on the death of Socrates; this year, it's *Championship Wrestling After Roland Barthes*. The basic point Barthes makes in his amusingly pedantic essay "The World of Wrestling" is that wrestling is not a sport but a spectacle; it belongs to the theatre, and like the theatre, it deals in "the intelligible representation of moral situations." Morris doesn't present a morality play. Since, according to Barthes, wrestling already is that, Morris focuses on the details of the way wrestlers look and act; he uses wrestling as a dance spectacle. The result is very different from Johanna Boyce or Molissa Fenley attempting to present sports as dance, and it's different from the various sports ballets, in which sports can't really exist. There is no tennis in *Jeux*, no skating in *Les Patineurs*. But everything about wrestling exists in *Championship Wrestling* except that no one gets bruised. As a parody, the dance is practically one on one with its subject. Even point-scoring can be eliminated, because, if Barthes is right, what matters in wrestling is not the excellence of the contestants but their participation in a universal drama—"the great spectacle," as he puts it, "of Suffering, Defeat, and Justice." Wrestling (like dancing) has no hidden code of meaning; what you see is all there is to it. On with the show.

Morris designed the piece for five men and five women, and he has men fighting women as well as women fighting women and men fighting men. He doesn't try to make any of it beautiful; it's all as indefensibly stupid as it is in the arena, only—because of witty staging and impeccable comic timing   a thousand times funnier. The clinches, the body blows, the crashes to the floor are as finely engineered as the mayhem in vintage Tom and Jerry cartoons. In the most outlandish sequence, two antagonists supported by two teams are maneuvered against each other in slow motion. On contact, each delivers a blow—in slow motion. One punches the other's head precisely ten times, is punched back, and by dozens of grappling hands is turned head over heels slowly and excruciatingly, over and over and on and on. Herschel Garfein, the composer, has provided a half-documentary, half-cartoon score, filled with crowd noises and electronic whammies. The dancers, men and women alike, take their macho poses and hunker around with brute authority; they manage to look svelte and squat at the same time. As the lights go down, they are lying all over the stage, slapping the floor with their hands in order, as Barthes says, "to make evident to all the intolerable nature of [their] situation."

—*December 17, 1984*

An American in Paris

—

George Balanchine's ballet to Gounod's first symphony, unperformed for twenty years, has been recovered in a lustrous New York City Ballet revival. Why it was discarded has never been clear; Lincoln Kirstein, in his book on New York City Ballet, lists it among "losses regretted by those who prize delicacy of texture or quiet sweetness of expression." Perhaps the ballet was too quiet for audiences who heard resemblances in the music to Bizet's Symphony in C and expected a ballet as brilliant and exciting as the one Balanchine had staged to that score. Maybe now we can begin to appreciate the qualities that Kirstein mentions and to assign the ballet a place in history.

Gounod Symphony, which had its première on January 8, 1958, is the forerunner of *Emeralds* and *Le Tombeau de Couperin*. In the chronology of Balanchine works, its nearest antecedent is *Scotch Symphony*, especially the last movement, with its steadily unfolding choral symmetry. The great stage and the spectacular corps de ballet of the Paris Opéra were the direct inspiration of all these works. Balanchine himself acknowledged the influence on *Gounod* of a Paris Opéra classic, *Soir de Fête*, choreographed in 1925 by Léo Staats to excerpts from Delibes's *La Source*. Balanchine could have seen it in the twenties and again in 1947, when he was a guest choreographer at the Opéra for six months. It was then that he produced, as *Le Palais de Cristal*, his ballet to the Bizet symphony. The inception of New York City Ballet the following year called forth the American production, retitled *Symphony in C*, and after that Balanchine kept a Paris Opéra wing in repertory, consisting of his own impressions of Opéra style. These he usually set as full-scale pieces to French music, but not always. *Scotch Symphony* is by Mendelssohn; so is *A Midsummer Night's Dream*. *Chaconne* is the Paris Opéra of Gluck's day. *La Source* is a small-scale divertissement to Delibes's music, as is *Ballo della Regina* to the music of Verdi. The quality that all these Opéra pastiches hold in common is femininity; sooner or later, the stage is flooded with women. *Walpurgisnacht Ballet*, the only other Gounod piece in the company's repertory, says it all, both in its pulchritudinous finale and in the dances that come before, which barely permit the passage of the single male in the cast. In *Gounod Symphony*, Balanchine uses a corps of twenty women and ten men. The ballerina has a cavalier who partners but seldom dances.

Gounod Symphony is a companion piece to *Symphony in C*, deliberately chosen as such. Besides the creative challenge of distinguishing between two closely related pieces of music, besides the undoubted pleasure of having a sumptuous new exhibit to add to the Opéra wing, the making of *Gounod* served Balanchine with a polemical purpose in his ongoing struggle for acceptance. Reviewing the première of *Symphony in C* for the *Times*, John Martin had written, "Mr. Balanchine has once again given us that ballet of his, this time for some inscrutable reason to the Bizet symphony."

The charge that all his ballets were alike was the biggest weapon in the arsenal of Balanchine's critics. There weren't many people around who were prepared to concede that the ballets looked alike only because, as Martin later came to admit, they were so unlike anybody else's. By creating a completely different work—different in expression, different in rhythm and contour, in style and spirit—to music that matched the Bizet score in its basic strategy and formal progressions, and even in some of its features (the fugue in the second movement, the droning bass in the third), Balanchine was hoping to respond to his critics, refuting the charge that he had no choice but to repeat himself. He was making a little musical lesson out of his twin Bizet-Gounod ballets—a lesson that began in the perception that, though they dealt with similar material, the two symphonies were differently conceived, by two different musical intelligences. (Bizet had, in fact, closely studied Gounod's symphony before, at the age of seventeen, writing his own; being Bizet, he had achieved fresh and distinctive results.)

I think Balanchine was also saying that no true musical intelligence repeats itself without meaning to. Not even Sousa, whom he regarded as America's Offenbach, ever composed two marches exactly alike. To bolster his point, Balanchine produced *Stars and Stripes* that same season and included an extended quotation from the opening of *Pas de Dix*, a Glazunov suite he had recently made to selections from *Raymonda*. In that ballet and in "Stars and Stripes Forever," he had the dancers enter with the identical steps. One can almost hear him murmuring to himself as he set this up, "See, I'll repeat myself on purpose and no one will notice." And no one did. He proved that the same steps set to different music are different in effect, just as in *Gounod* he proved that he was not compelled to treat same-sounding music in the same way.

The closer one looks at *Gounod Symphony* and its auspices, the more it appears to be part of a campaign. Balanchine was interested in making his style in ballet the American style. To do this, he would have to persuade the public that an authentic American dance tradition existed on which he—and he alone—could build. He had for years fought the inclination of Americans to regard ballet as ever and exclusively Russian. (Kirstein complained that "balletrusse" was one word.) He seems to have projected the winter of 1957–58 as his make-or-break season. Along with *Gounod Symphony*, he presented *Square Dance*, *Agon*, *Stars and Stripes*, and a major revival of *Apollo*. The new ballets weren't designed with the sole intention of displaying Balanchine's versatility. Their apparent differences were transcended by the common aim of clarifying and forwarding American classicism. Yes, it was a campaign; Balanchine even used the word to designate the separate sections of *Stars and Stripes*. And, to a great extent, this campaign of his succeeded. The links between the two Stravinsky ballets, *Apollo* and *Agon*, were noted at the time. Those between *Square Dance* and *Stars and Stripes* were strengthened by Balanchine's use in the former ballet of a caller to holler out square-dance combinations while the dancers executed classical steps and figures that were actually derived from seventeenth-century dance forms—a cultivated version, in other words, of the steps and figures of traditional American country dancing. In a subsequent revival, the caller was deleted, and *Square Dance*, set to string music by Corelli and Vivaldi, emerged more specifically linked to the old court dances that had inspired both *Apollo* and *Agon*. Balanchine's message to his 1957–58 public was succinct. *Apollo* predicted the classical style that he would develop in America and consolidate in *Agon*, *Square Dance* demonstrated the Americanism of classicism, and *Stars and Stripes* outrageously celebrated it.

Where did *Gounod Symphony* fit in all this? The conclusion then and for years to come was that it didn't fit and wasn't meant to. The historic season of 1957–58 is on record as one in which Balanchine, exercising his powers to the greatest capacity ever seen, abundantly and irrefutably made the case for American ballet and for himself as its master, and still found time to write a love letter to the Paris Opéra. But why should Balanchine have chosen to do so much at once? If he had wanted to, he could surely have put off work on the outré Gounod ballet to the next season, when the piece might have won more of the critical attention it deserved. True, he held a commission from Paris. But *Symphonie*, as the piece is called there, wasn't staged by the Paris Opéra Ballet until March 4, 1959. The ballet was done a year in advance because, as I see it, Balanchine *wanted* it included in the American season. His creative juices were stimulated by the other works he was doing and the connections among them, which extended to *Gounod*. Moreover, as soon as the season ended, the company would leave on a five-month Asian tour, and Balanchine would not be going along. Even if he were to go, his time would be taken up with official functions and the exigencies of the tour; he would not be able to rehearse a new ballet. Those creative juices were already flowing in the direction of a spectacular tribute to the French classical tradition, and he simply couldn't wait.

The relevance of *Gounod* is easier to see now than it was then. Its splashiness and prettiness (which relate it superficially to *Stars and Stripes*) may have concealed the formal integrity of a scheme based firmly on the music. Gounod planned all four movements around dance forms that he drew from the same Baroque sources that underpin the music of *Apollo*, *Agon*, and *Square Dance*. The first movement

of the symphony is a gavotte, the second a bransle, the third
a minuet, and the fourth a rigaudon that opens with a pavane. Balanchine's choreography is a free fantasy on those
models; he doesn't evoke court dances, as in *Agon* and
Square Dance; his subject is the Paris Opéra as an institution
with the Baroque as its heritage. He envisioned a stage fully
dressed and filled with women and their consorts, all repos-
ing in clusters as symmetrical as the flower beds in the Lux-
embourg Gardens, then launching themselves in profuse
demonstrations of *la danse d'école*. Every man in the corps
has two women to support. What that leads to—two lines
of women, each holding a balance as a line of men crosses
between them; repeated instances of this, with variations,
until finally the lines link together and dissolve in a maze—
must be seen to be believed. Kirstein has likened the ballet's
imagery to the ornamental gardens of Versailles. Then,
there are the quasi-military formations—diagonals, wheels,
and so on—that are the mainstay of spectacle in any large
megalopolitan opera house. At one point, the lines form up
so as to suggest the radial spokes of the avenues leading
from the Arc de Triomphe. (Balanchine didn't have quite
enough dancers, but you get the idea.) Throughout the ballet, there is a witty tension between grandiosity of scale and
daintiness of detail, between frivolity and *gravitas*. Like
America, France has a lively vernacular dance tradition;
when the gavotte of the opening movement changes into a
galop, the dancers burst into the emboîté hops associated
with the cancan. Balanchine, to whom coincidences mattered, would have been interested to know that Offenbach
opened his Bouffes-Parisiens in 1855, the year of Gounod's
symphony; *Orphée aux Enfers* was produced there three
years later. Probably he did know it, just as he knew that
Sousa (who was born in 1854) played in Offenbach's orches-

tra when the French composer toured the United States. The second number of *Stars and Stripes* is "French"—the girls do an entire cancan routine in the coda. So Sousa and Gounod are made to exchange a salute to Offenbach, because of whom, Balanchine once said, "Americans walk fast." The American march was driven by French tempos.

Ballets created in the same moment bear a watermark that time makes plain. All through *Gounod* are traces of things done in *Square Dance* or *Stars and Stripes*. We recognize in the blocky evolutions of the corps and in the lavish use of canon a phase in Balanchine's work which was soon to close. The long pas de deux of the second movement is notably short of wind; the adagio phrases that Balanchine would demand of his ballerinas in the sixties—phrases unthinkably fine and invisibly linked—are starting to blossom in *Gounod*, not in the pas de deux but in the pavane danced by the corps. The only quotation from *Symphony in C* I have been able to spot occurs in that pas de deux, in the sequence of slow finger turns in piquée attitude lengthening into piquée arabesque. On each arabesque, the ballerina pauses in profile, just as she does in the Bizet adagio, but without bending her supporting knee. Other mementos of the Bizet ballet are written into the role of the corps and are all but buried beneath the myriad elaborations to which Balanchine submits them. The stately entrance of the ballerina in the Bizet second movement is here done en masse; the Bizet's "country reel" is expanded into the swarming maze of the Gounod's marvelous allegro vivace finale.

The original première of *Gounod Symphony* marked the tenth anniversary of *Symphony in C* (another reason Balanchine may have been eager to get it on early). Martin, by then a supporter, was a *Gounod* enthusiast. Edwin Denby, to whom the revival is dedicated, wrote of the "autumnal richness of *Gounod Symphony*, hovering over a stately score, its steady four-bar phrases punctuated in thirty thousand ways, all correct." This hints at a regularity in the music which Balanchine had to find ways of overcoming. Other critics, less admiring, found the piece overambitious, both too large for the City Center stage and too difficult for the dancers. The ballet was given during NYCB's first year at the State Theater, then it made way for *Brahms-Schoenberg Quartet*, which, though not its equal, covered the vast stage without being too hard for the corps to dance. Since then, the company has matured; it handles with authority the slow parades and promenades that Balanchine made for it a generation ago on faith.

Gounod always belonged to the corps. Originally, the third movement was danced entirely by groups. Balanchine, after a season or two, inserted two entrées for the principals, and these are the only parts of his choreography that have been lost. Peter Martins made new choreography that passes for authentic Balanchine. The rest of the ballet has been staged from a choreographic script of her own devising by Vida Brown Olinick, who in 1958 was Balanchine's ballet mistress, and who also staged the Paris première. (*Gounod* has long been defunct in Paris; *Le Palais de Cristal* was recently revived.) Besides Mrs. Olinick's script, the company had only a silent 16-millimeter film of the corps in rehearsal and the principals in performance. Maria Tallchief and Jacques d'Amboise danced the 1958 première. Tallchief's place was soon taken by Diana Adams (who was in the record film), then by Allegra Kent. Most of the company's ballerinas had their day in *Gounod*; Violette Verdy, now a teaching associate, is especially well remembered. All the current performances have been danced by Merrill Ashley with Sean Lavery. Ashley is at a peak of strength these days, and she has kept on expanding artistically. In the season's single performance of *Symphony in C*, given on opening night, she danced the adagio with fresh musical insight and fullness of phrase. But in the Gounod second movement she has problems finding the right punctuation for the four-bar phrases Denby spoke of—problems that have kept her, despite Lavery's excellent partnering, from bringing the long dance to a climax.

Karinska's costumes have been retained with subtle modifications. The Degas cut and coloring of the women's dresses, the old-gold brocade of the men's doublets are still exactly right (though the ballerina's tutu should be fuller). A new décor, by Robin Wagner, depicts an indoor arboretum with glass walls and a vaulting glass roof. The Crystal Palace that was Balanchine's original metaphor for the Paris Opéra was among other things a hothouse for the nurturing of delicate plants. In *Gounod Symphony*, he was showing the American public how classical ballet flourishes in an institutional setting. In its initial season, it was at once the most old-fashioned and the most forward-looking of the four new ballets. It was the ballet that tied together past and future and said, "See what happened in Paris? It can happen here."

—February 25, 1985

Double Vision

"He has a boyish delight and trust in Things: there is always on his lips the familiar, pragmatic, American 'These are the facts'—for he is the most pragmatic of writers and so American that the adjective itself seems inadequate; one exclaims in despair and delight: He is the America of poets." So might Randall Jarrell, writing on William Carlos Williams, have described the man who is the most pragmatic of choreographers. Merce Cunningham's respect for the facts has colored his modernist sensibility with the convictions of a classicist. (And has helped make America the commodious haven for classical dancers that it is now.) He has no use for hidden meanings: "For me, it seems enough that dancing is a spiritual exercise in physical form, and that what is seen is what it is." The first thing one sees in *Doubles* is Catherine Kerr or Patricia Lent (the piece, designed for seven dancers, has two almost completely different casts) standing alone in the middle of the stage performing the kind of scrupulous, slow-motion développés and sustained balances that one might see in class. This is discipline as observable phenomena and as ritual—the dancer's daily ordinance. The slowness of the movement carries the eye from one incident to another: the mobilization of the thigh in développé, the tiny shift of weight that recenters control in equilibrium. This quality of clean-limbed power and clear detail is characteristic of the entire piece. We sense the pleasure of things accomplished for pure discipline's sake, and we sense, too, the existence of forms and objects moving beneath the surface of routine. I don't mean that the shapes and poses are evocations, though the boys in their rearing and bucking leaps, the girl who lies down and turns up her face like a sunbather—these say what they say. It's a more tenuous connection in moods and in the timing of events and their displacement by other events that makes us believe in *Doubles* both as a formal progression and as a picture of reality. Twice the stage empties completely; mysteriously, the drift of things continues. Cunningham manages it all without languor, without irony, without even those small touches of the irregular and the exotic that composed the "fugitive" atmosphere of *Summerspace*. Yet one thinks of *Doubles* in the same breath as *Summerspace*. It is perhaps an urban pastorale—Central Park rather than Arcadia. It is grittier, less ceremonious than *Summerspace*. But ceremony, "spiritual exercise," is the occupation of both pieces.

Though they often perform the same steps as the men, the women of Cunningham's company have a quaintly well-bred, collegiate look, while the men are untamed, impulsive, even feral. (This suggests that whereas the women try to do the movement objectively, the men look to Cunningham himself as a model.) The two interpretive styles are vivid in *Doubles*, where they seem to fit in with other sets of contrasts to make up a total dynamic configuration. The good thing about Cunningham, of course, is that he can deploy a pattern unpredictably. These sets of contrasts (stillness/motion, staccato/legato, alertness/indolence) aren't stuck together; they are variously combined. There can be passive and active stillnesses, for example. And Cunningham can use sectors of the stage dynamically. One thinks of the two women who make a gradual upstage cross and later make another cross downstage in the same disparate manner, each in her own way, pacing or swaying gently, while the action continues around them. The women are the only dancers in the piece who do not have a solo, a fact that seems organically related both to their crossings of the stage and to the individualized ways in which they cross it. The five solos are the heart of the piece. Each seems wonderfully shaped to the talents of the dancer you see doing it. (The double casting of the roles accounts for the title, which might with equal accuracy have been *Singles*.) Within the range of masculine or feminine style, each dancer finds his or her own quality of emphasis.

Ideally, a solo should be a process of self-realization for the dancer who does it. It is one of the hard truths of classicism that the more stress dancing lays on the "self," on personal vanities and habits of expression, the farther from self-realization it gets. This may be what Cunningham meant by "a spiritual exercise in physical form." He hasn't made it easy for his soloists, particularly the men. The three male solos, which are split into nonconsecutive segments, are constructed of viselike imperatives, and they're not so dissimilar in material as to bring out easy distinctions in the men's individual styles. No, the material makes these men brothers (just as the double casting makes them twins), and like real brothers, they have to fight for an identity. The result of this pressure is that each dancer has been brought to extend his range surprisingly. Chris Komar and Alan Good, normally opposites, are made to trade virtues: Komar becomes larger, less febrile; Good's lankiness acquires shape and tension. In the thrusting off-center leaps that are one of the choreography's motifs, Good really throws his body in two directions at once, and without buckling in the middle—he bends in the air like a sapling. Neil Greenberg has often seemed too eager, even violent; in the Komar role he is steady, composed, precise. If there is one principle of attack common to all these roles, it is élancé. It is a revelation to see Greenberg's blunt power in élancé next to Good's lyrically attenuated version next to the more naturally dartlike force of Komar or Robert Swinston or Rob Remley. And in another recurrent step—a low hop with one foot kicking up to the back—it is simply amazing to see the imprint of so many personal variations. Swinston and Remley (who are alternates) have unusually strong feet. They get to do a whole series of these low hops in place, and they charge the step with a pistonlike energy. Swinston gets an élancé shading into the hop, while Remley has the back kick of a mule.

As for the women, Kerr and Lent, in their perfect placement and firm command of their outspreading limbs in adagio, are both wonderful to behold. Helen Barrow's responsiveness in repose makes her, too, a pleasure to watch, and one got to watch her, along with Good (their alternates had both left the company), in every performance. *Doubles* isolates its dancers and lets us see them away from the flux of group presentation. Cunningham hasn't made a piece like it in a long time. That he can do so now with two casts is an indication of the company's current strength.

—April 1, 1985

The Fire This Time

The revival of *Firebird* by New York City Ballet brings back
a famous décor, by Marc Chagall, and a famous piece of
choreography—the role of the Firebird as set by George
Balanchine for Maria Tallchief. Chagall's designs, originally
executed in 1945, are among his most successful works for
the theatre. His enchanted forest has an iridescent glow that
matches the colors in the music, and there has never been
anything in this repertory—or in many another—to equal
the impact of the vibrant ruby reds in the throne room
when, to the spaced hymnlike chords of the finale, the curtain rushes up and reveals them. There are also two front-
cloths painted with themes and motifs from the ballet and
from Chagall's imaginary world; these have not lost their
fascination. Chagall's fantasyland and Balanchine's choreography were not created together, and there has always been
a degree of tension between them. Balanchine in 1949 took
over the décor from its owner, S. Hurok, and staged within
it a likable but disconcertingly whimsical and modest little
ballet. The staging expressed not a personal vision so much
as the lack of one; Balanchine appeared to be saying that

this wasn't, of course, *his* ballet—it was Fokine's and Stravinsky's, and now it was Chagall's, too. The only part of the show that seemed to interest him deeply was the ballerina role, but even the Firebird, even in 1949, was not a Balanchinean conception. Chagall's view of this mythological creature takes several forms; Balanchine ignored them all and presented Tallchief straight out as a virtuoso ballerina in a flame-red tutu. This was also the conception embodied in Diaghilev's revival of 1926, with the Gontcharova sets and costumes—the revival repudiated by Fokine. Fokine saw his creation (which had had overtones of the bayadère) reduced to a "ballerina stereotype." Balanchine, however, filled the stereotype with new content. The Firebird of the fifties danced steps that could never have been imagined in 1926. In Tallchief's depiction, the element of fire was conveyed by bravura—by qualities of force and speed in her technique, of intensity in her temperament.

In 1970, Balanchine redid the ballet as an extravaganza, with new choreography, enlarged sets, and costumes based by Karinska on Chagall's drawings. One of these, showing the Firebird in a short gold tunic with panniered wings jutting from her hips and, on her head, a little cockade trimmed with a spray of feathers, inspired the costume for Gelsey Kirkland. Her dances were filled with dainty beats and with jumps of all kinds, notably gargouillades. Balanchine was evidently searching for something different from the demonic strength he had found in Tallchief; he wanted an airy, impersonal, twinkling Firebird. I don't think he got it, but in any case the Kirkland version of the role was soon eliminated and a whole new set of characteristics was introduced. The dancer (Karin von Aroldingen) was now tall and statuesque. The costume was a long gown of mottled blue-and-white silk with big white wings sticking out of the shoulders and a train trailing behind. It was another Chagall inspiration, but it was not a dance costume, and comparatively static choreography was designed to accommodate it. When Kyra Nichols took the part, she was given an all-gold version of this confining outfit. "The Firebird," said Balanchine, "is *zhar*: incandescent, gold, like the sun." And that was his last word on the subject.

The music for Balanchine's ballet is the "ballet suite" arranged by Stravinsky, some seventeen minutes shorter than the original score. The current production includes the Firebird's waltz variation (she goes straight into it on entering, without first crossing and recrossing the stage, as in the Fokine version), her pas de deux with Prince Ivan, and her long solo in the Lullaby—all this in the Tallchief choreography of 1949—together with the Scherzo and Round Dance of the Maidens, the monster scene, and the finale, from the revival of 1970. What with Stravinsky's musical cuts, the ballet resembles more than ever the *Highlights from "Firebird"* that it always essentially was. The monster scene has choreography by Jerome Robbins in his best musical-comedy manner—lively, detailed, satirical. At its height, the Firebird appears, thrown upward from the center of a huddling group and holding high the sword with which the Prince will kill the enchanter Kastchei. As the music continues to build, she makes her exit in a circle of ever-higher split jetés. This passage was created for Kirkland; Tallchief's exit was a streaking line of déboulés. The original Balanchine version followed the original Fokine in making the Firebird the only character who dances on pointe. As a magical benevolent being, she opposes the magical evil being Kastchei, who at the sound of the climactic ostinato in the Infernal Dance rises onto his toes and scuttles sidewise in diabolical bourrées. In 1970, the Princess and the Maidens were also put on pointe. It makes a difference in the spirited Scherzo but none whatever in the grounded steps of the Round Dance. (Is this the reason, perhaps, that Balanchine's 1970 Round Dance is less inspired than his 1949 one? With no apparent motive, he appears to have changed it for change's sake.) The fact that the Princess now appears on pointe, however, strengthens her identification with the Firebird and suggests a duality similar to that depicted in the two-headed Bird-Bride creature who appears on Chagall's front-cloth. And the duality is borne out at the end of the ballet, when the cast takes its bows and the Prince is flanked by the Firebird, in her flame-red costume, and the Princess, in her garnet-and-ruby velvet gown. If you are lucky, you see Lourdes Lopez as the Firebird and Hélène Alexopoulos as the Princess—two handsome brunettes of Chagallian sensuousness. What it all means, though, should not be thought about too deeply, at least from Balanchine's standpoint. If the Firebird and the Princess are "sisters," surely it's because all the women in every Balanchine ballet are sisters. His work is innocent of psychology, and he was impatient with certain kinds of symbolism, as his experiments with the Firebird costume would indicate. Interviewed by Nancy Reynolds for the book *Repertory in Review*, he came down heavily on the idea of *Firebird* as a ballet: "Right from the beginning, it didn't work. You can never make it convincing that the ballerina really is fire—she's just a dancer in a red tutu."

The two characteristics that are immediately striking in Tallchief's role are its variety and its womanliness. The dynamic variety of the pas de deux—the push-pull oppositions of the bird's struggle with her captor, the taut and then the loosened, relaxed line of her poses as she coils about him—is derived from Fokine. But the rhythmic drama of these dynamics seems to me pure Balanchine: the way the tensions shift to the music, following it like light in a dark tunnel. A sharp turn, a convoluted one, a spasmodic one may be followed by a full recovery on balance; a delicate flutter is the preamble to a direct rush. Then, there is the wide-ranging vocabulary. The bird's strategy (for it is she who dominates the pas de deux) is devious, "Oriental"; step by step, she pits her strength and cunning against the man's. The step that does it best, for me, is the lunge on pointe braced by him from behind. This pose, with the legs in profile and the torso turned front, seems to *say* "strength and cunning." It's related to the wonderful moment that comes when the bird is completely lulled and bound over to the man—when, again standing on pointe and braced from behind, her arms intertwined with his, she slowly and deeply bends and straightens both knees together, moving her body in a languorous S-curve. (And isn't *that* related to the "Oriental" pas de deux in *Symphony in Three Movements*?) A couple of times, the bird flies at the Prince feet first through the air, like a deadly projectile. Another time, held by one hand, body arched and fully extended in a split, she is swung around and around in a huge circle. These acrobatic-adagio effects, souvenirs of the nightclubs that New York was then full of, are what Balanchine would have called "calculated vulgarity." The instant or two of flashiness that they supply are as immensely invigorating to the ballerina's classical demeanor as the rippling "Hindu" port de bras that Balanchine gives her at one point. If the Firebird is not made of fire, perhaps she is made of mercury. She is many beasts, shapes, and colors. She is bird but also cobra and jaguar. She is woman, not girl, and for this reason we may see the encounter with the young Prince as a sexual one, providing for him a rite of initiation, for her a lesson in tenderness.

In his subsequent revisions, Balanchine steered away from the "woman" aspect of the Firebird; he may have felt that he had closed that chapter with Tallchief. The Firebird was only the most spectacular of the roles that Balanchine made for her—roles that in many instances were reconceived versions of the canonical ballerina roles. Tallchief was also Balanchine's Odette, his Sugar Plum, his Sylphide, his Raymonda. She was "woman in ballet," and she became herself the ballerina archetype of her generation.

The Firebird's choreography is still difficult. The balance is often off center, with the upper body canted far forward or backward over the pointes. Step follows step without pause in a continual, scrolling Art Nouveau line. It doesn't look old-fashioned—not when one thinks that it is now nearly as old as Fokine's choreography was when it was made. Lopez, the ballerina who fits into it best, was given one performance, impressive in every way but somewhat too cautious. She needs to show more freedom of accent, more relish. Joseph Duell was a strong and serious Ivan. He understood the naïveté of the character and only once failed to project it—in the monster scene. The production was directed by Robbins; Violette Verdy, Rosemary Dunleavy, Francisco Moncion (Tallchief's Ivan), and Tallchief herself all had a hand in the reconstruction. The Firebird costume, beautifully cut, with a small tutu, was supervised by Dain Marcus.

—June 10, 1985

Tango

We have feet, two of them, although it is the fantasy of certain dance forms to pretend otherwise. Classical ballet keeps removing one foot from the ground or both together, as if to suggest that the classical dancer's element is other than earth. In tap-dancing, the body has multiple feet covering ground; in flamenco, its compressed bipedal force drills to the center of the earth. But the triumph of bipedalism is in social dances like the waltz and the tango. Here the illusion is of four feet pretending to be two. The waltz, with its three-beat phrase, makes a drama of balance. Weight is continually suspended, as if it could somehow be abolished, leaving us free to float. The tango, in two or four beats, offers no such incentive to keep moving. As an image of destiny, it is tragic rather than poignant, a dance in which we confront our mortality, luxuriate in it, but do not transcend it.

More than any other Latin dance, the tango exalts sensuality and sexual energy. But its eroticism—that cruel, insinuating grace made famous in thousands of theatrical portrayals—has been much exaggerated. The tango is a

magical, captivating dance, as capable of laughter and socia-
bility as it is of deep erotic emotion. Its variety was the subject of *Tango Argentino*, a show from Buenos Aires by way
of Paris that appeared at the City Center for one week at the
end of June and set off an uproar at the box office.

Strictly speaking, *Tango Argentino* was a concert, not a
show. Number followed number with nothing in between;
there were no frills or diversions. The only spectacle was the
tango, flowing like a river through endless permutations,
provocative and discreet, hot and cool, riotous and austere.
The dancers were all professional ballroom-style dancers,
and they worked most of the time in teams. Each team had
its own style and repertory, evolved from a common base.
Some of the basic steps were familiar; many were not. The
most unfamiliar, because censorable, aspect of the tango is
the use of legwork to involve partners below the waist. Men
and women alike do slow ronds de jambe that sweep along
the ground and invade the leg space of the partner, or rapid
ones that whip the air, pausing for an instant as the legs
hook together. Since it's the so-to-speak legless tango that
has been approved for worldwide popular consumption, it
was something of a revelation to see this leg language in
fully developed form—to see how articulate and graceful,
how sensual without being salacious it is.

Tango Argentino was unstintingly first-rate in every
department. Four *bandoneones*—Argentine accordions—
poured their hoarse, corrugated sound into some thirty
compositions, elegantly arranged against a background of
strings. The format for the dances was a historical survey
conducted without a shadow of pedantry. It began with
women in bustles and men in flat-brimmed hats and white
silk scarves meeting in a spotlight. All the costumes, from
the chemises and tuxedos of the twenties to modern-day

ballroom dress, were strikingly beautiful; the colors were black, white, gray, and silver. The designers, Claudio Segovia and Héctor Orezzoli, were also the producers of the show, which explains its exceptional unity of taste. For the twenties segment, the choreographer Juan Carlos Copes staged a tango drama about a girl from the slums who, seduced by a local bravo, ends in a brothel where tangoistas of every type, including a lesbian madam, await her. Amazingly, this vignette is played wholly for its dance values and gets away with it, reaching a kind of metallic perfection that stands apart from yet blends in with the rest of the show's style.

The tango is said to have originated in the working-class districts of Buenos Aires toward the end of the nineteenth century. Whatever it may be to the world, to Argentines it is a national art form, and it is a song as well as a dance. The singers in the show, uniformly spellbinding, were mature, substantial-looking individuals who sang inconsolably of shame and pain and despair and plain bad luck: "When you want to put the last bullet in your pistol into your head, it won't fire." The greatest of all tango singers, Carlos Gardel, has been dead for fifty years and is still a national symbol. His most famous line, uttered in a movie, is "My life is a bad script." A current idol (to judge by the audience's response), the venerable Roberto Goyeneche, came on late in the evening and sang three songs in a row. The last: "Life is an absurd wound." These bitter pills of tango philosophy are dispensed as nuggets of wisdom, and toward the end of Goyeneche's seminar I began to gag. The songs are the raw heart of the tango, and the dances are its heart's blood, racing through the body, hot with life.

—*July 22, 1985*

Hard Facts

Natalia Makarova retired from dancing the other day. To those for whom her glory years really began in 1970, when she defected from the Kirov Ballet, the career seems all too short. Yet fifteen years is a long time for a dancer to have been a star—especially a dancer who had already reached the age of thirty. Makarova's career in the West was a triumph against the odds. She never did accumulate the new personal repertory she must have hoped for, and no one's career better illustrates the fact that a ballerina without new choreography to amplify and specify her powers has no modern vocation to speak of. Though Makarova modernized her technique, her style was focused on the nineteenth-century classics, and it remained what it was when she left Russia. That she succeeded in imposing her style on American versions of those classics is a testament as much to her personal qualities as to the quality of her training. And when she applied her personal qualities to the modern repertory as she found it (at American Ballet Theatre and then at the Royal Ballet and other European companies), so strong was her impact that her influence and originality are unquestioned. But the inevitable decline of physical powers is easier for a dancer to face if she has a personal repertory. Then she can, from intimate acquaintance with her roles, readjust and even recompose their more troublesome features, and no one (or almost no one) will be the wiser. Makarova's last vehicles came from the hand of Roland Petit and were increasingly trivial—already adjusted downward, so to speak. And Makarova looked increasingly ineffective in them.

Dancers of Makarova's caliber don't usually fade away. They're out there performing for all they are worth, and then, the next season, they're gone. They know how to conceal the evidence of the chronic injuries that are wearing them out. But finally there is the kind of injury that skill alone cannot reach. A dancer who is injured beyond hope of recovery goes from day to day, dancing a little better or a little worse, all depending on the state of injury, on the role, and also, if the dancer is a ballerina, on the partner. Dancing takes on the aspect of a game of chance. (Makarova, after Petit's *Blue Angel* ballet, must have decided that on this level the game was not worth playing.) It is a precarious existence, and the pain is too frightful to think about, but it is less precarious the more one performs—at least, that is what I have always heard. Performing under extreme pressure of this kind, with adrenaline a temporary buffer against pain, actually enlarges the possibilities of performance. One can't know in advance, by rehearsing, what one will actually be able to do. How much technique have I got left? the dancer asks. Is the glass half empty or half full? Different performances and different ballets can give different answers, and some answers are encouraging. All this explains why certain dancers are still onstage at a time when even their most fervent admirers wish them off it. They may—these diehards—

be feeling a thrill in sheer performance that isn't coming through in their dancing.

Dancers used to have longer careers. Danilova, Markova, Ulanova, Fonteyn, Alonso danced into their fifties. Kolpakova, a contemporary of Makarova's who never left Russia, is still dancing at fifty-two. But the Western ballerina repertory has changed in the past twenty years. Today's dancers must meet steeply increased technical demands, and that takes a toll on longevity. Men may partner when they can no longer dance. Jacques d'Amboise's last role, created in 1980, was as Suzanne Farrell's partner in *Robert Schumann's "Davidsbündlertänze"*; he performed it till 1984, when he retired, having been a star for thirty years. But male endurance is measured by virtuoso standards, and—thanks to Villella, Nureyev, Martins, Baryshnikov, and their heirs—these standards, too, have climbed astronomically since the sixties.

Baryshnikov, at thirty-eight, is having to contend with the effects of a knee operation. If the press gave dancers the same coverage it gives athletes, the public would now be hearing as much about Baryshnikov's knees as it once heard about Joe Namath's. And there would be daily bulletins on Suzanne Farrell's hip joint, the condition of which colors her every move. But these matters aren't covered even in the dance press; they're either taken for granted or thought to be too personal. Balanchine did not like his dancers discussing their injuries with the press, and no management is going to start making pre-performance announcements of the infirmities among the cast (although this is commonly done for singers when they are suffering from colds). But Farrell and Baryshnikov are national treasures; dancing—to distinguish it for a moment from choreography—is the great theatre art we in America know today largely because of their contributions to it. So it is natural that what affects their performance should concern us and should lead us to consider the broad question of dancers' responsibility to their art.

I thought I detected a note of bitterness in some of the local press commentary on Baryshnikov when he had to withdraw from ABT's New York season last fall; it was nearly as if he'd injured himself on purpose to frustrate New York. Baryshnikov customarily gets a resentful press except when he's performing—either dancing or acting. The general feeling is that he has failed in the job of artistic director, and he is criticized for having inflicted policies on ABT that are against its grain ("There are no stars"), when in fact it is the times that are against ABT's grain. Baryshnikov has made mistakes; so has Peter Martins at New York City Ballet. But New York City Ballet has become something of a sanctuary since Balanchine's death; no bad news is ever spoken. The silence about Farrell's injury is falsely conceived homage to a great dancer. I think we see more of what she is doing when we know that she is doing it under great stress. And there is simply no way to speak about her current performances of her classic roles without referring to the disrepair that may in fact be the final consequence of the physical forces that enabled her to undertake those roles in the first place. How serious it all is only she can say, just as only she can know, with that second sight which many performers possess, how much of the problem is visible to the audience. What one can see is that Farrell has lost a certain amount of extension and rotation in her right hip; the superhigh battement is gone, the great arabesque no longer appears as regularly and as flowingly as it used to. But when you have subtracted these undeniably famous and precious attributes from Farrell's technique there is still a lot left over. Her timing, her flexibility, and her inspiration, which have always allowed her to expand beyond prediction the possibilities of performance at the moment of performance—these qualities are still there and are rising to support her now.

Lucky for us, because Farrell, even more than Baryshnikov, represents a line of creative thought. Watching New York City Ballet these days, you sense that the combination of her example and Balanchine's vision is very much on its mind. It is possible to see Farrell's example in the consistency and purity with which all the most talented of the company's ballerinas and younger soloists have been dancing since Balanchine's death. Merrill Ashley, Maria Calegari, and Kyra Nichols, among others, have actually gotten better, and while some of this improvement is attributable to Martins's direction, much of it is simply infectious suggestion. Several of Farrell's most personal roles have been passed around—*Chaconne*, *Walpurgisnacht Ballet*, and the Rondo alla Zingarese in *Brahms-Schoenberg Quartet*. Calegari even did *Mozartiana*, relieving Farrell a few seasons ago in Saratoga, and this season she took over the Farrell role in the *Davidsbündlertänze*, while Farrell went into the more domestic Karin von Aroldingen part, opposite the ravaged Schumann figure, danced by Adam Lüders. (Calegari's partner was a noncommittal Leonid Kozlov.) The colossal span of the Farrell arabesque was replaced by the V-shaped arabesque of Calegari—it was like seeing the Winged Victory where for years we had had the Arch of Triumph; but the singularity, vitality, and daring of the Farrell character (who represents Schumann's muse) were successfully captured in Calegari's dancing.

As Clara the wife, Farrell will take some getting used to. Right now, with her old performance fresh in memory—

fresher than anything she has been able to get out of her
new role—there seems to be a resemblance rather than a
contrast between Wife and Muse which forms the dramatic
fulcrum of the ballet. But this has its fascination, and there
is no question that Farrell understands her new part and
projects it faithfully. Nichols, new to the Rondo in *Brahms-
Schoenberg*, filled out the steps with a hardiness that put the
role over; she excelled in the sheer exuberance, scale, and
precision of her dancing, whereas Farrell, who did the part
herself this season, relied, more effectively than you would
think, on bravura presentation—the single element missing from Nichols's performance. Greater than individual
achievements, though, is the new cohesiveness of the principal women. Roles that were unique to Farrell have become
(with her consent and cooperation) a common birthright.
Everybody shares; there isn't only one "Farrell successor."
As a group, the ballerinas are closer than they have ever
been to achieving the unanimity of style which, along with
diversity of physique, was a primary Balanchine objective.

Farrell is not alone in what she is still able to show of the
accomplishments of a senior ballerina. Patricia McBride is
right there beside her. McBride was never the company fig-
urehead that Farrell was from the start, and she isn't responsible for so large and crucial a segment of the repertory,
although she, too, has the incomparable advantage of special roles that Balanchine either tailored or retailored for
her. She is physically and stylistically unorthodox—something that was less easy to see in the days when physical diversity among the ballerinas was more extreme than it is
now—and she has an unorthodox method of rendering her
old parts: she secretes herself in a "through" current of
energy and lets it (and a good partner) carry her. The
method—if that is what it is—works, but compared with

last year's *Liebeslieder Walzer*, the McBride of this year's *Brahms-Schoenberg Quartet* is noticeably more recessed. McBride is a few years younger than Makarova and a few years older than Farrell. Now that her technique is fraying, we see how deep her strength lies. It is the kind of strength that Balanchine relied on to shape the ballerina repertory. And as we watch McBride and Farrell maneuver inside their roles we see not only strength but the imagination that also played a part in the process. In *Brahms-Schoenberg*, which was made in 1966, both ballerinas are actually recapitulating and commenting on their roles in dance history.

But the most critical lesson to be learned from these two artists is the importance of performing. Darci Kistler, injured on the threshold of a major career, was off the stage for nearly two years. Now that she is back, she hardly ever performs, although she is scheduled frequently enough. And she is missed. It's my impression that her cancellations are the most deeply felt and hungrily discussed by the subscribers. To this large and loyal audience, Kistler's absences really matter. And the mystery that surrounds them—the company, of course, says nothing—has given rise to a lot of talk about permanent damage and a career destroyed. After twice dancing a role in *Divertimento No. 15* in the pre-*Nutcracker* season, she canceled both of her appearances in *Brahms-Schoenberg Quartet*, in which she was scheduled to dance the Andante with Jock Soto. Then she canceled *Nutcracker*. When she finally got on, in the next-to-last of the *Brahms-Schoenberg*s, she'd been off the stage for eight weeks—enough time for the clouds of suspicion to have regathered. On she came, dancing with a transparent ease and a plenitude of being that dispelled all doubt. Her dancing still has the unmistakable plushy texture of youth, and it is sophisticated dancing, too—dancing that summarizes and extends meanings, that clears a space for itself. And Kistler

has the wonderful extra gift of making her audience happy.
Why isn't she making us happy more often? Aren't the long
vamping-till-ready periods offstage bound to dissipate energy that should be used up in performance?

The trauma of injury in a young dancer can affect the direction of the career. In Kistler's case, it seems to have deep-
ened an already marked commitment to long and careful
preparation. She has been back a whole year and has yet to
find a satisfactory ratio of rehearsal to performance; eight
weeks in the studio to ten minutes on the stage simply isn't
professional dancing. The example of Farrell is just now
in extremis, but it shows that if a ballerina's first obligation
is to her art, then she must perform, because the art of
dancing is perfected, if not actually discovered, in performance. Then, there are such things as company morale
and audience gratification. The repertory needs Kistler, and
the audience needs reassuring that she's not just a guest
artist. I have the feeling that for Kistler a performance is a
precariously held-together illusion each separate second
of which must be predetermined and delivered in a set form.
Performance then becomes something to be endured, a
pleasant ordeal like holding your breath underwater. Yet
when Kistler dances she looks utterly spontaneous. Is this,
too, a dreamed-up effect? Gelsey Kirkland had the same
look of spontaneity, and she held to the same overfastidious
methods of preparation, and her career, the single most
promising one of the seventies, was over before the end of
the decade. I don't say that Kistler is Kirkland all over again;
I say that a provably bad method cannot be made good even
if every other factor in the equation is different. One would
prefer that, with the repertory she stands to inherit, Kistler
spent more time in the world where it was made.

—*February 3, 1986*

The Dreamer of the Dream

In *Tchaikovsky's Ballets* (Oxford) Roland John Wiley discusses all three of Tchaikovsky's ballet scores in detail, and describes first performances, covering both the original and the revised edition of *Swan Lake*. His scholarly equipment includes knowledge of the essential languages — Russian and Stepanov choreographic notation — and he isn't afraid to do primary research in the archives, just as if no one had been there before him. When Wiley tells us that certain facts are missing from the record, he isn't just passing on a supposition, he's looked for them. And on the ballets themselves Wiley's performance is first-rate. He knows how to illuminate musical procedures in a way that makes the ballets come alive as theatre. And his work has already had an effect on current theatre practice. Peter Wright, who produced the Sadler's Wells Royal Ballet *Sleeping Beauty* before Wiley's book was published, depended greatly on Wiley's researches both for *The Nutcracker*, presented by the sister company at Covent Garden, and for a new *Swan Lake*, to be presented in 1987.

It is tempting to read Wiley's chapters on *The Sleeping Beauty* as a corrective to the Wright production. Wright is not the first producer to impose interpretation on a ballet that needs none; nor is this the first time he has done so. When the Covent Garden Royals brought a new "Arthurian" *Beauty* here in 1970, I reviewed Mr. Wright as Mr. Wrong. I still think he's wrong, even though his current production, at the Brooklyn Academy, is cast in a more acceptable time frame (seventeenth to eighteenth century). And, having seen his Wiley-influenced *Nutcracker* on tape (a Thorn EMI/HBO videocassette is available here), I believe that Mr. Wright will go on being wrong about Tchaikovsky. The only thing that has changed since 1970 is the reason for attacking the unmusical Mr. Wright in the first place. Then he spoiled the perfect picture being created by the dancers. Now he's the whole picture—there's nothing else to see. The pellucid musical phrasing of the great ballerinas, from Fonteyn and Beriosova to Sibley and Seymour, has become blank routine. It's a sad spectacle, and I don't wish to dwell on it. (British dancing does bring one quality to *The Sleeping Beauty*—stylistic unity. But all this meant in Brooklyn was that everyone was bad in the same way.) What British custodianship of the Tchaikovsky classics amounts to is an insistence on nondance values— theories of interpretation and visual design and fancy renovation—and a willingness to spend money on them. And even these things it gets wrong.

Of the three ballets, *Swan Lake* is the most difficult to mount in four-act form, because Tchaikovsky's intentions are not always clear. It is *The Sleeping Beauty*, strangely enough, which is or should be the easiest. To understand why the most popular of the ballets is hard to produce and the greatest but least known (because prohibitively expensive) all but produces itself, we have to do some compare-and-contrast work in the Wiley manner.

The main difference between *Swan Lake* and *The Sleeping Beauty* is that in the earlier ballet Tchaikovsky is teaching himself to write ballet music and transforming ballet music at the same time. In the later one, he demonstrates an enlarged perception of what a ballet score can be: not only a serious dramatic structure but a self-enclosed, self-illuminating world, each of whose parts carries some charged relationship to the whole. Like *Swan Lake*, *The Sleeping Beauty* is based on a central image, but Tchaikovsky has by now found a way to fill the entire score with insights into and permutations of this image. Large sections of *Swan Lake* are enigmatic and diffuse; it is a noble, baffling, enrapturing work. If your knowledge of it was, like mine, acquired piecemeal, starting with the second act and then moving on to this and that portion of the other three acts, you probably found yourself thinking time and again, So this, too, is *Swan Lake*! The extended terrain is fascinating. But further excerpts from *The Sleeping Beauty* only give you more *Sleeping Beauty*. Listening to the score in sequence, you go deeper into its mysteries, and you also experience the pull of its momentum; the wonder of how such a thing can exist at this depth may be the greatest mystery of all. In *Swan Lake*, the central image (Odette and her eternal separation from her mortal love) does not permeate the ballet; it is isolated within the ballet, and it is mobilized in the continuity between Acts II and IV. But *The Sleeping Beauty* is all forward movement, all imperceptible change. Drop the needle at any point in a recording and you know exactly where you are. The light that shines on Aurora's birthday is not the same as the light on her wedding.

The construction of the ballet is appropriate to a story the major—the *only*—events of which (the casting of the spell, the lifting of the spell) are separated by a span of a hundred years. As Wiley notes, the story is essentially static; the outcome is never in doubt. By analyzing aspects of the score, particularly its harmonic structure, Wiley shows how Tchaikovsky imbued the story with theatrical elements (activity, expansion, suspense) while retaining the static purity of the central image. *The Sleeping Beauty* is true music drama, and every note of it can be staged. Wiley doesn't actually declare *Swan Lake* unstageable, but he refutes arguments that the music is continually responsive to the libretto (without, however, saying what it *is* responsive to). He persuades us that it is "a score of carefully chosen tonalities," yet in the end the purpose of these tonalities is elusive. Tchaikovsky may have wanted to secure a harmonic unity against the whims of ballerinas and ballet masters, but "the coherence provided in the score by tonality is not so much recondite as subliminal." Producers of *Swan Lake* have to do quite a bit of mind reading. And they do, they do.

The method of deducing meaning from an analysis of tonalities, which Wiley employs throughout the book, can lead to confusion as well as revelation. Wright's notion that Carabosse (the evil fairy in *The Sleeping Beauty*) should enjoy equal status with the Lilac Fairy (the heroine's godmother and the giver of all good) probably has its origin in the fact that Tchaikovsky identifies Carabosse with the key of E minor and Lilac with E major. They are sisters but not, Wiley cautions, look-alikes—not Odette and Odile. In Wright's version, the destiny of Aurora is the subject of a protracted struggle between two equal forces, Good and Evil. In the orchestra, though, there is no struggle; Aurora's destiny is resolved in the Prologue the moment the Lilac Fairy countermands Carabosse's prophecy. Wright has Carabosse hanging around during the second act, determined to have a showdown. She doesn't give up until the kiss of awakening is actually bestowed. It is all Manichaean farce, played to music that denies that any such dualism could possibly exist.

The idea that Carabosse holds power equal to that of the Lilac Fairy is carried out with a kind of nutty logic in Act I, when the presenter of the lethal spindle turns out to be not Carabosse in disguise but a genuinely innocent little old lady who is dragged off to the executioner's block. (Carabosse actually can control Aurora's fate, you see, so she needn't turn up as she used to in the first act, poking a spindle out of a long black cloak. But if the malefactor is not to be Carabosse, then why is it an old party in a black cloak?) The designer, Philip Prowse, makes Carabosse and Lilac all but identical figures, one in black and one in white or silver-gray. The casting of Carabosse with a woman instead of with a man *en travesti* I find less offensive than the idea of a Lilac Fairy without lilacs; she wears neither the flower nor the color.

Carabosse is indeed a principal character, but if Tchaikovsky had meant the two fairies to continue their duel in Act II, he would have retained their key associations from the Prologue. His meaning is exactly what Wiley says it is: "Carabosse is no longer a threat at this point; E major is no longer necessary as an antidote to E minor." So the Panorama, so richly suggestive of the world of the Lilac Fairy, unfolds in G major ("the key of resolution"), and the action eventually works itself around to a triumphant conclusion in E-flat major, the principal key, significantly, of Act II. Carabosse's limited function is clear even apart from the tonalities. Wiley doesn't analyze scenarios with the diligence he applies to scores. If he did, he might not have written that "as a theatrical work the story of *Sleeping Beauty* is unusual" in that its outcome is revealed early by means of a prediction. The figure of Carabosse is patterned on Madge, the witch in *La Sylphide*. Denied a place in the hero's wedding celebrations, Madge not only predicts his ruin but actively brings it about—a little too actively in some productions. Not letting Carabosse help fate along deprives the story of what little tension it has. And it has just enough. The cosmogony of the ballet is such that Florestan's realm may be tilted temporarily from its axis, but it cannot remain off balance for a hundred years—the Lilac Fairy sees to that. The whole idea of balance lost and regained is expressed in miniature in the overture. What the staging should tell us is that the world of the Lilac Fairy, which we visit in the second act, is the spirit world and may not be threatened by another spirit, however evil she may be. The world that the Lilac Fairy guards, however, is mortal and vulnerable. Philosophically as well as musically, *The Sleeping Beauty* is an advance from *La Sylphide*; it represents a world held in balance by divine force. In that respect, it is an advance, too, from *Swan Lake*. The ballet it most resembles is *Giselle*, where a divine force is palpable whether the production centers it in the power of the cross or in the love that Giselle bears Albrecht from beyond the grave. Was it this connection, I wonder, which caused Balanchine to observe, in that charming but insufficient book of interviews called *Balanchine's Tchaikovsky*, that *The Sleeping Beauty* is "the best of the old ballets, second only to *Giselle*"? Certainly he can't have meant musically!

The superior stageability of *The Sleeping Beauty* is often attributed to the controlling vision of the ballet master Petipa, whose collaboration was not available to Tchaikovsky on *Swan Lake*. Wiley thinks Tchaikovsky often disregarded Petipa's instructions, which were none too specific to begin with. (Full texts are included in appendixes. However, Wiley also includes a statement by the first Aurora, Carlotta Brianza, testifying to the composer's behavior in rehearsals: "Tchaikovsky met the wishes of the ballet master halfway, shortening, supplementing, and changing the music according to the dances.") The value of Petipa's preliminary instructions may have lain in the mere fact that they existed; the composer only needed to be made aware of certain demands and constraints for his imagination to do its work.

Vzevolozhsky drew up the picture of a fantasy Versailles which served his collaborators as inspiration. For Florestan's realm, parallels were found in Baroque arts and manners. A musician of the dance could have imagined no greater Golden Age than that of Lully and Rameau. A choreographer needed no better incentive than the chance to invoke the spirits of Camargo and Sallé, Angiolini and Vestris. The result was a masterpiece of world theatre, a ballet that both celebrates the birth of the classical tradition as we know it and symbolizes its endurance. Aurora is the reigning symbol: the world's first ballerina, Dance itself, born on a May morning in France, put to sleep by the deadly ministrations of the Paris Opéra, awakening to a Russian spring. Petipa's choreography is also a succession of choice tonalities. But the true and irreplaceable author of the ballet, Wiley leaves no doubt, is Tchaikovsky. It is he who tells us why *The Sleeping Beauty* is a ballet and not an opera. *Swan Lake* might be unsatisfactory as an opera, but it is not unimaginable as one; it has its Wagnerian side, and some of its love music was originally composed for an opera that Tchaikovsky abandoned. But *The Sleeping Beauty* is Tchaikovsky's dream of ballet, its storied and privileged past, its perishability, its prismatic technique and human radiance.

In an article published in *Dance Research*, "On Meaning in *Nutcracker*," Wiley uses the Russian word *duma* to describe the vision of the Land of Sweets. *Duma* means something between daydream and meditation: it allows fantasy to penetrate reality; it dissolves rational distinctions between what is real and what the imagination feels is true. More than any other composer, Tchaikovsky understood ballet as a happening out of this world and time. Each of his ballets is an extended *duma*, is both irrational and sane, and is, however personal its auspices, immediately the possession of whoever hears it. There were other good dance composers before him and after. But Tchaikovsky discovered the consciousness of the medium. In his music, time is space, sound is shape, thought is deed. Listening, we see, we touch, until we hardly know whether it is the tympani we hear or the hammering of our own hearts.

—*February 24, 1986*

Spanish from Spain

Flamenco Puro, the new show at the Mark Hellinger, is just what the title says it is: an entire evening of undiluted flamenco, presented without embellishment or commentary. For the New York audience, whether Hispanic or non-Hispanic, it is an evening of attentive looking and listening. The cast consists of seven dancers (four female, three male), seven singers, and six guitarists, all of whom are Spanish from Spain and many of whom are also Gypsies from Andalusia. To say that their knowledge of flamenco lies deep in the blood is to state a premise implicit in the word *puro*. And these performers do not compromise their art; they shake the dust of Andalusia in our faces. The printed program includes a glossary of song and dance forms which is none too helpful, and the English translations of the song lyrics only intensify their mystery. No matter; the show's staging makes everything accessible. It begins with hand-claps and shouts (as in the opening of *The Three-Cornered Hat*), and the curtain rises with the whole company on-stage, presenting its principal members one by one in brief solo turns (bulerías). The lights then go down, and the evening's few formal elements are introduced: one singer in a spotlight, followed by one guitarist, followed by three guitarists and three singers. By the time the dancers step out of the shadows, wearing austere gray costumes, the stage has been prepared by ritual incantation for ritual gesture.

Flamenco is to Spanish dance what the blues are to American jazz. The blues are incantatory; as Whitney Balliett was saying here the other week, "You can almost chant them."* So it is with flamenco; *cante jondo*, or deep song, is nothing if not soul music. And the distinction Balliett went on to make between blues singing and ballad singing—"The emotions in blues singing are primary, and the emotions in ballad singing are kaleidoscopic"—holds true for the flamenco of the Gypsies and the more objectively developed salon style of Spanish dancing which is featured in other touring companies. The primary emotions of flamenco make it by nature a soloist's art, one that disdains the stylizations and accessories of a more sociably theatrical recitalist tradition. Pure flamenco dancing is done without castanets, without partners (in the sense of a pas de deux), and without formal choreography. It is autobiographical. The dancer is provoked to confession by the music; nothing comes between the dancer and his "song." (In *Flamenco Puro*, the proscription extends even to other dancers. Only once, in a number called "Tarantos," do we see two or more dancers moving together.)

What happens, of course, is that as the evening goes on this radical concentration of means gives rise to kaleidoscopic impressions. Personalities blossom or contract, backgrounds are filled in, the range of the rhetoric starts to widen, and gradually a vista opens on the whole flamenco

*"Two in One," by Whitney Balliett, *The New Yorker*, October 27, 1986.

tradition: it becomes a metaphor of human fate. At least, that is the possibility which the evening holds out to us. The rewards of flamenco are a gamble. Its passions are spontaneous and dramatic rather than artful and lyrical. It is not meant to be served up in predictable form night after night. I think the producers of *Flamenco Puro* must have had this unpredictability in mind when they designed the program. After a leisurely progression of solos, to which we give the intensest scrutiny, they close with another bulerías, just like the first. But now as the performers step out one by one, we see them in the perspective of their art—we see how their art has transformed them, or else failed to. We see flamenco as a volatile process and art as a catalyst.

The producers, Claudio Segovia and Héctor Orezzoli, are the team who presented *Tango Argentino* last year. Segovia and Orezzoli are a new breed of producer; they may even be unique. They aren't living in the golden age of the art forms they present, and their concern seems to be with preservation—with isolating the essence of the art form's vitality even as the tradition that supports it diminishes and dies. (Their next show, significantly enough, is about the American blues tradition.) The tango was a revelation to American audiences; to Argentines it is a cliché perpetuated by middle-aged addicts. No one pretends that the flamenco clubs of Seville are bursting with talent; as if to prove the point, *Flamenco Puro* contains no outstandingly gifted dancers—no firebrands who ignite the art form and in effect re-create it. But if none of the dancers in the show are noticeably young and daring, none are licentious, either. With great talent there often comes violent change; the danger is that the art form will be re-created in the image of one all-powerful personality. *Flamenco Puro* is flamenco stabilized as much as possible; it is a picture of the forces that preserve the art against predatory star performance on the one hand and touristy reductions on the other. And in its solid, equable way it is exciting.

Manuela Carrasco and Eduardo Serrano would probably be stars in a more theatrically exploitative setting. Here they are the dancers who draw us the furthest into an understanding of the natural elegance of the style. Carrasco is a large, handsome woman with magnificent carriage. Blessed with a strong presence, she employs the widest plastic contrasts and in her footwork makes the biggest sound I have ever heard from a woman flamenco dancer. Though Serrano isn't a small man, his sound is comparatively delicate, and its tonal variety is astonishing. In pure flamenco, men and women dance the same steps, but one is hardly ever aware of the fact, so diversified is the style. The men tend to excel in line, the women, lifting Picasso arms, in plastique. Angelita Vargas and José Cortes are dancers of the same order of accomplishment as Carrasco and Serrano but less even in delivery. One night, Vargas was finely tuned but mousy; another night she was sensationally vivid, while her husband, Cortes, who can crackle with good spirits, was merely precise. Many of the performers in *Flamenco Puro* are related, and most have sobriquets. Cortes is El Biencasao (well married). El Farruco is a vigorous older party, evidently legendary, who dances with a hat and cane. His two daughters, La Farruquita and La Faraona, seem to be the comediennes of the troupe—one sweet, the other salty. The first time I saw the show, all the women let their shawls down under their bottoms and ground away at the audience. The second time, only La Faraona chose to do this, but she was prodigious. (In recital flamenco, needless to say, this isn't done at all.) Moments later, we had the pearly soleares of Serrano (El Guito), which he dances against shadows of himself projected on the backdrop, and this was followed by Carrasco's version, in which, wearing a white gown and beautiful to behold, she seemed to burst the skin of the style and dance out of herself, becoming for a moment rawly, even awkwardly sensual.

Flamenco Puro is a women's show. As in *Tango Argentino*, the musicians are the heartbeat of the performance. All of them are male except the singers Adele Chaqueta and Fernanda de Utrera, and these two flamenco matriarchs all but steal the show. When Fernanda de Utrera sings her soleares, she improvises the lyrics, and you seem to hear each stanza as it pops into her head. She comes on at a point in the evening when our concentration is at its peak. Nothing distracts us from her song, and if as we listen we are struck by the way the sense of it meshes with its sound and with the stress and intricacy of the dancing we have just seen, it may very well be because the flamenco experience is designed in this show to be grasped as an entity. Flamenco does have a systemic consistency; it is one language articulated in sound and spectacle. Segovia and Orezzoli have perceived this, and they've used marvelous stagecraft to bring out the mutually reflecting facets of the form. The simplest things interact—the ruffle on a dress, the rippling of a guitar—and seem to give off meaning.

—November 17, 1986

Post-Modern Ballets

Twyla Tharp was the first to put an end to barefoot dancing, and now that she has a company of young dancers,
some of whom are classically trained, she could be the first
to acquire pointe technique and make something new of it.
Her earliest use of pointes, in *As Time Goes By*, had a primitive charm that reminded me, at the time, of Nijinska. First
danced by the Joffrey in 1973, this enchanting Haydn ballet
is now in the Tharp-company repertory, and it retains its
freshness. Tharp—or the ballet dancers she worked with—
managed to blend elastically resilient pointework with
Tharpian dynamics. The gravitational pull of the body as it
spun off center, the driving force of the legs were somehow
enhanced; pointe technique seemed on the verge of categorical redefinition. This was integral expression, not the to-
kenism we see now in the Glass ballet *In the Upper Room*,
where the legwork is done on little stilts and one feels no
connection between the poised foot and the plunging instep
or between the foot and the leg. And though Tharp's
dancers are now all completely turned out, one feels no control from their turnout. In classical dancers, the impulse that

ends in the pointed foot begins in the hip socket and radiates outward even when the step is turned in. I don't know why this is so; I only know that without clear motivation from the hip the foot on pointe looks like an Eleanor Powell novelty. It's a mysterious business, pointework, and I don't doubt that Twyla Tharp will soon master it.

There's distinct progress in *Ballare*. At first, the women seem to be doing nothing but bobbing and spinning in place or maneuvering from place to place. The movement looks constricted, not like that of ballet dancers or Tharp dancers, either. This goes on until the third section, where a synthesis occurs. Each girl has a solo that covers ground, and each looks natural and free. The piece ends happily, a real breakthrough. One is ready to forgive the crudity of *In the Upper Room*, where the pointes are only a means of advertising the newly constituted company and what it can do. (Just to make sure you get the message, the girls wear red socks and red toe shoes as part of their Norma Kamali costumes.)

Lincoln Kirstein's complaint about modern dance—that it is narcissistic and lacking in continuity—comes into your mind when you see a stageful of Twylas, and when you see them going up on pointe you may agree with his assertion to W. McNeil Lowry that modern dance has in fact disintegrated because "the so-called post-postmodernists are all embracing ballet."* Kirstein cited *Bach Partita*, created in 1983 by Tharp for American Ballet Theatre, as an example of the classical ballet's ability to absorb "bastard variations, mutations, conversions, perversions" and thus perpetuate itself, whereas modern dance cannot absorb ballet or perpetuate itself, because it is inherently anti-academic. In an article

The New Yorker, December 15, 1986.

called "The Curse of Isadora," published a few weeks before in the Sunday *Times*, Kirstein located the fatal flaw in the democratic cult of self-expression. The moribund academy of her time left Isadora Duncan no other option, he wrote, and though she exercised it gloriously ("In dry seasons she poured rich wine"), her legacy was doom: "She certified modern dance with its dwindling succession." Kirstein has been saying these things for years. Why, on the eve of his eightieth birthday, with the School of American Ballet faithfully nourished by private donations and government grants, does he still say them? Might it not be time for another essay, called "The Curse of Balanchine," in which it would be shown how the great choreographer created twentieth-century ballet and put it off-limits at the same time? He incorporated into the mainstream everything there was to incorporate—jazz, Bauhaus, twelve-tone music, American pop; yes, even the modern dance—and left the academy at a peak of virtuosity, with nothing further to express. Balanchine's progeny rework his accomplishments; they can honor his precedents, but they can add nothing to what he has said.

I gather that Kirstein thinks that reworking Balanchine is better than letting those whom he calls "dance dilettantes" get at his company. He seems to see academic training as a guarantee against anarchy and hazardous experimentation. New York City Ballet's latest première, Paul Mejia's *Sinfonia Mistica*, must therefore have been a bitter disappointment to him. Mejia, a graduate of the School of American Ballet, produced choreography that was not only hazardous but theatrically naïve to a degree that would have embarrassed an SAB workshop production. It didn't use "the lexicon"—it didn't know how. Luckily, the company also presented this season two new ballets by Peter Martins, who may be said to represent the academy at its most purely and zestfully proficient. I like best those ballets of his which extend the dancers' virtuosity, so I liked *Les Petits Riens*, to Mozart's music, better than *Ecstatic Orange*, a big, boomingly hollow work to a minimalist-Stravinskyan score by Michael Torke, executed in Martins's Broadway-show style. The average age of the four boys and four girls in *Les Petits Riens* matches that of the dancers who have recently joined Twyla Tharp. The fact that Martins was able to hold these young people to the virtuoso standard he himself embodied as a dancer without having them mimic his dancing proves Kirstein's point about self-expression. But was it so very long ago that New York City Ballet was going through its spasm of Suzanne Farrell imitations, not only under Balanchine's very eye but seemingly at his behest? Critics were heard then to complain that Farrell was outside the classical tradition; now, at the moment of her retirement, they celebrate her centrality to the classical tradition as Balanchine has developed it. And who is to say that what Farrell gave Balanchine was not "self-expression"? But for her meeting with Balanchine, might she not have been another Isadora?

Farrellism was the last of Balanchine's great acquisitions. Today, the process of incorporation begun by that acquisition goes on, but subliminally, like the jazz in *Concerto Barocco* and the square dancing in *Square Dance*. I think the mistake many outsiders make when they look at Balanchine's ballets is to confuse Balanchine's language with the neutral academic "lexicon." Karole Armitage recently launched a new company on the strength of this confusion. I imagine she thought she was extending Balanchine's territory in her Webern-Stravinsky ballet, when she was really quoting or parodying him. Armitage, who had ballet lessons but gained her fame as a Merce Cunningham dancer, has taken to wearing toe shoes; she calls her company the Armitage Ballet, and her guest artists in her opening season at the Joyce were Stephanie Saland and Robert La Fosse. Without the sense these two dancers made of an Armitage pas de deux, the evening would have been chaos. Armitage has a more reflexive understanding of pointework than Tharp does. With Armitage, pointes look self-conscious but not artificial. (She herself looks a lot like Farrell in Béjart's choreography.) But she's doing what Kirstein accuses the dilettantes of doing—souping up her performance with ballet stylization. I can only assume that the skillful choreography she made for ABT in *The Mollino Room* was the result of her working, like Tharp, with experienced classical dancers.

One of Balanchine's Louis Quatorze utterances might well have been "*L'académie, c'est moi.*" His usages have become standard. His Baroque is *the* Baroque. He even thought up his own heresies, so in order to rebel against him a choreographer has to risk being completely incoherent. (Maybe this was Mejia's plan.) In *Ballare*, Tharp is not guilty of ballet stylization, or even Balanchine stylization; she's trying for straight classical expression in flowing white costumes. Yet something—maybe the combination of pointework and intricate Mozart piano music—throws off her rhythm. Can there be anything more difficult for a choreographer than making classical ballets in the Age of Balanchine? Kirstein is right: there is a void in American dance, and there has been a rush to the ballet, and it could be dangerous.

In England, where there has not until recently been a native modern dance, a new tradition has been formed by blending English classical schooling with an aesthetic derived from Cunningham. The choreographer and company responsible for the blend, Richard Alston and Ballet Rambert, passed through New York on a North American tour. Compared with what is going on here, they are only moderately progressive, but they gave pleasure. The English dance delightfully, in three dimensions, with grown-up manners. Alston doesn't duplicate the Cunningham formula for presenting dance; he uses sound and choreographs to its pulse. Or, less compellingly, he choreographs in silence. Sound, whether verbal or musical, is something more than aural décor; sometimes, as in *Java*, a piece to Ink Spots records, it's a text. The matching of movement to sound is so ritualistically precise I'm only sorry Alston didn't lay any comic stress on the Spots' own rituals — that same eight-bar vamping introduction, that same high tenor who sings the song, that same dolorous basso who speaks it.

So amiable, unstrained, and limply lyrical a piece as *Java* is unimaginable in the climate of American dance. And I can't imagine Alston or any of the other Rambert choreographers recycling their work, as Americans do, making it new, then more new. In *In the Upper Room*, not only do you see Twyla in just about everything the dancers do but you see the sources of her material — aerobics, karate, jogging, boxing, break dancing, and of course ballet — and you see them more clearly than in the 1983 piece called *Fait Accompli*, which used similar material in a similarly striking format but used it less obviously and more tendentiously. *Fait Accompli* was in two sections, one starring the company, the other starring Tharp; it had a "crisis" subtext, a David Van Tieghem score, and neoexpressionistic cathedral lighting by Jennifer Tipton. Tipton more or less reproduces her plot in *In the Upper Room*; as before, dancers enter and exit upstage, behind a curtain of golden mist. Arranged in nine sections, designed as a full-company vehicle without stars, *In the Up-*

per Room is unambiguously a dance suite, and I had an almost intolerably mixed reaction to it. Just when I was ready to dismiss it as designer choreography given a megalomaniacal production, it would veer back to being genuine, and I'd rub my eyes and see that it was probably closer to being Tharp's Olympiad than *Fait Accompli* was. It's also a huge audience hit—a gift to the aerobics generation. Glass's music, with its tootling ostinatos and keening strings, contributes exactly the supercharged atmosphere that Tharp wants here, although it's easy to see why she has not collaborated with Glass before. He sets a properly frenetic pace but builds no momentum; each dance is pinned in its own gridlike cage of sound. Compared with David Byrne's score for *The Catherine Wheel*, the Glass makes almost no rhythmic or textural demands on Tharp.

And she doesn't seem to want them. Breaking in a new company, holding the line at the box office, laying the groundwork for artistic conquests of a kind never before seriously associated with her—these seem to have been the priorities that shaped Tharp's current season. The Glass ballet was a predetermined success; with it, Tharp reaches a new public and takes out insurance for her experiments in classicism. Unlike *Fait Accompli*, *In the Upper Room* will probably last a couple of seasons. As the piece in which aerobics are made cosmic, as the proclamation of Twyla Tharp Dance II, it may not become a classic, but who can deny its significance?

—February 23, 1987

A Dance to Spring

American Ballet Theatre opened its spring season at the Met with the largest advance sale in its history and eight performances of *The Sleeping Beauty*. It rained that week, but the house was always full, its spirits undampened. For the Saturday matinee, women and children were there in droves; they folded dripping umbrellas, cheerfully shook out plastic rain bonnets, and got themselves settled well before the start of the overture. On Wednesday afternoon, women had come without kids, straight from the hairdresser's. The orchestra floor was a sea of pale permed heads, through many of which there undoubtedly played fond memories of other rainy Aprils when lilacs were being sold on the city streets and *The Sleeping Beauty* was at the Met. In those days, it was English dancers from Covent Garden filling the house with lilac fragrance, and it was the glad young Margot Fonteyn who tiptoed out under the arches of Act I, greeted the audience in arabesque, and then, after a wild moment in which she seemed to have disappeared even as the applause built, suddenly burst back upon us, the quintessential Aurora, the personification of youth and spring.

This year, along with the English weather, there was a new production by Sir Kenneth MacMillan, who once danced in the Act III pas de trois called Florestan and His Two Sisters. He has now chosen to abolish these characters in favor of a Jewels pas de cinq featuring a Gold danseur, a Diamond solitaire, and Silver triplets. But there was little else in the way of innovation to startle a nostalgic audience. The production, impeccably traditional, is both English and Russian in pedigree: staging and choreography by MacMillan, based on the classic Petipa texts as preserved by Nicholas Sergeyev; costumes and scenery by MacMillan's favorite designer, Nicholas Georgiadis; dancing in the classic "Kirov" style—long-lined, clean-limbed, technically meticulous—to which Americans are physically well suited and to which the dancers of Ballet Theatre are by now well accustomed. Cast as fairies, cavaliers, courtiers, forest nymphs, and friends of the ballerina, they danced throughout with a stylistic unity never before attained by this company in this ballet. That may seem a modest achievement; in fact, it is essential to the success of a ballet in which purity of schooling is the mirror of virtue and manners reflect morality. The welded ensembles of ABT project the sense of an *école*, and for this we must thank Baryshnikov as well as MacMillan.

The triumph of the production at the moment is this collective security, which the company exhibited through nightly top-to-bottom changes of cast. Anyone looking for the complete theatrical experience that *The Sleeping Beauty* can be will not find it here yet. MacMillan's staging gets the show on in decent fashion, but it doesn't solve the problem of how to keep the action rising in the sections leading up to and away from the Vision scene. Act III, with its storybook-character suite of dances, falls flat. And the

scenery is unworthy. Georgiadis has also employed a unified approach, which is to say that the same white columns
and canopies and crumpled swags, the same sepia parch-
ment borders (vaguely suggesting bookplates), the same
heavy gold accents appear in every scene. Vast curvilinear
forms load down the upper air. In the Prologue, people-size
gilded angels sit in cloud banks; in the Wedding, lamps
hang low. The enchanted forest is a tangle of vines (with
not a lilac in sight). And the omnipresent columns suggest
that Prince Désiré, when he enters, has already reached the
grounds of Aurora's castle, leaving him no place to go in the
Panorama. (And he goes no place. The Lilac Fairy's barge
makes one circuit of the stage and exits; a scrim blots out
the scene.)

This is Georgiadis's second treatment of *The Sleeping
Beauty*, MacMillan's third, and their first together. They
have collaborated eleven times before. All this experience
doesn't seem to have yielded a recognizable viewpoint for
this richest of classical ballets. The decision to elide Acts II
and III is a mere cost-wise maneuver, not a theatrical opportunity. Anxiety sets in the minute the plot is over. The
Awakening takes place, and the orchestra begins tossing
away pages of music. Instead of an onstage transition to the
Wedding, we sit looking at the same scrim painted with
vines which we have seen before, but now the orchestra is
playing the march to cover the backstage clatter. It must
pain MacMillan, a musical choreographer, and Stewart Ker-
shaw, an able conductor, to use orchestral parts with tactless
cuts. (If I'm not mistaken, these parts also accompanied the
failed production staged by this company in 1976.)

The scheme of the ballet divides the Prologue and the
first two acts into scenes of mime and scenes of dance. In
general, Ballet Theatre's dancers are much more comfort-

able dancing than acting, and yet the single all-dance act—
Act III—is the most dismally presented of all. The problem
is not (as it was in 1976) unstylish dancing; the problem is
unstylish and untheatrical dancing compounded by unstylish and untheatrical direction. I believe it is a mistake to adhere to Petipa's idea of jewel fairies. This starts the dance
suite off with an overfamiliar and illogical gambit. If there
are fairies in the realm who weren't at the Christening, then
Carabosse wasn't the only uninvited one after all. Florestan
and His Two Sisters was a substitution that made sense;
they were a fresh and welcome sight, and the audience took
to them at once.

The failure of the current Bluebirds and of Puss in Boots
is harder to explain. The influence of the purists for whom
dancing means technique unclouded by imagination can be
felt throughout the production, but these Bluebirds are not
only glacial; they're unmusical, too. The whole first half of
their adagio looks like the Odette pas de deux crammed into
the wrong music, and the rest of the number staggers fit-
fully along, teasing us with hints of the great charmer it can
be. The bits of vestigial mime—flying, listening, calling—
are scrimped, while in Puss in Boots the clawing and flounc-
ing are emphasized until the dance becomes nothing more
than a petulant tizzy, about as delightful to look at as two
drunks fighting over a check. While the dancing is the best
part of this *Sleeping Beauty*, it is dancing that is much too
narrowly conceived. The stylistic modes in which Petipa re-
joiced—classical, character, demi-caractère, and all shades in
between—are erased and resorted into two purist categories: dance or mime. This is the price paid by *The Sleeping
Beauty* for the new, purebred company image that Ballet
Theatre is able at long last to put before us.

It follows that the touchstone of the role of Aurora is no

longer that great pas d'action the Rose adagio but the Vision scene. It is beautiful, and is extremely well done, but who ever thought in the fifties that in the eighties our dancers would be exalting the scene that makes Aurora resemble every other romantic-ballet heroine instead of the scene that makes the audience love her? In the Rose adagio, Fonteyn and her generation rushed to embrace life—every pirouette was a new opportunity, every proffered rose held a different promise. The Kirov's Kolpakova and Sizova, as I recall, were no less vibrant. Today's Auroras—sagacious veterans like Martine van Hamel as well as debutantes like Amanda McKerrow—sail through the steps with scarcely a hint of their poetic import. The steps are, in fact, no longer the test of the ballerina's mettle that they used to be. Plumb balances without support have become corny clichés, and the Rose adagio is full of them. Cantilevered balances were easy *then*. (But since that is the case, perhaps it is time to restore the Petipa passage of Aurora taking her flat-footed arabesques penchées with one hand on the shoulder of each of four kneeling friends in turn. It wouldn't detract from our impression of Aurora's sovereign gifts, and it would explain what her friends are there for.)

When technical hurdles in a masterpiece are too low, the steps may become overarticulated and underexpressed. This is what seems to have happened to the fairy variations in the Prologue. Like the Bluebirds and like Aurora, the fairies are equipped with a poetic rationale for the steps they do, but all that most of these dancers do is steps. They lift their letter-perfect legs not as if they were paragons of elegance bestowing their personal attributes on the royal infant but as though they were pupils whom someone was waiting in the wings to whack with a ruler. We're meant to see these attribute dances as a growing profile of the princess-to-be, so perhaps we're not altogether surprised when she turns out, on her sixteenth birthday, to be a bit of a cold fish.

McKerrow, young and talented (and far too thin this season), dances Aurora like a *Theme and Variations* fish out of water. For dancers of her generation, the height of classical style is represented less by the role of Aurora than by the fantasia that Balanchine made of it and other *Sleeping Beauty* material in *Theme and Variations*. You can turn Aurora into a modern ballerina—at least, you can if you are Balanchine—but you can't turn the clock back. McKerrow's strong but uninflected technique gets her through Balanchine; Petipa, though, suffers from too much abnegation and scrupulosity. I saw Deirdre Carberry in several supporting roles in *Beauty*. She, too, is a strong technician, and she's also an avid performer. In her début in *Theme*, though, she was closer to what an Aurora should be than she'd ever been as a Bluebird or a Diamond or a Fairy of Benevolence. The reason, I think, is that the technique kept her too busy to impose "personality" on the part.

Anyway, success in classical dancing lies not in what the dancer imposes on the steps but on what she extracts from them. And from the music. About the only dancers in ABT's *Beauty* who are at present giving—and getting—full value are the men. Kevin McKenzie is a vivid Désiré, technically keen, poetically striking. His performance is an example of how a good classical dancer extracts meaning from steps, for he has precious few of them and little to work with in the way of characterization. Désiré is still the solitary loiterer he always was. The extra solo he is nowadays given in Act II, a sort of brooding soliloquy, is a stylistic solecism committed by choreographers to keep male dancers happy. MacMillan's version is done to the Sarabande, extrapolated from Act III; McKenzie focuses it by seeming to be addressing it to a woman who isn't there. Later, his excited runs toward and away from the Vision of Aurora (when Lilac first discloses it) lift the whole ballet. In the character parts, John Taras is an excellent pouter-pigeon Cattalabutte, and Victor Barbee and Michael Owen give serious noncamp performances as Carabosse. This travesty role is still a bit unwieldy for American dancers. Storming around in a black and gold-lace dress and red fright wig modeled by Georgiadis on Elizabeth I, Carabosse can easily become more flamboyant than absolutely necessary. But Barbee, in one electrifying performance that I saw, managed instead to give the role a soft insinuating feline malice. (Opening his mouth like the Chinese Conjurer in *Parade* I thought a mistake.)

In Petipa's day, men's roles in ballets like *The Sleeping Beauty* were largely the creations of their interpreters, who relied on their own ideas of what a Désiré or a Carabosse would do. In a sense, the women's roles must now be performed the same way. Unless they're fleshed out with sentiment, they look skeletal. The role of Aurora is not dramatically beyond the capacities of our dancers. Petipa designed it for the twenty-three-year-old Carlotta Brianza, who no one ever claimed was a great actress. And Fonteyn, our greatest Aurora, did not *act*. Her triumph was to realize that Aurora is not a special and distinct person—she is all young dancers. One wishes that the ballerinas of ABT who are searching for clues to a character would look no farther than the nearest mirror. You're sixteen, it's your birthday, and you've got on a new pair of toe shoes—now take it from there.

—*May 25, 1987*

Risky Business

Mythologies, a trilogy by Mark Morris, was suggested by the writings of Roland Barthes on popular culture which were published in a book of the same title in 1957; a translation appeared in 1972. Barthes wrote, as only French intellectuals can, about the iconography of soap powders and detergents, the ritual of the striptease and the wrestling match, and other pop phenomena. In adapting Barthes's themes to the theatre, Morris and his composer, Herschel Garfein, have evolved their own iconographies and rituals. In *Striptease* and *Championship Wrestling* they extend rather than illustrate Barthes's point. In *Soap-Powders and Detergents* they are elaborately beside the point, but they make such a ruckus that we're entertained anyway.

Mythologies doesn't represent the elegantly lyrical side of Morris's talent; it shows instead his gift for detached observation and impersonal satire. When he gives us quivering bubbles and regimented wavelets in *Soap-Powders* (the piece goes straight through the wash cycle), he isn't being unfair to Doris Humphrey's *Water Study*—he's just being the Spirit of Modernism. When big white laundry sheets keep parting and revealing figures frozen in poses, one doesn't respect Martha Graham's *Clytemnestra* any the less. The use of fabric is Morris's main design element, and it's pure Denishawn, just as the abstract groupings in serried Art Deco formations are pure post-Denishawn.

But Morris is only coping in *Soap-Powders and Detergents*. In *Striptease* and *Championship Wrestling* he is at or near his peak. The latter piece is a one-of-a-kind creation. Morris doesn't stylize wrestling the way stage fights stylize fisticuffs; he gives us the same brutal, exaggerated nonsense we see in the arena. He takes wrestling on its own terms as the theatre Barthes said it was. "Art" meets "sport" on the same phony turf. You can't believe that Morris could be getting so much out of this one-on-one overlay, or that, having succeeded here, he could possibly do it again. Yet *Striptease* goes beyond *Championship Wrestling* in explicit representation.

Between a Morris parody of a sensational or obscene spectacle and the spectacle itself there is a very fine line. Morris doesn't just allude to stripteasers or wrestlers—he drives us to confront the harsh physical facts. But his arrangement of those facts is such that we are absorbed and enlightened by what we see—never cheaply implicated, never dehumanized, and never immunized, either. I don't know which I admire more—Morris's refusal to play down to his material or his refusal to play up to his audience. He uses trash fastidiously. In this he reminds me of Bette Midler or Joe Orton, artists who practiced outrage and placed themselves at great risk of being misunderstood. To keep on doing this, you have to have a sturdy sense of self as well as a precise and flexible sense of where reality ends and parody begins. (I deliberately put Bette Midler in the past tense because, alas, after years of keeping her balance on the fine line she now seems to be losing it.) There's no hostility in Morris; he's much too various and large-spirited for that. In *Lovey*, a piece seen here a couple of years ago which dealt with murder and child molestation, he took us to hell laughing all the way and brought us back crying. Now, in *Striptease*, he and his company of dancer-mimes go to Nighttown. There are four female and four male strippers (including Morris), and they're so far off balance for so long that they seem to be out of control. Then, in the last thirty seconds of the piece, they make the miracle that transforms scabrous entertainment into a work of art.

This is a remarkable company. I saw *Lovey* with rotating casts; it was always extraordinary. For *Striptease* the cast is set; each dancer plays a character of fantasy or one with strong fantasy overtones, and each character—cowboy, dominatrix, motorcyclist, bimbo, construction worker, Oriental fan-dancer, bride, punk—is fully worked up in terms of drag and shtick. Rob Besserer, Ruth Davidson, Tina Fehlandt, Susan Hadley, Donald Mouton, Keith Sabado, Teri Weksler, and Morris come at us one at a time, strike a pose, remove a bit of gear, flaunt a piece of anatomy, and stride off. On the next round, they carry the process a stage further. You think they can't, but they can. Morris is the sleaziest of all; wearing a black suit, a dangling earring, and ringlets falling over one bloodshot eye, he oozes and jerks his way down to the footlights like an ejaculating jellyfish. He gets down to skin. They all do. There is a silence as they hold themselves in character, strutting in a red light, freezing in silhouette. Then, suddenly, the show is over and we see them having to pick up their clothes and get off the stage.

In the declension of the striptease, Barthes said, we see that nudity is not the point—dressing up (and undressing) is. Nudity has leveled all these raging individualists; it has canceled the process of revelation. If Morris had pulled the curtain at the climax, he would simply have succeeded in putting on a strip show, but, like Barthes, he has produced an essay on stripping, and his sad little anti-climax is the ultimate comment on truth games in the theatre. You think he can't get beyond stripping, but he can.

—June 8, 1987

Zeitgeist

Antony Tudor's great ballets were all made before 1950. He was born five years after George Balanchine and Frederick Ashton, but his work is actually closer to the time and spirit of Léonide Massine and Kurt Jooss. His masterpiece, *Jardin aux Lilas*, was created in 1936. After he moved from England to America, in 1939, he became famous as the choreographer of a new type of dramatic ballet (*Pillar of Fire*, *Undertow*), which could be discussed in the clinical language of pop psychology, but his finest work of this period may well have been *Romeo and Juliet*, to music of Delius—a return to the delicate characterization and mute pathos of *Jardin aux Lilas*. The advent of Tudor in America coincided with large-scale developments in the career of Martha Graham. In their different ways, each evolved a brand of expressionism powerfully responsive to the cultural climate of the forties. Though Tudor's creative impetus died and Graham's lived on, she is his closest American contemporary.

Exactly why Tudor's invention ceased is a matter of debate. His dramas of socially frustrated sexual passion went out of style, but their qualities of theatrically intelligent

physical movement, emotional refinement, and musical audacity made them interesting to watch even when you
didn't find their subject matter engaging. Tudor was one of
the self-styled aristocrats who founded British ballet on an
image of royal succession, changing their names to suit the
image. Miriam Ramberg became Marie Rambert, Edris
Stannus became Ninette de Valois, William Cook became
Antony Tudor. Like the rest of his generation, he was
forced to improvise the skills that academy-trained Russian,
French, or Danish dancers took for granted, and as outsiders sometimes do, he saw more in the language of classical ballet than those who spoke it as a native tongue. In
Jardin aux Lilas he converted the discipline of ballet into a
metaphor for social constraint, and this expressionistic use
of ballet took its place in his vocabulary of elaborately en-
coded naturalistic movements and gestures. No choreographer ever studied the science of pantomime more closely.
Tudor worked with taste and intuition. What he lacked in
schooling he made up in imagination. His then-limited ballet technique probably did him less harm than the expressionistic uses to which he put it. Next to the sleek classical
ballets of Balanchine, Tudor's began to look coercive and
sentimental. And as the popularity of ballet grew in America
it gave rise to a master race of dancers whom even Balanchine referred to as "monsters of perfection." Tudor reflected the trend in his work. But using ballet as direct
expression seemed to reduce him to anonymity. *The Leaves
Are Fading*, a late addition to his canon, is a wistful attempt
at a long, lyrically transporting "pure" ballet. As a composition it is full of prowess. As a drama it is very timid Tudor.

Tudor taught and coached a generation of dancers, and
he saw his repertory staged with fidelity by this generation
even though the times were out of joint and few interpreters

arose to continue what Nora Kaye, Hugh Laing, and Alicia Markova had begun. *Pillar of Fire* lasted into the seventies on the strength of Sallie Wilson's performance. Natalia Makarova arrived from Russia to cast a new light on Tudor ballets, and when Gelsey Kirkland joined American Ballet Theatre, Tudor was moved to compose new work. *The Leaves Are Fading* was danced this season at the Met (though without Kirkland), along with *Pillar of Fire* and *Dark Elegies*. Tudor himself, at the age of seventy-eight, had cast and rehearsed all three. He died the day before the season began. He had survived his greatest American ballerina, Nora Kaye, by two months; he himself is survived by Hugh Laing, who more than any ballerina incarnated the Tudor aesthetic and focused Tudor's creative drive. Laing had no successors. Not even Anthony Dowell, as the Boy with Matted Hair in *Shadowplay*, elicited the kind of poetry from Tudor that Laing did. Tudor's ballets were dark webs threaded with erotic tension and a kind of heroic fatalism. Without being directly about Laing, they took their color from him; he was their exponent and, perhaps, their one true inspiration.

I felt Tudor's presence at ABT this season not in his own work so much as in Paul Taylor's *Sunset*, which ABT was staging for the first time. This piece about soldiers meeting girls in a public park is one of the strangest, saddest, and most haunting that Taylor has ever made; the banality of the idea (it's like a tragic and infinitely becalmed *Fancy Free*) is not transcended but embraced. A war memorial, an elegy for dead young men, a study of sexual relations (men and men as well as men and women), an essay on loneliness and group identity, a meditation on the past: *Sunset* is all those things, and it is also a long look at a side of Taylor—a defenselessly emotional side—that doesn't often emerge. Taylor was a student of Tudor's (and he later became a Graham dancer), but I wasn't struck by the resemblances to Tudor in *Sunset* until I saw it done at ABT, where its shimmering aura of memory and bursts of throttled eloquence seemed almost an act of homage. There was even a technical link to Tudor, in the constant shifting of the action from the literal to the nonliteral and back again, which suggested the continuity in *Pillar of Fire*.

Sunset leaves a great many things unsaid, and one feels it's not because they are unsayable in dance but because Taylor respects the inarticulateness and the discretion of his characters too much to tell stories about them. A full-scale narrative ballet is something he just wouldn't dream of. For this production of *Sunset*, he appears to have made a few small changes. A sequence in which one of the soldiers is extensively coddled and carried about by the girls seemed less prominent than it once did. At the Met, the dying of the light on the Alex Katz set had a pallor it didn't have at the City Center, but I assume this was an effect Jennifer Tipton did not intend. *Sunset* is hardly the kind of Taylor piece a ballet company normally chooses to do. (San Francisco Ballet is the only other company to have attempted it.) It wouldn't have been a surprise to see the whole production fail, but though the dancing of the ABT cast was ballet-style Taylor, it was not at all bad, and the acting, projected with a little extra force, was quite good. Lila York reconstructed the choreography. Her former role—that of the little girl who walks on the men's backs—was taken by Dana Stackpole, and Kathleen Moore was unexpectedly vivid in Kate Johnson's role. (She hadn't been a very interesting Hagar in *Pillar of Fire*.) Robert Hill, John Summers, and the other men were less individually distinctive than Taylor's dancers, but their esprit was perfect.

Ballet Theatre also produced a first effort at chore-ography by one of its principal dancers, Clark Tippet. The title, *Enough Said*, led you to expect a jokey piece, but though Tippet's choreography was frequently nimble, even witty, it didn't crack a smile, or if it did it was a thin, wintry Clint Eastwood kind of smile. Clark Tippet has for years been one of ballet's best partners, and his ballet deals with men meeting and partnering women in various combina-tions: a woman and three men, a man and three women, one long pas de deux followed by several brief ones per-formed at the same time. In the final section, the cast runs through a new set of orderly permutations, and then the principal couple ends the game with a neutral handclasp. The structure of *Enough Said* may be derived from *Agon*. Tippet's music is the Serenade No. 3 by George Perle, the central movement of which is dedicated to George Balan-chine. The choreography's blend of gymnastics and classical dancing, the spareness and logic of its exposition, the cool-cat dance manners—these suggest *Agon*, too. But, as John Martin noted in his *Times* review thirty years ago, *Agon* does smile.

Tippet's atmosphere is the changed climate of male-female relations in the eighties, and his ballet is closer to Pe-ter Martins's newest piece, *Ecstatic Orange*, than either of them is to anything by Balanchine and Stravinsky. Martins's music is also by a contemporary American—Michael Torke, whose compositions are inspired by colors. For New York City Ballet's spring season, Martins choreographed Torke's "Green" and "Purple," and presented both sections with the *Ecstatic Orange* he had shown last winter in costumes by Stephen Sprouse. This time, the dancers wore plain black leotards and tights, but the choreography still had the lethal ferocity it had when they were in Sprouse's headbands and loincloths. The two other sections, also performed in black leotards and tights, were in the same spirit; the whole ballet is Beyond Thunderdome.

If the sexual atmosphere in Tippet's piece is glumly neutral, in Martins's it is primitivistic. Though Torke's music has a certain jagged neo-Stravinskyan vein running through it, Martins seems to hear it as anti-classical. He may be right. Just as Stravinsky incorporated popular elements, Torke represents a style of pop-based composing which incorporates Stravinsky. Martins's choreography emphasizes slashing limbs and thrust pelvises; principals and corps are as turned in as a Broadway chorus. "Purple" is a disjointed tango of the type Martins has several times choreographed to Stravinsky's music. To Torke's specially commissioned music he puts Heather Watts and Jock Soto through a series of tortuously evolving maneuvers that seem designed to top anything he's done before: lifts in which Watts goes over Soto's back and between his legs or is spun in the air or is held upside down while she does splits; absurd poses including a reclining one with only the top of her head and one point touching the ground. It is in the Watts and Soto roles that Martins expresses a fang-and-claw vision of sex. Soto, with the physique of a wrestler, can partner anything, and Martins keeps the zingers coming. The pas de deux ends with Watts kneeling on Soto's thigh, gripping her ankles (like the Siren in *The Prodigal Son*), being lowered by him to the floor, and there being turned knee to knee until the music runs out. This cheaply mechanistic role for Watts is a reduction rather than an extension of the other roles Martins has made for her. Unattractive as many of those roles made Watts out to be, they were analytical rather than exploitative. And Soto, whose career got under way in Martins's ballets, has become her gruntingly acquiescent caveman partner. He's a good dancer, Watts in the right ballets is a useful performer, and Martins has become a choreographer who commands wide respect, but they seem to bring out the worst in each other.

A successful first ballet is not hard to pull off. What's hard is the second, the third, the fourth. Tippet's début was unusually promising, but until he makes more ballets no profile of Tippet the choreographer can be drawn. Clearer than Tippet's prospects, though, is the trend at ABT toward ballets bearing the stamp of New York City Ballet. Tippet's was not the first that looked as though it could or should have been danced by the company across the way at Lincoln Center: Twyla Tharp's *Bach Partita* and Karole Armitage's *The Mollino Room* had "Balanchine" written all over them, and ABT since Baryshnikov took it over has produced a string of Balanchine's ballets; the latest, *Stravinsky Violin Concerto* is being unveiled this season in Washington. Meanwhile, Peter Martins produces an aggressively "modern" ballet and announces a three-week festival of choreography featuring American music, with guest choreographers drawn from the same modern-dance circuit that has been providing Baryshnikov with premières. To top it off, in the near future NYCB plans to produce *The Sleeping Beauty*; ABT has just done it.

Perhaps the two companies are drawing closer together because it is in the spirit of the times that they do so. But perhaps they are being forced onto the same path from having year after year to compete for the same audience in New York. When Balanchine ran City Ballet, and it played every spring and summer opposite Ballet Theatre at the Met, the competition was seen by many observers to be between his "neoclassicism" and its standard brand of classicism. One could disagree with those terms, but whatever the content of each company's offerings was said to be, it accounted in most people's minds for the division in taste which then really seemed to exist. If you liked Balanchine, you were not lured by Ballet Theatre. If you wanted big-name stars in three-act ballets, or simply the prestige of the Met, you did not attend City Ballet. Now, with Balanchine gone, the divide between NYCB and ABT appears to be closing, and the ballet audience is being forced to choose more arbitrarily what it will see. The booking policies that pit our two greatest companies against each other annually in New York were always deleterious, but their worst effects were mitigated as long as there was a clear aesthetic choice. What, though, if NYCB and ABT were to become as indistinguishable in the public mind as CBS and NBC? Surely then the fact that they play every year at the same time in the same place would be the least of their worries.

—July 6, 1987

The Bolshoi Bows In

New Yorkers who went to the Bolshoi Ballet this summer at the Met were put through an elaborate security net. Standing in long lines, they submitted to having their handbags searched and their persons surveyed by metal detectors, then to being penned inside the Met for the entire performance: no going out-of-doors into Lincoln Center Plaza during intermissions, not for an ice-cream cone, not even to smoke. When the performance started again, every ticket stub was rechecked in case someone had got into the building without a ticket. Since the Met has four thousand and sixty-five seats and every one of them had been sold (at a top of sixty dollars), the security procedures were a great bother, especially during the congested intermissions, but they were preferable to the type of assault on the audience which had taken place on the first night of the Moiseyev Dance Company's season at the same theatre last fall, when members of the Jewish Defense League released tear gas inside the house. On the first night of the Bolshoi season, a bomb scare caused the curtain to be delayed for an hour. The security checks that went on thereafter added considerably to the running time of every performance, but no one seemed to mind getting out late. Many people even stayed on to applaud, whipped up as much, no doubt, by the tension of the occasion as by the performance.

And by the Bolshoi mystique. This mystique, the joint creation of balletomanes, PR men, and politicians, has at its root a fixed belief in the supremacy of Russian ballet and the benefits of cultural exchange. Applauding Soviet dancers—letting them know we approve of and understand their art—is supposed to be good not only for one's own cultural health but for the health of nations. The Bolshoi mystique has always been a factor in the company's success here. People gripped by it don't just applaud dancing; they applaud demonstratively, caringly, as if casting a vote. They *come* to applaud, and this being the first Bolshoi visit in eight years, they sounded off with an enthusiasm that would not be dampened—not by bomb scares and security checks and boosted ticket prices, not by a heat wave that blanketed the city, not even by the ballets of Yuri Grigorovich. Every night, they rushed to the opera house, passed their security test, and cheered the cause of art and peace.

So eager was the response of these good citizens that it became disruptive, constantly anticipating cues for applause. And the Bolshoi dancers are very particular about cues. When the applause wasn't forthcoming at the right moment, the fact that it had already been granted made no difference; they demanded it anyway. When it died, they walked out and revived it by bowing some more. They bowed between the acts of a ballet, taking half-risen audiences by surprise, and they bowed during the coda of a classical grand pas de deux, rudely cutting off the music to do so. Plainly, the Bolshoi is used to an applause *routine*. Dancers with so little audience rapport that they can't adjust a simple curtain call are very strange to see, but the failing is symbolic of the insecurity and the lack of finesse that have afflicted the Bolshoi command all these years. (I don't mean to exempt the Kirov, in whose dancers the same bad habits are ingrained; but the Kirov has consistently held itself more aloof from the public than the Bolshoi.)

The great treasure of the Bolshoi has long lain in the talent of its dancers, not in its choreographers or musicians, and not, God knows, in its designers. (Actually, there is only one—Simon Virsaladze, who does both scenery and costumes. His stylistic signature—slapdash washes and glitter dust for the backdrops, particolored arms and legs for the costumes—is scrawled across every ballet with a heavy hand.) And the whole-souled passion of its dancers was the Bolshoi's gift supreme. In the first two decades of the American tours—the sixties and the seventies—one tended to take their talent for granted. The largest ballet company on earth, with the greatest supply of dancers to choose from— it stood to reason that Bolshoi casts were the pick of the crop. But the sixties and the seventies were a period of self-conscious renewal for the Bolshoi, during which it strove to meet the objections of Western critics that it was old-fashioned. Grigorovich's regime has largely silenced the critics; one no longer sees mime gesticulation in Bolshoi productions, either in the new ballets or in the classics. And one notices an attempt to conform to Western standards of classical style and breeding, especially in the female corps. The Bolshoi never was a classical company in the same sense as the Kirov or the great companies of the West; its expressive strength lay in a romantic ardor that, to Western eyes, recalled the *danse moderne* of Fokine and Isadora Duncan. This *was* old-fashioned, and it was keyed to mime expression as necessarily as classical dancing is keyed to pure

rhythmic and architectural expression. But it was real
enough. That old style had no great poetic radiance, but it
did have vitality; it had conviction. The dancers could believe in it and could communicate their belief. The closest
they've ever got to communicating belief under the Grigorovich regime is in his ballet *Spartacus* (1968), which incorporates the old-style heroic romanticism as the content of a
new-style "story" ballet without mime. *Spartacus* doesn't really have a story; it's an exercise in formalism—a sequence
of set pieces (like a typical sixties "Highlights" program)
linked by references to a story.

Spartacus, one act of which was on the "Highlights" bills
this season, remains Grigorovich's only feasible solution to
the problem faced by the new Bolshoi: how to put across a
socialist-realist message and look modern at the same time.
The latest Grigorovich ballet, *The Golden Age*, restates the
dilemma in more openly competitive terms, trying for jazzy,
Western-style elegance. It makes no more narrative sense
than *Spartacus*, but in addition to being directionless it is incoherent. Grigorovich doesn't tell stories, he untells them.
You can sense what the untold story of *Spartacus* is; in *The
Golden Age*, though, every scene is like a scramble to find
out who's concealing the point of it—the stalwart hero, his
tango-dancing girlfriend, her partner, or her partner's girlfriend. (Grigorovich's ballets always have four principals;
he's as superstitious about that as David O. Selznick was
about his four-word titles.) The music, from a once suppressed ballet by Shostakovich, has been rearranged by
committee; it includes Shostakovich's orchestration of "Tea
for Two" and movements from two of his piano concertos.
The libretto tosses around references to agitprop theatre
and popular art, crooks and Komsomol youth, but you get
nowhere by trying to follow any of it. It's Grigorovich un-

telling a story of the twenties, trying to be smartly nostalgic about the NEP years and yet trying to fill a socialist-realist prescription, too. (The Virsaladze décor, with its cynically superficial allusions to Constructivism, tells which side the ballet's heart is on.)

Grigorovich can't tell a story because his reformative impulse is negative—anti-mime, not pro-dance. He took the company off the mime standard and substituted steps for plastique. Technically speaking, his idea of Western neoclassical style comes from the Paris of Petit and Béjart, not the New York of Balanchine and Robbins. The real problem with *The Golden Age*—the real problem with the Bolshoi—is that its dance regimen doesn't engage the dancers the way the old mime regimen did, because it's a choreographer's medium, with meanings of its own to express. And when one choreographer rules a company, sooner or later every ballet comes to be danced in the style of that choreographer. The Petipa ballet *Raymonda*, diffuse and dramatically inert, virtually invites the Grigorovich treatment, but it was designed for a Russian classical company, not a neo-French institution with an identity crisis, an agenda to defend at home, and a mystique to promote abroad.

Grigorovich's policies have been periodically attacked by factions of dancers. According to a report this spring in the Manchester *Guardian*, the younger dancers are beginning to criticize "male chauvinism" in ballets like *Spartacus* which "give the best roles to male dancers." This goes to the heart of the Petipa matter. Without a cultivated classical style for women, a company can't dance Petipa ballets. The *Raymonda* has no lyricism, no precision in lightness, no variable speed, no intricacy, no repose. When, over the years, dancers with these gifts emerged, their gifts weren't used. Lyudmila Semenyaka, enchanting a decade ago, has become mannered and dreamy. Nadezhda Pavlova isn't on the American tour. I can't help thinking it a reflection of her absence, and of her wasted potential, that in the many grand adagios of *Raymonda*, and especially in the ensemble adagio of the third act, the dancers would rather hold poses than sustain a line. They build toward a climax not gradually but all in one rush, usually with a furious en-dedans spin-pirouette. Adagio thus becomes something that doesn't quite happen between two extremes of movement.

Male dancing suffers from a corresponding deficiency in the number of good character roles. The new Bolshoi seems to know only one kind of character—brutal. And he appears throughout the repertory. As the sheikh Abderakhaman in *Raymonda*, he is also supposed to be sexy, but Grigorovich's attempt to stylize his mime (so it doesn't look like mime) made him appear hysterical. The worst blow, though, came in the mazurka and czardas of Act III; this was "Hungarian" demi-caractère dancing that could not have withstood a challenge from New York City Ballet or American Ballet Theatre. In classical dancing, the middle rank of Bolshoi men is stronger than the middle rank of women. When the male quartet takes the stage in the double-tour variation in *Raymonda*, you get a glimmer of the style that made the Bolshoi so interestingly a men's company even before *Spartacus*. Even now, when the top line is made up of mostly earnest, unadventurous young men, you see a dignity, a weight, an amplitude that might still be the envy of the rest of the world. Unfortunately, you also see some beefy amateurs, who have the conscripted look of the porteurs on the early tours—men whose chief business was lifting women.

On the closing night of the season, the performance ended with all the principal dancers, led by Grigorovich, coming out in their street clothes and taking a final bow.

The ballet had been *Giselle*, danced by Semenyaka with the season's two most publicized dancers, Irek Mukhamedov and Nina Ananiashvili, as Albrecht and Myrtha. An injury to the company's senior ballerina, Natalya Bessmertnova, had prevented her from dancing Giselle, but she was on-stage bowing, and so were Galina Ulanova, the Giselle of the first Western tours, and Marina Semyonova, another legendary figure of the past, whom New York never saw and who now, like Ulanova, coaches the younger dancers. It would have seemed wrong if this bowing event of the season had followed any other ballet. *Giselle* still has its traditional form. Grigorovich has revised the old Leonid Lavrovsky version that so influenced the West (in ways both good and bad), but except for rearranging the entrance of the royal party to include some absurd dance steps he hasn't altered it in any significant way. True, ABT does a better Act I, and the Kirov a better Act II. Nevertheless, *Giselle* was the only production we saw all season that wasn't *poshlost* or cabaret classicism; it was the only ballet with developed adagio passages that displayed women, and the only link to the freely lyrical, impassioned performing style of the grand old days. The ballerina who came the closest to embodying that link was Nina Semizorova, whose high-voltage energy and sharpness of definition, wildly misplaced in the "Highlights" programs, worked in an attractively risky way for her Giselle. Ananiashvili deserved her publicity. She showed off her lovely figure and strength of form in role after role. At twenty-four, she lacks edge and discrimination, and her mask of self-satisfaction—the Bolshoi's official-first-lady look—is firmly in place. Probably, she can do a lot more than she knows. My guess is she won't get the chance.

It's the male dancing at the Bolshoi that tantalizes the general public. The most impressive dancer on the tour is

Mukhamedov. At first, in *The Golden Age*, I took him for an athlete rather than a dancer, the Bolshoi brute as hero; later I saw his virtuoso gifts. Though much about the Bolshoi has changed, its style of expression still seems to take its cue from men. Bolshoi dancing is easy to read. It focuses on one thing at a time; it prepares visibly and follows through. It employs the large contrasts and exaggerations of popular entertainment. The fact that it is simplified ballet, which can only repeat and multiply its effects, is not a disgrace. Simplified and serious is not a bad thing to be. Simplified and mediocre is.

—July 27, 1987

The Last Waltz

Vienna Waltzes, for all the wealth and glitter of its setting, is a ballet that brings the spectator very close to the stage. In the final scene, the stage is backed by giant mirrors that reflect the audience. Thus enclosed by spectators, the dancers perform the first waltz sequence from *Der Rosenkavalier*. The production of *Vienna Waltzes*, in 1977, was the climax of Balanchine's career at the State Theater, and the sense of the breathless occasion that the ballet was then returned last month when Suzanne Farrell, the star of the "Rosenkavalier" sequence, made her first appearance in the role following an eighteen-month absence from the stage. In that time, she had undergone surgery for the hip injury that had crippled her—an injury so severe that it was thought she would never dance again. This winter, she danced five performances with an artificial-hip implant—the first ballerina to accomplish such a thing.

Making medical history as well as dance history, Farrell was taking a great risk, but then risk-taking has been the hallmark of her style. Since her discovery by Balanchine in the mid-sixties, standards of virtuosity have risen to ever-higher levels of precision, and this is largely because Farrell has been willing to take chances—to go off balance, to dare the extra pirouette, to perform spectacular steps not as isolated feats an audience would applaud but as part of the fabric of choreography. At the time, she seemed an insular phenomenon; she even seemed a little perverse. Now, at New York City Ballet and elsewhere, the Farrell canon— *Diamonds, Chaconne, Mozartiana*, among other ballets—is considered the acme of ballerina style. The choreography is the liveliest of challenges to the ballerina aspirant and is likely to remain so for several generations.

The artificial hip joint is not made that can perform a Farrell arabesque, a Farrell développé or grand rond de jambe en l'air. Among her earliest contributions to technique were her enlargement of the scale on which big movements are done and her telescoping of the speed of change from big to small movements. In the extremes of its range, her technique was hair-raising; it seems safe to say we shall never see anything like it again. The "Rosenkavalier" role is not one of those in which the extremes are sensationally depicted. When Farrell, after a five-year hiatus, returned to Balanchine, in 1974, the ballets he composed for her bravura style featured long dance passages in which she really didn't seem to be doing much—in which she was *all* style. The opening solo in *Tzigane* was one example of this radical, stripped-down Farrell; the finale of *Chaconne* was another. "Der Rosenkavalier" is reminiscent of *Tzigane* in that it seems a self-involved fantasy, with no technique to speak of—just Farrell alone with herself and the mirror. That's dancing enough, Balanchine seems to be saying; she doesn't have to hit the ceiling with a battement.

And so this season when Farrell stepped out from the downstage-right wing (the wing from which Balanchine was accustomed to watch performances) and advanced to

center, and when she knelt, curtsied to her imaginary partner, and began to dance, really to dance, one couldn't shake
off one's wonder at whatever operative necessity had caused
Balanchine in 1977 to compose for Farrell an entire canonical role in which none of the canonical specialties were on
view. Balanchine, of course, always liked to see how far Farrell could go with how little support—from him, from partners, from custom or habit. Whatever his instinct may have
been, on this night it felt like prescience—the choreographer's final legacy to the dancer who had so enriched his last
quarter-century. The "Rosenkavalier" role is a portrait of
Farrell in her maturity; it is, if you like, a character role, but
a "white" character role that contains and purifies the colors
of her boldest characterizations—the rash young-blood
Gypsy of *Brahms-Schoenberg Quartet*, the stupendous, all-
conquering Tzigane. When she shades her eyes with her
forearm or bends backward in a trance over Adam Lüders's
arm, when she sketches the steps of some half-remembered
czardas, the sentiment of it hits us like a valediction: this is
farewell.

Farrell danced this performance of *Vienna Waltzes* and
four others with full control of the dynamics of scale and
impetus. It was not in every particular the same performance she used to give—it was lighter and gayer in tone,
and maybe a little more consciously dramatic—but it was an
unadulterated Farrell performance, with enough of the old
touchstones in place to hold us awestruck: the languishing
in her partner's arms, the contrapposto ripple through the
body when she sweeps a leg up in battement croisé, the
swiftness of the attack in the violin cadenza (akin to
sforzando in music), the sudden quiet melt to the floor as
the big melody is about to enter and her partner comes to
claim her, and, finally and unforgettably, the back-bent exit
into the wings "on fire," as the lights blaze and the stage is

filled with waltzing couples. I was happy to see again my favorite "nothing" moment—when, waltzing and turning face to face with her partner, she several times offers him her hand and then withdraws it so that she may on each turn switch her train from hand to hand behind her back. The switching of the train becomes the motif we are meant to enjoy here, not the turning, or even the offering of the hand. The emphasis, so oddly sensual, is pure Farrell and pure truth in dancing. Farrell's wit, which is so closely allied to her musical sense, gives her little bons mots like this. And it gives her the freedom to include a moment I don't recall ever seeing before. Her partner comes in for the first time, dances her through that first brief passage of introspection; then, after he has left her alone, she comes far downstage and gazes out over the audience. This, I think, is an extension of what we used to see: Farrell looking into the mirror of the audience. These performances of *Vienna Waltzes* were special occasions on which the dancer and her public came together as never before. We were celebrating her return and she was acknowledging that. The family-party atmosphere was real every time; it did not degenerate into hard-ticket New York ritual.

The physical misfortune that has overtaken Farrell's career is one we shall never cease to regret, for it cannot be certain that she will dance another role, and no other Balanchine role seems possible. (Unlike *Vienna Waltzes*, the others are all on pointe or involve jumping.) And, at forty-two, Farrell is still very strong. It was her physical strength that allowed her extremes to be consistently in full play; we saw it in ballet after ballet. That must have been the strength that brought her through her recent ordeal. The week of her return to *Vienna Waltzes*, Farrell's story was broadcast on the *MacNeil-Lehrer Newshour*. A surgeon (not Farrell's doctor) explained how hip implants work and what can go wrong if extreme care is not taken. The details were appalling. She was seen on crutches before the operation, then in recuperation, taking class and working out with her therapist. Farrell had intended not to sign a release for this footage to be shown unless she actually made it back onto the stage. The reason, she said, was that she did not care to become the latest victim claimed by those who think that ballet destroys dancers.

Her point, I believe, is not that she hasn't suffered destruction but that "ballet" is not the cause. Ballet is, after all, the creation of dancers, and it survives and progresses because of dancers, not because of inhuman regimes or dictatorial ballet masters. Balanchine gave classes in pointework so that he could learn from his girls. Commenting on the ballerinas that his system produced, one of the most respected teachers at the School of American Ballet has said, "We didn't teach them; they taught us." And she named Allegra Kent, Suzanne Farrell, Patricia McBride, and Gelsey Kirkland. Technique spreads like an infection among the young. Creativity is not without violence. But institutionalized violence is not what ballet is about. Another teacher of renown, visiting New York recently, remarked that today's SAB graduates were incomparably better trained than the dancers of a generation ago. Farrell danced on the largest scale from the smallest base seen up to that time. But she was a pathfinder. Her early training wasn't adequate to the strains of her technique. Today, it is possible to train girls to absorb those stresses. This is Farrell's own legacy, lodged in the canonical roles. And it will be dislodged only when the next Farrell comes along.

—February 22, 1988

Dimming the Lights

The New York City Ballet season that closed last week was not lacking in drama. A great star whose career had ended returned in glory to a beloved role; a rising young dancer stepped out of the corps, took over a major role on short notice, and danced it like a ballerina; the leading young prima of the Bolshoi Ballet made guest appearances, mastered the intricacies of a Balanchine adagio, and surged to victory in *Symphony in C*. None of these against-the-odds triumphs could have been predicted when the post-*Nutcracker* repertory season began. None were even scheduled to take place. Suzanne Farrell's long-hoped-for comeback performances were in doubt until she actually stepped onto the stage in *Vienna Waltzes*. Margaret Tracey had danced a few prominent roles and was beginning to be spoken of as a ballerina candidate, but without a cancellation in *Square Dance* she might not have had a chance this season to show what she could do with a big Balanchine role. The new cultural climate in the Soviet Union allowed Nina Ananiashvili and Andris Liepa to apply for permission to stage *Apollo*, which they had learned on videotape. They came to New York—another unheard-of freedom—to learn Balanchine style, and found themselves cast twice together in *Raymonda Variations* and twice separately in *Symphony in C*. No one expected more of them than a polite, newsmaking effort; milestones of this sort are irrelevant if not actually impertinent to the way NYCB conducts its affairs. And Liepa's performances were not in fact much more than politely enthusiastic. He learned a fair number of steps, a modicum of style, and firmly pushed away the rest, a dinner guest on a diet. Ananiashvili, though, attacked her roles, especially that of the second-movement ballerina in *Symphony in C*, like a starved cat with a platter of crème fraîche. She danced every step, and did it as well as she could in the Balanchine style, giving herself over completely to a different tradition, a new aesthetic. Evidently, Ananiashvili is not the complacent Bolshoi beauty she seemed to be—she's a real artist in desperate need of stimulation.

These revelations—Farrell, Tracey, Ananiashvili—are what the record-keepers will remember the season by. There were other events: Kyra Nichols's return to *Allegro Brillante*, her spectacular performance in *Diamonds*, her continuing brilliance in *Walpurgisnacht Ballet*, *Raymonda Variations*, and other repertory roles; Maria Calegari's important débuts in *Chaconne* and the second movement of *Symphony in C*, bringing to those ballets glamorous presence and illuminating style; Peter Boal's quietly elegant dancing and partnering of Tracey in *Square Dance*, making him a likely Apollo; the apparently unending appeal of Patricia McBride's performing in her old roles—wild, willful, spotty, but always alive, powered (as it sometimes seemed) by nothing more than a rapturous love of dancing. It would be a rare NYCB season that did not bring forth its quota of promising débuts and impressively sustained good performances in roles major and minor; I will mention some later. One measures seasonal progress by how closely related such gratifications appear to be to the ongoing work of the company: do they spring out of that ongoing work like flowers blooming from a carefully tended garden, or are they anomalies with no apparent logical connection to one another or to the things the company stands for?

Farrell's appearances were an undeniable thrill. But while it was wonderful to have her back, dancing in a way that confirmed her importance to the company and its life-line of style, it was also apparent that her performances had no great bearing on the way the company is dancing now. They were significant to Farrell's career and its symbolism. In the same way, McBride's performances belonged only to McBride. What is broadly significant just now is the extent to which the younger generation—the last dancers who were developed by Balanchine and who now lead the com-pany—has been able to assimilate and standardize the precedents that Farrell, McBride, and other great dancers contributed to the making of company style. Such standard-ization is necessary if there is to be new growth, and now, in Balanchine's absence, much depends on the creative intu-ition of the dancers who have inherited the repertory. Kyra Nichols's success in this regard was the mainstay of the win-ter season. Other principal women—first Merrill Ashley, then Calegari and Darci Kistler—succumbed to injury or in-disposition. And while we could be grateful for Nichols's steadfastness we could also thank the string of cancella-tions and uncertainties that made possible Calegari's two big débuts, Tracey and Boal in *Square Dance*, and such sel-dom seen spectacles as Nichols and Calegari together in *Brahms/Handel* and *Kammermusik*. What is creative intu-ition without the freedom to exercise it? Nichols in *Dia-*

monds—the performance of the season—was a replacement. Were it not for an emergency, would we have seen it at all? More striking, even, than these events was the fact of their taking place by chance, against an increasingly blurred and grayish background of routine. The fortuitous or anomalous nature of nearly every good thing that happened this winter at NYCB makes the entire season seem an anomaly in retrospect. For the first time since Balanchine's death, the company didn't appear to know how it got where it is, or where it was going.

The business of a ballet company is not to keep dancers busy dancing; it is to keep them dancing in a right relation to the repertory, so that each generation serves as a model of style for the next. This is true even in companies that haven't as much at stake stylistically as NYCB. The strangeness of the casting during the past season was a subject of much comment among ballet regulars. Balanchine's own casting policy was amply recalled. Of course, Balanchine didn't really have a policy—he had judgment and taste, and he had an aesthetic. He never went in for the typecasting favored by other companies, and his creative anti-typecasting made us patient with his experiments. Often a square plug would be cast in a round hole in order to soften the edges; Balanchine would temporarily sacrifice a ballet to get a better dancer. Sometimes he would square the hole—make over a role for the differing capacities of dancers he liked. And sometimes his choices were simply inscrutable. He would let an outrageous performance go on and on, until the only possible conclusion seemed to be that he didn't care, either for the ballet or for the dancer. (A more reasonable explanation is that he saw the problem in a complicated way and couldn't solve it by merely removing the dancer.) But nothing Balanchine did in his most perverse moments resulted in more than minor harm or passing self-contradiction. His casting was centered in values, consistently so; if you were shocked by his use of this or that dancer in certain roles, his next use of that dancer—or his principled nonuse—would usually clarify the situation. Assuming that the company is still operating on Balanchine's model, let us look at some of the more peculiar casting of the season:

Merrill Ashley in *Chaconne*. The Balanchine who cast Ashley experimentally and, as it turned out, productively in *Swan Lake* and *Emeralds* and also in such Farrell roles as *Diamonds* and *Union Jack* might plausibly wonder what she is doing here. The sensuousness of the first pas de deux, the wit of the second one, and the rococo rounds of the variations are things Ashley converts into dry stylistic exercises. The simplicity of the choreography in the finale defeats her. Ashley was the first of the company's ballerinas to see that taking over a Farrell role successfully didn't mean imitating Farrell, or even developing a different "interpretation"—it meant listening to the music. But here Balanchine's musical impulses as expressed through Farrell have reached their end point of ineffability. The forthright power of Ashley can do nothing with them. She is right, though, to have insisted on making the experiment. Current casting tends to relegate dancers to blandly suitable roles. Ashley gets the "steppy" ones—*Gounod Symphony*, *Concerto Barocco*, *Kammermusik*. And she responds appropriately. But any dancer of mettle longs to be liberated from appropriate roles.

Maria Calegari in *Suite No. 3* (Élégie) and *Variations pour une Porte et un Soupir*. Two "appropriate" roles, and minor ones at that. Calegari is the great romantic ballerina of her generation, with potentially the broadest range, but her career remains uneasily suspended between soloist and bal-

lerina roles. I thought she gave an uncharacteristically distracted performance in *Liebeslieder Walzer*, but that could
have been from the strain of her hastily scheduled début in
Chaconne, which she danced the same night. And by then
she was having bad luck. A new conductor had ruined her
first *Agon* of the season (she was dancing the pas de deux,
for a change); then Otto Neubert, her partner, nearly ruined her début in the second movement of *Symphony in C*.
She made a fine showing despite Neubert and the fact that
she'd been dancing off form since *The Nutcracker*. She was
even more persuasive in *Chaconne*, but it was the last *Chaconne* of the season. A début in a role of this magnitude deserves a sequel. And the role deserves Calegari performing
from strength.

Otto Neubert in *Symphony in C*, *Concerto Barocco*,
Walpurgisnacht, *Emeralds*. David Otto in *Emeralds* and *The
Nutcracker*. Current casting policy calls for leaving dancers
in roles forever whether they are successful or not. And
there is apparently a clause called "Politique des cavaliers"
(subclause "des Ottos"), which holds that men who can't be
soloists must be made to partner even though they aren't
good partners. Neubert has made life perilous for every ballerina in the company, and like David Otto he remains ob-
stinately detached while he partners, a man made of wood.
The Balanchine cavalier does more than walk a woman
through her part. He must know her moves as well as or
better than she knows them herself, and must place himself
intelligently and imaginatively as well as functionally at her
service. The whole man participates; in the course of a single pas de deux (see *Agon*) or a single ballet (see *Emeralds*),
he can be anything from dream lover to sexual counselor to
wise and forbearing friend. The ballet stage is like real life:
girls grow up more quickly than boys and have to wait for

partners to mature. The problem is exacerbated by the complexity of Balanchine's partnering roles, which he was creating right up to the end; and when you add in the loss over the past five years of the men who used to dance those roles—Peter Martins, Helgi Tomasson, Joseph Duell, Jacques and Christopher d'Amboise, and now Sean Lavery—you get a state of chronic emergency. To fill the void, experienced young men are regularly brought in from distant parts and put through fiery baptisms (*The Nutcracker* or *Theme and Variations* as a rule) while company cadets slowly, slowly grow up. One reason for the delay may be that straight partnering roles are disdained; they fall by default to the lunks. But, whether he dances or not, the male partner in Balanchine must have unusual finesse. Lindsay Fischer, the latest young import, is more responsive—he's plastic wood. And perhaps there is hope for Neubert since he brought Ananiashvili through *Symphony in C*. Adam Lüders, currently the partner of choice, looked overworked and underpowered nearly every time I saw him this season. It would be dramatic to say that he has sacrificed his dancing to his partnering, but that, alas, is not the case.

Lauren Hauser in *Rubies*. The soloist role was made on a tall, long-limbed, high-tension dancer, Patricia Neary. It contains an extended exit that is all lines and angles. Hauser is so thoroughly miscast—physically, technically, and temperamentally—that it is hard to see how the experience could be of any benefit to her. Except for Nichols's resplendent *Diamonds*, it was a bad year for *Jewels*. *Emeralds* receded into obscurity, and *Rubies* finally collapsed. Ib Andersen has loosened up a lot since he first took the Villella role, but his elfin charm seemed ground under by the ballet's velocity and force. McBride's worst imprecisions occurred in *Rubies*. She kept things large and lively, though;

you could see the sense of the choreography—something you couldn't do in the performance of her alternate.

Heather Watts in *Rubies*, *Agon*, *Stravinsky Violin Concerto*, *Bugaku*. Watts performs all these mostly Stravinsky roles as if they were forerunners of *Ecstatic Orange*. Until Peter Martins gave her a hit in this modishly brutal pop-style piece, it was possible to see Watts more or less as she seemed to see herself: loyal, hardworking, unfairly maligned (because of her close long-time friendship with Martins). If she wasn't the most interesting dancer in the company, she wasn't a threat, either. Even after Martins made her a star with his Stravinsky Centennial ballet, in 1982, she could still dance with responsibility and taste, if not much scope or allure, and since she was dancing a lot of Balanchine parts one waited to see what she would do with them. Watts is just the kind of smart nervy dancer who can be so affecting when touched with divinity in Balanchine's ballets. But I waited in vain for the tongue of flame to descend upon the head of Heather Watts. What she began doing with her Balanchine roles was leaving out steps, simplifying what she couldn't put over. Then she began interpreting the ballets, usually according to some sexy stereotype or other. Soon she was a mannered, facile "star," no longer just a limited dancer in beyond her depth.

As the winter season showed, Watts performs so many roles so often that she has been able to effect what amounts to a wholesale change in the repertory, reducing the roles to suit her qualifications. *Rubies* and *Agon* are complex and delicate creations that Watts has made over into glib personal vehicles. When, as sometimes happens, another dancer performs *Agon*—Calegari or Stephanie Saland—you can still see the shrunken shape and coarse texture that Watts has given it. Watts used to be rather good in *Rubies*, back in the days when she was dancing it with Baryshnikov, though she never suggested the showgirl innocence that McBride did and still does. Now she brings to it an insolence, a cheesiness worthy of the Paris Opéra or Béjart. Even *Bugaku*, which might well have been a Balanchine gift to the Opéra or to Béjart, is drained of its fragile vagrant ironies and made to sell a fanged feminist message. Watts's nerviness doesn't really extend to her dancing. She's good at sniffing out the subtext of a ballet and brandishing "meanings" in place of an honest dance performance. In "Voices of Spring" (in *Vienna Waltzes*), the moment of angst when she repeats pas couru, dragging one foot and covering her eyes, is absurd, especially compared with the utterly weightless emotion McBride gives it. (The gesture is no more angst-ridden here than in other McBride roles—*Brahms-Schoenberg Quartet* and *A Midsummer Night's Dream*.) In *Bugaku*, Watts uses the hyperextended joints that got her this Allegra Kent role to suggest that the geisha's contortions are a metaphor for sexual subjugation. In Kent's performance, extreme hyperextension was a comment on and a further source of her extreme delectability of movement. One wouldn't expect the same effect of Watts, but one might have hoped for a version that wasn't so insistently reductive of the tensions inherent in the role. With Watts, you "read" the ballet in terms of one earnestly titillating metaphor. It's persuasive in its simpleminded, point-scoring way—so much so that no newcomer I talk to believes Balanchine's ballet could ever have been any different. Ironically, the subtleties that have been drained away made it a more powerfully feminist as well as a more powerfully erotic work.

And then there was *Stravinsky Violin Concerto*, in the worst shape I have ever seen it, with Watts and Lourdes

Lopez and Jock Soto and Lüders. This was dancing of a kind and quality we aren't used to at New York City Ballet. As for the Watts versions of *Concerto Barocco* and *Symphony in C*, one must start with the fact that she isn't strong enough physically for the long classical adagios. Even if she were a more musical dancer than she is, she would be unable to fill out time and space on the scale to which this choreography is accustomed. And as her most recent performances show, her turnout is now so slack that she's expressionless below the waist. She dances *Rubies* as if turnout didn't matter, but it does matter to the inflected turned-in positions that are all through the piece, the source of much of its humor. Watts's winter-season repertory was the largest of any ballerina's except Nichols's, with Watts getting the greater share of the best roles—*Agon*, *Concerto Barocco*, *Symphony in C*, *Liebeslieder*, and *La Sonnambula*. There wasn't one that she left alive.

Of course, all this implicates Martins and must discredit him in the eyes of his dancers, who can see perfectly well that Heather Watts is not the equal of Kyra Nichols, and who see also that while Nichols and the other principal women wait for decent partners Watts has Jock Soto playing up to her in nearly every ballet (very often to the detriment of his own performance). For those of us on the outside, trying to understand what is going on isn't like reading Balanchine's old tea leaves. Balanchine had his pets, but none of them were ever as egregious as Heather Watts. Yes, it was Balanchine who appointed her a principal dancer in the first place. Thinking back to those days, though, I seem to recall that Watts functioned mostly as a utility ballerina, much as Lopez does today. Because Watts never got injured, she amassed a huge repertory. And she still never gets injured. A harassed company director needs depend-

able dancers. Perhaps he also needs to believe that Solo-
monic solutions exist to perpetual problems of casting. It
looks as though the prize roles of the Balanchine repertory
have been parceled out to the top ladies according to seniority or to fixed notions of type. And these ladies have exclu-
sionary rights, at least until they get injured. But what does
this do to the ballets? A casting policy may solve problems
for the director, but it isn't necessarily the most creative way
to run a company. Evening after evening went by this winter without excitement, without surprise, because the casting was so dull. The company hardly ever appeared at full
strength the way it used to—all evening long, several
evenings a week. I had the continual feeling that a good
portion of its riches were sunk somewhere out of view, perhaps to surface the next night, or next week, or next season.
New soloists were still being produced; wonderful dancing
was still being done at corps level. And it was all as if none
of it really mattered.

The closing night of the winter season has been for the
past few years a benefit for the Dancers' Emergency Fund.
This year, the program brought out many of the season's
good dancers: Judith Fugate, who had done well in "Voices
of Spring" and *Emeralds*; Carlo Merlo, who had been in
Emeralds and *La Sonnambula*; Nichol Hlinka and Lauren
Hauser and Melinda Roy, of *Walpurgisnacht*; and the entire
cast of *Raymonda Variations*. The *Corsaire* pas de deux with
the Bolshoi guest stars got the most applause. This was a
hard moment to sit through in the State Theater, with Balanchine's company waiting in the wings. The final movement of *Diamonds* closed the bill, with Nichols partnered by
Lüders and with Robert Irving conducting. New York City
Ballet style—complex musicality, simple presentation—is
just the opposite of the Bolshoi's. And Nichols, who is our

"Russian" ballerina, could not have been more nobly authoritative. In glittering white, she rose toward us on a stream of music from a stage filled with people. And we looked at her as we were meant to, and as we will again and again—with hope.

—March 7, 1988

Crises

In a 1948 essay called "The Crisis of the Easel Picture," the art critic Clement Greenberg described the change in pictorial composition in modernist painting in terms that some people now think are too narrow. However that may be, they are terms that are analogous to dance and helped at the time to explain (and possibly to influence) certain developments in choreography. The easel picture, Greenberg begins by saying, "subordinates decorative to dramatic effect. It cuts the illusion of a boxlike cavity into the wall behind it, and within this, as a unity, it organizes three-dimensional semblances." The tendency of the Impressionists, he went on, was to reduce depth and to treat every part of the picture "with the same kind and emphasis of touch." But, though the pictures went on getting shallower, Cézanne, van Gogh, Gauguin, Bonnard, and Matisse retained the convention of dominant shapes and light-dark color contrasts. This—the sine qua non, Greenberg said, of the easel picture—was what was threatened by Monet's later painting, "and now, twenty years after Monet's death, his practice has become the point of departure for a new tendency in painting." Greenberg didn't call this new tendency Abstract Expressionism; he called it American-Type Painting, a title under which, in another essay, he discussed the work of Gorky, de Kooning, Hofmann, Motherwell, Pollock, and others.

Substitute for the "boxlike cavity" the classical proscenium stage. Substitute for Cézanne & Company certain passages in Fokine (the orgy in *Schéhérazade*, the fair in *Petrushka*) and the ballets of Nijinsky (*L'Après-midi d'un Faune*, *Le Sacre du Printemps*). The result is the beginning of a parallel that culminates in the radical aesthetic of the Monet of dance, Merce Cunningham. The relationship of Cunningham's *Summerspace* (1958) to *Faune*, a ballet in which Nijinsky actually reduced stage depth and flattened the body to a silhouette, was underlined by Robert Rauschenberg's stippled backcloth and costumes—as clear a reference to Impressionist painting as Bakst's landscape for *Faune* was to Fauvism. Cunningham's dancers were made to inhabit an Impressionist landscape (what Greenberg described as an "evenly and tightly textured rectangle of paint"), and although Cunningham's stage was not without depth, it was remarkably without perspective in the classical sense. The classic stage box-picture has a front-and-center focus. Cunningham gave all parts of the stage equal emphasis—the choreographic equivalent of painting's shift from drama to something "close to decoration." Decentralization in choreography had already occurred—to little or no historical effect, as it turned out—in *Le Sacre*. Nijinsky's inspiration appears to have been rhythmic repetition, the main decorative element in primitive folk art. Cunningham's first spatial experiment was carried out forty years later, in *Suite by Chance*. He was then becoming interested in having his decisions as a choreographer ruled by chance—by the literal tossing of coins—and he has since written how "in applying chance to space I saw the possibility of multidirection." He has had a great many followers but no real successors. If there has been any Abstract Expressionism in dance, it has been by no one but Cunningham. In order to go beyond him, dancers had to get off the stage.

The crisis of the easel picture was the same as the crisis of the proscenium-stage picture. During the sixties and seventies, Cunningham held the stage while two generations of Cunningham-influenced radicals abjured it entirely. Whether out of principle or out of necessity hardly matters, since the whole avant-garde involvement with nonspecialized dancing in nonproscenium spaces is now dead, for the most part, or subsumed in performance art. On conspicuous and frequent occasion Cunningham himself chose to appear in nontheatrical places, thus beating his epigones at their own game. Still, one cannot help wondering how different the past quarter-century of American-type dancing would have been if more choreographers had had access to decent stages. The easel picture, as later events showed, managed to keep from falling off the wall only by becoming the wall itself—by expanding hugely in scale or evolving what Leo Steinberg has called "the flatbed picture plane." Dance, when it fell off the stage, had no recourse other than to climb back on, looking a little sheepish about its various survival strategies, such as being bracketed with star designers and star composers or being produced by ballet companies, for whom the crisis of the proscenium stage never existed.

Though Cunningham does not perform to music, his special mastery of abstraction has often depended on quasi-musical structure—on the recurrence of elements and their apt progression or variation within set limits. The limits vary from piece to piece, but usually his control of them has been strict; when it has been *very* strict, as in *Duets* or *Quartet* or *Pictures* or *Fabrications*, we say "That's a real *piece*," meaning that we sense in it a consistency of design and a quality—a kind of consciousness—that is whole and distinct. The Cunningham season just past offered three new works. By abandoning strict quasi-musical methods of composition, Cunningham destroyed the unity of each of his new pieces and drew our attention to the connections between them. In *Five Stone Wind*, *Cargo X*, and *Field and Figures*, events seemed to overflow from one piece into another, and these were not merely formal events or ways of moving that one is used to seeing in Cunningham's work; they were specific and unusual "created" events and uncustomary ways of moving. I found my concentration being stretched to the breaking point, especially by *Five Stone Wind*, which is fifty-five minutes long. This ruminative work isn't dense or heavy—not at all. Moment by moment, it is Cunningham at his most playful. In a particularly charming trio (Victoria Finlayson, Robert Swinston, Alan Good), the men take turns steadying the woman in balances, then hopping away like hares, with a curious switch of the feet in the air. A moment later, Kimberly Bartosik, a slight but strong, youthful-looking dancer, covers the stage with tiny running steps. She is succeeded by Emma Diamond, moving sideways at the same speed and scooting along on one toe. By the time Carol Teitelbaum enters, in rapid chassés, you know you are seeing one of Cunningham's special events. And, indeed, the "wind devils," as I came to call them, recurred not only in *Five Stone Wind* but in *Field and Figures*. But when they recurred, it was without emphasis and without reference to any other repetitions or gestures of unification. Something less than a motif yet something more than passagework, they were fragments of a puzzle which I had only begun to put together when the season ended. In memory, though, the three new pieces seem very like a triptych, and Cunningham's whole operation seems very like that of a painter who spreads his latest work before us—work in which current obsessions move from one canvas to the next.

The "five" in *Five Stone Wind*, Cunningham has said, is the five directions in which the choreographer focuses movement on the stage (or off it); "stone" and "wind" refer to notions of fixity and velocity. The work was conceived in two overlapping parts and was first presented in its entirety last year, on the outdoor stage at Avignon. For interior performances, Mark Lancaster designed a simple hanging of colored ropes against a softly glowing purple drop. Without a designer of Lancaster's subtlety and originality, I think, not even Cunningham would have dared such slow Monet-like mutation and attenuation for such a length of time. As an exercise in duration, it is the most deliberate challenge that Cunningham has yet issued; it may be his *Water Lilies*. Buttressed and amplified, as it seems to be, by the two other works, it yet stands apart—from them and from the repertory as a whole.

You can see all of a painting at once; you can't see all of a dance at once. In *Field and Figures*, you'd get to watch one thing—a trio, say—just long enough to form an impression; then you'd jump to another trio or a quartet. Frequently, there would come "washes"—the rest of the company rushing in and out, leaving one unit working. *Field and Figures* has a painter's title and a painterly décor reminiscent of *Summerspace*, with dancers and scenery blending into each other. The backcloth's horizontal gray stripes and vertical red bands were echoed in the costumes (the designers were Kristin Jones and Andrew Ginzel). The jumpy continuity of the piece wasn't so unusual for Cunningham that one couldn't adjust to it. What was unusual was the powerful presence of one trio and one dancer (Finlayson, who was very much a key dancer this season), and the refusal of the piece to give itself over to that presence. At one point, after we have seen her repeatedly collapsing between Robert Wood and David Kulick, Finlayson is carried on by them in an angled "crucified" position. The entrance, which is impressively staged and obviously important, corresponds to nothing else in the piece. But, like the wind devils, it is corroborated in another part of the triptych—in *Cargo X*, which contains a series of crucifixion images. *Cargo X* also contains, by way of décor, a stepladder on which the dancers place flowers. The ladder could be an altar or a burial mound, and the "X" in the title could stand for the Cross or for Christ. The martyr here is not Finlayson but Bartosik or Kristy Santimyer: both are lifted in suggestive stiff-bodied poses and one—Bartosik—is actually abused. And it may not be irrelevant that the sound score for this piece, wordless solo and choral chanting overlaid with maracas, invoked a ritualistic, prayerful, Latin American atmosphere.

Parallels to Cunningham's choreographic practice are as easily found in painting as parallels to Balanchine's are in music, but not until this season had I noticed in Cunningham a tendency to reduce or revoke temporal values in the construction of a piece. It almost seemed as if not being able to see all of a dance at once meant not seeing all of it *at all*—or not until some other dance was also seen. I've never felt more befuddled at the end of a Cunningham evening or more aware of just how unremittingly visual an experience it is. And how hard the dancers work! At the same time that

Cunningham seems to be dissolving temporal structure in his pieces, he is building up static definitions of space. The dancers who race like the wind are required to hold fixed positions of enormous difficulty, to initiate and stop movement without transition, to look simultaneously galvanized and still. It's not stasis; it's a kind of negative kinesthetics. Cunningham dancers have always had this capability, only now so much more depends on it.

Robert Rauschenberg was Cunningham's artistic adviser and main scenic designer from 1954 to 1964. It was he who, in relating Cunningham's multidirectional use of space to modernist painting, first gave Cunningham theatre the weight and authority it enjoyed for so long in the art world. (For a while, Cunningham's artistic adviser was Jasper Johns, the artist whom Leo Steinberg primarily identifies with the flatbed picture plane.) Rauschenberg is now designing for Trisha Brown's company, which followed Cunningham's with a week of repertory at the City Center. Brown, a major post-Cunningham figure, is not a former Cunningham dancer; her style has nothing of his emphasis on lifted carriage and articulated feet, and her ideas about space are ambivalent. She is Cunningham's disciple, however, in her method of collaboration with painters and composers.

There is a musical tradition in modern dance—it extends from Paul Taylor to Twyla Tharp to Mark Morris—but Brown has never been part of this or of the pseudo-musical minimalist tradition, either. She worked mainly in silence and commissioned her first score in 1981. For Brown music is entirely ancillary. She came to it, she says, because "not having music reduced the audience's ability to see the work. I knew it and kept asking myself: Do you want them to see the work?" But this viewer isn't always helped by Brown's music. On the contrary, it's because I *can* hear them that I can't see the pieces with scores by Robert Ashley or Peter Zummo. I can get through *Set and Reset* (Laurie Anderson), and silence isn't so bad; this was the season that I fell in love with *Opal Loop*. Brown's latest piece, *Astral Convertible*, sounds like Andrew Lloyd Webber with teeth; it has music by Richard Landry coming from somewhere and interacting with elements of the set, which is by Rauschenberg.

It's hard to tell whether, generally speaking, Brown has absorbed or rejected the idea of multidirectional focus. In her group pieces she uses a little bit of space here, a little there; the stage is a grid webbed by runs or long traveling lifts. The broad planes and distances of Cunningham are not for her. Brown matured as a choreographer during the anti-proscenium years, dancing, like so many of her colleagues, in lofts, churches, gyms, and parks. (Cunningham, so far as I know, never said to these people, "You are all a loft generation," but he might well have.) Rauschenberg's function, and that of other designers Brown has worked with, seems to have been mostly to define her space for her or take up what she doesn't use. Donald Judd's décor for *Newark* (*Niweweorce*) is a set of drops that descend at different times, reducing or expanding the space Brown has to move in. These "visual presentations" have a life of their own, and in Rauschenberg's case "visual" doesn't begin to cover it. He uses lights, movies, sound; he stages an independent attraction. In *Astral Convertible* he put aluminum scaffolds around the stage and rigged them with lights and sensors that were supposed to react to the dancers' movements. As these things so often do, the set turned out to have more force as an idea than as an experience. Nevertheless, it was a striking, a daunting, affair, and what's interesting is that

Brown's contribution wasn't overwhelmed by it. And her choreography was organized in such a way as to make more use of the stage, with broader contrasts in the size and shape of movement, with clear foreground and background distinctions, and even a bit of soloist-and-corps diversity. (Brown, following Cunningham, has tended to treat all her dancers as soloists.) Yet it was still pure Trisha Brown. One wonders whether her work would have looked anything like this fifteen years ago if she'd staged it in theatres. (In 1975, in one of her loft concerts, she presented *Locus*, a six-sided examination of cubic space.) One wonders, too, whether the practice of the last few years, bringing choreographers of talent but scant theatrical technique to work on big proscenium stages, hasn't actually changed our way of seeing movement in that kind of space and opened up further possibilities within the conventional stage picture. Wouldn't it be strange if, after more than thirty-five years of Cunningham virtuosity, it turned out to be the multidirectional stage that was in crisis?

—April 3, 1989

Sun and Shade

In 1987, having worked on it for six years, Paul Taylor published his autobiography, *Private Domain*. It was a highly professional job, like all Taylor productions, and gratifying in many respects. Without exactly explaining the phenomenon of Paul Taylor, it told us much about his interior life and about some of the external circumstances that may have affected the direction of his work. But to anyone who knows that work there was a certain discomfort with the book's level of talk. Some choreographers who regularly publish their writings—Agnes de Mille, Murray Louis— flourish their critical opinions. Taylor submerged his. As a writer, he was more of a novelist; his main energies went into the construction of scenes and conversations, into character sketches and tart, keep-it-lively descriptions. He handled the introspective stuff less well and made only the most dutiful connections between his life and work. He doesn't really know why he became a dancer, he says, but he recalls having a "flash" as he was devising nonvocal dialogue for a puppet theatre he was given as a boy. Jiggling the strings of his marionettes would produce an agitation that he thinks may have paved the way for the unbearable spasms that shake his dancers in *Last Look*. (As if this weren't prosaic enough, Taylor refers to *Last Look* as "a dance of alienation.") More striking is the thrill he tells us he felt whenever he raised the puppet theatre's cardboard curtain: "The expectance was like that felt on picturing the future of some exotic flower's bud before full bloom exposes it to the realities of aphids." No one but Taylor could have written that frighteningly extended sentence. Just as it is Taylor's hand that jiggles the marionettes' strings, it is Taylor's eye that sees flowers blooming only to be devastated by aphids.

Well do we know the workings of that eye: *Private Domain* (the dance), *Big Bertha*, *Dust*, *Nightshade*, *Last Look*, and now *Speaking in Tongues*, the latest addition to the catalogue, encompass terrors that no other choreographer has set before us. Taylor's book, a mixture of conscious art and offhand revelation, is a tricky thing to negotiate. What one takes away from it is the impressions Taylor worked to convey—the dog's life he endured in twenty years of touring, the time he nearly froze to death on the street after a glamorous opening night, the ordeal he underwent as his dancing career came to an end. It wasn't until I read the book a second time that I noticed that Edgewater Beach, the Maryland community where he summered as a child, is divided into two sections, Sunnyside and Shadyside. The author tells us this in passing, but mightn't the same be said of his sensibility? The black works that I've cited are balanced by innumerable bright and buoyant pieces, mostly set to Baroque music. And between the brightest and the blackest comes the whole range of middle Taylor, in which sun and shade are mixed in unpredictable amounts. Even at the black end of the scale, Taylor is sometimes able, as in *Big Bertha*, to show us the whole flower before it is ravaged by aphids. Rarely—*Last Look* is the greater for being so exceptional a vision—does he show us no bloom at all.

Speaking in Tongues is also an exception to the run of Taylor's work, but not in the way you might think. When I heard that Taylor had made an hour-long piece about Jimmy Swaggart, I thought, Uh-oh, Taylor must have something up his sleeve. Religion, bodied forth in symbols or cloaked in movement metaphors, is a subject he has explored before, often satirically. But Taylor has never been flippant about religion, and the peculiar dualism of his moral imagination seemed more than accommodating to Swaggart and his troubles. It is a question whether his musical imagination was stimulated by Matthew Patton's tape score. A young composer previously unknown to Taylor, Patton blends sonics and instruments in a sleekly impressionistic style that sounds to me like high-grade movie music. Chords burst and drift, prepared pianos plunk out hymn tunes, a shimmering haze of evocation envelops each of the score's eleven episodes. The titles for these episodes—"Loomings," "In December," "Book of Wishing"—appear not to have played a part in Taylor's calculations, but a prominent feature of the score is the half-audible voice of Swaggart rising out of the sonic mists together with crowd noise and applause. He repeats a sentence that we never hear distinctly and that wouldn't make sense if we could hear it: "Their blood will I require at your hands." In similarly cryptic fashion, Santo Loquasto has designed a backcloth of horizontal yellow planks densely hand-lettered with what seem to be biblical slogans or quotes from Swaggart's speeches. They aren't there to be read, and anyway you can't read them and watch the dancing at the same time.

All this is meant, I think, to suggest an abiding but not awesome mystery—a kind of senselessness that passeth understanding. And Taylor's choreography can't be said to probe too deeply into the murk. Although in his book Taylor professes to have no interest in religion, in his art he has expressed a religious world view. The sense in which I apply the word "dualism" to his work is the theological sense: the theory of good and evil existing as equal forces in the world. *Speaking in Tongues* offers us the usual Taylor compound of light and dark—the Man of the Cloth, who is at the center of things, is neither hero nor villain—but it's the darkness at the heart of the ballet's conception that is the real mystery here. The piece doesn't penetrate because it is too literally conceived as a study of a man and his congregation.

Taylor, a genius of figurative compression, has here all but abandoned metaphor and gone in for a newfangled expressionism that fills the stage with recognizable character types. The trouble is, they *stay* types. Since Taylor forswears his usual poetic concision for this new-old mode, we expect him to develop depth by means of dramaturgy, and he doesn't really do that. It's as if he had entered the world of Eugene O'Neill and then cautiously backed out. The preacher divided against himself, the confused flock with depraved or disturbed members and one bright angel who succors them all—the subject may be right for expressionistic treatment, but by Taylor? *Speaking in Tongues* sounds platitudinous as I describe it, and coming from this complex and inscrutable poet, this maestro of the infernal, it *is* platitudinous. I feel about it the way I feel whenever Ted Koppel takes up TV evangelism on *Nightline*. Not that Koppel's reporting isn't shrewd and sagacious. But it's easy for him to be shrewd and sagacious on this subject, and it's easy for Paul Taylor to get theatrical effects out of the same subject. Could Taylor be consciously working in the "writerly" mode in which he produced his book? Would I believe *Speaking in Tongues* if it had some such subtitle as "A Choreographer's Notebook"? I would if I thought that Taylor habitually choreographed by refining raw material to arrive at a statement, as Martha Graham appears to have done. As a statement, though, *Speaking in Tongues* flounders. Taylor hasn't managed, over the long haul (the piece actually runs fifty-two minutes), to pull the clichés inside out. Length and repetition and insistent variation don't work for him as those same strategies could work for O'Neill—to transfigure the material and irradiate it with meaning.

Of course, Taylor isn't really telling stories. He's building his own kind of illogically logical narrative, one that comes full circle, ending as it began, with a barn dance that tells us nothing, after which each member of the cast lies flat on the floor under a folded chair, which tells us nothing but that in the end we die. Because Taylor is working here with incidents and "significant" movement in place of images, his deliberate skirting of issues that crop up in the course of the piece strikes us as an evasion, and his use of violence is upsetting in the wrong way. I was stunned to see Karla Wolfangle yank Mary Cochran around, and the semistylized rape of Linda Kent by Joao Mauricio was another shock. That Taylor, of all choreographers, should be settling for graphic depictions! The enormities he can imagine are a thousand times more awful to contemplate than the ones he can report. In the same way, he can commit non sequiturs all over the place because of the brilliant subterranean sense his figurative patterns make. But *Speaking in Tongues*, the first nonfigurative drama I've known him to attempt, has nothing going for it underneath. It's an experiment that Taylor has had to suppress his daemon to make.

The Taylor company has a lot of new or newish male dancers this season, and until the men break all the way in the women are having to carry most of the dancing. They're doing beautifully. Johnson, Cochran, and Cathy McCann, who give glowingly faithful performances in *Speaking in Tongues*, also appear in *Brandenburgs*, a Bach ballet new last year. Both times I saw the piece, it seemed that none of the

three had ever danced better in her life. Each of them is a
muse to Christopher Gillis's Apollo (*Brandenburgs* is a Taylor variation on the theme of Balanchine's *Apollo*), and Mc-
Cann in particular established herself as a fount of fresh and
easy lyricism—something she has no opportunity to do as
the bright angel in *Speaking in Tongues*. Apes outnumber
and outdance angels in that piece, and normally I would
have said that they do so in any Taylor piece. But, watching
Brandenburgs, I began to think of Taylor's Baroque ballets
as his view of heaven. If *Last Look* is a vision of damnation
lying at one extreme end of the Taylor spectrum, surely it is
Esplanade that lies opposite, with its vision of communal joy
expressed in dance terms as elementary as those in *Last Look*.
In *Last Look*, people shudder and thrash, minimal souls all,
too horribly shriveled to dance. In *Esplanade*, it is the expansive purity of the movement vocabulary that exalts the
dancers; they step serenely or run, fall, roll, and slide with
all their might. Taylor has reduced movement metaphor to
mere locomotion in *Esplanade*, bare convulsion in *Last Look*,
and just these simple things are polar expressions of good
and evil.

Gillis and Elie Chaib are now Taylor's only veteran men,
and they alternated in the role of the Man of the Cloth—
Chaib more or less an ape, Gillis more or less an angel. If
I preferred Gillis, it's because his air of innocence driven
to desperation allowed for more color in the preacher's
makeup. But Chaib's baleful presence was very powerful, especially when he made a sudden entrance through the door
in the yellow wall, and the yellow seemed to blacken and
char at his appearance.

—May 1, 1989

Family Secrets

The New York City Ballet season just past broke down into two parts. The first five weeks were dominated by the spirit of Balanchine. *Mozartiana* and *Tchaikovsky Piano Concerto No. 2* and *Episodes* and *Symphony in Three Movements* cast their glow over the entire season. If these ballets hadn't been as handsomely danced as they were, the last four weeks, in which the company indulged in self-celebrations of one sort or another, would have seemed hollow.

The company doesn't always put itself forth at top strength. I'm not exactly sure why, but I think Peter Martins, as the man in charge of artists and repertory, must be bedeviled by all the top-tier ballets that have large numbers of principal roles; he has to fill those roles or else drop the ballets. It is standard New York City Ballet practice to put a number of stars in one ballet. Martins himself made *Echo* this season for four ballerinas, all of them stars; and the partners of all but one of them were principal dancers. Balanchine began this practice, of course, but what Balanchine meant by "stars" was dancers who interested him, and they could be promising corps kids as well as principals. Martins seldom jumps a corps dancer or a soloist over the head of a principal unless scarcity compels him. As a choreographer, he does little more, these days, than assert the status quo. If the four ballerinas in *Echo* had been Wendy Whelan and Santhe Tsetsilas and Kathleen and Margaret Tracey instead of Darci Kistler and Heather Watts and Kyra Nichols and Suzanne Farrell, not only wouldn't it have mattered to *Echo*, it wouldn't have mattered to the dancers, except in terms of prestige. Yes, Farrell with her artificial hip joint danced on pointe, but that, I'm afraid, was the only novelty the ballet had to show for itself. In everything else, it was willfully, even defiantly, unoriginal, a set of variations on a variation, a study in sameness and symmetry. When Balanchine or Robbins put several ballerinas into one ballet, he tried to make them all look different. But what the heck, says *Echo*, why shouldn't we celebrate how much *alike* they are? Individuality is less important than conformity to a type.

Echo came in the last weeks of the season, amid the injuries and cancellations that inevitably occur at the end of a long run of repertory. But the emotional tone had been prepared for it by the celebrations of the previous weeks. The bridge between the Balanchine series and what lay beyond was an evening devoted to a beloved ballerina, Patricia McBride, who had just announced her retirement. The occasion was a dramatic contrast to the restaging of Martins's ballet *A Fool for You* for a "Live from Lincoln Center" telecast. *A Fool for You* had been the climax of last summer's American Music Festival, with which the company marked its fortieth anniversary, but in *A Fool for You*, New York City Ballet itself was not the subject. As in so many of the festival's special events, the company stepped aside and let something else take the spotlight—American Music, American Painting, American Modern Dance—and then Martins

ended it all with a forty-minute ballet to Ray Charles songs,
sung and played by Ray Charles in person, backed up by his
band and his singers, the Raeletts. Martins wished, he said,
to commemorate the music he had grown up with, so
Charles delivered songs he had recorded twenty and thirty
years ago. The telecast commemorated Martins's commemoration; once again, an exhausted and spiritless Charles re-
hashed the hits of his prime, and classical dancers scooted
about like the juveniles they were not and never had been.
(When Charles recorded "Hit the Road Jack" and "What'd I
Say," Heather Watts and Judith Fugate and Stephanie Saland were lined up at the barre practicing tendues.)

On both sides of *A Fool for You* were Balanchine ballets—*Episodes* and *Cortège Hongrois*—which weren't tele-
vised. To the officials at PBS, this wasn't a New York City
Ballet event; it was a Ray Charles event. It brought into the
theatre an audience that had also grown up with Ray
Charles and that left the minute his act was over. The nearly
four-hour-long tribute to McBride brought in an audience
that had grown up at New York City Ballet, that recognized
each of her former partners as he walked out onstage and
presented her with flowers (a long list headed by Martins,
Edward Villella, Mikhail Baryshnikov, and Jean-Pierre
Bonnefoux, McBride's husband), and that stayed and applauded through call after call taken by the ballerina as red
roses rained from the galleries. If last year the company
opened its gates and let everybody in "to see how things
might look," as Martins put it to the interviewer John
Gruen, this year it closed itself off and gazed inward. The
annual spring gala honored Jerome Robbins, and it included a family joke: the "Mistake Waltz," from *The Concert*, danced by the company's leading ballerinas. The big
Robbins event of the season, though, was Nichols's début

in *In Memory of . . .* , turning what originally (in 1985) seemed to be an idiosyncratic Farrell role into a dramatically powerful personal statement. Farrell's presence throughout much of this moistly elegiac piece had undermined its conventionality; Nichols's presence elevated it. Lacking Farrell's extremes, she endowed the role with a calmly expansive center, an even, unelliptical, onrolling force. The ballet became less a metaphysical vision and more a drama about a heroic woman who is the last to succumb to some unspecified universal catastrophe. Unfortunately, with Nichols looking palpably alive and well, the seraphic final scene seemed frailer than ever, depriving her of the ovation she deserved.

Ballerina technique may actually be at a higher level now than it was when Balanchine was alive. Watching Nichols in this latest début, watching Kistler in *Swan Lake* or Merrill Ashley in *Ballade* and *A Midsummer Night's Dream*, I see each of them working to integrate head, arms, and torso in more continuously vivid terms relative to the lower body. When this next stage in the development of technique is consolidated, it will have been the ballerinas themselves who, feeling about in their roles, made it possible; neither Robbins nor Martins choreographs for that sort of thing.

Partners are still a problem. Robert Hill, formerly of American Ballet Theatre, has been signed to partner Nichols; the two appeared together in *Echo*, while Kistler was paired with Jeppe Mydtskov, the *very* tall Danish dancer who joined the company a couple of years ago. Hill and Mydtskov partner well, but not like men who can keep up with their forward-looking ballerinas. The company is growing up. It no longer waits for obvious interpretive goals to be set for it by its directors. Along with technique, there has been an improvement in company morale. You can see it in *Western Symphony*; the high-spirited choreography is once again getting its full due from the dancers. (For years, *Western* was a like a party where the host, Balanchine, was the only one having fun.) The sheer sensuous pleasure that dancers take in dancing is a pleasure for the audience, too.

Sensuous pleasure in dancing is Kistler's personal discovery, or so it seemed this season. As Alastair Macaulay wrote here last summer, "her dancing has a subtle and fascinating range of contrasts: blushing audacity, delicacy and hugeness, grandeur and intimacy, sweetness and abandon."* And she is now twice as strong, varied and surprising as she was then. This was Kistler's season. Until now, her position among the company's ballerinas had been something of a puzzle. Was she going to break the mold or ignore it? Kistler's mold-breaking potential gave her performances this season a breathlessly suspenseful quality. She would carry us beyond the limits of the corporate ballerina style and then quietly return; she would plunge ahead to some radiantly indeterminate future or draw back and reclaim the past. Kistler could go on tantalizing us this way for years—it would be wonderful. But it would be even more wonderful if new choreography could help show her the way. Kistler at the moment does what she does by herself.

If the dancers are starting to show some initiative, it may be because they no longer feel the weight of authority looming over them. Robbins rehearsed Nichols in *In Memory of . . .* , although he is officially on a leave of absence. This puts Martins in complete charge of the company and the company's new choreography, but as I contemplate what that may mean an image from a Robbins ballet comes

The New Yorker, July 11, 1988.

to mind. Toward the end of *Interplay*, the two competing teams of dancers send their women spinning downstage— four women, each tossing off a perfect string of chaînés, while the men behind them sweep the air forward, urging them on. In *Echo* Martins does something like that. He sends all of his ballerinas out on the same little chaîné trip, only he has them do it one at a time and at widely spaced intervals. In between, they do a lot of other similar things, similarity being the keynote of the ballet. The reason the chaîné sequences are so noticeable is that the dancers have to turn their legs out to do them, and just about every other movement they make is turned in. *Echo* tells us that Martins thinks of his ballerinas as girls who come out of the same mold all looking alike. But why do they all look like *this*? Is Martins trying to accommodate a ballerina with an artificial hip, or is he trying to remake the mold?

The American Music Festival received the worst reviews in the company's history. By commissioning pieces from outsiders, like Paul Taylor, Lar Lubovitch, Eliot Feld, Laura Dean, and William Forsythe, Martins had hoped, as he also told Gruen, to show off his dancers' versatility. Perhaps he thought, too, that each of these choreographers would present him with a different view of the company—would reappraise the gifts of NYCB dancers in fresh terms. Instead, the outsiders elected to produce self-portraits, coopting NYCB dancers for choreography that could just as easily have been produced elsewhere (and has been, in some cases). Along with all this designer-label choreography, Martins has retained his own *Black & White* and Richard Tanner's *Sonatas and Interludes*, two ballets that featured the familiar team of Heather Watts and Jock Soto and the chic attitudes that Watts and Soto specialize in projecting. To dance historians I leave the task of deciding which came first, Martins's chicken or Tanner's egg. The same two choreographers were involved in the creation of *Calcium Light Night*, back in 1977—the ballet that set Martins's future as a choreographer and Watts's style as a ballerina, and served as the (possibly unconscious) inspiration for the entire American Music Festival. But by the time of the festival Watts's technique had become something other than what it had been in 1977. Whatever else the saucy attitudes stood for, they were now a cover for technical infirmities. Watts turned her legs in and angled her knees and flipped her wrists, and she had Soto for the long, oversupported partnering sequences that everybody said were so sexy.

It's unlikely that any of the outsiders' ballets, or even his own other festival pieces, hold the same place in Martins's estimation that *Black & White* and *Sonatas and Interludes* do. These two ballets were his and Tanner's attempts to put Watts and Soto over as company figureheads, incredible as that may seem. I can't believe that Martins really thinks Watts and Soto are today what he and Farrell were in Balanchine's day. But what choice do I have? Any ballet with Watts and Soto in it, especially any Martins ballet with Watts and Soto in it, especially any Martins ballet to Michael Torke's music with Watts and Soto in it, presents itself as a link in the great chain going back to Balanchine. Watts and Soto were in *A Fool for You*. The link there was to the Balanchine of *Who Cares?* The link in all the Watts-Soto-Torke ballets—*Ecstatic Orange* and *Black & White* and now *Echo*—is to what Lincoln Kirstein once called "the master's advanced manner." Not that these pieces have anything real in common with those Stravinsky-Hindemith-Webern ballets in which the dancers turned their legs in and flexed their feet; what for Balanchine was a living process of disarticulation is for Martins a mere look, a pose, an advanced mannerism. By the same token, the Stravinskyan strain in Torke's music is less an indication of affinity than of what the post-modernists call appropriation. Torke, Martins's Stravinsky, writes bad music. His score for *Echo* repeats a short-phrase pattern obsessively in a kind of hiccupping rhythm for about eight minutes; then, with minor differences, it repeats that three times. Music like this strikes New York City Ballet at its very heart. *Echo* is a ballet that begs legitimacy, revealing family secrets and showing us twisted lines of descent. As an image of how ballerinas are formed, it belies its own bloodlines. Would a Farrell ever have come out of a mold like this? Would a McBride ever have got in?

—July 3, 1989

THE NINETIES

Classical Values

The New York ballet season, once a thing of marvels and inventions, has slipped into somnolence, and the condition is dangerous. Symptoms that in other arts could be passed off as post-modernist torpor or even simple fatigue are life-threatening to dance, which lives in the moment. Is dance really alive when nearly everything that happens is a version of something that has already happened? Specifically, can classical ballet, with its tradition of recapitulating the past in terms of the present, survive the contradictions of stasis and stale imitation?

The season still runs from late April through July, and New York City Ballet and American Ballet Theatre still launch it, playing side by side at Lincoln Center. The slump hasn't affected box-office for the simple reason that it hasn't affected standards of execution; these remain spectacular enough, and individual careers (Damian Woetzel's, Julio Bocca's and, on a higher level, Darci Kistler's) are booming. But the events that used to justify such prolonged seasons— débuts, premières, the vicissitudes of talent being tested in the highest reaches of the art—have become few and far between. ABT presented the most distinguished première, Twyla Tharp's *Brief Fling*, on the second night of its run, and not again for three weeks. New York City Ballet has offered one new ballet, a piece by Peter Martins in his by now official minimalist-formalist mode. This time, Martins used a score by John Adams rather than one by Michael Torke, and the result was less abrasively lean and mean. With that difference, the ballet was a fairly predictable affair, and so was the NYCB season as a whole; what with seniority casting and a Balanchine repertory largely held over from last winter, dance watchers found that they could pretty well dope it out in advance, like racetrack touts. The main event was a two-week Jerome Robbins retrospective: nothing new there, and only one revival of note—*Watermill*, with its original star, Edward Villella, returning to the State Theater stage after eleven years.

Now fifty-three, Villella inadvertently became part of a "fifty-something" trend set by ABT's guest stars when Carla Fracci revisited *Jardin aux Lilas* and Ekaterina Maximova and Vladimir Vasiliev danced—or, rather, demonstrated—*Giselle*. Though Vasiliev threw himself about with undiminished zeal, these were really token appearances, served up for an audience that had felt itself deprived during Baryshnikov's administration of the big stars who made the seventies shine. Villella, as big a star as any, had the advantage, at least, of performing a role he had come to late in his career, one designed in part as a relief from virtuoso dancing. *Watermill*, a protracted slow-motion "Japanese" pantomine steeped in the mortuary gloom of Robert Wilson, seemed shorter this time, with fewer and less showily provocative incidents. That Oriental moon waxed and waned, the wind rustled through the marsh grass, and tiny, tinkling ineffabilities rained down. But the audience didn't boo, as it had in

1972—it cheered, mostly because of Villella, whose magnetism and control had actually increased. It happens that he is the same age that Robbins was when he made the piece. If *Watermill* has a meaning (Robbins intended to show a man coming to terms with the past, and in view of his resignation from the company, last winter, the revival could be taken for a valediction), it is the meaning that Villella now gives it, with his mature craftsmanship and unassertive, unmelancholy ease of concentration.

The older of the two biggest American companies, Ballet Theatre, is celebrating its fiftieth anniversary. But though dance technique and dance medicine march on, no way has yet been found to make fifty-year-old dancers effective in the roles of their youth. Age is not the only debilitating factor. The new ABT management also brought back Fernando Bujones and teamed him with the Bolshoi ballerina Lyudmila Semenyaka in *The Sleeping Beauty*. He is thirty-five, she thirty-eight, but they seem older because of their blighted careers. Semenyaka, a dancer of exquisite breeding, looked sadly pinched. Flashes of her former delicacy still illumine her Aurora, but the net effect of her Bolshoi regimen has been the trivialization of her greatest gift—the ethereal combination of strength and daintiness. The very quality of her energy has been Bolshoivized—it's become both coarse and faint. As for Bujones and *his* gifts, he long ago surrendered them to a notion of marketability, and now offers tired surefire routines in place of a performance. He was to have danced *Beauty* with Cynthia Gregory. When she canceled, management saw fit to bring Semenyaka all the way from Moscow, even though she is to appear in New York with the Bolshoi in July, and even though ABT has under contract young and vital American Auroras who dance the role better.

This was to have been Baryshnikov's tenth and final year as artistic director. He began his tenure with the idea that ABT should be an American company able to dance the classics with authority, not an international gathering of performers with inconsistent and inorganic notions of style. Another idea was that the highest priority should be the development of talent. There's a common saying that it takes ten years to make a ballet company. Had Baryshnikov not resigned prematurely last year, he would now be presiding over a season that is seeing his policies finally pay off. Ballet Theatre's younger ballerinas weren't very interesting when they began dancing this version of *The Sleeping Beauty* three seasons ago. Though they'd been very well trained, right up to last spring they weren't interesting in any of the classics. It looked as if, without the kind of stimulus that Baryshnikov's dancing had provided for the men, there would never be an authentic ballerina presence at ABT. The blossoming of a new, lyrical, soft yet exacting style is most noticeable so far in the dancing of Susan Jaffe and Cheryl Yeager, Baryshnikov's two most conspicuous groomed-from-the-ground-up ballerina candidates. The force behind the change is Irina Kolpakova, former prima ballerina of the Kirov, whom Baryshnikov brought in as a coach when *glasnost* opened the way. The company is wise to retain this great artist. The pure classicism which she teaches is the same as that taught and practiced for years by great Russian dancers in the West; it is poetic dancing, not abstract discipline. I didn't notice a Kolpakova influence in *Swan Lake*, but in the Prologue to *The Sleeping Beauty* I thought I saw it all down the line—or the beginning of it, anyway. What a lovely thing to encounter in the ballet's centennial year. What a consuming thought, that one of Baryshnikov's last official acts may turn out to be his most significant.

The Sleeping Beauty is a ballet that cannot be revived; it can only be rediscovered. It's about the enduring values of classicism, and a correct performance is an act of faith. The orchestra this season murdered the music. The dancers fought back valiantly, especially Jaffe, whose taut serenity in the Rose adagio was a refreshing surprise. Partnered by Kevin McKenzie, she was again triumphant in the Wedding pas de deux. But no ballerina should have the responsibility of building up a ballet that collapses as soon as the Vision scene is over. From here to the end of the act, Kenneth MacMillan's staging is out of scale with the music. Carabosse is melodramatically overexposed, and the Lilac Fairy (whether the wooden Christine Dunham or the puddingy Leslie Browne) is too vaguely drawn to counteract the menace. The divertissement, beginning with MacMillan's Jewel quartet, had no coherence. The Bluebirds either failed to ignite or, danced by Bocca and Alessandra Ferri, flared up out of control, a discordant flash act.

Bocca's excesses are less of a puzzle to me than Ferri's. His stem from exuberance, brute capacity, and simple indifference to style; they're the flaws of a young, unpolished dancer trying to thrill his public. Tharp harnessed him in *Brief Fling*. Otherwise, only the role of Albrecht seemed to quell the beast in Bocca; his point-of-death variation was responsive to the music and the dramatic moment. But Ferri is a real oddity: a sensitive actress who lacks subtlety as a dancer. No single role resolves her contradictions; she appears of a piece only when accompanying Bocca through some slam-bang exercise in audience manipulation. And even then it's not a *whole* piece. Pyrotechnics don't suit Ferri. (Yeager is more at home with them.) Her fans adore her in *Giselle*, particularly in Act I. She can act the peasant girl in love better than most, but she's too much the peasant in Act II; the elegance of the inner woman doesn't show in this girl with the brawny port de bras and mushy feet. But when she dances a variation in *Birthday Offering* it does show. Somehow, the Royal Ballet schooling to which the choreography is tuned brings it out.

Ashton's *Birthday Offering* is also tuned to Petipa; it's half a tribute to *Beauty* and half a commemoration of *temps perdu*. Ashton endowed the seven female variations with the airs and graces of his mother's generation, and André Levasseur's costumes reinforce the image with their hints of whalebone and plush velvet. As each dancer comes forward, you want to give her a Mauve Decade name: Letitia, Maud, Ivy, Zuleika . . . But Ashton was also a pure-water classicist, and for him the ballet was foremost a study of the Royal ballerinas of the fifties. If you're a veteran Royal fan, the names that come to mind are Beryl, Nadia, Rowena—members of the original cast. Above all, you long to see through the past to the soul of the present, to these women dancing *now*, and the view is obscure. It's not just a matter of bloodlines; I daresay ABT dances the choreography better than the Royal today would. Revived this season, the ballet has been attentively coached by Georgina (Georgina!) Parkinson, like Ferri a former Royal Ballet dancer. Fonteyn was also brought in for some coaching sessions. But it's a rare revival that can recapture an original transparency.

For Ballet Theatre this has been very much a transitional season, planned by Baryshnikov, executed by his successor, Jane Hermann. Formerly the Met's director of presentations, Hermann came to ABT with a reputation as a tough-minded businesswoman who could control costs. She spoke of battering down the deficit acquired during the Baryshnikov years. The question was how she intended to go about it—whether artistic gains would have to be sacrificed.

From some of the choices Hermann has made so far—
bringing on old grads and various dubious Russians—it
looks as if she would rather appeal to the audience's weaknesses than to the company's strengths. The most pandering
and pointless decision has been the hiring and casting of the
Kirov dancer Faruk Ruzimatov. Bad enough that he danced
La Bayadère with a full complement of snake-charmer tor-
sions and poses. He brought the same plastique to *Stravinsky Violin Concerto.* In *Theme and Variations,* he focused on
one half of the ballet—his own—and by inept partnering
undermined Cynthia Harvey's half. But why put him in
these Balanchine ballets in the first place?

The real excitement of the season was *Brief Fling.* For
Tharp it was a return to form after a stumble last spring,
and also an exhilarating statement of classicism reengaged.
Few nonacademically trained choreographers have been so
fascinated by classical ballet or so keen on mastering its
technique. But Tharp always seemed to have reservations
about what Stravinsky called "the beauty of its *ordonnance.*"
She preferred a semblance of anarchy to one of constraint.
Except when she worked with Baryshnikov, she resisted the
notion of hierarchy. She built grids of all-over equalized activity instead of pyramids with virtuoso declensions moving
through the ranks from one or two soloists at the top.
Tharp had nothing against soloists or against their tendency
to come in pairs, but in common with so many ballet choreographers of the eighties she always used two or more couples and promoted a kind of equilibrium between them.
Brief Fling is the first ballet in which she has used just one
ballerina, just one premier danseur. True, she gives us her
demi-soloists and her corps in sequential units instead of
placing them behind the principals in contrapuntal support,
as Balanchine would have done, and she gives us a fourth

unit consisting of Tharp dancers matching the classical dancers feat for feat. For whole stretches, it seems as if she has choreographed four different ballets. But *Brief Fling* is a four-in-one construction. Its four sections run concurrently, are interpenetrating, and are finally made to cohere in a vision of vernacular/academic parallelism as persuasive as the last act of *Raymonda* or—the more evident source of Tharp's inspiration—*Union Jack*. The pleasure of the ballet as you watch it is the willed integration of recalcitrant material. The pattern of integration is jagged, even jarring, but unity does come about. It's really a victory of Tharp over her own recalcitrance and ambivalence—her need to make ballet accommodate her, and her refusal to give in to its dictates.

Originally, she wanted, I think, to democratize ballet—to knock the coronets off the heads of the principal dancers. But that idea went against the classical principle of unified construction. The idea of a ballet as a piece of architecture evolving in time, defining its expressive goals more and more distinctly, is directly analogous to the way dancers evolve through training. Principal dancers are ultimate definition. A ballet without them isn't just a house without a cupola—it's more like a house without a roof. *Brief Fling* comes to a peak in the dancing of Bocca and Yeager. The steps are "compounded"—virtuoso classical combinations with Tharpian boosters. Tharp makes more of Bocca than the Baryshnikov clone he makes of himself (even adopting the 1970s Misha haircut, which doesn't go well with his nose); and Yeager's terrier tenacity is enlarged into bold wit. Circling high in the air over Bocca's head, sliding down his back as he exits, or echoing him in tightly coiled "skating" spins, she is the classical counterpart of the colloquial Shelley Washington and every bit as fearless. Isaac Mizrahi has dressed the piece schematically in Scottish tartans. As a reflection of the ballet's all-in-one design, the three men who support Washington wear different parts of a single kit. Mizrahi's only mistake is dark-blue and crimson tights, which make the dancers' legs hard to see.

Balanchine showed that a ballet could have more than one lead couple. But the preference of the eighties for split-focus ballets was a defeat for Balanchine and also for Petipa, from whose *Sleeping Beauty* the idea of progressive articulation clearly derives. In other words, a defeat for classical values. In *Stravinsky Violin Concerto*, and more radically and strangely in *Kammermusik No. 2*, Balanchine split the focus between two ballerinas and their partners. These are among his least characteristic works, but for the majority of choreographers who have followed his example they are the most influential—you'd almost think he'd done nothing else. Since his death, the repertory at NYCB has filled up with pieces of this type; Martins's latest, *Fearful Symmetries*, stands for what has now become a genre.

Martins's case is especially harrowing because it seems related to NYCB's failure to develop a star ballerina since Darci Kistler, whose advent year was 1980. As long as Kistler is there, dancing gloriously, as long as Merrill Ashley's renaissance continues, as long as Kyra Nichols returns fully healed and good impressions are made by the likes of Nichol Hlinka and Hélène Alexopoulos, this great vacancy will be covered, and Martins's penchant for making multiple-ballerina vehicles can be perceived as a simple in-ability to choose among riches. In *Fearful Symmetries* he paired Ashley with his perennial leading lady, Heather Watts, and while it was painful to see Ashley's dancing reduced, for symmetry's sake, to the etiolated level of Watts's, there was consolation in the presence of Margaret Tracey,

who, along with Jeffrey Edwards, was given some nice things
to do. The role didn't advance her as much as *Tchaikovsky
Pas de Deux* did, but the point about these occasional
promising débuts is that they're not followed up with further performances or further débuts, so as to be of real value
to the dancers. Each gain is followed by a lapse, and signs of
disintegration start to set in. Kelly Cass and Wendy Whelan,
once prime candidates to succeed Ashley and Nichols, now
look tough rather than strong. The thing I miss most in
NYCB's operations is the feeling of somebody's—anybody's—eye scanning the field, plotting careers. Damian
Woetzel's rise has been the company's one real success in all
this time; instructively enough, it followed the old route of
development through repertory. Two talented long-legged
and very young dancers, Ethan Stiefel and Yvonne Borree,
danced a single performance of *The Steadfast Tin Soldier* and
were so good that one wanted to pass a petition: Give them
Coppélia, give them *Harlequinade*. The odds are that they
won't even do *Steadfast* again—ask any tout.

The company is stagnating on the musical front, too.
The orchestra this season frequently sounded overmiked
and underrehearsed. A great blow was the sudden death of
Ashley Lawrence, who of all the guest conductors functioned best. But these are days of drift and inanition for
what has been the world's most creative ballet company.
Coming at such a time, Robbins's resignation is both
poignant and perilous. The festival of his works brought
out one of his best and most underrated pieces—*Ma Mère
l'Oye*, to Ravel's music. How extraordinary a piece it really is
and how hard it must have been to get the little tales told
with exactly the right combination of dryness and sweetness
become apparent when a debacle like *Puss in Boots* takes
place. Perhaps too much had been expected of this original
ballet to a commissioned score, the featured event of the an-

nual School of American Ballet performances. The choreographer, Robert LaFosse, had done well with pure-dance ballets, and this was to be a story ballet, drawn from a libretto by Lincoln Kirstein. But the choreography, the music by Larry Spivack, and the décor by Gary Lisz all failed for the same reason: instead of being emotionally innocent and technically sophisticated, they were the reverse.

One would have liked to think that Robbins had passed on to LaFosse some of his choreographic secrets. A former Baryshnikov protégé, LaFosse was brought to NYCB by Robbins, and he has become an exceptionally fine Robbins dancer; his performance with Kistler of *In G Major* is the best the ballet has seen. As a Balanchine dancer LaFosse has difficulty submerging himself in his roles; he'd rather winkle out the subtext and add little touches, like the hand-twirling gesture that says "Dance," quite needlessly, in *Who Cares?* But he has enormous depth of commitment, and he's a heroic partner. He got Kistler smoothly through *Who Cares?* in spite of the fact that she was dancing a role three sizes too small for her. Like Suzanne Farrell and Merrill Ashley before her, she opted for the part created for Patricia McBride. And she came breathtakingly close to re-creating it, lifts and all. Kistler is unstoppable; her performances this spring took place a world away from the company's troubles. So—almost—did those of Maria Calegari in *Chaconne* and *Violin Concerto*. After several seasons of dancing erratically, she has reached a state that I can only describe as subdued turbulence. It's exciting and beautiful, but it's alarming, too. Calegari is in obvious need of a new role; she's like a racehorse in the starting gate. Happily, *Brahms/Handel*, in which she is the Tharp ballerina, returned just in time to release some of her energy.

Tharp's other contribution to the season was her marvelous *Nine Sinatra Songs*, from 1982, with an ABT cast that danced it to the hilt. In spite of all that *Brief Fling* accomplishes and should be cherished for, it does not satisfy the way *Nine Sinatra Songs* does. Tharp's ballet-company ballets engage and challenge the classical tradition, they drive dancers to go beyond themselves, but they don't roll out of the azure of pure inspiration, like the pieces to Fats Waller and Willie (the Lion) Smith. To call "Nine Sinatra Songs" a classical ballet might strike even Tharp as impertinent, and yet as an experience it is for me closer to *Who Cares?* than *Brief Fling* is to anything of Balanchine's, including *Union Jack*. As the seasons pass and we watch our choreographers wrangle through this thing of being classical, of being George, of being beside, against, or beyond him, it helps to remember that his favorite dancer was Fred Astaire; he said so, he was perfectly serious, and his ballets all showed it. For Balanchine, Astaire was as true an example of classical style as *The Sleeping Beauty*. A classical tradition with no touchstones in the present is a tradition nobody understands.

—July 2, 1990

Multicultural Theatre

There used to be only one place a nondancer could learn about dance the theatre. Now there's the college classroom, too: at its best, a forum for the lively discussion of things seen and sensed in the theatre; at its worst, a refuge for theatrephobes and intellectual diddlers, and a source of Newspeak. The latest buzzword is "multiculturalism"—the term educators have been using to define the vogue in curriculum reform. In dance circles, multiculturalism means the political advocacy of other than Western (or non-"Eurocentric") forms of dance. Those of us who are educated in the theatre may well wonder what there is to be political about. Multiculturalism exists and has always existed in American dance; there is scarcely an American choreographer of note who has not been influenced both by the pluralism of our society and by the way dance just naturally soaks it up. Pinning a label on a simple thing like that is something only an academic would want to do. And only political academics would want to isolate the elements of pluralism in such a way as to aggrandize some and stigmatize others.

The multiculturalists who cite recent trends in immigration have a case. There may be a need to promote the accessibility of Asian, Hispanic, and African dance companies, many of which lead a marginal life with few bookings. But the dance forms themselves are hardly inaccessible—they're part of every dance tradition the West knows. At their purest (assuming that one can find village and street festivals that are uninfected by television and tourism), they still speak a rhythmic language intelligible to all who love dance. To argue otherwise fits in with certain divisive notions of culture popular in the universities; it also fits in with theories of curriculum reform.

But the discussion of multiculturalism among dance people has a peculiar urgency. What the academic partisans of Asian and Hispanic and African dance are really telling us is that ballet is in decline and the creative impetus in modern dance has finally petered out; therefore, we'd better pay attention to these other styles or we have no dance to talk and write about. The key word is "other" (it's another buzzword); the assumption is that these styles lie outside the mainstream and are kept there by mainstream prejudice. And what the pols want (and, given their weight in academic quarters, seem certain to get) is the creation of special-interest groups that need special-interest, academically fostered insights in order to be understood.

The Dance Critics Association, which often serves as an academic sounding board, has announced a conference on "Critical Imperatives in World Dance," to be held later this summer in Los Angeles. At the same time, the Los Angeles Festival will offer dance presentations consisting of—according to the DCA flyer—"ensembles from the Pacific Islands, Asia, Australia, Central and South America, Mexico and Indonesia, as well as performances by distinguished American artists." Presumably, by American the flyer means

United States–based or United States–bred artists. In any case, one of the scheduled ones was Mark Morris, whose Brussels-based company has just completed its annual summer engagements in this country. Morris was dropped when the festival finances got too tight. Los Angeles will miss seeing what the festival could have taken pride in sponsoring as a genuine expression of world dance. The dancers Morris employs are of every color and physical description, and are cast without regard to race, rank, or sex. The choreography is a blend of styles Western and Eastern. Though it may not advertise itself this way, the company is, in fact, a multicultural microcosm. I saw it in Boston, in Brooklyn, and at Jacob's Pillow. As a dance spectacle, it seemed to have matured over the past year. I was fascinated not only by its abundance and variety but by its elegant distillation, its emphasis on *this* world in *this* grain of sand. It was what every great dance company—ethnic, classical, or modern—has always been: a vision of the universe and the individual's place in it.

Morris's company stresses the individual, though, in ways that other companies don't. Men and women make powerful impressions, but they hardly ever do so together, or in relation to one another, or by themselves in relation to the group. Though partners exist in Morris's universe, their existence is circumscribed and qualified by the group; they step out of a human panorama and fall back into it without asserting themselves for more than a few seconds as a unit. I'm describing a general tendency, not a hard-and-fast rule. But certainly none of the pieces I saw this summer included the pas de deux as a preferred form, even when the form could have been mandated by the subject, and even when it might have been given single-sex treatment. (That possibility existed, as it always does, on Morris's stage.)

In his version of Purcell's *Dido and Aeneas*, the lovers do not make love; the ceremonial nature of the proceedings all but precludes it, and anyway, the more important duo is Dido and the Sorceress, both of whom are danced by Morris, in an unnervingly suggestive double portrait. Aeneas, resplendently portrayed in a stylized "still" performance by Guillermo Resto, is really the fulcrum of Dido's passion, the means by which she meets her destiny in death. In his setting of Brahms's *Liebeslieder Walzer,* Morris avoids the pas-de-deux form almost entirely. The music, of course, is the basis of one of the great Balanchine ballets, in which the vast majority of the dances are danced by couples, and monogamous couples at that. Morris's version of the waltzes (like Balanchine, he has choreographed both books, for a total of thirty-three dances) involves trios and quartets more than duets. Trios reform themselves into couples, then back into trios. Couples "make love" two pairs at a time and freely interchange partners—at least, they do in that half of the ballet which was choreographed in 1982. The other half, which Morris made last year, is another story.

In his dances Morris often tells us what he thinks of another artist's work, judging it against his own view of the world. The intensity of Balanchine and his vision of deepening erotic mystery are things that Morris doesn't even try for. Instead of romantic poetry he composes a kind of stumblebum ode to adolescence, all crude energy and confusion. He builds dances out of ultra-simple "folk" movement, with rough edges. The beauty of the art songs flows around and through the movement in emotional counterpoint. For some reason, Morris choreographed the second set of Brahms's song cycle first, and it was presented first on the Boston program. It opens with a single dancer, the robust, big-boned Ruth Davidson, rushing forward, springing into an air turn, and landing with a bang in second position.

That image turns out to characterize the piece, both its orgiastic spirit (love as appetite, as the life force) and its tragic spirit, seen in the eventual loss of the eager-hearted solitary ones, trampled in the crowd.

The sequel, Brahms's (and Balanchine's) prequel, is not only more restrained; it's more graceful. The clodhopping movement style is pared down, and Morris has more control; he no longer lustily bites off more music than he can chew or gets unwanted laughs. As in the Balanchine version, the tone of the dancing is more recreational, with less complicated feelings. The sexual confusion continues, the partners yearning toward and away from each other at the same time. But the only actual face-to-face dancing is the ballroom waltz. The odd-man-out theme dwindles to one scene of a boy trying to escape from his (family?) circle and being gently but insistently restrained until he is finally given up. In the last dance, Keith Sabado, whom Morris often uses symbolically, waltzes the other dancers one by one off the stage, then walks off himself.

In the Balanchine Part One, the couples leave the stage one by one to return transfigured in Part Two. The way Morris clears the stage of couples—the finality of it—tells us that this is really the end of the ballet; there's no going on, no reversing the parts back to Brahms's order. Read as a commentary on contemporary sexual realities, the confinement, the openly social tone, the new spareness in the dance style are poignant and yet bracing in their awareness. We feel the sensitivity of Morris's response to the AIDS plague, and his hardheadedness, too. Opening with a bang, he has done all he can to keep from ending with a whimper.

At Jacob's Pillow, there was another new piece about social manners, the hilarious, satirically coarse-grained *Going Away Party*. Three couples, and they are unmistakably couples, have a heavy Saturday-night date to the music of Bob Wills and the Texas Playboys—eight selections in all, including the title number, "Yearning," "My Shoes Keep Walking Back to You," "Milk Cow Blues," and "When You Leave Amarillo, Turn Out the Lights." Morris makes broad jokes, such as having the men constantly go upstage to pee, but he doesn't vulgarize his dance idiom—if anything, it's prettier and dancier than the idiom of the Brahms pieces. It's also exactly suited to the music, not ironically opposed, as in the Brahms. Morris uses this idiom to portray an earlier America and characters who are slightly older and who live, somewhat cynically, by convention—brash, sexually aggressive kids. In the world of *Going Away Party*, love is only something you hear about in songs. I have carried away a memory of that world made of the repeated parallel lunges on the opening phrase of "Yearning (Just for You)." Side by side, a man and a woman twice lunge forward on one foot, with heads bent and arms swinging, as if they were taking low, hungry bites out of the air. They move, callously, on the downbeat. These are tough gals and horny guys, sure of getting what they want from each other. Meanwhile, Morris as the loner in their midst, the good-ole-boy bachelor host of the party, tries—literally—to keep his footing. (When he slumps to the floor, the others walk right over him—an incident repeated from *New Love-Song Waltzes*.) Wearing a silver spangled Western outfit, a ponytail, and a hearty grin, Morris is both the central and the most peripheral figure in the piece. We get the feeling that he's the soft-touch big brother and the dreamer and the goat, but, like the others, he keeps fading back into the group life, with its group values. He may be the most underprivileged of the characters that Morris has invented for himself to perform; in his solo, he even looks as if he isn't much of a dancer. And yet without him the whole piece would lack focus and definition.

As a picture of cowtown dating rituals, *Going Away Party* may be a little too wicked, especially to the women, who thump the men's heads to keep them in line. We see how the sexes use each other, but (and here is Morris's superiority as a choreographer and a social observer) we also see their fun, and it really isn't as simple as it looked at first. When Morris brings the dancers out in solos, we see the gleaming sexual energy that has charged them up for this big night. And when the Texas Playboys sing about women as "milk cows" Morris lets the scathing lyric stand without comment; it explains a lot about cowtown girls.

Morris had a good season as a performer. He also appeared in *Tamil Film Songs in Stereo*, at the Pillow, and a mime solo, *Ten Suggestions*, in Boston. In the ineffable *Tamil Film Songs*, Morris lifts a singing lesson from the sound track of an Indian movie musical and interprets it as a dance lesson that a foppish pedant administers to a quaking pupil (Penny Hutchinson). The lesson gets hung up on an absurdly complex movement phrase, which Morris has to demonstrate over and over, and the way he does it makes the audience weak with joy, beginning with the fop's mincingly precise dictation of the phrase. His imperial anger at having to repeat it to the little fluffball doesn't die down, it just becomes a frame for transitions: covert pleasure in his own silky execution gives way to sheer self-gratification, with the now impossibly magisterial phrase unrolling as if by itself and the pupil all but forgotten. First choreographed in 1983, *Tamil Film Songs in Stereo* remains the funniest comic turn in dance today. The epilogue—master and pupil reconciled in the rosy glow of her recital, for which he has reserved a large and dearly cherished pink tutu—is as fine in its way as the lesson itself. (The piece is billed as *The "Tamil Film Songs in Stereo" Pas de Deux*, but the title doesn't fool us any more than it does the winsome and resourceful Hutchinson.)

Ten Suggestions is little charades in which Morris appears in pink silk pajamas and amuses himself with, in turn, a hoop, a chair, a hat, and a pair of scissors. His musical timing is pointedly mickey-mousy (the music is Tcherepnin's "Ten Bagatelles"), with punch lines delivered smack on the beat. This is the kind of performance piece that the performer blows up around himself like an inner tube. Though Morris did not fall prey to improvisation, that temptation clearly exists in the material. *Ten Suggestions* is an enjoyably inconsequential excursion into, and possibly a spoof on, mime—the depressed-Pierrot school of street meem.

Another of Morris's favorite themes is coexisting opposites. His ecstatic doubling of the roles of Dido and her Nemesis in Purcell's opera was not female impersonation but a representation of the duplicitous forces that lie within the heart of Dido and drive her to her doom. The basis for the dual characterization may have been a decision to create a split personality in dance terms, with the Queen as the adagio and the Sorceress as the allegro half of one character. But the dignified Dido and the daft, malignant Sorceress are not really equals. The Sorceress and her band are schoolgirls, and they dance to obstreperous schoolgirl music. (Literally schoolgirl; Purcell composed the opera for performance by the ladies' seminary that had commissioned it.) Watching Morris writhing and squatting and knuckling his eyes in derision made me think that the monster was not Dido's alter ego but her child, spawn of the love she bore Aeneas, and the embodiment of her pent-up passion for self-annihilation. Morris's *Dido* is a disturbing work; beneath the folly and the grandeur of it lie reverberant intimations of sadomasochism. Its seed is *One Charming Night*, which Morris choreographed a few years ago to Purcell hymns. The subject was the seduction of a virgin by a vampire. Morris played the vampire, and his slow, insinuating dance with Teri Weksler was a pas de deux in every sense. For a vampire's victim, love and death are one and the same, and love and death exert equal claims on Dido: that is her tragedy. Aeneas brings about her destruction, but the force behind him is the diabolical "child" that she has created with him in her own image.

Only Morris, or the Martha Graham of forty years ago, would have conceived such an idea or had the courage to present it so dispassionately. The production, in fact, reminds me of *Clytemnestra*, with its clean design and echoes of archaic theatre. The choruses of lascivious witches and drunken sailors are operatic conventions, pointing up the domestic tragedy. Morris and his company had excellent support from the Philharmonia Baroque Orchestra and the Concert Chorale of New York, conducted by Nicholas McGegan.

Mark Morris was born in Seattle. There and in another port city, New York, he found teachers of dance in the various forms that influence his choreography: flamenco at first, then Balkan, Israeli, and Russian folk dance. Javanese and Hindu dance inform the court scenes in *Dido*; the mime portions make liberal use of the deaf-mute vocabulary of signs. Morris speaks so many languages that it comes as a surprise when, from time to time, he creates a work that has no trace of an accent—that is just "pure" movement. In between the two sets of Brahms lieder in Boston came *Behemoth*, as stark a work as Morris has yet conceived, heightened by being danced in silence. Morris without music is still a musical Morris, however. The thirty-four minutes and ten sections of *Behemoth* are concisely executed in suite form, with blackouts. One thinks of the Jerome Robbins of *Moves*. All the steps are organically related. The dynamic range is comfortingly wide, with speeds that go from headlong runs down to nothing, to absolute motionlessness. One thinks of the darker side of Cunningham. There is even sound: handclapping, the beating of limbs on the floor. It is the sound of the void.

Behemoth, named for its unusual length and weight (fifteen dancers), is about the individual and the group. But the story it tells is elusive. The dancers' movements are integrated but unresolved, assembled in such a way as to keep us seeking, guessing, dreading their outcome. As *Behemoth* unfolds, the sense of a crushing arbitrary force develops. People aid but don't see each other. Unseeingly, they catch each other's hands. Stage space is unstable, divided in radical ways: oddly angled floor patterns, a bit of activity far downstage or over against the wings, a huge mass of people covering the stage, draining it, then returning while one or two stationary soloists labor. The lights frequently go out at a peak of tension; then they come on, and the scene, though changed, is still at that peak.

The tragic core of the piece is, I think, not dramatic so much as it is sensuous. To follow the action is to experience something like a new method of sensitization; you're off balance, hanging in there. *Behemoth* is new in what it is willing to expose of human suffering without offering a collateral emotion for it. Behind these images of disaster is a kind of cogent sympathy, the weightlessness of conviction in the void, and that's *all*. It's as if a new range of feeling had come into the world just in time for Morris to explore it.

The diversity of Mark Morris is a legend. But where he

gets it all we'll never really know. In him a gift of prove-
nance and a gift of expression are indistinguishable. All we
can say is that he's a true dance artist. In dance, high art has
always needed to be nourished by folk art, and folk art has
always needed the mediation of the theatre. Without the
theatre, dance isn't a medium; it's the preserve of anthropol-
ogists, not of artists.

—July 23, 1990

Waking Up *The Sleeping Beauty*

In the ballet business, *The Sleeping Beauty* is a white elephant. You have to spend money on it, and you have to be able to dance it and maintain it in repertory, and few companies can, although many try. Last year, the ballet's centenary, there were several ambitious productions. The most prominent, by the San Francisco Ballet, had its merits, chief among them a brilliant début in the title role, but the production itself was undermined by the notion that the ballet would be much better off set in Russia than in France. It is always a mistake to let the designer rule the ballet and substitute visual for musical interest; if Tchaikovsky is not in charge of the show, it all goes wrong. The designer in this case, Jens-Jacob Worsaae, substituted a whole new conception for the image of civilization that Tchaikovsky had in mind. There are no Kremlinesque equivalents of the music and manners of the French Baroque era; at least, the choreographer, Helgi Tomasson, was unable to find any.

It would be too much to expect Tchaikovsky to be in charge of the production, new this spring, by New York City Ballet; as soon as you walk into the theatre, the covered orchestra pit tells you that this is going to be a visual more than a musical experience. The first thing we see when the ballet begins is a leafy allée leading us, in a series of dissolves, up to the door of the royal palace. Most of the projections that dominate David Mitchell's visual design (and have to be protected from the lights in the pit) work well enough in the cause of the music, and most of the stage action, choreographed by Peter Martins, works even better, so that Tchaikovsky's storytelling power becomes known and is in force throughout the evening.

Because ballet has no reliably recordable history, it must prove itself anew to each generation of theatregoers, and *The Sleeping Beauty* has problems the other classics don't have: not only must it evoke an image of luxury which is also an image of beauty, and not only must it live up to the music that is and always will be its most precious asset; it must also tell a story that every single person in the audience, young or old, knows in advance—the story of the princess who pricks her finger on a spindle and sleeps a hundred years to be awakened with a kiss. *Swan Lake* and *The Nutcracker* and *Coppélia* and other family-audience favorites have stories you learn in the theatre; *The Sleeping Beauty* tells you a story you know. And the story of *The Sleeping Beauty* is what attracts the kind of business that alone justifies the effort of mounting and maintaining a serious and costly production. The cardinal virtue of the New York City Ballet production is that it tells the story, tells it well, and in record time.

Much nervous apprehension has attended Martins's editing of the ballet down to two acts, as if this could only result in a stripped-down, speedy "NYCB" version, in defiance of tradition. Christening, birthday, hunt, and vision are combined in one act, and time in between—sixteen years, then a century—is shown passing by means of overlapping projections. Above the turrets of the castle, the wheel of the zodiac turns toward Aurora's fatal birthday. When the Lilac Fairy puts the castle to sleep, we see the same allée we saw at the beginning growing over with brambles and sinking from view. A moment's silence, and then another castle appears in the distance, among hills surrounded by lakes. Act I ends with Prince Désiré leaving for the sleeping castle in the Lilac Fairy's boat. The single intermission is followed by the panorama, staged uncut against changing views of a winding river (which allows the boat to cross the stage in two directions). Next comes enough of Tchaikovsky's symphonic entr'acte to get the prince ashore and up to the bedroom, slashing at vines as he goes. Then, as in the two historic Western productions, by Diaghilev in 1921 and the Royal Ballet in 1946, the Awakening gives way to the Wedding in an onstage transition.

These feats of elision aren't accomplished without a struggle. Because the music is intensely visual, the worst moments in the production are those that try to enlist Tchaikovsky's cooperation in scenic effects that he did not anticipate. (Only the zodiac really works, using for "cover" the final portion of the knitting-women scene, which Martins does not stage.) The great achievement is the avoidance of anticlimax in the Wedding scene. When the kiss has been bestowed and the castle restored, the arc of the evening is still rising. The audience that watches the Wedding suite of dances is an alert, unbored audience. We take in a lot at one sitting (the first act runs seventy-five minutes, the second just under an hour), but we are always moving forward, going somewhere. The old story retells itself in terms that gratify and nourish the appetite for fantasy which it has awakened in us.

An old story well told is a new story, and in that sense this *Sleeping Beauty* is new; it is not High Concept, it is not Post-Modern. It is not even particularly original. Barring those pace-setting elisions and certain other adjustments that are the prerogative of a good ballet master (for example, the filling out of the steps in the traditional Prologue variations, and the creation of new Wedding dances to go with the old ones), Martins has contributed very little of his own. He has used standard Petipa-based choreography, freely mixing the best elements of Royal and Kirov productions, modifying, tidying, enhancing, never intruding unless needed, a true metteur en scène. In only one instance has he made a questionable choice—Kirov Bluebirds. I would have picked Royal. I would also have preferred a man in the part of Carabosse, as in the original production. Tchaikovsky's music for the bad fairy is grotesquerie, very different from the kind of music that he would have written for a woman. But Martins's choice may be the right one for now. The 1990s have already seen more than their share of drag-queen performing, and there is much in the ballet's performance history that is worse than casting a woman as Carabosse. (There is putting her on pointe.) And it is to performance history that Martins continually turns for his guidelines.

The ballet that our century knows as *The Sleeping Beauty* is not the ballet that was produced in St. Petersburg. Marius Petipa would probably disown a good deal of it. Even though our productions stem from notation that was based on his production, they also incorporate the changes that intervening generations saw fit to make in order to bring Petipa abreast of contemporary dance style and make him viable in the face of contemporary economics. Sometimes it's hard to tell which kind of change is operative in what we see today. In the Rose adagio, Martins produces the standard text, unmodified by so much as a single petal. (All of the ballerina role is the standard, authorized King James Version.) But when Aurora performs the sequence of flat-foot balances in arabesque penchée, is she doing it unsupported because this production can't afford the liveried violinists whose shoulders she leaned on originally, cupping her ear on each balance? Or is it because Margot Fonteyn long ago not only did without violinists but did brilliantly without support of any kind? Whatever the reason, a passage that Petipa had imagined as a genre scene à la Watteau was converted—as was the rest of the Rose adagio—into a study in unsupported balance.

Martins sees to it that Aurora's destiny is worked out to the letter. The Lilac Fairy mimes that the princess will be awakened by a prince wearing a feather in his hat, and, sure enough, when Désiré appears he is wearing a feather in his hat, a big blue one. The hunt scene is actually not a hunt but a picnic, and the prince is late. "What can be keeping him?" mimes the countess. "You know how he is," an aide replies, but the countess, whose party this evidently is, is impatient. By the time the prince walks on, to the low-key reprise of his entrance music, we know that he doesn't want to be here, and soon we hear the hunting horns that signal the end of the scene. The prince bids the party join the hunt without him, and everyone picks up and leaves, taking along half of what used to be the second act. It is all smoothly, even wittily, done, with Martins accomplishing the mime equivalent of Fonteyn's penchée balances and making a virtue of necessity. The change is organic: as supported balances change to unsupported ones, a prince who doesn't want a party doesn't have one. Martins has understood, too, that just as Aurora is chiefly a dance character Désiré is chiefly a mime one. The sarabande soliloquy usually inserted at this point has nothing to do with Petipa's scenario. Instead of dancing about under the trees, the prince waits alone for a long moment on an empty stage and is a hundred times as eloquently lonely.

What can ail thee, knight-at-arms? The question, which Tchaikovsky surely would have wished to ask in *Swan Lake*, had his collaborators been willing, is asked and answered in his next ballet. As the Lilac Fairy approaches the lost figure of Désiré, she brings with her the yearning, the anxiety and intoxication of the Romantic ballet. From eighteenth-century court dance to nineteenth-century ballet blanc: we are sped from one dance era to the next. Désiré's world of reasoned and refined passion is suddenly overcome by magnificent wish-fulfilling dreams: nymphs leap from the trees; all nature is spellbound. By cutting Désiré's court dances, Martins leaves this part of the ballet's meaning cursorily expressed, but the music, so abundantly alive to all aspects of the libretto, easily sustains the prince on his journey through space and time. Désiré doesn't really enter the nineteenth century; he only beholds a vision of it—he looking forward, Petipa looking backward, each seeing Aurora as the young Taglioni and himself as her contemporary. Too much fuss can be made over period correctness in *The Sleeping Beauty*. The action spans the grand siècle, but Tchaikovsky's larger point is that dance eras don't succeed one another in an orderly progression through time so much as they are annihilated by time and are contained one inside another, the past eclipsed by an eternal present.

It is in this scene—the Vision scene—that the production works most tellingly on three levels: choreography, scenery, and music. As Désiré threads his way among the nymphs in pursuit of Aurora, they form themselves into lanes and tiered groups that recall the allée or the fountain in the palace garden out of which, at one point, the Lilac Fairy rose. Now she is present to guide and restrain the headlong emotions of the prince. When Martins brings the scene to a climax, it's with the mime speech of Désiré to Lilac—an impassioned "Take me to her, I implore you," delivered on one knee as the strings take the melody into crescendo. When the Vision ends and he's again alone, he bounds exultingly about in a solo to the agitato reprise of the Rose adagio theme, music that binds his destiny to Aurora's. It's a moment that calls for dance.

Mitchell's palace sets are adapted from the great châteaus of France. The throne room where the Christening takes place is modeled, in part, on the bedroom at Blois of Catherine de Medici—she who imported ballet from Italy to France. Look closely and you'll see arms sticking out of the wall holding candelabras, a detail previously borrowed from Chambord by Christian Bérard for Cocteau's *Beauty and the Beast*. But Mitchell isn't really comfortable with fantasy. His palace exteriors are cold and without mystery, and Mark Stanley's lighting doesn't do much for them. The setting for the Rose adagio, the garden at Villandry, is far too literal, with some decidedly odd-looking topiary. And it's strange that visual projections set the style of the production but aren't used full force when they're really needed—after the Panorama, in the prince's approach to the castle. Following Tchaikovsky's mobile camera through the woods and up the dust-covered stairs to the cobweb-laden bed is what Mitchell has prepared us to do, and perhaps one day we will get to do it.

For now, it's more important that the two most awkward scenic transitions be corrected. As the Lilac Fairy casts her spell, brambles close in from both sides of the stage and vines travel upward, but so slowly that the music must be painfully dragged out. Then the music, with its beautiful diminuendo, is smothered by applause when the scrim is lowered and the projections take over. But this is nothing compared with the revving and vamping that must take place after the Awakening, when the music of the Wedding polonaise is already under way and the bed refuses to disappear. (As it slowly moves upstage, unseen hands not designed by Bérard snatch away the bedclothes.) Martins crams the Awakening scene so full of action—uniting the lovers, reviving the court, blowing up Carabosse—that he kills it and loses the payoff for all his good work. What's needed here is what Petipa requested of Tchaikovsky when he wanted to stretch the panorama—yard music. In the American Ballet Theatre version of 1987, which also elided Awakening and Wedding, Kenneth MacMillan resorted to a blackout and a stage wait. Martins wants the exhilaration of going from peak to rising peak. He wants to end the story but not the excitement. But he can afford to extend this scene, maybe with the aid of some transposed music. Speed mustn't be confused with momentum. Time is on the production's side, and it hardly ever is at this point in the ballet.

Martins sees Carabosse as young and handsome, a fallen angel among the good fairies at the Christening. Two of the performances were persuasive, amazingly so when you consider how underdeveloped the acting at New York City Ballet has always been. (Martins, of course, grew up in the Royal Danish Ballet, the company with the best mime tradition in the world. It's a background that all too seldom comes into play in his work.) Merrill Ashley is a pale, shrill, and somehow charming witch. In her black net evening gown and little black feathered tricorne, she demands justice with her pointy chin stuck well forward and her elbows stuck well back. She's fun mainly because she's Ashley, and we've not seen her like this before. Lourdes Lopez is not fun. We've never seen her like this, either: she's still and deadly, a black widow emerging from her web of evil, and I imagine she scares the children in the audience to bits. (Surely a reason to play the role in travesty is not to scare the children.) Ashley looks like Katharine Hepburn as Mary of Scotland, but Lopez is a living, sneering Velázquez, whose beauty only adds to the disaster she wreaks upon the court.

Like threads in a tapestry, every detail in *The Sleeping Beauty* carries its weight of meaning. Martins pulls one of these threads when he excises Carabosse's dialogue with the other fairies. Especially now that from the way she looks we can imagine Carabosse once being *good*, we want to know more about her condition. And, because Tchaikovsky particularizes every scrap of moral as well as psychological information, every gesture counts. The little court not only must be seen to be protected by a benevolent Lilac Fairy, it must deserve to be protected; its king and queen must not be haughty, languorous creatures, its Catalabutte must not be silly or too feckless. The overall mime frame of the production is just now a little thin. It needs heavier gilding to support the impasto of the dancing.

Patricia Zipprodt has designed serviceable costumes in rich materials. The colors follow no scheme, and some are dreary or garish. Aurora's birthday tutu is bright apricot; her nymphs' costumes are phlegm green. Balanchine's Garland Dance, with sixteen small girls augmenting the corps, is so blanketed in pea green that the audience does not see the children making their enfilade entry until they are all the way downstage. The ensembles look crowded; the late entry of the eight extra girls isn't the burst of excess that I remember. Probably, if Balanchine had known there was going to be a set with stairs, he would have allowed for it.

The company has changed a lot since Balanchine's death. The hardest change of all is the decline in musical standards. The orchestra, roofed over and miked as it never was in Balanchine's—and Robert Irving's—day, cannot have been happy, but after two weeks it was still playing the score crudely, with a brass section that blatted and flatted. Of the three conductors, Hugo Fiorato drew the best sound from the orchestra and the best performances from the dancers. Gordon Boelzner, an excellent musician, is not yet a master of orchestral technique. Maurice Kaplow's inflexible beat lashed the dancers about the stage.

It is strange to encounter musical problems at New York City Ballet, but then it is strange to see New York City Ballet dancing *The Sleeping Beauty*. How does one watch it, exactly? When I watch from the point of view of *Sleeping Beauty* style, comparing this production with others, I'm impressed. When I watch from the point of view of NYCB style, and think what that has meant to me over the years, I lose heart for the future. Despite the wonderful work of Kistler, Nichols, and other dancers in key roles, and despite a consistently excellent corps de ballet, this is stylistically a backward-looking production. Dancers are allowed to fake their technique and punch out steps the way other companies do. Yes, they dance on the music, but not, as in the old days, on *behalf* of the music. And in the Rose adagio the company is praying to a false god. The touchstone of American ballerina technique in the nineties is balance-imbalance as a constant dynamic. Does the company think that this hallmark of Balanchine was just a Suzanne Farrell specialty? It was not only the hallmark of Balanchine long before Farrell, it was exciting dancing long before Balanchine. When NYCB ballerinas go for that first series of piqué balances in attitude, they look like dutiful dolls giving us exciting posing.

Kyra Nichols, with her exquisitely slow multiple pirouettes, proves, if proof is needed, that she has the authority
to impose herself on "Petipa" the way Fonteyn did and
Maria Tallchief did in Balanchine's *Nutcracker*. I don't mean
that Nichols has to rip tradition apart. In the *Nutcracker*
adagio, there is a hair-raising unsupported pirouette in
which the ballerina turns toward then away from her partner; at the last second, he catches her by the wrists. There
are also Aurora-like promenades in arabesque. This is a
good example of how Balanchine treated traditional material, preserving the best of the old, embracing the new. And
what of ballerinas outside New York City Ballet? Balanchine's *Nutcracker* can be excitingly danced by Miami City
Ballet because the choreography is still fresh, but the San
Francisco's Elizabeth Loscavio, at twenty-one already an authoritative Aurora, hasn't much to look forward to in a role
that poses no further challenges. When Petipa created Aurora as Taglioni, he did not give her Taglioni's steps—he
gave her the most beautiful steps he could think of, and
probably the hardest ones, too.

New York City Ballet's production was an eighty-fourth
birthday salute to Lincoln Kirstein, born May 4, 1907.
Kirstein was twenty-six years old when he brought Balanchine to New York to found the School of American Ballet
and, ultimately, New York City Ballet. Balanchine's name
day, the feast of St. George, falls on April 23. April 24 was
the opening night of *The Sleeping Beauty*, a ballet he had
often talked of producing. Kirstein stepped before the curtain with Martins, and the two of them drank a toast to
Tchaikovsky, Petipa, and Balanchine. While the ballet was
running at the State Theater, Carnegie Hall celebrated its
centenary. A hundred years ago, on May 5, Tchaikovsky was
there to open the hall. On his fifty-first birthday, May 7, he

conducted his Suite No. 3, which was to become a Balanchine ballet with a finale, *Theme and Variations*, that pays homage to *The Sleeping Beauty*. It was Tchaikovsky's first and only visit to America.

What this strange alignment of ballet, composer, and company suggests to me is that the present revival means something it would not have meant if it had occurred last year, as one of several centennial productions. New York City Ballet has always had a rendezvous with *The Sleeping Beauty*. Whether the powers there think they have already kept it or have some way to go—that's for them to know and us to find out.

—*May 27, 1991*

Agnes and Martha

Agnes de Mille's *Dance to the Piper* has deservedly been called a classic. An autobiography published in 1952, it told a spunky-American-girl success story, but with a twist: the girl was rich and well connected, and she struggled in a world where none of that mattered; she had to learn spunk before she could succeed. De Mille, a skillful and spontaneous writer, mingled exhilaration and irony in just the right proportions. The opening sentence caught the spirit of the whole book: "This is the story of an American dancer, a spoiled egocentric wealthy girl, who learned with difficulty to become a worker, to set and meet standards, to brace a Victorian sensibility to contemporary roughhousing, and who, with happy good fortune, participated by the side of great colleagues in a renaissance of the most ancient and magical of all the arts."

A dozen more de Mille books have followed, their contents enlarging on the terrain of *Dance to the Piper*: personal and professional adventures, dance history, family and friends, Old Hollywood, personalities in the arts. De Mille's writing still has panache, and it has acquired dimension.

Last year, in *Portrait Gallery*, she published fuller accounts
of some of the people who had figured in *Dance to the Piper*.
There was a priceless record of Sol Hurok's table talk, and
some family secrets were exposed, among them the discomfort of her uncle Cecil Blount De Mille at having had a Jewish mother. Now, in *Martha: The Life and Work of Martha
Graham* (Random House), de Mille expands and deepens
her profile of the woman who was the greatest of the "great
colleagues" in *Dance to the Piper* and the most vivid figure in
the book, apart from de Mille herself. *Martha* may actually
have been intended as a companion volume. The book
jacket features twin portraits of Graham and de Mille by the
same painter, and the first sentence of the book recalls the
beginning of *Dance to the Piper*, only instead of a dissonant
fanfare it is an absolutistic gong stroke: "This is the story of
a genius, of a woman who made a greater change in her
art—in the idiom, in the technique, in the content, and in
the point of view—than almost any other single artist who
comes readily to mind." It doesn't sound half as interesting
as the story of the spoiled egocentric, and it's debatable besides. De Mille doesn't mean that Graham made the greatest
change in the modern dance; she means that Graham was
the greatest, or almost the greatest, of all artists who made
changes in any art. Possibly Wagner was her equal, but not
Picasso. (His changes affected only painting.) And after
Graham the revolutionary genius there's Graham the institution, which in de Mille's view can be compared only with
the Grand Kabuki—favorably! For the Grand Kabuki took
two hundred years to evolve, while Graham's theatre was
the product of a single lifetime.

If all of *Martha* were in this maniacal-monumental vein,
the book would not be worth mentioning in the same
breath as *Dance to the Piper*. To be sure, that is where the

claims and the effusions about Graham originate, but the role that Graham plays in *Dance to the Piper* is that of a goddess; and a goddess who inspires, goads, and chastens the heroine is a dramatic necessity. Without that Martha Graham, de Mille's life story would have been like *Hamlet* without the ghost.

The Martha Graham of *Martha* is a much more lifelike creation. De Mille writes out of love, awe, bewilderment, exasperation. She has a Hollywood-shrewd way of dealing with legends, particularly in the later stages of the book, when the Graham operation comes under strange new management:

> Now, under the guidance of Ron Protas, there was an attempt to charge royalties for all usage, not only of composed dances, but of actual technique: an impossible project . . . Every program and announcement bore the assurance that the Graham technique had been designated and registered as an official trademark . . . The presentation hinted of Lourdes, all the external trappings were being enshrined and worshiped. And sold. This was called "public relations."

De Mille's heart goes out to the Graham, crippled and frail, who daily met her obligations to the Graham industry. But she also uses her own emotional investment in Graham's career as a legitimately intrusive biographical device. Seventy-odd years of memories existed to be drawn on, including an encompassing, for de Mille, friendship. This friendship, which began in 1929, ended in 1986, when de Mille lectured at Graham's school and Graham received her courteously but distantly. Their careers had never intersected, but they had once been close, or so de Mille thought. "One does not domesticate a prophetess," de Mille had warned herself in *Dance to the Piper*, and in *Martha* she speculates on Graham's attitude toward her. "She must have liked me, yet very possibly I was also at times a burdensome nuisance in my constant pleading for advice, my talents manifesting themselves in such a comparatively frivolous manner and in such a derivative style." (One may speculate, in turn, whether frivolous-and-derivative, as in *Oklahoma!* and *Carousel*, would have bothered Graham half as much as solemn-and-derivative, as in *Fall River Legend*.)

There was no cooperation on the book from Graham. "She said tartly that she was going to write her own autobiography and changed the subject," de Mille informs us. Not wishing to offend, she withheld publication until after Graham's death, which occurred last spring amid talk of Graham franchises and subleasing contracts. The book speaks for many others who invested emotionally in Graham and remain uncowed by the latter-day House of Graham mystique. De Mille does not trouble herself with this mystique. Her approach is very simply to tell us everything she knows about the woman. It works, and *Martha* is a triumphantly unruly and truthful book, because, for all de Mille's settled opinions on what Graham stands for, her information and her insight keep flowing. "Keep the channel open" was Graham's own advice to de Mille at the end of *Dance to the Piper*. She has followed it.

De Mille's Victorian sensibility was one of several things that she may have felt she had in common with Graham. Both had had a privileged upbringing, a pretty and orderly family life shattered by the loss of an idol-father. Both were seduced onto the stage by the sight of a female star—Ruth St. Denis in Graham's case, Anna Pavlova in de Mille's. Both endured years of hardship in their professional lives. The reader of *Dance to the Piper* will see the resemblance in

Martha; de Mille doesn't point it out. She doesn't ever confuse herself with Graham, but she responds viscerally to the
strain that Graham was under and is quick to register quirks
and shadings in her temperament. Graham's bohemianism
when she was a young woman always shocks her, because
she knows about Graham's propriety. And she cannot
fathom the Graham who in old age becomes a fixture on the
celebrity circuit. When this Graham, lying in the hospital,
lets her hair go white, it is de Mille—de Mille of Broadway
and Hollywood—who urges her to leave it that way. "The
hell I will," the great artist says, and calls in a colorist. (The
incident is also recounted in *Blood Memory*, the "autobiography" issued by Graham the celebrity as her crowning contribution to the commercialization of her empire.)

Graham was such an original spirit, so dangerous to be
near, and so Sphinx-like in her final years, that we may be
surprised to discover how involving her life was to those
who knew her. De Mille brings us very close to the Presence—she even has some intimate knowledge of Graham's
sex life—yet she is content to interpret Graham as an obsessed artist, a woman who gave up her life for her work,
who wanted love but could never have it. Perhaps Graham's
banality was her mystery. Perhaps most women artists covet
the life of an ordinary woman, especially in relation to men,
and Graham was no exception. De Mille tells how Graham
nearly wrecked her company trying to establish Erick
Hawkins as co-star and co-creator. "Pearl [Lang] went to
Martha's dressing room. 'Martha,' she said, 'he's not worth
one of your tears. You are the greater artist. You are carrying our flag.' Martha raised her ruined face and with streaming eyes said softly, 'But I love him.' "

It hardly matters that de Mille can't seem to decide
whether Graham was a masochist, a martyr to feminism, or
"the last of the sacrificial females, a nineteenth-century

victim." None of that engages us the way Graham's daily personality does, or her actual behavior (much of it unspeakable), or her conversation, which de Mille is so good at transcribing. She also gives us Graham as she was seen by others—what would the Hero be without the Chorus? A shifting cast of Graham-watchers crowds the book. Every move Graham makes on or off the stage is discussed, weighed, worked at. Graham herself has one confidante, a Mrs. Wickes, who is a Jungian lay analyst. How she must have needed Mrs. Wickes! But was she under analysis or what, and, if not, why? The more inscrutable and intransigently private the woman gets, the heavier the talk gets. You have the feeling that this is just the way it was in life, with marathon phone calls keeping everyone up on news of Martha. You sense the emotions of dozens of people feeding on each burst of gossip—the elation, the nausea. Out of pages of analytical turmoil and post-facto dramatization, out of masses of ungovernable detail, a life grows, and it grows beyond the rationales; de Mille does not try to restrain it. The fact that she can't ultimately explain Graham to us gives her book a tragic authority.

Graham was born in Pittsburgh in 1894, de Mille in New York in 1905, and both had girlhoods in California. When they met—in New York, in 1929—Graham was not young; she was thirty-five years old. She'd had her own studio and her own professional life for only about four years, and she was living in poverty in a brownstone walkup. But this wasn't as late a start as it seems to us. Doris Humphrey, who was a year younger than Graham, produced her first independent dances two years after Graham produced hers. The two had spent their youth in Denishawn, which at the time was the only college of dance in America. (Graham did have a late start as a dancer; she took her first dance lesson, at Denishawn, at the age of twenty-two. De Mille, also a late starter, began ballet at fourteen.) Modern dance was still a new idea, and with the emergence of Graham and Humphrey it was right on schedule.

But it was very much an older woman's art form. St. Denis had always danced like a lady. De Mille's opinion of St. Denis's way of moving—"It just was not interesting enough"—tells us what Graham must have secretly felt about it. (Her loyalty to Miss Ruth would have prevented her from speaking out.) When Graham discovered that she had the power in her to transform dance as it was then known, she was well into her maturity as a performer. The possibilities that would have been open to a young body were denied her. As a teacher, she had pupils who were fifteen years younger, de Mille says, "but even while she was standing beside them and dancing publicly with them, she insisted on out-dancing, out-running, out-performing every other woman on the stage, every other woman in her profession." I think that Graham's belated discovery tortured her, and compelled her to create for herself those magnificent reformative roles—roles that were youthfully delicate or youthfully heroic. De Mille notes how Graham, in many of her earlier pieces, surrounded herself with stalwart young women; she looked like an orchid amid cactus. She didn't begin to play tragic queens until she was in her fifties. She didn't double-cast her roles and share them with young women (the Four Marys, the young Judith) until her sixties, or parcel out the bulk of her personal repertory until her seventies. She left the stage at seventy-five, long after the time had come.

No woman ever regretted old age more, no dancer ever fought her dying body harder than Martha Graham. I saw her for the first time, in *Clytemnestra*, when she was sixty-three. She was still doing hinge drops onto the back of her neck, still kicking high and falling flat, and scuttling across the floor on her feet or knees. The feet had arthritis, so she punished them. The hands, too, were gnarled, so she flaunted them. She was, as de Mille confirms, in agony, and drinking heavily. "Die while you're still beautiful," she advised one of her dancers during her last, miserable years onstage. When the power to move on cue left her, she still had incurable stamina, and was forced to lead that half life which all performers but most especially dancers dread worse than death. Turning ninety, she had not forgotten what it was to live as a dancer, to have a body: "As a dancer, you take that body and you train it, almost like a little animal—you discipline it, care for it, feed it, and you adore it. It's a symbol of your life; it is your life." She had six more years to go.

Some of de Mille's chronology is off. She says that Graham danced her last performance in 1968; it was in 1969, and it was a year later (not in 1967) that her retirement became official, with a page-one announcement in the *Times*. Apparently, no one had told Graham about it. She was scheduled to appear on the stage of the Brooklyn Academy the following evening to accept the Handel Medallion, New York City's highest cultural award. She did so, then dryly discredited the *Times* story, saying, "When I retire, I'll probably go to a Greek island, and you'll know nothing about it." De Mille states that she was drunk. I didn't think she was, but then Graham fooled a lot of people. And she never did dance again. Not long afterward, she was hospitalized with what de Mille informs us was cirrhosis of the liver, and told that she was dying. The history of Graham's alcoholism is vague. Although de Mille says that Graham when she first knew her did not drink, she also reports Louis Horst's telling people that Graham relied on a daily dose of whiskey before she ever had a company. Horst, Graham's music director, had been her lover before being displaced by Hawkins. Nobody ever displaced Hawkins. He and Graham were together from 1940 to 1950; the last two years, they were legally married. His leaving Graham was probably what triggered her drinking problem.

Horst, who had been her mentor, was ten years older than Graham; Hawkins was about fifteen years younger. Even to outsiders, it was obvious that the Graham-Hawkins partnership was a replay of Ruth St. Denis and Ted Shawn. De Mille reinforces the parallel, starting with the disparity in their ages and going right down the line: her talent, his lack of it; her indulgence, his abuse of it; her need of his managerial abilities, his need of power, his ambition, his conceit. In love, as in all things, Graham outdid her model. St. Denis could occasionally restrain Shawn's more deluded aspirations with a quiet "No, Teddy, no." She didn't mind that he was homosexual. But Graham was sexually dependent on Hawkins; de Mille hints at undertones of sado-masochism in their union. And Graham was desperately determined that her husband have artistic success. Horst, who might have seen Hawkins coming, moaned, "This is Shawn all over again, and she swore it would never happen in her life." Ruth and Ted, Martha and Erick—their fatal symmetry is the skeleton key to *Clytemnestra*. Graham, with her usual resourcefulness, mentally cast two Denishawn generations as the House of Atreus.

Sex, dancing, and life were for her, as for most great dance artists, indivisible. An earlier biographer, Don Mc-Donagh, quoted her explanation of why a dancer turns her legs out: "The thing that makes you turn . . . is the desire to turn, first, so that everything comes out in desire; and where does desire reside but between the legs, for most people." The gynecological aspects of Graham symbolism became more fraught as she aged. De Mille does not go deeply into this. She does say that Graham's sexual vulnerability was profound, that sex was "the key root to her dynamic organization." And, presumably, to its breakdown. I believe that in some of Graham's late pieces what was on view was a woman's outraged sexuality. Because her bodily anguish was not relieved by creation, Graham let her art become a fount of curses. You simply couldn't look at the stage. When the spirit wasn't present, it was awful; when it was, it was worse. And not just because of the drinking.

Graham and de Mille belong to a generation of enlightened anti-Victorian women for whom sex tends to be a totem. Graham expressed the attitude of this generation most explicitly in *Phaedra* (1962), the piece that riled members of Congress. *Phaedra* was about phallic worship and male superiority from the viewpoint of the undernourished woman. (Paul Taylor, Graham's Theseus, later wrote, "Sometimes I think she views us men onstage as giant dildos.") De Mille was delighted by it; all right-thinking women were supposed to be—it was the truth! But you had only to compare it with *Dark Meadow* (1946) to see how far Graham had descended from holy awe. *Phaedra* wasn't erotically charged; it was angry. This was the spiteful Martha, the Martha who bullied her girls and flirted with her boys.

Theatrically accomplished women of the anti-Victorian generation were powerfully motivated by their sexuality, their talent, and their anger. When these women became stars, their talent carried them part of the way, and then their anger drove them. The bigger the star and the longer the career, the deeper and more corrosive the rage. Elders of the stage and screen, they "hang around getting into trouble," as de Mille says. They collect our tributes, and they don't count the cost. De Mille—called by Elia Kazan "the most strong-minded stage artist I've known"—has been fortunate. She became a choreographer and an author. She has grown old and venerable without corroding in the spotlight.

When Graham was told that she was dying of alcoholism, she decided to quit drinking and get well. Then she went back to work and fired everybody. De Mille writes:

> One by one Martha and Ron [Protas] rid themselves of all the faithful workers and the board members—relentlessly, brutally, and finally. It was almost Russian in its thoroughness. No quarter was given and no respect paid to any memories. Onlookers were amazed and even considerably frightened. She or Ron, or she together with Ron, cleaned out the entire Graham organization.

By the end of 1973, Bertram Ross and Mary Hinkson, billed as associate directors, were gone. By the end of the seventies, Graham had begun a new life. She redyed her hair, had face-lifts, accepted luxurious gifts, and attended openings and parties—"even, God save us, discothèques," wails de Mille—and it was all for business purposes. There was the Blackglama-mink ad: Graham appeared with Margot Fonteyn and Rudolf Nureyev, shocking the old grads to the core, shocking even the ballet fans. She got a mink coat and the school got a donation. De Mille does not begrudge her her pleasures, but the change was unsettling: "She looked like a little Oriental deity, a little goddess, an empress, like a miniature Japanese doll. She was tiny and costly, rare and superb. And very remote. How unlike the plain girl we used to know, with the thunder in her head!"

Maybe the plain girl had been too plain. At Denishawn,

she had failed to attract the eye of her heroine, St. Denis. Doris Humphrey was the favorite, and Graham was pushed off on Shawn, to become his protégée. (De Mille says that St. Denis secretly feared a dangerous rival.) In *Blood Memory* Graham relates how she would have to tend St. Denis's addled mother or help St. Denis wash her hair. Not that she minded—Miss Ruth remained ever perfect. And Graham remained forever transfixed by her. Just as Graham's entire career can be read as a corrective of St. Denis, its postlude can be seen as a capitulation to her. In the twilight of her life, Graham became the true and complete Miss Ruth, floating, with her "Oriental" remoteness, above the media circus, neither in it nor out of it. St. Denis and Shawn had been aesthetic snobs, intolerant of kitsch, although they were formed by it and were not above turning a profit in vaudeville. Ruth St. Denis's epoch-making dreams of an exotic nonclassical dance style had actually been inspired by a cigarette poster. When Graham posed for Blackglama or appeared on *Entertainment Tonight*, she was returning as Miss Ruth to her source. She was finishing what St. Denis had begun, and she saw to it that the end of modern dance was in its beginning. Kitsch was flowing back to kitsch.

Meanwhile, there were great changes in the Graham company. New pieces, when they were not parodies of old ones, were ill-conceived, with uncharacteristic choices of subject and music. Everything was designed by Halston, who had replaced the Graham fabric-and-costume department. Of this period, de Mille writes half the time as an outsider taking down the testimony of the disaffected. When she is being a direct observer, her focus is uncertain and her views are ambivalent, and she is much bedeviled by change as an inevitable factor in the preservation of the repertory. She takes heart from the return of some of the old grads to teach, and from the rise of new dancers who reinterpreted the old roles and got good reviews. In the new works produced in the eighties Graham "continued to be herself, composing and directing and bringing to our stage her unmatched instinct, her impeccable taste, her boldness." "Continued to be herself" in such pieces as *Andromache's Lament*, *The Rite of Spring*, and *Maple Leaf Rag*? De Mille does not say that the level was as high as ever; individual works had flaws, Halston was deplorable, and the dancers were, on the whole, poor substitutes for the artists who had performed with Martha. Still, what today's dancers perform is recognizable to her as Graham: "Chopin played by a beginner is still Chopin and still an experience to cherish." Yes, if the beginner is talented and well trained. I remember some of the Graham dancers whom de Mille names as artists, and to me there is not the slightest resemblance between them and the current Graham "stars"; and there is not a shred of continuity between the performance style of the sixties—or even the seventies—and that of the Protas era.

Although de Mille says that "Martha's literature" is now being preserved, I don't think the company ever recovered from the blow that Graham and Protas dealt it in 1973. People were right to be alarmed by Protas and Halston and Blackglama. This was not just a new period in Graham's life; it really was a new life. I have sometimes thought that Graham's "rebirth" (her own word) was made possible only by a complete break with her former life, and this entailed the elimination of the Graham image from her company's performance. Graham believed that she could never be replaced in her great roles—that it was better to destroy the mold than present weak copies. She did not intend to let the wonderful dancers whom she'd developed be her successors. They had to be sacrificed and their example expunged, so that the only Grahamites left would be pure products of the school or hybrids trained in Graham technique by others. A Graham company without Graham was going to be a sham anyway; let it be a deliberate sham.

Let it be a completely new company, true to its idea of Graham, not hers. She didn't really have to set her hand to any destructive policy. Once she'd broken the chain of succession, she merely had to let the inevitable take place and resign herself to functioning as a CEO. Naturally, she would look after the choreography, but as she had never considered herself a choreographer to begin with ("I only choreograph so as to have dances to perform"), this was a task she could accept as part of her new regime.

All that is one theory. Another is that she simply wasn't responsible. She was leading the half life of a retired dancer with the brain of a reformed drunk. She was old and still unwell. She kept herself alive with work, supporting the business out of sheer ego. Ron Protas wanted things a certain way, and she complied. And who is Protas? Originally, he was a fan of the company who wanted to make himself useful. He was there in the hospital during Graham's "terminal" illness, and she thought he saved her. Soon he was casting her ballets and masterminding her purges, or so de Mille was informed. He is now, with Linda Hodes, running the Graham company, and it is he who retains the right to make final artistic decisions.

The Protas story is not greatly different from the stories of other dedicated young strangers who have helped bring about profound changes in the lives of aging artists. In some cases—Graham's, Picasso's—the stranger reordered the artist's life. In Stravinsky's case, it was only the art that changed. But in all instances it was the intrusion of a new person with a new program which enabled the artist to go on producing. The story of Protas's rise, as de Mille tells it, has never before seen print. Too many people do not know what to make of him. They want above all to protect the Graham organization. But for some old and scarred Graham-watchers this organization is Graham's in name only. It is a husk, like the empty shell of the queen's dress which is left standing by itself at the end of *Episodes*. The queen, Mary Stuart, had a motto: "In my end is my beginning." Life, for Graham, had come full circle, and art had reverted to fancy dancing, more or less as she had found it.

—*October 14, 1991*

Miami's *Jewels*

George Balanchine's three-part *Jewels*, often billed as the world's first full-length "abstract" ballet, was a hit from the moment of its première, in 1967—a fact that may prevent us from seeing that it is actually one of his most delicate creations, so intricately engineered that it easily crumbles in performance. Balanchine himself had to shore up *Emeralds* when he lost his two first-cast ballerinas, Violette Verdy and Mimi Paul, but *Emeralds* over the years has proved to be only slightly more fragile than *Rubies* and *Diamonds*. All three ballets rely on a complex interworking of structure and style; without a sense of how *Jewels* operates, it cannot be done, either in whole or in part. When it was last seen, a year ago, New York City Ballet's supposedly definitive production was nearly two-thirds destroyed, with only corps work and, less dependably, the performing of the *Diamonds* ballerina to carry the whole thing off. (All too often, you got the wrong ballerina.) The qualities that *Jewels* requires—precision of execution, musical intelligence, energy, and taste—happen not to exist in abundance anywhere in the world today. The failure of Balanchine's own company adds one other scarce quality to that daunting list of requisites: nerve.

Miami City Ballet is not a great company; it is merely one of the most daring and rewarding of the younger companies now on the rise throughout the country. Its director, Edward Villella, has perception as well as ambition. When he produced *Rubies*, two and a half years ago, he knew from having danced it for Balanchine that high spirits were not enough. Determined to acquire the entire trilogy, he depended on an excellent staff and some talented dancers to help him bring off a coup. At this point in their development, the Miamians are finding out what it takes to turn a company into an institution. The complete *Jewels* was to have crowned seven years of steady growth; instead, its première last month, at the Kravis Center for the Performing Arts, in West Palm Beach, was a triumph, precisely, of nerve. For Miami City Ballet, 1992 has been a year of setbacks. Like every other company, it was troubled by the recession, but it also had bad luck: an engagement in Los Angeles canceled because of the Rodney King riots and, four months later, the Florida hurricane. Although only the company's wardrobe department suffered actual storm damage, the disaster wiped out important funding sources and threw a heavy damper on ticket sales.

For a luxury operation like ballet, this was hell, nor is the company out of it. But there is a venturesomeness about the Miamians that reminds me of New York City Ballet in its City Center years. Last month's *Jewels* went on with an orchestra threatening to strike (very NYCB, this). The storm hadn't kept the resident designer, Haydée Morales, from coming through with a complete set of Karinska-inspired costumes. On the eve of the première, however, the scenery for *Diamonds*, which had to move on cue, still hadn't been tried out.

But the première, a gala benefit, was a sellout, and in spite of everything the coup happened on schedule. The conductor was Akira Endo, formerly of American Ballet Theatre. As the *Diamonds* cast swung into the finish, the audience blasted off, and it was pure madhouse for ten minutes after the curtain fell. Not since the last great performances of Suzanne Farrell and Peter Martins had the ballet gone over like this. But, of course, Miami City Ballet does not possess the likes of Suzanne Farrell and Peter Martins— or Violette Verdy or Patricia McBride. Or Edward Villella. What the Miami production proved was that *Jewels* can exist without the stars it once showcased so memorably. A company with a secure enough sense of structure and style can present this elusive ballet—can make it seem possible again for another generation of dancers in an America irrevocably changed by what Balanchine wrought back in the sixties and seventies.

In the principal roles, the company gave performances ranging from the well-drilled and workmanlike through the movingly conscientious to the surprisingly apt. There were no great personal revelations along the way (those will come), but the ballets were revelation enough: stopped clocks started ticking again. *Rubies* is a real job of restoration. No one performs the Villella role better today than the Romanian dancer Marin Boieru; he lacks only Villella's spontaneity and sense of mischief to be perfect. Maribel Modrono, a McBride-in-the-making, evaded none of the difficulties that lay in her path. That is the way to grow and to keep the ballet growing. The beginning of the end for New York City Ballet's *Emeralds* came when its ballerinas decided that the Verdy choreography was too subtle, too hard, or "too Violette," and only the Farrell role really mattered anyway. Marielena Mencia is not the dancer to restore the Verdy role—she's not even remotely a Balanchine dancer—but her mettlesome performance of the wonderful "bracelets" solo was a rebuke to the elaborate faking we see at NYCB. Mencia and Iliana Lopez are Villella's two senior ballerinas and were already formed stylistically when he hired them. Lopez, with the same disadvantage of being untrained in Balanchine style, knew what to aim for in the *Diamonds* adagio. Partnered securely by her husband, Franklin Gamero, she succeeded in adding scale and consequence to her dancing and heightening the soft luster she has by nature; I have never admired her more.

The company is beginning to show us a ballerina lineup. In Maribel Modrono and in her twin sister, Mabel, who danced in the *Emeralds* pas de trois, School of American Ballet virtues gleam. Below principal level, there is a uniform elegance of bearing and an amplitude that looks new. The freedom of movement in the upper back is a special joy; it's another thing I recall seeing in the City Center company. Villella's dancers aren't the new breed of overcorrect T-square classicists who sap the dance meaning from Balanchine's ballets. And the best of them aren't all men, although along with Boieru there was Arnold Quintane, outstanding in the *Emeralds* pas de trois. The most exciting dancer in *Jewels*, the most exuberant and the wittiest, was Myrna Kamara. Other dancers may have performed both the bighearted, space-straddling showgirl of *Rubies* and the role I think of as Melisande's in *Emeralds*, but not usually in the same performance, and not like this. Kamara has recreated both characters; her natural energy unleashes something new on the ballet stage, and Villella is giving her chances she has never had before. She spent five years in New York City Ballet getting nowhere. Now, suddenly, she has a future.

One hopes that the company does, too—that its misfortunes won't continue into next year. This *Jewels* marks a very evident new stage in the maturing of a company style. The production, the only complete *Jewels* besides New York City Ballet's, goes into repertory in Miami on February 27, by which time the scenery problem, which is conceptual as well as functional, will presumably have been solved. Where does *Diamonds* take place? Robert Darling's frosted ocher pennants against dark-blue drapes suggested nothing to me. Pairs of stalactites lowered at the start of the chorale were dramatic but confusing: were we in an ice cavern? But the illuminated green-disk constellations of *Emeralds* and the red ones of *Rubies* were perfectly okay.

—*December 28, 1992–January 4, 1993*

The Balanchine Show

What did Balanchine really expect would happen to his ballets when he died? In 1974, he answered the question this way: "People dance while I'm here, they dance a certain way. When I'm gone, they will continue dancing, but somebody will rehearse them different and it will all be a little different, with different approach, different intensity. So a few years go by and I won't be here. Will be my ballets, but will look different." At the time, that didn't seem such a bad thing to look forward to. The ballets had already changed; the technique was different in the seventies from what it had been in the fifties. For Balanchine to offer us as the worst that could happen "different approach, different intensity," for him to indicate that what was in store might just be a more radical version of the process of change that is built into the art, meant, I think, that he was seriously considering, probably for the first time, the matter of a successor. He was not harboring any unrealistic hopes. "Memories are short; also, bodies are lazy." He said that, too, in 1974, and in the same interview; he was very fond of saying it. It didn't quite fit into the picture he drew of a post-Balanchine world in which all that is missing is Balanchine himself, but the statement as a whole, while typically enigmatic (one wonders how different the ballets could look and still be his), was a far cry from the terrible finality of what he usually said about the future of his repertory: "When I go, it goes." The future sounded almost tolerable, almost interesting. If this was a rare moment of optimism, what had caused it?

For Balanchine, 1974 was late in the day; he had turned seventy. The previous year, he had been in Germany filming fifteen of his ballets, not for commercial but for archival purposes. The man who cared nothing for posterity was not above taking certain precautions. He went on filming or videotaping right to the end. Also, in 1974 his company was coming back to strength after a fallow period; his school was pouring out talent; his audience, which had begun to drift away and had been recaptured only by the superhuman effort of the Stravinsky Festival of 1972, was now caught up in something the press called "the ballet boom"—it filled the State Theater nightly, breathless with expectation. Balanchine rewarded it with the burst upon burst of glory that marked his final decade of creativity: *Chaconne*, *Union Jack*, *Vienna Waltzes*, *Mozartiana*. The choreographer's health was breaking down, but his creation, New York City Ballet, was sound.

Was it in the euphoria of the moment that Balanchine calculated the longevity of his ballets once he was gone, and gave an estimate of twenty years? Twenty years! The figure stuns us with its generosity. Yet when we consider that twenty years for a repertory without its master was a life span that could have been predicted for Petipa's ballets— and Petipa did not have his ballets on film—we begin to understand Balanchine's thinking. Probably, he was basing his estimate on the condition of those old ballets as he first encountered them, in the teens of this century. His own case, he must have reckoned, corresponded to Petipa's. *His* descendants, passing along their secrets, would be able to keep his ballets alive, in some sort of "different" but recognizable form, until at least the first decade of the next century.

We know now that, so far as New York City Ballet's caretaking capacities are concerned, this is not going to happen. The company is in the midst of an eight-week Balanchine retrospective marking the tenth anniversary of his death and the catastrophically swift decline of his repertory under Peter Martins. Five years ago, the ballets were still there. They haven't been put to the test of time and changing circumstance, changing tastes; they haven't deteriorated the way Balanchine had a right to expect them to—as a natural consequence of his not being there to rehearse them and despite the best efforts of those in charge. That kind of deterioration would be heartbreaking, but it would be in the nature of things: ballets aren't like sculptures or paintings. (Even paintings die after thirty years, Marcel Duchamp said.) Those of us who have been around long enough to see Balanchine's ballets when they were new would give anything to see in them now the qualities that Balanchine predicted for them in 1974: "different approach, different intensity." But Martins's treatment of them cannot be said to embody anything so conscious as an approach. There is no new point of view, no sense of rediscovery or impress of conviction, not even a shift in tone. The ballets have had their hearts torn out. They hold the stage not through any lingering or newly arrived-at "intensity" but through their own irreducible merit as constructions and— might as well admit it—their cachet as Balanchine products. They live not as ballets that have changed but as empty demonstrations of formerly meaningful spectacles. Where the company used to put on *Apollo*, it now puts on *The Apollo Show*. It puts on *The Four Temperaments Show*, *The La Valse Show*, *The Jewels Show*.

Balanchine was famously indifferent to the ultimate fate of his ballets; this is not to say he didn't care who would be rehearsing the company on the day of his death. History teaches the crucial importance of the immediate successor. Petipa had Nicholas Legat, Bournonville had Ludwig Gade, followed by Hans Beck. Without those men, nothing at all of the nineteenth century would have remained to atrophy. Balanchine trained Peter Martins carefully, supervised his ballets, did what he could to educate his taste. He must have seen that Martins would not be his Legat, but he was a religious man on his deathbed, and such things were in the hands of God. As for Martins, he talked impressively about preserving the "legacy," but he also talked about not being just a curator (as if Balanchine's work had gone out of date when the old man died) and about the need for change and innovation (as if he were the creative force that could produce it). It's a question whether preservation was ever a priority with Martins. Because of Legat, Lopukhov, and other Maryinsky ballet masters (and because of Diaghilev, who loved *The Sleeping Beauty*), Balanchine was able to reclaim Petipa. Harald Lander by a similar route could reclaim Bournonville. But if the process of descent is disrupted right at the beginning, if the inheritance is squandered by the first generation, there can be no hope of eventually reconstituting it. The possibility that there would be at least one unborn generation that would come to know Balanchine's art pretty much as he intended it to be known—that possibility is denied.

Like the Columbus quincentennial, the Balanchine Celebration contains the seeds of its own destruction. Already vulnerable, Martins's regime is calling up reserves of ineptitude its worst enemies didn't know it had. Memory is not so short that images of the great performances of the past cannot be called to mind as a judgment upon the present. (Some of the greatest performances were being given as recently as 1991.) Inexplicably, the company helps us out with film clips of the golden years or with *Serenade* or *Symphonie Concertante* danced by School of American Ballet students. These teenagers had only to take the stage to put their elders to shame. But the elders convicted themselves, not only in the regular repertory, which they regularly misrepresent, but in revivals of long absent works, like the *Valse Fantaisie*, the *"Sylvia" Pas de Deux*, and the two pas de trois to Minkus and Glinka, all of which Balanchine made in the fifties for the likes of Eglevsky, Tallchief, Le Clercq, Adams, Hayden, and Wilde. Some of these pieces had actually been rehearsed or supervised by members of the original casts. Since the "text" was true, the failure of the new casts was all the more visible. You didn't have to wait for the dancers to fall off pointe or out of their turns—the facial expressions were enough. Instead of the smiling mastery one might have remembered from Eglevsky and Tallchief, one saw tension and fear or the bravado of insecurity. Choreography that had been designed to show dancers off now showed them up.

There is a widespread belief in the profession that today's standards of technique are way above those of a generation ago. Before we discredit this belief, let's ask whether today's NYCB truly represents the highest standards of technique. Standards did rise, and they also changed. But I daresay that at no time would the company under Balanchine have been incapable of the petit allegro required for the Glinka pas de trois or the dangerously unmoored pirouettes of the Tallchief coda variation in *Sylvia*. By the seventies, the technique had branched out, but it branched from the same tree that Balanchine had been cultivating since the beginning. The company has now taken an axe to that tree.

Technique changes, but style, the soil that nourishes technique, never changes. Many of us were shocked by what the past decade gradually but unmistakably disclosed—that Peter Martins was not an adept of the style, not Balanchinean, not a believer, and didn't want to be. There are some talented répétiteurs on his staff, and here and there one sees small triumphs for which these répétiteurs must be responsible—a skeletal passage suddenly fleshed out with tantalizing detail, a soloist briefly endowed with wit and fantasy. If one could seize and analyze these moments, one would see that they are made of simple virtues: constancy of articulation, musical fidelity, and, simplest and rarest of all, moral commitment. These are mutually dependent virtues, and they add up to what we have been accustomed to think of as Balanchine style.

There is no great mystery to the style; children understand it. Among the many Balanchine seminars held during the season was one on the staging and teaching of Balanchine. Kay Mazzo, a former principal dancer now an SAB instructor, had a young student demonstrate fundamentals and the principles behind them: the tightly crossed fifth position, the resilient plié ("go down to go up"), the tendus extended from the center of the body. Everything the student did revealed the Balanchinean ideal: a focused, intelligent, forward-and-upward dancer overflowing with energy. Mazzo reminded the audience that in the well-known Cartier-Bresson photograph of Balanchine teaching class he is demonstrating tendu. Everyone knew what she was talking about; whether out of ignorance, fatuity, or self-reproach, the company has been using the photograph all season in its ads. I think that Balanchine, whose downward-extended palm is aligned with his right heel, is also telling his dancers to press the heel forward. Who is telling them that now? Balanchine's ballets were meant to project from deep inside the cubic space of a classic opera-house stage. That's why the tight fifth position is so important: it unlocks the body's ability to occupy and animate space in depth. Seeing the company now is like looking at a bas-relief or trying to read a half-open book. And along with the sensation of deep space we lose the sensation of transfigured time. Balanchine's technique is the only known technique that prepares a dancer for the intricacies of Mozart or Stravinsky. The very first stroke of battement tendu (the foot generally goes out on *and*, in on the count of *one*) is an intimate response to music. It is through strength of technique that the body stays in possession of music. Balanchine would make his dancers repeat tendu until they nearly went mad. When he had a stageful of women do it in *Symphony in C* he was alerting us all, dancers and audience, to what matters most. Lose the space-time continuum and you have lost Balanchine.

In the old days, when Balanchine was considered controversial, there used to be reasoned arguments against him, mostly from the Cecchetti camp, but also from an enclave within his own company, who preferred other teachers to him. In all the turbulence of that period, I never once heard any of those Balanchine dissenters challenge the basics of his teaching, and I see no rationale behind what the company is doing now. Lazy bodies have lazy minds. The criterion of performance is defined not by what should be done with this phrase to this music but by what So-and-so did with it last time. Martins is easily insulted by criticism, and he responds by accusing critics of wanting to turn the clock back to some previous set of standards which the company has outgrown. Isn't it Martins himself who is turning the clock back, to a pre-fifties world where full-blown Balanchine expression is as yet unknown? He resisted the idea of cooperating with former Balanchine principals who know the older ballets, because, he said, there are too many different versions of *Concerto Barocco* around. But *his Concerto Barocco* isn't even the *Concerto Barocco* in which he used to partner Gelsey Kirkland or Suzanne Farrell. A true festival version of *Concerto Barocco* would be one that united the best features of all the versions that are available, with Martins making the decisions. But this would have meant restudying the ballet and refreshing the NYCB production, thereby admitting that it had a few flaws.

The Celebration could have been marvelously restorative; instead, the whole thing is being run at status quo level. The revivals of Balanchine discards are all taken over from companies that had them first and did most of them better. Though the ballets are being presented chronologically, no opportunity was taken to revive the 1951 *Swan Lake*, the 1957 *Square Dance*, or the *Pas de Dix* (1955), which is not the same ballet as *Cortège Hongrois*. We got a truncated *Gounod Symphony*, a *La Sonnambula* with the wrong ending, and a *Theme and Variations* without the musical overture that Balanchine drew from the last movement. This last may seem a trivial omission, but it's an example of theatrical gaucherie which Balanchine would never have tolerated. Nor would he have thought much of the idea of chronological presentation. Balanchine redid many ballets and updated many more; presenting them in sequence serves no visible theory of creation and makes for dull programming. And then there is the matter of how the ballets *look*. We got no new décor to replace Benois's hideous *Theme*, nor are there any plans to dress the dressable ballets that Balanchine was forced to produce on a budget of five dollars—*Stravinsky Violin Concerto* and *Symphony in Three Movements* and *Le Tombeau de Couperin*. The new décors that were provided for some of the ballets during the first years of Martins's tenure were not all of them wonderful, but they showed a curatorial discrimination which Martins was unable to extend to choreography, reviving (and then dropping) the third movement of *Western Symphony* and the Paul Taylor solo in *Episodes*. Curating does not mean worshipping relics; it often means the opposite. Was a new production of *Bourrée Fantasque* (1949) needed to prove yet again that the first movement just doesn't work anymore? Created for two great comedians, Le Clercq and Robbins, on the intimate scale of the City Center stage, it cannot begin to explain why audiences of the time were left, in the words of one reviewer, "limp with laughter." I am sorry for whatever inhibition has kept Martins or, better, Robbins from replacing it, for the two other movements are worth saving. Legat and Beck would not have hesitated.

If Balanchine had any secret, it was one that has endured through two hundred years of classical ballet. It is that dancing correctly in three dimensions, on the music, creates the fourth dimension of meaning. Ballet becomes metaphysical not by aspiring beyond its material parts but, paradoxically, by being humblingly, gruelingly, systematically materialistic, working every technical fine point into the body until it becomes second nature. It may be the metaphysical plane in Balanchine's ballets that is throwing his epigones into confusion. They don't see that there's a direct connection between transcendence and fifth position. They've translated simplicity into superficiality. Over and over, when I watch these reductions of Balanchine prepared by Martins and Company, the thought that occurs to me is: They think it's easy. Of course they do work hard. Martins is very proud of being able to give more rehearsal hours to the ballets than Balanchine could afford. He says the company is dancing better, as a result, than it did under Mr. B. Can he really believe that x number of rehearsal hours equals great performance?

From the look of *Swan Lake* and *Symphony in C* and *Gounod* and the other big-corps works, those hours of rehearsal go mainly into straightening the lines, getting the dancers to keep together. Balanchine cared less about straight lines than about musically expressive, vital dancing. The fact that Balanchine's dancers didn't move as one, like the Royal's or the Bolshoi's, was unimportant; the point was they *moved*. Now NYCB has a synchronized corps, one without rigor, without life. As for the principals, what do they offer us in place of living performance? Balanchine's "Don't think, dear, do" is useless to dancers who carry nothing in their heads but steps and counts. Do what? Phrase how? *Symphony in C*, Balanchine's greatest show-piece, has become the mechanical ritual his detractors always said it was; it's hours of steps and counts executed in two dimensions. Nor does a ballet with a story make any difference. Here we may see dancers thinking, but their ideas about *Apollo* aren't interesting, and their "acting" in *Swan Lake* and *La Valse* is perfectly dreadful. The vacuity of *Orpheus*, the retrospective's low point so far, stands as a grim beacon pointing the way to what a post-Martins generation will bring: performances that are complete nullities, dancers who can neither think nor do.

Martins's misunderstanding of the technique required

to dance Balanchine was apparent long ago in the way he cast the ballets, and he still seems unable to analyze the requirements of the roles and the abilities of the dancers well enough to bring the two together successfully more than half the time. This analysis starts in the classroom; by the time the dancer is in the rehearsal studio trying to learn a part, it's too late. And Martins's myopic casting had the inevitable dire result. The less accurate the performance, the less scrupulous the training needed to maintain it. A couple of years ago, it began to be obvious that something had gone terribly wrong in company class. Balanchine used to welcome incoming SAB graduates to company class by saying, "Now you will learn to dance." But the school and the company have changed places; the school teaches Balanchine, and the company unteaches him.

Balanchine's system was ecological. Technique, style, discipline, morale are all under attack today not because Martins has deliberately targeted these elements but because they are all interrelated parts of a single organism—New York City Ballet. To tamper with one element is to risk systemic injury. I have spoken only of the bad dancing, but the music in which the dancing is rooted is just as bad. Here we touch on something that is the inmost treasure of Balanchine, the basis of his art, and yet the most difficult loss to account for. Like Hermione in *The Winter's Tale*, I feel it gone but know not how it went. Distorted tempos are part of the overall dark picture of inefficiency which the company presents, yet even when the tempo is reasonable the sound of the orchestra cannot be borne. Just why this formerly polished instrument should be sending up clouds of pollution I cannot say, but it is humiliating to hear *Swan Lake* played better at American Ballet Theatre. Lest we forget his impact on the musical world, it was Balanchine, not

Massine, who reconciled serious musicians to the use of symphonic scores for ballet and gave them steady jobs in his orchestra. But music is only one of the problems that the Martins regime seems helpless to solve.

The Martins issue is splitting what remains of Balanchine's audience in New York. Martins's defenders are hailing the box-office success of the Balanchine Celebration and saying that audiences are enjoying themselves. But these people want it both ways: if the season succeeds, Martins gets the credit; if it doesn't, Balanchine gets the blame. Then there are the horrified observers who would like to indict Martins for cultural vandalism. Some of them see him as a kind of prodigal son, reacting spitefully against a father figure. Still another group sees a troubled artist they must protect for the sake of his art. These people are wrong: if Martins is an artist, it is only his own artistic interests, not those of New York City Ballet, that are at stake. But Martins is not a cultural vandal. The great mistake of the last ten years was in leaving him in sole charge of the company, in thinking that he, or anyone else, could do all the jobs that Balanchine did. It is not a crime to fail to fill Balanchine's shoes, although no one would think to blame Martins if he himself hadn't insisted so doggedly on doing just that *and* on being the company's champion fund-raiser besides. In the process, his own career as a choreographer has suffered. He is leaching Balanchine from the repertory and replacing it with nothing.

For five years after Balanchine's death, the company kept going on the impetus he had given it. In 1987–88, the first signs of collapse appeared; yet so strong was that impetus that the company held together even under the battering of an ill-conceived modern-dance jamboree (billed as the American Music Festival) in the spring of '88. Today, the ruin is all but complete. The ballets are still Balanchine's in the sense that they are as yet no one else's (though *Haieff Divertimento*, a relic of 1947, was danced in a style more appropriate to a Martins ballet). Balanchinean dancers are disappearing and being replaced by un- or anti-Balanchinean dancers. Too late, we remember the overhopeful climate of the late seventies and recognize in it the seeds of our delusion that the transition from Balanchine to Martins was a logical one. The inevitability of Martins, accepted by all, accepted (however ambivalently) by Balanchine himself, can no longer be justified.

—June 7, 1993

Behind White Oaks

Since ideological barriers crumbled in the seventies, aging ballet stars have sought an alternative outlet in the modern dance, but none have done so with the success of Mikhail Baryshnikov. Baryshnikov was lucky to have come along at a moment when American modern dance could offer him a playground for his kind of technique. If Twyla Tharp hadn't been willing to open herself up to the challenge of ballet virtuosity and opera-house scale, all those other nonballet or ballet-cum-modern roles of his would be simply long-lost experiments. With Tharp, Baryshnikov began transforming himself, becoming the American Baryshnikov. He joined Balanchine's company for a year or so, and by 1980, when he took over the direction of American Ballet Theatre, he was fully naturalized.

Another piece of luck: the company Baryshnikov currently heads, the White Oak Dance Project, was founded by him in collaboration with Mark Morris, who was there to succeed Tharp as the ballet master of modern dance. Though the company is directed by a ballet star, its aesthetic reflects the modern-dance companies that most of its dancers come from: Morris's company and Tharp's and Lar Lubovitch's and Paul Taylor's. The main advantage to Baryshnikov, who is now forty-six, is that modern dancers start later and go on longer than ballet dancers, so he is able to surround himself with soloists of rank who are not kids. White Oak dancers, by and large, have already made their reputations, and some of them, like Rob Besserer and Kate Johnson, have followings almost as big, in their sphere, as Baryshnikov's.

White Oak presents itself modestly. Baryshnikov is listed as one of eight dancers, and his name leads all the rest only because the listing is alphabetical. Top billing is given to the choreographers whose work is on display. Besides Tharp and Morris, they included Merce Cunningham, Hanya Holm, and Jerome Robbins—the left, the center, and the right of the American dance spectrum—and two newcomers, the American Kevin O'Day and the German Joachim Schlömer. Anthology companies are by nature conservative, and the idiomatic variety of American modern dance virtually presupposes small chance of artistic success. To the extent that White Oak succeeds in reconciling Merce Cunningham and Hanya Holm, it does right by neither. And yet if its revivals had been all Cunningham or all Holm they wouldn't have worked any better. The strong idiomatic content of Cunningham's *Signals* (1970) is something I daresay even Cunningham's current company couldn't recapture. His recent revival of *RainForest*, a piece from the same period, looked like thin ballet. It was all too long ago, and everybody these days seems to have a ballet body, Mark Morris notwithstanding. Still, when White Oak makes a collective artistic impression it is usually because the dancers have been working directly with Morris or have some of his method in their blood, or else some of Tharp's method.

White Oak's lineage doesn't really extend back beyond these two masters.

In Holm's *Jocose*, the company was going back only to the eighties; it was one of the last pieces to come from Holm before her death a year ago at the age of ninety-nine. The dancers put it across, but on the basis of personal authority and not stylistic penetration. Substance was reduced to atmosphere. Since the atmosphere was that old standby amorous, the audience liked *Jocose* very much. And it went wild for Kevin O'Day's *Quartet for IV*, a kind of *Jocose* for today. Unlike Holm, O'Day laid out his shifting combinations of number and gender without arch references to love's roundelay. His approach was strictly formal, never veering into anecdote, and, as strict form will, it told a fresh and interesting story about men and women.

I may have made the Holm piece sound quainter than it is. Actually, the most old-fashioned of the seven works presented was the one by Schlömer, *Behind White Lilies*, a stolidly hieratic affair in which dancers dressed in Egyptian sarongs trundled opacities on and off the stage for the duration of a string trio by Schoenberg. It was a bit of a shock to learn that Schlömer is the same age as O'Day, thirty-one— much too young to have absorbed so many clichés of the expressionistic era. *Behind White Lilies* (actual urns with bouquets were on the stage, a cliché of more recent vintage) was Baryshnikov's only out-and-out mistake as artistic director, but one could forgive it for the way the Schoenberg Opus 45 was played. White Oak musical standards are high. Five years ago, this fact would not have been especially worth noting, but live musical performance at dance events has become a rarity.

I'm told that wherever White Oak appears across the country a portion of the audience arrives in black tie, even when the performance is in a gym. White Oak is a class act. There is a good nervous feeling of anticipation in the house, there is seriousness on the stage, there is civility in the air. I felt no urgency in anything the company did; its edge doesn't cut. But I did feel a strong sense of honor and, occasionally, the lash of passion. Cutting edges you can buy on Canal Street.

Baryshnikov as a dancer is in fine shape. Everyone knows he no longer does *Giselle* or *Apollo* or *Push Comes to Shove*; he communicates on an entirely different wavelength. I think that people who are just catching up to the movies *The Turning Point* and *White Nights* will have no trouble recognizing him; it's as if he'd just exchanged a tight military uniform for a slouchy sweater. On the White Oak programs in New York, he gave himself one group appearance and one solo spot every night. And though the week seemed to take a toll on his bad knee, he always came through.

In *Pergolesi*, arranged for him by Twyla Tharp, he is supercasual—noodling, dawdling, goofing off—and then he explodes into a sextuple pirouette. Some of the movement may be improvised; a lot of it was surely based on improvisation, just as a lot of *Push Comes to Shove* was. And *Push* material is recycled in *Pergolesi*: the *Swan Lake* hops in arabesque, the bits of mime ("I you marry"), the jokes about ballet versus normal behavior. Just when it gets a little too cozy and coquettish, he brings on an invisible partner (a reference, don't you suppose, to the solo's having originally been a duet with Tharp). This recharges his batteries, and he's off on a new tangent. The abrupt switches in mood, the contrasting Mishas (diffident then demonic) recall an early solo of his called *Vestris*; so does the eighteenth-century music. But *Pergolesi* mostly recalls the moment of Twyla and Misha, eighteen years ago.

Robbins's Bach suite is not nostalgic; it is all about Baryshnikov today. And it is deep-structure choreography, probing areas that only the most gifted dancing could clarify. The theme is dynamic relationships: a circle of turning hops will gradually diminish in scale but not in tempo; while the pulse still flickers, the step converts itself into large open swings of the leg. In a series of low leaps and beats in triple time, the dancer is asked to define minimum-contrast shapes clearly and fluently. In a saraband beginning with one foot decorously crossed over the other, he lifts and cantilevers his weight through the foot; the dance is almost a study in relevé. A particularly fine passage occurs when Bach sounds like a country fiddler and Baryshnikov responds by marching downstage and up a dozen times or more, each time embroidering his path with skips, with pirouettes, with turned-in knees, with robotlike rockings on his heels, and, of course, with every combination thereof.

Through all this the balance of rigor and relaxation never ceases to fascinate. Likewise the mood of the solo: it is neither antic nor pedantic. Whom to thank for this miracle of equilibrium, the dancer or the choreographer? It is clear that Baryshnikov still contains, in himself, the arsenal of virtuosity. Having fired all his rockets, he dazzles us with slingshots and popguns. Robbins magnifies the achievement by never exaggerating it. He counts as much on Baryshnikov's skill, humor, and severity as he counts on his own, and in the end it's impossible to tell where he begins and Baryshnikov leaves off. The dancer has been brilliantly challenged, and the choreographer has challenged himself.

—March 28, 1994

Discussing the Undiscussable

I have not seen Bill T. Jones's *Still/Here* and have no plans
to review it. In this piece, which was given locally at the
Brooklyn Academy, Jones presents people (as he has in the
past) who are terminally ill and who talk about it. I understand that there is dancing going on during the talking, but
of course no one goes to *Still/Here* for the dancing. People
are asking whether Jones's type of theatre is not a new art
form. Dying an art form? Why, yes, I suppose dying can be
art in a screwily post-neo-Dada sense. (Dr. Kevorkian, now
playing in Oregon . . .) But this is not the sense intended by
Bill T. Jones, even though he had his origins as a choreographer in the Dada experimentation of the sixties. If I understand *Still/Here* correctly, and I think I do—the publicity
has been deafening—it is a kind of messianic traveling medicine show, designed to do some good for sufferers of fatal
illnesses, both those in the cast and those thousands more
who may be in the audience. If we ask what a show does
that no hospital, clinic, church, or other kind of relief
agency has so far been able to do, I think the answer is obvious. If we consider that the experience, open to the public
as it is, may also be intolerably voyeuristic, the remedy is

also obvious: Don't go. In not reviewing *Still/Here*, I'm sparing myself and my readers a bad time, and yet I don't see that I really have much choice.

A critic has three options: (1) to see and review; (2) to see and not review; (3) not to see. A fourth option—to write about what one has not seen—becomes possible on strange occasions like *Still/Here*, from which one feels excluded by reason of its express intentions, which are unintelligible as theatre. I don't deny that *Still/Here* may be of value in some wholly other sphere of action, but it is as theatre, dance theatre, that I would approach it. And my approach has been cut off. By working dying people into his act, Jones is putting himself beyond the reach of criticism. I think of him as literally undiscussable—the most extreme case among the distressingly many now representing themselves to the public not as artists but as victims and martyrs.

In theatre, one chooses what one will be. The cast members of *Still/Here*—the sick people whom Jones has signed up—have no choice other than to be sick. The fact that they aren't there in person does not mitigate the starkness of their condition. They are there on videotape, the better to be seen and heard, especially heard. They are the prime exhibits of a director-choreographer who has crossed the line time and again between theatre and reality—who thinks that victimhood in and of itself is sufficient to the creation of an art spectacle.

The thing that *Still/Here* makes immediately apparent, whether you see it or not, is that victimhood is a kind of mass delusion that has taken hold of previously responsible sectors of our culture. The preferred medium of victimhood—something that Jones acknowledges—is videotape (see TV at almost any hour of the day), but the cultivation of victimhood by institutions devoted to the care of art is a menace to all art forms, particularly performing-art forms.

In writing this piece, I enter a plea for the critic and risk being taken for a victim myself. But the critic is part of the audience for art that victimhood also threatens. I can't review someone I feel sorry for or hopeless about. As a dance critic, I've learned to avoid dancers with obvious problems — overweight dancers (not fat dancers; Jackie Gleason was fat and was a good dancer), old dancers, dancers with sickled feet, or dancers with physical deformities who appear nightly in roles requiring beauty of line. In quite another category of undiscussability are those dancers I'm *forced* to feel sorry for because of the way they present themselves: as dissed blacks, abused women, or disfranchised homosexuals — as performers, in short, who make out of victimhood victim art. I can live with the flabby, the feeble, the scoliotic. But with the righteous I cannot function at all. The strategies of victim artists are proliferating marvelously at the moment. There's no doubt that the public likes to see victims, if only to patronize them with applause. The main type of victim art (the type that I think gave rise to all the others) is a politicized version of the blackmail that certain performers resort to, even great performers, like Chaplin in his more self-pitying moments. Instead of compassion, these performers induce, and even invite, a cozy kind of complicity. When a victim artist finds his or her public, a perfect, mutually manipulative union is formed which no critic may put asunder. Such an artist is Pina Bausch. Such an audience is the Brooklyn Academy's Next Wave subscription list, which also welcomed Bill T. Jones.

What Jones represents is something new in victim art — new and raw and deadly in its power over the human conscience. Jones's personal story is none of my concern.* His

*An autobiography, *Last Night on Earth*, was published by Jones in August 1995.

career, however, intersects vitally with cultural changes since the sixties that have formed an officialdom, a fortress of victim art. Bill T. Jones didn't do this all by himself; in fact, he probably didn't mean to do it at all.

Where it all began is not difficult to see. The arts bureaucracy in this country, which includes government and private funding agencies, has in recent years demonstrated a blatant bias for utilitarian art—art that justifies the bureaucracy's existence by being socially useful. This bias is inherent in the nature of government, although it did not seem to be when I was on a National Endowment for the Arts panel in the late seventies. In those years, art and art appreciation were unquestioned good things to support, and "community outreach" had its own program. Jones, who came along at that time, was one of our favorites because he seemed to be uninterested in conforming to the stereotype of the respectable black choreographer. By the late eighties, the ethos of community outreach had reached out and swallowed everything else; it was the only way the NEA could survive. The private funders soon knuckled under to the community- and minority-minded lobbies—the whole dynamic of funding, which keeps the biggest government grants flowing on a matching-funds basis, made the knuckling under inevitable. But ideology had something to do with this. When even museum directors can talk about "using art" to meet this or that social need, you know that disinterested art has become anathema. (Disinterested art: you have to understand that there's no such thing.) The ideological boosters of utilitarian art hark back to the political crusades of the sixties—against Vietnam, for civil rights. The sixties, in turn, harked back to the proletarian thirties, when big-government bureaucracy began. And now once again after a thirty-year lapse we are condemned to repeat history.

I'll say one thing for the sixties: the dance profession flourished in a climate of aesthetic freedom it hasn't enjoyed since. Jones's main connection to the sixties experimenters was to the power they'd claimed to control the terms on which they could be artists and be written about as artists. This, it turns out in retrospect, was their lasting legacy, and Jones has been their most conspicuous legatee. Members of the sixties generation, seeing themselves as picking up where Merce Cunningham's revolution left off, had decided that walking and other forms of nondance locomotion were in fact dancing. Their authority was John Cage more than it was Cunningham (who continued to use pure-dance movement), and for a few years there was lively controversy in New York over the direction of the new post-modern (as it was then not yet called) modern dance. It seemed to many that this kind of dance had a built-in resistance to criticism—not to writing but to criticism. There were critics who specialized in this art, or antiart, but few of them went beyond description. They hardly ever wrote about conventional dancing, but then writing about conventional dancing is hard. It's easier to describe actions that can be "danced" by you and me and require no formal evaluation.

Quite a number of the practitioners of the new dance assumed that because they abjured formality of expression they were beyond criticism—I don't know why. Dance critics have traditionally interested themselves in all sorts of "movement theatre"—puppets, skating, the circus. Theoretically, I am ready to go to anything—once. If it moves, I'm interested; if it moves to music, I'm in love. And if I'm turned off by what I see it's seldom because of the low-definition dance element. It was still possible in the sixties and seventies to unearth values in post-modern dance and write about those values as if they were the legitimate concern of the choreographers. Motion is motion; the body is the body. Multimedia theatre, a big thing then, enforced its own disciplines; you could write about it. The concerts that Bill T. Jones gave with his partner, Arnie Zane, were different from the ones he gave after Zane's death, though both were fairly typical of the post-sixties atmosphere of "conceptual" dance. Talking and singing were mixed with dancing; dancing was mixed with nondancing. It was Jones who split the mixed media from the message, with his baiting of the audience. This was an aggressively personal extension of the defiant anticonventionalism of the sixties, when you were manipulated into accepting what you saw as art. With Jones, you were actually intimidated.

At first, I saw the intimidation as part of the game that post-modernists played. Choreographers as different as Kenneth King and David Gordon and, later, William Forsythe had fun heckling the critics—anticipating or satirizing the reviews. Jones also did this. When I blasted an early work of his with the phrase "fever swamps," he retaliated by using the phrase as the title of a piece. It wasn't long before the Jones company became openly inflammatory. Politically provocative, accusatory, violent, it was a barely domesticated form of street theatre. And it declared war on critics, the most vocal portion of the audience. Jones's message, like Forsythe's, was clear: No back talk! Anything you say not only will be held against you but may be converted into grist for further paranoid accusation.

Many writers who discovered dance in the sixties and seventies felt as if they'd stumbled into the golden age of the art. All the way up and down the line, the most wonderful dancing, the most brilliant choreography were all about dance. What happened to politicize it? The promotion, for one thing, of the new arts-support networks, which began to stress the democratic and egalitarian aspects of nonformal movement. Academics, teaching newly accredited dance-history courses, also laid heavy stress on these aspects. By the eighties, when the culture wars got under way and the NEA was targeted by pressure groups left and right, it had become painfully clear that New York–centered, disinterested, movement-game, do-your-own-thing, idealistic post-modern dance was doomed. It was élitist. It had no audience. It produced no repertory. Most fatally, it did not establish itself in the universities and influence the coming generations. The sixties, it turned out, had been not the golden dawn but the twilight of American modern dance, and suddenly there was Pina Bausch and Butoh. And AIDS.

The kind of dance that was against criticism because it was "against interpretation" wound up a dependent of taxpayers who wanted a say in the art forms they were supporting. But didn't the problem really originate in the self-awarded privileges of the sixties radicals? The kind of "innovation" that seeks to relieve critics of their primary task of evaluation is always suspect. In the sixties, if you didn't like the rules you made your own; you fought the critics because they impinged on your freedom. In the eighties, you fought the critics because they hampered your chances of getting grants. Criticism had always been an issue in post-modern dance. I'm not sure that criticism wasn't *the* issue: the freedom of the audience to judge versus the freedom of the artist to create. In the visual arts, Warholism had pretty well demolished the need for serious criticism. And the same kind of trash-into-art transformations in dance tempted lesser talents than those who had thought them up in the first place. "It's art if I say it is," the Humpty-Dumpty war cry of the sixties, was a pathetic last-ditch attempt to confound the philistines, but now the philistines are likely to be the artists themselves. From the moment that Bill T. Jones declared himself HIV-positive and began making AIDS-focused pieces for himself and members of his company—from that moment it was obvious that the permissive thinking of the sixties was back, and in the most pernicious form. Actually, I'm not sure who came first: Jones the AIDS victim or Mapplethorpe the AIDS victim. But Jones and Mapplethorpe, parallel self-declared cases of pathology in art, have effectively disarmed criticism. They're not so much above art as beyond it. The need for any further evaluation, formal or otherwise, has been discredited. Where will it go from here? If an artist paints a picture in his own blood, what does it matter if I think it's not a very good picture? If he mixes the blood with Day Glo colors, who will criticize him? The artist is going to bleed to death, and that's it.

Painting pictures in their own blood was, metaphorically speaking, what many artists of the nineteenth century were doing. Even when they weren't mentally unsound or dying of syphilis or tuberculosis, they were preoccupied with death—their own or that of the Beloved. One's personal disease and impending death were unmentionable—Keats wrote no "Ode to Consumption"—but through art the individual spirit could override them both. Even in music, which can name nothing, which can only attract names (the Funeral March), and which can therefore speak freely, it is the surging spirit of Chopin that calls out, not the raging bacillus. One man, one death, one art. And what an art. After two world wars and the other unspeakable terrors of our century, death is no longer the nameless one; we have unmasked death. But we have also created an art with no power of transcendence, no way of assuring us that the grandeur of the individual spirit is more worth celebrating than the political clout of the group.

A few weeks ago, I attended a seminar on Schumann and mental illness. The psychiatrists who spoke were unanimous in the conviction that though Schumann's ailments were clinically real and debilitating, they were not accountable for the generally perceived decline in his later music. Because Schumann went mad, we think the madness must have told in his art. But the later Schumann is not deranged; it is dry. The composer had exhausted himself in the rigors of his music. Drained of inspiration, he thought he heard themes being sung to him by angels, and they turned out to be variations on themes he had already composed. The depletion experienced by Schumann is haunting the world of art in which we live today. We are all, artists and nonartists alike, survivors and curators, shoring up the art of the past, rummaging among its discards for new ideas. The nineteenth century and its wealth of art almost can't be comprehended; the bravura individualism that drove Schumann on is almost alienating. Personal despondency is not so easily sublimated today, nor do we look to sublimate it. Instead, it's disease and death that are taking over and running the show. As in the old woodcuts of Famine and Plague, a collective nightmare descends from which no one may be spared. And the end of twentieth-century collectivism is the AIDS quilt. The wistful desire to commemorate is converted into a pathetic lumping together, the individual absorbed by the group, the group by the disease.

The morbidity of so much Romantic art is bearable because it has a spiritual dimension. The immolation of the body leaves something behind: it's like a burning glass through which we see a life beyond life—not "the afterlife" but an animation of spirit, a dream life more abundantly strange and real than anything we know. The Romantics did not use art, they were used by it, consumed by it as much as by killer diseases. The mass-produced art of the twentieth century, art that has no spiritual dimension, is art that you can use. In fact, the potential of mass-produced art, whether for general enlightenment or gross dehumanization, was a prime topic of intellectual debate for most of the century. It wasn't so very long ago that people were arguing the merits of "educational" TV. They don't do that anymore. The last quarter of our century, which has seen the biggest technological advances in mass communications since the first quarter, hasn't sensitized us to the uses of mass-produced art; it has simply canonized as art that which is mass-produced. And it's the mass-production sensibility operating in terms of high art that's so depressing today—in these grisly high-minded movies like *Schindler's List* (showered with Oscars while the Serbian genocide goes on and on), these AIDS epics, these performance-art shockers like *Still/Here*. Artists today, whether their medium is popular art or not, work in a climate dominated by TV and the passive narcissism of the TV audience. The quasi-clinical attention to suffering that is the specialty of the TV talk shows may be a sham, but it's not such a sham as pretending to tell us how terminal illnesses are to be borne or what to make of Schindler and his list. And can we really displace the blame for our cultural deprivation on the wars, the death camps, and the bomb? It's worth remembering that most of the masterpieces of art and literature of this century were created by exiles or by those who worked on despite evil conditions in their homeland.

And, despite everything that is being done to discourage them, good artists are at work today. *The Family Business*, a play written by David Gordon and his son Ain Gordon, which will return for an extended New York run next spring, deals with sickness and dying in cathartic terms that are the polar opposite of those employed in *Still/Here*. The main character, a helpless, ranting, shrewd old woman around whom the other characters form a death vigil, is played by David Gordon himself, in a housedress, with a foolish-looking barrette in his hair. There are no videos, no testimonials, no confessions, yet every word seems taken from life. How David Gordon, one of the original radicals of post-modern dance, escaped being trapped by the logic of sixties permissiveness and Bill T. Jones did not is a question that can't be answered by some presumed cultural advantage that Jews have over blacks. Jones, caught up in his own charisma, didn't seem to hear the trap being sprung. But there was also a more invidious logic at work, in the campaigns of the multiculturalists, the moral guardians, and the minority groups. Together with entertainment-world evangelism and art-world philistinism, they made up a juggernaut that probably no one in Jones's position could have escaped.

Bill T. Jones seems to have been designated by his time to become the John the Baptist of victim art. (His Christ was Arnie Zane, who died of AIDS in 1988.) For me, Jones is undiscussable, as I've said, because he has taken sanctuary among the unwell. Victim art defies criticism not only because we feel sorry for the victim but because we are cowed by art. A few years ago, a jury in Cincinnati acquitted a museum director who had been charged with obscenity for putting prints from Mapplethorpe's "X," "Y," and "Z" portfolios on public display. Members of the jury told reporters afterward that they had based their verdict on "expert" testimony that the photographs were art. Art sanctifies. The possibility that Mapplethorpe was a bad artist or that good art could be obscene seems not to have occurred to anyone. Naturally not, since this is a subject for critics to discuss, not juries.

I do not remember a time when the critic has seemed more expendable than now. Oscar Wilde wrote that the Greeks had no art critics because they were a nation of art critics. But the critic who wishes to restore the old connection between the artist and his audience appeals in vain to readers who have been brought up on the idea of art as something that's beneficial and arcane at the same time. People for whom art is too fine, too high, too educational, too complicated may find themselves turning with relief to the new tribe of victim artists parading their wounds. They don't care whether it's an art form. They find something to respond to in the litany of pain, and they make their own connection to what the victim is saying. Of course, they are all co-religionists in the cult of Self. Only the narcissism of the nineties could put Self in place of Spirit and come up with a church service that sells out the Brooklyn Academy.

—December 26, 1994–January 2, 1995

Our Dancers in the Nineties

The central fact of ballet history of the last decade is the disintegration of the company and of the company style. It has happened everywhere, and to companies with once invincible reputations: the New York City Ballet, the Royal Ballets of Britain and Denmark, the Bolshoi, the Kirov. Such companies were fortresses of style; they absorbed change, withstood adversity, challenged each other for world domination, and through it all maintained a healthy local accent and native vigor that inspired civic pride even in the nonballetgoing public. Who knew then that they would fade so soon (some sooner than others—the Bolshoi was already disappearing) and become as obsolete as ocean liners in the age of jet travel?

The companies of the eighties and nineties resemble the fortress companies of the sixties and seventies in name only: they are dance collectives that operate more or less as corporations do; they are business companies. This is true even in Russia, where all business used to be run by the state. Just ten years ago this summer, the Kirov Ballet made its last tour of America as a fortress company. It had an exciting

new generation of dancers headed by the rising young ballerina Altinay Asylmuratova. Insofar as talent could be
equated with prosperity, the future looked bright; there was
no sign of the company's forthcoming internal dissolution
such as could be seen in the Bolshoi. *Perestroika* was a crushing blow to the unity of the Russian companies, maintained
more by iron discipline than by aesthetic choice. In the
West, the survival of Balanchine's New York City Ballet after his death was a beacon—illusory, as it turned out—to
other companies in search of a new direction. By the end of
the eighties, Balanchine's ballets had become a prime com-
modity in the world market even as Balanchine's company
suffered the same fate as all the rest—loss of leadership, ensuing loss of identity, technical collapse, an artistic program
composed of defeatist solutions to the threatened extinction
of the classical tradition. Each company has its own "solution": New York City Ballet has new ballets that ask less and
less of its dancers' hard-won classical technique; the Royal
British has scenery; the formerly Soviet companies freshen
up the repertory with Diaghilev revivals eighty years late.

These companies are responding to internal crises with
external remedies: a greater infusion of funds, a more rapid
audience turnover. Corporate decision-making is serving as
a cover for inept artistic direction. Is there a connection between this development and the fact that most of the artistic
directors are former premiers danseurs whose only previous
experience in directing a company may have been a few off-
season runouts? In exchange for the reassuringly masculine
presence in a supposedly unserious feminine art form, the
boards who elect these guys may be getting zero capacity
and a bundle of hard-to-handle temperament to boot; the
typical male star is notoriously a worse prima donna than
any ballerina. In any case, artistic direction, which used to

mean the careful matching of dancers' capabilities to a progressive standard and the keying of both factors to audience psychology, is now indistinguishable from marketing strategy; the only things that progress are the audience's ignorance and the prices it will pay.

Marketing strategy was a necessity recognized by company directors in the sixties and seventies, the years of the so-called ballet boom. What was being marketed then was prestige. You bought a ballet ticket and stepped up in class; ballet dancers gave you a glimpse of something rare and costly, aesthetically as well as financially. Ballet dancers conferred class on Ed Sullivan; in return, an Ed Sullivan booking cleared ballet of charges of élitism, a term not then in use. (The terms in use were much worse.) Today I have the impression that élitism, the negative of prestige, is something the marketeers themselves accept as the truth about ballet, and their strategies are aimed at trying to fit ballet into popular culture.

Last year, NYCB brought in a *West Side Story* suite; that it was done well is less significant than that it was done at all. This year, the audience that was attracted to the company by *West Side Story* was treated to some new ballets in ballet newspeak, which means a large admixture of aerobics. The question these strategies bring to mind is the one Henry James answered when he stopped trying to write plays; he said that he had to throw the cargo overboard to save the ship. But NYCB can't seem to give up its show-biz connection. To get the season under way, it put ten of its female dancers on the David Letterman show. Wearing costumes from Balanchine ballets, the dancers twirled one by one into camera range and uttered lines composed by Letterman's writers: "You gonna finish those cheese fries?" "Baseball players can scratch themselves, why can't we?"

"When I have to jump really high, I pretend there's a ferret biting me in the ass." These were supposed to be things no ballerina would ever say—a list devised, as was the whole presentation, by the Letterman staff. Nobody was invited to *dance* on the Letterman show. That, presumably, would have spoiled the fun.

Dancer abuse takes many forms. For nearly a decade, the majority of the plum roles in the NYCB repertory were cast with aging ballerinas or aging would-be ballerinas while talented young dancers were sidelined. Now that the elders are getting out of the way and Darci Kistler is on maternity leave, young dancers are being tossed into roles for which, through no fault of their own, they are technically underprepared. They've inherited standards of execution adjusted to the demands of forty-year-old dancers. The company prepares them by teaching them the steps, but steps to a dancer are no more than words on a page to an actor. A measure of the talent of the young Maria Kowroski was her ability this season to dance leading roles in *Apollo* and *Agon* and *Swan Lake* and *Symphony in C* without an adequate support system. There is nobody on the teaching staff who has ever danced those roles under Balanchine and who might have explained their intricacies to her. Relying on her own sense of style and the partnering of Igor Zelensky, Kowroski established her claim to stardom. But she could have done much more.

What one sees in Kowroski is the magnificence of her attributes—a large, lovely face and body, a theatrical sensibility, a softness, an intuitive musicality—and also the technical deficiencies, which keep the attributes from adding up. She dances on a big scale, but it could grow bigger still and more pliable. It could be an event rather than a fact—a verb (as Martha Graham liked to say) rather than a noun. For that to happen, she would need a lot more strength in turnout, a less retracted pelvis, an altogether more forward placement, and active épaulement. In the old days, she would have acquired all this in class. She would have been kept from making beginners' mistakes: going to extremes, repeating her effects, focusing on something up in the flies. In *Swan Lake* and *Symphony in C*, she looked like a Kirov dancer (Zelensky, a former Kirov star, may have had something to do with that), and Kirov is a long way from Balanchine.

Kowroski's faults can all be corrected, which is not to say that they will be. The alternative to becoming a Balanchine-style ballerina is becoming a ballerina in a business company, carrying on in star roles without really dancing them. This could happen to Kowroski (it happened to Margaret Tracey and Wendy Whelan), or she could simply disappear, as to all intents and purposes Monique Meunier and Jenifer Ringer have disappeared. The company's failure to make principal dancers of these two extraordinary young women is not explained by the stories that one hears about their problems, particularly Meunier's problems, which at different times were said to include being too young, too weak, too fat, seriously ill, or psychologically blocked and generally helpless. Some of these stories have come from Meunier herself and may be true. Her star rose in the 1989 School of American Ballet Workshop and has been rising and falling ever since. Jenifer Ringer's seasons were 1993–95; those of us who saw her performance of the Intermezzo in *Brahms-Schoenberg Quartet* are not likely to forget it or her impact in smaller roles. Meunier and Ringer, still under twenty-five, are the most notable of the several ballerina candidates who have appeared and vanished since Balanchine's death, trailing apologies for their weakness, young-ness, fatness, etc. It's my experience that dancers who are being properly nurtured do not disqualify themselves in these ways. It's also my experience that iron women who can dance the hell out of anything are not necessarily ballerinas—witness Stacey Calvert, Yvonne Borree, and Miranda Weese. Borree, once a logical choice for the Patricia McBride roles that Margaret Tracey was failing to fill, sat around too long; she's still scraping the rust off. In Weese the company has the kind of dancer—fluent, aggressive—normally found among the men, but this doesn't mean she's strong. NYCB doesn't produce strong dancers anymore; it produces coarse ones. The advent of Kowroski is interesting not because she's strong but because she's elegant—large and fine-grained at the same time.

Strong dancers in the Balanchine tradition are still being produced by the School of American Ballet. Every spring in the annual workshop performance, you see two or three. Then, once they go into the company, you lose them. Two years pass, then five. A certain amount of bench-sitting is unavoidable in a big company crowded with talent; yet, as I've said, it isn't talent that's being served. A lot of other things—politics, nepotism, the egos of first dancers, the needs of subscribers—can get ahead of talent. A ballet company adds one evil to the standard forms of institutional venality, and that is that most of the victims are too young to understand the system. They wonder why, when they work so hard and do everything they're told, they're still not getting anywhere. There were times when, watching Balanchine, we on the outside would wonder the same thing and study the company for signs of a pattern, but the old Kremlinology doesn't work on the new regime. Kowroski, after only a year in the company, is in danger of being used up before her time. Why, having handed her all these big roles, has the company given her no opportunities to develop in them? Not until the last week of the season did Kowroski get more than one or two performances a week. If I can't figure out company behavior, how can a nineteen-year-old? On the same program as Kowroski's *Swan Lake* we were given Margaret Tracey in *Chaconne*, a piece of miscasting so colossal that I stayed to watch it. The result was amazing: she danced every step, or nearly every step, but so thinly, so weightlessly, and so inconsequentially that the outcome wasn't *Chaconne* at all. The great old galleon had turned into a paper sailboat. Was it a purposeful transformation, yet another demonstration of the defeatist way of saving something by changing it into its opposite? Were we now going to get *Eastern Symphony* and *Prodigal Daughter*?

It's a crazy but perhaps accurate supposition that this fetishism of doing-the-steps in order to give-a-performance is the company's way of being true to Balanchine. He was famous for telling his dancers "Just do the steps, dear." (What he meant was "Do them the way I taught you. Speak the speech *as I pronounce it to you*.") When today's dancers look at the last of the ballerinas bred under Balanchine (if, indeed, they ever look at her)—when they see Kyra Nichols at the top of her form—they probably don't see the form, only the steps she's dancing and the effect she's having on the audience. Nichols has now reached the privileged moment in a dancer's career when she is doing less and giving more. I remember that moment in Fonteyn, in Tallchief, in Kolpakova, in Farrell; it's the ultimate refinement of classical style, the crowning achievement of a lifetime in dance. At thirty-eight, Kyra Nichols is too remote from the needs and concerns of insecure young dancers for them to be able to learn from her: she's not a model for steps; she's a vision of dance. An artist of sterling technique and shadowless temper, she is passing just now through unaccustomed territory: the romantic side of Balanchine—*La Sonnambula*, *Swan Lake*, the "Rosenkavalier" section of *Vienna Waltzes*. And the rarefied state she's in makes her seem the ideal dancer for these ballets.

Of the generation of ballerinas born by the end of the sixties, Kyra Nichols is the only one with a completely formed, articulate technique and a distinguished repertory in which to deploy it. She ripened on the vine while her two great NYCB contemporaries, Darci Kistler and Maria Calegari, and the Kirov's Asylmuratova, the Bolshoi's Ananiashvili, the Paris Opéra's Sylvie Guillem, and the Royal Ballet's Darcey Bussell all suffered disruptions and cancellations of one sort or another. To the emergence of the business company we owe the phenomenon of the disaffiliated ballerina—the dancer who seeks artistic completion by freelancing or by guest-starring all over the world. Nichols is a disaffiliated star who never left her home company. One could say that it left her, but there has been no actual rupture between Nichols and Peter Martins. Since they've stopped working together, she has if anything found more freedom to maneuver and more challenge and inspiration in her roles. The splendid isolation of Kyra Nichols can even be a dramatic statement. When she enters in *Vienna Waltzes*, it's on a note of high resolve: "Alone, then!" Head up, erect as only Kyra Nichols can be, she walks into the darkened ballroom.

Nichols isn't completely alone as a Balanchine loyalist; Nichol Hlinka and Ethan Stiefel are also stylistically exemplary, and so is Peter Boal when he is well cast. (As Tracey's partner in *Chaconne*, he tried so hard to get some energy into the movements that he ruined his own performance.) Merrill Ashley is trying to maintain two careers, a fading one as a dancer and a budding one as a teacher, but she must be counted a distinct asset. And then there is the School of American Ballet. This spring, it put on its esteemed productions of *Concerto Barocco* and *Valse Fantaisie*, and took a fling at *Rubies*, which failed (not for kids). Among the dancers were the usual prospects. How long before they stop appearing? Since most of the school's teachers are former members of the company, it can only be a matter of time before the current knowledgeable generation is replaced by people who come from another world—the world of NYCB in the nineties.

When remarkable young dancers like Kowroski and Paloma Herrera become stars without having been trained up to the level of the roles they will have to carry, it isn't just a damn shame and an abuse of talent; it's an affliction—it means actual physical hardship. Paloma Herrera, who comes from Buenos Aires, was an SAB Workshop star in 1991, when she was fifteen. She signed with American Ballet Theatre, having spent six months in the school. Last year, she was promoted to principal dancer, and is now the biggest female box-office attraction ABT has had since Gelsey Kirkland. Herrera's technical problems are worse than Kowroski's, but her drive, her youthful energy, and her sheer animality override them; she's a true beast of the theatre. And the ABT management seems to think she can do anything. At one end of her range this season lay Kitri in *Don Quixote*, a role which has maybe three steps; at the other lay Polyhymnia in Balanchine's *Apollo*, and his *Tchaikovsky Pas de Deux* and *Ballet Imperial*, in the latter of which she danced both principal and soloist roles. Both had her breathing a little hard. Her one attempt at the tremendous ballerina role was brave but inconclusive; mainly, it revealed that Jose Manuel

Carreno is a better partner for her than Angel Corella, and that the ballet easily accommodates what is already a wonderful Latin softness and plasticity in his style and, incipiently, in hers. (Balanchine himself staged the ballet for the Colón, her hometown theatre.) But without careful supervision Herrera could turn into iron.

The aesthetic inconsistencies and the physical perils that Paloma Herrera deals with every day are an old ABT story. Of all the major companies, it has changed least; it always was a business company, more concerned with selling tickets than with developing the art. In the eighties, Baryshnikov's regime raised the level of taste and extended the capacities of the corps and the middle-rank soloists, but it created few stars for the public to adore. Now, with talented dancers looking for work the world over, the company can put together a roster and a repertory that function more pleasurably as ballet entertainment than the strained offerings of the more brightly endowed companies. It can be dumb-ballet entertainment, like the Rose adagio, a pas d'action from *The Sleeping Beauty* lifted out of its normal setting and done as a stunt, or Ben Stevenson's *Cinderella* instead of the Frederick Ashton version it was obviously modeled on. Or it can be not so dumb. To rehearse *Ballet Imperial*, the company brought in Merrill Ashley, her first such assignment. The result of her coaching was that ABT now has something to show besides a more "imperial" alternative to the NYCB production. At the same time, because the management insisted on having multiple casts, many of the big moments that eventuated in the performances were moments the dancers had had to work out for themselves. Amanda McKerrow and Wes Chapman evoked a kind of understated sentiment that I identify with an earlier era in ballet. Their dancing was not the grandest that this ballet has seen, but it was immaculate, like all their work. On other occasions, Ashley Tuttle, with Chapman or Guillaume Graffin, made a thing of coherence and fascination out of Kevin McKenzie's scrappy *Nutcracker* pas de deux. ABT dancers have a long tradition of self-reliance. In that respect, too, they're ahead of the competition.

Corella, at twenty, is better off as a character dancer than as a classical virtuoso. Keith Roberts can be both, even though he's not nearly so gifted or so well built as Corella. Roberts understands and projects the paradoxes of classical style—the contrapposto, the two-things-at-once oppositions. Corella is by comparison flat and facile; he lacks only Julio Bocca's force to become what Bocca has become, a dance performer rather than a dancer. Corella's sweetness and hair-in-the-eyes boyishness are endearing to the audience, just as Bocca's fury does. Part of Vladimir Malakhov's charm is that it isn't there when you expect it. He makes no extra move toward the public, does not ingratiate himself. He is as pure a dancer, in his own terms, as Kyra Nichols is in hers. In the bizarre *Apollo* tournament that was held this season between NYCB and ABT (nine performances with eight changes of cast), Malakhov faced Ethan Stiefel for first-place honors. I would not care to choose between them. Both men were making débuts in this role, and both are already closer to the elemental, fiery quality that is the most elusive part of Apollo's magic than anyone has come since Baryshnikov danced the part.

This may be seen as a greater triumph for Malakhov, who was trained in Moscow, than for the American Stiefel, who has danced Balanchine all his life. Yet the *way* Stiefel dances Balanchine is completely his own. His *Apollo* was born in the marvelous dynamics of his performance earlier in the season of the third movement of *Symphony in C*. The easy play of the torso against the jackknife precision of the legs and feet, the spaciousness, the elastic rhythm made a spectacle unlike anything else in that performance. Stiefel is the NYCB's only young star, the only really first-rate classical dancer to develop under the Martins regime; and he is now leaving the company for the Zurich Ballet, where he has previously spent time. He will appear with ABT next spring in New York. It is a disconcerting trend, this leaving home. Dancers cannot float indefinitely untethered; they cannot make careers for themselves on their grasp of an academic tradition that by defi-nition depends on the handful of institutions that have cultivated it in this century. However, when the tradition is being actively undermined by the institutions themselves, it's every man for himself.

—July 8, 1996

On *Beauty* Bare

Revivals of historic pre-Revolutionary productions have become a specialty of the Kirov Theatre, the Maryinsky of St. Petersburg. Last year, a Silver Age *Ruslan and Lyudmila*, with designs by Konstantine Korovin and Alexander Golovin and ballets by Michel Fokine, was the hit of the Kirov Opera season in New York. This summer, the Kirov Ballet brought us another and more ambitious restoration—the original 1890 *Sleeping Beauty* of Tchaikovsky and Petipa, staged according to notation dating from 1903, the year the ballet passed its hundredth performance. The efficacy of dance notation is very much on people's minds these days, along with the whole questionable business of dance curatorship; also, the state of Russian art and culture has been a subject of curiosity since the collapse of the Soviet Union. The ballet was once the jewel of that culture, and the jewel of the ballet was *The Sleeping Beauty*. It was only a matter of time before the process of recovery in which the Russians seem currently engaged would bring them to it.

To anyone who has not felt its magic in a live ballet performance, it is probably impossible to convey a sense of the uniqueness of *The Sleeping Beauty*, of its distinction as a dance masterpiece, and of where it stands among the masterpieces of lyric theatre. There is no other ballet like it, although several of Balanchine's give us concentrated doses of its essence. There is no opera like it, although, if one could imagine a *Magic Flute* which came after Wagner and not before, one might be close to the truth. The best testimonials to *The Sleeping Beauty* are the careers of the artists who came under its spell and for whom it had the power of conversion. It was this ballet that made Balanchine a choreographer, Pavlova a dancer, and Diaghilev a balletomane. The impact of the first production upon Diaghilev's generation of artists and intellectuals, a generation enthralled by Wagner, Nietzsche, and the principle of the *Gesamtkunstwerk*, has been borne out in a number of memoirs. "For three hours I lived in a magic dream," Leon Bakst has recalled. In common with other celebrants of that production, Bakst seemed to think the music was written just for him. "All my being was in cadence with those rhythms, with the radiant and fresh waves of beautiful melodies, already my friends." For Alexandre Benois, the music was "something infinitely close, inborn, something I would call *my* music."

Perhaps, as Benois in his eighties insisted, it really was his personal passion for ballet, rekindled by *The Sleeping Beauty* and communicated to his colleagues in the World of Art, that inspired the formation of the Ballets Russes. However, the general experience of that moment was one of personal revelation. The principle of the *Gesamtkunstwerk* involves not only the combining of the arts but the intermingling of the senses. The music, by setting off precisely that *dérèglement de tous les sens* of which Rimbaud had spoken, had plunged each listener into a profound state of trance-like subjectivity. It can still do that, of course, although without Petipa's choreography to direct your thoughts, without the actual scenes for which Tchaikovsky had provided the setting, you probably can never really hear *The Sleeping Beauty*.

The script of the ballet turns the fairy tale into a parable of divine intervention. What plot there is, is played out or foretold in the Prologue. Fairies bring christening gifts to the infant Princess Aurora. An uninvited fairy, Carabosse, storms in and condemns the infant to death on her sixteenth birthday, but the Lilac Fairy revokes the curse, changing death to sleep. In the next three acts, fate simply takes its course. The parable of divine intervention in human affairs becomes a revelation of the divinity within human nature which lies in the capacity for art. The unmentioned gift of art, for which ballet itself becomes the metaphor, stands revealed in the final scene (the apotheosis), when Apollo descends to confer his blessing on Aurora's wedding.

The allegory of *The Sleeping Beauty* is porous; you can find anything in it you like: a defense of monarchy, a myth about the earth's renewal, a love story, the Incarnation. Fundamentally, though, it is a meditation on itself. It sees art as a kind of miracle which is truly possible in human life. It *was* a kind of miracle that happened in the life of Marius Petipa. At the age of seventy, after some forty years of choreographing to the music of hacks, he was handed the opportunity to work with Tchaikovsky. Petipa the formalist seized the chance to clothe form in meaning. The format of the ballet is unswervingly consistent for three acts. Each act builds up to a pas d'action in the form of an adagio with variations. The story unfolds inside these parallel structures—the fairies' gift-giving, the royal rite of courtship on Aurora's sixteenth birthday (the Rose adagio), Prince Désiré's vision of Aurora. The last act, the Wedding, is a divertissement of fairy tales.

The whole scholastic point of *The Sleeping Beauty* is a display of the classical arts of mime and dance—not in rigidly specialized compartments but in free sequences of gestural exchange flowing throughout the ballet. Even in the Rose adagio, where the steps may still be a technical challenge to today's dancers, one wants to see a ballerina exhibit the range of meaning they possess in the context in which Petipa sets them: a slightly flustered but gracious young princess being courted by four boys at once. The ingenuity of the Rose adagio is its contextualization of technique—one kind of protocol (social) explains, or is exchanged for, another (dance). All too often the number is presented as an echoless exercise in technique.

How the Rose adagio is danced today is not how it was danced in Petipa's day. Ballets change in performance. The only way to revive choreography is by magic empathy. "Petipa" is not an author or even a text but a climate of inspiration, like Auden's Freud. It would be wonderful to be able to report the restoration, in this sense, of Petipa's contribution to *The Sleeping Beauty*, but the Kirov worked strictly from the record, and the record is fragmentary. We were given stopgap inspiration, some of it unavoidable. It was no fault of the Kirov's that the Panorama, comprising the prince's journey by boat and his approach by land to the sleeping castle, could not be staged at the Met. Instead, as a bridge to the awakening of the princess, the entr'acte with the violin solo was played to a drop curtain. Very nice, but untrue to 1890. (Discarded by Petipa, the entr'acte provided Tchaikovsky with the motif for Christmas-tree music and wound up in Balanchine's *Nutcracker*.) But, compared to the music and the décor, the choreography seems to have been insecure from the start of the notating process in or around 1903. That was the year of Petipa's dismissal; the venerable ballet master's rehearsals were now in the hands of Nicholas Sergeyev, a régisseur who was also one of several Maryinsky functionaries working in Stepanov notation to transcribe the repertory. (Vladimir Stepanov, a curious figure who combined anatomical and anthropological research with dance studies, had evolved a system for notating movement keyed to music, which he managed to have accepted by the Imperial Theatres before dying, at thirty, in 1896.) The likelihood that the notators of *The Sleeping Beauty* never worked from a rehearsal conducted by Petipa, and the fact that the notation was never completed, did not keep it from becoming the master score of that ballet and, when Sergeyev left Russia in 1918, the basis of the two most meritorious and influential Western productions, both staged in London: Diaghilev's in 1921 and the Sadler's Wells's in 1946.

Petipa, isolated from his art, died in 1910, an embittered man. Did he foresee that Sergeyev ("that malicious régisseur Sergeyev," as he called him) would be making a living peddling Petipa ballets around Europe? What is important for us to note is that Sergeyev was not a choreographer. Lacking in stage sense and unmusical "to a degree bordering on eccentricity," according to Ninette de Valois, he actually posed a threat to the productions he oversaw. As she tells it, de Valois had to circumvent him in order to save the ballet:

He always carried a blue pencil, and would carefully pencil out a bar of music, which, for some reason, wearied him. The offending bar would receive a long, strong blue cross through it. This would mean that I must phone [the music director] Constant Lambert who would come down in the lunch break and put the bars back. Sergueeff [sic] would return, and because, in his absence, I had extended some small choreographic movement to cover Mr. Lambert's tracks, he would be unaware that the position was musically where it had been before the onslaught of the blue pencil!

By these surreptitious means, de Valois and Lambert in 1939 contrived to put on a musically distinguished production of *The Sleeping Beauty* starring the young Margot Fonteyn, and after the war they redid it, again with Fonteyn, and with embellishments and interpolations by Frederick Ashton, performing essentially the same service of rehabilitation that Nijinska had performed for Diaghilev in 1921. It was the Diaghilev version, a failure in its time, that the British artists held in mind, and it was their success at Covent Garden and then at the Met in New York that established the fame of Russian ballet's greatest classic.

The presence of that classic and of a half-dozen others brought from Russia to London by Sergeyev virtually guaranteed not only that the cream of the Russian repertory would be accurately performed in the West but that its creators' contributions would be recognized and analyzed by historians. Dance is the art without a past. Our knowledge of the three Tchaikovsky ballets and the process by which they were made is based largely on Sergeyev's trunkful of dance scores and related memorabilia, which since 1969 has been stored in the Harvard Theatre Collection. Without this source material we should have had to reinvent a crucial part of the nineteenth century, and Petipa's genius would have remained as shadowy and indistinct as that of his fellow choreographers Perrot and Saint-Léon.

Sergeyev was an odd duck who gained a place in history from an ability to reproduce the steps and configurations of many different ballets. His proficiency was sorely tested by Tchaikovsky's music and by the poverty of British ballet in

1939; where Petipa had eighty dancers for the Garland Dance, Ninette de Valois had maybe sixteen.* But manipulating numbers is part of a régisseur's job. In the Kirov reconstruction, large numbers are revealing when they not only swell the scene but activate it. All the little maids and pages, each group with a moment of dancing to do, were charming to see, and were called for, too, by the repeats in the music. But a régisseur only provides the plan of action; a choreographer—a Nijinska or de Valois or Ashton—revives the ballet. It was never the aim of Sergeyev and the other Maryinsky notators to record Petipa's masterpieces for posterity. Rather, with Petipa's long reign over, they needed to assure themselves of a way of carrying on without him.

Roland John Wiley, the American dance historian who has made the closest study of Sergeyev's papers, believes that the choreographic scores were mainly intended as a practical tool, "an aide-memoire for those who already know the choreography." As might be expected, the notators concentrated on the dances, minutely transcribing steps, counts, and accents. They also wrote out descriptions of the stage action, drew diagrams of floor plans, and set down mime scenes in dialogue form. Production details in *The Sleeping Beauty*, such as entrances and exits, were left

---

*That figure of eighty needs some explanation. The Garland Dance packed forty-eight dancers, including eight pairs of children, onto the Met stage, which is bigger than the Maryinsky's, yet at the Maryinsky the number of dancers, we have been told, is seventy-two. I was unable to find out from Kirov personnel whether all seventy-two are ever on the stage at one time. If in fact the dancers come and go in units with some units not reappearing, we have the explanation for the Maryinsky's capacity and the solution to the puzzling photograph of the 1890 Garland Dance in the *Sleeping Beauty* program, which shows dancers in costumes different from the ones we saw on the stage.

blank, as was a large portion of Act II, including the Panorama, the sleeping castle, and the awakening of the princess—in other words, the heart of the ballet from the dramatic point of view. Among the supplementary material carried off by Sergeyev, the most important items were the ballet master's plan prepared by Petipa, various scenarios, and a batch of heavily marked music scores used in rehearsal. Besides this trove of documents from Harvard, the Kirov reconstructors delved into archives in St. Petersburg for stage photographs and for scenery and costume designs. Probably the most precious local resource was a textbook on Stepanov's work by Sergeyev's confrère Alexander Gorsky, which enabled the chief reconstructor, Sergei Vikharev, to decipher the notation.

What Vikharev and his team have put on the stage is a régisseur's work of art. Like a dinosaur skeleton, it stands, it moves, it exists as history. But it is minimal, inert theatre. The costumes by Ivan Vzevolozhsky constitute the principal attraction. Vzevolozhsky was the director of the Imperial Theatres and the key figure in the creation of *The Sleeping Beauty*, dreaming up the idea, planning the mise-en-scène, commissioning the score from Tchaikovsky, and writing the libretto with Petipa's help. His costumes were reservedly commended by Benois, and Benois was right, particularly about the jarring colors: maroons, browns, crimsons, and deep blues jostle dainty pastels. But the costumes for the fairies and their attendants in the Prologue would grace any production today, and the Lilac Fairy (portrayed by Marie Petipa, the choreographer's daughter) got a number of changes, a fact which explains the contradictory photographs taken of her in 1890. The standard of workmanship in clothes, masks, and wigs throughout the present production is impeccable. One hundred and nine years after opening night, Vzevolozhsky is finally getting his due as a costume designer.

In Vzevolozhsky's conception, not Princess Aurora but the Lilac Fairy is the ballet's kingpin, and lilacs are the leitmotif of the décor. The frontcloth shows a bouquet of lilacs on a balustrade. The Fairy's attendants have sprays emblazoned on their costumes, and wave fans made of leaves. In Act II, she carries a tall staff bound with bunches of lilacs at one end. The branches that cover the castle are lilac branches. We are supposed to smell this ballet. Through synesthesia, the symbolism becomes palpable: lilacs, spring, Aurora, dawn, youth, renewal, reawakening, renaissance.

The hundred years' sleep falls between the sixteenth and the seventeenth centuries—between the Valois and the Bourbon kings. Appearing in the second act, Désiré is a fantasy version of the young Louis XIV, young Apollo, the Sun King. Under the director's supervision, five scenic designers raised credible facsimiles of Fontainebleau and Versailles (which are less well reproduced than the costumes). Benois, who in his own art cherished the *grand siècle*, lamented the change that came about in his favorite ballet when the epochs were moved forward eighty years by Korovin, the designer of Sergeyev's revival of 1914. Korovin's scheme celebrated the Bourbons at the wrong end of the line, making nonsense of Tchaikovsky's quotation of the hymn "Vive Henri Quatre" at the very end of the ballet.* Bakst's scenery for Diaghilev in 1921 substituted for real locales Baroque stage sets after the Bibienas; his costumes for

---

*The ballet was timed to coincide with the signing of a Franco-Russian pact. Russians who, like the ballet's makers, considered themselves enlightened monarchists would consciously have aligned the tsarevich Nicholas with the dauphin Louis and his grandfather Henri IV, the first of the Bourbon kings and the most liberal of French monarchs.

the second half of the ballet were unequivocally Louis XV. Oliver Messel's décor for Sadler's Wells followed suit.

Meddling with the epochs has since become a scene designer's prerogative. I have seen transitions from the eighteenth to the nineteenth centuries, even from the nineteenth to the twentieth. What difference does it make? Well, the Russians understood *The Sleeping Beauty* as an allegory, and a young girl's sexual awakening was the least of it. Primarily the ballet was about ballet—its flowering in the French courts of the Baroque era and its resurgence under Romanticism at the Paris Opéra. France was Petipa's homeland; Vsevolozhsky had been a member of the French legation in Paris. For their scenario, they drew on their memories of the *féeries* of French theatre as well as on the backlog of Opéra ballets about the sleeping princess and/or the evil fairy. One of these was a *Belle au bois dormant* of 1829, in which the young Taglioni danced as a naiad. In 1890, they looked backward to Renaissance dance and, in a momentous Vision scene, forward to the "modern" ballet of the Romantic era. Historically speaking, Aurora in Act I is the embodiment of Mlle La Fontaine, the first ballerina of the Paris Opéra; in Act II, she is Taglioni, appearing to the prince as a naiad of the river of time. In the third-act mazurka, Aurora is a Petersburg ballerina.

The Russians saw themselves as ballet's rescuers, bestowing the kiss of life on an art that lay moribund in Paris. When Korovin moved the ballet into the eighteenth century, it was probably to bring it closer to the Russian experience of ballet, which began with the founding of the St. Petersburg school in 1738 by a French ballet master, the first of a long line culminating in Marius Petipa. In Petipa's own production, the Russianization of French ballet is the grander for being implicit.

The Kirov production clarifies the allegorical sweep of the ballet, but it leaves other questions unsettled, leading us to conclude either that a fair amount of confusion reigned over the ballet at its inception or that exigencies of the initial seasons got locked in as sacred writ. Who is giving gifts in the Prologue? The action shows the fairies giving gifts to the infant Aurora several times over. The libretto states that they also receive gifts from the king, but we never see this. The crux seems to occur between the waltz (No. 2) and the adagio (No. 3). The waltz commences with the pages of the court, who have been parading about with objects on pillows (the king's gifts) — and the fairies skillfully blend themselves with the waltzers. The fairies then dance the adagio, joined at one point by their own pages. The difference between the two sets of pages and the more important difference in tone between the secular waltz and the divine adagio are not made clear in the staging. We never get the point that the fairies' gifts of qualities and talents (beauty, wit, song, dance, etc.) are of an order entirely different from anything they could receive from the king of the realm. The last gift, sleep, is given by the Lilac Fairy to countermand the evil fairy's prophecy of death, but the wonderful irony of this gift's having been the result of a last-minute interruption is missing.

In the Vision scene, the Kirov characterizes Aurora and her retinue as naiads. It even restores the ancient device of Venus' seashell, on which Aurora takes an arabesque balance at the close of the adagio. But it obscures the symbolism of the river and of the naiad as Venus-Aphrodite, the source. When the prince is offered a glimpse of the sleeping Aurora, she isn't in her rocky niche at the fountainhead, posing with face averted and eyes downcast; she's at home, lying prosaically on her satin bed — a painting is slid out from the wings. (This may be staged differently at the Maryinsky.) All the I'm-here-but-not-here declarations of the ectoplasmic Aurora's dancing in this act are compromised. The solo is set to music transferred by Petipa from Act III rather than to the music written for it—why can only be guessed at. Wiley speculates that the transferred number (Gold, from the suite of Jewels and Precious Metals) was easier for the ballerina to dance. But by 1903, thirteen years after the première, several ballerinas had danced it besides the original, Carlotta Brianza. Retaining the Gold waltz in the wrong place meant that an awkward segue had to be written into Tchaikovsky's score. Why would Petipa have clung to this arrangement? I can only theorize that the symbol for gold in the table of elements, *Au*, suggested to him Aurora and, perhaps, Aumer, the choreographer of that 1829 *Belle au bois dormant* from which he borrowed his naiads. Naiads in turn suggested the Rhine maidens and the Rhine gold. (Wagner's *Ring* was not given in full locally until 1889, the year *The Sleeping Beauty* was in preparation. Like many another Petersburger, Petipa may have fallen under its spell.)

Finally, does Carabosse come to the wedding or not? Astonishingly, she does, carried in on a chair like other fairies from the Prologue. But nothing is made of her presence, ostensibly because her original interpreter, Enrico Cecchetti, appeared in the Wedding scene as the Bluebird and her arrival had to be faked by a double. Again, this seems a poor excuse. By 1903, Cecchetti was in Warsaw. Had Petipa taken the notated rehearsals, he would probably have revised Carabosse's perfunctory entry in the Wedding.

In *The Sleeping Beauty*, Russian ballet went back to the source and moved ahead; to return is to advance. When Balanchine was a young dancer in Petrograd, participating in

Fyodor Lopukhov's revival of 1922, the watchword was "Forward toward Petipa!" (This, of course, was before social realism crushed classicism.) In 1928, Balanchine and Stravinsky did go forward toward Petipa and Tchaikovsky by creating *Apollo*. One of the things I wondered whether I might see in the 1890 ending (the apotheosis) was a connection with the 1928 ending of *Apollo*. A photograph of the 1939 London production has the fairies arrayed on a staircase in the manner of Apollo and the Muses in Balanchine's ballet. Petipa's apotheosis hadn't been notated, so somebody—Sergeyev or de Valois or Ashton or the fairies themselves—staged it from memory. But a memory of Petipa's ending or Balanchine's? Or was it Balanchine's memory of Petipa (or Gorsky or Lopukhov)? No one connected with the 1939 apotheosis now recalls where it came from, and the Kirov's apotheosis has no staircase. (The scene, very likely staged from a photograph, is hard to make out: Apollo in his quadriga, crudely painted on the backcloth, surmounts scalloped tiers of clouds with live cherubim sticking their heads out, playing harps.)

Ballet can be reduced to notation, but it really exists in the interplay between memory and the imagination. We are interested in, even fascinated by, the curio the Kirov has presented, because we love *The Sleeping Beauty*. But we do not love it as given here. Scene for scene, dance for dance, we (that is, I and a few other fossils) have seen it better done. We have seen it better done by the Kirov in the 1960s. In those days, the Kirov had no choreographers, but the choreographers it has today are like ours—self-starters with no interest in the classical tradition, no belief in it as something that steadily evolves, redefining itself against a changing background of times and customs.

At the end of a century it has mostly had to sleep

through, the Kirov wakes to find itself in the same predicament as every other classical company, but it has options the others don't have. One is to absorb the Balanchine ballets that are the century's masterpieces, part of the legacy from Petipa. As for *The Sleeping Beauty*, with the best will in the world, the company can only give us the Wagnerian side, not the Mozartean side. When it can dance that, the ballet will wake up, too, and recognize Maître Petipa in whatever guise he has come, and speak to him the words of the old tale: "Is it you my Prince, you have waited a great while."

—August 12, 1999

Index